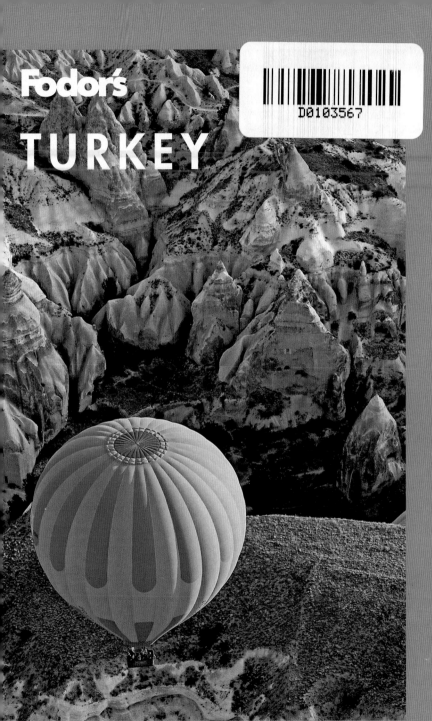

Fodor's
TURKEY

WELCOME TO TURKEY

In modern Turkey, the legacy of centuries of history coexists with progressive and contemporary culture. Its exciting capital, Istanbul, spans Europe and Asia: here, upscale eateries and swanky nightclubs are squeezed between Byzantine and Ottoman structures, with calls-to-prayer from city mosques sounding above the city. The Aegean and Mediterranean coasts mix ancient Roman ruins with stunning beaches and resorts. Still, the real cultural lessons come from the Turkish people, always welcoming and eager to share their homeland's fascinating past and present.

TOP REASONS TO GO

★ **Istanbul:** The Aya Sofya, Blue Mosque, Topkapı Palace, plus fabulous food and shopping.

★ **History:** Greco-Roman ruins such as Ephesus, Ottoman palaces, World War I battlefields.

★ **Local Eats:** Kebabs and *meze* are essential, along with regional and cutting-edge fare.

★ **Natural Wonders:** Cappadocia's fairytale rock formations, Pamukkale's travertine pools.

★ **Shopping:** Markets and bazaars brim with treasures from carpets to fragrant spices.

★ **Seaside Serenity:** Beautiful beaches, charming coastal towns, memorable Blue Cruises.

Fodor's TURKEY

Publisher: Amanda D'Acierno, *Senior Vice President*

Editorial: Arabella Bowen, *Editor in Chief*; Linda Cabasin, *Editorial Director*

Design: Fabrizio La Rocca, *Vice President, Creative Director*; Tina Malaney, *Associate Art Director*; Chie Ushio, *Senior Designer*; Ann McBride, *Production Designer*

Photography: Melanie Marin, *Associate Director of Photography*; Jessica Parkhill and Jennifer Romains, *Researchers*

Maps: Rebecca Baer, *Senior Map Editor*; Mark Stroud (Moon Street Cartography) and David Lindroth, *Cartographers*

Production: Linda Schmidt, *Managing Editor*; Evangelos Vasilakis, *Associate Managing Editor*; Angela L. McLean, *Senior Production Manager*

Sales: Jacqueline Lebow, *Sales Director*

Marketing & Publicity: Heather Dalton, *Marketing Director*; Katherine Fleming, *Senior Publicist*

Business & Operations: Susan Livingston, *Vice President, Strategic Business Planning*; Sue Daulton, *Vice President, Operations*

Fodors.com: Megan Bell, *Executive Director, Revenue & Business Development*; Yasmin Marinaro, *Senior Director, Marketing & Partnerships*

Copyright © 2014 by Fodor's Travel, a division of Random House LLC

Contributors: Jennifer Hattam, Vanessa Larson, Aidan McMahon, Scott Newman, August Siena Thomas

Editors: Amanda Sadlowski (lead editor), Penny Phoenix, Susan MacCallum-Whitcomb

Production Editor: Evangelos Vasilakis

9th Edition

ISBN 978-0-8041-4191-8

ISSN 0071-6618

All details in this book are based on information supplied to us at press time. Always confirm information when it matters, especially if you're making a detour to visit a specific place. Fodor's expressly disclaims any liability, loss, or risk, personal or otherwise, that is incurred as a consequence of the use of any of the contents of this book.

SPECIAL SALES

This book is available at special discounts for bulk purchases for sales promotions or premiums. For more information, e-mail specialmarkets@randomhouse.com

PRINTED IN COLOMBIA

10 9 8 7 6 5 4 3 2 1

CONTENTS

CONTENTS

MAPS

ABOUT
THIS GUIDE

Fodor's Recommendations
Everything in this guide is worth doing—
we don't cover what isn't—but exceptional sights, hotels, and restaurants are
recognized with additional accolades.
Fodor's Choice★ indicates our top recommendations; and **Best Bets** call attention to
notable hotels and restaurants in various
categories. Care to nominate a new place?
Visit Fodors.com/contact-us.

Trip Costs
We list prices wherever possible to help
you budget well. Hotel and restaurant
price categories from $ to $$$$ are noted
alongside each recommendation. For
hotels, we include the lowest cost of a
standard double room in high season.
For restaurants, we cite the average price
of a main course at dinner or, if dinner
isn't served, at lunch. For attractions,
we always list adult admission fees; dis-
counts are usually available for children,
students, and senior citizens.

Hotels
Our local writers vet every hotel to recom-
mend the best overnights in each price cat-
egory, from budget to expensive. Unless
otherwise specified, you can expect pri-
vate bath, phone, and TV in your room.
For expanded hotel reviews, facilities, and
deals visit Fodors.com.

Restaurants
Unless we state otherwise, restaurants are
open for lunch and dinner daily. We men-
tion dress code only when there's a specific
requirement and reservations only when
they're essential or not accepted. To make
restaurant reservations, visit Fodors.com.

Credit Cards
The hotels and restaurants in this guide
typically accept credit cards. If not, we'll
say so.

Top Picks
★ Fodor's Choice

Listings
⊠ Address
⊠ Branch address
☎ Telephone
🖷 Fax
⊕ Website
✉ E-mail
💳 Admission fee
🕓 Open/closed times
Ⓜ Subway
✛ Directions or Map coordinates

Hotels & Restaurants
🛏 Hotel
🛏 Number of rooms
🍴 Meal plans
✗ Restaurant
🍴 Reservations
👔 Dress code
🚫 No credit cards
$ Price

Other
⇨ See also
☞ Take note
🏌 Golf facilities

EXPERIENCE
TURKEY

WHAT'S WHERE

Numbers correspond to chapters.

2 Istanbul. Straddling Europe and Asia, Istanbul is the undisputed cultural, economic, and historical capital of Turkey. There are enough monuments and attractions, as well as enticing restaurants, shops, and museums, to keep you busy for days.

3 The Sea of Marmara and the North Aegean. The battlefields of Gallipoli are one of the main reasons travelers visit this part of Turkey, but the area is also a destination for beach lovers and those looking for pleasant places to hike. The archaeological site of ancient Troy is here, too.

4 The Central and Southern Aegean Coast. The heart of what was once known by the ancient Greeks as Asia Minor, this area has been drawing visitors since the time of, well, Homer. The heavyweight attraction these days is the Roman city of Ephesus but there are also many beach destinations, ranging from glitzy to relaxed.

5 The Turquoise Coast. The beaches along Turkey's Mediterranean shores—dubbed the Turquoise Coast—are some of the best in the country, and the ruins here are spectacular. With unspoiled seaside villages and charming hotels and *pansiyons*, this is very

close to paradise. Steer clear of the megaresorts though, which have invaded many towns, particularly around Antalya.

6 Cappadocia and Central Turkey. In magical Cappadocia, wind and rain have shaped soft volcanic rock into a fairy-tale landscape, where conical outcroppings were centuries ago turned into churches and homes. Southwest of Cappadocia is Konya, home to a museum

and tomb dedicated to the 13th-century founder of the whirling dervishes. Ankara, Turkey's capital, is also here, though it ranks fairly low on most visitors' itineraries.

7 The Far East and Black Sea Coast. It may not have the resorts, boutique hotels, and upscale restaurants of western Turkey, but there are impressive sites—both natural and man-made—including picturesque mountain villages; historic monasteries and churches; the ancient city of Ani and the towering Mt. Ararat, believed by some to be the resting place of Noah's Ark; and the fascinating Mt. Nemrut. In all these places, you're certain to get a taste of a different and rewarding Turkey.

TURKEY TODAY

Politics

In June 2011, the Justice and Development Party (AKP) won a decisive victory, giving the conservative party, led by Prime Minister Recep Tayyip Erdoğan and President Abdullah Gül, a third term. Since its accession to power in 2002, the AKP has sparked alarm among diehard secularists who assert that the party seeks to erode the secular legacy of Mustafa Kemal Atatürk. Some even contend that the AKP seeks to impose Sharia (strict Islamic day-to-day religious law) on the country, pointing to its efforts to remove restrictions on headscarf wearing and Erdoğan's vocal opposition to alcohol and tobacco use, though party leadership denies this.

Under the AKP, Turkey has moved toward greater political and economic engagement with the Arab world, as well as with developing countries in other regions, though the government says it remains committed to joining the EU. Most member states are in favor of Turkey's accession, but there are some strong opponents, and the talks have made only halting progress as Turkey faces criticism on several issues. Continued Turkish occupation of Northern Cyprus (which only Turkey recognizes as a sovereign nation) is one major stumbling block; another is the Turkish government's refusal to label the deaths of several hundred thousand Armenians during World War I as genocide. Domestically, critics cite criminal laws that punish anyone found guilty of insulting "Turkishness" (amended in 2008 to insulting the Turkish nation) and pressures on the media as further obstructions.

Simmering tensions between the AKP and its critics boiled over in the summer of 2013, when the heavy-handed police response to a peaceful sit-in at a central Istanbul park sparked weeks of antigovernment protests in Istanbul, Ankara, and elsewhere around the country. The two sets of elections scheduled for 2014 local elections in March and a first-ever popular vote for the country's president in August—will be watched carefully to see if the opposition from various segments of society can be turned into a real challenge to the AKP at the ballot box.

The Economy

The AKP's greatest bargaining chip in recent elections has been the upsurge of the Turkish economy since the aftermath of the 1999 Marmara earthquake, but this trend has shown signs of faltering in recent months. The country still enjoys a diverse economy: self-sufficient agricultural production, a massive textile industry, and a growing electronics sector, not to mention impressive tourism figures, with the number of foreign visitors nearly tripling between 2000 and 2010. International faith in the economy has driven considerable foreign investment, which has strengthened the Turkish lira. Inflation, which for 30 years led to the counting of the lira in millions, dropped low enough to allow the government to lop six zeroes from the old lira in 2005. But while Turkish annual GDP growth averaged more than 6% throughout most of the 2000s and hit 8.9% in 2010, it slowed sharply to 2.2% in 2012. Meanwhile inflation began to rise again in 2011, nearing 9% in summer 2013, and the lira's value against the dollar weakened to an all-time low. These trends, combined with Turkey's greatest economic liability—a sizable trade deficit, driven largely by the country's need to import foreign oil—and concerns about an overheating economy, have caused some renewed jitters among foreign investors.

Religion

In Istanbul they sell a T-shirt with the name of the city spelled using a crescent, a cross, and a Star of David. Turks pride themselves on their tolerance of other religions, a legacy of the Ottoman Empire, which governed people of all faiths. Turkey is a secular republic, however the population is overwhelmingly (99%) comprised of Muslims; the remaining 1% are Christians (mostly Greek Orthodox and Armenian Apostolic) and Jews. One reason for the relative harmony between people of different faiths may be the more relaxed approach toward religion found in much of Turkey. Many Turks drink alcohol and smoke cigarettes, and on any given day in Istanbul you're as liable to find as many scantily clad fashionistas walking down the street as women wearing headscarves (many of whom are plenty stylish themselves).

The Arts

Turkey has made many recent contributions to the art world—no surprise from a country that boasts such stunning antiquity. The Istanbul Film Festival will be in its 33rd year as of 2014: held every April, the festival awards prizes for both Turkish and international films. The country's most well-known creative mind may still be novelist Orhan Pamuk, who garnered Turkey's first Nobel Prize in 2006 for his dreamy yet historical novels, though the stars of other authors—as well as filmmakers, designers, and musicians—are on the rise as well. Additionally, Turkey's status as a large textile exporter has helped ensure the nation a place in fashion design, and Istanbul's Nişantaşı district is a maze of small boutiques selling imported and Turkish clothing. In the visual arts, Turkey is most famous for its ceramics and porcelain, especially handmade Kütahya and İznik tiles.

Sports

Turkey is a diehard soccer nation (they call it football), and heated rivalries run strong. Turkey's clubs boast lots of homegrown talent along with some players imported from Europe and South America. The Turkish national football team has enjoyed sporadic success in international play. In the last decade, the team reached the semifinals in the 2002 World Cup and 2008 European Cup. Basketball is also an increasingly popular sport in Turkey, which hosted the 2010 FIBA World Championship—and cheered its national team of "12 giant men" to a second-place finish.

Media

Turkish media seems to always be on people's lips, mainly because of Article 301 and the Turkish government's penchant for closing down, fining, or otherwise applying pressure on outlets that offend its sensibilities or offer criticism that is deemed too harsh. Until 2008, Article 301 forbade anyone from insulting "Turkishness," under pain of criminal prosecution (as mentioned above, the crime has now been changed to insulting the Turkish nation). Most cases are dropped but many notable Turks, including Orhan Pamuk, have been prosecuted. Frequent shutdowns of popular Internet sites, most prominently YouTube, have raised concerns about freedom of speech, as have recent detentions of journalists and the 2007 murder of Armenian-Turkish journalist Hrant Dink. Despite these controversies, the Turkish press remains large and vibrant, with a variety of voices represented.

TURKEY PLANNER

When to Go

Most tourists visit Turkey between April and the end of October but July and August are the busiest—and hottest—months. April through June and September to October offer more temperate weather, and crowds are smaller; hotel prices are usually lower, too.

Istanbul tends to be hot and humid in summer, cold and rainy in winter. The Mediterranean (Turquoise) and Aegean coasts have mild winters and hot summers; you can swim along either coast from late April into October. The Black Sea coast is mild and damp, with a rainfall of 90 inches per year. Central and Eastern Anatolia can be extremely cold in winter, with roads and mountain passes closed by snow; summers bring hot, dry weather, but cool evenings.

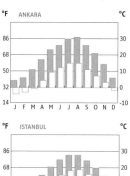

Getting Around

In Turkey you can travel by plane, car, bus, or train. With the advent of several new domestic airline companies in recent years, competition has increased and the cost of domestic flights has come down, so if your aim is to see several different areas of the country in a short time, you may want to fly between destinations.

Turkey has an extensive bus network, with buses serving all the major cities and even the smallest towns. Buses are generally safe, reliable, and surprisingly comfortable, making them an excellent way to travel around the country.

Renting a car allows you greater flexibility than traveling by bus and the chance to see places that are more off the beaten path, as well a glimpse of small-town Turkish life. Although major roads are generally in good condition, minor roads can be rough and badly paved, and it's wise to avoid driving at night. Traffic in large cities, particularly Istanbul, can be nightmarish. If you don't want a stick shift, reserve well in advance and specify automatic transmission.

Although they can be cheaper than buses, trains tend to be far slower and do not serve many areas of the country. High-speed rail lines run between Ankara and Konya, Ankara and Eskişehir, and Eskişehir and Konya, but for other routes it's not usually worth taking the train. ⇨ *For more detailed information, see the Travel Smart chapter and the specific regional chapters.*

What to Pack

For women, it's advisable to bring a scarf or shawl that will cover the hair (and shoulders, if you are wearing a sleeveless shirt) when entering mosques. If you're planning to visit Cappadocia, a flashlight can be useful for exploring cave churches and underground cities. If you're going anywhere with beaches or archaeological ruins, it's wise to bring sunscreen. An umbrella is a good idea if you're visiting Istanbul in the rainy winter months, though cheap ones are readily available for sale on city streets.

Festivals in Turkey

Istanbul is the country's festival capital, with events devoted to a wide variety of films, musical styles, and performing arts. Many of the biggest and most well-known events are put on by the Istanbul Foundation for Culture and Arts (İKSV), including the annual Istanbul Film Festival (April), Istanbul Music Festival (June), and Istanbul Jazz Festival (July), as well as the biannual Istanbul Biennial (to be held next in September and October 2015). The summer months are busy with rock music festivals, while film festivals tend to pick up in the fall, winter, and spring.

Festivals in other cities don't tend to draw as many big names but often feature performances in stunning settings such as the ancient theaters in Antalya (Aspendos International Opera and Ballet Festival) and Side (Side Culture and Art Festival). Many smaller cities and towns have festivals celebrating local crops and arts, such as the Kiraz Festivalı (Cherry Festival) in Tekirdağ each June or the Karagöz Festival held every November in Bursa, where traditional shadow puppets are believed to have originated.

To experience Turkey's unique take on wrestling, check out the country's top oil wrestlers contending for the oil wrestling championship each summer (typically late June or early July) just outside Edirne, where the greasy sport (known in Turkish as yağlı güreş) is said to have been invented by Ottoman soldiers back in 1361. Camel wrestling (deve güreşi) is also very popular, with tournaments held every winter during the animals' mating season, and primarily along the Aegean, with the largest event in Selçuk, near Ephesus. Watching the massive beasts heave themselves into each other is only part of the attraction—camel wrestling bouts are festive events with roving musicians, picnicking families, and rakı-drinking men cheering their favored animals on from the sidelines.

Another event that's a big draw for travelers is the Mevlâna Festival, held each December in Konya to mark the death of Mevlâna, or Rumi, the 13th-century Sufi saint whose followers are often known as whirling dervishes. Book festival tickets and accommodations well in advance.

Mosque Etiquette

The Turks are quite lenient about tourists visiting mosques and most are open to the public during the day, but there are some rules of etiquette:

It's best not to enter a mosque during the five daily prayer sessions, especially at midday on Friday, when attendances are higher.

Immodest clothing is not allowed but an attendant by the door will lend you a robe if he feels you aren't dressed appropriately. For women, bare arms and legs aren't acceptable, and men should avoid wearing shorts. Women should cover their heads before entering a mosque.

Shoes must be removed before entering a mosque; there's usually an attendant who watches over them, or you can put them in your backpack or handbag, or use the plastic bags often provided near the entrance.

It's considered offensive for a non-Muslim to sit down in a mosque.

It's also advisable to show respect by talking only in whispers.

Don't take photographs inside the mosque, particularly of people praying.

A small donation is usually requested for the upkeep of the mosque. The equivalent of about $3 is appropriate.

TURKEY
TOP ATTRACTIONS

Topkapı Sarayı

(A) Topkapı Palace was the home of the Ottoman sultans and the heart of the empire. Its grassy courtyards once buzzed with the comings and goings of soldiers, ambassadors, eunuchs, and pashas, while in the private chambers of the Harem, dripping with lovely blue tiles, the sultan's women schemed to bring a son to the throne. Former storerooms overflow with gold thrones, gigantic diamonds, and the holiest relics of Islam.

Aya Sofya

(B) Hagia Sophia was, for nearly a thousand years, the greatest church in Christendom. Built by the emperor Justinian in the 6th century, it's one of the few buildings of its age, size, and grandeur to survive today. Its giant dome shelters numerous historic artworks, from Byzantine mosaics to Islamic calligraphy.

Basilica Cistern

(C) Dark basements with serious damp problems aren't normally tourist attractions, unless they happen to be evocative Byzantine cisterns, held up by ancient columns that are reflected in water teeming with fish. Built 1,500 years ago as part of a system to preserve the city's water supply through siege and drought, Yerebatan Sarnıcı is a peaceful, surreal escape from the heat of an Istanbul summer.

The Blue Mosque

(D) Elegant, cascading curves and a central location make the Blue Mosque (aka Sultan Ahmet Camii) the most famous mosque in Istanbul. Inside is a spectacular coating of blue İznik tiles, which gives it its nickname.

Ephesus

(E) Ephesus was the metropolis of Asia Minor and archaeologists have revealed a treasure trove of ancient streets once walked by Alexander the Great and St.

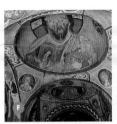

Paul. The houses, theaters, temples, toilets, even a brothel, and the columned facade of the Library of Celsus are in remarkably good condition.

Göreme Open-Air Museum

(F) The unique lunar landscape of Cappadocia is honeycombed with Byzantine churches cut from the rock in the Middle Ages, many decorated with beautiful frescoes. The most famous and easily accessible place to visit is the collection of churches and dwellings known as the Göreme Open-Air Museum.

Mt. Nemrut

(G) Atop a lonely mountain overlooking the Euphrates, this ancient shrine to the megalomania of one man is an extraordinary archaeological site. The oversize heads of King Antiochus and a pantheon of gods litter the ground beside a great burial mound.

Olympos

These jungle-entangled ruins in a valley by one of the Mediterranean's most beautiful beaches are overlooked by the natural eternal flame of the Chimaera. Few places combine so many of Turkey's many attractions as does Olympos.

Pamukkale

(H) Stunning white travertine pools of water cascade down a hillside in the hinterland of the Aegean coast: this unique rock formation was created over eons by mineral-rich water and has attracted tourists for millennia, although the rock pools are smaller, and not as pristine as they once were.

TOP TURKEY EXPERIENCES

Take a Boat up the Bosphorus

A boat ride along the Bosphorus is one of the most enjoyable ways to see the sprawling, magnificent city of Istanbul. From the ferry's vantage point, you'll see landmarks like the Dolmabahçe and Çırağan palaces; Ortaköy Mosque, perched right on the water's edge; and exquisite waterfront mansions, called *yalıs*, that were summer homes for the Ottoman elite. You'll also pass under the waterway's two suspension bridges, which connect Asia and Europe. While on board, sip a glass of Turkish tea and listen to the calls of the seagulls as you contemplate this beautiful meeting of two continents.

Scrub Down in a Turkish Bath

Before the era of indoor plumbing, going to a *hamam*, or public bath, was a central element of Turkish life. Today many beautiful centuries-old hammams are still in use, by both locals and tourists. In the hammam's steam room, you can relax on the heated marble platform in the center and rinse yourself at one of the marble washbasins. If you choose, you'll also be lathered, scrubbed, and massaged by a hammam attendant, whose goal seems to be to remove every last dry skin cell from the surface of your body. You'll emerge ultraclean, refreshed, and having taken part in an age-old Turkish tradition.

Stay in a Cave Hotel

Where but in Cappadocia can you sleep like the Flintstones while having all your creature comforts? Few of Cappadocia's inhabitants still live in traditional homes carved out of the soft tufa stone, but in recent years the area's hoteliers have been converting more and more of these "cave" dwellings into hotels, which range from basic inns for backpackers to upscale lodgings with plush furnishings, modern lighting, and fully equipped bathrooms, some even with Jacuzzis. Surrounded by Cappadocia's magical landscape, tucked cozily into your cave room at night, you'll feel almost as if you're on another planet.

Watch the Dervishes Whirl

Turkey is famous for its "whirling dervishes," a sect of Sufi mystics, the Mevlevi, who believe that ritual spinning in circles will bring them to union with God. This trancelike whirling is just one element of the *sema*, a highly symbolic religious ceremony that also includes music and Koranic recitation. Despite the fact that these dervish ceremonies have become increasingly tourist-oriented in recent years, attending a *sema* can still be a powerful and mesmerizing experience. Seeing the dervishes whirl is one of the main draws of the festival commemorating Rumi in Konya each December; there are also regular dervish performances (although not all of them terribly authentic) in Istanbul and elsewhere in Turkey.

Take a Blue Cruise

One of the most popular and relaxing ways to experience Turkey's Aegean and Mediterranean coasts is to take a Blue Cruise aboard a *gulet*, or wooden fishing vessel. Usually lasting several days (or longer), these cruises take passengers along the rugged coastline, with stops to visit ruins or villages. Away from the beach crowds, you'll enjoy the simple pleasures of swimming in remote coves, eating fresh-caught fish, and sleeping on your boat in a wooded inlet.

Quench Your Thirst Like the Locals

A trip to Turkey isn't complete without sampling certain quintessentially Turkish beverages. You can barely go anywhere without being offered a glass of *çay*, or tea: the lubricant for every social

and business encounter, it's consumed in Turkey at one of the world's highest rates per capita. The famous Turkish coffee, a thick, unfiltered brew made with extremely finely ground coffee beans, is in fact drunk far less often—primarily just on special occasions and as a digestive after meals. For something cold, try the ubiquitous *ayran*, a frothy, salted yogurt drink that's a refreshing accompaniment to a spicy meal of kebabs. Another unique beverage is *salep*, a sweet, milk-based hot drink served during the winter months. And don't forget to taste the anise-flavored national liquor, *rakı*.

See Cappadocia from Above

Taking a trip in a hot-air balloon is a thrilling way to see the amazing scenery of Cappadocia; for many people this is a highlight of their visit to the area. As your balloon follows the natural contours of the terrain, you'll look down into scenic valleys and sail right past "fairy chimneys" and unusual rock formations that seem almost close enough to touch. Flights leave at dawn, when the air is calmest and safest for flying, and end with a champagne toast.

Wander Among Ruins

With so many civilizations having occupied the land that is now Turkey, it's no surprise that the country is sprinkled with ancient ruins. The remains of Roman and Greek cities, with their impressive theaters, temples, stadiums, and colonnaded streets, compete with even older sites dating back to the Hittites. From beachside Patara and Olympos, to Termessos high up in the mountains, to the inland Aphrodisias, each spot is uniquely picturesque. At the best-preserved sites like Ephesus and Troy, you'll be among many visitors marveling at the ruins, but at places that are more off the beaten path, you'll be free to wander and explore with virtually no one else around.

Travel the Country by Bus

Taking an intercity bus in Turkey is a lot like taking an airplane in other countries. Since most Turks travel this way, bus terminals are as heavily trafficked as airports, and house a myriad of different companies with buses departing around the clock for every corner of the country. Seats are assigned, with unrelated males and females usually not seated together. During the ride, a uniformed bus attendant will regularly come around distributing snacks, water, and tea and coffee for no extra charge; he'll also offer you lemon-scented cologne to refresh your face and hands. Long-haul buses break every few hours at a rest stop so passengers can smoke, use the toilet, or just stretch their legs.

Experience and Appreciate Different Religions

Turkey is a cultural crossroads where the world's three Abrahamic religions have coexisted for centuries, and one of the most surprising things for many visitors is the way these religions are juxtaposed. Particularly in Istanbul, but in other places as well, you'll see ancient churches and synagogues right around the corner from mosques. This is an excellent opportunity to learn about different religious traditions as you listen to the Muslim call to prayer, visit Istanbul's Jewish Museum, or gaze at Eastern Orthodox iconography in a Byzantine church.

QUINTESSENTIAL TURKEY

Markets and Bargaining

A highlight of any trip to Turkey is a stroll through one of its markets; they provide the chance to experience the country at its most vibrant and colorful. The grand-daddy of them all is, of course, Istanbul's Grand Bazaar, a must-see simply for its size and historical significance. Though touristy, this is the most convenient place to stock up on souvenirs—inlaid wood backgammon sets, colorful ceramic bowls, and of course, rugs.

Remember, in nearly all of Turkey's markets, bargaining is the norm. Every vendor (and every buyer, as you will soon discover) has his or her own style, but some general rules govern the interaction. The seller will undoubtedly offer you a high initial price, so don't feel embarrassed to come back with a price that's much lower—try half, for starters. And remember, it's your money that's being spent, so feel free to walk out at any time—though

it's both bad manners and bad business to bargain aggressively or to decline to buy once the seller has accepted your offer. And don't shop in a rush: bargaining takes time.

Mezes

Good things come in small packages, and the Turkish tradition of serving appetizers known as mezes—the local version of tapas—is proof. Mezes originated when simple dishes—usually a slice of tangy, feta-like sheep's milk cheese with honeydew melon and fresh bread—were brought out to accompany rakı, the anise-flavored spirit that many call Turkey's national drink. From its humble origins, though, the meze tradition has developed into something quite elaborate. Today, in the *meyhanes* (literally "drinking places") of Istanbul and other restaurants throughout Turkey, waiters will approach your table with a heavy wooden tray loaded down with sometimes more than 20

For many Westerners, visiting Turkey is an exotic experience, but it's incredibly easy to get drawn into the everyday rituals that make life here such a pleasure. Eat, drink, shop ... you'll quickly understand the allure of the country and why the Turks are renowned for their hospitality.

different kinds of small dishes—smoky eggplant purée, artichoke hearts braised in olive oil, slices of cured fish, perhaps—for you to choose from. Just point at whatever looks good and the dish will be placed on your table.

Rakı

Typically served with fish, mezes, or a simple plate of melon and cheese, Turkey's favorite alcoholic beverage (similar to the Greek *ouzo* or Lebanese *arak*) is best consumed with water and ice, which give rakı the cloudy white color that inspired its nickname, "lion's milk." At up to 90 proof, be sure to pace yourself and don't worry if you can't keep up with the locals.

Tea

Visitors who come to Turkey expecting to be served thick Turkish coffee at every turn are in for a surprise—black tea is the hot beverage of choice and you'll be offered it wherever you go: when looking at rugs in the Grand Bazaar or when finishing your meal in even the humblest restaurant. Tea, called *çay*, is grown domestically along the slopes of the Black Sea coast. Flavorful and aromatic, it's not prepared from tea bags, a concept that horrifies most Turks; instead, it's made in a double boiler that has a larger kettle on the bottom for heating up the water and a smaller kettle on top where a dark concentrate is made using loose tea leaves. The resulting brew—strong and rust-colored—is usually served in a small, tulip-shaped glass, with two or more cubes of sugar (but never, Allah forbid, with milk or lemon). If you want your tea weak (light), ask for an *açık çay*.

Most teahouses will also carry a range of herbal teas, which are also popular, especially *ada çayı* (sage tea) and *ıhlamur çayı* (linden flower tea). *Elma çayı* (apple tea), usually made from a synthetic powder, is often served to tourists.

IF YOU LIKE

Ancient Sites

Turkey, a sort of bridge between Europe and Asia, has been a cultural crossroads for thousands of years. Numerous civilizations—Greeks from the west and Mongols from the east—settled or moved through the (vast) area at one point or another, leaving lasting and impressive reminders of their sojourns. As a result, virtually every region in Turkey has a bounty of stunning ancient ruins.

Ani: The abandoned former capital of a local Armenian kingdom, this haunting city in the middle of nowhere is filled with the ruins of stunning churches.

Cappadocia's underground cities: A marvel of ancient engineering, these subterranean cities—some reaching 20 stories down and holding up to 20,000 people—served as a refuge for Christians under siege from Arab raiders.

Ephesus: This remarkably well-preserved Roman city has a colonnaded library that seems as if it could still be checking out books and an amphitheater that appears ready for a show.

Mt. Nemrut: At the top of a desolate mountain, this 2,000-year-old temple—a collection of larger-than-life statues facing the rising and setting sun—is a testament to the vanity of an ancient king.

Termessos: This impregnable ancient city is set dramatically high up in the mountains above Antalya; even Alexander the Great and the Romans found it too difficult to attack.

Beaches

With 8,000 km (5,000 miles) of coastline, it's no wonder that Turkey is home to several world-famous beaches, and you can find all kinds: from pristine, remote coves to resort hotel beaches with water sports and all sorts of amenities.

İztuzu: A nesting ground for sea turtles, the beach here stretches for 5 sandy kilometers (3 miles) close to Dalyan, with a freshwater lagoon on one side and the turquoise waters of the Mediterranean on the other.

Kilyos and Şile: These beaches just outside Istanbul are among the nicest stretches of sandy shoreline along Turkey's Black Sea coast. Since both are relatively easy escapes from the city, they are often crowded on summer weekends. The water here is cold year-round, and swimmers should watch out for the powerful waves.

Ölüdeniz: This stunning lagoon near Fethiye boasts azure waters—which, like elsewhere along the Mediterranean, stay warm well into October—backed by white sand.

Patara: The 11-km (7-mile) stretch of unspoiled beach here is one of Turkey's best, with fine white sand and dunes. The picture-perfect coastline is reached by walking through a field scattered with ancient ruins, and has been spared the overdevelopment that has become a problem in some parts of the Mediterranean.

Sarımsaklı: The long stretch of sand here has made this one of the most popular beach destinations on the Aegean coast, with a row of inexpensive beach clubs running along the water parallel to a row of high-rise hotels and apartments on the shore. Take a *dolmuş* (shared taxi) from Ayvalık to Badavut Plajı (Badavut Beach) for a bit more peace and quiet.

Monuments

The Byzantine and Ottoman empires may be long gone, but they left behind some truly striking monuments: churches, mosques, and palaces that still hold the power to take your breath away.

As the former capital of both empires, Istanbul has the lion's share of Turkey's most famous structures, but there are also impressive ones to be found in every other part of the country.

Aya Sofya: The monumental church built by the emperor Justinian some 1,500 years ago continues to be an awe-inspiring sight—arguably the most impressive one in Istanbul or even all of Turkey.

Blue Mosque: With its cascading domes and shimmering tiles, this exquisite Istanbul mosque is one of the Ottomans' finest creations.

İshak Paşa Sarayı: In Turkey's far east, near the legendary Mt. Ararat, this 18th-century palace seems as if it was transported straight out of a fairy tale.

Kariye Museum: The former Chora Church, a 12th-century Byzantine structure on the periphery of Istanbul's Old City, is much smaller and less known than the Aya Sofya, but is filled with glittering mosaics and stunning frescoes that are considered among the finest in the world.

Topkapı Sarayı: The former home of the Ottoman sultans is a sumptuous palace with stately buildings, tranquil gardens, and the must-see Harem.

Museums

The country's wealth and depth of history guarantee that Turkey has lots of artifacts for its museums—even if there has been a problem with other countries shipping the booty off to foreign lands. The best and biggest museums are in Istanbul, where you can spend your days hopping from one fascinating exhibit to the other.

Istanbul Archaeology Museums: This sprawling institution near Topkapı Palace holds discoveries from digs throughout the Middle East.

Istanbul Modern: Stylish with a stunning waterfront location, this museum has a good collection of modern Turkish art and a photography gallery featuring adventurous contemporary work, and plays host to large, well-curated temporary exhibitions.

Gaziantep Zeugma Mosaic Museum: Opened in 2011 in Turkey's southeast, this museum is one of the country's best, with a world-class collection of Roman-era mosaics that were uncovered in the vicinity.

Museum of Anatolian Civilizations: Found in a restored 15th-century covered market in the capital city of Ankara, this museum holds masterpieces spanning thousands of years of local history.

Mevlâna Museum: Konya, in central Turkey, is home to this fascinating museum dedicated to the founder of the whirling dervishes and located inside what used to be a dervish lodge.

Museum of Underwater Archaeology: This unusual museum is located in a 15th-century castle in Bodrum on the southwestern Aegean coast and displays booty found in local shipwrecks.

ISLAM

Islam and Muhammad

Islam is an Abrahamic religion—one of the three largest (and somewhat interrelated) monotheistic religions in the world. The prophet Muhammad is believed to be descended from Ishmael, son of Abraham, through a union with his wife Sarah's handmaiden, Hagar. Abraham also sired Isaac, who was one of the patriarchs of Judaism and Christianity. Thus, many of the prominent figures in Judaism and Christianity—Adam, Moses, and Jesus—are also revered as prophets in Islam.

Muhammad was born in Mecca on the Arabian Peninsula (near the Red Sea in present-day Saudi Arabia). He became a religious figure in 610 AD when, according to Islamic tradition, while meditating in solitude he began to receive visions from the angel Gabriel. The words of these visitations became the *shuras* (verses) of the Koran, the holy book of Islam. When Muhammad first began preaching the new religion he was met with hostility by pagan tribesmen and forced to flee to Medina (also in Saudi Arabia) in 622 AD.

After converting the people of Medina to Islam, Muhammad returned to Mecca and converted his hometown, and by the end of the 6th century, Islam was the dominant religion in Arabia. In the subsequent centuries Muslim armies would sweep across North Africa and into Spain, throughout the Levant and eastward into Central Asia and Persia. Turkic peoples were converted to Islam sometime during their journey across Asia, and when the Seljuks swept through Byzantine territory in Asia Minor, they brought Islam with them. After the rise of the Ottoman Empire, Muslims crossed the Dardanelles into Eastern Europe, where the Turks conquered as far as Vienna. Today there are 1.6 billion Muslims throughout the world.

Islam Today

Islam is a comprehensive religion and its tenets touch all aspects of life. Devout Muslims pray five times a day: at sunrise, midday, in the afternoon, at sunset, and in the early evening—exact times are determined by the sun's passage. One of the first things visitors to Istanbul notice is the sound of the call to prayer—called the *ezan*—wafting from the minarets of local mosques. The focal point of Muslim prayer is the Sacred Mosque in Mecca, at the center of which is the Kabaa, a shrine said to have been built by Abraham and rebuilt by Muhammad. One duty of able-bodied Muslims is to make the pilgrimage, or *hajj*, to Mecca at least once in their lifetime.

Despite a lot of praying, modern Turks tend to have a relaxed approach to their religion. Many drink alcohol and smoke cigarettes—both of which are forbidden by strict interpretations of Islam. They typically don't, however, eat pork. While the Koran expressly forbids eating all carnivores and omnivores, pigs are especially abhorrent. Turkish men can be shameless flirts and modern women often dress in contemporary and revealing couture, though such behavior is not in keeping with Islamic ideas of modesty. There are, however, a great many conservative folks, too, and in the modern Turkey, the role of religion in society is hotly debated as the political old guard fights with the young, often more religious majority, over Atatürk's definition of secularism.

Islam and Art

Turkey enjoys a proud tradition of contributing to Islamic art. Ottoman mosque architecture incorporated many of the

Byzantine design elements that Mehmet II's armies found in Constantinople. Ottoman mosques with their spacious courtyards and mammoth domes, notably the Sultan Ahmet Camii, are essentially variations on Aya Sofya. Ottoman art also boasts some of the most elaborate and colorful tile designs in the world. The best Ottoman tiles were created in İznik during the 16th and 17th centuries and sport dazzling geometric and floral designs, which adhere to the Islamic prohibition on depicting human figures. This ban (which scholars believe inspired the iconoclastic period during which the Byzantines actually destroyed their own icons), came out of a desire to discourage idolatry. When Mehmet II conquered Istanbul, the first things to go were the mosaics and frescoes. He recognized, however, that the Christian images were works of art created by talented artists and, rather than having the images scratched out, he merely had them painted over. The Sultan's foresight has allowed restorers to uncover many of the Byzantine images that adorned the walls of the city's churches before 1453.

Ramadan

The Islamic holy month of Ramadan, called "Ramazan" in Turkish, lasts for 30 days and is an especially pious time. During it, observant Muslims abstain from eating, drinking, smoking, and sexual relations, from dawn to sunset; this self-denial teaches restraint and humility and is meant to bring one closer to God. Those who are fasting start each day with a predawn meal called *sahur*. At sundown, the fast is broken with a meal called *iftar*, which traditionally includes dates, soup and bread, olives, and other foods. Many restaurants offer special iftar fixed menus during Ramadan. In small towns and conservative parts of Turkey it may be hard to find restaurants open during the day during Ramadan, but in most cities and tourist areas it's not an issue. Though it's understood that non-Muslims will not be fasting, it's respectful to avoid eating in public (such as on the street or on public transportation) during Ramadan. You should also be prepared for the fact that in many places, even touristy areas like Sultanahmet in Istanbul, it's customary for drummers to walk around in the wee hours of the morning to wake people for the sahur—which can make for a rather startling, and early, awakening. The end of Ramadan is celebrated with a three-day holiday called Ramazan Bayramı or *Şeker Bayramı* ("sugar holiday"), during which people visit family and friends and plentifully consume sweets.

Another festival, *Kurban Bayramı* (feast of the sacrifice), requires Muslims to sacrifice an animal—typically a sheep or a cow—for their faith, honoring Abraham's willingness to sacrifice his firstborn son to God and God's last-minute substitution of a ram for the boy. Today, many Turks purchase vouchers that empower a professional butcher to make the kill in their name. Ramazan Bayramı and Kurban Bayramı are national holidays, and schools and many businesses are closed for the duration; museums and other attractions generally close only for the first day of the holiday.

TURKEY FOR BEGINNERS

Is Turkey cheap?

It depends on where you go. Istanbul, coastal towns in high season, and other tourist locations, like parts of Cappadocia, are quite a bit more expensive than elsewhere in Turkey. Hotels, especially in Istanbul, can be expensive—even along the lines of Paris or New York—though there are budget options. Anything imported is also expensive, so a cup of coffee at Starbucks in Istanbul will cost about the equivalent of $3 and a burger meal at McDonald's can cost as much as $8. Anything you buy at the Grand Bazaar or on İstiklal Street, in Istanbul, will be much more expensive than the same wares purchased off the beaten track.

How do I change money?
Does Turkey use the euro?

The Turkish word for change office is *döviz*. In Istanbul and most other tourist hubs, they seem to be everywhere. The fees for changing money aren't usually too outrageous, even in tourist locales; however, your best option is to use your ATM card, with which you usually get that day's exchange rage. Turkey doesn't use the euro (and beware sellers who insist you pay in foreign currency, which is illegal). The currency in Turkey is the Turkish lira. At the time of this writing, $1 = 1.91 TL and €1 = 2.55 TL, but the current economic situation means that the exchange rate is constantly in flux.

Will it be hard to find an alcoholic beverage in a Muslim country?

The anise-flavored spirit rakı is the traditional accompaniment to a meal of mezes and fish. In large cities like Istanbul and İzmir, and in resort towns along the coast, rakı is consumed quite liberally, as is Efes, the national beer. However, in smaller towns and more conservative parts of the country (particularly Central Anatolia), don't be surprised if alcohol is not for sale in restaurants or shops. Because of high taxes, alcoholic drinks, particularly those that are imported, are a fair bit more expensive in Turkey than they are in North America or Europe. Under a new law expected to go into effect in September 2013, retail outlets such as grocery stores and corner shops will not be able to sell alcoholic beverages between the hours of 10 pm and 6 am.

Is Turkish food spicy?

Not really. Turkish cuisine is similar to Greek and Hungarian food, with many dishes consisting of roasted meat, boiled or roasted vegetables, and rice. Turks often add red pepper on the side, but even heaped generously on your food, it generally won't set the mouth afire. The only thing that might take you by surprise is a roasted pepper, which often comes as a side with kebab dishes. Any food with too much heat is easily disarmed with a ubiquitous Turkish favorite—yogurt.

Will Ramadan affect my visit?

Ramadan, the month of fasting between sunrise and sunset, is one of the most exciting times to be in Turkey because after sunset, most Turks party down. It's rumored that your average Istanbullu actually gains weight during the fast. Elsewhere in Turkey, the degree of adherence to the fast typically increases in proportion to how far east you venture. In Istanbul and other tourist destinations it's not a problem to find restaurants that are open during the day, although in smaller and more conservative towns the profusion of closed eateries and cafés might make it more difficult to get a bite to eat, but it's by no means impossible.

Do I need to cover up?

No man or woman on the street is ever forced to wear a headscarf, turban, or veil, though many Turkish women do. Due to Turkey's official secularism, there are some government institutions where the covering of women is banned. In mosques, however, all women—including tourists—are expected to wear headscarves and all visitors must remove their shoes. In Istanbul and in many coastal cities you will see women dressed provocatively and even wearing bikinis, while in more conservative cities such behavior is frowned on. Female tourists anywhere who don't want to draw undue attention to themselves should err on the side of modesty.

Are the people friendly?

Yes! Turks are renowned for their hospitality and any local will gladly tout this reputation. In Istanbul you might find some cosmopolitan snobbishness, depending on the neighborhood, but just about everywhere else throughout the country Turks are friendly, talkative, and passionate, and often sport large grins along with a hidden mischievous side. As long as you are polite and avoid insulting the nation, its symbols, or its politics, you'll do just fine and in all probability you'll be awed by how kind and friendly Turkish people are.

What if I don't speak Turkish?

As in any European nation, it benefits salespeople and waiters in tourist hot spots to speak English, and many young professionals and students also make it a priority to learn the language. Some schools even have their instruction entirely in English. There's a good chance that the proprietors of your hotel, and perhaps the restaurant servers that you meet will speak perfectly adequate English. Outside of these groups, and in more remote locations, your average Turk has a less firm grasp of the language, but even still you probably won't have too big a problem, though learning a few key phrases is a good idea before traveling (F*See the vocabulary lists at the back of this book*). Turkish is an easy language to read as it is written in the Latin alphabet and is entirely phonetic. For the most challenging of linguistic tangles, pointing in a dictionary or trying the same word in a few other languages will often suffice.

Should I be afraid of terrorism?

Terrorism does, unfortunately, seem to be a part of the world we live in today and there is a certain amount of risk inherent in traveling anywhere. In Istanbul the risk of being the victim of a terrorist attack is not much higher than in any European capital: London and Madrid have both been host to terrorist attacks far greater in magnitude than anything in Istanbul. Elsewhere in Turkey the threat level depends on where you are. In the tourist-friendly cities of the Mediterranean and Aegean regions as well as Cappadocia the risk is negligible. In the east, where the government is still fighting Kurdish separatists, a bit more caution might be called for, though most of the violence takes place in remote areas where visitors are unlikely to venture. The key thing is to stay informed, keep a low profile, and bear in mind that while terrorist attacks are dramatic you still have better odds of being struck by lightning.

GREAT ITINERARIES

BEST OF TURKEY, 8 DAYS

A week in Turkey will only give you a taste of what the large and varied country has to offer, from the big-city buzz of Istanbul to the surreal natural landscape of Cappadocia. Regardless, this busy itinerary makes sure you hit the big sights and whets your appetite for a return visit.

Days 1–3: Istanbul

Arrive in Istanbul and check into a hotel in Sultanahmet, the neighborhood close to the major sites. If you have time, visit the Aya Sofya, the Blue Mosque, and the Basilica Cistern, all within a stone's throw of each other. The Aya Sofya is one of the world's largest and most important religious monuments, as well as one of the most widely regarded examples of Byzantine architecture. The Blue Mosque and its 20,000 shimmering blue-green İznik tiles showcase the grandeur of Ottoman architecture while the Basilica Cistern is a stunning example of an ancient underground waterway and a quiet place to relax amid the chaos of the city above.

Start your second day with a visit to Topkapı Palace, home to the Ottoman sultans for nearly 400 years, and explore the gorgeously tiled rooms of the Harem and the palace collections of weaponry, religious artifacts, and jaw-dropping jewels. In the afternoon, cross the Galata Bridge and head up to the waterfront art museum Istanbul Modern, where you can browse artwork from both local and international contemporary artists. Continue your journey into the city's contemporary culture at the numerous art galleries and other exhibition spaces along İstiklal Caddesi, winding up at one of Beyoğlu's many meyhanes for a dinner of mezes and rakı.

On your last day, be sure to check out any of the major sites you missed on day one. Then make a stop at the famous Grand Bazaar to try your hand at haggling and pick up some classic Turkish souvenirs.

Day 4: Ephesus

Take an early flight from Istanbul to İzmir (roughly one hour) and rent a car at the airport to drive the 84 km (52 miles) to Ephesus, a well-preserved ancient Roman city that is one of the most popular tourist attractions in Turkey. Explore the marble-paved streets and partially reconstructed buildings and monuments. Depending on your forward travel schedule, you can either return to İzmir for the night or stay near Ephesus in the town of Selçuk or the attractive mountain village of Şirince, 10 km (6 miles) away from the ruins. Either way, if you have an extra day, detour to the Çeşme Peninsula on your way back to İzmir for some quality beach time.

Day 5: Ankara

Take an early flight from İzmir to Ankara, Turkey's capital city, where you won't want to miss the Museum of Anatolian Civilizations, with its ancient treasures going back nearly 10 millennia, and Anıtkabir, the mausoleum of Mustafa Kemal Atatürk, the revered founder of the modern Turkish Republic.

Days 6 and 7: Cappadocia

Rent a car or buy a bus ticket for the approximately 4½-hour drive to Göreme, the most convenient base for a short visit in Cappadocia. Stay at one of the comfortable boutique hotels fashioned out of the area's many old cave homes and spend the afternoon exploring the Göreme Open-Air Museum, a breathtaking complex of cave monasteries and rock-cut churches full of brightly colored frescoes.

Greet the sunrise on your second day in Cappadocia from an early morning hot-air balloon ride, one of the most popular ways to take in the area's fantastical rock formations. In the afternoon, visit the Kaymaklı or Derinkuyu underground city, both mazes of rooms descending deep into the earth that once sheltered up to 20,000 people. Close out your trip with a meal and some local wine at one of the growing number of fine restaurants in nearby Ürgüp.

Day 8: Return to Istanbul

You can fly back to Istanbul from Nevşehir, about a 30-minute bus ride away. If your flight is later in the day, go for a morning hike in the Rose Valley before departing Göreme.

GREAT ITINERARIES

CROSSROADS OF FAITH, 9 DAYS

Once home to powerful Christian and Muslim empires, the area that makes up modern Turkey has played a crucial role in the development of both religions. This tour takes you to some of the most important religious sites in Turkey, places that still poignantly convey spirituality.

Days 1 and 2: Istanbul

Arrive in Istanbul and check into a hotel in Sultanahmet. If you have time, visit two of the quintessential Istanbul sites: the Aya Sofya and the nearby Blue Mosque.

Start your second day with a visit to the Süleymaniye Mosque, one of the greatest achievements of Mimar Sinan, the Ottomans' favorite architect. Then head to the western edge of Istanbul's old city walls, where you'll find the Kariye Museum in what was the Byzantine Chora Church. It's filled with glittering mosaics and beautiful frescoes that are considered among the finest in the world. End your day in Eyüp Camii, a historic mosque complex on the Golden Horn that is one of the holiest areas in Istanbul.

Day 3: Konya

Take a morning flight from Istanbul to Konya and pick up a rental car at the airport. In Konya you'll see the magnificent Mevlâna Museum and tomb, dedicated to the life and teachings of Rumi Celaleddin, the 13th-century mystic who founded the order of the whirling dervishes. The city's 13th-century Alaaddin Mosque is also worth a visit. In the evening, catch a live dervish performance at the cultural center behind the museum if they're performing.

Days 4 and 5: Cappadocia

After Konya, head east toward the lunar landscape of Cappadocia, where the volcanic rock outcroppings and cliffs were used by local Christians centuries ago as churches, monasteries, and homes. One of the best places to see these unique structures is in the village of Göreme. Spend the night in one of the hotels built into the stone caves. Ürgüp has what is regarded by some as the best collection of boutique hotels in Turkey.

The attractions in Cappadocia are above ground and below it. Under siege from Arab invaders in the 7th through 10th centuries, local Christians built a series of underground cities—some going down 20 stories and capable of holding 20,000 people—where they sought refuge. The ruins in Kaymaklı and Derinkuyu are marvels of ancient engineering. Get an early start if you want to beat the summer crowds, and bring a flashlight.

If you have time, consider a visit to the Ihlara Valley, a deep gorge that has numerous monasteries and churches cut into its cliffs and a lovely green river running through it.

Days 6 and 7: Cappadocia to Antakya

From landlocked Cappadocia, head south to the Mediterranean Sea and the city of Antakya, formerly known as Antioch, which played an important role in the early days of Christianity. It's a long drive of 482 km (300 miles), so plan on spending most of the day on the road. Fortunately, there's a highway for most of the way. If you get to Antakya early enough, head to the Church of St. Peter, in a cave on the outskirts of town. Blackened by 2,000 years' worth of candle smoke, this is perhaps the oldest church in the world,

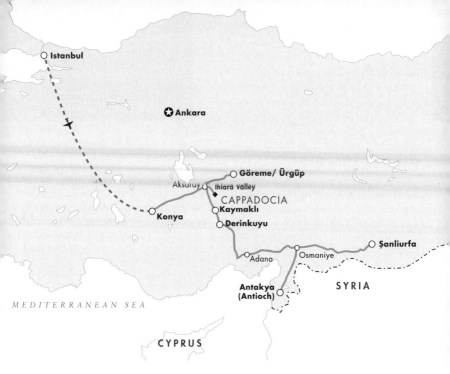

where the apostle Paul preached to his converts.

The next day, spend the morning walking through the narrow lanes and the lively bazaar of Antakya's old town. Then visit the Archaeological Museum, which has an excellent collection of Roman and Byzantine mosaics and other artifacts. Antakya is famous for its Syrian-influenced cooking, so have lunch at one of the restaurants serving local dishes (Antik Han or Hatay Sultan Sofrası are two good options). After lunch, begin your 351-km (218-mile) drive to Şanlıurfa, where you can stay in one of several grand old stone houses that have been converted into small hotels.

Day 8: Şanlıurfa

Many Muslims believe the biblical patriarch Abraham was born in Şanlıurfa, and a fascinating and peaceful pilgrimage site has developed here, with mosques and a park with spring-fed pools filled with sacred carp. After lunch, make the quick drive to the small village of Harran, 45 km (28 miles) southeast of Şanlıurfa.

Harran is mentioned in the Bible as a place where Abraham lived for a period, and the village, with its ancient stone walls and unique beehive-shape houses, has the look of a place that hasn't changed much since biblical times. Another worthwhile side trip is the archaeological site of Göbekli Tepe, 15 km (9.3 miles) northeast of Şanlıurfa, and thought to be the world's first temple—6,000 years before Stonehenge.

Day 9: Şanlıurfa and Return to Istanbul

You can fly back to Istanbul from Şanlıurfa, or from nearby Gaziantep (145 km [90 miles] away). If you have a flight from Şanlıurfa later in the day, take some time to explore Şanlıurfa's bustling and authentic bazaar, where coppersmiths hammer and tailors work on foot-powered sewing machines. If your flight is out of Gaziantep, consider driving there in the morning in order to have lunch at one of that city's famous restaurants. Imam Çağdaş, which has great kebabs and heavenly baklava, is your best bet.

GREAT ITINERARIES

BEST BEACHES AND RUINS, 10 DAYS

It's fairly safe to say that the main features that attract visitors to Turkey are the beaches and the magnificent archaeological sites. This itinerary covers the best of both, along the two major coastlines. Adding a couple of days in Istanbul at the beginning or end makes a perfect trip.

Days 1 and 2: Istanbul

Arrive in Istanbul and head to one of the charming small hotels in Sultanahmet (the Empress Zoë and the Sarı Konak Oteli are two good options). If you have time, go to see the awe-inspiring Aya Sofya and the nearby Blue Mosque.

The next day, visit Topkapı Sarayı to get a sense of how the Ottoman sultans lived (make sure to take a tour of the Harem). From there, go to the nearby Archaeological Museum, displaying Roman and Greek artifacts that come from many of the sites that you'll soon be visiting. In the evening, head by taxi to one of the little neighborhoods along the Bosphorus, such as Ortaköy or Arnavutköy, for a fish dinner by the waterside (if you time it right, you can take one of the limited Bosphorus commuter ferry services there, though none go back down to the Beyoğlu or Sultanahmet areas at night).

Day 3: Ephesus

On the morning of Day 3, take the roughly one-hour flight to İzmir and rent a car at the airport to make the quick 84-km (52-mile) drive down to the ancient Roman city of Ephesus. If you get an early flight out, you should be here by lunch. The site is one of the most popular tourist attractions in Turkey, and you'll see why: the buildings and monuments are remarkably well preserved and easily give you

the sense of what life must have been like in this important trading city 2,000 years ago. After Ephesus, visit the nearby Meryemana, a pilgrimage site for both Christians and Muslims where the Virgin Mary is believed to have spent her final years. You can spend the night in Selçuk, which is right on the doorstep of Ephesus, but better yet, head 10 km (6 miles) into the mountains above Selçuk and stay in the tranquil village of Şirince, surrounded by fruit orchards and vineyards.

Day 4: Priene, Miletus, and Didyma

Start off your day with a visit to Priene, an ancient Greek city that sits on a steep hill looking out on a valley below—it's about 62 km (38½ miles) from Şirince. From there continue 16 km (10 miles) south to Miletus, another Greek city, where a spectacular theater is all that remains of its former glory. Twenty kilometers (12 miles) south of here is Didyma and its magnificent Temple of Apollo, its scale as grand as the Parthenon, with 124 well-preserved columns. To keep yourself from burning out on ruins, continue another 5 km (3 miles) to the white-sand beach of Altıkum (this is not the same as the similarly named beach near Çeşme) and take a dip in the warm water, then have a meal at one of the numerous fish restaurants lining the shore. Drive back to the busy seaside resort town of Kuşadası, where there are several small *pansiyons* (guesthouses) at which you can spend the night.

Day 5: Aphrodisias

Get an early start for the drive to the ruins of Aphrodisias, a Roman city named in honor of the goddess of love, Aphrodite. High up on a plateau and ringed by mountains, Aphrodisias has a spectacular setting and as much to offer as Ephesus, although with significantly fewer crowds;

there are many ancient sites in Turkey, but Aphrodisias in quite evocative, especially after you've visited Ephesus. From here work your way down to the coast and the quiet town of Dalyan, where you can spend the next two nights in one of several riverside *pansiyons*.

Day 6: Dalyan, İztuzu Beach, and the Rock Tombs of Kaunos

At Dalyan's riverside quay, you can hire a boat to take you to the ruins of ancient Kaunos, a city dating back to the 9th century BC and famous for its collection of tombs cut into the surrounding cliffs. Watch for the herons and storks idling in the river's reeds when you stop to take a look at the ruins. Continue your day cruise to the famed İztuzu Beach, a 5-km (3-mile) stretch of undeveloped sand that's also a nesting ground for sea turtles. There are a few snack bars at the beach, but you might want to consider bringing a picnic lunch along.

Day 7: Letoon, Patara, and Kaş

The mountainous coastal region south of Dalyan is the home of ancient Lycia. An independent and resourceful people, the Lycians built a series of impressive cities whose ruins are sprinkled throughout the area. To get a good glimpse of one of these Lycian cities, drive from Dalyan to Letoon, a UNESCO World Heritage site with three fascinating temples dating back to the 2nd century BC. From here continue to Patara, another Lycian ruin that has the added bonus of being right next to one of Turkey's finest and longest beaches. You can spend the night in the relaxing little seaside town of Kaş, which has several good lodging and eating options. If you have an extra day, take the three-hour boat trip out of Kaş through the beautiful Kekova Sound and its fascinating underwater Greek and Roman ruins.

Day 8: Olympos

On your eighth day (ninth if you spend an extra day in Kaş), drive to the Lycian ruins of Olympos, which have a small river running through them that ends at a beautiful crescent beach backed by mountains. Stay in the little village of Çıralı, a good spot for an evening visit to the legendary Chimaera, small flames of ignited gas that shoot out of the rocks of a nearby mountain.

Day 9: Antalya/Termessos (or Aspendos)

Spend your last night in the rapidly growing resort city of Antalya, but before going there head up into the rugged mountains above the city to visit the dramatic site of Termessos, an impregnable city that both

Alexander the Great and the Romans decided not to attack. (Alternatively, continue 48 km [30 miles] past Antalya to visit Aspendos, a spectacular Roman theater that is still in use today.) Return to Antalya in the afternoon and stay in one of the renovated old Ottoman houses in the Kaleiçi, the city's charming old town.

Day 10: Return to Istanbul

If you have time before your flight back to Istanbul, use the morning to walk around the narrow streets of the Kaleiçi and then visit the city's large Archaeological Museum. If you need to stock up on souvenirs before your return, head to Antalya's bazaar before going to the airport.

TIPS

Roads are mostly in good condition, though rarely wider than two lanes or lit at night, so driving after sunset isn't recommended.

These itineraries take you through some of the most popular spots in Turkey, so book lodgings in advance.

Consider doing one of the itineraries in the fall: prices will be lower, the crowds will be gone, it won't be baking hot, and the ocean will still be warm enough for swimming.

Many towns have fabulous weekly markets, when farmers and craftspeople from the area come to sell their goods; try to time some of your trip around one of them. Many markets are held on Saturday, but check locally.

TURKEY THROUGH THE AGES

According to an ancient saying, "Turkey is a man running West on a ship heading East." Today this adage is more apt than ever; amid growing tensions over the current government's Islamic leanings, the nation is still seeking EU membership. The ambivalence here underscores the country's age-old search for identity. Few can deny that Turkey is once again trying to remake itself.

Situated at the point where the continents of Europe and Asia come together, Turkey has served as the stomping ground for sundry migrations of mankind. Hittites, Persians, the armies of Alexander the Great, Romans, Byzantines, and Ottomans all have their place in the intriguing history of this land, whose early inhabitants, living on the vast Anatolian plain, created many of civilization's most enduring myths.

Ancient Troy, immortalized in Homer's *Iliad*, is located on Turkey's Aegean coast, while in Phrygia, it is said, Alexander the Great split the Gordian knot with his sword, fulfilling the prophecy that this feat would make him king of Asia. These colorful legends are no match for the plain facts of history, but together they make Turkey one of the most fascinating places on earth.

| TIMELINE | 25,000 BC Paleolithic humans inhabit Karain Cave in Anatolia | 7000 BC Anatolians begin to grow crops and raise livestock | 6500 BC Çatal Höyük thrives as the world's earliest urban settlement |

| Prehistory | 7000 BC | 6000 BC | 5000 BC |

Top: Archaeologist discovers obsidian objects in a Çatal Höyük house.
Right: Entrance to Karain Cave, Antalya.
Far right: Statues from Hacılar.

25,000 BC–3000 BC

The Earliest Cultures

The history of the lands that comprise modern Turkey began to unfold as long as 25,000 years ago, on the plains of Anatolia (Asia Minor), where bones, teeth, and other evidence of early humans have been unearthed in the Karain Cave near Antalya. Some of the most fascinating finds include Göbekli Tepe (in southeast Turkey), the world's oldest known shrine, whose monolithic pillars and templelike structures were erected by hunter-gathers around 9500 BC. Then there are the first signs of agricultural life, from about 7000 BC, which have been found at Hacılar, near Bur-

dur. And by 6500 BC, Çatal Höyük, (near Konya)—often considered the world's first city—was at its height; evidence suggests that as many as 8,000 inhabitants lived in flat-roofed, one-story mud-brick houses, grew crops, and fashioned clay figurines representing a mother goddess. By 3000 BC the residents of many such Anatolian settlements were wielding tools and creating figurines hammered from gold, silver, and copper, and trading them with Mesopotamians to the east and Mediterranean cultures to the west.

■ Sights to see:
Karain Cave, Antalya
(⇨ Ch.5).
Çatal Höyük (⇨ Ch.6).

2000 BC–1200 BC

The Hittites

Ushering in the Bronze Age, the Hittites arrived from lands north of the Black Sea around 2000 BC to establish a powerful empire that flourished for almost 800 years. They expanded their holdings as far east as Syria and, c.1258 BC, made an accord with Egypt's great Pharaoh Ramses II—the world's first recorded peace treaty. The Hittites adopted a form of hieroglyphics, developed a pantheon of deities, established a complex civil code, and built shrines and fortifications, many of which have been unearthed at such sites as Alacahöyük, Hattuşa and Kültepe.

c. 1258 BC Hittites make
the world's first peace accord,
with the Egyptians

| 4000 BC | 3000 BC | 2000 BC | 1000 BC |

1

IN FOCUS TURKEY THROUGH THE AGES

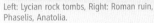

Left: Lycian rock tombs, Right: Roman ruin,
Phaselis, Anatolia.

During this time, colonies were settled on the west coast of modern-day Turkey by Achaeans and Mycenaeans from Greece, who went on to wage a famous war against the Anatolians in Troy (c. 1200 BC), later immortalized by Homer in *The Iliad*. After their victory, not all Achaeans rushed back home.

■ Sights to see:
Troy (⇨ *Ch. 3*).
Museum of Anatolian Civilizations, Ankara (⇨ *Ch. 6*).

1200 BC–600 BC

Invaders & Home-grown Kingdoms

With the passage of time, the Hittite society began to fall to encroaching civilizations. Lycians, Mycenaens, and other early Greeks sailed across the Aegean to establish Ephesus, Smyrna, and other so-called Ionian cities on the shores of Anatolia. The Phrygians also migrated to Anatolia from Thrace, flourishing for a mere century or so, until 690 BC—though long enough to leave the legends of kings Gordias and Midas: Gordias, of the intricate knot that could not be unraveled until Alexander the Great slashed through it with a bold stroke of his sword,

and Midas, of the touch that turned everything to gold. The Lydians emerged as a power in the 7th century BC by introducing the world's first coinage. With their vast gold deposits, they became so wealthy that the last of the Lydian kings has forever since been evoked with the term "rich as Croesus."

■ Sights to see: Lycian tombs at Fethiye and Carian tombs at Dalyan (⇨ *Ch. 5*). Greek ruins at Phaselis (⇨ *Ch. 5*).

Far left: Alexander the Great, King of Macedon, fighting, at Battle of Issus, mosaic, circa 100 BC.
Top: Arch at Ephesus.
Left: Temple of Trajan, built to honor Trajan, the Roman Emperor (98-117).

550 BC–50 BC
Persians & Alexander the Great

The Persians invaded Anatolia in 546 BC and controlled the area for two centuries, until Alexander the Great swept across Asia. The young warrior's kingdom died with him in 323 BC, and Anatolia entered the Hellenistic Age. Greek and Anatolian cultures mixed liberally amid far-flung trading empires. None of these kingdoms were more powerful than Pergamum (present-day Bergama). Adorned with great sculptures such as the Laocoön and an acropolis modeled after that of Athens, it was one of the most beautiful cities of the ancient world.

■ Sights to see:
Pergamum (⇨ Ch. 3).

100 BC–AD 100
Romans & Early Christians

By the middle of the 1st century BC, Roman legions had conquered Anatolia, and Ephesus had become the capital of the Roman province of Asia Minor. As Christianity spread through the empire, it was especially well received in Anatolia. Saint John is said to have come to Ephesus, bringing Mary with him, and both are allegedly buried nearby. Saint Paul, a Jew from Tarsus (on Turkey's coast), traveled through Anatolia and the rest of the empire spreading the Christian word for 30 years, until his martyrdom in Rome in AD 67.

■ Sights to see:
Ephesus (⇨ Ch. 4).

306–563
The Rise of Constantinople

Constantine the Great became Roman emperor in 306 and made two momentous moves: he embraced Christianity and re-established ancient Byzantium as the capital of the increasingly unwieldy Roman empire. With the fall of Rome in AD 476, the Byzantine Empire ruled much of the Western world from its newly named capital Constantinople. The Byzantines reached their height under Justinian I (527–563), whose accomplishments include the Justinian Code (a compilation of Roman law), and such architectural monuments as the Aya Sofya.

■ Sights to see:
Aya Sofya, Istanbul (⇨ Ch. 2).

527 Byzantine Empire flourishes under Emperor Justinian	1071 Seljuks defeat the Byzantines	1300 Ottoman Empire established	1520 Ottoman Empire enters Golden Age
650 AD	**950 AD**	**1250 AD**	**1550 AD**

1

IN FOCUS TURKEY THROUGH THE AGES

Top left: Map of Constantinople.
Above: Wall tiles, Topkapı Palace, Istanbul.
Bottom left: Byzantine mosaic of Jesus, Aya Sophia, Istanbul.
Left: Süleyman the Magnificent.

The First Turks

1071–1300

Around the 8th century, the nomadic Turkish Seljuks rose to power in Persia and began making inroads into Byzantine lands. The defeat of the Byzantine army in 1071 ushered in the Great Seljuk Empire and Seljuks converted their new subjects to Islam. In turn, Pope Urban II launched the First Crusade to reclaim Byzantium in 1097. Armies from Western Europe clashed with Seljuk forces for the next two centuries. The Mongols, under Genghis Khan, swept down from the north and put an end to the weakening Seljuks.

■ Sights to see:
Mevlana Museum, Konya
(⇨ *Ch.6*).

The Rise of the Ottomans

1300–1500

By 1300, the Seljuk lands had been divided into independent states, known as the ghazi emirates. Osman I was one of the leaders, and began to expand what would come to be known as the Ottoman Empire, establishing a capital at Bursa. By the 14th century the Ottomans had extended their rule over most of the eastern Mediterranean. Constantinople, the last Byzantine holdout, fell in 1453 and became the new Ottoman capital, which it would remain until the founding of modern Turkey.

■ Sights to See
Topkapı Palace, Istanbul
(⇨ *Ch.2*).

The Golden Age of the Ottomans

1520–1566

By the time of the reign of Süleyman the Magnificent, the Ottomans controlled lands stretching east into Persia, through Mecca and Medina (Islam's holiest cities), south into Egypt and west into central Europe. The empire entered its Golden Age under Süleyman, himself a poet and author of civil laws. Literature, music, and craftsmanship thrived, while Süleyman's architect, Sinan, built beautiful shrines such as the Süleymaniye Mosque in Istanbul.

■ Sights to see:
Süleymaniye Mosque, Istanbul (⇨ *Ch.2*). Blue Mosque, Istanbul (⇨ *Ch.2*).

TIMELINE

| 1876 Abdülhamid II becomes Sultan | Late 19th c. Ottoman Empire begins massacre of Armenian populations | 1915 Gallipoli campaign | 1923 Turkish Republic is established |

1875   1900   1925

1571–early 1900s

The Long Decline

The defeat of the Otto-
man navy in 1571 by a
coalition of European
forces at the Battle of Lepanto, off the western coast
of Greece, heralded the end
of Ottoman supremacy in
the Mediterranean. Incompe-
tent leadership plagued the
empire almost continually
over the next several centuries, and the empire shrank.
Abdülhamid II supported
liberal reforms when he
became Sultan in 1876, and
effectively Westernized many
aspects of public works,
education, and the economy.
He also turned his energies
to reinvigorating Islamic
identity, aiming to unite the
increasingly restive ethnic
groups of the empire. Most
infamously, he suppressed
Armenian revolutionary
groups and an estimated
300,000 Armenians were
killed under his regime. A
movement of revolutionary
societies grew throughout
the country and one in particular, the so-called Young
Turks, rose up in revolution
in 1908, deposing the Sultan.
By the early 20th century,
the days of the once great
empire—now known as the
"Sick Man of Europe"—were
clearly numbered.

■ Sights to see:
Dolmabahçe Palace, Istanbul
(⇨ Ch. 2)

WWI–1938

The Birth of the Republic

World War I, during
which the Ottomans
sided with the Axis
powers, put an end to what
was left of the Ottoman
Empire. In a key battle in
1915, the Allies landed at
Gallipoli but were eventually repulsed with heavy
losses. In 1920, the Treaty
of Sèvres turned Ottoman
lands over to France, Italy,
Greece, and other vic-
tors, but a nationalist hero
had come onto the scene:
Mustafa Kemal formed the
first Turkish Grand National
Assembly in Ankara and led
the forces that routed Greek
armies, pushing across
Anatolia to reclaim lands
once part of the Byzantine

1

IN FOCUS TURKEY THROUGH THE AGES

Top left, opposite: Battle of Lepanto. Bottom left, opposite: Süleymaniye Mosque. Bottom right, opposite: Sultan Abdülhamid II. Left: Mustafa Kemal Atatürk Above: Pera Palas Hotel, Istanbul, Turkey: Atatürk's bedroom preserved as a museum.

Empire. In 1923 the Treaty of Lausanne banished foreign powers and established the boundaries of a Turkish state with its capital in Ankara. Kemal—who took the name Atatürk (literally "Father of the Turks")—reinvented Turkey as a modern nation. Turkey embraced secularism and instituted widespread reforms that replaced religious law with secular jurisprudence, advanced education, implemented universal suffrage, and introduced a Western style of dress, abolishing the fez as a symbol of Ottoman backwardness.

■ Sights to see:
Gallipoli (⇨ Ch.3).

1938–Present

After Atatürk

Turkey has largely allied itself with the West since Atatürk's death in 1938, though the balance between secularization and the religious right has at times been precarious, with the military often stepping in to ensure the country's Western leanings. A military coup in 1960 removed a Democratic Party government that had reinstituted the call for prayer in Arabic and instituted other right-wing reforms. The military seized control in two other coups, in 1971 and 1980, while the government of Turgut Özal from 1983 to 1993 ushered in widespread legal and economic reforms.

First elected in 2002, the Islamic-rooted AKP deftly led the country through the first years of the new millennium, reinvigorating the economy, reinvigorating Turkey's candidacy for EU membership, and forging economic and political relationships with once-contentious neighbors. But the future looks a bit less rosy as EU talks have stalled, fresh conflicts have broken out in the region, the economy has weakened, and domestic opposition to the AKP has become more vocal.

■ Sights to see:
The Anıtkabir (Atatürk's Mausoleum), Ankara (⇨ Ch.6).

ISTANBUL

WELCOME TO ISTANBUL

Çiçek Pasajı

TOP REASONS TO GO

★ **Change continents:**
Spend the morning in Europe and the afternoon in Asia, with just a ferry ride in between; how cosmopolitan is that?

★ **Cruise the Bosphorus:**
Taking a boat ride up the strait, past scenic waterfront neighborhoods and forested slopes topped with fortresses, is quintessentially Istanbul.

★ **Haggle in the bazaars:**
Bargain like the locals do as you make your way through the Grand Bazaar and Spice Bazaar—it may be a bit touristy, but it's fun.

★ **Marvel at ancient domes:** From the stunning Aya Sofya to the graceful Süleymaniye Mosque, the city's greatest works of imperial architecture never cease to impress, especially from the inside as you look up.

★ **Ogle at opulence:** With their sumptuous decor and fascinating harem quarters, the Topkapı and Dolmabahçe palaces offer a glimpse of the splendor of the Ottoman Empire.

1 **Sultanahmet.**
The Blue Mosque, Topkapı Palace, Aya Sofya, and the Istanbul Archaeological Museums are just some of the impressive attractions in this historic (but crowded) Istanbul neighborhood.

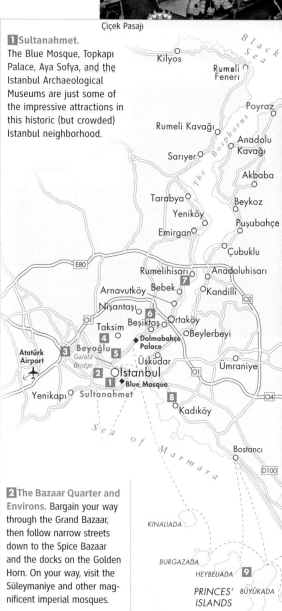

2 **The Bazaar Quarter and Environs.** Bargain your way through the Grand Bazaar, then follow narrow streets down to the Spice Bazaar and the docks on the Golden Horn. On your way, visit the Süleymaniye and other magnificent imperial mosques.

Grand Bazaar

3 **The Western Districts.** A gem of Byzantine art, the former Chora Church is the highlight of the western districts, which also include the historically Greek and Jewish neighborhoods of Fener and Balat.

4 **Beyoğlu.** With its elegant 19th- and early-20th-century apartment buildings, Beyoğlu is the place to see for yourself that "new" is a relative term in this city. The main pedestrian thoroughfare off Taksim Square, İstiklal Caddesi, is lined with shops and cafés.

5 **Galata and Karaköy.** These ancient, rapidly gentrifying neighborhoods are home to both historic sites and new attractions like the Istanbul Modern.

6 **Beşiktaş and Nişantaşı.** Dolmabahçe Palace—the lavish home of the last Ottoman sultans—and Istanbul's naval and military museums are among the attractions in these parts of town, which also include the city's high-fashion district.

7 **The Bosphorus.** Hop on a ferry and zigzag back and forth between Asia and Europe, past grand palaces, ancient fortresses, fishing villages, and beautiful old wooden villas.

8 **The Asian Shore.** The pleasant neighborhoods on Istanbul's Asian side have fewer "sights" but there are interesting enclaves to explore, away from the throngs of tourists.

9 **Princes' Islands.** This nine-island archipelago in the Sea of Marmara has pine forests, beaches, and a welcome absence of motorized traffic—the perfect antidote to the noise and chaos of the big city.

GETTING ORIENTED

Istanbul is a city divided. The Bosphorus—the 31-km-long (17-mile-long) waterway joining the Black Sea to the Sea of Marmara—separates the European side of the city from the Asian side. The European side is itself divided by the Golden Horn, an 8-km-long (5-mile-long) inlet that lies between historic Sultanahmet to the south and the new town, known as Beyoğlu, to the north. In Beyoğlu, the 14th-century Galata Tower dominates the hillside that rises north of the Golden Horn; just beyond, high-rise hotels and other landmarks of the modern city radiate out from Taksim Square, not far above the Bosphorus-side neighborhood of Beşiktaş. To the north, European suburbs line the western shore of the Bosphorus. The Asian suburbs are on the eastern shore.

Sabiha Gökçen Airport

Kartal

Pendik

0   4 mi

0   4 km

Ortaköy

Dolmabahçe Palace

ISTANBUL STREET FOOD

As much as Turkish people love to sit down for a leisurely dinner, they're also serious snackers, day and night, so finding a quick bite to eat is never a problem. The only challenge is choosing among the numerous tempting options.

Street food is not an afterthought in Turkey. Turks are quite demanding when it comes to eating on the run, expecting what is served to be fresh and made with care. Although McDonald's and other chains have made inroads in Turkey, many people still prefer their country's original "fast food," which sometimes is not so fast at all. Rather, some of Turkey's most popular street food dishes require some tender loving care in preparation, and frequently will be cooked or assembled right before your eyes, though there are also simple things like roasted chestnuts available.

In Istanbul and other large cities, snack bars and food stalls are open from early morning until late into the night. Look for the crowded places: chances are they're the local favorites.

FOR THE ADVENTUROUS

Fancy a grilled intestine sandwich or stomach soup? To make *kokoreç*, seasoned lamb intestines are wound up into a long, fat loaf, grilled over charcoal and then chopped up with tomatoes and served on a half loaf of crusty bread. *Işkembe* is a soup made out of tripe—cow stomach—and flavored with garlic and vinegar. It's usually sold in small eateries that serve nothing but this soup, said to be the ultimate way to prevent a hangover. For many late-night revelers in Turkey's big cities, a night out isn't complete without one of these pungent Turkish street food staples.

BÖREK

This is the name given to a wide range of flaky filo dough pastries. The windows of *börek* shops usually display their freshly baked goods, long coils of rolled-up filo dough stuffed with ground meat, potato, spinach, or cheese and baked until golden brown. *Su böreği* is a börek made of buttery egg noodles layered over crumbles of tangy white cheese and baked in a deep dish.

DÖNER

This cheap and filling sandwich *(Fbelow)* is Turkey's most popular street food. Meat, usually lamb or chicken, is grilled on a rotating vertical spit, shaved off in paper-thin slices, and served in a pocket bread called *pide* or rolled up in a tortilla-like flatbread into a wrap called a *dürüm*. For many Turks, a döner sandwich, downed with a glass of refreshing *ayran* (a drink made of salted, watered-down yogurt), is a meal in itself.

KUMPIR

Think of this as a baked potato on steroids. At *kumpir* stands, massive spuds are taken hot out of the oven, split open, and filled with an almost overwhelming assortment of toppings. Options include everything from grated cheese to chopped pickles, olives, and hot dog bits. It's not unusual for people to ask for six or more ingredients. The kumpir-maker then mixes it all up into

a glorious mess and puts it back in the potato skin.

MIDYE

In Turkey, mussels *(Fabove)* truly deserve to be called street food. They're usually sold by roving vendors carrying big baskets filled with glistening black shells that have been stuffed with a combination of mussels, rice, and herbs and spices. As tempting as it may be to buy these delicacies on the street, however, the risk of food poisoning from shellfish means it's better to err on the safe side and eat *midye* only at snack bars or restaurants, where there are higher standards of hygiene. Some specialty snack bars serve mussels coated in batter and deep-fried, in addition to the stuffed form.

SIMIT

Sort of the Turkish answer to the bagel, or a New York street pretzel, these humble sesame-coated bread rings are found all over Turkey. They're the ultimate street food: cheap, satisfying and—when fresh from the oven—delicious. And they're available all day long, from pushcarts found on almost every street corner. The *simit* has gone slightly upscale in recent years, with the appearance in Istanbul and other Turkish cities of several chains that serve simits and other baked goods.

Updated by
Vanessa H.
Larson

The only city in the world that can lay claim to straddling two continents, Istanbul—once known as Constantinople, capital of the Byzantine and then the Ottoman Empire—has for centuries been a bustling metropolis with one foot in Europe and the other in Asia. Istanbul embraces this enviable position with both a certain chaos and inventiveness, ever evolving as one of the world's most cosmopolitan crossroads.

It's often said that Istanbul is the meeting point of East and West, but visitors to this city built over the former capital of two great empires are likely to be just as impressed by the juxtaposition of old and new. Office towers creep up behind historic palaces, women in chic designer outfits pass others wearing long skirts and head coverings, peddlers' pushcarts vie with battered old Fiats and shiny BMWs for dominance of the noisy, narrow streets, and the Grand Bazaar competes with modern shopping malls. At dawn, when the muezzin's call to prayer resounds from ancient minarets, there are inevitably a few hearty revelers still making their way home from nightclubs and bars.

Most visitors to this sprawling city of more than 14 million will first set foot in the relatively compact Old City, where the legacy of the Byzantine and Ottoman empires can be seen in monumental works of architecture like the brilliant Aya Sofya and the beautifully proportioned mosques built by the great architect Sinan. Though it would be easy to spend days, if not weeks, exploring the wealth of attractions in the historical peninsula, visitors should make sure also to venture elsewhere in order to experience the vibrancy of contemporary Istanbul. With a lively nightlife propelled by its young population and an exciting arts scene that's increasingly on the international radar—thanks in part to its stint as the European Capital of Culture in 2010—Istanbul is truly a city that never sleeps. It's also a place where visitors will feel welcome: Istanbul may be on the Bosphorus, but at heart it's a Mediterranean city, whose friendly inhabitants are effusively social and eager to share what they love most about it.

PLANNING

WHEN TO GO

Summer in Istanbul is hot and humid. Winter usually hits around October and lasts until April, and the months from November and February see a fair amount of rain. All the surrounding water generally keeps the temperature above freezing, but a cold wind blows off the frozen Balkans and there's an occasional dusting of snow. May and September are pleasant and the most comfortable times for exploring.

FESTIVALS

Istanbul Film Festival. Every April for two weeks, the Istanbul Film Festival presents films from Turkey and around the world, giving film buffs a great opportunity to see contemporary Turkish cinema subtitled in English. Screenings are held mainly in Beyoğlu, as well as in Nişantaşı and Kadıköy. Make sure to purchase tickets in advance, as seats are reserved and the festival is extremely popular. ⊕ *www.iksv.org.*

April also sees Istanbul's **Tulip Festival**, when parks all over the city become a riot of color.

The well-regarded **Istanbul Music Festival**, held during several weeks in June, features mostly classical music performed by world-class musicians.

The **Istanbul Jazz Festival** is generally held in the first two weeks of July and brings in major names, new and old, from Turkey and around the world.

In the fall, the **Istanbul Biennial** is held in odd-number years, while the Istanbul Design Biennial is held in even-number years; both showcase cutting-edge work in venues around the city

Istanbul Foundation for Culture and Arts. Tickets for all these events can be ordered online through Biletix (⊕ *www.biletix.com*) or by contacting the Istanbul Foundation for Culture and Arts (İKSV). At press time, the İKSV had plans to move to a new, yet-to-be-determined location. ⊠ *Istanbul Kültür Sanat Vakfı, Sadi Konuralp Cad. 5, Şişhane* ☎ *212/334–0700* ⊕ *www.iksv.org.*

PLANNING YOUR TIME

Istanbul is one of the most unique cities in the world and with two continents of treasures, three days will hardly do it justice. A week will give you time to enjoy the sights, sounds, and smells with a little leisure. Make sure to see the main sites like Topkapı, Aya Sofya, the Blue Mosque, the palaces, and the bazaars, then seek out more of what you like: there are plenty more Ottoman mosques and Byzantine monuments. Or you can just chill out, *çay* (tea) in hand, by the waters of the Bosphorus.

The **Museum Pass Istanbul** allows single entry into eight state-run museums over a period of 72 hours; the five most significant of which are the Aya Sofya, Topkapı Palace (including the Harem), the Istanbul Archaeological Museums, the Mosaic Museum, and the Kariye Müzesi. At 85 TL, it's a significant savings over the cost of paying for all these museums individually, and it also includes discounts off entrance fees at the private Rahmi M. Koç and Sabancı museums and 10% off purchases at all of these museums' gift shops. The other advantage of the museum pass is it allows you to bypass entrance lines, which will save time—a commodity you'll certainly need if you're going to pack in so many museums in just three days.

GETTING HERE AND AROUND

AIR TRAVEL

Most international and domestic flights arrive at Istanbul's Atatürk Airport, although an increasing number of both domestic and international flights on low-cost carriers fly into the newer Sabiha Gökçen Airport on the Asian side of the city.

There is a slow metro directly from Atatürk Airport to the Aksaray neighborhood, where you can then catch a tram to Sultanahmet, but you'll have to walk a short way between these two rail lines, as they don't actually connect. It's considerably less of a hassle to take one of the regular shuttle buses operated by the Havataş company (10 TL to Taksim) or a taxi. Taxis and shuttle buses can be found at the main exit from the terminal building. There is no rail link to Sabiha Gökçen Airport, so you'll need to take a Havataş shuttle bus (13 TL to Taksim) or a taxi (⊕ *www.havatas.com.tr*).

BOAT TRAVEL

It's no surprise that Istanbul is well served by ferries. With the exception of the leisure-oriented Bosphorus cruises, ferries are most useful for crossing the Bosphorus (rather than going up and down it) and for getting to the Princes' Islands. The main docks on the European side are at Eminönü and Karaköy (on either side of the Galata Bridge) and at Kabataş, while Üsküdar and Kadıköy are the most important docks on the Asian side. Traditional large ferry boats operated by Şehir Hatları (⊕ *www.sehirhatlari.com.tr*), as well as smaller, faster-moving ferries run by two private companies (Turyol and Dentur Avrasya), crisscross the Bosphorus day and night, and cost about the same as land-based public transport. The Princes' Islands are served both by Şehir Hatları and by İDO, which operates "sea bus" catamarans that are faster, sleeker, and completely enclosed (⊕ *www.ido.com.tr*).

Taking a ferry is also one of the best ways to get in and out of Istanbul. "Fast ferries," some of which carry cars, leave from Yenikapı, which is south of Aksaray and a short taxi ride from Sultanahmet, to various ports on the southern side of the Sea of Marmara. The most useful routes are the ferries to Yalova, Bursa, and Bandırma, for travelers heading to İznik, Bursa, and Çanakkale, respectively.

BUS TRAVEL

Bus service within Istanbul is frequent, and drivers and riders tend to be helpful, so you should be able to navigate your way to major tourist stops like Eminönü, Taksim, and Beşiktaş. You must have an İstanbulkart *(Fsee İstanbulkart section below)* to board, and the fare is 1.95 TL.

For travel around the country, Turkey has an extensive system of intercity buses, and Istanbul's large, chaotic Esenler Otogar is the heart of it. Esenler itself is a bit out of the way, though easily accessible by metro from Aksaray. Alternatively, most of the major bus companies have offices located near the top of İnönü Caddesi (which winds down from Taksim Square to Kabataş), from which they operate shuttle buses, known as a *servis*. These take passengers either to Esenler or to their own ministations on the main freeway, allowing you to avoid making the trek out to Esenler via public transport.

A second, smaller bus station, at Harem on the waterfront on the Asian side of the Bosphorus, is easily accessible by ferry from Eminönü.

CAR TRAVEL

If you're entering or leaving Istanbul by car, E80 runs from the Bulgarian border and through Turkish Thrace to Istanbul, continuing on to central Anatolia in the east; this toll road is the best of several alternatives. Getting out of the city by car can be challenging, as the signs aren't always clear. It's always useful to have a driving map.

Istanbul is notorious for congested traffic, a cavalier attitude to traffic regulations, poor signposting, and a shortage of parking spaces. In short, don't even think about renting a car for travel in the city.

DOLMUŞ TRAVEL

A **dolmuş**, or shared taxi, is a cross between a taxi and a bus: they run set routes, leave when full, and make fewer stops than a bus, so they're faster. Most dolmuşes are bright yellow minibuses. Dolmuş stands are marked by signs but you can sometimes hail one on the street; the destination is shown on a roof sign or a card in the front window. Dolmuşes mostly head out to the suburbs, but visitors may find a few routes useful, including those that go from Taksim to Beşiktaş and from Taksim to Nişantaşı/Teşvikiye (for both routes, dolmuşes leave from the top of İnönü Caddesi near Taksim Square, and the fare is 2.25 TL). Dolmuşes also run between Taksim and the Kadıköy neighborhood (5 TL) on the Asian side, which is useful if you are coming back at night after the last boat.

FOOT TRAVEL

Istanbul is a walker's city, and the best way to experience it is to wander, inevitably getting lost—even with a good map, it's easy to lose your way in the winding streets and alleyways. When in doubt, just ask. Particularly in the old part of the city, most of the main sites are within a short distance of each other, and the easiest way to get to them is on foot.

FUNICULAR AND METRO TRAVEL

Istanbul's two short underground funiculars are convenient for avoiding the steep, uphill walk from the Bosphorus waterfront to Beyoğlu; each takes less than two minutes to ascend. The historic Tünel, in operation since 1875, connects Karaköy and Tünel Square. The ultramodern funicular from Kabataş (the end of the tram line) to Taksim is also convenient. The city has two underground metro lines: one starts in Şişhane (near Tünel), passes through Taksim, and continues north to the business districts, while the other connects Aksaray, west of Sultanahmet, with the airport and Esenler Otogar. Fares for each line are 3 TL for a token or 1.95 TL with an İstanbulkart *(Fsee İstanbulkart section below)*.

THE İSTANBULKART

The İstanbulkart is a prepaid "smart card" that you can swipe to pay for buses, trams, the funiculars and metro, and most ferries. The 6-TL nonrefundable fee for the card may not be worth paying if you're only in town briefly, but it can save you money if you plan to take public transportation a fair bit (especially if you're in a group, as up to five people can use the same card). With an İstanbulkart, fares are 1.95 TL—versus 3 TL for a single-ride token—and there is a discount on transfers within a two-hour period; you'll also save yourself the hassle of buying tokens for each ride. The İstanbulkart can be purchased at major transit stops such as Taksim and Eminönü and theoretically reloaded at most stops. In practice, however, the machines are not always working, but most newsstands are able to upload credit as well. The municipality eventually plans for cardholders to pay for taxi rides and museum entrance fees with the card but so far, aside from transport, it can only be used to pay for some public toilets.

MARMARAY TRAVEL

The long-awaited and much-delayed Marmaray—a 13.3-km-long (8.5-mile-long) rail tunnel extending under the Bosphorus from Sirkeci on the European side to Üsküdar on the Asian side—finally opened on October 23, 2013, the 90th anniversary of the Turkish Republic. The Marmaray is expected to revolutionize transport in Istanbul, linking up with new and existing rail lines to create a 76-km (46-mile) commuter rail line connecting the city's farthest-flung suburbs and allowing passengers to cross under the Bosphorus in just four minutes.

TAXI TRAVEL

Taxis are metered and relatively cheap—a ride from Sultanahmet to Taksim is about 15 TL. Many drivers don't speak English, so it may be helpful to write your destination on a piece of paper, and to bring the business card of your hotel with you so you don't have problems getting back later. Ask your hotel to call a taxi or find a stand in front of a hotel—you'll be more likely to get a driver who won't take you the long way around.

TRAIN TRAVEL

Istanbul has two main train stations: Sirkeci, near the Eminönü waterfront in Old Istanbul, and Haydarpaşa, on the Asian side of the Bosphorus. Trains in Turkey are known for being slow, but as of this writing, a high-speed train connecting Istanbul with Ankara and Konya was expected to launch within a few months after the opening of the Marmaray rail line under the Bosphorus.

TRAM TRAVEL

There are several tram lines in Istanbul, but the one most useful to visitors runs from Kabataş (below Taksim) along the Bosphorus to Karaköy, across the Galata Bridge to Eminönü, and then to Sultanahmet and Beyazıt/the Grand Bazaar before heading out to the western part of the city. The fare is 3 TL for a token, or 1.95 TL if you have an İstanbulkart, and trams run from around 6 in the morning to just before midnight. There is also a slow but atmospheric historic tram that runs along İstiklal Caddesi between Tünel and Taksim; tokens have traditionally been sold on board, but once the İstanbulkart comes into wider use that may no longer be possible.

TOURS

Names of tour companies and their itineraries change frequently so it's best just to make arrangements through a travel agency or your hotel; the offerings are all pretty similar. If you join a group, a "classic tour" of the Aya Sofya, Blue Mosque, Hippodrome, and Grand Bazaar should cost about 90 TL for a half day. For a full-day tour that also includes the Topkapı Palace and Süleymaniye Camii, as well as lunch, expect to pay about 180 TL. Bosphorus tours include a cruise and excursions to sights like Rumeli Hisarı and the Dolmabahçe or Beylerbeyi palaces. Rates for private tours with a guide and driver are higher, and more cost-effective if you have a large party; for two people, expect to pay at least 250 TL per person for a full day, and about a third less per person if you have four or more people. Keep in mind that admission fees and meals are generally not included in private tour rates, so this alternative ends up being considerably more costly.

VISITOR INFORMATION

There are several tourism information offices in Istanbul run by the Turkish Ministry of Culture and Tourism, including at both airports, in Sultanahmet (✉ *Divanyolu Cad. 3* ☎ *212/518–1802)*, just outside the entrance to the Sirkeci train station, near Eminönü (☎ *212/511–5888)* and next to the Atatürk Culture Center in Taksim (☎ *212/233–0592)*. They are open every day from 9 to 6 in summer and 9 to 5 in winter.

EXPLORING

SULTANAHMET

Sultanahmet is the heart of Old Istanbul, where many of the city's must-see attractions are located: an incredible concentration of art and architecture spanning millennia is packed into its narrow, winding streets. At the eastern edge of the Old City, Topkapı Palace—the center of Ottoman power and the residence of sultans for centuries—sits perched on the promontory overlooking the Bosphorus and the mouth of the Golden Horn. Behind the palace rise the imposing domes and soaring minarets of the Blue Mosque and Aya Sofya, two of Istanbul's most famous landmarks.

As you walk through the Hippodrome, explore the underground Basilica Cistern, and view the Byzantine mosaics displayed in the Mosaic Museum, you'll also get a feel for what the city of Constantinople looked like more than a thousand years ago, well before the Turks conquered it in 1453. The three buildings that compose the Istanbul Archaeological Museums showcase an incredible collection of artifacts going back even further in time, left by ancient civilizations that once thrived in Anatolia and around the region. When the call to prayer echoes from Sultanahmet's great mosques, pause for a moment to soak up the atmosphere here; nowhere else in Istanbul do you get such a rich feel for the magic of this ancient and mysterious city.

TOP ATTRACTIONS

Fodor's Choice
★

Aya Sofya (*Hagia Sophia, Church of the Holy Wisdom*). This soaring edifice is perhaps the greatest work of Byzantine architecture and for almost a thousand years, starting from its completion in 537, it was the world's largest and most important religious monument. As Emperor Justinian may well have intended, the impression that will stay with you longest, years after a visit, is the sight of the dome. As you enter, the half domes trick you before the great space opens up with the immense dome, almost 18 stories high and more than 30 meters (100 feet) across, towering above look up into it and you'll see the spectacle of thousands of gold tiles glittering in the light of 40 windows. Only Saint Peter's in Rome, not completed until the 17th century, surpasses Hagia Sophia in size and grandeur. It was the cathedral of Constantinople, the heart of the city's spiritual life, and the scene of imperial coronations. It was also the third church on this site: the second, the foundations of which you can see at the entrance, was burned down in the antigovernment Nika riots of 532. Justinian then commissioned a new church and, in response to his dictum that Aya Sofya be the grandest place of worship ever built—far greater than the temples whose columns were incorporated in the church—his master architects devised a magnificent dome. New architectural rules were made up as the builders went along, though not all were foolproof, since the dome collapsed during an earthquake just two years after the church was completed. The church stood a shell until a new architect built a steeper dome, and the aged Justinian finally reopened the church on Christmas Eve 563. Subsequent repairs and such structural innovations as flying buttresses ensured the dome remained firmly in place, making it the prominent fixture it is on the Istanbul skyline to this day. Over the centuries Hagia Sophia has survived additional earthquakes, looting Crusaders, and the conquest of the city by Mehmet the Conqueror in 1453.

Mehmet II famously sprinkled dirt on his head before entering the church after the conquest as a sign of humility. His first order was for Hagia Sophia to be turned into a mosque and, in keeping with the Islamic proscription against figural images, mosaics were plastered over. Successive sultans added the four minarets, *mihrab* (prayer niche), and *minbar* (pulpit for the imam) that visitors see today, as well as the large black medallions inscribed in Arabic with the names of Allah, Muhammad, and the early caliphs. In 1935, Atatürk turned Hagia Sophia into a museum, and a project of restoration, including the uncovering of mosaics, began.

Recent restoration efforts have, among other things, uncovered the large, beautifully preserved mosaic of a seraph, or six-winged angel, in the northeast pendentive of the dome, which had been plastered over 160 years earlier. The 9th-century mosaic of the Virgin and Child in the apse is also quite impressive: though it looks tiny, it is actually 16 feet high. To the right of the Virgin is the archangel Gabriel, while Michael, on the left, is almost totally lost.

The upstairs galleries are where the most intricate of the mosaics are to be found. At the far end of the south gallery are several imperial portraits, including, on the left, the Empress Zoe, whose husband's face and

Istanbul: History in Architecture

CLOSE UP

Byzantium was already 1,000 years old when, in AD 326, Emperor Constantine the Great began to rebuild it as the new capital of the Roman Empire. On May 11, 330, the city was officially renamed "New Rome," though it soon became known as Constantinople, the city of Constantine. Constantine's successors expanded the city and gave it new walls, aqueducts, and churches.

Under the emperor Justinian (ruled 527–65) Constantine's capital reached its apogee, with the construction of the magnificent Hagia Sophia, or Church of the Holy Wisdom (known as Aya Sofya in Turkish) on the site of a church originally built for Constantine. This awe-inspiring architectural wonder still dominates Istanbul's skyline. Constantinople became the largest, wealthiest metropolis the Western world had ever seen.

The Byzantine Empire began to decline toward the end of the 11th century and a devastating blow came in 1204, when the Western Europeans of the Fourth Crusade, who were supposed to be on their way to recapture Jerusalem, decided that instead of going another thousand miles to fight a load of Muslims, they'd instead sack and occupy the Eastern Orthodox Christian city of Constantinople. The members of the Byzantine dynasty were forced to flee to Trabzon on the Black Sea coast, and although they eventually regained control of Constantinople, in 1261, neither the city nor the Byzantine Empire recovered.

Constantinople in the late Byzantine period was more a collection of villages set among ruins than a city. Byzantine artists set to work, however, to restore and redecorate the damaged churches, and in their work in the mosaics and frescoes of the Church of the Holy Savior in Chora, we can see the first breath of the Renaissance that would later be carried west to Italy by artists and intellectuals fleeing the arrival of the Turks.

The Ottoman sultan Mehmet II, known as Fatih (the Conqueror), conquered the much-diminished Constantinople in 1453, rebuilt it, and made the city once again the capital of an empire. The Turks named the new city Konstantiniyye, but in time Constantinople seems to have been shortened to "Stanbul" by the Greeks and Westerners, and to "Istanbul" by the Turks. Another explanation says the name Istanbul is derived from the Greek *eis tin polin*, meaning "in the city" or "to the city"—for the Byzantines, "The City" was truly one and only.

In 1459 Mehmet II began building a palace on the hill at the tip of land where the Golden Horn meets the Bosphorus. Later sultans embellished and extended the complex until it grew into the fabulous Topkapı Palace. Most of the finest Ottoman buildings in Istanbul, however, date from the time of Süleyman the Magnificent (ruled 1520–66), who led the Ottoman Empire to its highest achievements in art and architecture, literature, and law. Süleyman and his court commissioned the architect Sinan (circa 1491–1588) to design buildings that are now recognized as some of the greatest examples of Islamic architecture in the world, including the magnificent Süleymaniye Mosque, the intimate Sokollu Mehmet Paşa Mosque, and the exquisitely tiled Rüstem Paşa Mosque.

name were clearly changed, as she went through three of them. On the right is Emperor John Comnenus II with his Hungarian wife Irene and their son, Alexius, on the perpendicular wall. Also in the upper level is the great 13th-century Deesis mosaic of Christ flanked by the Virgin and John the Baptist, breathing the life of the early Renaissance that Byzantine artists would carry west to Italy after the fall of the city to the Turks—note how the shadows match the true light source to the left. The central gallery was used by female worshippers. The north gallery is famous for its graffiti, ranging from Nordic runes to a complete Byzantine galley under sail. On your way out of

> ## A COLUMN OF LUCKY CHARMS
>
> The marble-and-brass **Sacred Column**, in the north aisle of Aya Sofya, to the left as you enter through the main door, is laden with legends. It's thought that the column weeps water that can work miracles, and over the centuries believers have worn a hole as they caress the column to come in contact with the miraculous moisture. It's also believed that if you place your thumb in the hole and turn your hand 360 degrees, any wish you make while doing so will come true.

the church, through the "vestibule of the warriors," a mirror reminds you to look back at the mosaic of Justinian and Constantine presenting Hagia Sophia and Constantinople, respectively, to the Virgin Mary. ⊠ *Aya Sofya Sq., Sultanahmet* ☎ *212/522–1750* 🖻 *25 TL* ⊗ *Tues.–Sun. 9–7 in summer; Tues–Sun. 9–5 in winter.*

Fodor'sChoice ★ **Blue Mosque** (*Sultan Ahmet Camii*). Only after you enter the Blue Mosque do you understand the name. The inside is covered with 20,000 shimmering blue-green İznik tiles interspersed with 260 stained-glass windows; calligraphy and intricate floral patterns are painted on the ceiling. After the dark corners and stern faces of the Byzantine mosaics in Aya Sofya, this mosque feels gloriously airy and full of light. Indeed, this favorable comparison was the intention of architect Mehmet Ağa (a former student of the famous Ottoman architect Sinan), whose goal was to surpass Justinian's crowning achievement (Aya Sofya). At the behest of Sultan Ahmet I (ruled 1603–17), he created this masterpiece of Ottoman craftsmanship, starting in 1609 and completing it in just eight years, and many believe he indeed succeeded in outdoing the splendor of Aya Sofya.

Mehmet Ağa actually went a little too far though, when he surrounded the massive structure with six minarets: this number linked the Blue Mosque with the Masjid al-Haram in Mecca—and this could not be allowed. So Sultan Ahmet I was forced to send Mehmet Ağa down to the Holy City to build a seventh minaret for al-Haram and reestablish the eminence of that mosque. Sultan Ahmet and some of his family are interred in the *türbe* (mausoleum) at a corner of the complex, although the tombs are closed for renovations until 2015.

From outside the Blue Mosque you can see the genius of Mehmet Ağa, who didn't attempt to surpass the massive dome of Aya Sofya across the way, but instead created a secession of domes of varying sizes to cover the huge interior space, creating an effect that is both whimsical and uplifting. ⊠ *Sultanahmet Sq., Sultanahmet* ⊙ *Daily 8:30–12:15, 2–4:30, and 5:45–6:30 (closed to tourists during prayer times).*

FAMILY
Fodor'sChoice
★
Istanbul Archaeology Museums (*İstanbul Arkeoloji Müzeleri*). Step into this vast repository of spectacular finds, housed in a three-building complex in a forecourt of Topkapı Palace, to get a head-spinning look at the civilizations that have thrived for thousands of years in and around Turkey. The main museum was established in 1891, when forward-thinking archaeologist and painter Osman Hamdi Bey campaigned to keep native antiquities and some items from the former countries of the Ottoman Empire in Turkish hands. The most stunning pieces are sarcophagi that include the so-called Alexander Sarcophagus, found in Lebanon, carved with scenes from Alexander the Great's battles, and once believed, wrongly, to be his final resting place. An excellent exhibit on Istanbul through the ages has artifacts and fragments brought from historical sites around the city that shed light on its complex past, from prehistory through the Byzantine period.

Exhibits on Anatolia include a display of some of the artifacts found in excavations at Troy, including a smattering of gold jewelry. A significant recent addition to the museum's collection is a 2nd-century AD Roman mosaic of Orpheus from Edessa (the modern-day Turkish city of Şanlıurfa) that the Dallas Museum of Art returned to Turkey in 2012 after it was determined to have been looted decades earlier. ⚠ **The main building's south wing, which has an extensive collection of classical sculpture, is closed for renovations until at least summer 2014.**

Don't miss a visit to the **Çinili Köşk** (Tiled Pavilion), one of the most visually pleasing sights in all of Istanbul—a bright profusion of colored tiles covers this one-time hunting lodge of Mehmet the Conqueror, built in 1472. Inside are ceramics from the early Seljuk and Ottoman empires, as well as brilliant tiles from İznik, the city that produced perhaps the finest ceramics in the world during the 16th and 17th centuries.

In summer, you can mull over these glimpses into the distant past as you sip coffee or tea at the café in the garden, surrounded by fragments of ancient sculptures.

The **Eski Şark Eserleri Müzesi** (Museum of the Ancient Orient) transports visitors to even earlier times: The vast majority of the panels, mosaics, obelisks, and other artifacts here, from Anatolia, Mesopotamia, and elsewhere in the Arab world, date from the pre-Christian centuries. One of the most significant pieces in the collection is a 13th-century BC tablet on which is recorded the Treaty of Kadesh, perhaps the world's earliest known peace treaty, an accord between the Hittite king Hattusili III and the Egyptian pharaoh Ramses II. Also noteworthy are reliefs from the ancient city of Babylon, dating to the era of the famous king Nebuchadnezzar II. ⊠ *Gülhane Park, next to Topkapı Sarayı, Sultanahmet* ☏ *212/520–7740* ⊕ *www.istanbularkeoloji.gov.tr* ☏ *10 TL (total) for the 3 museums* ⊙ *Apr.–Oct., Tues.–Sun. 9–7; Nov.–Mar., 9–5; ticket sales until an hr before closing.*

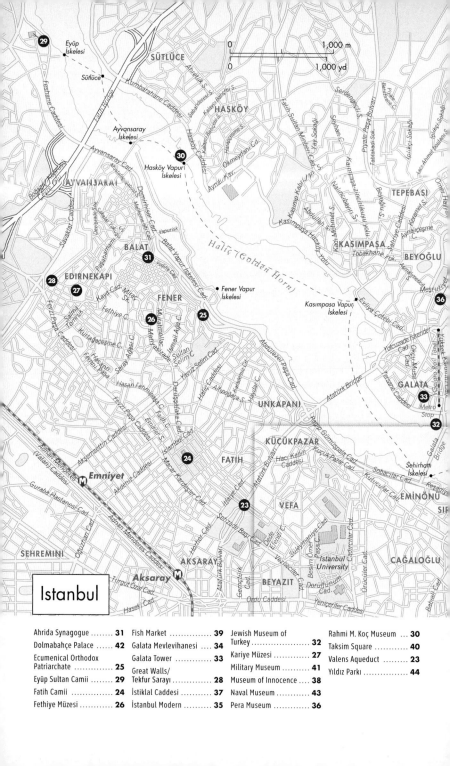

Istanbul

KURTULUŞ **41**

NIŞANTAŞI
TEŞVİKİYE

Hüsrev Gerede Caddesi

Abdi İpekçi Caddesi

Yıldız Parkı **44**

HARBİYE Ufade

Spor Caddesi

Kadırgalar Caddesi

Barbaros Bulvarı

Ortabahçe Cad.

Çırağan Caddesi

BEŞİKTAŞ

Maçka Parkı

Maçka Cad.

Beşiktaş Vapur İskelesi **43**

Taşlık Parkı

Dolmabahçe Caddesi

İnönü Stadium

42

Taksim Gezi Parkı

İstanbul Teknik University

TAKSİM **40** ℹ

Cumhuriyet Caddesi

Mete Cad.

İnönü Cad.

KABATAŞ

GALATASARAY **39**

İstiklal Caddesi

Tarlabaşı Bulvarı

Kabataş Vapur İskelesi

(Boğaziçi)

37

38

FINDIKLI

Meclis-i Mebusan S.

CİHANGİR

Tomtomkaptan S.

Tophane Square

Necatibey Cad.

35

KARAKÖY **34**

TOPHANE

KEY

Ferry Stops
Ferry Lines
Ⓜ Metro Stops
ℹ Information

Bosphorus

Üsküdar Vapur İskelesi

Sahil Yolu

Uncular Cad.

ÜSKÜDAR

Deniz Otobüsü İskelesi

Karaköy Vapur İskelesi

Kız Kulesi

Doğancılar Caddesi

Halk Caddesi

Eminönü İskelesi

Sirkeci Feribot İskelesi

Sirkeci Station

Statue of Atatürk

Gülhane Parkı

Topkapı Palace

Kennedy Caddesi (Sahil Yolu)

Üsküdar Harem Sahil Yolu

Harem Feribot İskelesi

see Sultanahmet map

Aya Sofya **1 – 22**

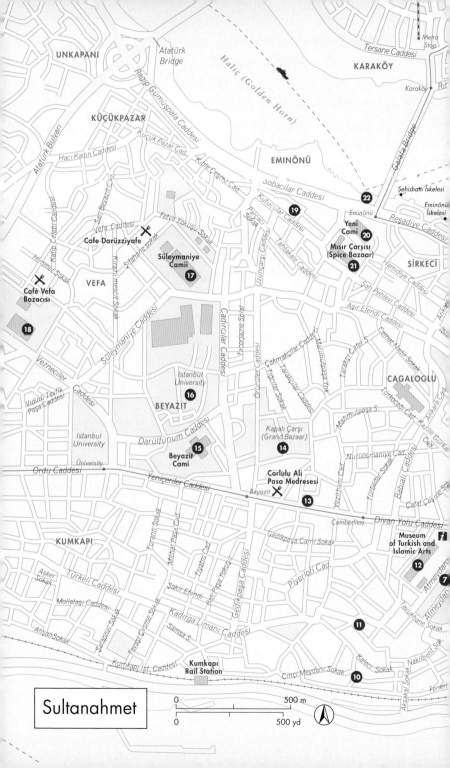

UNKAPANI

Atatürk Bridge

Haliç (Golden Horn)

Metro Stop

Tersane Caddesi

KARAKÖY

Karaköy Rıh

Galata Bridge

Ragıp Gümüşpala Caddesi

KÜÇÜKPAZAR

Küçük Pazar Cad.

Kıble Çeşme Cad.

EMINÖNÜ

Sobacılar Caddesi

Şehirhattı İskelesi

Atatürk Bulvarı

Hacı Kadın Caddesi

Kutucular Caddesi

19

Eminönü İskelesi

Reşadiye Caddesi

Şair Baytar Cad.

Vefa Caddesi

Fetva Yokuşu Sokak

Kıztaşı Mescit Sokak

22

Eminönü

Yeni Cami

20

SIRKECI

Cafe Darüzziyafe

Şifahane Sokak

Süleymaniye Camii

17

Uzunçarşı Caddesi

Tahtakale Caddesi

Mısır Çarşısı (Spice Bazaar)

21

Hamidiye Caddesi

Himmet Sokak

Katip Çelebi Caddesi

VEFA

Şah Pehlevi Caddesi

Café Vefa Bazaçısı

Aşır Efendi Caddesi

18

Süleymaniye Caddesi

Cadırcılar Caddesi

Taçorjane Sokak

Oruçcular Caddesi

Çakmakçılar Caddesi

Mahmutpaşa Yok.

Tarakçılar Caddesi

Tarakçı Cafer S.

Cemal Nadir Sokak

CAGALOGLU

Veznecile

Vidinli Tevfik Paşa Caddesi

Istanbul University

BEYAZIT

16

Mahmutpaşa S.

Türkocağı Cad.

Kazım Gürkan

Ankara Cad.

Kapalı Çarşı (Grand Bazaar)

14

Nuruosmaniye Cad.

Hacı Sokak

Babıali Caddesi

Istanbul University

Darülfünum Caddesi

Beyazit Cami

15

Yeniçeriler Caddesi

Ordu Caddesi

Üniversite

Çorlulu Ali Paşa Medresesi

Yıldızhan Cad.

Türbedar Sokak

Çatal Çeşme Sok.

Bayazit

13

Divan Yolu Caddesi

Çemberlitaş

KUMKAPI

Gedikpaşa Cami Sokak

Museum of Turkish and Islamic Arts

12

i

Turanlı Sokak

Mithat Paşa Cad.

Tiyatro Cad.

Gedikpaşa Caddesi

Piyerloti Cad.

Atmeydan

7

Türkeli Caddesi

Asker Sokak

Şakir Efendi

Bali Paşa Yokuşu

Atmeydan Sokak

Tavukhane Sokak

Mollataşı Caddesi

Kadırga Limanı Caddesi

11

Aksaray Sokak

Nakilbent Sok.

Afşar Sokak

Yalçıngül Sokak

Samsa S.

Tavaşı Çeşme Sokak

Kaleci Sokak

Kumkapı İst. Caddesi

Cinçi Meydanı Sokak

10

Kumkapı Rail Station

Fenerti

Sultanahmet

| 0 | | 500 m |
| 0 | | 500 yd |

2

KEY

Ferry Stops

Ferry Lines

Ⓜ Metro Stops

🛈 Information

Tramway

Hammams

A favorite pastime in Istanbul is to spend time in one of the city's hammams, or Turkish baths, some of which are in exquisite buildings more than 500 years old. Hammams were born out of necessity—this was how people kept clean before there was home plumbing—but they also became an important part of Ottoman social life, particularly for women. Men had the coffeehouse and women the hammam as a place to gossip and relax. Now that people bathe at home, hammams have become much less central in Turkish life. There are still bathhouses dotted throughout Istanbul, but many wouldn't survive without steady tourist traffic.

Most hammams have separate facilities for men and women. Each has a *camekan,* a large, domed room with small cubicles where you can undress, wrap yourself in a thin cloth called a *peştemal,* and put on slippers or wooden sandals—all provided. Then you'll continue through a pair of increasingly hotter rooms. The first, known as the *soğukluk,* has showers and toilets and is used for cooling down at the end of your session. The centerpiece of the bath is the *hararet,* also known as the *sıcaklık,* a steamy, softly lit room with marble washbasins along the sides, where you can douse yourself by scooping water up

from one of the basins with a copper bowl. In the middle of the room is the *göbektaşı,* a marble platform heated by furnaces below and usually covered with reclining bodies. This is where, if you decide to take your chances, a traditional Turkish massage will be "administered."

The masseur or masseuse (who traditionally has always been of the same gender as the person receiving the massage, although in some tourist-oriented hammams this is not the case) will first scrub you down with a rough, loofa-like sponge known as a *kese.* Be prepared to lose several layers of dead skin. Once you're scrubbed, the masseur will soap you up into a lather, rinse you off, and then conduct what will probably be the most vigorous massage you'll ever receive. Speak up if you want your masseuse to use a lighter hand.

After you've been worked over, you can relax (and recover) on the *göbektaşı* or head back to your changing cubicle, where you'll be wrapped in fresh towels and perhaps massaged a bit more, this time with soothing oils. Most cubicles have small beds where you can lie down and sip tea or juice brought by an attendant. Before you leave, it's good etiquette to tip your masseuse.

FodorśChoice **Topkapý Sarayý** (Topkapı Palace). *See the highlighted feature in this*
★ *chapter.*

FAMILY **Yerebatan Sarnıcı** (*Basilica Cistern*). The major problem with the site
FodorśChoice of Byzantium was the lack of fresh water, and so for the city to grow,
★ a great system of aqueducts and cisterns was built, the most famous of which is the Basilica Cistern, whose present form dates to the reign of Justinian in the 6th century. A journey through this ancient underground waterway takes you along dimly lit walkways that weave around 336 marble columns rising 26 feet to support Byzantine arches

Like the Cağaloğlu Hamamı, most Turkish hammams have separate facilities for men and women.

and domes, from which water drips unceasingly. The two most famous columns feature upturned Medusa heads. The cistern was always kept full as a precaution against long sieges, and fish, presumably descendants of those that arrived in Byzantine times, still flit through the dark waters. A hauntingly beautiful oasis of cool, shadowed, cathedral-like stillness (with Turkish instrumental music playing softly in the background), the cistern is a particularly relaxing place to get away from the hubbub of the Old City. Come early to avoid the long lines and have a more peaceful visit. ⊠ *Yerebatan Cad. at Divan Yolu, Sultanahmet* ☎ *212/522–1259* ⊕ *www.yerebatan.com* ✉ *10 TL* ☉ *Apr–Oct., daily 9–6:30; Nov.–Mar., daily 9–5:30.*

WORTH NOTING

FAMILY **Gülhane Parkı.** Istanbul has precious few public green spaces, which makes this park—once the private gardens of the adjacent Topkapı Palace—particularly inviting. Shaded by tall plane trees, the paved walkways, grassy areas, gazebos, and flower beds make this a relaxing escape from the nearby bustle of Sultanahmet. Walk all the way to the end of the park for excellent views of the Bosphorus and Sea of Marmara. The Istanbul Museum of the History of Science and Technology in Islam is inside the park, as are a municipal-run café and a couple of places serving tea and snacks. ⊠ *Alemdar Cad., Sultanahmet.*

Hippodrome. It takes a bit of imagination to appreciate the Hippodrome—once a Byzantine stadium for chariot racing with seating for 100,000—since there isn't much here anymore, though the hawkers selling guidebooks, snacks, and boat tours create a hint of the atmosphere that must have prevailed during chariot races and circuses. Notably

THE ISTANBUL PROTESTS

In the early summer of 2013, central Istanbul was swept with a wave of antigovernment protests when the mildly Islamist Justice and Development Party (AKP), led by Prime Minister Recep Tayyip Erdoğan, began a campaign to raze Gezi Parkı—a small public park just off Taksim Square and one of Istanbul's few green spaces—and replace it with a shopping mall. What began as a small-scale sit-in created to draw attention to the government's approach to urban planning and commercialization of public spaces, quickly sparked the largest mass protest movement in Turkey in over a decade.

Shortly after citizens gathered in the park, police staged a crackdown against the peaceful demonstrators that included the use of tear gas and water cannons. In the weeks that followed, a diverse swath of the middle class joined the rallies, which spread to the capital, Ankara, and dozens of other Turkish cities. A total of five people lost their lives in often tumultuous clashes with security forces. By summer's end, with Erdoğan's government having made no concessions and resorting to intimidation tactics to cow opposition leaders into silence, the "Gezi movement" had lost steam; meanwhile, the fate of the park, embroiled in legal battles, is still unclear.

While it remains to be seen what will happen in the months leading up to, and after, nationwide municipal elections scheduled for March 2014 and a presidential election slated for August 2014, travelers should nonetheless feel at ease about visiting Turkey and its largest metropolis. Istanbul is remarkably safe for a city of its size and even when protests do happen, they are generally concentrated in one or two neighborhoods—Taksim/Beyoğlu and occasionally Beşiktaş—so visitors spending most of their time near the tourist attractions of the Old City are unlikely to have any chance of exposure to the turmoil.

It's also worth keeping in mind that although the Turkish police's use of force can be indiscriminate and it's therefore best to avoid getting too close to demonstrations, protestors themselves are often eager to share their grievances and are unlikely to show any hostility towards sympathetic foreign visitors. Still, it's a good idea to check news reports and the U.S. State Department website before a trip, and if there is a developing situation, it may be wise to choose accommodations outside of the Beyoğlu area.

absent are the rows and rows of seats that once surrounded the track and the life-size bronze sculpture of four horses that once adorned the stadium—the Venetians looted the statue during the Fourth Crusade, and it now stands above the entrance to St. Mark's Basilica in Venice. You can, however, see several other monuments that once decorated the central podium. The **Dikilitaş** (Egyptian Obelisk), from the 15th century BC, probably marked the finish line. Theodosius I had it shipped over from Egypt in the 4th century AD and commissioned the reliefs on the base, which show the emperor in his royal box, which stood opposite, under what is now the Blue Mosque. The very partial **Yılanlı Sütun** (Serpentine Column) was taken from the Temple of Apollo at

Delphi in Greece, where it was dedicated after the Greek victory over the invading Persians in the 5th century BC. The **Örme Sütun** (Column of Constantine Porphyrogenitus) was once entirely covered with gilt bronze, which was stripped off by vandals during the Fourth Crusade. Down the hill to the southeast, along Nakılbent Sokak, you can see the giant southern foundations of the Hippodrome. Closer to the tram stop is a much more recent addition: a neo-Byzantine fountain that was a gift from the German government in 1901, commemorating Kaiser Wilhelm II's visit to Istanbul three years earlier. ⊠ *Atmeydanı, Sultanahmet, Sultanahmet* ⊜ *Free.*

Istanbul Museum of the History of Science and Technology in Islam (*İstanbul İslam Bilim ve Teknoloji Tarihi Müzesi*). On the western side of Gülhane Parkı, this museum, located in the former stables of Topkapı Palace, chronicles the significant role played by medieval Muslim scientists, inventors, and physicians in advancing scientific knowledge and technology while Europe was still in the Dark Ages. Exhibits cover subjects such as astronomy, navigation, mathematics, physics, warfare, and medical expertise. Unfortunately, almost none of the items on display are actual historical artifacts, but the models and reproductions built especially for the museum are interesting nevertheless. ⊠ *Gülhane Parkı, Sultanahmet* ☎ *212/528–8065* ⊕ *www.ibttm.org* ⊜ *5 TL* ⊗ *Wed.–Mon. 9–7 in summer; Wed–Mon. 9–5 in winter.*

Küçük Aya Sofya (*Little Aya Sofya*). Built by Justinian as the Church of Sergius and Bacchus (patron saints of the Roman army), this church is commonly known as the "Little Aya Sofya" due to its resemblance to the great church up the hill. In fact, it was built just before Aya Sofya, in the 530s, and the architects explored here many of the same ideas of the larger church but on a smaller scale. The church was converted to a mosque around the year 1500 by Hüseyin Ağa, Beyazıt II's chief eunuch. Though the mosaics are long gone, a Greek inscription dedicated to Justinian, his wife Theodora, and the saints can still be seen running along the cornice of the colonnade. The marble and verd antique columns with their delicate, ornate capitals are also quite impressive, and you can climb the stairway to the upper-level gallery for a closer look. ⊠ *Küçük Aya Sofya Cad., Sultanahmet* ⊗ *Daily, sunrise–sunset except during prayer times.*

Mosaic Museum (*Mozaik Müzesi*). One of Istanbul's more fascinating sights, the small but well-done Mosaic Museum is reached via an entrance halfway through the Arasta Bazaar and houses an excellent display of early Byzantine mosaics—some presented in situ—from the Great Palace of Byzantium, the imperial residence of the early Byzantine emperors when they ruled lands stretching from Iran to Italy and from the Caucasus to North Africa. This enormous residence reached from here all the way down to the sea and consisted of several terraces, with various palaces, churches, and parks, almost all of which are now gone. Only scant ruins remained by 1935, when archaeologists began uncovering what is thought to have been the floor of a palace courtyard, covered with some of the most elaborate and delightful mosaics to survive from the era, most dating to the 6th century. They include images of animals, flowers, hunting scenes, and mythological characters—idylls far

Continued on page 74

TOPKAPI
SHOWPLACE OF THE SULTANS

Like Russia's Kremlin, France's Versailles, and China's Forbidden City, Istanbul's Topkapı Sarayı is not simply a spectacular palace but an entire universe unto itself. Treasure house of Islamic art, power hub of the Ottoman Empire, home to more than twenty sultans, and site of the sultry Seraglio, the legendary Topkapı remains a world of wonders.

Astride the promontory of Saray-burnu ("Seraglio Point")—"the very tip of Europe"—Topkapı Sarayı has lorded over Istanbul for more than 5 centuries. As much a self-contained town-within-a-town as a gigantic palace, this sprawling complex perches over the Bosphorus and was the residence and center of bloodshed and drama for the Ottoman rulers from the 1460s to the 1850s. At one time home to some 5,000 residents—including a veritable army of slaves and concubines—Topkapı was also the treasure house to which marauding sultans brought back marvels from centuries of conquest, ranging from the world's seventh-largest diamond to the greatly revered Mantle of the Prophet Muhammad.

Today's visitors are captivated by the beauty of Topkapı's setting but are even more bewitched by visions of the days of ruby wine and roses, when long-ago sultans walked hand-in-hand with courtesans amid gardens lit by lanterns fastened to the backs of wandering giant tortoises.

As privileged as it was, however, Topkapı was rarely peaceful. Historians now recount horrifying tales of strangled princes, enslaved harem women, and power-mad eunuchs. Just in front of the main Gate of Salutation (from which decapitated heads were displayed centuries ago) stands the Fountain of the Executioner—a finely carved bit of onyx stonework where mighty vassals once washed the blood of victims from their hands in rose-petaled water. It is history as much as beauty that rivets the attention of thousands of sightseers who stream through Topkapı.

When you've had your fill of the palace's bloody yet beautiful past, venture to one of its marble-paved terraces overlooking the Bosphorus. Islands, mosques, domes, crescents shining in the sun, boats sailing near the strand: here shimmer the waters of the strait, a wonderland as seen by a thousand romantic 19th-century travelers—the Constantinople, at last, of our dreams.

Left: Imperial Hall in Harem

FOUR CENTURIES OF BLOOD & POWER

Stretching through times of tragedy and triumph, the story of Topkapı is a saga worthy of Scheherazade. Built between 1459 and 1465 by Sultan Mehmet II, the palace was envisioned as a vast array of satellite pavilions, many topped with cupolas and domes (Turkish architectural conservatism liked to perpetuate the tents of the nomadic past in stone). Over the centuries, sultan after sultan added ever more elaborate architectural frills, until the palace acquired a bewildering conglomeration of buildings extending over four successive courtyards, each more exclusionary than the last.

Sultan Mehmet II

MANSION OR MAUSOLEUM?

While Topkapı became the power center of the Ottoman Empire—it grew to contain the **state mint, the arsenal,** and the *divan* (chamber of the judicial council)—its most fearsome aspect was the **sultan's court.** Many of its inhabitants lived their entire adult lives behind the palace walls, and it was often the scene of intrigue and treachery as members of the sultan's entourage plotted and schemed, sometimes even deposing and assassinating the sultan himself.

A SURFEIT OF SULTANS

Set with stained-glass windows and mother-of-pearl decorations the **"Gilded Cage"** was where the crown prices lived in strict confinement—at least after the old custom of murdering all possible rivals was abandoned in the 17th century (the greatest number of victims—19 brothers—were strangled in 1595 by order of the mother of Mehmet III; seven of his father's pregnant concubines were drowned, to boot). House arrest in this golden suite kept the internal peace but deprived the heirs to the throne of interacting with the real world. After Süleyman II spent 39 years in the Gilded Cage he proved so fearful that, in 1687, he nearly refused the sultanate. Indeed, many sultans who ascended the throne were, in effect, ruled by their mothers, the all-powerful *Valide Sultans* (Queen Mothers). The most notorious was Kösem, whose rule over two sultan sons ended in 1651 when she was strangled upon orders of a vengeful daughter-in-law. As much to escape this blood-stained past as to please visiting European royalty, Topkapı was finally abandoned in 1856 when Abdülmecid I moved his court to Dolmabahçe Palace.

Procession of Constantinople in the Hippodrome (detail)

⊕ Babihümayun Caddesi, Gülhane Park, near Sultanahmet Sq.

☎ 212/512-0480

⊕ www.topkapisarayi. gov.tr

▧ Palace: 25TL; Palace & Harem: 40TL

☉ Palace: Wed.–Mon. 9–7 from April to Oct., 9–5 from Nov. to March (last entry one hour before closing time). Harem: Wed.–Mon. 9–6 from April to Oct., 9–4 from Nov. to March

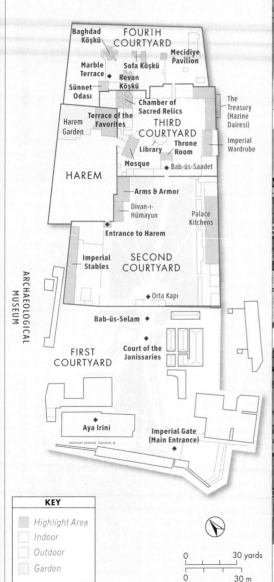

Topkapı Sarayı

Baghdad Köşkü

FOURTH COURTYARD

Mecidiye Pavilion

Marble Terrace

Sofa Köşkü

Revan Köşkü

Sünnet Odası

Chamber of Sacred Relics

The Treasury (Hazine Dairesi)

Terrace of the Favorites

THIRD COURTYARD

Harem Garden

Imperial Wardrobe

Library

Throne Room

HAREM

Mosque ◆ **Bab-üs-Saadet**

Arms & Armor

Divan-ı-Hümayun

Palace Kitchens

Entrance to Harem

Imperial Stables

SECOND COURTYARD

◆ **Orta Kapı**

Bab-üs-Selam ◆

ARCHAEOLOGICAL MUSEUM

◆

FIRST COURTYARD

Court of the Janissaries

Aya Irini ◆

Imperial Gate (Main Entrance) ◆

KEY

- *Highlight Area*
- Indoor
- Outdoor
- Garden

0   30 yards
0   30 m

Imperial Gate

Harem garden

The Tiled Hall

OF RICHES UNTOLD: TOPKAPI HIGHLIGHTS

THE FIRST COURTYARD

Upon arriving from Istanbul's noisy streets, the magic city of an Oriental tale stretches before you. Also known as the First Courtyard, the **Court of the Janissaries** has always been freely accessible to the public. In the shade of its plane trees, the turbulent Janissaries— the sultan's armed guard—prepared their meals and famously indicated their discontent by overturning their soup kettles: a dreaded protest followed, several times, by the murder of the reigning sultan. Looming over all is the **Aya Irini** church, dating from the time of Justinian; it's believed to stand on the site of the first church of Byzantium but, uniquely for Istanbul, has never been converted to a mosque. To the left is the imposing **Archaeological Museum,** housing treasures from Ephesus, Troy, and other ancient sites.

Archaeological Museum

Gate of Salutation

GATE OF SALUTATION

You begin to experience the grandeur of Topkapı when you pass through **Bab-üs-Selam** (Gate of Salutation). Süleyman the Magnificent built the gate in 1524; only a sultan was allowed to pass through it on horseback. Prisoners were kept in the gate's two towers before they were executed next to the nearby Executioner's Fountain. The palace's ticket office is on the walkway leading to this gate.

THE SECOND COURTYARD

A vast rose garden shaded by cypress trees, the second, or **Divan,** courtyard was once the veritable administrative hub of the Ottoman empire, often the scene of great pageantry when thousands of court officials would gather before the sultan's throne. On the far left is the entrance to the Harem. Also on the left is the **Divan-ı-Hümayun,** the strikingly ornate open-air Assembly Room of the Council of State. Occasionally the sultan would sit behind a latticed window, hidden by a curtain, so no one would know when he was listening. On the right of the yard are the **Palace Kitchens,** where more than 1,000 cooks once toiled at immense ovens. The cavernous space now displays one of the world's best collections of porcelain, amassed over the centuries by Ottoman rulers. The Yuan and Ming celadon pottery were especially prized for their alleged ability to change color if the dish held poisonous foods.

Gate to the Divan

Kitchen area of the palace

THE THIRD COURTYARD

As you walk through the **Bab-üs-Saadet, or Gate of Felic-ity**, consider yourself privileged, because only the sultan and grand vizier were allowed to pass through this gate. It leads to the palace's inner sanctum, the Third Courtyard, site of some of the most ornate of the palace pavilions. Most visitors here only got as far as the **Arz Odası**, the Audience Hall, or Throne Room, where foreign ambassadors once groveled before the sultan. Here, too, is the fabled **Treasury (Hazine Dairesi)**.

İznik tiles

CHAMBER OF SACRED RELICS

On the courtyard's left side is the Hasoda Koğuşu, housing the Chamber of Sacred Relics (1578), which comprises five domed rooms containing some of the holiest relics of Islam. Pride of place goes to the Mantle of the Prophet Muhammad, kept in a gold casket (exhibited behind shatter-proof glass). Nearby are the Prophet's Standard, or flag; hairs from his beard; his sword; a cast of his footprint; and teeth. Other relics, including the "staff of Moses" and the "cooking pot of Abraham," are also on view.

Dome atop Gate of Felicity

THE IMPERIAL WARDROBE

An impressive collection of imperial robes, spanning many generations of the Ottoman dynasty, is displayed in a hall on the right side of the Third Courtyard. The sultans' oversized caftans and other garments, and the tiny costumes worn by the crown princes, are made of splendid silks and brocades and are stiff with gold and silver thread, tooled leather, and even jewels.

THE FOURTH COURTYARD

More of an open terrace, this courtyard was the private realm of the sultan, and small, elegant pavilions are scattered amid tulip gardens overlooking the Bosphorus and Golden Horn. The loveliest of the pavilions, the **Baghdad Kiosk** (covered with İznik tiles), was built by Murat IV in 1638 after his conquest of Baghdad. Off the wishing-well terrace is the **Circumcision Room (Sünnet Odası)**, also famed for its lavish tiling.

Interior Baghdad Kiosk

On the right side of the courtyard are steps leading to the 19th-century rococo-style Mecidiye Pavilion, now **Konyalı Restaurant** (open Wed.—Mon., 10:30 to 7), which serves excellent Turkish food and has a magnificent vista of the Sea of Marmara. On a terrace below is an outdoor café with an even better view. Go early or reserve a table to beat the tour-group crush.

Circumcision Room colonnade

PLEASURE DOMES: THE HAREM

Evoking the exoticism and mystery of the Ottoman Empire, the Harem is a maze of 400 terraces, wings, and apartments. These were the quarters of the sultan's courtesans, mostly Circassian women from the Caucasus (Muslim women were forbidden to be concubines).

Seeing the forty rooms that have been opened to the public reminds us that the Harem (the term means "forbidden" in Arabic) was as much about confinement as it was about luxury. Of the 1,000 women housed in the harem, many finished their days here as servants to other concubines.

Imperial Hall

Built around grand reception salons—including the Imperial Hall, the Crown Prince's Pavilions, and the Dining Room of Ahmet III—the Harem was studded with fountains, whose splashes made it hard to eavesdrop on royal conversations.

WOMEN'S QUARTERS
Adjacent to the Courtyard of the Black Eunuchs (most of whom hailed from Africa's Sudan), the first Harem compound housed about 200 lesser concubines in tiny cubicles, like those in a monastery. As you move deeper into the Harem, the rooms become larger and more opulent; the four chief wives lived in grand suites around a shared courtyard.

Ornate ceiling in Harem

Most concubines were trained in music and poetry, but only those who achieved the highest status were given access to the sultan.

APARTMENTS OF THE SULTANS
The sultan's own apartments are, not surprisingly, a riot of brocades, murals, colored marble, wildly ornate furniture, gold leaf, fine carvings, and, of course, the most perfect znik tiles. Nearby is the Gilded Cage, where the crown princes were kept under lock and key until they were needed.

Dining Room of Ahmet III

APARTMENTS OF THE VALIDE SULTAN

The true ruler of the Harem was the *Valide Sultan*, the sultan's mother, and her lavish apartments lay at the heart of the Harem complex. For the young women of the Harem, the road to the sultan, quite literally (using a hallway known as the "Golden Way") ran through his mother.

DO YOU LOVE EMERALDS? DON'T MISS TOPKAPI'S TREASURY

If you love jewels, you're in luck—at the **Topkapı Treasury (Hazine Dairesi)** you can admire three of the world's most wondrous emeralds, which are embedded in the hilt of the fabulous Topkapı Dagger. Crafted in 1747, it was meant as a gift for the Shah of Persia; he could well have used it but it arrived too late—he was assassinated as the dagger was en route to him. Here also are two of the world's largest extant emeralds: uncut, they each weigh about eight pounds. Now displayed behind glass, they were originally hung from the ceiling as spectacular "lamps." Amazingly, even these mammoth gems were outshone by the 86-carat Spoonmaker's Diamond which, according to legend, was found by an Istanbul pauper glad to trade it for three wooden spoons. These are but six of the many jewels found here.

A true cave of Aladdin spilling over four rooms, the treasury is filled with a hoard of opulent objects and possessions, either lavish gifts bestowed upon generations of sultans, or spoils garnered from centuries of war. The largest objects are four imperial thrones, including the gold-plated Bayram throne given to Sultan Murat III by the Khedive of Egypt in 1574. Also on display is the throne sent to Istanbul by the same unfortunate shah for whom the Topkapı Dagger was intended. All is enhanced by the beautiful display of turban crests and jewel-studded armor, with every possible weapon encrusted with diamonds and pearls—all giving testimony to the fact that, before the 18th century, it was the man, not the woman, who glittered like a peacock.

There are trinkets, chalices, reliquaries, and jewels, jewels, jewels. Ladies, be sure to hide your engagement rings—they will be overwhelmed in comparison!

Sultan headgear

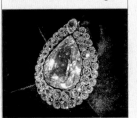

Spoonmaker's Diamond

ROCK STARS

The most glamorous jewel heist film ever, *Topkapi* (1964) is director Jules Dassin's dazzling homage to Istanbul, diamonds, and his famous *Never on Sunday* blonde (and wife), Melina Mercouri. Playing jet-set mastermind Elizabeth Lipp, she seduces a troupe of thieves into attempting to steal the Topkapı Dagger. Rooftop high jinks, a script scintillating with wit, the Oscar-winning performance by Peter Ustinov, and an eye-popping credit sequence make for a film almost as intoxicating as a visit to the Treasury itself.

Topkapı dagger

removed from the pomp and elaborate ritual of the imperial court.

As you walk the streets of Sultanahmet, you'll see many fragments of masonry and brickwork that were once part of the palace, and several cisterns have been found under hotels and carpet shops, some of which are open to visitors. New excavations on property owned by the Four Seasons Hotel are supposed to open as an archaeological park. Down by the water, there are extensive, overgrown remains of the facade of the **Bucoleon Palace,**

> ### MUSEUM TIMING
>
> Check opening days when you plan your outings. Most museums in Istanbul are closed Monday, with a few exceptions: Topkapı Palace is closed Tuesday, the Kariye Müzesi is closed Wednesday, and Dolmabahçe Palace is closed both Monday and Thursday. The military and naval museums are closed both Monday and Tuesday.

the private quarters of the emperors from the 6th to 11th centuries, which are gradually being shaken apart by the passing train line. ⊠ *Arasta Çarşısı, Kabasakal Cad. 103, Sultanahmet* ☎ *212/518–1205* 🕾 *8 TL* ⊙ *Apr.–Oct., Tues.–Sun. 9–6; Nov.–Mar., Tues.–Sun. 9–4:30.*

Sokollu Mehmet Paşa Camii (*Mosque of Sokollu Mehmet Pasha*). Built in 1571 for Sokollu Mehmet Pasha, a grand vizier to three successive sultans, this small mosque is not as grand as the Süleymaniye Camii, but many consider it to be the most beautiful of the mosques built by master Ottoman architect Sinan. Here, Sinan chose not to dazzle with size but to create a graceful, harmonious whole, from the courtyard and porticoes outside to the interior, where floral-motif stained-glass windows and gorgeous, well-preserved İznik tiles with both floral patterns and calligraphic inscriptions are set off by white stone walls. Inside, the *minbar* (pulpit), delicately carved in white marble and crowned with a tiled conical cap, is particularly noteworthy. ⊠ *Şehit Mehmet Paşa Yokuşu, Kadırga, Sultanahmet* ⊙ *Daily sunrise–sunset except during prayer times.*

THE BAZAAR QUARTER AND ENVIRONS

The area between the Grand Bazaar and the Spice Bazaar was historically the city's center of business and trade, and the streets here still teem with tradespeople and shoppers. You could easily spend hours exploring the Grand Bazaar, and the Spice Bazaar also has its charms. But take time to wander outside them, too, whether along Nuruosmaniye Caddesi with its upmarket jewelry, antiques, and carpet boutiques, or through the narrow, somewhat run-down streets—lined with stores and stalls selling all manner of everyday items at bargain prices, primarily to locals—that lead from the Grand Bazaar down toward the Golden Horn.

Even though most of the old Byzantine and Ottoman buildings have long disappeared, the area gives an impression of what the city must have been like when it was the bustling capital of a vast empire. The beautiful Süleymaniye Mosque, one of the architect Sinan's masterpieces, is grandly situated on a hilltop just a stone's throw from the

SINAN THE ARCHITECT

The master architect Mimar Sinan, the greatest of the Ottoman builders, is said to have designed more than 350 buildings and monuments throughout Turkey. His genius as an architect lay in his use of proportion, and as an engineer he mastered the use of buttresses and other elements to create vast, open spaces. He was born in a Greek or Armenian village near Cappadocia and at about the age of 22 he was recruited through the *devşirme* (conscription) system to serve the sultan; these Christian conscripts were raised Muslim and trained to become the army and bureaucracy that formed the backbone of the empire. Sinan spent the next several decades of his life as a military engineer, before being appointed chief imperial architect at the age of 50. He then worked into his nineties building more than 80 mosques—some 50 in Istanbul alone—as well as religious schools, palaces, bridges, and caravansaries. Among the works attributed to Sinan are the Sokollu Mehmet Paşa, Süleymaniye, and Rüstem Paşa mosques, parts of the kitchens at Topkapı, two of the minarets at Aya Sofya, and the Selimiye Camii in Edirne. His tomb is beside his most important Istanbul mosque, the Süleymaniye.

Grand Bazaar and is worth a detour. The Rüstem Paşa Camii and Yeni Cami, both located near Eminönü on the waterfront, are also particularly striking. When exploring this area, it's a good idea to start at the Grand Bazaar and work your way downhill to Eminönü—it's a rather stiff climb the other way.

TOP ATTRACTIONS

Fodor'sChoice **Grand Bazaar** (Kapalı Çarşı). *See the highlighted Bazaars feature in this* ★ *chapter.*

Rüstem Paşa Camii (*Rüstem Pasha Mosque*). Tucked away in the backstreets just west of the Spice Bazaar, this Sinan masterpiece was built in the early 1560s for Rüstem Pasha, a grand vizier and son-in-law of Süleyman the Magnificent. Though it's unassuming from the outside, this is one of the most highly ornamented of the Ottoman mosques, and you're in for a treat when you step into the interior, where almost every surface but the dome is decorated with gorgeous İznik tiles in a magnificent array of colors and patterns. The mosque—raised on a high terrace that's surrounded at street level by a warren of small shops—is reached via flights of interior stairs in the corners that lead up to a courtyard and portico, the facade of which is also lined with beautiful tiles. ⊠ *Hasırcılar Cad., south of Sobacılar Cad., The Bazaar Area and Environs* ⊙ *Daily sunrise–sunset except during prayer times.*

Spice Bazaar (Mısır Çarşısı). *See the highlighted Bazaars feature in this chapter.*

Fodor'sChoice **Süleymaniye Camii** (*Mosque of Süleyman*). Perched on a hilltop opposite ★ Istanbul University, Süleymaniye Camii is perhaps the most magnificent mosque in Istanbul and is considered one of the architect Sinan's masterpieces. The architectural thrill of the mosque, which was built between 1550 and 1557, is the enormous dome, the highest of any Ottoman mosque. Supported by four square columns and arches, as well as exterior walls with smaller domes on either side, the soaring space gives the impression that it's held up principally by divine cooperation. Sinan was guided by a philosophy of simplicity in designing this mosque and, except for around the *mihrab* (prayer niche), there is little in the way of tile work—though the extremely intricate stained-glass windows and baroque decorations painted on the domes (added later) more than make up for that. Thanks to a multimillion-dollar restoration project completed in late 2010, the Süleymaniye can now be seen in its full glory. The tomb of Sinan is just outside the walls, on the northern corner, while those of his patron, Süleyman the Magnificent, and the sultan's wife, Roxelana, are housed in the cemetery adjacent to the mosque. The *külliye*, or mosque complex, still includes a hospital, library, hammam, several schools, and other charitable institutions that mosques traditionally operate, so take a stroll around the beautiful grounds—and don't miss the wonderful views of the Golden Horn. ⊠ *Süleymaniye Cad., near Istanbul University's north gate, The Bazaar Area and Environs* ⊙ *Daily sunrise–sunset except during prayer times.*

NEED A BREAK?

Darüzziyafe Restaurant. The former soup kitchen of the Süleymaniye Camii has been returned to its original use, serving traditional *zeytinyağlı* (vegetables cooked in olive oil) dishes and a range of Turkish and Ottoman meat entrées in the leafy courtyard and cool, stone halls. ⊠ *Şifahane Cad. 6, The Bazaar Area and Environs* ☎ *212/511-8415* ⊕ *www.daruzziyafe. com.tr.*

Yeni Cami (*New Mosque*). A dominant feature of the Istanbul skyline, thanks to its prime spot on the Eminönü waterfront, the "new mosque" is known as much for its history as its architecture. Its location, rising out of the Golden Horn, presented formidable engineering challenges to the former apprentice to Sinan who laid the waterlogged foundations in 1597. Due to sultans' deaths and complicated harem politics, it was not until 1663 that the project was finally completed, by the queen mother at the time: Turhan Hatice (who is buried in a mausoleum behind the mosque with her son, Mehmet IV, and several succeeding sultans). The entrance to the courtyard from the main square offers a marvelous view of the small domes and semidomes—66 in all—that appear to cascade down around the main dome, flanked by two minarets. Inside, almost every square inch of the interior is decorated—from the elaborate, multicolored İznik tiles to the intricately painted domes and gilded minbar—while numerous windows, including in the wall of the mihrab, fill the mosque with light. ⊠ *Eminönü waterfront, The Bazaar Area and Environs* ⊙ *Sat.–Thurs. sunrise–sunset except during prayer times; Fri. open after midday prayer.*

WORTH NOTING

Beyazıt Camii. Inspired by Aya Sofya and completed in 1506, this domed mosque holds the distinction of being the oldest of the Ottoman imperial mosques still standing in the city. Though the inside is somewhat dark, it has an impressively carved mihrab and the large courtyard has 20 columns made of verd antique, red granite, and porphyry that were taken from ancient buildings. ⚠ Most sections of the mosque, except for a small area open for worship, will be closed until at least summer 2014 for an extensive restoration project. ⊠ *Beyazıt Meyd., Beyazıt, The Bazaar Area and Environs* ☉ *Daily sunrise to sunset; usually closed during prayer times.*

The Column of Constantine (*Çemberlitaş*). This column stood at the center of what was a large circular marketplace or forum where Constantine formally rededicated the city on May 11, 330. Carved out of blocks of a reddish-purple stone called porphyry that was especially prized by the ancient Romans, the column is 35 meters (115 feet) high and was once topped by a golden statue of Apollo, to which Constantine added his own head. Constantine was said to have placed various relics under the column, including an ax used by Noah to make the ark, a piece of the True Cross, and some of the leftover bread from the miracle of the loaves and fishes. ⊠ *Yeniçeriler Cad. and Vezirhan Cad., The Bazaar Area and Environs.*

Eminönü. The transportation hub of Old Istanbul, Eminönü teems with activity. There are docks for traditional ferry boats (including both short and day-long Bosphorus cruises) and faster "sea bus" catamarans that cross the Bosphorus, as well as the Eminönü tram stop, the Sirkeci train station, and the departure area for buses headed to Istanbul's western districts. Thousands of people and vehicles rush through this bustling, frenetic neighborhood by the hour, and the many street traders here do a quick business selling everything from trinkets to designer knockoffs. From Eminönü, you can cross the Galata Bridge on foot or via the tramway to Karaköy, the gateway to the "New Town." ⊠ *The Bazaar Area and Environs.*

Fatih Camii (*Fatih Mosque*). This complex consisting of a mosque, religious schools, and other buildings of a pious nature was the largest in the Ottoman Empire, and is still one of the most culturally important mosques in the city. Today it remains the heart of Fatih, Istanbul's most religiously conservative neighborhood. The original mosque, which was destroyed by an earthquake in 1766, was built from 1463 to 1470 by Mehmet the Conqueror on the site of the demolished Church of the Twelve Apostles, the burial church of Byzantine emperors from Constantine on. The 18th-century replacement, which recently underwent a complete restoration, is quite attractive—particularly the extensive stained-glass windows—though probably very little of what you're seeing is original. Behind the mosque is the reconstructed baroque-style tomb of the Conqueror himself, along with the far plainer tomb of his wife Gülbahar. On Wednesdays, the area just north of Fatih Camii is taken over by one of the city's largest street markets, packed with locals buying everything from produce to clothing and housewares. It's best to avoid visiting the mosque at prayer times. ⊠ *Fevzi Paşa Cad., Fatih, The Bazaar Area and Environs* ☉ *Daily sunrise–sunset.*

Istanbul University. The main campus of Turkey's oldest institution of higher learning originally served as the Ottoman war ministry—hence the magnificent gateway arch facing Beyazıt Square and the grandiose, martial style of the main buildings, which surround a long greensward filled with giant plane trees. The stone 85-meter (279-foot) **Beyazıt**

Tower, built in 1828 by Mahmud II as a fire-watch station, is the tallest structure in the Old City and is still one of the most recognizable landmarks in the area. At night, it is lit up with LED lights in different colors indicating weather conditions. Though it can no longer be climbed, it's worth seeing up close. ■TIP→ **Because of its history as a nexus of political activism over the past several decades, the campus is not very publicly accessible, though in theory tourists are allowed entrance from 10 am to 3 pm on weekdays during the school year and until about 4 pm during the summer.** Proceed along the main drive and past the rectorate building to the garden behind it, from which there is a stunning view overlooking the Süleymaniye Camii. ⊠ *Fuat Paşa Cad., Beyazıt, The Bazaar Area and Environs.*

> ### TEA HOUSES
>
> Istanbul is filled with teahouses—many with shady gardens—where people spend long hours quietly sipping glass after glass of tea. Sitting down at one of these teahouses—particularly if it has a nice view, like the one by the waterfront in Gülhane Parkı—is one of the simple pleasures of Turkish life.

Şehzade Camii. The medium-sized Şehzade Camii was built for Süleyman the Magnificent's eldest son, Prince Mehmet, who died of smallpox in 1543 at age 22. This was the great Ottoman architect Sinan's first imperial mosque and he called it his "apprentice work." The result is quite attractive, although less spectacular than the nearby Süleymaniye. The tranquil gardens contain several imperial tombs—including that of Prince Mehmet—decorated with some of the best İznik tiles in Istanbul. As of this writing the tombs were being restored, after which it is hoped they will be open to the public. ⊠ *Şehzadebaşı Cad., Fatih* ☉ *Daily sunrise to sunset; usually closed during prayer times.*

Valens Aqueduct. A Roman city needed its aqueduct, and Constantinople, which seriously lacked drinking water, finally got one in 375 under Emperor Valens. The aqueduct, which was just one element of a well-engineered water distribution system that extended for miles, was restored in the 16th century by the Ottoman architect Sinan and continued to function well into the Ottoman era. The best and most dramatic surviving section is that near Şehzade Mosque, where Atatürk Bulvarı, a major urban thoroughfare, passes through the great arches of the aqueduct—still one of Istanbul's most significant landmarks. ⊠ *The Bazaar Area and Environs.*

WESTERN DISTRICTS

The historical peninsula's western districts are farther off the beaten path than the heavily tourist-trod Sultanahmet and bazaar areas, but the rewards of visiting are a number of interesting sights and a more authentic atmosphere. Just inside the ancient city walls, the former Chora Church, now Kariye Müzesi, contains a wealth of gorgeous Byzantine mosaics and frescoes whose splendor surpasses those in the Aya Sofya. The Great Walls themselves, sections of which have been restored, give an idea of the scale of the ancient city and of how

Constantinople successfully resisted so many sieges before finally falling to the Ottomans in 1453. Along the water, Fener and Balat—once predominantly Greek and Jewish neighborhoods, respectively—are home to several historic churches, including the Greek Orthodox Patriarchate, as well as the city's oldest synagogue. Farther up the Golden Horn, the Eyup Sultan Mosque complex is an important Muslim pilgrimage site.

TOP ATTRACTIONS

Eyüp Sultan Camii (*Eyüp Sultan Mosque*). Muslim pilgrims from all over the world make their way to the brightly colored, tile-covered tomb of Eyüp Ensari (Ayyub al-Ansari)—a companion of the Prophet Muhammad who served as his standard-bearer—at this mosque complex on the Golden Horn. Ensari was killed during the first Arab siege of Constantinople (AD 674–78), and the eternal presence of a man so close to Muhammad makes this the holiest Islamic shrine in Turkey. His gravesite was visited by Muslim pilgrims in Byzantine times and "rediscovered" during Mehmet the Conqueror's siege of Constantinople. After the conquest, Mehmet monumentalized the tomb and built a mosque, where investiture ceremonies were held for successive sultans; the mosque currently on the site was built after the original edifice was ruined in the earthquake of 1766. The plane-tree-shaded courtyards and large numbers of visitors—particularly at midday Friday prayers—imbue Eyüp Sultan Camii with a sense of peace and religious devotion not found in many other parts of this often frenetic city. A vast cemetery has grown up around the mosque, including the grand tombs of many other distinguished departed. It's best to avoid visiting at prayer times. ⊠ *Cami Kebir Cad., Eyüp* ⊗ *Daily.*

The Great Walls. The walls of Constantinople were the greatest fortifications of the medieval age and, although they were severely damaged by Sultan Mehmet II's canon in the siege leading up to the Ottoman conquest of the city in 1453, large sections still stand more or less intact today. The walls were built in the 5th century after the city outgrew the walls built by Constantine, and they stretched 6.5 km (4 miles) from the Marmara Sea to the Golden Horn. The "wall" was actually made up of a large inner and smaller outer wall, with various towers and gates, as well as a moat. Parts have been restored and you can even climb around on top; the easiest section on which to do this is near Edirnekapı, a short walk uphill from Chora Church.

From Edirnekapı, if you walk along the inside of the walls for a few hundred yards north in the direction of the Golden Horn, you will come to what is known in Turkish as the **Tekfur Sarayı** (⊠ *Hoca Şakir*

VIEW FROM THE BRIDGE

The Galata Bridge, or Galata Köprüsü, connects Old Istanbul to the so-called New Town on the other side of the Golden Horn. The bridge was finished in 1994, replacing the old pontoon bridge that had been around since about 1010, when horses, oxs, and mule-drawn carriages rattled across it for a fee. The bridge itself isn't much to look at, but it offers a postcard-worthy view of the main sights of the Old City, and is a particularly nice vantage point from which to watch the sun set.

Anastasis fresco, artist unknown, Kariye Müzesi

Cad.), a large three-story building that has an impressive facade and is built into the city walls. This 13th-century edifice represents the only significant remains of the multibuilding Palace of Blachernae, which served as the Byzantine emperors' primary residence after they recaptured Constantinpole from the Latin Crusaders in 1261. The Tekfur Sarayı is supposedly being restored and as of this writing, entrance to the site is prohibited.

Fodor's Choice ★ **Kariye Müzesi** (*Kariye Museum or Church of the Holy Savior in Chora*). The dazzling mosaics and frescoes in the former Church of the Holy Savior in Chora are considered to be among the finest Byzantine artworks in the world. Most of the mosaics, in 50 panels, depict scenes from the New Testament and date from the 14th century. They are in splendid condition, having been plastered over when the church became a mosque in the 16th century and not uncovered until the 1940s. "Chora" comes from the Greek word for countryside; the original church here was outside the city walls that were built by Constantine the Great, but at the beginning of the 5th century AD Theodosius built new fortifications to expand the growing city, which brought the church inside the walls. The current edifice is believed to have been built in the 12th century.

The modern entrance is off to the side of the church but it's best to head straight to the original front doorway, in the outer narthex. Here, over the entrance, a large mosaic of Christ Pantocrator bears the phrase "I am the land (Chora) of the Living." This door leads to the inner narthex, where you can see the mosaic of Theodore Metochites, a kind of Byzantine prime minister, presenting the church to Christ. Metochites was responsible for the restoration and redecoration of the church after the damage wrought by the Fourth Crusade. To the left is a series of mosaics depicting the early life of the Virgin, based on the apocryphal gospel of St. James: moving clockwise, the series starts at the far end with her parents, Joachim and Anne, her first steps, her service in the temple, her marriage to Joseph, and, finally, the Annunciation. Above in the dome are the ancestors of the Virgin. The story continues in the outer narthex with the infancy of Christ, starting again at the far left end with the journey of Mary and Joseph to Bethlehem. It continues clockwise around the outer narthex, with the Nativity, the wise men before Herod, and the flight to Egypt. At the far right end is the massacre of the innocents, which continues gruesomely over several scenes, with the cycle ending with the return from Egypt and the presentation of the young Jesus in the temple. The ceiling vaults show various scenes from the ministry of Christ, including his temptation by the devil, the multiplication of loaves, and the transformation of water into wine. These continue in the south side of the inner narthex, with scenes of Christ healing the sick and a vast wall mosaic, known as the Deesis, which depicts Christ and the Virgin, along with two tiny imperial figures.

The nave itself is light and airy but has lost most of its decoration, though a mosaic of the Dormition (Assumption) of the Virgin survives over the door, as well as a small mosaic of Mary and Jesus. The large side chapel was used for burials and contains several large tombs including, on the left, that of Theodore Metochites, which is surrounded by frescoes of saints and stories from the Old Testament. In the apse is an arresting image called the Anastasis, or "Resurrection"; it's one of the masterpieces of Byzantine art, showing Christ raising up Adam and Eve from their tombs at the end of time. The fresco in the vault shows the Second Coming: Christ sits enthroned with the saved, while the damned are taken down to hell and an angel rolls up the heavens like a scroll.

The easiest way to reach Kariye Müzesi is by taxi (about 10–15 TL from Eminönü), or take an Edirnekapı-bound bus from Eminönu or Taksim Square. The tree-shaded café outside the church and Asitane Restaurant next door are both pleasant spots for lunch before you trek back into town. ⊠ *Kariye Türbesi Sokak, (a short walk north of Fevzi Paşa Cad., near Edirnekapı in Old City walls)* ☎ *212/631–9241* 🖾 *15 TL* ⊙ *Apr.–Oct., Thurs.–Tues. 9–7 (ticket sales until 6); Nov.–Mar., Thurs.–Tues. 9–4:30.*

WORTH NOTING

Ahrida Synagogue. Located in Balat, the city's historically Jewish district, Istanbul's oldest synagogue is believed to date back to the 1430s, when it was founded by Jews from the town of Ohrid in what is today Macedonia. The synagogue was extensively restored in 1992 to the Ottoman baroque style of its last major reconstruction in the 17th century. The most interesting feature of this Sephardic place of worship is the boat-shape wooden *bimah* (reading platform), whose form is thought to represent either Noah's Ark or the ships that brought the Jews from the Iberian Peninsula to the Ottoman Empire in 1492. To visit, you must apply by email (preferred) or fax at least four business days in advance to the Chief Rabbinate (follow the directions on their website). ✉ *Kürkçü Çeşmesi Sok. 9, Balat* ☎ *212/293–8794* ⊕ *www. turkyahudileri.com* ☉ *Can be visited weekday mornings at 10.*

Ecumenical Orthodox Patriarchate (*Church of St. George*). After being kicked out of Aya Sofya after the Turkish conquest of the city, the Greek Orthodox Patriarchate wandered among several churches before settling here in the Church of St. George in 1601. Rebuilt after a fire in 1720, the church is a relatively simple basilica, though the (rather dark) interior has a refined atmosphere. Sarcophagi with the remains of some famous Byzantine saints, a Byzantine-era patriarchal throne, and two very old mosaic icons on the right side of the elaborate iconostasis are considered the most noteworthy features of the church. The main front gate of the compound has been welded shut ever since Sultan Mahmud II had Patriarch Gregory V hanged from it in 1821 as punishment for the Greek revolt. This small church is theoretically the center of the Orthodox world, though some Turks would like to claim that it serves only the dwindling community of Istanbul Greeks. ✉ *Rum Patrikhanesi, 342 20 Fener-Haliç* ⊕ *www.ec-patr.org* ☉ *Daily 9–4; check website for service times.*

Fethiye Müzesi (*Church of Theotokos Pammakaristos*). Thought to date to the 12th century, this church served as the seat of the Orthodox Patriarchate from 1456 to 1587 and a few years later was converted into a mosque, Fethiye Camii. While the main church building continues to function as a mosque, the beautiful side chapel has been turned into a small museum, with well-restored, impressive mosaics. The dome shows Christ Pantocrator ("ruler of all") surrounded by Old Testament prophets, while figures of Christ, saints, and patriarchs adorn the walls. In this chapel, Mehmet the Conqueror would talk religion and politics with his hand-picked patriarch, Gennadius. ✉ *Cami Avlusu Sokak off Fethiye Cad., Fatih* ☎ *212/635–1273* 💳 *5 TL* ☉ *Apr.–Oct., Thurs.–Tues. 9–6; Nov.–Mar., Thurs.–Tues. 9–4:30.*

FAMILY **Rahmi M. Koç Museum.** Housed on the grounds of an Ottoman-era shipyard on the shore of the Golden Horn, and in an adjacent foundry where anchors were cast for the Ottoman fleet, this museum complex was founded by one of Turkey's leading industrialists. The wonderful, eclectic collection includes aircraft, boats, a submarine, a tank, trucks, trains, a horse-drawn tram, motorcycles, antique cars, medieval telescopes, and every type of engine imaginable. Along with the many vehicles and machines, interactive displays on science and technology, as well as recreations of a sawmill and a 1920s olive oil factory, are of special appeal to children. There are several food and beverage venues on the premises, including Café du Levant, a Parisian-style bistro with art nouveau furnishings, and the waterfront Halat Restaurant. Take a Golden Horn ferry, a bus from Şişhane, or a taxi to get here. ✉ *Hasköy Cad. 5, Hasköy* ☎ *212/369–6600* ⊕ *www.rmk-museum.org.tr* 💳 *12.50 TL* ☉ *Apr.–Sept., Tues.–Fri. 10–5, weekends 10–8; Oct.–Mar., Tues.– Fri. 10–5, weekends 10–6.*

BEYOĞLU

Beyoğlu, the neighborhood on the hill above Galata, has traditionally been thought of as the "new town," and this is where you will feel the beating pulse of the modern city: the district is a major destination for eating and drinking, shopping, and arts and culture. "New" is of course a relative term in Istanbul, and many of the grand, European-style buildings you'll see here date from the late 19th century, when Beyoğlu—then known as Pera—was one of the city's most fashionable areas, home to large numbers of the city's non-Muslim minorities and the foreign diplomatic community. After a period of decline in the latter decades of the 20th century, Beyoğlu was revived around the turn of the millennium, as Istanbullus rediscovered the elegant old buildings and incredible views.

At the southern end of the neighborhood, Tünel Square marks the start of İstiklal Caddesi (Independence Avenue). Istanbul's main pedestrian street, İstiklal is lined with shops, cafés, and nightlife venues; allow some time to stroll along this bustling thoroughfare and simply take in the scene. İstiklal climbs gently uphill through Beyoğlu and across Galatasaray Meydanı (Galatasaray Square) to Taksim Square, the center of modern Istanbul. The Galata Mevlevihancsi (Galata dervish lodge), historic Fish Market, and private art museums and art galleries, including the Pera, are also in this area.

TOP ATTRACTIONS

İstiklal Caddesi (*Independence Avenue*). Running for almost a mile between Taksim Square and Tünel Square, İstiklal Caddesi is the heart of modern Istanbul. The street was once known as "La Grande Rue de Péra," after the Pera neighborhood. (The name "Pera" means "across" in Greek, and it was used because the area was on the other side of the Golden Horn from the city proper.) In the 19th century, palatial European embassies were built here, away from the dirt and chaos of the Old City. The wealthy city folk soon followed, particularly after the short funicular called the Tünel—the first underground urban rail line in continental Europe—was built in 1875 to carry them up the hill from their workplaces in the banks and trading houses of Karaköy. The area was traditionally non-Muslim, and the Greek, Armenian, Catholic, and Protestant churches here are more prominent than the mosques. The impressive building behind the massive iron gates halfway down the street is Galatasaray, a French-language high school founded in 1868 that for a time was the most prestigious institution of learning in the Ottoman Empire.

Today İstiklal is a lively pedestrian thoroughfare, filled with shops (an increasing number of them international chains), restaurants, cafés, and one or two cinemas. Turks love to promenade here, and at times it can turn into one great flow of humanity; even in the wee hours of the morning it's still alive with people. This is the Istanbul that never sleeps. ✉ *İstiklal Cad., Beyoğlu.*

**NEED A
BREAK?**

Mandabatmaz. On a tiny alleyway off İstiklal Caddesi, Mandabatmaz makes what many regard as the thickest, tastiest Turkish coffee in Istanbul—indeed, the shop's name roughly translates to "so thick even a water buffalo wouldn't sink in it." Seating is at tiny wooden tables and stools that line the alleyway. This being Turkey, tea is served also. ✉ *Olivya Geçidi 1/A (on alleyway across from St. Antoine Church on İstiklal), Beyoğlu, Istanbul* ⏱ *Daily 10 am–midnight.*

Museum of Innocence (*Masumiyet Müzesi*). Nobel Prize–winning Turkish novelist Orhan Pamuk's Museum of Innocence is one of the most unusual museums in Istanbul—and, perhaps, in the world. Opened in 2012 in the gentrifying Çukurcuma neighborhood in a former town house dating to the late 19th century, it's based on Pamuk's eponymous novel chronicling a decades-long story of unrequited love. On display are thousands of everyday objects, from vintage silverware and clothing to lottery tickets and matchbooks—obsessively "collected" over the years by the novel's main character—that present a portrait of daily life in Istanbul over the second half of the 20th century. The quirky, intimate museum is a must-see for anyone familiar with Pamuk's work or interested in Turkish social history, though some may find it esoteric. Audio tours available in English offer context. ✉ *Çukurcuma Cad., Dalgıç Çıkmazı 2, Beyoğlu* ☎ *212/252–9738* ⊕ *www.masumiyetmuzesi. org* ⏱ *Tues.–Thurs., Sat., and Sun. 10–6, Fri. 10–9.*

Pera Museum. A small private museum housed in a grand 1893 building (the former Bristol Hotel), the Pera showcases a diverse range of exhibits. It's best known for its permanent collection of Orientalist paintings by both European and Ottoman artists, dating from the 17th to 19th centuries and including panoramas of the city and court life; *The Tortoise Trainer* by Osman Hamdi Bey—a late-Ottoman painter who also founded the Istanbul Archaeological Museums—is particularly famous. Two smaller permanent exhibits focus on Kütahya ceramics and on the history of Anatolian weights and measures from the Hittite period to the early 20th century. The upper three levels house well-conceived temporary exhibits featuring local and international artists. ✉ *Meşrutiyet Cad. 65, Tepebaşı, Beyoğlu* ☎ *212/334–9900* ⊕ *www.peramuzesi.org. tr* 🎫 *10 TL* ⏱ *Tues.–Sat. 10–7, Sun. 12–6.*

WORTH NOTING

Fish Market (*Balık Pazarı*). Located just off İstiklal Caddesi next to the entrance to the Çiçek Pasajı, the Balık Pazarı is a bustling labyrinth of streets filled with stands selling fish, produce, spices, sweets, and souvenirs, and there are a couple of eateries specializing in *kokoreç*, or grilled lamb intestines: it all makes for great street theater. The adjacent Second Empire–style arcade, known as **Çiçek Pasajı**, was one of Istanbul's grandest shopping venues when it was built in 1876. In the early 20th century, it was gradually taken over by flower shops run by White Russian émigrés—earning it the name "Flower Arcade." In later decades, the arcade became dominated by famously boisterous *meyhanes*, or tavernas. The passage reopened in 1988 after a major restoration that rebuilt a collapsed section, and though it's still quite pretty, it feels more than like a reproduction. It now houses about a dozen rather touristy meyhane-style restaurants offering mezes and fish. For a more authentic local vibe, continue toward the end of the Fish Market and turn right on narrow **Nevizade Sokak**, a lively strip of bars and meyhanes, all with tiny sidewalk tables packed with locals in summer. ⊠ *Sahne Sok., Beyoğlu.*

Galata Mevlevihanesi (*Galata Mevlevi Lodge Museum*). Istanbul's oldest Mevlevi dervish lodge, which served as a meeting place and residence for "whirling dervishes" (followers of the Sufi mystic Celaleddin Rumi), was founded on this site in 1491 and rebuilt after a fire in 1765. Recently restored, it now houses a small but interesting museum with displays of dervish garments, handicrafts, and other artifacts, along with background information about the Mevlevi order and Sufism more generally. The biggest draw are the *sema* ceremonies (popularly known as whirling dervish ceremonies) that are performed by different Sufi groups at 5 pm each Sunday in the lodge's ceremonial hall. A sign out front explains how to book tickets; make arrangements in advance because performances can sell out. ⊠ *Galip Dede Cad. 15, southeast of Tünel Sq., off İstiklal Cad., Beyoğlu* ☎ *212/245–4141* ⊕ *www.galatamevlevihanesimuzesi.gov.tr* ☜ *5 TL, sema ceremonies 40 TL* ⊙ *Apr.–Oct., Tues.–Sun. 9–7, Oct.–Apr., Tues.–Sun. 9–4:30.*

Taksim Square (*Taksim Meydanı*). At the north end of İstiklal Caddesi, Istanbul's largest public square was once essentially a chaotic traffic circle and public transportation hub, but the Istanbul municipality has recently embarked on a project to completely pedestrianize the area (by rerouting traffic through underground tunnels) and create a true open plaza. The redevelopment of Taksim has been controversial, with some critics saying the ambitious makeover will end up dehumanizing the space. Meanwhile, plans by the government to likewise redevelop Gezi Parkı, next to the square, sparked major antigovernment protests in summer 2013 (⇨ *see Istanbul Today section*). At the time of this writing, redevelopment of the area was still under way.

The entrance to the Taksim Square station, from which both the metro and the funicular going down to Kabataş can be reached, is located in the square, so you'll probably end up here at one point or another. The open area at the top of İstiklal is dominated by the Monument of the Republic, built in 1928 and featuring Atatürk and his revolutionary cohorts. Also facing the square are Atatürk Cultural Center—the city's main concert hall —and the high-rise Marmara Hotel. Cumhuriyet Caddesi, the main street heading north from the square, is lined with travel agencies and airline ticket offices. Further up Cumhuriyet, Vali Konağı Caddesi splits off from the avenue and veers right, taking you to Nişantaşı, the city's high-fashion district. ⊠ *Beyoğlu.*

GALATA AND KARAKÖY

Just across the Galata Bridge from Eminönü, Karaköy was formerly a major port and its busy trading houses and banks made the neighborhood the economic hub of the late Ottoman Empire. Today, only ferry boats and cruise ships stop here, but the area still has a historic feel to it: Ottoman mosques line the waterfront, and Istanbul's Jewish Museum is also here. The Istanbul Modern, nestled among the mosques in a former shipping warehouse near the Tophane tram stop, is the city's leading art museum. Tophane is also one of the most popular spots in Istanbul for *nargile* (water pipe) smoking, featuring a long row of cafés filled with customers puffing away. In the last few years, Karaköy has started to become gentrified, with cafés, art galleries, and a few boutiques and hotels elbowing out dingy hardware stores and import-export offices. Galataport, a massive redevelopment project slated for the area, is likely to further revitalize the shoreline but also erase much of its historic character.

Just uphill from Karaköy is Galata, one of Istanbul's most ancient neighborhoods, dominated by the 14th-century Galata Tower about halfway up the slope. Like Karaköy, Galata has become increasingly popular and gentrified in recent years, though the neighborhood's long history is still palpable. Serdar-ı Ekrem, one of the main streets leading off the square around the Galata Tower, is lined with cafés and cutting-edge fashion designers' boutiques.

NEED A BREAK?

Karaköy fish sandwiches. Restaurants and cafés line the Karaköy waterfront by the passenger ferry landing, but for a truly delicious, cheap snack, the no-frills sandwich known as *balık ekmek*—literally "fish in bread"—may be one of your most memorable seafood meals in Turkey. The recipe is simple: take a freshly grilled fillet of fish and serve it in a half loaf of crusty white bread, perhaps with onion and/or tomato slices. What makes balık ekmek, though, is the setting—in Istanbul, the best sandwiches are served alfresco from small boats that pull up to the atmospheric quays near the Galata Bridge, smoke billowing from their onboard grills.

TOP ATTRACTIONS

Galata Tower (*Galata Kulesi*). The Galata area was a thriving Italian settlement both before and after the fall of Constantinople, and the Genoese built this tower as part of their fortifications in 1348, when they controlled the northern shore of the Golden Horn. The hillside location provided good defense, as well as a perch from which to monitor the comings and goings of vessels in the sea lanes below. The 67-meter (220 feet) tower later served at times as a jail and at others as a fire tower and now houses a restaurant at the top. The viewing gallery, which offers fabulous panoramic views of the city and across the Golden Horn and Sea of Marmara, is accessible by elevator and open during the day, for a rather steep fee—though it bears noting that similar views can be had at rooftop cafés and restaurants around the area. ⊠ *Büyük Hendek Cad., Galata* ☎ *212/293–8180* 🎫 *13 TL* ⊙ *Daily 9–8:30.*

Fodor's Choice ★ **Istanbul Modern.** Housed in a converted warehouse on the shores of the Bosphorus, the Istanbul Museum of Modern Art showcases modern and contemporary painting, sculpture, photography, and works in other media from Turkey and around the world. The permanent collection tells the story of modern Turkish art from its late-19th-century beginnings up through the present day, while a top-notch program of temporary exhibitions features significant local and international contemporary artists, with one gallery devoted exclusively to photography. A free guided tour (Thursdays and Sundays at 5 pm; reservations required) can give you a good introduction to the art scene in Turkey. The museum also has a sculpture garden, small cinema, and design store, while the Istanbul Modern Restaurant offers beautiful views of the Sea of Marmara and the Old City. ⊠ *Meclis-i Mebusan Cad. Liman İşletmeleri Sahası, Antrepo No. 4* ☎ *212/334–7300* ⊕ *www.istanbulmodern.org* 🖾 *15 TL* ⊗ *Tues., Wed., and Fri.–Sun. 10–6, Thurs. 10–8,*

WORTH NOTING

Jewish Museum of Turkey. The history of the Jews in Turkey is much more extensive and colorful than the size of this small museum housed in the 19th-century Zulfaris Synagogue might suggest. Nevertheless, the museum provides a fascinating glimpse into the lives of Turkish Jews, whose presence in Anatolia is traced back to as early as the 4th century BC. In 1492, the Spanish Inquisition drove Sephardic Jews from Spain and Portugal, and Sultan Beyazıt II welcomed the refugees to the Ottoman Empire. A large Jewish population thrived here for centuries, and some older Turkish Jews still speak a dialect of medieval Spanish called Ladino, or Judeo-Spanish. Today, Turkey's Jewish community numbers about 23,000, most of whom live in Istanbul, which has 18 active synagogues (three of which are on the Princes' Islands). The museum exhibits, most of them based on items donated by local Jewish families, include photographs, documents, and an ethnographic section with changing exhibits on subjects such as marriage traditions. There are also religious items brought from some very old (no longer active) synagogues in other parts of Turkey. ⊠ *Karaköy Meydanı, Perçemli Sok. 1(off Tersane Cad. Perçemli is small street on your right as you come out of Tünel exit of underpass)* ☎ *212/292–6333* ⊕ *www.muze500.com* 🖾 *10 TL* ⊗ *Mon.–Thurs. 10–4, Fri. and Sun. 10–2.*

BEŞIKTAŞ AND NIŞANTAŞI

A short ways up the Bosphorus from Karaköy is one of Istanbul's most visited attractions outside the Old City: the stunning neoclassical Dolmabahçe Palace, each room more ornate and over-the-top than the last. Nearby Beşiktaş is home to attractions like Yıldız Parkı and the recently reopened Naval Museum, which showcases an impressive collection of Ottoman artifacts in a specially designed venue overlooking the water. Most of Istanbul's luxurious Bosphorus-side hotels, including a couple that are housed in former Ottoman palaces, are likewise found in and around this area. A major transit hub, Beşiktaş is also the gateway to the Bosphorus neighborhoods to the north, and a departure point for ferries to Istanbul's Asian side.

Up the hill from Beşiktaş is Nişantaşı, the city's high-fashion district, home to the flagship stores of internationally known luxury brands as well as some local talent; the upscale hotels, restaurants, and cafés here also make it a great area for people-watching. The Military Museum is just a short walk away on Cumhuriyet Caddesi, which then leads back to Taksim Square.

TOP ATTRACTIONS

Fodor'sChoice **Dolmabahçe Palace** (*Dolmabahçe Sarayı*). The name Dolmabahçe means
★ "filled-in garden," from the fact that Sultan Ahmet I (ruled 1603–17) had an imperial garden planted here on land reclaimed from the sea. Abdülmecid I, whose free-spending lifestyle later bankrupted the empire, had this palace built from 1843 to 1856 as a symbol of Turkey's march toward European-style modernization. He gave father and son Garabet and Nikoğos Balyan—from a prominent Armenian family of late-Ottoman architects—complete freedom and an unlimited budget, the only demand being that the palace "surpass any other palace of any other potentate anywhere in the world." The result, an extraordinary mixture of Turkish and European architectural and decorative styles, is a riot of rococo: marble columns with gilt Corinthian capitals, huge mirrors, trompe l'oeil painted ceilings, inlaid parquet floors, rich brocade. Abdülmecid's bed is solid silver, the tub and basins in his marble-paved bathroom are translucent alabaster, and more than 200 kilos (420 pounds) of gold were used throughout the palace. European royalty helped contribute to the splendor: Queen Victoria sent a Bohemian crystal chandelier weighing 4½ tons (still the largest in Europe), while Czar Nicholas I of Russia provided polar-bear rugs. The result is as over-the-top and showy as a palace should be, and every bit as garish as Versailles.

Dolmabahçe is divided into the public "Selamlık" and the private "Harem," which can only be seen on separate, oversized guided tours, which together take about 90 minutes. The Selamlık is far more opulent, befitting its ceremonial purpose, while the Harem shows how traditional social hierarchies and living arrangements continued despite the outwardly European decor. Atatürk, the founder of the Turkish Republic, spent his last days here, and visitors are shown his deathbed in the Harem; all the clocks in the palace remain permanently stopped at 9:05 am, the hour of his death on November 10, 1938.

After the tour(s), take time to stroll along the palace's nearly ½ km (¼ mile)-long waterfront facade and through the formal gardens. Two small buildings set back from the palace can be visited without a tour: the ornate Crystal Pavilion, which boasts a crystal piano and glass conservatory with a crystal fountain, and the Clock Museum, which has some of the most elaborate clocks you have ever seen. ■TIP→ **The palace has a daily visitor quota, so call the reservation number, 212/327–2626 (open Mon.–Sat.), at least a day in advance to reserve tickets and to avoid lines of up to an hour long at the ticket booth.** ⊠ *Dolmabahçe Cad., Beşiktaş* ☎ *212/236–9000* ⬚ *Selamlık 30 TL, Harem 20 TL, joint ticket 40 TL* ☉ *Tues.–Wed. and Fri.–Sun. 9–4. Last tickets sold at 3.*

WORTH NOTING

FAMILY **Military Museum** (*Askeri Müze*). This large and fascinating museum boasts an extensive collection of swords, daggers, armor, and other weaponry, but it's not just for those interested in military history. Exhibits on the history of Turkic armies going back to the Huns, the Ottoman conquest of Istanbul, and more recent Turkish military engagements show the importance of military strength in shaping Ottoman history and modern Turkish society. Two gorgeously embroidered silk tents used by the Ottoman sultans on campaigns are particularly impressive. And don't miss the section of the great chain that the Byzantines stretched across the Golden Horn in 1453 during the Ottoman siege of the city. Atatürk was educated in this former military academy, and one room is a re-creation of his classroom. The highlight is the *Mehter*, or Janissary military band, which performs 17th- and 18th-century Ottoman military music in full period costume in a special auditorium at 3 pm when they're in town (most days). Watching this 55-member-strong ensemble, with their thunderous kettledrums and cymbals, will certainly give you an idea of why the Ottoman army was so feared in its day. ⊠ *Valikonağı Cad., Harbiye, Nişantaşı* ☎ *212/233–2720* 💷 *5 TL* ☼ *Wed.–Sun. 9–5.*

FAMILY   **Naval Museum** (*Deniz Müzesi*). Founded in 1897 and located here since 1961, Istanbul's Naval Museum reopened in late 2013 with a huge, state-of-the-art new wing that impressively showcases its large collection of Ottoman-era boats and maritime paraphernalia. The multistory, hangar-like structure was built to house more than a dozen *kayıks* (caiques)—long, slim wooden boats, rowed by oarsmen, that served as the primary mode of royal transportation in Istanbul for several hundred years. These graceful boats are decorated with gorgeous painted patterns and intricate carvings and figureheads covered with gold leaf; most also have an equally ornate curtained wooden pavilion that was built for the sultan, his wife, or his mother. The only extant Ottoman galley— a 40-meter ship dating to the 16th century that was used for warfare and rowed by 144 oarsmen—as well as an array of smaller boats and ship models are also on display. The underground level houses several exhibits of paintings, naval coats of arms, and other objects that give a good sense of the Ottoman Empire's onetime supremacy at sea. In the square just beside the museum are the tomb (usually locked) and a statue of Hayreddin Pasha, or "Barbarossa," the famous admiral of the empire's fleet in the Ottoman glory days of the early 16th century. ⊠ *Beşiktaş Cad., Beşiktaş* ☎ *212/327–4346* ⊕ *www.denizmuzeleri.tsk. tr/en/idmk* 💷 *5 TL* ☼ *Wed.–Sun. 9–5.*

Yıldız Parkı. The wooded slopes of Yıldız Parkı once formed part of the great forest that covered the European shore of the Bosphorus from the Golden Horn to the Black Sea. In the waning years of the Ottoman Empire, the park was the private garden of the nearby Çırağan and Yıldız palaces, and the women of the harem would occasionally be allowed to visit, secluded from prying eyes as they wandered among acacias, maples, and cypresses. Today the park is still beautiful, particularly in spring when the tulips and other flowers bloom, and in fall when the leaves of the deciduous trees change color.

At the top of the park (a 15–20-minute walk from the entrance) is the relatively modest (by Ottoman standards) **Yıldız Şale** (Yıldız Chalet), where the despotic Sultan Abdülhamid II (ruled 1876–1909) spent most of his time. It also served as a guesthouse for visiting heads of state, from Kaiser Wilhelm II to Charles de Gaulle and Margaret Thatcher.

The chalet, which can be visited on a guided tour only (30–40 minutes), is often blissfully empty of other tourists, which makes a visit all the more pleasurable. From the ornate French-style furniture to the huge, gilded Rörstrand porcelain stoves, the European influence is perhaps more obvious here than at any other Ottoman imperial residence, yet the elaborate mother-of-pearl inlay work in the dining room and the enormous Hereke carpet in the Ceremonial Hall are distinctly Turkish. Also in the park is the **Malta Köşkü**, a late 19th-century Ottoman pavilion that now houses a restaurant with period decor and views of the Bosphorus. ⊠ *Çırağan Cad., Beşiktaş* 🕾 *212/261–8460 for park, 212/259–4570 for chalet* 🎫 *Chalet 10 TL* ⊙ *Park: Apr–Oct., daily 8–10; Nov–Mar., daily 9–9; chalet: Apr–Oct., Tues., Wed., and Fri.– Sun. 9–5; Nov–Mar., Tues., Wed., and Fri.–Sun. 9–4:30.*

THE BOSPHORUS

Whether explored in person or seen from the vantage point of a boat on the water, the Bosphorus shores are home to some of the prettiest parts of the city. Both sides of the strait are dotted with palaces, fortresses, and waterfront neighborhoods lined with old wooden summer homes, called *yalıs* (waterside mansions), which were built for the city's wealthier residents in the Ottoman era. As you cruise up the Bosphorus, you'll have the chance to disembark at some of these waterside enclaves for a stroll.

Anadolu Kavağı. At the upper end of the Asian shore, Anadolu Kavağı is the final destination on the full Bosphorus cruises. A pretty little fishing village, it gets enough tourists to have a wide range of seafood restaurants, waffle stands, and ice cream shops. The main attraction is the dramatically situated **Byzantine Castle**, a 15-minute walk uphill from the village past more restaurants and cafés. The hill was once the site of a temple to Zeus Ourios (god of the favoring winds), which dates back, legend has it, to the days when Jason passed by in search of the Golden Fleece. The castle, built by the Byzantines and expanded by their Genoese allies, is today in a fairly ruined state, but it's worth climbing up to it for the spectacular views over the upper Bosphorus to the blustery Black Sea.

Arnavutköy. This picturesque neighborhood just below Bebek is a pleasant place for a stroll. The waterfront is taken up by a row of beautiful 19th-century wooden yalıs, some of which now house fish restaurants. Up the hill from the water, narrow streets are lined with more old wooden houses, some with trailing vines.

Bebek. One of Istanbul's most fashionable suburbs, Bebek is especially popular with the affluent boating set, thanks to the area's pretty natural harbor. The neighborhood has a number of cafés and restaurants on both sides of the main coastal road and a few upscale boutiques selling clothing and jewelry; there's also a small, shaded public park on the waterfront. The stretches of coastline both north and south of Bebek are perfect for a promenade. Bebek is about 20–30 minutes by taxi from central Istanbul.

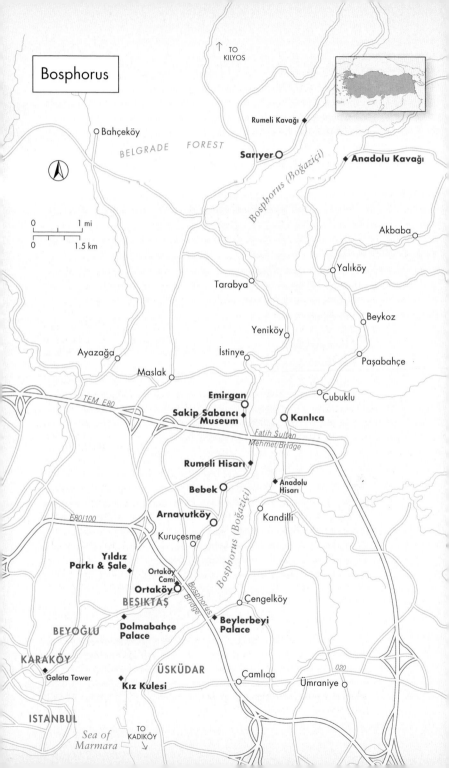

Bosphorus

↑ TO
KILYOS

Rumeli Kavağı ◆

BELGRADE   FOREST

○ Bahçeköy

Sarıyer ○

◆ Anadolu Kavağı

Bosphorus (Boğaziçi)

0   1 mi
0   1.5 km

Akbaba ○

○ Yalıköy

Tarabya ○

○ Beykoz

Yeniköy ○

Ayazağa ○

İstinye ○

○ Paşabahçe

Maslak ○

TEM E80

Emirgan ○

○ Çubuklu

Sakip Sabancı
Museum ◆

◆ Kanlıca

Fatih Sultan
Mehmet Bridge

Rumeli Hisarı ◆

E80/100

Bebek ○

◆ Anadolu
Hisarı

Arnavutköy ○

○ Kandilli

Kuruçesme ○

Bosphorus (Boğaziçi)

Yıldız
Parkı & Şale ◆

Ortaköy
Cami

Ortaköy ○

BEŞİKTAŞ

○ Çengelköy

BEYOĞLU

Bosphorus Bridge

◆ Beylerbeyi
Palace

Dolmabahçe
Palace ◆

KARAKÖY

ÜSKÜDAR

Çamlıca ○

020

◆ Galata Tower

○ Çamlıca

Ümraniye ○

Kız Kulesi ◆

ISTANBUL

Sea of
Marmara

TO
KADIKÖY
↓

Mini Dondurma. This tiny ice cream shop on Bebek's main street has repeatedly been rated the best in town since it opened back in 1968. Their 22 flavors include the distinctive *güllü lokum* (rose-flavored Turkish delight) ice cream. The shop is open March through November. ⊠ *Cevdet Paşa Cad. 38A, Bebek* ☎ *212/257-1070.*

Beylerbeyi Palace (*Beylerbeyi Sarayı*). Built as a summer residence for Sultan Abdülaziz in 1865, Beylerbeyi is a bit like a mini-Dolmabahçe that incorporates a similarly eclectic mix of European and Turkish styles but is smaller, less grandiose, and has more of a personal feel. Beylerbeyi boasts ornately painted ceilings, Baccarat crystal chandeliers, gold-topped marble columns, and intricately carved wooden furniture; the central hall has a white-marble fountain and a stairway wide enough for a regiment. The magnolia-shaded palace grounds are also pleasant, while two waterfront bathing pavilions (one was for men, the other for women) stand out for their bizarrely fanciful architecture. You must join a tour to see the palace. ⊠ *Çayırbaşı Durağı, Beylerbeyi* ☎ *216/321-9320* ✆ *20 TL* ☺ *Tues.–Wed. and Fri.–Sun. 9–5 in summer, 9–4 in winter.*

Emirgan. The quiet suburb of Emirgan is best known for its large, attractive public park, **Emirgan Korusu**—formerly an estate owned by the Khedive of Egypt—which has flower gardens, a small pond, walking paths, and picnic areas. Three 19th-century wooden pavilions in the park have been restored, and house restaurants and cafés. During Istanbul's annual Tulip Festival in April, visitors flock to Emirgan Korusu for its striking flower displays—each year, a million or more tulips of dozens of different varieties are planted in this park alone. The flower, which takes its name from the Turkish word *tülbend* (turban), was most likely introduced to Europe in the late 16th century via the Ottoman Empire, setting off the famous "tulip craze" in the Netherlands. Emirgan is also where the **Sakıp Sabancı Museum** is located.

Kanlıca. Just north of the second Bosphorus bridge, the village-turned-suburb of Kanlıca has been famous for its delicious yogurt for at least 300 years, and small restaurants around the square by the quay serve this treat. Nearby, white 19th-century wooden villas line the waterfront. Kanlıca is the first stop on the Asian shore on the full Bosphorus cruises leaving from Eminönü.

Ortaköy. The charming neighborhood of Ortaköy is popular with both locals and visitors and is a lovely spot to spend a summer afternoon or evening. Restaurants and cafés are clustered around the small square on the waterfront, which is dominated by the iconic silhouette of **Ortaköy Camii** (closed for restoration as of this writing), an elegant 19th-century Ottoman mosque designed by the same Armenian architects who built the Dolmabahçe Palace. The mosque is perched directly overlooking the water, with the imposing sight of the Bosphorus Bridge (built 1973) looming behind it. On Sundays, the narrow, cobblestoned surrounding streets are lined with stalls selling jewelry, scarves, trinkets, and small antique items. Ortaköy is also considered the best place in Istanbul to try the street food called *kumpir* (basically giant baked potatoes for

CLOSE UP

Planning a Bosphorus Day Cruise

This ferry is leaving the Eminönü docks near Sultanahmet to cross the Bosphorus.

One of the most pleasant experiences in Istanbul—and an easy way to escape the chaos of the city—is a trip up the Bosphorus by ferry. If you want to go all the way to the mouth of the Black Sea, and have the time to make a day of it, you can take a "full Bosphorus cruise." These boats leave from Eminönü and zigzag up the Bosphorus with set stops, arriving in the middle of the day for a three-hour break at either **Rumeli Kavağı (European side)** or **Anadolu Kavağı (Asian side)**, two fishing villages with fortresses at the opening to the Black Sea. Then they zigzag back down to Eminönü. Operated by Şehir Hatları, the ferries depart daily from the first quay on the Bosphorus side of the Galata Bridge (look for the sign that says "Boğaz İskelesi") at 10:35 and 1:35 in the summer months (approximately early June to mid-September) and at 10:35 in the winter. A one-way ticket is 15 TL, while the round-trip costs 25 TL. On Saturday nights in summer, a "Sunset Cruise" follows the same route, leaving Eminönü at 6:25 and returning around midnight (20 TL). The Dentur Avrasya company recently launched its own boat rides to Anadolu Kavağı from Kabataş (departing 11:15) and Ortaköy

(departing 11:30), for a round-trip fare of 15 TL; as of this writing, it's not clear whether these will continue year-round.

If your time is more limited, you can take a short cruise with no stops, lasting two hours or less, which goes to the second Bosphorus bridge before turning around. Two private companies operate frequent daily trips: Turyol, on the Golden Horn side of Galata Bridge, has a set timetable (12 TL), while Boğaziçi Yoltur, on the Bosphorus side, operates in a more ad hoc fashion (10 TL).

Alternatively, several commuter ferries leave from Boğaz İskelesi between 5 and 7 pm every day (more frequently on weekdays than weekends) and zigzag up the Bosphorus for a mere 3 TL—but you'll have to catch a bus or taxi back later, as there are no return ferries until the morning. A number of buses run up and down both sides; most useful on the European side are the 25E (Kabataş to Sarıyer) and 25T (Taksim to Sarıyer). On the Asian side, several buses run from Üsküdar past Beylerbeyi, Anadolu Hisarı, and Kanlıca to Beykoz, from where the 15A continues up to Anadolu Kavağı.

which you can choose all sorts of fillings): look for the row of about a dozen food stands—selling kumpir, waffles, and other snacks—all competing for customers' attention.

FAMILY **Rumeli Hisarı** (*Castle of Europe*). Built on a hill overlooking the water, Rumeli Hisarı is the best preserved of all the fortresses on the Bosphorus and well worth a visit. Constructed in just four months in 1452, these eccentric-looking fortifications were ordered built by Mehmet the Conqueror directly across from Anadolu Hisarı, at the narrowest point of the strait. This allowed the Ottomans to take control of the waterway, and Mehmet and his troops conquered Constantinople the following year. The real fun here is in climbing on and around the towers and crenellated walls, which offer fabulous views of the Bosphorus and the nearby Fatih Sultan Mehmet Bridge. ⊠ *Yahya Kemal Cad. 42, Rumelihisarı* ☎ *212/263–5305* 🎫 *5 TL* ☉ *Thurs.–Tues. 9–7 in summer, 8:30-6 in winter.*

Sakıp Sabancı Museum (*Sakıp Sabancı Müzesi*). The Sakıp Sabancı Museum is one of Istanbul's premier private museums, thanks to its world-class exhibits and stunning location in a historic villa overlooking the water in the leafy suburb of Emirgan. The permanent collection includes an excellent display of late-19th-century Orientalist and early Republican Turkish paintings, rare examples of Ottoman calligraphy, and antique furnishings such as exquisite Sèvres vases, all from the private collection of the industrialist Sabancı family. The biggest draws, though, are the temporary installations—of a caliber equal to that seen at top museums around the world—which range from retrospectives on major artists like Picasso and leading contemporary names such as Anish Kapoor to exhibits on Anatolian archaeology and masterpieces of Islamic art. Housed in the museum, Müzedechanga restaurant is a foodie destination in itself. The beautiful grounds, which boast 150-year-old monumental trees and a variety of rare plants from around the world, are perfect for a stroll after viewing the art. ⊠ *Sakıp Sabancı Cad. 42, Emirgan* ☎ *212/277–2200* ⊕ *muze.sabanciuniv.edu* 🎫 *15 TL; free on Wed.* ☉ *Tues. and Thurs.–Sun. 10–6, Wed. 10–8.*

Sarıyer. One of the northernmost settlements on the European shore of the Bosphorus, Sarıyer, centered on a small harbor and backed by a row of seafood restaurants, still has the feel of a fishing village. As you stroll along the Bosphorus with the hustle of the big city at arm's length, you'll see majestic old *yalıs*—some of which are beautifully kept up, and others that have been abandoned and are in a sad state of deterioration. Sarıyer is one of the stops on the full Bosphorus cruises that leave from Eminönü, and is a nice place for a fish lunch.

THE ASIAN SHORE

Spread out along the shoreline of the lower Bosphorus and the Sea of Marmara, the main residential districts on the Asian side have few "sights" as such but offer a pleasant change of pace from the faster tempo of the European side—as well as a welcome escape from the tourist crowds. Üsküdar has several Ottoman imperial mosques and presents a slice of Istanbul life that is more traditional than what visitors generally see across the water. Farther down the coast, Kadıköy has a youthful, relaxed vibe; the pedestrian-only area off the waterfront and lively nightlife are among its top draws. From Kadıköy, a short taxi or dolmuş ride takes you to the beginning of Bağdat Caddesi, or "Baghdad Avenue," a 6-km-long (3.7-mile-long) boulevard that is the Asian side's ritziest avenue. Lined with elegant apartment buildings, upscale designer boutiques, and trendy restaurants, it gets increasingly posh as you get farther away from Kadıköy towards Suadiye.

Kadıköy. Though there's no visible evidence of its beginnings as the ancient Greek colony of Chalcedon, the relaxed, suburban neighborhood of Kadıköy is a pleasant area to explore on foot. As you approach by ferry, look for the beautiful neoclassical-style Haydarpaşa train station, built out over the water on piles at the north end of the harbor. Built in 1908, the terminal is one of the most notable pieces of architecture on the Asian side and a classic Istanbul landmark. You can get off here, at the tiled Ottoman-era quay, or stay on the boat for a few more minutes until it reaches Kadıköy proper.

The area just up from the Kadıköy dock, to the south of busy Söğütlü Çeşme Caddesi, is known as the Çarşı, or "market"—a grid of narrow, pedestrian-only lanes filled with a small open-air food market, shops, cafés, nightlife venues, and a few modern churches. Güneşlibahçe Sokak, home to an assortment of fish restaurants and some bars, is particularly lively. Several streets up and farther to the right, Kadife Sokak, dubbed Barlar Sokağı, or "bars street," is the center of Kadıköy's nightlife, lined with small, wooden rowhouses occupied by bars with a casual, laid-back vibe. A few streets north of Kadife Sokak toward Söğütlü Çeşme Caddesi, Osmancık Sokak (just off Serasker Caddesi) is another popular nightlife street that becomes a sort of mini version of Beyoğlu's Nevizade Sokak in the summer, lined with small bars with sidewalk seating.

General Asım Gündüz Caddesi, which runs perpendicular to Söğütlü Çeşme Caddesi, has branches of well-known Turkish and international clothing stores, movie theaters, and some eateries. On Tuesdays, near the intersection of these two streets (look for the bronze sculpture of a bull), there begins a lively, open-air street market, selling mostly food and clothes. A tiny nostalgic tram runs in a clockwise direction up General Asım Gündüz, from where it loops down to the lovely waterfront neighborhood of Moda before stopping at the Kadıköy dock. If you've come this far on foot, it's nice to ride the tram back to the dock. ⊠ *Asian Side.*

Kız Kulesi (*Maiden's Tower*). Fortified since Byzantine times, this little islet off the Asian shore guarded the busy shipping lanes and, now, restored and lit up, it's the star of the lower Bosphorus. The name Leander's Tower, as it was known in antiquity, associates the island with the legend of Leander, who was said to have swum the strait each night guided by the lamp of his lover, Hero—though this myth in fact took place in the Dardanelles to the southwest. The Turkish name "Maiden's Tower" comes from a legend associated with several offshore castles: as the story goes, a princess is placed on an island after a prophecy that

2

she will die of a snakebite, but it happens anyway, when a snake comes ashore in a basket of fruit. The current tower, which dates to the 18th century, now houses an expensive but not all that impressive café and restaurant. Boats ferry visitors at regular intervals from Kabataş on the European side and Salacak (near Üsküdar) on the Asian shore. ☒ *Asian Side* ☎ *216/342-4747* ⊕ *www.kizkulesi.com.tr* ✉ *20 TL for round-trip boat ride from Salacak or Kabataş for daytime visitors; boat transfers free in evening for restaurant customers (reservations essential)* ☉ *Daily 9–6:30 for visitors; 8:15pm–midnight for dinner and bar.*

Üsküdar. One of the oldest inhabited areas on the Asian shore, Üsküdar takes its name from the 7th-century BC settlement of Scutari, though nothing now remains of that ancient town. Today, Üsküdar is a conservative residential district with a handful of noteworthy Ottoman mosques. The waterfront looks set to change dramatically with the opening of the long-awaited Marmaray, a rail tunnel under the Bosphorus that is to transport passengers from Üsküdar to Sirkeci in just four minutes. The ferry landing is dominated by Sinan's pretty, if somewhat dark, Mihrimah Sultan Camii, also known as the İskele Camii (built 1548). The large Yeni Valide Camii from 1710 and another Sinan mosque, the small, beautifully situated Şemsi Paşa Camii, are a short walk southwest along the waterfront.

The most architecturally significant mosque in the district, Sinan's Atık Valide Camii from 1583, is a 20-minute gradually uphill walk from the waterfront on Hakimiyeti Milliye Caddesi and then on Dr. Fahri Atabey Caddesi. There's a pleasant tea garden in the mosque courtyard, and several other buildings in the complex are in the process of being restored. Another couple hundred yards to the left and then up Çavuşdere Caddesi is the 17th-century Çinili Cami, or "Tiled Mosque," which has splendid İznik tiles. Though the mosque itself is usually kept locked to protect the tiles, it's possible to access the porticos and peak in through the windows. ☒ *Asian Side.*

WHERE TO EAT

Updated by
Vanessa H.
Larson

This city is a food lover's town and restaurants abound, from humble kebab joints to fancy fish venues, with a variety of excellent options in between. Owing to its location on the Bosphorus, which connects the Black Sea to the Sea of Marmara, Istanbul is famous for its seafood. A classic Istanbul meal, usually eaten at one of the city's rollicking *meyhanes* (literally "drinking places"), starts off with a wide selection of tapas-style cold appetizers called *mezes,* then a hot starter or two, and then moves on to a main course of grilled fish, all of it accompanied by the anise-flavored spirit rakı, Turkey's national drink. The waiter will generally bring a tray over to your table to show off the day's *mezes* and you simply point to what you'd like. Note that the portions you get are often larger than the samples shown on the tray, so don't over-order; you can always select a second—or third—round later. When it comes to the main course, fish can be expensive, so check prices and ask what's in season before ordering. In Istanbul, fall and winter are the best seasons for seafood.

Although Istanbul's dining scene, though diverse, was once mostly limited to Turkish cooking, a new generation of chefs is successfully fusing local dishes with more international flavors. Some are trained in the United States and Europe and bring home the contemporary culinary techniques they've learned abroad, and the result is a kind of nouvelle Turkish cuisine. Interest in little-known specialty foods and regional dishes from around Turkey is also taking hold, as chefs increasingly look at home, rather than abroad, for inspiration. Over the past few years, a handful of restaurants have opened where the chef-owner defines the vision and personality of the venue—though this may be old hat in Europe or North America, it represents an exciting new trend in Istanbul.

Istanbullus take their eating seriously, holding establishments to a very high standard; they expect their food to be fresh and well-prepared at even the most basic of eateries, and are likely to feel that few places can hold a candle to "Mom's cooking." That said, at restaurants catering to a trendier, more upscale crowd, style sometimes seems to pass for substance, and consistency can be elusive; the fanciest venues may not necessarily offer the best food.

Sultanahmet might have most of the city's major sights and many hotels, but sadly, these places cater mostly to tourists and are the ones most likely to let their standards slip. Save for a few standouts, the area is sorely lacking in good dining options, and you'll have much better luck if you head across the Golden Horn, where the lively Beyoğlu district has everything from holes in the wall serving delicious home cooking to some of Istanbul's sleekest restaurants, while Karaköy and Galata also have an increasing range of dining options. Or head to some of the small, charming neighborhoods along the Bosphorus, which are famous for their fish restaurants; while these establishments tend to be more upscale and expensive, there are some affordable options as well.

Since Istanbullus love to go out, reservations are essential at most of the city's better restaurants. In summer, many establishments move their dining areas outdoors, and reservations become even more important if you want to snag a coveted outside table. For the most part, dining is casual, although locals enjoy dressing smartly when they're out. You may feel terribly underdressed if you show up in a restaurant dressed in shorts and a T-shirt, even in summer.

Despite Islamic proscriptions against alcohol, beer, wine, and the local spirit rakı are widely available, and at more upscale venues you can also find cocktails. Because of high taxes, however, alcoholic drinks—particularly anything imported—tend to be considerably more expensive than in North America or Europe. The national lager Efes is the most widely available beer; venues may carry two or three other domestic and international labels, but don't expect a wide selection. Yeni Rakı, a state-run monopoly until not long ago, has remained the most popular rakı brand despite a recent proliferation of new companies producing the spirit. Wine consumption in Turkey has traditionally lagged far behind that of beer and rakı, but that's been slowly changing in recent years as the quality of local wines has started to improve. The local wine

2

industry is still in its fledgling stages compared to other parts of the world, but there are some very drinkable domestic wines on the market, most priced at only a fraction of what you'd pay for an imported label. Turkish wines are made from foreign grapes as well as indigenous varietals, of which the most noteworthy are the reds Öküzgözü, Boğazkere, and Kalecik Karası and the whites Emir and Narince.

During the Islamic holy month of Ramadan, restaurants that cater primarily to tourists, and most venues in cosmopolitan parts of Istanbul such as Beyoğlu, continue to operate normally. In more traditional neighborhoods some restaurants close altogether or change their hours of operation. In recent years, it has become increasingly popular to go to restaurants for *iftar*—the evening meal that breaks the daily fast—instead of having it in the home, as was traditionally done.

Prices in the reviews are the average cost of a main course at dinner, or if dinner is not served, at lunch.

USING THE MAPS

Throughout the listings, you'll see mapping symbols and coordinates (such as ⊹ 1:A2) after property names or reviews. The first number after the ⊹ symbol indicates the map number. Following that is the property's coordinate on the map grid.

SULTANAHMET

$

TURKISH

✕ **Doy-Doy.** *Doy-doy* is a Turkish expression for "full" and, unlike many other places in tourist-filled Sultanahmet, you can indeed fill up for a reasonable sum at this no-frills spot. The place serves a fairly standard array of kebabs and *pide*—a type of Turkish pizza baked in a wood-burning oven—with different toppings, but at lunchtime, it's also frequented by local workers, who come for the cheap daily specials, such as meat-and-vegetable stew or baked beans (displayed on the steam table to the left of the entrance). The two-level rooftop terrace, open in summer, has fine views of the area—but don't expect to savor them with a drink in hand, as no alcohol is served. Ⓢ *Average main: 16 TL* ✉ *Şifa Hamamı Sok. 13* ☎ *212/517–1588* ⊕ *www.doydoy-restaurant. com* ⊹ *2:B5.*

$$$$

SEAFOOD

Fodor'sChoice

★

✕ **Giritli.** Popular with locals and visitors alike, Giritli offers a prix-fixe multicourse dinner menu of well-prepared Cretan specialties that includes unlimited local alcoholic drinks (wine or *rakı*). At least 15 different cold mezes—such as sea bass ceviche, herb-covered cubes of feta cheese with walnuts and olives, and various uncommon wild greens—are followed by hot starters like fried calamari or octopus leg in olive oil. The main course is a choice among several grilled fish, followed by dessert. With its whitewashed walls, colored lights, and blue trim, the restaurant's relaxed garden feels like a slice of the Greek islands in Istanbul. A limited lunch menu is also available. Ⓢ *Average main: 125 TL* ✉ *Keresteci Hakkı Sok.* ☎ *212/458–2270* ⊕ *www.giritlirestoran. com* ⚐ *Reservations essential* ⊹ *2:C5.*

$$

TURKISH

✕ **Khorasani.** One of Sultanahmet's most outstanding restaurants emphasizes the Arab- and Kurdish-influenced cuisine of southeastern Turkey, from where the restaurant's owners hail. This translates to delicious

BEST BETS FOR ISTANBUL DINING

With so many restaurants to choose from, how to decide? Fodor's writers and editors have chosen their favorites, by price, cuisine, and experience. In the lists below.

Fodor's Choice ★

Çiya, $, p. 115
Giritli, $$$$, p. 99
Gram, $, p. 108
Kantin, $$, p. 113
Lokanta Maya, $$$, p. 112
Mikla, $$$$, p. 110
Münferit, $$$, p. 110
Müzedechanga, $$$$, p. 114
NAR Restaurant, $$, p. 106
Yeni Lokanta, $$$, p. 111

By Price

$
Çiya, p. 115
Doy-Doy, p. 99
Fıccın, p. 108
Gram, p. 108

$$
Kantin, p. 113
Karaköy Lokantası, p. 112
Khorasani, p. 99
NAR Restaurant, p. 106

$$$
Asitane, p. 107

Lokanta Maya, p. 112
Münferit, p. 110
Yeni Lokanta, p. 111

$$$$
Giritli, p. 99
Mikla, p. 110
Müzedechanga, p. 114
Seasons, p. 101

By Cuisine

CONTEMPORARY
Changa, $$$$, p. 107
Gile, $$$$, p. 113
The House Café, $$, p. 114
Istanbul Modern Restaurant, $$$, p. 111

KEBABS
Akdeniz Hatay Sofrası, $$, p. 106
Antiochia, $, p. 107
Khorasani, $$, p. 99
Zübeyir Ocakbaşı, $$, p. 111

MEZES
Karaköy Lokantası, $$, p. 112
Meze by Lemon Tree, $$$, p. 110
Münferit, $$$, p. 110

REGIONAL SPECIALTIES
Akdeniz Hatay Sofrası, $$, p. 106
Çiya, $, p. 115
Fıccın, $, p. 108
Giritli, $$$$, p. 99

SEAFOOD
Adem Baba, $, p. 114
Giritli, $$$$, p. 99
Karaköy Lokantası, $$, p. 112
Sıdıka, $, p. 113
Sultanahmet Fish House, $$, p. 101

TRADITIONAL OTTOMAN
Asitane, $$$, p. 107
Tuğra, $$$$, p. 115

By Experience

FINE DINING
Asitane, $$$, p. 107
Gile, $$$$, p. 113
Mikla, $$$$, p. 110
Seasons, $$$$, p. 101
Tuğra, $$$$, p. 115

GREAT VIEW
Hamdi Restaurant, $$, p. 106
Istanbul Modern Restaurant, $$$, p. 111
Mikla, $$$$, p. 110
Müzedechanga, $$$$, p. 114

OUTDOOR DINING
Asitane, $$$, p. 107
Giritli, $$$$, p. 99
The House Café, $$, p. 114
Müzedechanga, $$$$, p. 114

TRENDY VIBE
Gram, $, p. 108
The House Café, $$, p. 114
Istanbul Modern Restaurant, $$$, p. 111
Lokanta Maya, $$$, p. 112
Meze by Lemon Tree, $$$, p. 110
Münferit, $$$, p. 110

mezes like hummus, *muhammara* (hot pepper and walnut spread), and thyme salad, as well as tasty kebabs like the lamb shish. Interesting non-kebab main dishes include lamb stew, which has chunks of meat in a thick sauce of onions, carrots, and prunes. Diners can sit outdoors on the cobblestoned sidewalk or get a table inside to watch the chefs prepare kebabs over the large charcoal grill. [$] *Average main: 30 TL* ✉ *Ticarethane Sok. 39/41* ☎ *212/519–5959* 🌐 *www.khorasanirestaurant.com* ✍ *Reservations essential* ✦ *2:B4.*

$$ INTERNATIONAL 🍴 **Mozaik.** This restored late-19th-century house with small, sun-dappled dining rooms, cozy furniture, and creaky wooden floors is a delightful refuge in the midst of busy Sultanahmet. But it's not just the setting that's noteworthy; the vast menu at this friendly venue ranges from a variety of kebabs and other Turkish specialties to salads, pastas, steaks, schnitzel, and other international fare. The food here is well above average for this part of town, and in summer, seating spills out into the alley beside the restaurant, creating a lively atmosphere. [$] *Average main: 31 TL* ✉ *İncili Çavuş Sok. 1* ☎ *212/512–4177* 🌐 *www.mozaikrestaurant.com* ✦ *2:B4.*

$$ TURKISH 🍴 **Rumeli Café Restaurant.** This charming spot on a quiet side street off Divanyolu offers a range of Turkish specialties, including unusual Armenian and Greek options such as *papaz yahnisi,* a Byzantine stew of lamb, potatoes, and pumpkin cooked in a terra-cotta dish. International classics include a variety of salads, pastas, and steaks. The cozy interior, formerly the site of a book bindery, has Ottoman and Byzantine-style architectural details and hand-painted frescoes on the exposed brick walls. In summer you can sit outside at tables on the sidewalk or on the intimate roof terrace (with a partial view). [$] *Average main: 30 TL* ✉ *Ticarethane Sok. 8* ☎ *212/512–0008* ✦ *2:B4.*

$$$$ TURKISH 🍴 **Seasons.** A delightful gazebo-like glass pavilion in the middle of the manicured garden courtyard of the Four Seasons is the ritziest restaurant in Sultanahmet (and also the most expensive). The dinner menu highlights Turkish dishes—made with ingredients sourced locally from around the country—ranging from cold and hot mezes to grilled meats and fish, including a boneless lamb shank cooked for eight hours. The lunch menu is broader, featuring sandwiches and brick-oven pizzas in addition to meat and seafood dishes. On Sunday, the restaurant's brunch buffet (140 TL; no buffet during Ramadan) draws crowds from across Istanbul. [$] *Average main: 70 TL* ✉ *Tevkifhane Sok. 1* ☎ *212/402–3150* 🌐 *www.fourseasons.com/istanbul/* ✍ *Reservations essential* ✦ *2:C4.*

$$ SEAFOOD 🍴 **Sultanahmet Fish House.** There are no obsequious waiters at Sultanahmet Fish House and no fancy dress code—just good, well-prepared seafood served in a friendly atmosphere. The mainly seafood mezes include sardines, octopus, and mackerel in olive oil, while mains comprise a range of fish and a few kebabs. Fish preparations go beyond the standard grilling and frying: sea bass with saffron, cooked in a terracotta casserole, is a particular standout. Light blue and yellow walls, multicolored antique lamps hanging from the ceiling, and colorful nomad textiles create an inviting atmosphere. There is also a small section of sidewalk seating out front. [$] *Average main: 34 TL* ✉ *Prof. İsmail*

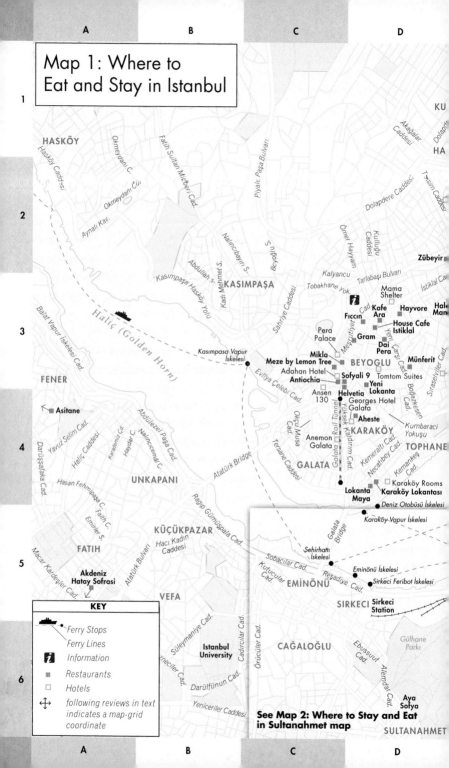

Map 1: Where to Eat and Stay in Istanbul

HASKÖY

Hasköy Caddesi

Okmeydanı C.

Okmeydanı Cd.

Aynalı Kav.

Fatih Sultan Mehmet Cad.

Piyale Paşa Bulvarı

KU

Akadalar Caddesi

Dolap

HA

Tesvin Caddesi

Dolapdere Caddesi

Kulluğu Caddesi

Ömer Hayyam

Beyoğlu'u S.

Nalıncıbayrı S.

Abdullah s.

Kadı Mehmet s.

Kalyancu

Tarlabaşı Bulvarı

Tobakhane yok.

Zübeyir

İstiklal Cad

KASIMPAŞA

Satırye Caddesi

Kasımpaşa Hasköy Yolu

Mama Shelter

🛈

Kafe Ara Cad

Hayvore

Hale Man

Ficcin

House Cafe İstiklal

Haliç (Golden Horn)

Kasımpaşa Vapur İskelesi

Pera Palace

Gram

Yeni Çarşı Cad.

Dai Pera

Münferit

Mesrutiyet Cad.

Evliya Çelebi Cad.

Mikla

Meze by Lemon Tree

BEYOĞLU

FENER

◀ **Asitane**

Adahan Hotel

Antiochia

Sofyali 9

Tomtom Suites

Yeni Lokanta

Sıraselviler Cad.

Boğazkesen Cad.

Ansen 130

Helvetia

Georges Hotel Galata

□

Yüksek Kaldırım Cad.

Aheste

Anemon Galata □

Galata Rail Tunnel

KARAKÖY

Kumbaracı Yokuşu

TOPHANE

Abdülezel Paşa Cad.

Yavuz Selim Cad.

Haydar C.

Karabaşı Cd.

Nalıncıemal C.

Okçu Musa Cad.

Atatürk Bridge

Tersane Caddesi

GALATA

Kemeraltı Cad.

Necatibey Cad.

Kemankeş Cad.

Darüşşafaka Cad.

Hasan Fehmipaşa C.

Fatih C.

Emirler S.

Macar Kardeşler Cad.

UNKAPANI

Ragıp Gümüşpala Cad.

Lokanta Maya

□ **Karaköy Rooms**

Karaköy Lokantası

● Deniz Otobüsü İskelesi

Galata Bridge

Karaköy-Vapur İskelesi

KÜÇÜKPAZAR

Hacı Kadın Caddesi

Şehirhattı İskelesi ●

Sobacılar Cad.

Kutucular Cad.

Reşadiye Cad.

EMİNÖNÜ

Eminönü İskelesi

Sirkeci Feribot İskelesi

FATİH

Atatürk Bulvarı

Akdeniz Hatay Sofrası

SIRKECİ Sirkeci Station

VEFA

Süleymaniye Cad.

Cadırcılar Cad.

Istanbul University

Örücüler Cad.

CAĞALOĞLU

Ebussuut Cad.

Gülhane Parkı

Alemdar Cad.

Yeniçeriler Caddesi

Darülfünun Cad.

See Map 2: Where to Stay and Eat in Sultanahmet map

Aya Sofya

SULTANAHMET

KEY

🚢 ● Ferry Stops

Ferry Lines

🛈 Information

■ Restaurants

□ Hotels

⬌ following reviews in text indicates a map-grid coordinate

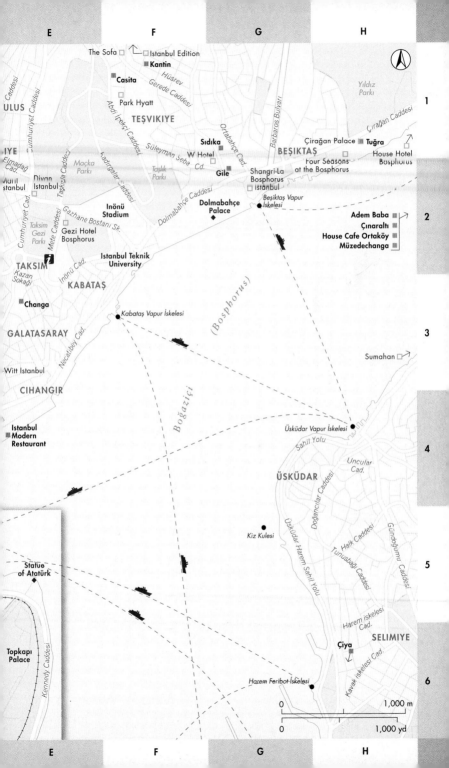

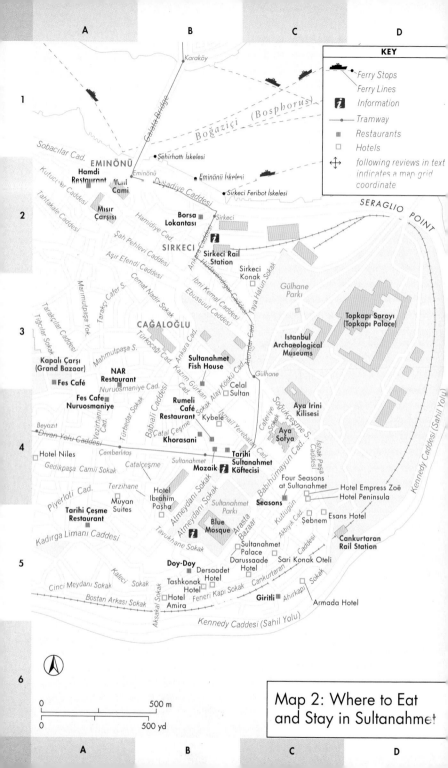

KEY

- Ferry Stops
- Ferry Lines
- *i* Information
- Tramway
- ■ Restaurants
- □ Hotels
- ⬌ following reviews in text indicates a map grid coordinate

Karaköy

Boğaziçi (Bosphorus)

Sobacılar Cad.

EMINÖNÜ

Şehirhattı İskelesi

Eminönü

Hamdi Restaurant

Yeni Cami

Kutucılar Caddesi

Eminönü İskelesi

Sirkeci Feribot İskelesi

SERAGLIO POINT

Tahtakale Caddesi

Mısır Çarşısı

Hamidiye Cad.

Rüsdiye Caddesi

Borsa Lokantası

Sirkeci

SIRKECI

i

Sirkeci Rail Station

Şah Pehlevi Caddesi

Aşır Efendi Caddesi

Sirkeci Konak

Gülhane Parkı

Topkapı Sarayı (Topkapı Palace)

Marmutpaşa Yok.

Tarakçı Cafer S.

Cemal Nadir Sokak

Tava Hatun Sokak

Taraklılar Caddesi

Tiğcılar Sokak

CAĞALOĞLU

Türkocağı Cad.

Ankara Cad.

İbni Kemal Caddesi

Ebussuut Caddesi

İstanbul Archaeological Museums

Kapalı Çarşı (Grand Bazaar)

Mahmutpaşa S.

NAR Restaurant

Nuruosmaniye Cad.

Sultanahmet Fish House

Kazım Gürkan Cad.

Gülhane

Kemal Alay Köşkü Cad.

Fes Café

Fes Cafe Nuruosmaniye

Vezirhan Cad.

Türbedar Sokak

Babıali Caddesi

Rumeli Café Restaurant

Çatal Çeşme

İsmail Yerebatan

Kybele

Celal Sultan

Aya Irini Kilisesi

Cafenre

Soğukçeşme S. Sokak

Aya Sofya

Beyazıt

Divan Yolu Caddesi

Khorasani

Çemberlitaş

Sultanahmet

İshak Paşa Caddesi

Kennedy Caddesi (Sahil Yolu)

□ **Hotel Niles**

Gedikpaşa Camii Sokak

Çatalçeşme

Mozaik

Tarihi Sultanahmet Köftecisi

Babıhümayun Cad.

Four Seasons at Sultanahmet

Hotel Empress Zoë

Hotel Peninsula

Piyerloti Cad.

Terzihane

Muyan Suites

Hotel İbrahim Paşa

Atmeydanı Sokak

Sultanahmet Parkı

Seasons

Kutlugün

Akbıyık Cad.

Esans Hotel

Tarihi Çeşme Restaurant

Kadırga Limanı Caddesi

Tavukhane Sokak

Atmeydanı Sokak

Blue Mosque

i

Arasta Bazaar

Şebnem

Cankurtaran Rail Station

Doy-Doy

Sultanahmet Palace

Darussaade Hotel

Sari Konak Oteli

Cankurtaran Caddesi

Kaleci Sokak

Cinci Meydanı Sokak

Dersaadet Hotel

Tashkonak Hotel

Feneri Kapı Sokak

Bostan Arkası Sokak

Hotel Amira

Aksakal Sokak

Giritli

Ahırkapı Sokak

Armada Hotel

Kennedy Caddesi (Sahil Yolu)

0   500 m

0   500 yd

Map 2: Where to Eat and Stay in Sultanahmet

Gürkan Cad. 14 ☎ *212/527–4441* ⊕ *www.sultanahmetfishhouse.com* ✛ *2:B3.*

$ ✕**Tarihi Çeşme Restaurant.** Just a short walk from the area's major tour-
TURKISH ist attractions, Tarihi Çeşme is a rare find in Sultanahmet, offering
good food at very reasonable prices, genuinely friendly service, and a
congenial atmosphere that appeals to both visitors and local residents.
The menu includes a fairly typical range of mezes and kebabs, as well
as *pide,* or flatbread baked with different toppings—the Turkish version of pizza. There's a simple yet pleasant indoor seating area, but the
biggest attraction is the lovely streetfront patio, shaded by vines and
decorated with hanging lanterns. $ *Average main: 16 TL* ✉ *Kadırga
Liman Cad., Küçük Ayasofya Camii Sok. 1* ☎ *212/516–3580* ⊕ *www.
tarihicesmerestaurant.com* ✛ *2:A5.*

$ ✕**Tarihi Sultanahmet Köftecisi.** Like pizza for New Yorkers, humble *köfte*
TURKISH (grilled meatballs) inspire countless arguments among Istanbullus about
who makes the best. Some of the most highly regarded are served on
a simple menu—meatballs, lamb kebab, *piyaz* (boiled white beans in
olive oil), and salad—that has remained virtually unchanged since 1920.
Service is somewhat perfunctory, and this bustling place is not somewhere to linger, but the location just steps from the Blue Mosque and
Aya Sofya makes it ideal for a quick and affordable lunch. ■**TIP**➔ There
are imitators with similar names on the same street, but Tarihi Sultanahmet Köftecisi ("Historic Sultanahmet Köftecisi") is considered the real
deal. $ *Average main: 12 TL* ✉ *Divanyolu Cad. 12* ☎ *212/520–0566*
⊕ *www.sultanahmetkoftesi.com* ▭ *No credit cards* ✛ *2:B4.*

THE BAZAAR AREA AND ENVIRONS

$ ✕**Borsa Lokantası.** This simple spot is part of a small chain of self-ser-
TURKISH vice, cafeteria-style eateries that has been in business since 1927 and
it continues to attract a hungry crowd that comes to eat inexpensive
yet well-prepared food. The offerings change daily, and include dishes
like stuffed artichokes and baked lamb with eggplant purée. There is
also an appealing selection of desserts, so you might want to leave
room. Borsa is close to Eminönü, making it convenient for a quick
meal before or after a boat ride on the Bosphorus or a shopping excursion in the Spice Bazaar. $ *Average main: 10 TL* ✉ *Yalıköşkü Cad.,
Yalıköşkü Han 60–62* ☎ *212/511–8079* ⊕ *www.borsaselfservis.com*
☾ *Closed Sun.* ✛ *2:B2.*

$ ✕**Fes Café.** Funky black-and-white Lucite chairs and fresh flowers on the
CAFÉ wooden tables provide a shot of modern style in the heart of the Grand
Bazaar. Squeezed into a former market stall, the small kitchen turns out
simple sandwiches, salads, excellent fresh lemonade and fruit juices,
homemade desserts, and other American-style fare. It's a great place
to sit back and watch the comings and goings of the bazaar. A second,
larger branch just outside the Bazaar on Ali Baba Türbe Sokak offers a
fuller menu that includes salads, pastas, and meat dishes. It also houses
a small boutique selling products by sister company Abdulla, along
with interesting housewares and jewelry from young Turkish designers. $ *Average main: 16 TL* ✉ *Halıcılar Cad. 58–62, Grand Bazaar*
☎ *212/528–1613* ⊕ *www.fescafe.com* ☾ *No dinner; closed Sun.* ✛ *2:A3.*

$$ TURKISH 🍴 **Hamdi Restaurant.** This longtime grillhouse is an Istanbul institution, with its huge selection of kebabs, as well as appetizers like mini *lahmacun* (thin flatbread topped with spicy ground meat). Although the food may not be too different from other kebab houses, Hamdi's three dining floors still tend to be packed with both tourists and locals. This makes for a lively, even boisterous, atmosphere, and service can be a bit harried; make sure that you get—and pay for—exactly what you order. Reserve a table on the restaurant's terrace level, which has wonderful views of the Golden Horn and the Bosphorus. **TIP→ For a calmer dining experience, have dinner on the early side.** [$] *Average main: 27 TL* ✉ *Kalçın Sok. 17* ☎ *212/528–0390* 🌐 *www.hamdi.com.tr* ✍ *Reservations essential* ✣ *2:A2.*

TURKISH COFFEE

Tea might be the beverage of choice in Turkey these days, but those in need of a coffee fix need not worry. Most teahouses serve Turkish coffee, although you may find a better cup by going to a more upscale café, which will probably use better coffee and take the time to prepare it properly. Well-made Turkish coffee should be thick and almost chocolaty, with espresso-like foam on top. Turks drink their coffee three ways: *sade* (plain), *orta* (medium sweet), and *şekerli* (extra sweet). It's usually served with a small glass of water and, frequently, a little piece of *lokum* (Turkish delight).

$$ TURKISH Fodor's Choice ★ 🍴 **NAR Restaurant.** Focused on preserving traditional, authentic recipes from around Turkey, NAR ("Natural and Regional") Restaurant is located on the top floor of the Armaggan boutique and is the only fine dining establishment in the Grand Bazaar area. Signature dishes include the incredibly tender lamb *tandır*, cooked in an underground oven. The best deal is at lunchtime, when diners can assemble a meal from several daily small dishes—options might include cured salmon or stuffed zucchini blossoms, or an entree of meatballs with sour cherry stew. There's a vast array of delectable desserts made on-site by a master confectioner, and an extensive wine list has over 100 established and up-and-coming Turkish wines. [$] *Average main: 33 TL* ✉ *Armaggan Nuruosmaniye, 5th fl., Nuruosmaniye Cad. 65, Fatih, The Bazaar Area and Environs* ☎ *212/522–2800* 🌐 *www.narlokantasi.com* ⏲ *Closed Sun.* ✣ *2:A3.*

WESTERN DISTRICTS

$$ TURKISH 🍴 **Akdeniz Hatay Sofrası.** Popular with locals, this restaurant specializes in the Arab-influenced cuisine of Hatay (originating near Turkey's border with Syria), which features delicious mezes like hummus, baba ghanoush, *muhammara* (a spread of mashed chili peppers and walnuts), a spicy version of tabbouleh called *kısır*, and a wide range of uncommon kebabs. The venue's famous "meter kebab" serves several people and requires advance ordering, as does the salt-shell-baked chicken and lamb. No alcohol is served, but there are sherbets (fruit drinks) and rich local desserts like *künefe* (a sweet cheese pastry). Located in Akarsaray, the venue is a short taxi ride from Sultanahmet or a short walk from

the Haseki tram stop. [$] *Average main: 26 TL* ✉ *Ahmediye Cad. 44/A, Fatih* ☎ *212/444–7247* 🌐 *www.akdenizhataysofrasi.com.tr* ⊕ *1:A5.*

$$$ TURKISH 🍴 **Asitane.** One of Istanbul's most distinctive restaurants serves seasonally changing menus based on the traditional cuisine of the Ottoman court, which the venue's owners have carefully researched over the past two decades. Dishes feature unusual combinations of ingredients, such as eggplant stuffed with quail, or baked melon with a pilaf and ground meat filling. The historical versions of more familiar contemporary Turkish dishes, like stuffed grape leaves with sour cherries, also make appearances. The atmosphere is elegant, service exceptional, and there's a pleasant, shaded courtyard open in summer. Asitane is conveniently located next to the Kariye Müzesi. [$] *Average main: 36 TL* ✉ *Kariye Camii Sok. 6, Edirnekapı* ☎ *212/635–7997* 🌐 *www.asitanerestaurant.com* ✍ *Reservations essential* ⊕ *1:A4.*

2

BEYOĞLU

$ TURKISH 🍴 **Antiochia.** This restaurant in the popular Asmalımescit area of Beyoğlu offers specialties of Turkey's Arab-influenced southeastern Hatay province at reasonable prices. The short menu comprises fewer than 10 types of mezes and just a few kebabs, but the dishes all have intense flavors and are served with Antiochia's uncommonly tasty chili pepper–rubbed flatbread. Unfortunately, due to the tiny venue's popularity, the waitstaff tends to "help" diners (especially those unfamiliar with the cuisine) decide what to order and to rush service to ensure quick turnover—so this is not the place for a long and leisurely meal. [$] *Average main: 20 TL* ✉ *Asmalı Mescit Mah. Minare Sok. 21* ☎ *212/292–1100* 🌐 *www.antiochiaconcept.com* ✍ *Reservations essential* 🕓 *Closed Sun. No lunch Sat.* ⊕ *1:C3.*

$$$$ ECLECTIC 🍴 **Changa.** The sister venue of Müzedechanga occupies a three-story, early-20th-century art nouveau town house near Taksim Square and is only open mid-October through May. Innovative, fusion-style dishes combine flavors and ingredients from Turkey and around the world, presented with aesthetic flair. A large circular "skylight" cut into the ground floor reveals the bustling basement-level kitchen below. [$] *Average main: 54 TL* ✉ *Sıraselviler Cad. 47* ☎ *212/249–1348* 🌐 *www.changa-istanbul.com* ✍ *Reservations essential* 🕓 *Closed Sun. and June–mid-Oct. No lunch* ⊕ *1:E3.*

$$ ECLECTIC 🍴 **Dai Pera.** Proprietor and chef Arzu Gürdamar likes experimenting with food, and her menu includes traditional Istanbul-style mezes like *muska böreği* (a triangular meat-stuffed pastry), as well as her own tasty creations, such as zucchini in strained yogurt with crushed almonds. The entrées are mainly Turkish "home-style" dishes reinterpreted to please a contemporary palate and include Dai's signature caramelized steak and delicious sliced lamb and artichokes in a creamy sauce, served with cinnamon-dusted rice. The cozy, laid-back atmosphere—plain wooden furniture, posters and artwork on the walls, funky jazz music playing—makes up for the sometimes overly casual service. [$] *Average main: 28 TL* ✉ *Yeni Çarşı Cad. 54* ☎ *212/252–8099* 🌐 *www.dairestaurant.com* ⊕ *1:D3.*

Drinks with a View

In recent years, venues in Istanbul have been aiming high, literally, as an increasing number of savvy entrepreneurs take advantage of the city's greatest natural asset—its spectacular views. The proliferation of open rooftop dining and nightlife spots has been especially pronounced in the Beyoğlu neighborhood, which sits on a ridge overlooking the Bosphorus, the Golden Horn, and the sights of Sultanahmet.

With the notable exception of **Mikla**, an upscale restaurant and sophisticated roof bar at the top of the 18-story Marmara Pera Hotel that is one of the city's best, most of the venues offering panoramic views of the city tend to fall flat when it comes to food. But they make great places for a pre- or post-dinner drink—where else in the world can you gaze at two continents with a martini in hand?

In Beyoğlu, **Leb-i Derya** has two branches where you can watch the sun set over the Bosphorus. The Leb-i Derya at the top of the Richmond is fully enclosed, while the one on Kumbaracı Yokuşu has an upper level with a breezy, roofless terrace that's open in summer. The open-air (and therefore summer-only) **NuTeras** is a chic lounge that serves finger food and looks out on the Golden Horn, while **5. Kat** in Cihangir is a restaurant and lounge offering excellent views of the Bosphorus from both its indoor section and summer-only upper-level deck. Also in summer, the open-air terrace on the top of **Mama Shelter Hotel** on İstiklal Caddesi houses a restaurant and bar with a fun, happening vibe and excellent views all around.

$ ✕ **Ficcın.** Occupying a number of rooms and storefronts on both sides of
TURKISH   narrow Kallavi Sokak, this down-to-earth restaurant is best known for Turkish standards and specialties of the Circassian kitchen. The latter include the signature *ficcın*, a savory pastry filled with ground meat; a regional variation of *mantı* dumplings stuffed with meat or potatoes; and "Circassian chicken," a cold spread of shredded chicken in a creamy walnut sauce. The menu, which changes daily, always includes a range of mezes—many of them vegetarian—as well as a handful of simple meat and fish dishes, and prices are extremely reasonable. $ *Average main: 14 TL* ✉ *Kallavi Sok. 13/1* ☎ *212/293–3786* ⊕ *www.ficcin. com* ✛ *1:D3.*

$ ✕ **Gram.** Opened in Şişhane by the chef-owner of Lokanta Maya, Didem
TURKISH   Şenol, this casual restaurant and bakery is a delightful place to stop
Fodor's Choice   for breakfast, lunch, or dessert. The fresh, well-prepared lunch spe-
★   cials change daily but always include a half-dozen or so cold items like smoked eggplant with tahini sauce or beetroot salad with avocado; you can sample two or four on a plate. The handful of hot dishes might include ox tongue with caper sauce or chicken with rosemary mashed potatoes. Gram's delightful baked goods and desserts are worth a special trip. Seating in the small, tastefully decorated venue is around a couple of large, communal wooden tables next to an open kitchen. $ *Average main: 17 TL* ✉ *Meşrutiyet Cad. 107/D* ☎ *212/243–1048*

⊕ www.grampera.com ⚓ Reservations not accepted ⊘ Closed Sun. No dinner ⊹ 1:D3.

$ ✕ **Hala Mantı.** As its name suggests,
TURKISH   this restaurant on a side street not far from İstiklal Caddesi specializes in ravioli-like *mantı*, small pockets of pasta filled with ground meat; *hingal*, a variation eaten in the Caucasus with a cheese and potato filling, is also served. *Gözleme*, a type of very thin flatbread filled with ingredients such as cheese and spinach, then cooked on a huge griddle as you watch, is very good here; other options include tasty home-style soups and vegetable and meat dishes. With traditional Anatolian-style decor and paper napkins, the atmosphere is simple but homey. No alcohol is served. $*Average main: 13 TL* ✉ *İstiklal Cad. 137A* ☎ *212/292–7004* ⊹ *1:D3.*

$ ✕ **Hayvore.** This informal restau-
TURKISH   rant just off İstiklal Caddesi turns out hearty specialties of Turkey's Black Sea at very affordable prices. There's no menu, but the daily offerings (just point to what you want) usually include several items with anchovies—a mainstay of the region's cooking—as well as meat dishes like lamb stew and vegetarian alternatives made with chickpeas, baked beans, bulgur pilaf, and pickled vegetables. The black cabbage soup is also especially good, as is the dense cornbread that comes with it. The unassuming venue is brightly lit, with simple wooden tables and framed photos of the verdant Black Sea region. $*Average main: 14 TL* ✉ *Turnacıbaşı Sok. 4* ☎ *212/245–7501* ⊕ *www.hayvore.com. tr* ⊹ *1:D3.*

$ ✕ **Helvetia.** The menu at Helvetia changes daily but there are always
TURKISH   at least a dozen home-cooked dishes on offer at this very affordable restaurant. They range from meat dishes like curried chicken or meatballs in tomato sauce to plentiful vegetarian options (cooked without meat stock), such as stewed vegetables, sauteed eggplant, chickpeas in sauce, potato salad, and bulgur pilaf. The atmosphere is laid-back and the easiest way to order is to simply point at what you want from the day's specials, which are displayed in front of the open kitchen; ask for a mixed plate if you'd like to try several small portions. No alcohol is served. $*Average main: 11 TL* ✉ *General Yazgan Sok. 8/A* ☎ *212/245–8780* ⊘ *No lunch Sun.* ⊹ *1:C3.*

$$ ✕ **Kafe Ara.** This popular, cozy hangout, named after famous Turk-
CONTEMPORARY   ish photographer Ara Güler, whose black-and-white photographs of Istanbul line the walls (and who sometimes can be seen holding court

BEER IN TURKEY

For years, visitors to Turkey basically had one choice when ordering beer: Efes. These days, international brands are also brewed locally, and imports like Corona and Heineken are available, too. Efes itself has branched out and now makes several different brews (including Efes Dark and Efes Light), and also brews the somewhat maltier Bomonti—Turkey's first beer, recently revived as a nostalgic brand. And in the world of microbrews, Istanbul is now home to two brewpubs, the Bosphorus Brewing Company (✉ *Esentepe Mah., Yıldız Posta Cad. 1/1A* ☎ *212/288–6499*) in the Gayrettepe district *and* Taps (✉ *Cevdetpaşa Cad. 119* ☎ *212/263–8700*) on the Bosphorus, just north of Bebek.

here), is a nice place for a light meal or cup of coffee. The menu includes several Turkish meat dishes along with more international fare, such as grilled entrecôte with pommes frites or tagliatelle with salmon. The wide variety of salads (such as quinoa with chickpeas and avocado) are also good, as are the desserts. It's open late, though no alcohol is served. [$] *Average main: 25 TL* ⊠ *Tosbağı Sok. 2, Galatasaray* ☎ *212/245–4105* ⊕ *www.kafeara.com* ✛ *1:D3.*

$$$
TURKISH

✕ **Meze by Lemon Tree.** Mezes in this trendy and attractive spot change seasonally and even daily, and put a clever international spin on traditional favorites—a gazpacho-like, basil-infused version of *acılı ezme* (red pepper spread) is served in a shot glass—while others, such as sea bream with chickpeas and mustard sauce, are friendly chef-owner Gençay Üçok's unique creations. Though slightly overshadowed by the inventive mezes, main dishes include standouts like lamb sirloin with baked potatoes and beets and a delicious variation on sea bass cooked in paper. The popular venue seats just 38, so make reservations as far as a week in advance. [$] *Average main: 40 TL* ⊠ *Meşrutiyet Cad. 83B* ☎ *212/252–8302* ⊕ *www.mezze.com.tr* ✍ *Reservations essential* ⊗ *No lunch* ✛ *1:C3.*

$$$$
CONTEMPORARY
Fodor's Choice
★

✕ **Mikla.** With sleek, contemporary decor and a stunning 360-degree view of Istanbul from its perch on the top floor of the 18-story Marmara Pera Hotel, Mikla is the dramatic setting for prestigious American-trained Turkish-Finnish chef Mehmet Gürs's modern Anatolian cuisine. Sophisticated dishes of domestically sourced ingredients offer unique flavor combinations rarely seen in traditional Turkish cuisine, such as dentex served with artichokes, fennel, couscous, and lemon confit, or a dessert of sour cherry compote with bulgur wheat. One of Istanbul's most wide-ranging—though expensive—wine lists features some 40 pages of labels from Turkey and around the world. Diners can choose between a three-course prix-fixe menu (150 TL) or a seven-course tasting menu (225 TL), with or without wine pairings. [$] *Average main: 150 TL* ⊠ *Meşrutiyet Cad. 15* ☎ *212/293–5656* ⊕ *www.miklarestaurant. com* ✍ *Reservations essential* ⊗ *Closed Sun. in Nov.–Mar. and July–Aug. No lunch* ✛ *1:C3.*

$$$
TURKISH
Fodor's Choice
★

✕ **Münferit.** Owner Ferit Sarper's menu gives traditional meyhane fare a twist that's as contemporary as the upscale surroundings, creating dishes that are innovative and remarkable, but not too experimental. Traditional "Circassian chicken" is made here with duck breast, while feta cheese is served baked in paper with porcini mushrooms and truffle oil; other standout mezes include grilled jumbo shrimp with hummus and a sea bass carpaccio. The extensive wine list features both Turkish and international labels, and desserts are worth saving room for, particularly the house-made ice cream in flavors like tahini and sage. Seating is on the popular outdoor patio—if you can get a table—or in the chic, private-club-like interior. [$] *Average main: 40 TL* ⊠ *Yeni Çarşı Cad. 19* ☎ *212/252–5067* ✍ *Reservations essential* ⊗ *Closed Sun.* ✛ *1:D3.*

$$
TURKISH

✕ **Sofyalı 9.** With Greek music playing in the background, photographs of old Istanbul on the walls, and friendly, laid-back surroundings on a lively backstreet in Beyoğlu's Asmalımescit area, the classic meyhane food and quaint atmosphere here are well above average. Mezes, whether from the regular menu or the daily specials, are excellent; standouts include cubes of fried eggplant in a yogurt and tahini sauce and "Circassian chicken," a spread made with chicken and ground walnuts. A limited menu is served during lunch on weekdays. $ *Average main: 28 TL* ⊠ *Sofyalı Sok. 9* ☎ *212/245–0362* ⊕ *www.sofyali.com.tr* ⚐ *Reservations essential* ⊙ *No lunch Sat. and Sun.* ✛ *1:D3.*

$$$ ✕ **Yeni Lokanta.** Rising chef Civan Er (formerly of Müzedechanga) puts
TURKISH a unique and contemporary twist on traditional Turkish dishes, using
Fodor'sChoice ingredients sourced from local producers in different regions of the
★ country. The menu consists mainly of small plates that offer innovative flavor combinations, as in sweet-and-sour *kısır* (tabbouleh) made with a sour cherry infusion, or spicy, rustic *sucuk* sausage with walnuts and served on top of a barlotti bean purée. Dishes such as green beans with "burnt" yogurt are made in the venue's wood-fired oven, as is the sourdough bread. The decor blends a contemporary vibe with nods to Turkish culture, and service is above typical Istanbul standards. $ *Average main: 36 TL* ⊠ *Kumbaracı Yokuşu 66* ☎ *212/292–2550* ⊕ *www.lokantayeni.com* ⊙ *Closed Sun.* ✛ *1:3D*

$$ ✕ **Zübeyir Ocakbaşı.** This *ocakbaşı*, or grill house, is popular for its deli-
TURKISH cious food, authentic feel, and especially lively atmosphere. The wide variety of kebabs are cooked on a special grill over hardwood coals—part of the fun here is watching the chefs at work—and include some cuts of meat not found on the average kebab menu, such as *kaburga* (lamb ribs). The mezes are also particularly tasty, among them such unique dishes as *kabak ezmesi*, or pumpkin spread (available only in fall/winter), and Van-style *cacık*, a dip made from thick strained yogurt, cucumber, onions, and herbs. $ *Average main: 28 TL* ⊠ *Bekar Sok. 28* ☎ *212/293–3951* ⚐ *Reservations essential* ✛ *1:D2.*

GALATA AND KARAKÖY

$$ ✕ **Aheste.** On the main street of Galata's fashion and design scene, Aheste
ECLECTIC (meaning "slowly" in Persian) is a casual café by day and an inviting bistrolike venue by night. The small but appealing evening menu consists mainly of hot and cold mezes with some Persian, Ottoman, and Middle Eastern influences with contemporary twists; the smoked sea bass over sea beans and wild rice with currants and herbs is particularly tasty. The daytime menu has lighter fare, including a variety of healthy salads and bruschettas. Prices are a bit high for the portion size, but the friendly, laid-back service and hip-yet-cozy atmosphere make up for it. $ *Average main: 35 TL* ⊠ *Serdar-ı Ekrem Cad. 30/A, Galata* ☎ *212/245–4345* ⊕ *www.ahestegalata.com* ✛ *1:D4.*

$$$ ✕ **Istanbul Modern Restaurant.** Though it's a bit on the pricey side, the
INTERNATIONAL inventive menu, along with gorgeous waterfront views and stylish industrial-chic decor—think exposed air shafts and cement walls—warrant a visit whether or not you're interested in the art at the Istanbul Modern. A sleek, rectangular wooden bar dominates the dining room, which looks out onto Istanbul's Karaköy harbor (avoid visiting when there's a huge cruise ship obscuring the view); there is also seating on the waterfront deck. You can choose from a range of lighter fare—including a variety of pastas, salads, and pizzas—and more substantial dishes

This Istanbul street vendor is selling freshly roasted chestnuts.

like grilled lamb loin with sautéed spinach and pan-roasted salmon with fresh asparagus. $ *Average main: 42 TL* ⊠ *Meclis-i Mebusan Cad., Liman İşletmeleri Sahası, Antrepo 4, Karaköy* ☎ *212/292–2612* ⊕ *www.modernrestaurantbar.com* ⟁ *Reservations essential* ✢ *1:E4.*

$$
Karaköy Lokantası. This popular dual-format venue is a bustling day-
TURKISH time spot offering a changing menu of reasonably priced vegetable and meat dishes from the Turkish kitchen and a classy meyhane at night, serving an excellent variety of mezes, including octopus salad and salted, dried mackerel. The mainly grilled fish and meat entrées are equally well-prepared. The gorgeous two-level dining room features a wrought-iron spiral staircase, blue and turquoise tiles, old-fashioned lamps, and long mirrors. Service is professional but waiters can be brusque, particularly during the midday peak, when you may end up sharing a white-tablecloth-clad table with local businesspeople on their lunch break. $ *Average main: 23 TL* ⊠ *Kemankeş Cad. 37A, Kara-köy* ☎ *212/292–4455* ⊕ *www.karakoylokantasi.com* ⊘ *No lunch Sun.* ✢ *1:D4.*

$$$
Lokanta Maya. At her highly regarded restaurant, New York–trained
TURKISH chef Didem Şenol offers what could be called "nouvelle Turkish" cui-
Fodor'sChoice sine, based on seasonal, local, and primarily organic ingredients. A
★ daily-changing menu features a range of tasty appetizers, like grilled octopus with red onions and zucchini fritters with cucumber sauce, and a handful of main course options, such as caramelized sea bass with apricots. The wine list consists of Turkish labels, both established and new. Hip yet unpretentious, with contemporary furniture, light-colored woods, and warm lighting, it's located on one of the main streets in fast-gentrifying Karaköy. $ *Average main: 38 TL* ⊠ *Kemankeş Cad. 35A,*

Karaköy ☎ *212/252–6884* 🌐 *www.lokantamaya.com* ✍ *Reservations essential* ⏲ *Closed Sun.* ✥ *1:D4.*

BEŞIKTAŞ AND NIŞANTASI

$$ TURKISH

🍴 **Casita.** This charming little restaurant, established 30 years ago and now one of several branches in Istanbul, is best known for its *mantı*—a ravioli-like Turkish pasta traditionally stuffed with ground meat—and specifically "Feraye" (a name the restaurant has trademarked), a fried variation filled with cheese and spinach, potato and cheese, or chicken. The menu also offers café food with a modern Turkish twist, including meatballs, steaks, and a variety of salads; cheesecakes and other desserts are also available. The atmosphere is casual, and diners can either sit at sidewalk tables out in front or at tables looking onto a quiet garden in the back. [$] *Average main: 23 TL* ✉ *Abdi İpekçi Cad., Atiye Sok. 3, Nişantaşı* ☎ *212/327–8293* 🌐 *www.casita.com.tr* ✥ *1:F1.*

$$$$ CONTEMPORARY

🍴 **Gile.** In upscale Akaretler row, Gile is helmed by two rising chefs whose avant-garde Turkish cuisine incorporates sophisticated gastronomic techniques and ingredients sourced from around the country to create complex (often deconstructed) dishes for a seasonally changing menu. Standout appetizers include lamb loin wrapped in a delicate baklava phyllo dough and served with hummus and puréed eggplant, while ambitious mains include rock bass with a tomato sauce and creamy potato foam. Gile offers a diverse, primarily Turkish wine list, and there's a more casual menu at lunch. Original art pieces and custom-made ceramics by noteworthy Turkish artists complement the smart, intimate dining room. [$] *Average main: 55 TL* ✉ *Şair Nedim Cad. 14, Akaretler, Beşiktaş* ☎ *212/327–1166* 🌐 *www.gilerestaurant.com* ✍ *Reservations essential* ⏲ *Closed Sun.* ✥ *1:G2*

$$ TURKISH
Fodor's Choice ★

🍴 **Kantin.** A sort of Turkish Alice Waters, Şemza Denizsel finds the freshest ingredients for her daily menus, written on chalkboards, that feature simply prepared but delicious Turkish dishes emphasizing meat and vegetables. Prices are a bit high for the portion size, but you're paying for local, mostly organic foods, such as sourdough bread made with heirloom Anatolian wheat. The venue is especially popular at lunchtime with local professionals; if you can't land a seat in the upstairs dining rooms or on the pleasant backyard deck, consider making a picnic from the side dishes and delectable baked goods sold at Kantin's street-level food shop (entrance is separate from the restaurant). No alcohol is served. [$] *Average main: 24 TL* ✉ *Akkavak Sok. 30, Nişantaşı* ☎ *212/219–3114* 🌐 *www.kantin.biz* ✍ *Reservations not accepted* ⏲ *Closed Sun.* ✥ *1:F1.*

$ SEAFOOD

🍴 **Sıdıka.** An unassuming local favorite not far from posh Akaretler Row and downtown Beşiktaş, Sıdıka offers stellar Aegean-influenced starters and fish dishes at reasonable prices. Unique mezes include a delicious spread made from feta, pistachio, and garlic; seasonal daily specials could include artichoke hearts with fava bean purée. Simple but tasty main-course fish dishes, such as grilled sea bass fillets wrapped in vine leaves, are especially recommendable. The casual decor—bare wooden tables and chairs, tile floors, a chalkboard listing the specials—and a cheerful, welcoming ambience draw groups and families. The place can get pretty boisterous on the weekends. $ *Average main: 20 TL* ✉ *Şair Nedim Cad. 38, Beşiktaş* ☎ *212/259–7232* ⊕ *www.sidika.com. tr* ⚐ *Reservations essential* ⊘ *Closed Sun. No lunch* ✤ *1:G1.*

BOSPHORUS

$ ✕ **Adem Baba.** This place is the Turkish version of a New England fish
SEAFOOD   shack, with nets and crab traps hanging from the ceiling in three venues located around the corner from one other. Families and groups
come here to enjoy simple, fresh, and well prepared fish, at much less
than what they would pay at some of the fancier seafood restaurants
along the Bosphorus (it's cheaper in part because no alcohol is served).
A refrigerated display at the entrance holds the day's catch. To start,
order the fried calamari and the tasty *balık köftesi* (fish cakes); the
main course of *dil şiş* (skewers of sole) is also excellent. Adem Baba is
in Arnavutköy, a low-key Bosphorus neighborhood that's perfect for a
stroll before or after dinner. $ *Average main: 20 TL* ✉ *Satış Meydanı
Sok. 2, Arnavutköy* ☎ *212/263–2933* ⊕ *www.adembaba.com* ✤ *1:H2.*

$$ ✕ **Çınaraltı.** Named after the massive sycamore tree growing through
TURKISH   the center of the restaurant and shading the upstairs terrace, Çınaraltı
("under the sycamore") has been in business for three decades in the
same spot on Ortaköy's waterfront square. With its relaxed service,
spacious feel, and simple decor, it has remained refreshingly unpreten-
tious and reasonably priced in a neighborhood known increasingly
for its trendiness. The spring roll–like fish pastry is a highlight among
the wide but otherwise fairly standard selection of mezes, while fish is
mainly served grilled or fried (make sure the price quoted is per fish
or serving, not per kilo). $ *Average main: 23 TL* ✉ *İskele Meydanı 28*
☎ *212/261–4616* ⊕ *www.cinaralti.com* ✤ *1:H2.*

$$ ✕ **The House Café.** The largest and one of the most popular branches of
INTERNATIONAL   this chain of upscale eateries is directly on the waterfront, with chic fur-
nishings and two enormous open-air terraces. The international menu
ranges from starters like Asian-style crispy chicken fingers and salmon
ceviche to main-course salads, pastas, pizzas, steaks, and the signature
House Burger. Two long wooden bars are perfect for enjoying a predin-
ner drink from the excellent cocktail list. The chain has successfully
expanded to eight locations in Istanbul, including a branch on İstiklal
Caddesi in Beyoğlu that's trendy and happening, while the original
venue, in chic Nişantaşı, has a more laid-back vibe and a shady garden.
$ *Average main: 32 TL* ✉ *Salhane Sok. 1* ☎ *212/227–2699 Ortaköy,
212/259–2377 Nişantaşı* ⊕ *www.thehousecafe.com* ✤ *1:D3.*

$$$$ ✕ **Müzedechanga.** A beautiful, lush setting just a stone's throw from the
ECLECTIC   Bosphorus, a Mediterranean-inspired menu, and a sophisticated ambi-
Fodor's Choice   ence makes this restaurant in the Sakıp Sabancı Museum a draw in
★   its own right. Particularly recommendable are the small plates, which
include reinterpretations of traditional Turkish mezes, such as grilled
halloumi cheese in vine leaves or fried zucchini flowers stuffed with lor
cheese. Overseen by award-winning London-based chef Peter Gordon,
the menu also shows international influences, like the sea bass with
creamy basil sauce or catfish served with potato salad. The venue is
especially relaxing in summer, when seating is on the open-air terrace.

$ *Average main: 54 TL* ⊠ *Sakıp Sabancı Cad. 42, Emirgan* ☎ *212/323–0901* ⊕ *www.changa-istanbul.com* ⚞ *Reservations essential* ☉ *Closed Mon.* ✛ *1:H2.*

$$$$ ✕ **Tuğra.** Fitting for a restaurant housed in the Çırağan Palace, dinner
TURKISH here is a refined, luxurious affair, with formal service, rich Ottoman and Turkish specialties, and one of the most high-end wine lists in Turkey (Chateau Pétrus, anyone?). The quite pricey menu features a variety of cold and hot mezes, and entrées emphasize fish and meat, such as in the restaurant's signature *külbastı*, lamb escalope served with puréed eggplant. Reserve a table to dine alfresco in the small balcony, where marble columns flank a beautiful Bosphorus view, or ensconce yourself in the elegant interior, with its soaring ceilings, large mirrors, and hanging oriental lamps. $ *Average main: 100 TL* ⊠ *Çırağan Cad. 32* ☎ *212/326–4646* ⊕ *www.kempinski-istanbul.com* ⚞ *Reservations essential* 🎩 *Jacket required* ☉ *Closed lunch* ✛ *1:H1.*

ASIAN SHORE

$ ✕ **Çiya.** Three no-frills branches on the same street make up one of
TURKISH Istanbul's most popular foodie destinations, and the reputation is well-
Fodor's Choice deserved. Chef-owner Musa Dağdeviren, who hails from the southeast-
★ ern Turkish city of Gaziantep, is something of a culinary anthropologist, serving recipes from around Turkey that you're unlikely to find elsewhere. His original venue, Çiya Kebap, makes a range of top-notch kebabs, but the biggest draw is the selection of seasonal and daily specials—both meat-based and vegetarian—featuring unusual flavor combinations. Equally memorable desserts include candied olives, tomatoes, or eggplant, served with sweet clotted cream. Nearby Çiya Sofrası offers home-style dishes only, while Çiya Kebap 2 just does kebabs. Alcohol is only served at Çiya Sofrası; at the other locations, try the *şerbet*, a traditional drink made from various fruits. $ *Average main: 19 TL* ⊠ *Güneşlibahçe Sok. 48B, Kadıköy* ☎ *216/336–3013* ⊕ *www.ciya.com.tr* ✛ *1:H6.*

WHERE TO STAY

With the number of visitors to Turkey increasing every year, Istanbul's hoteliers are busy keeping up with the growing demand. New lodgings, from five-star hotels to smaller boutique inns, are opening all the time, while older establishments are busy renovating and expanding. This means there are plenty more options than there were in the past, but because Istanbul is such a popular destination, it's not the travel bargain it used to be. It's also worth noting that hotels in Turkey tend to quote their rates in euros, which makes what might look like a good deal something less than that when paying in U.S. dollars. Most lodgings, save four- and five-star hotels, include a full Turkish breakfast with the room rate.

The majority of visitors to Istanbul stay in the Sultanahmet area, where they are conveniently in walking distance to most of the city's major sights, including Aya Sofya, the Blue Mosque, Topkapı Palace, and the bazaars. Sultanahmet has a good selection of hotels, smaller family-run guesthouses, and some charmingly stylish inns, many of which are decorated in typical Turkish style, with traditional touches like kilim carpets or old-fashioned furnishings. The rooms here generally tend to be on the small side, and bathrooms often only have showers, but what's lacking in space tends to be more than made up for in character and atmosphere. The downside of staying in Sultanahmet is that at the height of the season, the area is overrun not only with tourists but touts who will approach you at every turn. On the upside, stiff competition in the area means that Sultanahmet usually has the best deals in town; some hotels even offer a 5% to 10% discount for payment in cash, or a complimentary airport transfer if you stay three or more nights.

For a wider range of hotel options in somewhat less tourist-oriented neighborhoods, head to the Golden Horn. The Beyoğlu district, only a 15- or 20-minute tram ride or cab ride from the sights of Sultanahmet, has recently emerged as an attractive alternative to the Old City. Entrepreneurs have caught on to the tourism potential of the historic area and are restoring elegant, century-old buildings and giving them new life as hotels. Staying near Taksim Square or in one of Beyoğlu's trendy sub-neighborhoods—such as Şişhane/Tünel, Cihangir, or Galata—puts you closer to Istanbul's best restaurants and nightlife spots and also gives you a chance to stroll through the area's lively backstreets.

For the most luxurious, indulgent accommodations, stay in one of the large, modern, high-end hotels that are mostly clustered in the upscale neighborhood of Nişantaşı and along the coveted strip of the Bosphorus between Beşiktaş and Ortaköy. You'll pay considerably more to stay in these digs but the perks can include incredible waterfront views, swimming pools and top-notch fitness facilities, and sophisticated dining options. Wherever you stay, you may notice that hoteliers are starting to embrace traditional Turkish styles and motifs; one new trend is to design hotel bathrooms like hammams. Though the setup may be less familiar than a traditional shower or bath, these bathrooms can be quite luxurious, with marble-lined tubs and heated floors.

Prices in the reviews are the lowest cost of a standard double room in high season. For expanded reviews, visit Fodors.com.

SULTANAHMET

$$ HOTEL **Armada Istanbul Old City Hotel.** These comfortable accommodations are a 10-minute walk from Istanbul's main tourist sites, and most rooms look out either to the sea or over the Old City—although one of the best views is at night from the hotel's rooftop Teras Restaurant, where you can see Aya Sofya and the Blue Mosque. **Pros:** amazing views of the water; professional service; in quiet area. **Cons:** somewhat steep uphill walk from hotel to the sights of Sultanahmet; smallish rooms; no fitness facilities. $ *Rooms from: $195* ✉ *Ahırkapı Sok. 24* ☎ *212/455–4455* 🌐 *www.armadahotel.com.tr* 🛏 *110 rooms* 🍴 *Breakfast* ✥ *2:C5.*

$$$ HOTEL **Celal Sultan.** Three conjoined, restored town houses make up this comfortable, well-maintained hotel that has new furnishings designed to look old-fashioned, and an inviting lobby with a cozy bar decorated with

2

BEST BETS FOR
FOR ISTANBUL LODGING

Fodor's writers and editors have chosen their favorite hotels, resorts, and B&Bs by price and experience. Fodor's Choice properties represent the very best, across price categories. You can also search by area for excellent places to stay; check out our reviews on the following pages.

LOCAL CHARACTER

Dersaadet Hotel, $$,
p. 118

Divan Istanbul, $$$$,
p. 121

Hotel Empress Zoë,
$$, p. 119

Hotel İbrahim Pasha,
$$, p. 119

MOST ROMANTIC

Four Seasons Hotel
Istanbul at the Bos-
phorus, $$$$, p. 124

Georges Hotel Galata,
$$$, p. 122

The House Hotel Bos-
phorus, $$$, p. 124

Sumahan on the
Water, $$$$, p. 125

Tomtom Suites, $$$$,
p. 122

Fodor's Choice ★

Çırağan Palace Kem-
pinski Istanbul, $$$$,
p. 123

Dersaadet Hotel, $$,
p. 118

Esans Hotel, $, p. 118

Four Seasons Hotel
Istanbul at Sultanah-
met, $$$$, p. 118

Hotel Amira, $$,
p. 118

Hotel İbrahim Pasha,
$$, p. 119

The Istanbul Edition,
$$$$, p. 124

Pera Palace Hotel
Jumeirah, $$$, p. 122

Sumahan on the
Water, $$$$, p. 125

Tomtom Suites, $$$$,
p. 122

Dersaadet Hotel,
p. 118

Hotel Amira, p. 118

Hotel İbrahim Pasha,
p. 119

$$$

Georges Hotel Galata,
p. 122

Pera Palace Hotel
Jumeirah, p. 122

Witt Istanbul, p. 122

$$$$

Çırağan Palace Kem-
pinski Istanbul, p. 123

Four Seasons Hotel
Istanbul at Sultanah-
met, p. 118

Sumahan on the
Water, p. 125

Tomtom Suites, p. 122

GREAT VIEWS

Anemon Galata, $$,
p. 122

Çırağan Palace Kem-
pinski Istanbul, $$$$,
p. 123

Four Seasons Hotel
Istanbul at the Bos-
phorus, $$$$, p. 124

Georges Hotel Galata,
$$$, p. 122

HISTORIC INTEREST

Çırağan Palace Kem-
pinski Istanbul, $$$$,
p. 123

Four Seasons Hotel
Istanbul at Sultanah-
met, $$$$, p. 118

Pera Palace Hotel
Jumeirah, $$$, p. 122

INTERIOR DESIGN

Karaköy Rooms, $$,
p. 123

The Istanbul Edition,
$$$$, p. 124

Martı Istanbul, $$$$,
p. 121

Witt Istanbul, $$$,
p. 122

BEST SERVICE

Hotel Amira, $$,
p. 118

Dersaadet Hotel, $$,
p. 118

Four Seasons Hotel
Istanbul at Sultanah-
met, $$$$, p. 118

Sirkeci Konak Hotel,
$$$, p. 120

TRUSTED BRAND

Four Seasons Hotel
Istanbul at the Bos-
phorus, $$$$, p. 124

Park Hyatt Istanbul–
Maçka Palas, $$$,
p. 123

Shangri-La Bospho-
rus, Istanbul, $$$$,
p. 123

By Price

$

Esans Hotel, p. 118

Hotel Niles, p. 119

Şebnem, p. 120

$$

Adahan, p. 121

By Experience

BEST B&Bs

Esans Hotel, $, p. 118

Hotel Peninsula, $,
p. 119

Sarı Konak Oteli, $$,
p. 120

Şebnem, $, p. 120

colorful Turkish rugs and kilims. **Pros:** hotel is on a quiet street; personable staff. **Cons:** standard rooms and bathrooms are small; some guests report poor sound insulation in rooms; rather high rates. $ *Rooms from: $325* ⊠ *Salkımsöğüt Sok. 16, Yerebatan Cad.* ☎ *212/520–9323* ⊕ *www.celalsultan.com* ⌨ *53 rooms, 2 suites* ⦿ *Breakfast* ✛ *2:B4.*

$$
HOTEL
⛺ **Darussaade.** This hotel (created by joining two 19th-century houses) offers old-world charm and comfortable rooms close to Sultanahmet's main sights. **Pros:** comfortable, nicely furnished accommodations; very helpful staff; rooms receive lots of natural light. **Cons:** some small rooms; extra charge for some breakfast items; breakfast served in windowless basement. $ *Rooms from: $160* ⊠ *Akbıyık Cad. 90* ☎ *212/518–3636* ⊕ *www.darussaade.com* ⌨ *21 rooms, 1 suite* ⦿ *Breakfast* ✛ *2:C5.*

$$
B&B/INN
Fodor'sChoice
★
⛺ **Dersaadet Hotel.** Dersaadet means "place of happiness" in Ottoman Turkish and this small, cozy hotel lives up to its name—rooms have an elegant, even plush, feel, with colorful rugs on the floor, antique furniture, and ceilings hand-painted with traditional motifs. **Pros:** extraordinary level of service; lovely terrace; good value. **Cons:** some rooms are on the small side; no view from rooms on lower floors; walls can be thin. $ *Rooms from: $150* ⊠ *Küçükayasofya Cad. Kapıağası Sok. 5* ☎ *212/458–0760* ⊕ *www.dersaadethotel.com* ⌨ *14 rooms, 3 suites* ⦿ *Breakfast* ✛ *2:B5.*

$
B&B/INN
Fodor'sChoice
★
⛺ **Esans Hotel.** The emphasis at this delightful family-run bed-and-breakfast is on guest satisfaction, and the eight rooms in the restored wooden house are decorated with thoughtful attention to detail, like lovely Ottoman-Victorian-style wallpaper, upholstery, and linens, real wooden floors and ceilings, and old-fashioned furniture. **Pros:** great value; located on quiet street; staff go out of their way to assist. **Cons:** no elevator; breakfast served in rather dimly lit reception area. $ *Rooms from: $130* ⊠ *Yeni Saraçhane Sok. 4* ☎ *212/516–1902* ⊕ *www.esanshotel. com* ⌨ *8 rooms* ⦿ *Breakfast* ✛ *2:C5.*

$$$$
HOTEL
Fodor'sChoice
★
⛺ **Four Seasons Hotel Istanbul at Sultanahmet.** What a rehabilitation success story: a former prison just steps from Topkapı Palace and Aya Sofya is now one of Istanbul's premier accommodations, where rooms and suites are luxuriously outfitted and overlook the Sea of Marmara, the Old City, or a manicured interior courtyard. **Pros:** historic building surrounded by major tourist attractions; luxurious accommodations; exceptional service. **Cons:** limited fitness facilities; no view from rooms on lower floors; expensive rates and food. $ *Rooms from: $690* ⊠ *Tevkifhane Sok. 1* ☎ *212/402–3000* ⊕ *www.fourseasons.com/istanbul* ⌨ *54 rooms, 11 suites* ⦿ *No meals* ✛ *2:C4.*

$$
HOTEL
Fodor'sChoice
★
⛺ **Hotel Amira.** An attractive atrium between two wings houses the lobby, and well-appointed rooms are furnished in an eclectic mix of Turkish and contemporary styles, from ornate Ottoman ceiling patterns and metal lampshades evoking the Istanbul skyline to modern rugs and plush upholstery. **Pros:** extraordinarily helpful staff; good value; guests feel pampered. **Cons:** some rooms not accessible by elevator; located on somewhat noisy corner; basement-level rooms can be dark. $ *Rooms from: $168* ⊠ *Mustafapaşa Sok. 79* ☎ *212/516–1640* ⊕ *www. hotelamira.com* ⌨ *31 rooms, 1 suite* ⦿ *Breakfast* ✛ *2:B5.*

$$ **Hotel Empress Zoë.** At what is now a Sultanahmet institution, rooms
HOTEL and suites are varied and charming—standard rooms, with colorfully canopied four-posters, nomad textiles, and dark woods, have an almost rustic feel, while suites are more fully furnished, and some have marble-lined bathrooms done up to look like mini hammams. **Pros:** quirky, bohemian atmosphere; location just steps from major sights; lovely garden oasis. **Cons:** no elevator; narrow spiral staircase and labyrinthine layout require a fair bit of climbing; some rooms and bathrooms small and basic. $ *Rooms from: $182* ⊠ *Akbıyık Cad. 10* ⊕ *www.emzoe.com* ⟳ *14 rooms, 12 suites* ⓘⓞⓘ *Breakfast* ✚ *2:C4.*

$$ **Hotel İbrahim Pasha.** What was once the home of an extended Arme-
HOTEL nian family offers comfortable, stylishly decorated rooms—a few look
Fodor'sChoice out toward the Sea of Marmara—with vintage-looking wood and
★ leather furniture, colorfully patterned Turkish carpets and textiles, and contemporary Middle-Eastern touches. **Pros:** location just off Hippodrome; personable staff; inviting public areas and roof terrace. **Cons:** standard rooms can be cramped; most rooms don't have a view; rates for standard rooms a bit high for what is offered. $ *Rooms from: $240* ⊠ *Terzihane Sok. 7* ☎ *212/518–0394* ⊕ *www.ibrahimpasha.com* ⟳ *24 rooms* ⓘⓞⓘ *Breakfast* ✚ *2:B5.*

$ **Hotel Niles.** The elaborate lobby—with its carved wooden columns
HOTEL and ceilings, plush antique furniture, chandeliers, and marble floors with Oriental rugs—could well be a film set, while the standard rooms are equally atmospheric, decorated in a "retro Ottoman" style that includes vintage-style lamps, decorative mouldings stenciled onto the walls, and reproductions of Ottoman miniature paintings on the glass bathroom doors and interior windows. **Pros:** great value; close to Grand Bazaar and tram stop; on-site gym. **Cons:** a little ways from other main sights; small bathrooms in standard rooms; a bit hard to locate amid somewhat unsightly nearby streets. $ *Rooms from: $130* ⊠ *Dibekli Cami Sok. 13, Beyazıt* ☎ *212/517–3239* ⊕ *www.hotelniles.com* ⟳ *29 rooms, 10 suites* ⓘⓞⓘ *Breakfast* ✚ *2:A4.*

$ **Hotel Peninsula.** One of the best values in Sultanahmet, the well-located
B&B/INN Hotel Peninsula offers comfortable and clean rooms, with nice decorative touches that include mirrors, small artworks, kilims, and gauzy draped fabric; three rooms have a partial sea view. **Pros:** great value; convenient location near major sights; service is genuinely friendly and accommodating. **Cons:** no elevator; loud call to prayer from mosque directly behind hotel; bathrooms a bit small and basic. $ *Rooms from: $90* ⊠ *Adliye Sok. 6* ☎ *212/458–6850* ⊕ *www.hotelpeninsula.com* ⟳ *12 rooms* ⓘⓞⓘ *Breakfast* ✚ *2:C4.*

$ **Hotel Tashkonak.** Occupying two adjacent Ottoman-style wooden
HOTEL houses on a quiet side street, Hotel Tashkonak has appealing rooms, friendly service, and a spacious, leafy garden patio that provides a calming oasis in busy Sultanahmet. **Pros:** on quiet street; lovely secluded garden is a gem; good value. **Cons:** rather small rooms; no elevator and lots of stairs. $ *Rooms from: $130* ⊠ *Tomurcuk Sok. 5, Sultanahmet, Istanbul* ☎ *212/518–2882* ⊕ *www.hoteltashkonak.com* ⟳ *27 rooms, 3 suites* ⓘⓞⓘ *Breakfast* ✚ *2:B5.*

$$ B&B/INN 🏨 **Kybele.** Named after an ancient Anatolian fertility goddess, this charming little inn is best known for the incredible profusion of antique lamps—4,000 at last count—that hang from the ceilings in the ornate, parlor-like lobby and small but imaginatively decorated rooms. **Pros:** unique decor and quirky charm; warm, friendly staff. **Cons:** no terrace, elevator, or TVs in most rooms; breakfast served in somewhat dim underground level; heavily ornamented, lamp-filled rooms may not appeal to everyone. [$] *Rooms from: $220* ✉ *Yerebatan Cad. 35* ☎ *212/511–7766* 🌐 *www.kybelehotel.com* 🛏 *16 rooms* 🍴 *Breakfast* ✥ *2:D1.*

$$ B&B/INN 🏨 **Muyan Suites.** The large rooms and suites at this cozy hotel on a quiet backstreet not far from the Çemberlitaş tram stop are attractively if a bit eclectically decorated, with brocade satin upholstery in Ottoman patterns, hanging Middle Eastern–style brass and cloth lamps, ornate mirrors, and kilims on parquet floors. **Pros:** good for families; very friendly, attentive staff; excellent breakfast. **Cons:** thin walls; some bathrooms showing wear and tear; currently no roof terrace or any area with views. [$] *Rooms from: $162* ✉ *Dizdariye Medresesi Sok. 13* ☎ *212/518–6061* 🌐 *www.muyansuites.com* 🛏 *8 rooms, 3 suites* 🍴 *Breakfast* ✥ *2:A4.*

$$ HOTEL 🏨 **Sarı Konak Oteli.** These bright, well-maintained accommodations in a converted Ottoman mansion have mainly modern furniture, though the decor also includes Turkish and period accents like brass lamps, antique mirrors, and Ottoman-era etchings; some rooms have original tiled floors. **Pros:** cozy, intimate feel; good value. **Cons:** standard rooms a bit small; no views from rooms. [$] *Rooms from: $168* ✉ *Mimar Mehmet Ağa Cad. 42–46* ☎ *212/638–6258* 🌐 *www.istanbulhotelsarikonak.com* 🛏 *18 rooms, 5 suites* 🍴 *Breakfast* ✥ *2:C5.*

$ B&B/INN 🏨 **Şebnem.** This lovely little inn near the main sights of Sultanahmet has bright, clean, and attractively decorated rooms—with dark wooden floors, burgundy curtains, and a few four-post beds that have embroidered canopies—and a pleasantly laid-back vibe. **Pros:** extraordinarily friendly staff; outstanding breakfast; lovely terrace. **Cons:** rather small rooms; no elevator; no safes in rooms. [$] *Rooms from: $130* ✉ *Adliye Sok. 1* ☎ *212/517–6623* 🌐 *www.sebnemhotel.net* 🛏 *15 rooms* 🍴 *Breakfast* ✥ *2:C5.*

$$$ HOTEL 🏨 **Sirkeci Konak Hotel.** The comfortable and inviting room decor emphasizes local character, while the bustling, ornate lobby and warm, helpful staff convey feelings of refined luxury. **Pros:** staff especially eager to please; excellent facilities; Gülhane tram station just steps away. **Cons:** lower-level rooms have lackluster views; poor soundproofing of rooms. [$] *Rooms from: $280* ✉ *Taya Hatun Sok. 5, Sirkeci* ☎ *212/528–4344* 🌐 *www.sirkecimansion.com* 🛏 *52 rooms* 🍴 *Breakfast* ✥ *2:C3.*

$$ HOTEL 🏨 **Sultanahmet Palace.** The sultans meet Las Vegas in this glitzy re-creation of an Ottoman palace, where grand marble stairways, columns, Greek statues, and fountains grace the public spaces, and rooms have touches like ornate ceiling mouldings, arched windows, and cushioned divans for reclining and gazing out the windows. **Pros:** prime location just behind Blue Mosque; elegant decor and feel; great views from restaurant. **Cons:** some small rooms; setup of hammam-style bathrooms can be awkward; no elevator. [$] *Rooms from: $220* ✉ *Torun Sok. 19*

☎ *212/458–0460* 🌐 *www.sultanahmetpalace.com* 🛏 *43 rooms, 2 suites* 🍴 *Breakfast* ✥ *2:B5.*

BEYOĞLU

$$ HOTEL 🏨 **Adahan.** An elegant apartment building from 1874 has been lovingly restored by architect-owner Sedat Sırrı Aklan and turned into a charming boutique hotel where no two rooms are exactly alike. **Pros:** highly atmospheric public spaces; excellent homemade breakfast; very comfortable beds. **Cons:** staff is a little inexperienced and could speak better English; no real minibar or room service available; poor Wi-Fi in rooms. [$] *Rooms from: $182* ✉ *General Yazgan Sok. 14* ☎ *212/243–8581* 🌐 *www.adahanistanbul.com* 🛏 *41 rooms, 8 suites* 🍴 *Breakfast* ✥ *1:C3.*

$$$$ HOTEL 🏨 **Divan Istanbul.** An Istanbul institution established in 1956, the Divan has been completely rebuilt and redesigned to offer grand luxury that brings together authentic Turkish style and contemporary design elements. **Pros:** first-class service; beautiful half-Olympic-size indoor pool; excellent breakfast (not included). **Cons:** fairly uninteresting views from most rooms; expensive food and beverages; fee for Internet use. [$] *Rooms from: $422* ✉ *Asker Ocağı Cad. 1, Taksim* ☎ *212/315–5500* 🌐 *www.divan.com.tr* 🛏 *149 rooms, 42 suites* 🍴 *No meals* ✥ *1:E2.*

$$$ HOTEL 🏨 **Gezi Hotel Bosphorus.** Contemporary, minimalist decor infuses a bit more personality than you'll find in most business-caliber hotels, and rooms in this 11-story building have views of the Bosphorus, the park, or the city. **Pros:** central location just across from Taksim's Gezi Parkı; classy atmosphere; helpful staff. **Cons:** most rooms and bathrooms are small; rooms on lower floors don't have much of a view; breakfast could be better. [$] *Rooms from: $285* ✉ *Mete Cad. 34, Taksim* ☎ *212/223–2700* 🌐 *www.gezibosphorus.com* 🛏 *56 rooms, 11 suites* 🍴 *Breakfast* ✥ *1:E2.*

$ HOTEL 🏨 **Mama Shelter.** Smack in the middle of Istanbul's entertainment district, the celebrated Philippe Starck–designed Parisian boutique hotel brand presents its first foray outside France: a hip, central base for travelers at an affordable price. **Pros:** good value; trendy, happening vibe; surrounded by dining, nightlife, and shopping possibilities. **Cons:** small rooms; music blasting on premises and nearby, particularly on weekend nights in summer; some showers leak. [$] *Rooms from: $103* ✉ *İstiklal Cad. 50–54* ☎ *212/252–0100* 🌐 *www.mamashelter.com* 🛏 *81 rooms* 🍴 *No meals* ✥ *1:D3.*

$$$$ HOTEL 🏨 **Martı Istanbul.** This centrally located hotel offers spacious rooms and suites in pleasing shades of blues, purples, and grays that bring together traditional Turkish decor and contemporary aesthetics. **Pros:** close to Taksim Square, entertainment, and transport; unique design with local touches. **Cons:** views from rooftop terrace and gym are only noteworthy; amenities not quite equivalent to its five-star billing. [$] *Rooms from: $397* ✉ *Abdulhak Hamit Cad. 25/B, Taksim* ☎ *212/987–4000* 🌐 *www.martiistanbulhotel.com* 🛏 *239 rooms, 31 suites* 🍴 *No meals* ✥ *1:D2.*

$$$ HOTEL Fodor's Choice ★ 🏨 **Pera Palace Hotel Jumeirah.** Extensive restoration has brought this Istanbul landmark—founded in 1892 to provide upscale accommodations for travelers arriving on the Orient Express—back to its former glory, with beautifully outfitted rooms and plenty of period decorations and antique furniture. **Pros:** historic venue; luxurious facilities. **Cons:** some rooms have small bathrooms; rooms on back side look onto street with lots of traffic; expensive food and drinks. [$] *Rooms from: $318* ✉ *Meşrutiyet Cad. 52, Tepebaşı* ☎ *212/377–4000* 🌐 *www.jumeirah.com* 🛏 *99 rooms, 16 suites* 🍴 *No meals* ⊕ *1:C3.*

$$$$ HOTEL Fodor's Choice ★ 🏨 **Tomtom Suites.** A restored 1901 residence that once housed Franciscan nuns offers superb accommodations and authentic character, with guest rooms furnished with warm woods, textiles in natural colors, high ceilings, and original artwork. **Pros:** historic building with romantic ambience; on quiet street; helpful, welcoming staff. **Cons:** only upper room categories have sea views; reached via steep streets; rather high rates, especially considering lack of fitness facilities. [$] *Rooms from: $416* ✉ *Boğazkesen Cad., Tomtom Kaptan Sok. 18* ☎ *212/292–4949* 🌐 *www.tomtomsuites.com* 🛏 *20 suites* 🍴 *Breakfast* ⊕ *1:D3.*

$$$ HOTEL 🏨 **Witt Istanbul.** All accommodations at this stylish boutique hotel in the popular Cihangir neighborhood are suites—essentially very large loft apartments with separate sleeping and living areas and (in most) "kitchenettes" with marble countertops—and the design is contemporary and überchic: hardwood floors, exposed concrete ceilings, neutral tones, and designer lamps and furniture. **Pros:** swanky design aesthetic; location in quiet residential neighborhood with trendy café scene; personalized service. **Cons:** steep uphill walk from nearby tram stop; venue is not that family-friendly; minimal public spaces. [$] *Rooms from: $298* ✉ *Defterdar Yokuşu 26* ☎ *212/293–1500* 🌐 *www.wittistanbul.com* 🛏 *18 suites* 🍴 *Breakfast* ⊕ *1:D3.*

GALATA AND KARAKÖY

$$ HOTEL 🏨 **Anemon Galata.** An attractively renovated, century-old building so close to the 14th-century Galata Tower that you can almost reach out and touch it, the Anemon Galata provides plenty of old-world charm. **Pros:** historic neighborhood; professional service. **Cons:** rooms facing the square can be noisy at night; some rooms small; reached on steep, winding streets. [$] *Rooms from: $200* ✉ *Büyükhendek Cad. 5, Galata* ☎ *212/293–2343* 🌐 *www.anemonhotels.com* 🛏 *21 rooms, 7 suites* 🍴 *Breakfast* ⊕ *1:C4.*

$$$ HOTEL 🏨 **Georges Hotel Galata.** Housed in a restored late-19th-century apartment building on a street lined with fashion designers' boutiques, the classy Georges and its minimalist yet old-fashioned rooms exude chic—think high ceilings and plain white walls with elaborate mouldings, teak wood furniture, and brass lamps. **Pros:** situated in a trendy yet historic neighborhood; attentive, personalized service; romantic setting away from the tourist fray. **Cons:** can be hard to find; unexciting views from some lower-category rooms; no on-site fitness facilities. [$] *Rooms from: $310* ✉ *Serdar-ı Ekrem Sok. 24, Galata* ☎ *212/244–2423* 🌐 *www.georges.com* 🛏 *20 rooms* 🍴 *Breakfast* ⊕ *1:D4.*

$$ ⚏ **Karaköy Rooms.** Owned and managed by the husband-and-wife team
B&B/INN behind popular restaurant Karaköy Lokantası (and located directly
above it), this intimate property offers impeccably maintained apart-
ment-style accommodations near the Karaköy waterfront. **Pros:** huge
rooms with sophisticated design; good value for location. **Cons:** no
real common areas; not suitable for families with children. $ *Rooms
from: $182* ⊠ *Kemankeş Caddesi, Galata Şarap İskelesi Sok. 10, Kara-
köy* ☎ *212/252–5422* ⊕ *www.karakoyrooms.com* ⬎ *12 rooms* ⦿ *No
meals* ✛ *1:D4.*

BEŞIKTAŞ AND NIŞANTASI

$$$ ⚏ **Park Hyatt Istanbul–Maçka Palas.** A restored Italian-style art deco 1922
HOTEL apartment building offers spacious, elegant rooms decked out in sleek
walnut with modern amenities alongside old-fashioned touches like
period chandeliers and black-and-white photographs of Istanbul. **Pros:**
large rooms; located in upscale shopping and nightlife area; staff is
friendly and efficient. **Cons:** most rooms have no view; spa rooms somewhat overwhelmed by their bathrooms. $ *Rooms from: $300* ⊠ *Bronz
Sok. 4, Nişantaşı* ☎ *212/315–1234* ⊕ *www.istanbul.park.hyatt.com*
⬎ *80 rooms, 10 suites* ⦿ *Breakfast* ✛ *1:F1.*

$$$$ ⚏ **Shangri-La Bosphorus, Istanbul.** Offering all the opulence and sophis-
HOTEL tication expected of this world-class brand, the Shangri-La Bosphorus
overlooks the water, with a glittering lobby that features a two-story
crystal chandelier, richly colored marble paneling, and gold-rimmed
furniture. **Pros:** plush, spacious rooms; extraordinarily attentive service; next to ferry dock. **Cons:** overlooks Bosphorus but no open-air
spaces or waterfront access for guests; location next to prime minister's
offices can mean heavy security presence; box-style hotel architecture
feels rather insular. $ *Rooms from: $637* ⊠ *Hayrettin İskelesi Sok. 1,
Beşiktaş* ☎ *212/275–8888* ⊕ *www.shangri-la.com* ⬎ *169 rooms, 17
suites* ⦿ *No meals* ✛ *1:G2.*

$$$ ⚏ **The Sofa.** Design is the emphasis here, with large rooms that have
HOTEL attractive contemporary textiles and furniture in neutral tones and
reds, as well as an eponymous trademark sofa. **Pros:** spacious, com-
fortable rooms; original design and hip feel. **Cons:** rooms can be noisy
due to rooftop restaurant and location on busy street; interior-facing
rooms rather dim; staff not as helpful as they could be. $ *Rooms from:
$338* ⊠ *Teşvikiye Cad. 41–41/A, Nişantaşı* ☎ *212/368–1818* ⊕ *www.
thesofahotel.com* ⬎ *65 rooms, 17 suites* ⦿ *No meals* ✛ *1:F1.*

BOSPHORUS

$$$$ ⚏ **Çırağan Palace Kempinski Istanbul.** Once a residence for the Ottoman
HOTEL sultans, the late 19th-century Çırağan Palace (pronounced chi-rahn) is
Fodor'sChoice Istanbul's most luxurious hotel, with ornate public spaces that feel abso-
★ lutely decadent and a breathtaking setting right on the Bosphorus—the
outdoor infinity pool seems to hover on the water's edge and most rooms,
full of Ottoman-inspired wood furnishings and textiles in warm colors,
have balconies overlooking the Bosphorus as well. **Pros:** grand setting
in incredible Bosphorus-front location; over-the-top feeling of luxury.

Cons: exorbitant price of food and drinks; high rates, especially for rooms that have no Bosphorus view. $ *Rooms from: $683* ✉ *Çırağan Cad. 32* ☎ *212/326–4646* ⊕ *www.kempinski.com/istanbul* ⇆ *282 rooms, 31 suites* ⦿ *No meals* ✛ *1:H1.*

> **BREAKFAST IN ISTANBUL**
>
> A Turkish breakfast of fresh bread, *beyaz peynir* (feta-like white cheese), tomatoes, cucumbers, and olives, and often jam or honey, is included at most hotels in Turkey, although not usually at the higher-end properties.

$$$$ 〒 **Four Seasons Hotel Istanbul at**
HOTEL **the Bosphorus.** This restored 19th-century Ottoman palace with two modern wings exudes luxury; rooms and suites, a quarter of which have Bosphorus views (others have garden and city views), are elegant yet understated, with soaring ceilings, muted tones, and Ottoman touches such as handcrafted mirrors. **Pros:** impeccable service; beautiful views and location; top-notch spa and fitness facilities. **Cons:** expensive food and drinks with little local flavor; underwhelming views from non-Bosphorus rooms, especially considering high rates. $ *Rooms from: $690* ✉ *Çırağan Cad. 80, Beşiktaş, Istanbul* ☎ *212/381–4000* ⊕ *www.fourseasons.com/bosphorus* ⇆ *145 rooms, 25 suites* ⦿ *No meals* ✛ *1:H1.*

$$$ 〒 **The House Hotel Bosphorus.** Most of the stylish accommodations in
HOTEL this restored late-19th-century waterfront mansion and the small annex just behind it have views of the Bosphorus, and some have private balconies; all are decorated in a chic, contemporary style—warm woods, neutral textiles, brass lamps, and engraved mirrors—with historical touches like high ceilings and floral moldings. **Pros:** hip hotel with intimate feel; waterfront location in charming Ortaköy; exceptionally attentive service. **Cons:** standard rooms and some bathrooms are small; located in popular nightlife area that can be loud at night. $ *Rooms from: $300* ✉ *Muallim Naci Cad., Salhane Sok. 1, Bosphorus, Istanbul* ☎ *212/327–7787* ⊕ *www.thehousehotel.com* ⇆ *10 rooms, 16 suites* ⦿ *Breakfast* ✛ *1:H1.*

$$$$ 〒 **The Istanbul Edition.** A sophisticated oasis in the city's bustling finan-
HOTEL cial district offers comfortable, spacious rooms that have a somewhat
Fodor's Choice masculine feel—sleek woods, minimalist decor, textiles in champagne
★ and cream tones—and feature the latest technology, with iPod docking stations and Bang & Olufsen adjustable flat-screen TVs. **Pros:** stylish, high-tech rooms; exceptionally attentive staff; luxurious spa and fitness facilities. **Cons:** hotel is far from sights (though located next to a metro station); in-house Cipriani restaurant is expensive; dining and public areas overlook a busy expressway. $ *Rooms from: $618* ✉ *Büyükdere Cad. 136, Levent, Istanbul* ☎ *212/317–7700* ⊕ *www.editionhotels.com* ⇆ *77 rooms, 1 suite* ⦿ *No meals* ✛ *1:F1.*

$$$ 〒 **W Istanbul.** An 1870s Ottoman block of row houses has been restored
HOTEL and enhanced with posh ultramodernity—sexy lighting, chic East-meets-West decor, and cool amenities like iPod docks and rainshowers. **Pros:** cool, trendy atmosphere; ultracomfortable beds. **Cons:** dim, nightclub-like lighting in public spaces may not suit all tastes; awkward bathroom layout in some rooms offers little privacy; service is hit or

miss. $ *Rooms from: $300* ✉ *Süleyman Seba Cad. 22, Beşiktaş, Istanbul* ☎ *212/381-2121* ⊕ *www.starwoodhotels.com* ⟿ *107 rooms, 29 suites* ⏏ *No meals* ✛ *1:G2.*

ASIAN SHORE

$$$$ 🏨 **Sumahan on the Water.** What was once a derelict distillery on the
HOTEL   Asian waterfront of the Bosphorus is now one of Istanbul's chicest and
Fodor's Choice   most original places to stay, with comfortable rooms and suites—all
★   with incredible views of the water and decorated in a contemporary
style with a few Turkish touches. **Pros:** stunning waterfront location;
stylish and inviting public areas; secluded, romantic atmosphere. **Cons:**
far from sights and commercial center; somewhat inconvenient to get
to without the launch. $ *Rooms from: $422* ✉ *Kuleli Cad. 43, Çengelköy* ☎ *216/422-8000* ⊕ *www.sumahan.com* ⟿ *11 rooms, 13 suites*
⏏ *Breakfast* ✛ *1:H3.*

NIGHTLIFE AND THE ARTS

NIGHTLIFE

Istanbul's nightlife still revolves, in many ways, around its meyhanes,
the tavern-like restaurants where long nights are spent nibbling on
mezes and sipping the anise-flavored spirit rakı. The atmosphere at these
places—mostly found in the lively Beyoğlu area—is jovial, friendly,
and worth experiencing. But there are lots of other options, too, again
mostly in Beyoğlu, which has everything from grungy American-style
dive bars to sophisticated lounges, performance spaces that host world-
class live acts, and dance clubs. In recent years, the trend in the neighborhood has been literally upward, with the opening of rooftop bars
that offer stunning views and fresh breezes.

As Istanbul's reputation as a hip city continues to grow, the quality of
the live acts that come to town has risen, too. Established and up-and-
coming performers now frequently include Istanbul on their European
tours, and the city has become a good place to catch a show for far less
than what you might pay in Paris, London, or New York. Note that
many live-performance venues close for part or all of the summer, when
school is out and the city's elite departs for vacation.

To experience Istanbul's most high-end nightlife, head to the neighborhoods along the Bosphorus, where chic (and pricey) nightclubs play
host to Istanbul's rich and famous and those who want to rub shoulders
with them. The vibrant dance club scene here, as well as at a few places
in Beyoğlu, is not for the faint of heart. Things typically get rolling at
around midnight and go until 4 or 5 in the morning. The city's most
upscale clubs tend to be expensive—admission fees can be steep on summer weekends—and there are no guarantees you'll get past the door-
man, whose job it is to make sure only Istanbul's best dressed get in.

Sultanahmet isn't known for its nightlife, but in summer, the strip of
tourist-oriented restaurants and dive bars at the end of Akbıyık Sokak

close to the Aya Sofya can be quite lively, with a young crowd that fills the sidewalk tables.

SULTANAHMET
BARS AND LOUNGES

A'ya Lounge. Sultanahmet doesn't have many noteworthy nightlife spots, but the open-air rooftop lounge at the Four Seasons Sultanahmet is an inviting place to have a drink. Relax on the comfortable deck furniture as you take in the spectacular views of the Aya Sofya and Blue Mosque lit up at night. The lounge closes at 11 pm. ⊠ *Four Seasons Hotel Sultanahmet, Tevkifhane Sok. 1* ☎ *212/402–3000* ⊕ *www.fourseasons.com/istanbul.*

CABARETS

Surviving strictly on the tourist trade, Istanbul's nightclub shows include everything from folk dancers to jugglers, acrobats, belly dancers, and singers. Rather than being authentically Turkish, the shows are a kitschy attempt to provide tourists with something exotic and Oriental. Typically, dinner is served at about 8, and floor shows start at around 10. Be aware that these are not inexpensive once you've totaled up drink, food, and cover. Reservations are a good idea; be sure to specify whether you're coming for dinner as well as the show or just for drinks.

BEYOĞLU
BARS AND LOUNGES

5. Kat. A rather pricey restaurant that turns into a trendy lounge/bar later in the evening, 5. Kat is on the fifth floor of an unassuming building in the quiet Cihangir neighborhood and offers wonderful views of the Bosphorus—along with great cocktails. With its wooden furniture and potted plants, the upper-level terrace (open only in warm months) makes you feel like you're passing the time on somebody's roof deck. ⊠ *Soğancı Sok. 7, Cihangir, Beyoğlu* ☎ *212/293–3774* ⊕ *www.5kat.com.*

Araf. Located on one of Istanbul's busiest nightlife strips, Araf is usually packed to the gills with a young, energetic, and unpretentious crowd that likes to dance their hearts out to funky beats. Sunday through Thursday nights generally feature live bands playing Turkish folk, Balkan/Gypsy, or reggae/ska music, while on weekends a DJ spins music from around the world. There's no cover charge. ⊠ *Balo Sok. 32, 5th fl., Beyoğlu* ☎ *212/244–8301* ⊕ *www.araf.com.tr.*

Balkon. A sixth-floor bar and lounge, Balkon has excellent views of the Golden Horn and a laid-back outdoor deck. Despite the location in the increasingly trendy Asmalımescit area, drink prices are

---

NARGILES

Nargiles (also known as hookahs) and the billowy smoke they produce have been an integral part of Istanbul's coffeehouses for centuries. Once associated with older men who would spend their days smoking, sipping strong Turkish coffee, and playing backgammon, the nargile is experiencing renewed popularity among younger Istanbullus. They are often used with a variety of flavored tobaccos, such as apple or strawberry. Because the smoke is filtered through water, it's cool and smooth, though it can make you light-headed if you're not used to it.

reasonable. ⊠ *Şehbender Sok. 5, Beyoğlu* ☎ *212/293–2052* ⊕ *www. balkonrestaurantbar.com.*

KV. Tucked into a late 19th-century open-air arcade, KV has a brasserie kind of feel that's perfect for a quiet drink; a piano or local musicians occasionally supply live background music. ⊠ *Tünel Geçidi 10, Beyoğlu* ☎ *212/251–4338* ⊕ *www.kv.com.tr.*

Fodor'sChoice **Leb-i Derya.** The reward for finding this sixth-floor rooftop restaurant
★ and bar—in an apartment building with only a small sign out front—is a magnificent view overlooking the Bosphorus and the Old City. The small venue is popular with an almost-too-hip crowd of locals and expats who come for the cocktails and the views, so you may have to wait for a table or stand by the bar if you show up without reservations. A second branch—at the top of the Richmond Hotel on İstiklal Caddesi—is more restaurant-like and a bit less "scene-y," catering to a slightly more mature crowd, and has superb views as well. ⊠ *Kumbaracı Yokuşu 57/6, Beyoğlu* ☎ *212/293–4989* ⊕ *www.lebiderya.com.*

Mama Shelter. The enormous rooftop terrace on the top of Mama Shelter Hotel houses a trendy restaurant/bar offering 360-degree views of the city, specialty cocktails and drinks, and a fun, lively atmosphere. Open in the warm months only, there's a buzzing bar section and several more casual lounge areas. In the winter, the venue moves inside to the building's fourth floor. ⊠ *Mama Shelter Hotel, İstiklal Cad. 50–54, Beyoğlu* ☎ *212/252–0100* ⊕ *www.mamashelter.com.*

Şahika. On a narrow street lined with basic beer joints and meyhanes serving mostly identical food menus, Şahika offers something more unusual. The lively, multistory venue has a different concept and ambience on each level, ranging from a pub atmosphere on the street level, to casual lounge areas on the middle floors, to a clublike vibe on the terrace, which also has excellent views of the Golden Horn. ⊠ *Nevizade Sok. 17, Beyoğlu* ☎ *212/249–6196* ⊕ *www.sahika.com.tr.*

DANCE CLUBS

Fodor'sChoice **NuTeras.** The rooftop of a historic building (known as NuPera) with
★ wonderful views of the Golden Horn is home to one of Istanbul's trendiest nightclubs. There's a chic bar and small dance floor, with sleek decor and a fashionable crowd to match the striking location. NuTeras is entirely open-air, so it's only open from late spring through early fall; as of press time the establishment was planning to open an indoor nightclub in the same building, to keep dancers happy during the winter months. ⊠ *Meşrutiyet Cad. 149, Beyoğlu* ☎ *212/245–6070* ⊕ *www. nupera.com.tr* ۞ *Closed mid-Oct–mid-May.*

JAZZ CLUBS

Nardis Jazz Club. One of Istanbul's few dedicated jazz venues, the well-regarded Nardis Jazz Club hosts mainly Turkish musicians and the occasional big name from abroad. The cozy, intimate space only has room for 110, so reservations are strongly recommended. The club is closed Sundays and during the entire month of August. ⊠ *Kuledibi Sok. 14, Beyoğlu* ☎ *212/244–6327* ⊕ *www.nardisjazz.com.*

Going out to hear Turkish music in Istanbul

MUSIC VENUES

Fodor's Choice
★ **Babylon.** This is Istanbul's top live music space, hosting world-famous performers in genres ranging from jazz, indie pop, and rock to world music and electronica. Despite being in a converted warehouse, the sound system is excellent—the friendly crowds take their music seriously. It's closed in summer, when Babylon Aya Yorgi opens in the beach town of Çeşme, near İzmir. ✉ *Şehbender Sok. 3, Beyoğlu* ☎ *212/292–7368* ⊕ *www.babylon.com.tr.*

Fodor's Choice
★ **Ghetto.** With an excellent sound system and attractively furnished premises on two levels, Ghetto brings in a diverse lineup of Turkish and international musical acts performing a varierty of genres. The club is closed Sundays. ✉ *Kamer Hatun Cad. 10, Beyoğlu* ☎ *212/251–7501* ⊕ *www.ghettoist.com.*

Hayal Kahvesi. One of Beyoğlu's longest-running live music venues, Hayal Kahvesi has been in operation for over 20 years, recently moving into a sleek spot two streets up from the original, far grungier location. The long, narrow space hosts nightly gigs by both well-known and up-and-coming Turkish bands and musicians, mostly playing rock, with the occasional blues, jazz, or pop in the mix. The main performance usually starts mid- to late evening, with a cover band coming on after midnight. ✉ *Büyükparmakkapı Sok. 19, Beyoğlu* ☎ *212/244–2558* ⊕ *www.hayalkahvesibeyoglu.com* ⊗ *Closed Aug.*

Salon İKSV. This top-notch performance space is housed in the headquarters and cultural center of the Istanbul Foundation for Culture and Arts (İKSV), one of the city's most important arts organizations. The concert lineup features both local and international acts spanning a wide range of genres, including jazz, rock, alternative, and world music. At the time of this writing, the İKSV had plans to eventually move to a new, yet-to-be-determined location. ✉ *Sadi Konuralp Cad. 5, Şişhane, Beyoğlu* ☎ *212/334–0841* ⊕ *www.saloniksv.com* ✆ *Closed mid-July–mid-Sept.*

BOSPHORUS

BARS AND LOUNGES

Bebek Bar. With its masculine interior decor that brings to mind a private club, and a breezy terrace directly overlooking the Bosphorus, Bebek Bar attracts a dressed-up crowd. There is a particularly wide selection of liqueurs, scotch, and other spirits, as well as classic cocktails, making it a perfect spot for a before-or after-dinner drink. ✉ *Bebek Hotel, Cevdet Paşa Cad. 34, Bebek* ☎ *212/358–2000* ⊕ *www.bebekhotel.com.tr.*

The W Lounge. The stylish yet comfortable lounge/bar in the W Hotel has plush divans, low tables, and signature cocktails, drawing a sophisticated, trendy crowd. There are DJs several nights a week during the winter months. ✉ *W Istanbul Hotel, Süleyman Seba Cad. 22* ☎ *212/381–2121* ⊕ *www.wistanbul.com.tr/en/wlounge.*

DANCE CLUBS

Anjelique. Overlooking the Ortaköy waterfront, Anjelique's classy atmosphere offers partiers a more intimate feel than the larger nightclubs farther up the Bosphorus. Dinner is served to a well-heeled crowd before the venue turns into a dance club. ✉ *Muallim Naci Cad., Salhane Sok. 5* ☎ *212/327–2844* ⊕ *www.anjelique.com.tr.*

Sortie. If you want to mingle with Istanbul's rich and famous (and the paparazzi that await them), swanky Sortie has a slightly less pretentious ambience and a friendlier door policy than its famously exclusive neighbor, Reina. In summer, a half-dozen of Istanbul's trendiest restaurants open up locations here to serve dinner. There's a steep entrance fee (70 TL or more) to get into the club on summer weekends. ✉ *Muallim Naci Cad. 54, Ortaköy* ☎ *212/327–8585* ⊕ *www.sortie.com.tr.*

ASIAN SHORE

BARS AND LOUNGES

Karga Bar. The longest-established and most popular venue on Kadıköy's so-called "Barlar Sokağı" ("bars street"), Karga takes up several levels of an old wooden house, whose many small rooms and intimate niches provide a perfect laid-back hangout. There is live music on weekends during the winter months and occasional art events. There's no sign out front but look for a building with a green facade and an emblem of a crow over the doorway (karga means "crow" in Turkish). ✉ *Kadife Sok. 16, Asian Side* ☎ *216/449–1725* ⊕ *www.kargabar.org.*

Lâl. The best thing about this low-key café/bar on Kadıköy's main nightlife street is the large courtyard in the back, where patrons can gather around tables and an old, distinctive tree. In cooler months, the rustic interior is a cozy place to chat. ✉ *Kadife Sok. 19, Kadıköy, Asian Side* ☎ *216/346–5625* ⊕ *www.kadyagrup.com.tr.*

ARTS AND ENTERTAINMENT

For upcoming events, reviews, and other information about what to do in Istanbul, pick up a copy of the monthly *Time Out Istanbul* or the bimonthly *Guide,* both of which are English-language publications with listings of restaurants, bars, and events, as well as features about Istanbul. The English-language *Hürriyet Daily News* and *Today's Zaman* are also good resources for listings and for keeping abreast of what's happening in Istanbul and in Turkish politics.

FILM

Several movie theaters along İstiklal Caddesi between Taksim and Galatasaray (a square at the midpoint of İstiklal Caddesi) show the latest from Turkey and Hollywood, with European movies occasionally thrown in. There is also a plush, modern theater at City's shopping mall in Nişantaşı. Most foreign films are shown with their original soundtrack and Turkish subtitles, although many children's films are dubbed into Turkish. Look for the words *İngilizce* (English) or *orijinal* (original language). Films in languages other than English will have subtitles in Turkish. When in doubt, ask at the ticket office whether the film is dubbed (*dublaj*) or subtitled (*altyazılı*).

PERFORMANCE VENUES

Akbank Sanat. Sponsored by one of Turkey's largest private banks, the six-story, multipurpose Akbank Sanat (Akbank Art Center) hosts regular classical music and jazz concerts, including the Akbank Jazz Festival, held annually over several weeks in late September and early October. More than 700 other events are held at the center each year, including modern dance performances, theater productions, film screenings, and art exhibitions. ⊠ *İstiklal Cad. 8, Beyoğlu* ☎ *212/252–3500* ⊕ *www.akbanksanat.com* ☺ *Closed Aug.*

Cemal Reşit Rey Concert Hall. Located off Cumhuriyet Caddesi between Taksim and Nişantaşı, Cemal Reşit Rey Concert Hall is run by the Istanbul Municipality and hosts a wide variety of performances, from classical music, opera, and the occasional jazz and pop concert to ballet and flamenco. ⊠ *Gümüş Sok., Harbiye, Nişantaşı* ☎ *212/232–9830* ⊕ *www.crrks.org* ☺ *Closed Jan. 1–15 and Jun.–Sept.*

Garajistanbul. Located in the basement of a parking lot near Galatasaray Square, Garajistanbul is an experimental venue that hosts contemporary dance and theater, as well as musical, literary, and artistic events. ⊠ *Yeni Çarşı Cad., Kaymakam Reşit Bey Sok. 11A, Galatasaray, Beyoğlu* ☎ *212/244–4499* ⊕ *www.garajistanbul.org* ☺ *Closed Jun.–Sept.*

WHIRLING DERVISHES

The Mevlevi, a Sufi brotherhood originally founded in Konya, are best known around the world as the whirling dervishes, mystics who believe ritual spinning will bring them closer to God. If you can't make it to Konya to see the *sema* ceremony in the place where it all began, there are a couple of places to see them in Istanbul. It should be noted that these ceremonies—at least in Istanbul—have essentially turned into performances staged for tourists, lacking much religious context. Nonetheless, seeing the dervishes whirl tends to entrance even the least spiritual of people, and gives a window onto a unique aspect of traditional Turkish culture.

Hodjapasha Culture Center. Housed in a nicely restored 15th-century hammam, the Hodjapasha Culture Center hosts whirling dervish ceremonies most nights of the week. The hour-long event starts with a performance of classical Turkish music before the dervishes whirl. Though some are captivated by the whirling, others may find it excessively slow and hypnotic, so consider whether this sort of cultural experience is your cup of tea. Note that photography is not allowed during the sema ceremony. Hodjapasha also offers two different dance shows that are considerably more lively; one features traditional Turkish folk dancing and the other is a theatrical performance that combines bellydancing and modern dance. Tickets are 60 TL for the dervishes and 70 TL for the dance shows. ⊠ *Hocapaşa Hamamı Cad. 3/B, Sirkeci, The Bazaar Area and Environs* ☎ *212/511–4686* ⊕ *www.hodjapasha.com.*

Mevlâna Education and Culture Society. A local dervish group, the Mevlâna Education and Culture Society (MEKDER), holds sema ceremonies one Sunday per month at the Galata Mevlevihanesi. The ceremonies last about an hour and include traditional Mevlevi music and ritual whirling. Tickets cost 40 TL. ⊠ *Galata Mevlevihanesi, Galip Dede Cad. 15, Beyoğlu* ☎ *216/336–1662* ⊕ *www.mekder.org.*

SHOPPING

Istanbul has been a shopper's town for, well, centuries—the sprawling Grand Bazaar, open since 1461, could easily be called the world's oldest shopping mall—but this is not to say that the city is stuck in the past. Along with its colorful bazaars and outdoor markets, Istanbul also has a wide range of modern shopping options, from the enormous new malls that seem to be sprouting up everywhere to small independent boutiques. Either way, it's almost impossible to leave Istanbul without buying something and some say you haven't truly experienced the city until you take a whirl through the Grand Bazaar or Spice Bazaar. Whether you're looking for trinkets and souvenirs, kilims and carpets, brass and silverware, jewelry, leather goods, old books, prints, and maps, or furnishings and clothes (Turkish textiles are among the best in the world), you can find them in this city. Shopping in Istanbul also provides a snapshot of the city's contrasts and contradictions: eastern Turkey migrants haggle with tourists and sell their wares on the streets while wealthy shoppers browse the designer goods found in plush, upscale Western-style department stores.

İstiklal Caddesi is a pedestrian-only boulevard with everything from global brands like Levi's and big-name Turkish companies like Mavi to small bookshops and old-school shoe stores—though, sadly, increasingly high rent prices mean there are fewer and fewer independent local stores located on İstiklal these days. Down the hill from İstiklal, Çukurcuma Caddesi is home to a miscellany of antique dealers carrying everything from small, Ottoman-era knickknacks to enormous antique marble tubs. Meanwhile, the character-filled Galata and Karaköy neighborhoods are becoming the places to find independent boutiques and intriguing shops selling clothing, jewelry, housewares, and objets d'art created by up-and-coming local designers.

The high-fashion district is the upscale Nişantaşı neighborhood, 1 km (½ mile) north of İstiklal Caddesi. This is where you'll find the boutiques of established Turkish fashion designers, such as Özlem Süer, Arzu Kaprol, and Atıl Kutoğlu, as well as the flagship stores of high-end international brands like Chanel, Prada, and Louis Vuitton—though because of high import taxes and unfavorable exchange rates, these labels are usually considerably more expensive in Turkey than they are in the United States.

Istanbul is also a good place to buy jewelry, as Turkey has a long tradition of jewelry making, and many jewelers are skilled at working with both gold and silver. While local brands often tend to copy European designs in their collections, recently there has been a trend towards creating beautiful pieces with a local flavor, using traditional motifs or taking Ottoman-era charms and setting them in silver or gold. The jewelry sold in the Grand Bazaar and in high-end boutiques in Nişantaşı tends to be fairly classic and high quality; if you're looking for something a bit more unusual or easier on the wallet, try the smaller-scale boutiques in Beyoğlu or Galata.

SULTANAHMET

BOOKS

Galeri Kayseri. If you're looking for books about Turkey, this is the place to visit. The two Galeri Kayseri shops (the storefronts simply say "Bookshop") are across the street from one another, and between them you'll find an outstanding collection of nonfiction books about Turkey in a variety of subject areas, as well as a selection of Turkish and Turkey-related novels and elegant coffee table books on Islamic art, architecture, and culture. Number 58 is the main store, No. 11 is across the street. ⊠ *Divanyolu Cad. 58* ☎ *212/516–3366* ⊕ *www. galerikayseri.com.*

CARPETS

Cocoon. Proprietor Şeref Özen has one of the best collections in Istanbul of antique and vintage tribal carpets, flatweaves, and textiles—primarily Central Asian rugs, tie-dyed ikats, and embroidered suzanis, though there are also some Turkish and Persian pieces—at his main shop not far from the Arasta Bazaar. A few doors up the street (at No. 13), a second Cocoon store sells a specially designed collection of colorful pieces made mainly from felt, including hats, slippers, pillowcases, and decorative items—perfect for anyone looking to pick up a unique souvenir or gift. ⊠ *Küçükayasofya Cad. 17* ☎ *212/638–6271* ⊕ *www.cocoontr.com.*

Gallery Aydın. The collection at Gallery Aydın includes high-end antique Turkish, Persian, Georgian, and Caucasian carpets dating back to as early as the 16th century. Dealer Adnan Aydın seriously knows his rugs, and also specializes in repairing and restoring antique pieces. ⊠ *Küçükayasofya Cad. 5/B* ☏ *212/513–6921* ⊕ *www. aorientalrugs.com.*

HANDICRAFTS

FodorsChoice **Tulu.** Istanbul-based American textile collector and designer Elizabeth
★ Hewitt carries her own designs at Tulu, along with a fascinating collection of textiles, housewares, and decorative items—both new and
antique—from Turkey and around the world. Her beautiful bed linens and other home textiles are made in India using traditional hand
blocking techniques. The third floor has a selection of new, vintage, and
antique carpets curated by Hewitt's husband, Hüseyin Kaplan, owner
of Karavan carpet shop in Konya. ⊠ *Binbirdirek Mah. Üçler Sok. 7/A*
☏ *212/518–8710* ⊕ *www.tulutextiles.com.*

MARKETS

Arasta Bazaar. Just behind the Blue Mosque, the Arasta Bazaar is a
walkway lined with shops selling items similar to those you'll find
at the Grand Bazaar (primarily carpets, ceramics, and other handicrafts), at sometimes lower prices. The atmosphere is also considerably
calmer and, unlike the Grand Bazaar, the Arasta is open on Sunday
and stays open later (till about 9pm). ⊠ *Arasta Çarşısı 143* ⊕ *www.
arastabazaar.com.*

SPAS

FodorsChoice **Ayasofya Hürrem Sultan Hamamı.** This hammam, which reopened in 2011
★ following a several-year, $10-million restoration after decades of dis-
use, is the sleekest and most luxurious in the Old City. It has a prestigious history, having been built by Ottoman architect Sinan in 1556
on the order of Sultan Süleyman the Magnificent, in honor of his wife
Roxelana (Hürrem). The setup here is more like that of a modern spa:
there is no self-service option, reservations are strongly encouraged, and
you'll certainly feel pampered (particularly by the redbud-scented bath
amenities). The prices are on par with this level of service—the cheap-
est treatment is a whopping US$110 (about 200 TL). In addition to
traditional hammam services, more modern treatments such as aroma-
therapy massage are offered. ⊠ *Babıhümayun Cad. 1* ☏ *212/517–3535*
⊕ *www.ayasofyahamami.com.*

Cağaloğlu Hamamı. Housed in a magnificent building dating to 1741, the
Cağaloğlu Hamamı has long been considered one of the best in Istanbul. Florence Nightingale and Kaiser Wilhelm II once steamed here,
and the clientele has remained generally upscale. Prices are on the high
side, starting at about $40 (about 75 TL) for a self-service visit; if you
want both a scrub and a massage from an attendant, it'll cost you about
$65 (about 125 TL). Unfortunately, in recent years the Cağaloğlu has
become fairly overrun by tourists and service has gone downhill; guests
complain of quick, perfunctory massages by attendants and persistent
demands for tips. If you want to experience this famous hammam, consider going the self-service route, so you can relax at your own pace.
⊠ *Prof. Kazım Gürkan Cad. 24, Cağaloğlu* ☏ *212/522–2424* ⊕ *www.
cagalogluhamami.com.tr.*

Çemberlitaş Hamamı. Built in 1584, Çemberlitaş Hamamı is famous for
its beautiful architectural design and has long been a favorite hammam

with visitors, as it's one of the city's most atmospheric. Nevertheless, it's become so heavily trafficked that service can be somewhat rushed and attendants can be aggressive in asking for tips. Fees for scrubbing by an attendant start at 80 TL. The self-service option, which gives you the chance to linger longer, is 54 TL. Avoid going between 4 and 8pm, which is the busiest time. ✉ *Vezirhan Cad. 8, Çemberlitaş* ☎ *212/522–7974* ⊕ *www.cemberlitashamami.com.*

Gedikpaşa Hamamı. In operation since 1475, this hammam is unique in that both the men's and women's sections have small indoor plunge pools and saunas added in modern times. The atmosphere here is somewhat less touristy than at other hammams, but standards of cleanliness seem a little less stringent than they are at more expensive baths. The most affordable of the hammams in the area, Gedikpaşa charges around 50 TL for self-service and about 65 TL for a professional scrub. ✉ *Hamam Cad. 65–67, Beyazıt* ☎ *212/517–8956* ⊕ *www.gedikpasahamami.com.tr.*

Süleymaniye Hamamı. Part of the complex of buildings around the Süleymaniye Camii, and built, like the mosque, by Sinan in the 1550s, the Süleymaniye Hamamı is unique in being the only coed hammam in the Old City. It caters specifically to couples and families—in fact, single travelers and single-sex groups cannot visit. Some may find the coed arrangement (with no nudity) preferable to going to a sex-segregated hammam, but it's no less touristy than the rest and women should note that there are only male masseurs. Rates are about 90 TL per person. ✉ *Mimar Sinan Cad. 20, Süleymaniye* ☎ *212/519–5569* ⊕ *www.suleymaniyehamami.com.tr.*

BAZAAR QUARTER AND ENVIRONS

ANTIQUES

Fodor's Choice ★ **Sofa.** One of Istanbul's most highly regarded antiques stores, Sofa is located on pedestrian-only Nuruosmaniye Caddesi. Two levels are filled with a fascinating collection of metalwork, original İznik and Kütahya ceramics, old maps and prints, calligraphy and miniatures, textiles, vintage jewelry, artwork, and assorted other treasures. ✉ *Nuruosmaniye Cad. 53/A, Cağaloğlu* ☎ *212/520–2850* ⊕ *www.kashifsofa.com.*

Ziya Aykaç Antikacı. One of the oldest antique stores in the Grand Bazaar, Ziya Aykaç Antikacı is filled floor to ceiling with antique fabrics, silverware, ceramics, watches, and other treasures. The pieces come from Turkey, Europe, and as far away as China. ✉ *Takkeciler Sok. 68–72, Grand Bazaar* ☎ *212/527–6082.*

BATH ACCESSORIES

Abdulla. This delightful boutique sells high-quality towels, tablecloths, throw rugs, and other traditional Turkish home textiles with a simple, modern aesthetic. The immensely appealing and stylish collection also includes luscious, all-natural olive-oil soaps. ✉ *Halıcılar Cad. 62* ☎ *212/527–3684* ⊕ *www.abdulla.com.*

Derviş. At Derviş, the emphasis is on handcrafted towels, bathrobes, soaps, and traditional Turkish bath accessories, as well as antique and vintage kaftans and robes from Anatolia. ⊠ *Keseciler Cad. 33–35* ☎ *212/514–4525* ⊕ *www.dervis.com.*

BOOKS

Sahaflar Çarşısı. Reached through a doorway just outside the western end of the Grand Bazaar, the Sahaflar Çarşısı is the traditional home of Istanbul's secondhand booksellers. The market now mainly houses bookshops selling new editions in Turkish, though a handful of secondhand and rare book dealers carrying books in English and other languages are still located here. The market is open every day.

CARPETS

Adnan & Hasan. One of Istanbul's most reputable carpet dealers, Adnan & Hasan espouses a "hassle-free shopping" policy and is favored by the diplomatic community. The company and its friendly staff offer a large selection of antique, semi-antique, and new carpets and kilims, mainly from Anatolia. ⊠ *Halıcılar Cad. 89–90–92, Grand Bazzar*☎ *212/527–9887* ⊕ *www.adnanandhasan.com.*

Dhoku. Design brand Dhoku stands out among the traditional carpet merchants of the Grand Bazaar for its radically different, contemporary styles, which include bold geometric designs and stylized floral patterns. The high-quality rugs are handmade near İzmir using organic handspun wool and natural dyes. Directly across the street is sister company Ethnicon (⊠ *Takkeciler Caddesi 49–51*), which pieces together different-sized squares of colorful rug material to create carpets reminiscent of American-style quilts. Both stores offer fixed prices; at Dhoku, pricing is by the square meter. ⊠ *Takkeciler Sok. 58–60, Grand Bazaar* ☎ *212/527–6841* ⊕ *www.dhoku.com.*

Odabaşı Halıcılık. Odabaşı, in the Babıali Carpet and Kilim Bazaar, specializes in rugs and kilims from Turkey and the surrounding region—particularly antiques, although there are some new pieces as well. Proprietor İsmet Odabasio is primarily a wholesaler of rugs with a busy export business to the United States, but he is happy to work directly with customers looking for special pieces at reasonable prices. ⊠ *Babıali Cad. Babıali Çarşısı No. 18 D. 22–42, Cağaloğlu* ☎ *212/511–5983.*

Şengör. Established in 1918 and now run by the fourth generation of the Şengör family, this experienced and trustworthy dealer has a large inventory of carpets from different regions of Anatolia. ⊠ *Takkeciler Sok. 65–83 and 98, Grand Bazaar* ☎ *212/527–2192.*

HANDICRAFTS

Fodor's Choice
★
Armaggan Nuruosmaniye. In a seven-story emporium with the cachet of a small boutique, the high-end design brand Armaggan offers limited-edition collections of housewares, carpets, naturally dyed garments, jewelry, accessories, and decorative objects with unique, contemporary designs inspired by traditional Turkish motifs and techniques. The venue also houses a gallery showing work by contemporary Turkish artists; in addition, it's home to NAR Restaurant and carries NAR's line of all-natural gourmet Turkish food products. ⊠ *Nuruosmaniye Cad. 65, Nuruosmaniye* ☎ *212/522–4433* ⊕ *www.armaggan.com*

Kaptan Bros. This store specializes in handworked copper and brass pieces, both old and new, and also sells stylish lanterns in traditional Middle Eastern and contemporary styles. ⊠ *Terziler Sok. 30, Grand Bazaar* ☎ *212/526–3650.*

Nick's Calligraphy Corner. One of the most unusual stores in the Grand Bazaar—indeed, anywhere—is Nick Merdenyan's tiny shop. The artist produces intricate calligraphic works and miniature paintings incorporating motifs and themes from major world religions, as well as universal nonreligious messages. Each small masterpiece is done on dried Dieffenbachia leaves, which he calls "Nick's missionary leaves of tolerance and peace." ⊠ *İç Bedesten Şerif Ağa Sok. 24* ☎ *212/513–5473* ⊕ *www.nickscalligraphy.com.*

JEWELRY

Bagus. In the Grand Bazaar's Cevahir Bedestani, Bagus sells the proprietor's own reasonably priced collection of handmade jewelry made with silver and semiprecious stones as well as intriguing pieces imported from countries including India, Nepal, Thailand, and Indonesia. ⊠ *Cevahir Bedestan 42–43* ☎ *212/528–2519.*

Horasan. There are piles and piles of antique rings, bracelets, necklaces, and earrings from Central Asia at Horasan, as well as walls covered in strands of colorful beads made out of precious and semiprecious stones from which the staff will help you create your own jewelry. Prices are fair. ⊠ *Terlikçiler Sok. 37* ☎ *212/519–3654.*

MARKETS

Nuruosmaniye Caddesi. One of the major streets leading to the Grand Bazaar, Nuruosmaniye Caddesi has a pedestrian boulevard section lined with some of the Old City's most stylish (and high-end) shops, with an emphasis on fine carpets, jewelry, and antiques.

SPECIALTY FOODS

Kurukahveci Mehmet Efendi. On a backstreet just outside the western entrance of the Spice Market is the tiny flagship store of Kurukahveci Mehmet Efendi, Turkey's oldest coffee producer (founded 1871), whose finely ground coffee—which can be seen being ground on the premises—is legendary. Customers can purchase either beans or ground coffee, which makes a good souvenir of a trip to Turkey. ⊠ *Tahmis Sok. 66* ☎ *212/511–4262* ⊕ *www.mehmetefendi.com.*

Ucuzcular Baharat. Located in the back wing of the Spice Bazaar, Ucuzcular Baharat not only has great prices, but it's also just about the friendliest and most hassle-free shop in the bazaar. It's run by the energetic Bilge Kadıoğlu, a U.S.–educated, fifth-generation spice purveyor who is the bazaar's first (and still only) female shop owner. Kadıoğlu prides herself on the shop's extremely fresh spices and specially prepared mixes—which she is happy to have you taste—as well as pure, alcohol-free essential oils and a variety of Turkish sweets. ⊠ *Mısır Çarşısı 51* ☎ *212/444–8289* ⊕ *www.ucuzcular.com.tr.*

TEXTILES

İgüs. With two shops in the Grand Bazaar, İgüs offers one of the widest selections of scarves and pashminas found anywhere in Turkey, along with reasonable prices. ⊠ *Yağlıkçılar Cad. 29 and 80, Grand Bazaar* ☎ *212/512–3528* ⊕ *www.igustekstil.com.*

BEYOĞLU

ANTIQUES

Fodor'sChoice **Alaturca.** Styled more like a grand private mansion than a store, Alaturca ★ has four floors that house a carefully selected—and very high-end—collection of antiques, including artwork, ceramics, metalwork, and Ottoman calligraphy. Just a small fraction of proprietor Erkal Aksoy's extensive collection of antique carpets and kilims is on display here. ⊠ *Faik Paşa Yokuşu Sok. 4, Çukurcuma, Beyoğlu* ☎ *212/245–2933* ⊕ *www.alaturcahouse.com.*

Artrium. A delightful shop located in a historic 19th-century arcade just off Tünel Square, Artrium has a range of antique items, including a fascinating collection of old prints and paintings, as well as some interesting ceramics, jewelry, and other handmade crafts. A second branch opposite the original boutique has a wide selection of mostly contemporary handicrafts and gift items. ⊠ *Tünel Geçidi 7, Beyoğlu* ☎ *212/251–4302* ⊕ *www.artrium.com.tr.*

Levant Koleksiyon. The maps, engravings, calligraphic works, and charming old postcards with photographs of Ottoman-era Istanbul sold here are quite affordable. The shop sells both framed and unframed pieces, and they do professional framing on the premises. ⊠ *Meşrutiyet Cad. 64/B, Beyoğlu* ☎ *212/293–6333* ⊕ *www.levantkoleksiyon.com/index. htm.*

Tombak. In two shops around the corner from each other, Tombak—one of the area's longest-established antique dealers—stocks an eclectic collection of antique metal objects, tablewares, lamps, paintings, clocks, jewelry, and other interesting finds. ⊠ *Faik Paşa Yokuşu 22/A, Çukurcuma* ☎ *212/244–3681.*

BOOKS

Denizler Kitabevi. This shop has a selection of antiquarian books—primarily in English and French, focusing on Turkish history and nautical subjects—along with old maps, prints, and a small section of new books. ⊠ *İstiklal Cad. 199/A, Beyoğlu* ☎ *212/249–8893* ⊕ *www. denizlerkitabevi.com.*

Homer Kitabevi. One of Istanbul's best bookstores, Homer carries an impeccable selection of English-language books, especially ones dealing with the politics and history of Turkey and the Middle East. ⊠ *Yeni Çarşı Cad. 12/A, Galatasaray, Beyoğlu* ☎ *212/249–5902* ⊕ *www. homerbooks.com.*

Pandora. One of Turkey's premier book sellers for more than two decades, Pandora has a dedicated English-language branch (located just across the street from its Turkish-language bookstore) and carries

The centuries-old practice of smoking tobacco in a *nargile*, also known as a hookah or water pipe

an impressive selection of books in all genres, with a particular emphasis on nonfiction. ⊠ *Büyükparmakkapı Sok. 8, Beyoğlu* ☎ *212/245–1667.*

Robinson Crusoe. A Beyoğlu institution, Robinson Crusoe is about as appealing as a bookstore can get, with two cozy levels lined floor to ceiling with a well-chosen selection of books, about a quarter of which are fiction and nonfiction in English. There is also a very good collection of magazines and journals. ⊠ *İstiklal Cad. 195/A, Beyoğlu* ☎ *212/293–6968* ⊕ *www.rob389.com.*

CLOTHING

Mavi. Turkey's homegrown jean company, Mavi, has come a long way since its founding in 1991, with stores now in dozens of countries. The flagship Istanbul store near the top of İstiklal Caddesi (there are two other, smaller, branches farther down the avenue) carries the brand's signature jeans and casual wear, as well as a collection of hip Istanbul-themed T-shirts created by different guest designers. ⊠ *İstiklal Cad. 123/A, Beyoğlu* ☎ *212/244–6255* ⊕ *www.mavi.com.*

HANDICRAFTS

Fodor'sChoice
★

İKSV Design. Run by the Istanbul Foundation for Culture and Arts and housed in the organization's headquarters, the İKSV Design boutique focuses on local designers' work and has the sophistication of a museum shop. The varied collection includes jewelry, accessories, and decorative items by emerging designers, as well as reproductions of artwork by several 20th-century Turkish painters on ceramic items, pillowcases, and the like. At the time of this writing, the İKSV had plans to move to a new, yet-to-be-determined location. ⊠ *Sadi Konuralp Cad. 5, Şişhane, Beyoğlu* ☎ *212/334–0830* ⊕ *www.iksv.org/en.*

JEWELRY

Mor. On a side street off İstiklal Caddesi, Mor displays the work of a brother and sister designer pair who make funky, bold jewelry that incorporates antique and ethnic elements into modern designs. The chunky pieces, mostly made using bronze and stones, are affordably priced. ⊠ *Turnacıbaşı Sok., Sarayhan 10/B, Beyoğlu* ☎ *212/292–8817.*

SPECIALTY FOODS

Hacı Bekir. Ali Muhiddin Hacı Bekir founded his sweets business back in 1777 and is considered the inventor of Turkish delight. Today, the Hacı Bekir stores run by his descendants are still among the best places to buy the delicacy, which comes in a variety of different types—including such uncommon flavors as pomegranate with pistachios—and is sold fresh by the kilo or prepackaged. The original location is in Eminönü, on a backstreet just east of the Yeni Cami, and there is also a branch on İstiklal Caddesi. ⊠ *İstiklal Cad. 83, Beyoğlu* ☎ *212/245–1375* ⊕ *www.hacibekir.com.tr.*

GALATA AND KARAKÖY

CLOTHING

Arzu Kaprol. One of Turkey's most successful fashion designers both domestically and internationally, Arzu Kaprol has a handful of boutiques in Istanbul and elsewhere in Turkey. Her atmospheric Galata store, housed on the ground floor of a century-old residence, carries the designer's collections of structured, avant-garde, and almost futuristic women's clothing, as well as shoes, bags, and other accessories. ⊠ *Serdar-ı Ekrem Sok. 22, Galata* ☎ *212/252–7571* ⊕ *www.arzukaprol.com.*

HANDICRAFTS

Sır Çini. On Galata's main street for design shops, Sır Çini is the workshop and showroom of Sadullah Çekmece, a craftsman and artist who makes both traditional and contemporary interpretations of İznik and Küthaya ceramics and sells them at reasonable prices. ⊠ *Serdar-ı Ekrem Sok. 38, Galata* ☎ *212/293–3661* ⊕ *www.sircini.com.*

JEWELRY

Aida Pekin. At her tiny Galata boutique, designer Bihter Ayda Pekin sells unique collections of whimsical jewelry under her label Aida Pekin. Many of the pieces incorporate motifs inspired by Istanbul, and prices are very affordable. ⊠ *Serdar-ı Ekrem 44/A, Galata* ☎ *212/243–1211* ⊕ *www.aidapekin.com.*

SPAS

Kılıç Ali Paşa Hamamı. Reopened in 2012 after a meticulous seven-year restoration, this is the only major Ottoman-era hammam above the Golden Horn, located just steps from the Istanbul Modern. Completed in 1583, it is one of Sinan's last significant works, with the second-largest dome of any hammam in Istanbul. The services at this beautiful bath don't come cheap—prices are 100 TL for self-service and start at 130 TL for a professional scrubbing—but it tends to be less crowded than the tourist-oriented baths in the Old City (at least so far).

Continued on page 150

SHOPPING IN ISTANBUL
The Grand Bazaar & the Spice Market

Istanbul, historically one of the most important stops on the Silk Road, which linked the East and West through commerce, is today still a fabulous place to shop. You can find everything from the quintessential woven carpet to cheap trinkets, from antique copper trays to faux Prada bags. At the center of it all is the sometimes chaotic Grand Bazaar, also known as the Kapalı Çarşı or "Covered Bazar," which in many ways can be considered the great-grandmother of the modern shopping mall: it's been around since the 15th century, has more than 20 entrances, covers about 65 streets, and is said to have some 4,000 shops. It can be a bit intense, but it's a must-see. The following pages will help you get oriented so the experience will be less daunting. For comparison, check out the Spice Market in Eminönü; it's also several centuries old but specializes in spices and food items and is much calmer. It's great place to find snack items and Turkish delicacies to take home (Turkish delight, anyone?).

THE GRAND BAZAAR

This behemoth of a shopping complex was built by Mehmet II (the Conqueror) in 1461 over several of the main Byzantine shopping streets and expanded over the years. Today it's almost a town unto itself, with its own restaurants, tea houses, mosques, banks, exchange bureaus, post office, police station, health clinic, and several bathrooms nestled among the myriad shops.

Streets in the bazaar are named after the tradespeople who traditionally had businesses there, with colorful names in Turkish like "slipper-makers street," "fez-makers street," and "mirror-makers street." Today, although there's little correspondence between street names and the shops now found on them, the bazaar is still organized roughly by type of merchandise: gold and silver jewelry shops line the prestigious main street, most of the leather stores are in their own wing, carpet shops are clustered primarily in the center, and souvenirs are found throughout. The amazingly polylingual sellers are all anxious to reassure you that you do not have to buy . . . just drink a glass of tea while you browse through leather goods, carpets, clothing (including counterfeit brand names), brass and copper items, furniture, ceramics, and gold and silver jewelry.

✉ Yeniçeriler Cad. and Çadırcılar Cad.
🕙 Mon.–Sat. 8:30–7

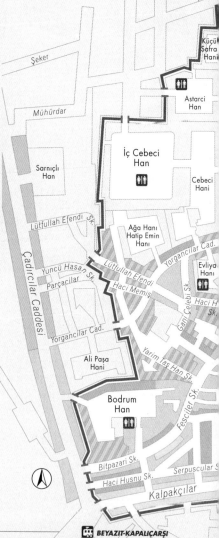

KEY	
▫ Gold	▫ Antiques
▫ Carpets	▫ Silver
▫ Denimwear	◂▮▸ Main Gates
▫ Copper	🚋 T1 Tram
▪ Fabric	🚻 Restroom
▫ Souvenirs	🍴 Restaurant
▫ Leather	

🚋 BEYAZIT-KAPALIÇARŞI

Grand Bazaar Shops

THE BEDESTEN

The domed *iç bedesten* (inner bazaar), aka the Cevahir Bedesteni, once a secure fortress in the heart of the market, is the oldest part of the bazaar and historically where the most valuable goods were kept. Today the *bedesten* is the place to find unique items: it's filled with tiny shops selling an array of antiques that are of generally better quality than the souvenirs sold in the rest of the bazaar. Here you can find anything from pocket watches to vintage cigarette tins, from jewelry to Armenian and Greek religious items. Look for the double-headed Byzantine eagle over the door and you'll know you've found the heart of the bazaar.

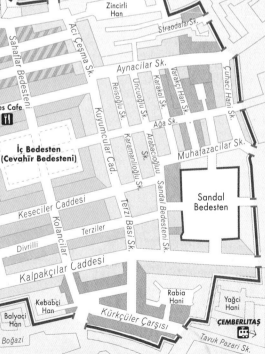

WHAT TO BUY

JEWELRY

There are over 370 jewelry shops in the bazaar, and you'll find as many locals in them as tourists. Gold and silver jewelry are sold by weight, based on the going market price plus extra for labor, so there's room for bargaining. Sterling silver pieces should have a hallmark. In terms of semiprecious stones, amber and turquoise are especially popular.

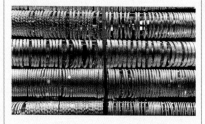

CERAMICS

Turkey's ceramics tradition goes back to Ottoman times. Today, the most important distinction is between İznik and Kütahya designs; traditional İznik designs, recognizable by the blue, red, and green colors on a white background, are more intricate and more expensive. You'll see gorgeous bowls and plates in both styles, but note that many are coated with lead glazes and are not safe for use with metal utensils or hot food. Medium-size bowls and plates go for between 50-100 TL. Decorative tiles can be made of either ceramic or quartz, with quartz tiles selling for two to three times more than ceramic tiles.

METALWARE (COPPER & BRASSWARE)

Turkey has a long tradition of metalworking, and you can find both new and antique copper and brass items engraved with elaborate designs. Round copper trays can run well into the hundreds of lira for large, intricately worked items if they're new, and into the thousands for antiques. Small serving trays can be acquired for around 100 TL. Most copper items are plated with tin to make them safe to eat from and therefore appear silver-gray in color. You can find pure copper items but these are suitable for decorative purposes only. Brass items like samovars and pitchers can be shiny if unoxidized or gray-black if oxidized. In general, brass costs more than copper because it's harder to work. Middle Eastern-style lanterns made of worked metal and glass are also neat to check out.

INLAID-WOOD ITEMS

You'll see a lot of wood items at the bazaar, beautifully inlaid with mother-of-pearl and different colored woods. Try to avoid imitation inlay: one clue that the inlay is fake is if the mother-of-pearl sections in the design are too uniform in color. You can also usually tell by weight and touch if a backgammon board is plastic. Price is also a dead giveaway: fake-inlay backgammon boards can be had for around 75 TL, whereas those made of walnut and real mother-of-pearl can go for 250-400 TL for a medium-size board. Prices vary based on the amount of inlay and intricacy.

LEATHER

Leather is a big industry in Turkey, and the Grand Bazaar has no shortage of stores selling leather jackets, bags, wallets, and, occasionally, shoes. When buying leather goods, look carefully at the quality of the workmanship, which can be assessed by examining seams, zippers, and linings. Imitation leather is, unfortunately, fairly widespread, and even dealers say they sometimes can't tell what's fake and what's not—one clue is that real leather is a bit softer than artificial leather. "Genuine fake" designer bags [i.e., imitation designer bags made with (supposedly) real leather] abound in the Bazaar and sell for around 250 TL.

SOUVENIRS AND GIFTS

The bazaar is chock-full of trinkets aimed at tourists—including ornaments featuring the ubiquitous evil-eye beads, Turkish tea sets, and fake designer clothing—but you can also find some nice souvenirs and gift items. Textiles like woven or embroidered pillow covers, and pashmina and silk scarves, are inexpensive (15-30 TL apiece) and come in many designs and patterns. Tiny jewelry boxes made of camel bone and decorated with Persian-miniature-style paintings sell for under 50 TL. Turkey is also famous for its meerschaum, a mineral that is used primarily to make pipes; prices range from about 75-250 TL based on the quality of the meerschaum and the intricacy of the carving.

▓ TIP → Exporting antiquities from Turkey is forbidden, and the ban is rigorously enforced. If you buy a carpet or other item that looks old, make sure you get certification from the seller that it's not an antiquity.

BUYING A CARPET

Carpet salesmen in the Grand Bazaar (Kapalı Çarşı)

It's almost impossible to visit Istanbul without making a detour into at least one rug shop, and you'll inevitably be poured a glass of tea (or several) while the salesman rolls out one carpet after another on the floor in front of you. Just remember, regardless of how many cups of tea you drink and how persistent the salesman, you are not obligated to buy anything.

The vivid colors and patterns of Turkish carpets and kilims, which are flat-woven rugs (without a pile), are hard to resist. Patterns and colors vary by region of origin, and in the case of kilims they often have symbolic meanings.

The Grand Bazaar is, without a doubt, the most convenient place in Istanbul to buy a rug, since the sheer number of rug dealers means there is a wide selection. That said, don't go to the Grand Bazaar looking for bargains—there are enough tourists coming through every day to keep prices on the high side.

When shopping for a carpet or kilim, the most important thing is to find a dealer you can trust. Avoid dealers who are pushy, and don't let anyone pressure you into buying something. It's best to look at merchandise at several different shops before buying anything, in order to get an idea of prices and see what's out there. Ask lots of questions, such as what a carpet is made of (wool or silk), what kind of dyes were used, and where it was made (many so-called Turkish carpets are now made in countries like Iran, India, and China). Note that silk carpets are considerably more expensive than wool ones, and kilims are generally less expensive than carpets because they involve less labor.

▪TIP→ The Arasta Bazaar, near the Blue Mosque, also has a number of good rug shops in a somewhat more relaxed environment.

GRAND BAZAAR TIPS

■ You may want to mentally prepare yourself for being aggressively pursued by merchants who are as shameless about making sales pitches as they are competitive over business; it can be overwhelming at first but underneath the hard sell most of the shop owners are quite friendly.

■ The Grand Bazaar is less crowded earlier on weekday mornings.

■ Once you're in the bazaar, spend some time getting your bearings and comparison shopping before you make any major purchases; this will help you get an idea of prices as well as narrow down what you'd like to buy.

■ Watch out for fakes, be they antique rugs, leather, or jewelry—if a dealer's price seems too good to be true, it probably is.

CARPET AND KILIM TIPS

■ Ask for a Certificate of Authenticity for rugs that are handmade or antique.

■ A new (non-antique) rug should sit flat on the floor when it's laid out, and the edges should be straight.

■ The number of knots per square inch is not the only thing to go by when choosing a carpet. A lower-knot carpet made with high-quality wool and dyes is worth more than a higher-knot carpet made with poor materials.

■ In Turkey, wool or wool on cotton warp carpets and kilims are your best bet. Silk carpets are traditionally made only in Hereke.

■ Try to buy a carpet directly from the store owner, not a third party.

■ If you have your rug shipped, get a receipt describing exactly what you bought (not just a serial number), and take a picture of the item.

BARGAINING AT THE BAZAAR

Prices at the Grand Bazaar can be high due to high rents and the never-ending stream of tourists, but the huge selection offered in the bazaar often makes it a good place to shop. Shop owners will expect you to bargain, so here are some tips.

■ Ask the price of several different items before focusing on the thing you really want, to get an idea of a store's prices and to make your intentions less obvious.

■ After the merchant quotes a price, make a counter-offer that's about two-thirds what they asked; then negotiate until you reach a price somewhere in the middle.

■ Do accept a shopkeeper's offer of tea. This gives you the chance to get familiar with the dealer. Accepting tea, however, does not obligate you to buy anything.

■ If you and the merchant can't reach a deal, starting to walk away often results in the merchant lowering the price.

■ The more items you buy from a merchant, the more you can bargain the price down.

THE SPICE MARKET

MISIR ÇARŞISI, OR THE EGYPTIAN BAZAAR

The 17th-century Egyptian Bazaar, also known as the Spice Market, in Istanbul's Eminönü neighborhood, is a riot of colors and fragrances. Although some of the spice shops have recently given way to stalls selling tourist souvenirs like you'll find in the Grand Bazaar, the Spice Market, with its mounds of *lokum* (Turkish delight), bags of spices, and heaps of dried fruit and nuts, is still a wonderfully atmospheric place to shop for spices and other delicious edibles.

For the most part prices at the Spice Market are clearly marked. Unlike in the Grand Bazaar, bargaining is discouraged here —if you're buying a lot, you might get the seller to come down by 10%, but don't expect much more.

✉ Yeni Cami Meydanı, Eminönü
🕓 Mon.–Sat. 8:30–7, Sun. 9–6:30

WHAT TO BUY

Lokum, or **Turkish delight**, in a wide variety of flavors, including rosewater and fruit-essenced, stuffed with pistachios or walnuts, or chocolate-covered. Merchants will enthusiastically ply you with free samples.

Herbs and spices, including cumin, sumac, turmeric, nigella ("black sesame") seeds, many varieties of pepper, and curry mixes. The best saffron (*safran*) found here comes from neighboring Iran, and although it's still not cheap it's less expensive than in the United States.

Dried fruits, particularly figs, dates, and apricots.

Nuts, including domestically harvested pistachios and hazelnuts.

Essential oils, including attar of roses, of which Turkey is one of the world's leading producers.

Black and herbal **teas** and finely ground **Turkish coffee.**

Caviar is also sold here for less than in the U.S. or Europe due to Turkey's proximity to its source, the Caspian Sea. Considering the serious endangerment of sturgeon, however, you might think twice about buying it.

You'll also see a variety of rather questionable-looking concoctions being sold as natural aphrodisiacs or "Turkish Viagra." Draw your own conclusions about their reliability.

Since there's just one bathing facility, there are separate visiting times for women (8–4) and men (4:30–11:30), and reservations are recommended. ☒ *Kemankeş Mah. Hamam Sok. 1, Karaköy* ☎ *212/393–8010* ⊕ *www.kilicalipasahamami.com.*

BEŞIKTAŞ AND NIŞANTAŞI

CLOTHING

Beymen. Istanbul's version of Bloomingdale's, Beymen has suited doormen and sells expensive, up-to-date fashions from well-known international brands and designers in its multistory flagship department store. The two underground levels house **Beymen Blender,** a hip store-within-a-store that carries clothing from trendy international designers and brands as well as jewelry by local Turkish designers. ☒ *Abdi İpekçi Cad. 23, Nişantaşı* ☎ *212/373–4800* ⊕ *www.beymen.com.*

Fodor'sChoice ★ **Gönül Paksoy.** Longtime designer Gönül Paksoy is known for her elegant and stunning women's clothing that reinterprets Ottoman and tribal designs. Her museum-like store shows off beautiful pieces created with vintage textiles, as well as new garments handmade using all-natural fabrics and dyes. There is also a collection of more casual (and less pricey) items including jewelry, bags, shoes, and other accessories, all crafted in Paksoy's characteristic style. ☒ *Atiye Sok.1/3, Nişantaşı* ☎ *212/236–0209.*

Fodor'sChoice ★ **Vakko.** One of Turkey's oldest and most elegant fashion houses, Vakko carries its own lines as well as clothing, shoes, and accessories from high-end international labels at its flagship department store in Nişantaşı. The company is particularly well known for its collection of silk scarves and ties in a variety of traditional and modern designs. It also sells its own signature chocolates. ☒ *Abdi İpekçi Cad. 33, Nişantaşı* ☎ *212/248–5011* ⊕ *www.vakko.com.*

JEWELRY

Armaggan Nişantaşı. The sister boutique to Armaggan in Nurusomaniye offers stunning (and pricey) collections of limited-edition jewelry that bring together traditional Turkish elements with a contemporary design aesthetic. The multilevel store also carries the brand's collections of all-natural textiles, accessories, and luxurious housewares and decorative items. ☒ *Bostan Sok. 8, Nişantaşı* ☎ *212/291–6292* ⊕ *www.armaggan.com.*

Urart. One of Turkey's most established jewelry companies, Urart makes re-creations, and also chic interpretations, of ancient Anatolian designs and motifs; there is an additional sales point in the Çırağan Palace Kempinski. ☒ *Abdi İpekçi Cad. 18, Nişantaşı* ☎ *212/246–7194* ⊕ *www.urart.com.tr.*

BOSPHORUS

CERAMICS

İznik Foundation. In the upscale suburb of Etiler is the flagship showroom of the İznik Foundation, dedicated to reviving and preserving the classic art of İznik ceramic and tile work. Operating as a kind of design studio for İznik tiles, the foundation has lately worked mainly on large-scale institutional projects—ranging from metro stations and mosques in Istanbul to Hermès window displays in Paris—but also designs tiles for private clients, and some individual pieces are for sale as well. Prices are high, but the quality is outstanding. ⊠ *Cengiz Topel Cad., Tuğcular Sok. 1/A, Etiler* ☎ *212/287–3243* ⊕ *www.iznik.com.*

SIDE TRIPS FROM ISTANBUL

PRINCES' ISLANDS

20 km (12 miles) off the coast of Istanbul from Sultanahmet.

The Princes' Islands—a cluster of nine islands in the Sea of Marmara, known simply as "Adalar" in Turkish—are everything that Istanbul isn't: quiet, green, and car-less. They are primarily a relaxing getaway from the noise and traffic of the big city, though they can be quite crowded on weekends, particularly in summer. Restrictions on development and a ban on automobiles help maintain the charmingly old-fashioned and quiet atmosphere —transportation here is only by horse-drawn carriage or bicycle. There are few real "sights," per se; the main attraction is the laid-back ambience and natural beauty of the islands, which are hilly and mainly wooded, with a fresh breeze that is gently pine-scented. Thanks to frequent ferries from the mainland, an excursion to the islands makes a fun day trip, or a pleasant overnight getaway from the city.

The islands have served various purposes for the people of Istanbul over the years. Back in Byzantine times, religious undesirables and deposed members of the royal family sought refuge here, while during the Ottoman Empire, the islands likewise provided a convenient place to exile troublesome princes and other notables—hence the name. By the mid-19th century, well-heeled Istanbul businessmen had staked their claim and built many of the Victorian gingerbread–style houses that lend the islands their charm. The islands became especially popular as summer residences for Istanbul's non-Muslim communities (Jews, Armenians, and Greeks), and were known for their cosmopolitan way of life. For several years in the 1930s, Büyükada, the largest of the islands, was the home of the exiled Leon Trotsky; the islands were considered to be safer than Istanbul, with its 35,000 hostile White Russian refugees.

Of the nine islands, four have regular ferry service, but only the two largest, Büyükada and Heybeliada, are of real interest to the general traveler, offering a variety of places to eat and stay and a few small beaches and other attractions. Two of the other inhabited islands are Kınalıada, long popular with the city's Armenians, and Burgazada, which has traditionally been more Greek. From the ferry you can see the larger two of the uninhabited islands, known in Greek and Turkish as the "pointy" Oxia/Sivri and the "flat" Plati/Yassı. Sivri's main claim to fame is that in the 19th and early 20th centuries Istanbul's stray dogs would be occasionally rounded up and dumped there, while Yassı was the site of the trial and execution of Prime Minister Adnan Menderes after a 1960 military coup.

GETTING HERE AND AROUND

From Katabaş, near Taksim at the end of the tram line, both atmospheric old ferry boats and more modern catamarans known as sea buses depart regularly for the islands, with more frequent service in summer. Ferries cost 5 TL for a token (3.50 TL with an İstanbulkart) and take around 90 minutes (⊕ *www.ido.com.tr/en*). The faster sea buses cost 9 TL for a token (7 TL with an İstanbulkart) and take about half as long, but don't run quite as late in the day (⊕ *www.sehirhatlari. com.tr/en*). On weekends in summer both the ferries and the islands themselves can be very crowded, so it's preferable to visit during the week. If you're planning on staying the night, most hotels also have cheaper rates on weekdays.

No cars are allowed on the islands, so you'll do most of your exploring on foot. The cost of horse-drawn carriage rides varies by distance. On Büyükada, a "short tour" (40–45 minutes) costs 70 TL and a "long tour" (70–75 minutes) is 80 TL, while a one-way ride to the Monastery of St. George is 30 TL. Fares on Heybeliada are 45 TL and 60 TL, respectively, for short and long tours. Renting bicycles (4–5 TL per hour; about 10 TL for the day) from one of the numerous bike shops on Büyükada and Heybeliada is also a fun (and more strenuous) way to get around. To get from one of the Princes' Islands to the other, hop aboard any of the several daily ferries or sea buses.

BÜYÜKADA

Büyükada is the largest of the Princes' Islands (about 5 square km, or 2 square miles) and generally the one with the most to offer. Just by the ferry docks is the main commercial center, filled with restaurants, shops, bike rental places, and a few hotels, as well as the boarding point for the horse-drawn carriages, which are known as *fayton* (phaeton) in Turkish. The island has a few tiny beaches, including **Yörük Ali Plajı**, located on the west side of the island and an easy walk from the harbor. An admission fee of 10–20 TL for the day at the island's beaches generally includes the use of a beach chair and umbrella.

Çankaya Caddesi, up from the clock tower and to the right, is home to the island's most splendid old Victorian houses, painted in pastel colors and with beautiful latticework. The carriage tour passes this way, winding up hilly lanes lined with gardens filled with jasmine, mimosa, and imported palm trees. After all of Istanbul's mosques and palaces, the frilly gingerbread-style houses come as something of a surprise. If you're on foot or a bike, turn off Çankaya Caddesi onto Hamlacı Sokak and go down to the end of the lane to see one of the houses Trotsky lived in while exiled here. Now almost in shambles, with crumbling brick walls and a caved-in roof, the house can only be viewed from outside the locked gate, but offers an interesting glimpse into the past.

The island's most significant attraction is the **Greek Monastery of St. George (Aya Yorgi)**, a 19th-century church built on Byzantine foundations at the top of Yücetepe Hill, with a view that goes on and on. It's a fairly steep 20-minute walk up from Birlik Meydanı, where your driver will

2

drop you off if you come by buggy. ■TIP→ Drivers charge a waiting fee and there are always numerous carriages for hire in the square, so it's cheaper to pay 30 TL each for two one-way rides than to do the "short tour." This is a popular Orthodox Christian pilgrimage site; as you walk up the path, notice the pieces of cloth, string, and even plastic that visitors have tied to the bushes and trees in hope of a wish coming true. The small church is open daily from 9 to 6.

NEED A BREAK?

Yücetepe Kır Gazinosu. The outdoor restaurant next to Aya Yorqi is known for its homemade wine, once made by the monks themselves, but now made by a family on the Aegean island of Bozcaada. There's a light menu consisting of a few simple appetizers and grilled meats, and amazing views all around from the rickety wooden tables. The venue stays open in the evening after the church closes. ⊠ *Yücetepe Mevkii 5 (next to Monastery of St. George on Yücetepe Hill)* ☎ *216/382–1333* ⊕ *www.yucetepe.com* ☾ *Daily in summer; weekends only in winter.*

WHERE TO EAT AND STAY

With one or two exceptions, there is little difference from one spot on Büyükada's row of waterfront fish restaurants to the next. The best bet is to look at a menu and ask to see the mezes and fish on offer that day. Food on the island is generally overpriced because everything has to be brought in from the mainland, and the heavy influx of tourists means venues have little incentive to stand out. Generally, prices are more expensive closer to the docks; the side streets further in have some cheaper cafés and eateries.

$$
SEAFOOD

✕ **Kıyı.** At the very end of the gauntlet of touristy seafood restaurants that line the waterfront of Büyükada's main ferry terminal is Kıyı, a tiny, almost ramshackle restaurant offering mezes and fish at slightly lower prices than its competitors and with far more charm. Uncommon mezes include the "Greek pastry"—thick slices of fried eggplant, topped with mild, crumbly *lor* cheese and dill—and, mainly in the winter and spring, several dishes of wild herbs collected on the island by Kıyı's owner. Main-course fish dishes are reliably well-prepared, and the selection, which is displayed in a glass case out front, is quite broad. $ *Average main: 30 TL* ⊠ *Çiçekli Yalı Sok. 2, Büyükada* ☎ *216/382–5606.*

$
B&B/INN

⌂ **Ada Palas.** Housed in a restored, late-19th-century building that was formerly a schoolhouse, this hotel and its dozen rooms are decorated in an old-fashioned Victorian style outfitted with modern lighting, bathrooms, and other conveniences. **Pros:** charming, intimate property; romantic garden; friendly staff goes out of their way to make guests feel at home. **Cons:** no views; rooms off the reception area may be noisy. $ *Rooms from: $125* ⊠ *Çiçeklıyalı Sok. 24, Büyükada* ☎ *216/382–1444* ⊕ *www.adapalas.com.tr* ↵ *12 rooms* ◎*Breakfast.*

$
HOTEL

⌂ **Splendid Palace Hotel.** This charming turn-of-the-century hotel (built in 1908) is the grande dame of Büyükada, with old-fashioned furniture, large rooms—including those in the front with stunning sea views—and a blend of Ottoman and art nouveau styles. **Pros:** peaceful, romantic setting; waterfront views can't be beat. **Cons:** could use some restoration; vintage ambience may not be to everyone's taste; no air-conditioning.

$ *Rooms from: $130* ✉ *23 Nisan Cad. 53, Büyükada* ☎ *216/382–6950* ⊕ *www.splendidhotel.net* ⇆ *66 rooms, 4 suites* ☉ *Closed Dec.–Mar.* ⏹ *Breakfast.*

HEYBELIADA

Heybeliada, the closest island to Büyükada and the archipelago's second largest, is similar in appeal, and the quiet, lovely surroundings attract similar boatloads of day-trippers in summer, some hoping to avoid the crowds on the "big island."

To the right of the dock are teahouses and cafés stretching along the waterfront. You can take a leisurely carriage ride or rent a bike, stopping, if the mood strikes, at one of the island's several small, sandy beaches—the best are on the north shore on either side of Değirmen Burnu (Windmill Point).

The big building to the left of the ferry dock is the **Deniz Lisesi** (Turkish Naval High School), founded in 1773. The island's most significant landmark is the **Haghia Triada Monastery**, built in the 19th century on Byzantine foundations and perched at the top of Heybeliada's highest hill. The building served as the Halki Seminary (Halki is the Greek name of the island), a theological school for Greek Orthodox priests, until it was shut down in 1971 by the Turkish government in a controversial move that, decades later, is still unresolved despite diplomatic pressure from the United States and Europe. The island is also home to a modern Greek Orthodox church and a synagogue, though they are usually closed.

THE SEA OF MARMARA AND THE NORTH AEGEAN

WELCOME TO THE SEA OF MARMARA AND THE NORTH AEGEAN

TOP REASONS TO GO

★ **Explore "Green Bursa":** Visit Yeşil Cami (Green Mosque), stroll the covered bazaar, and make sure to try the local kebab specialty, İskender kebap.

★ **Go back in time at Troy:** Visit the ruins of this 5,000-year-old city of Homer's *Iliad*, where more than nine layers of civilization have been uncovered.

★ **Pay respects at Gallipoli:** Tour the battlefields and memorials where one of the key campaigns of World War I was fought.

★ **Ramble through ancient Pergamum:** Explore this spectacular showcase of the classical period, second in Turkey only to Ephesus.

★ **Relax in Assos:** Enjoy the quiet of Behramkale village; marvel at the Greek ruins; and soak up the sun on nearby beaches.

★ **Shop for İznik tiles:** Watch craftswomen engrave the famous ceramics and buy some to take home.

Ruins of the Temple of Trajan Acropolis of Pergamum

A Canakkale war monument at Gallipoli

3

1 Sea of Marmara. You can still feel the Ottoman spirit in this part of Turkey, where you'll find some of the best examples of early Ottoman architecture, faithfully restored thermal baths, the surviving arts of tile making and silk weaving, and wonderful old bazaars.

2 The Dardanelles. The Gallipoli Peninsula, to the north of the straits connecting the Aegean and Marmara seas, is full of moving historical sites marking one of the bloodiest campaigns of World War I. Beautifully tended cemeteries stretch along the 35-km (22-mile) peninsula where so many soldiers are buried. Çanakkale is south of Gallipoli.

3 North Aegean. The combination of Greek heritage and Turkish rural life, set in an unspoiled natural setting of azure sea, curving coastline, and pine-clad hills, is perfect for unwinding. If you want to explore the ancient past, the ruins of Troy, Pergamum, and Behramkale (Assos) are within easy reach.

GETTING ORIENTED

A ferry ride across the Sea of Marmara from Istanbul will take you close to İznik, famed for its beautiful tiles, and the old Ottoman capital of Bursa. The historic World War I battlefields of the Gallipoli Peninsula are best visited from Çanakkale or Eceabat, on either side of the Dardanelle straits; Çanakkale is also the jumping-off point for visits to the fabled ancient city of Troy. Farther down the Aegean coast you'll find a scenic hilltop village and ruins at Assos (Behramkale), the laid-back harbor town of Ayvalık and its nearby sandy beaches, and (a short distance inland) the ancient ruins of Bergama (Pergamum).

Updated
by Aidan
McMahon

The ruins of Pergamum, Troy, and Assos, along with the Gallipoli battlefields, are the main draws of the region, but leisurely exploration is also rewarded with fresh air, a cool sea, great food, and havens in the wilderness.

The North Aegean and the Sea of Marmara areas are rich in history, spanning many centuries and empires. Civilizations rose and fell at Troy for 5,000 years, and the ruins of Pergamum date from the time of Alexander the Great. The bustling city of Bursa was the first capital of the Ottoman Empire, before Istanbul. The battlefields of Gallipoli bear testament to the more recent past, World War I, while the backstreets of Ayvalık still echo with the footsteps of the Greeks who lived there until early in the 20th century.

The beaches in this region tend to be more pebbly (and the water a touch colder) than they are in other parts of Turkey, but they're also frequently less crowded. You can see the whole of the region in a week or, if you're based in Istanbul, on separate, shorter journeys. Spend at least one evening watching the sun go down over Homer's wine-dark sea, and you'll agree that the North Aegean has a little bit of everything—and a lot you won't find anywhere else.

PLANNING

WHEN TO GO

The Southern Marmara and the North Aegean region are considerably cooler than the South Aegean and Mediterranean coast, but summer is still very hot. In July and August, the national park at Uludağ, in Bursa, remains refreshingly cool, and, with its skiing opportunities, is also an attraction in winter. If you're here in colder months, soaking in Bursa's thermal baths is a good antidote to the winter blues.

Travelers from New Zealand and Australia throng the Gallipoli Peninsula and nearby towns for the April 25 Anzac Day commemorations; other visitors may want to avoid the area at this busy time. Çanakkale, Gallipoli, and Troy—which Homer referred to as a windy city—can all be gusty in late summer and fall.

PLANNING YOUR TIME

You can see a bit of the Sea of Marmara on a quick one- or two-day trip from Istanbul: you could do just a day in İznik (make sure you leave Istanbul early), but you'll want to spend a night, at least, in Bursa. The ferry from Istanbul's Yenikapı terminal to Yalova takes about an hour; from there, you can catch a bus to İznik or Bursa. There are also direct ferries to Bursa (Güzelyalı) from Yenikapı, though you should allow an hour to get between the ferry terminal and the city center by public transportation.

An optimal way to spend two days around the Sea of Marmara is to leave Istanbul by ferry early enough to be in Yalova by midmorning, then catch a bus or drive to İznik and have lunch by the lake. Next head into the center of town to visit the Saint Sophia, the Lefke Gate, and some of the famous tile workshops. If you leave İznik by late afternoon, you'll be in Bursa in the early evening. Spend the second day sightseeing in Bursa—don't miss Yeşil Cami, the covered bazaar, Ulu Cami, and the Muradiye Tombs. For lunch, make sure to try the *İskender kebap*. If you have time, you can take the gondola lift up Uludağ and enjoy the view from the mountain's pine-covered slopes. Head down to the Bursa ferry station in the early evening and catch the last boat back to Yenikapı terminal in Istanbul.

You can visit Gallipoli in a long, rushed day trip from Istanbul (as many tour operators do) but you're better off spending the night in Çanakkale and seeing the ruins of Troy as well. If you have five or six days, you can pretty much see everything in the vicinity, visiting İznik, Bursa, and Çanakkale then continuing on to Behramkale (Assos) and Ayvalık, with a visit to Cunda, Ayvalık's main island, and the ruins of Pergamum. Be warned, though: once you get a taste of the area's natural beauty and relaxing vibe, you might want to stay longer.

GETTING HERE AND AROUND

AIR TRAVEL

There are several small airports in the area. Bora Jet operates four weekly flights between Istanbul's Sabiha Gökçen airport and Çanakkale airport. From Balikesir Koca Seyit Airport in Edremit, 50 km (31 miles) north of Ayvalık, Bora Jet flies to and from Sabiha Gökçen. Bursa, the largest city in the region, has an airport, but it is not served by direct flights from Istanbul.

BOAT AND FERRY TRAVEL

Fast ferries operate daily between Istanbul's Yenikapı terminal and ports in Yalova and Bursa and provide the quickest, most pleasant way to get to Bursa or İznik. The Yalova ferries run more frequently, approximately every two hours between 8:30 am and 8 pm, with fewer departures in winter. The journey takes just over an hour and costs about 15 TL to 20 TL each way for walk-on passengers and between 35 TL and 80 TL for a car including driver and one passenger (check the latest times and fares at ⊕ *www.ido.com.tr/en*). Boats also operate daily between Yenikapı and Bandırma, a good point from which to make your way to Assos or Ayvalık.

Since the Bandırma–Çanakkale road is normally less crowded than the Istanbul–Çanakkale road, when traveling to Gallipoli, you may want to take the boat to Bandırma and continue from there by car. Ferries from Istanbul to Bandırma run daily at 7 am, with an evening passenger ferry at 6:30 pm. Special timetables for religious holidays and summer are posted on ⊕ *www.ido.com.tr/en*. The journey takes two hours, and costs about 35 TL each way per passenger and 85 TL to 125 TL for a car including driver and one passenger. Reservations are essential during holidays and summer weekends, and advisable generally for weekends and anytime between June and August.

BUS TRAVEL

Buses are a good form of transport in this region, though the frequent stops on some routes, such as between Çanakkale and Edremit, can be frustrating. Most bus companies have branches both in the terminals and in the town centers. Several buses make the trip from Istanbul's Esenler terminal to Yalova (about four hours) and from there you can travel on to İznik or Bursa. The trip from Istanbul to Çanakkale is about six hours and costs about 50 TL. The trip from Bursa to Çanakkale is five hours and costs about 35 TL. From Çanakkale buses run almost every hour to İzmir, passing Ezine, Ayvacık, Edremit, Ayvalık, and Bergama on the way. The fare is about 35 TL.

CAR TRAVEL

The best way to explore this area is by car, especially if you're visiting Alexandria Troas and some of the other lesser-known sights and wish to forego organized tours of Gallipoli, which is quite spread out. Roads are quite good and well marked. There are several options for getting to the region from Istanbul: one is to take the E80 headed for Ankara. At İzmit take Route 130 to Yalova; Route 575 connects Yalova and Bursa.

TRAIN TRAVEL

Train journey in this region is not advisable: trains (and tracks) are old and painfully slow.

RESTAURANTS

Aegean cuisine is in many ways different from Turkish food elsewhere. The shared Turkish and Greek culture of the region's past, the climate and soil suitable for growing a wide range of vegetables, including tasty local greens and herbs, and the prevalence of olive trees and olive oil production have helped the region develop a much more varied way of eating that is healthier than in other Turkish regions. Olive oil replaces butter, and fish, rather than meat, is the star on most menus. The class of dishes generally called *zeytinyağlı* (literally "with olive oil") mostly comes from this region; these are usually comprised of tomatoes, onions, and other vegetables cooked in olive oil and served cold. Vegetarians will be in heaven.

Prices in the reviews are the average cost of a main course at dinner, or if dinner is not served, at lunch.

HOTELS

From simple, family-run *pansiyons* (guesthouses) in rural Assos, to luxurious, well-established palaces in Bursa; from garden retreats in Bozcaada to Greek stone houses in Ayvalık and Bergama, the Marmara and North Aegean areas have an impressive range of lodging options. In general, however, smaller boutique hotels that make the most of the region's alluring natural beauty are what define the best accommodations here. Many can be found in Bozcaada, Assos, and Ayvalık; breakfasts are fresh and made with herbs, fruit, and vegetables that are often sourced in the hotels' own gardens and orchards. Hotels in more rural towns like Bergama or İznik can also be your best sources for information, as local tourist offices have inconsistent opening hours and sometimes lack resources. Room rates drop significantly in the off season, and it is always a good idea to ask for a discount in quiet periods. As many of the destinations featured here are hubs for their rural hinterlands, weekends can fill up with wedding guests and other local visitors, so phone ahead to confirm that there are rooms. Advanced bookings are crucial if you are considering visiting the Gallipoli peninsula or Çanakkale around Anzac Day, and are advisable throughout the region in summer.

Prices in the reviews are the lowest cost of a standard double room in high season. For expanded reviews, visit Fodors.com

GALLIPOLI TOURS

If you have a car, you can tour the battlefields and memorials on your own, though a good guide can help bring the area's history to life. Hotels that offer tours will also often screen the feature film *Gallipoli* or the documentary *The Fatal Shore* before the trip to set the mood for the visit. Tours are conducted year-round out of Çanakkale and Eceabat, and typically run about 5½ hours, starting around noon in summer, 10:30 am in winter. (Tour companies operating out of Çanakkale will allow time to make the ferry trip to Eceabat before heading out on the peninsula.) Good walking shoes are advised and, in summer, a hat and water.

Hassle Free Travel Agency. The morning tours to Troy (32 TL) will get you back in time for their 11:45 tour to Gallipoli (110 TL); a practical choice if you're staying next door in the Anzac House. Hassle Free also organize boat trips around the beaches at Suvla bay, which offer a unique sense of the topography of the peninsula. All-inclusive overnight packages from Istanbul can be arranged. ⊠ *Cumhuriyet Meydanı 61, Çanakkale, Turkey* ☎ *286/213–5969, 533/240–7892* ⊕ *www. anzachouse.com.*

RSL Tours. Based at the Grand Eceabat Hotel, this company offers a number of popular tours around the area, including Cape Helles on the southern tip of the peninsula. Standard tours around the Kabatepe area are 70 TL, and overnights from Istanbul can be arranged, starting at 400 TL, with discounts possible for groups. ⊠ *Grand Eceabat Hotel, Cumhuriyet Meydani 2/D, Ismetpasa Mh., Eceabat, Turkey* ☎ *286/814–2458* ⊕ *www.rsltours.com.*

TJ's Tours. This company has been operating out of Eceabat on the Gallipoli peninsula for about 20 years. The midday tour to the main battlefields costs around 80 TL, and is ideal if you are staying in their impressive new hostel. Daily tours to Troy, and snorkeling/diving excursions to shipwrecks around the Gallipoli Peninsula are also available.

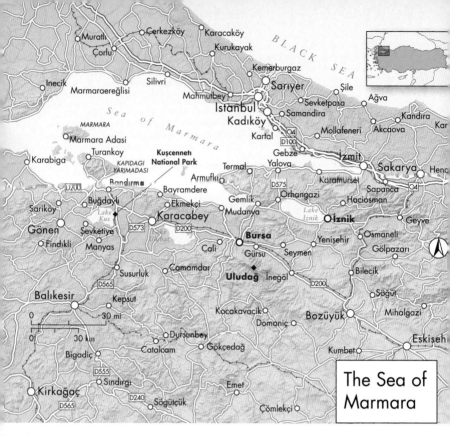

The Sea of Marmara

✉ *Kemalpaşa Mahallesi, Cumhuriyet Cad. 5/A, Eceabat, Turkey* ☎ *0286/814–3121* ⊕ *www.anzacgallipolitours.com.*

VISITOR INFORMATION

Each featured town in the region has a visitor information center, and although staffers are generally extremely helpful, the office opening hours vary depending on the number of tourists around, and as such are unreliable. Resources for self-guided tours in Gallipoli are detailed later in the chapter, but the new interpretive center at Kabatepe is worth visiting for more information. For much of the rest of the region, with the exception of Bursa, hotels serve as the primary sources of visitor information.

SEA OF MARMARA

Although quite close to Istanbul, the area around the Sea of Marmara is sometimes overlooked, but there is much here to attract visitors interested in history and beautiful landscapes.

İznik, a center of early Christianity and an important city for the Ottomans, contains historical sights from the Roman, Byzantine, Seljuk, and later periods; the town's beautiful tiles are another reason to visit Bursa, the first capital of the Ottoman Empire, boasts some of the finest examples of imperial architecture in its mosques and bazaars. You can visit either city as a day trip from Istanbul, though Bursa deserves at least an overnight stay. Both cities are, more or less, on the way to the Mediterranean, Central Anatolia, or even the North Aegean if you're traveling by ferry across the Marmara Sea.

İZNIK

190 km (118 miles) from Istanbul.

Nature has been generous to İznik, which is beautifully situated around the east end of İznik Lake. You can swim (though the water can be chilly), picnic, or rent a kayak or paddleboat, and you can also soak in centuries of history and witness the city's legendary tile-making tradition, in full revival today.

An important city in early Christian history, İznik (known in ancient times as Nicaea) was the site of the First and Second Councils of Nicaea, which drew up the Nicene Creed that outlines the basic principles of Christianity and set the church's stance on iconography. The city was put on the map in 316 BC when one of Alexander the Great's generals claimed it. The Seljuks made the city their capital for a brief period in the 11th century, and Byzantine emperors-in-exile did the same in the 13th century, when Constantinople was in the hands of Crusaders. The production of famous İznik tiles, unequaled even today, was launched not long after the Ottomans captured the city in 1331.

GETTING HERE AND AROUND

If you're driving, İznik is 190 km (118 miles) from Istanbul via Route 100 or E80 to İzmit and Route 130 to Yalova; it's 60 km (37 miles) east from Yalova via Route 595. Or take the ferry from Istanbul's Yenikapı terminal to Yalova (1 hour). The ferry trip lops 140 km (87 miles) off the journey.

In Istanbul, several buses (the 69A, 70KY, and 70FY are the most frequent) run from Cumhuriyet Caddesi (Republic Street) near Taksim Square to Yenikapı terminal.

Once you arrive in Yalova by boat, if you don't have your own car, exit the ferry port, turn right and walk about 50 meters past the police station to the minibus station. Destinations are clearly displayed in the bus windows, and you'll find the one to İznik near a series of buildings on your right. The trip from Yalova to İznik costs about 9 TL.

İznik is easy to navigate and the town's sights are all easily within reach on foot, and you should encounter the city's walls as you explore. The four main gates date back to Roman times, and the city's two main streets intersect each other and end at these gates. Running east–west is Kılıçaslan Caddesi; north–south is Atatürk Caddesi. Saint Sophia church is at the intersection of these streets.

ESSENTIALS

Visitor Information. This wooden booth downtown has a small selection of maps of the İznik area. If there's no one working inside, check at Saint Sophia next door. ⊠ *Atatürk Cad. and Kılıçaslan Cad.* ☎ *0532/665–0370*

EXPLORING

TOP ATTRACTIONS

Aya Sofya (*Saint Sophia, Aya Sofya Camii*). A primitive mosaic floor is believed to date from the church's construction in the 6th century, during the reign of Justinian. Wall mosaics were added as part of a reconstruction in the 11th century, after an earthquake toppled the original church, and some fine fragments of frescoes date from the Byzantine era. In a controversial move, authorities converted the museum into a mosque in 2011. Try to arrange your visit outside of prayer times, when you can explore the site freely and take photographs. ⊠ *Atatürk Cad. and Kılıçaslan Cad.* ⊡ *Free* ☉ *Daily dawn–dusk.*

Lefke Kapýsý (*Lefke Gate*). The eastern gate to the ancient city was built in honor of a visit by the Roman emperor Hadrian in AD 120 and is among the best-preserved remnants of the thick, sturdy fortifications that once encircled İznik. Some of the original inscriptions, marble reliefs and friezes remain intact. Outside the gray stone and faded brick gate is a leafy graveyard and the city's small but technically impressive aqueduct. ⊠ *At the eastern end of Kılıçaslan Cad.*

WORTH NOTING

İznik Müzesi. Artifacts such as Greek tombstones, Ottoman jewelry, pieces of Byzantine floor mosaics, and original Iznik tiles will be on display in this museum if it reopens as scheduled in early 2014. The high-domed white room was constructed in 1388 as a soup kitchen to serve food to the poor. In the same complex are two mosques, the smaller ªeyh Kutbuddin Camii and the larger Yeşil Camii, the latter notable for its colorfully tiled minaret and intricate stone-cutting work. ⊠ *Eşrefzade Mahallesi, Müze Sok. 11* ☎ *0224/757–1027* ⊡ *5 TL (anticipated price on reopening; call to check)* ☉ *Daily 8–noon and 1–5.*

Roman Theater. The Roman Emperor Trajan asked the governor Plinius to construct this theater in the early 2nd century. Today the site is little more than a pile of rubble, but it's easy to imagine its former grandeur. Extensive renovations are progressing slowly, and the theater may not reopen to the public until as late as 2015. ⊠ *West of bus station near lake, Kule Sok.*

Tomb and Mosque of Abdülvahap. If you're looking for a good spot to watch the sunset over İznik Lake, the tomb of Abdülvahap Sultan Sancaktarý, a hero of the battle in which the Ottomans captured the city in 1331, is well worth the trip for its sweeping view. From these monuments, on a clear evening the orange glow of sunset makes the surrounding mountains look like the backs of gigantic serpents sleeping in the lake. The spot—a short drive or a 30-minute walk (some of it uphill) from the city center—attracts couples young and old as well as extended families, many of whom bring dinner along to accentuate the experience. Take Kýlýçaslan Caddesi east through the Lefke Gate and then follow the ruins of the Roman aqueduct along the road on your right until you can see the large Turkish flag on the hilltop near the tomb. ⊠ *East of İznik Orhangazi Yolu/Sansarak Yolu.*

İznik's Tiled Beauty

İznik tile makers believe that their tiles have magical properties. There is one sound explanation for this (alongside any number of unsound ones): İznik tiles, made from soil that's found only in the area, have a high level of quartz, an element believed to have soothing effects. It's not just the level of quartz that makes İznik tiles unique, though. The original tiles also have distinctive patterns and colors: predominantly blue, then green and red, reflecting the colors of precious stones. The patterns are inspired by local flora—flowering trees or tulips. These days artists use different colors and designs as well as the traditional ones.

İznik became a center for the ceramics industry after the 15th-century Ottoman conquest of Istanbul. To upgrade the quality of native work, Sultan Selim I (ruled 1512–15) imported 500 potters from Tabriz in Persia. The government-owned kilns were soon turning out exquisite tiles with intricate motifs of circles, stars, and floral and geometric patterns, in lush turquoise, green, blue, red, and white. Despite the costliness of the tiles, their popularity spread through the Islamic world, until the industry went into decline in the 18th century.

İznik tiles are expensive—more so than those produced in the rival ceramics center of Kütahya, 120 km (72 miles) farther south. A single tile costs about 40 TL; a small plate starts at the same price, but prices can run into the hundreds of dollars. İznik tiles are made of better-quality stone with a higher quartz content than those made elsewhere, so they're heavier and more durable, making them ideal for decorating high-traffic spaces such as airports and mosques. They're all handmade, with no artificial colors, and

the designs tend to be more intricate and elegant than those of their rivals. The tile-makers' street (Salim Demircan Sokak), near the city center, is lined with small shops and workshops where you can see the tiles being made and buy the famous wares.

The İznik Training and Education Foundation. Founded in the 1990s to revive the art of tile making, this establishment fashions large orders, often for overseas delivery. Even if you are not commissioning a job, you can see the beautiful craftsmanship and wander in the lavender fresh gardens. They sponsor summer music courses also, which take place around the complex. ⊠ Sahil Yolu, Vakıf Sok. 13 ☎ 0224/757–6025 ⊕ www.iznik.com ⊘ Weekdays 8–6.

Süleyman Pa°a Medresesi. Once an early Ottoman theology school, this building now houses a tile and ceramic bazaar with 10 workshops. They're grouped around a peaceful courtyard where you can enjoy a cup of tea or a Turkish coffee. ⊠ Maltepe Cad. 27 ⊘ Apr.–Oct., daily 10–6:30; Nov.–Mar., daily 11–4 or 5.

OFF THE BEATEN PATH

Termal. A popular spa since Roman times, Termal is a good stop if you're en route between Yalova and either İznik or Bursa. The springs were used by the Ottomans, refurbished in 1900 by Sultan Abdül Hamid II, and regularly visited by Atatürk in the 1920s and 1930s. Termal is a self-contained resort with three hotels (Çamlýk, Çýnar, and Thermal), exotic gardens, a huge swimming pool, and four historic bath houses offer many options for soaking in the mineral-rich waters. The hotels also have private baths for guests only. Avoid summer weekends, when the place is absolutely packed and the crowds will probably outweigh the baths' relaxing properties—anyway, the hot baths are more appealing, and the rates cheaper, in other seasons. Also consider a walk in the pine forests, where you can enjoy a packed lunch. ✉ *About 70 km (42 miles) west of İznik; 12 km (8 miles) southwest of Yalova on the way to Çınarcık, Termal* ☎ *226/675–7400* 🌐 *www.yalovatermal.com.*

DINING IN İZNIK

The restaurants of the lakefront hotels are your best bet for drinks and dinner. While touring the sights, though, eat in the town center at any of the various establishments along or around Kılıçaslan Caddesi, where good *pide* (pizza-like flatbread), *lahmacun* (flatbread with ground meat on top, literally "meat with dough"), kebabs, and *esnaf* (home cooking) are easy to find and are low-cost options for a quick lunch. The many *çay bahçe* (tea gardens) along the lake offer cheap eats as well.

WHERE TO EAT

$ TURKISH 🍴 **Kenan Çorba & Izgara.** This popular spot just opposite the Aya Sofya specializes in soups and beans. *İşkembe* (tripe soup) is probably best for those who are into experimenting—you'll either hate it or love it—but the beans with sliced Turkish pastrami and rice, accompanied by tiny pickled peppers, is hard to beat. The restaurant opens early, at 5 am, but don't plan on a later dinner—it closes at 8 pm. [$] *Average main: 7 TL* ✉ *Atatürk Cad. 93/B* ☎ *0224/757–0235.*

$ TURKISH 🍴 **Köfteci Yusuf.** Turks love their *köfte* (meatballs), and almost every city in the country makes a claim to fame based on its own way of preparing them, including İznik. Locals fill the large, canteen-type tables of this casual bi-level eatery opposite İznik Lycee at almost all times of the day to enjoy İznik köfte, served with tomatoes, peppers, and onions. Other types of grilled meats are also on offer, with yogurt and salads as optional sides. Not for vegetarians. [$] *Average main: 10 TL* ✉ *Atatürk Cad. 73* ☎ *0224/757–3597, 0224/444–6162* 🌐 *www.kofteciyusuf.com.tr.*

WHERE TO STAY

$$$ HOTEL 🏨 **Çamlýk Motel.** The simple, clean rooms of the oldest hotel in İznik are not yet showing their age, and this quiet lakefront establishment is, after 30 years, still an excellent choice. **Pros:** nice location near the quietest part of the lake; good, reasonably-priced restaurant. **Cons:** fairly basic accommodations; only four rooms face the lake; no elevator. [$] *Rooms from: $220* ✉ *Göl Sahil Yolu* ☎ *0224/757–1362* 🌐 *www.iznik-camlikmotel.com* 🛏 *24 rooms* 🍴 *Breakfast.*

$$$ ⬚ **Grand Hotel Belekoma.** Modern, spotless facilities, a selection of fam-
HOTEL   ily rooms and suites, and an inviting courtyard pool make this lakeside
hotel a welcome addition to İznik's lodging options. **Pros:** friendly ser-
vice; good location; elevator; good choice of rooms with views. **Cons:**
limited English; noise from wedding parties on the weekend; busy
road between lake and hotel; lacks character. $ *Rooms from: $200*
✉ *M. Kemalpaşa Mh., Göl Sahil Yolu 8* ☎ *0224/757–1407* ⊕ *www.
iznikbelekomahotel.com* 🛏 *46 rooms* ❙◎❙ *Breakfast.*

$$ ⬚ **Hotel Aydýn.** This clean and simple spot, near the lake in the center of
HOTEL   town, is run by friendly cousins Barbaros and Sertaç, whose grandfather
opened the on-premises Aydo Patisserie, a café that serves justly famous
homemade ice cream. **Pros:** good location near Saint Sophia. **Cons:** a
few minutes from the lake; street noise in some rooms. $ *Rooms from:
$120* ✉ *Kılıçaslan Cad. 64* ☎ *0224/757–7650* ⊕ *www.iznikhotelaydin.
com* 🛏 *18 rooms* ❙◎❙ *Breakfast.*

$ ⬚ **Kaynarca Hotel and Pansiyon.** A fun, multilingual website sets the tone
HOTEL   for this homey hotel—the best choice for single travelers or couples on
a budget. **Pros:** free maps and travel advice; good place to meet other
travelers; satellite television. **Cons:** no a/c in rooms; basic accommodations; breakfast not included in room price; lake is 10-minute walk
away. $ *Rooms from: $35* ✉ *M. Gündem Sok. 1* ☎ *0224/757–1753*
⊕ *www.kaynarca.net* 🛏 *13 rooms* ▭ *No credit cards* ❙◎❙ *No meals.*

BURSA

240 km (150 miles) from Istanbul.

An important center since early Ottoman times, Bursa is today one
of Turkey's more prosperous cities (due to its large automobile and
textile industries) and is also a pleasing mix of bustling modernity,
old stone buildings, mosques, thermal spas, and wealthy suburbs with
vintage wood-frame Ottoman villas. Residents proudly call their city
Yeşil Bursa (Green Bursa)—for the green İznik tiles decorating some
of its most famous monuments, and also for its parks and gardens and
the national forest surrounding nearby Uludağ, Turkey's most popular
ski mountain.

Bursa became the first capital of the nascent Ottoman Empire after the
city was captured in 1326 by Orhan Gazi, and the first five sultans of the
Ottoman Empire lived here until Mehmet the Conqueror took Istanbul
and moved the capital there. Each of the sultans built his own complex
on five different hilltops, and each included a mosque, a *medrese* (theological school), a hammam, a kitchen house, *kervansaray*, and tombs.
It was in Bursa that Ottoman architecture blossomed, and where the
foundations were laid for the more elaborate works to be found in the
later capitals, Edirne and Istanbul. More than 125 mosques here are
on the list of historical sites kept by the Turkish Historical Monuments
Commission, and their minarets make for a grand skyline.

GETTING HERE AND AROUND

If you're driving, Bursa is 240 km (150 miles) from Istanbul via Route
100 or E80 to İzmit, Route 130 to Yalova, and Route 575 south from
Yalova to Bursa; the Yalova–Bursa part of the trip is 72 km (45 miles).

Bursa is 80 km (50 miles) from İznik.

From Istanbul, through Yalova, it's a four-hour bus trip to Bursa, including the ferry ride from Darýca to Yalova, and costs about 20 TL. A better option is to take the sea bus to Yalova or Bursa (Güzelyalý); near the quay in Yalova are buses to Bursa that cost about 10 TL and take one hour. From the Bursa ferry terminal, take the yellow bus to the Organize Sanayi metro stop then the metro to the Demirtaþpaþa Ýstasyon stop near the bazaar area downtown. The journey takes about an hour and costs 5 TL.

> **TAKE THE WATERS**
>
> Bursa has been a spa town since Roman times. Rich in minerals, the waters are said to cure a variety of ills, from rheumatism to nervous complaints. The thermal springs run along the slopes of the Çekirge neighborhood, and mineral baths are an amenity at many hotels in this area. The historical **Eski Kaplýca Hamamý** is now affiliated with the Kervansaray Termal Hotel, but open to the public at reasonable rates for a soak, scrub, or massage.

Bursa is a large city, stretching out along an east–west axis. The town square, at the intersection of Atatürk Caddesi and Inönü Caddesi, is officially named Cumhuriyet Alanı (Republic Square), but is popularly called **Heykel** (Statue), after its imposing equestrian statue of Atatürk. East of Heykel is the Yeşil neighborhood, with Yeşil Cami and Yeşil Türbe. To the northwest is Çekirge, the thermal spa district, with the city's fanciest lodging options.

Buses from outside the city center converge on Heykel, from where you can reach most sites. Shared taxis with white destination signs on top regularly ply the route between Heykel and Çekirge; hop in or out at signs marked with a "D" (for *dolmuş*). The main bus routes run about every 15 minutes during the day and roughly every 30 minutes at night. There are signs and posted schedules at most major stops.

ESSENTIALS
Visitor Information ✉ *Orhan Gazi Çarşısı 1, Heykel* ☎ *0224/220–1848.*

EXPLORING
TOP ATTRACTIONS

Fodor's Choice **Kapalý Çarþý** (*Covered Bazaar*). The vast complex here comprises many
★   adjoining *hans* (caravansaries, inns for merchants) surrounding a *bedestan* (the central part of a covered bazaar, which is vaulted and fireproofed). Bursa sultans began building bazaars in the 14th century to finance the construction or maintenance of their schools, mosques, or kitchen houses. The precinct was soon topped with roofs, creating the earliest form of covered bazaar, and late in the century Yýldýrým Beyazýt perfected the concept by building a *bedesten* with six woven parts connected by arches and topped by 14 domes. The complex was flattened by a massive earthquake in 1855, and parts were badly burned by fire in the 1950s, but Kapalý Çarþý has been lovingly restored to provide wonderful flavor of the past. ■ TIP→ Best buys here include silver and gold jewelry, thick Turkish cotton towels (for which Bursa is

famous), and silk goods. ⊠ *Behind Ulu Cami, between Atatürk Cad. and Cumhuriyet Cad.* ☉ *Mon.–Sat. 8–8.*

Muradiye Tombs. The complex around the Sultan Murat II Camii (built 1425–26) is probably the city's most serene resting place, with 12 tombs tucked amid a leafy park. Among those buried here are Murat (1404–51), the father of Mehmet the Conqueror, and Mustafa (1515–53), the eldest son of Süleyman the Magnificent, who was strangled in his father's tent. Murat's plain tomb was built in accordance with his will, with an open hole in the roof right above the tomb to let the rain in. The most decorated tombs are those of two grandsons of Murat, Çelebi Mehmet and Cem Sultan, which are kept locked most of the time—ask the caretaker to open them for you. The historical complex also included a nearby hammam, medrese (now the Uluumay Museum), and a kitchen house for the poor (now the restaurant Darüzziyafe). ⊠ *Muradiye Mahallesi, Muradiye Cad.* ☎ *0224/222–0868* ▭ *Free* ☉ *Daily 8–8.*

Ulu Cami (*Great Mosque*). This striking building opposite the northern end of Maksem Caddesi dates from 1399, when Sultan Beyazýt had it constructed after vowing to build 20 mosques if he was victorious in the battle of Nicopolis in Macedonia; he settled for a compromise, this one mosque with 20 domes. The interior is decorated with an elegantly understated display of quotations from the Koran in fine calligraphy. The fountain, with taps on the sides for ritual washing before prayer, is inside the mosque rather than outside the entrance —an unusual feature. ■ **TIP→** Ulu Cami draws huge crowds during prayer times, which you'll probably want to avoid. ⊠ *Atatürk Cad.*

Fodor's Choice ★ **Yeşil Cami** (*Green Mosque*). A juxtaposition of simple form, inspired stone carving, and spectacular tile work, this is among the finest mosques in Turkey. Work on the building was completed in 1419, during the reign of Mehmet I Çelebi (ruled 1413–21). Its beauty begins in the marble entryway, where complex feathery patterns and calligraphy are carved in the stone; inside is a sea of blue-and-green İznik tiles. The central hall rests under two shallow domes; in the one near the entrance an oculus sends down a beam of sunlight at midday, illuminating a fountain delicately carved from a single piece of marble. The *mihrab* (prayer niche) towers almost 50 feet, and there are intricate carvings near the top. On a level above the main doorway is the sultan's loge, lavishly decorated and tiled; a caretaker will sometimes take visitors up to see it. ⊠ *Yeşil Cad.* ▭ *Free* ☉ *Daily dawn–dusk.*

WORTH NOTING

Bursa Kent Müzesi (*Bursa City Museum*). At Heykel, in the city center right behind the statue, this is a showcase for local history and handicrafts. Among the exhibits are impressive re-creations of sections in a traditional bazaar, such as those for silk weavers and knife makers, artifacts relating to the history of Bursa and its first five sultans, and to Atatürk during the independence war. Clothing, household items, and dioramas of life at home, school, and in the hammam are also on show. The exhibits are in Turkish, so get one of the English-language headsets at the entrance, though the audio does not provide full narration.

✉ *Atatürk Cad. 8* ☎ *0224/220–2626* ⊕ *www.bursakentmuzesi.com*
💲 *1.5 TL* ☉ *Tues.–Sun. 9:30–5:30.*

Emir Sultan Camii (*Emir Sultan Mosque*). The daughter of Sultan
Yýldýrým Beyazýt built the Emir Sultan Camii in 1429 for her husband, Emir Sultan, and it sits amid cypresses and plane trees on a quiet
hilltop overlooking the city. The single-domed mosque was badly damaged in the 1855 earthquake and was almost totally rebuilt by Sultan
Abdülaziz. The two cut-stone minarets are considered great examples of
rococo, and the assemblage faces an attractive courtyard that houses the
tombs of Emir Sultan, his wife, and children. ✉ *Doyuran Cad.* 💲 *Free*
☉ *Daily dawn–dusk.*

Kültür Parký (*Culture Park*). Refreshingly green, this park is laced with
restaurants, tea gardens, a pond with paddleboats, and an amusement
park. It's always crowded and pleasantly animated, though it seems more
like a busy public gathering spot than a place of refuge. Amid the lawns
and boulevards is Bursa's recently reopened **Arkeoloji Müzesi** (Archaeology Museum), which hosts a range of finds from the surrounding region.
The **Atatürk Müzesi** (Atatürk Museum), just opposite, is housed in a
19th-century French-style mansion once offered as a gift to Atatürk,
and which contains old-fashioned furniture and a few exhibits on his
life. ✉ *Çekirge Cad. and Stadyum Cad.* ☎ *0224/234–4918 Archaeology
Museum, 0224/234–7716 Atatürk Museum* 💲 *Archaeology Museum 5
TL, Atatürk Museum free* ☉ *Museums open Tues.–Sun. 8–5.*

Türk Ýslam Eserleri Müzesi (*Turkish Islamic Arts Museum*). On the west
side of Yeşil Cami, this museum is housed in an attractive *medrese* (theological school), part of a complex that includes ⇨ *Yeşil Cami* and ⇨ *Yeşil
Türbe*. Displayed in small rooms around a cool courtyard are inlaid
wood, jewelry, calligraphy work, manuscripts, Turkish shadow puppets, carpets, coins, musical instruments, pottery, and traditional clothes
embellished with colorful embroidery. ✉ *Yeşil Cad.* ☎ *0224/327–7679*
💲 *Free* ☉ *Tues.–Sun. 8–12 and 1–5.*

Uludað Milli Parký (*Uludağ National Park*). To fully appreciate why Bursa
is called Green Bursa, take the 30-minute trip up the *teleferik* (gondola
lift), a 15-minute bus or *dolmuş* ride from Heykel, to **Sarıalan point**
in lush Uludað Milli Parký. This terminus has panoramic views and is
lively in summer, with restaurants and picnic areas. In winter it serves as
a staging point for skiers and night-clubbers heading to the mountain's
hotel area 7 km (4 miles) farther up (⇨ see ⊕ *www.uludaghotels.com* for
information). ■ TIP➤ **Take a sweater or jacket, as temperatures fall dramatically as you climb, even when it's warm downtown.** There are also
various walking paths up the mountain between Bursa and Uludað; the
hike takes about three hours each way. ✉ *Piremir Mahallesi, Teleferik
Teferrüç İstasyonu Yıldırım* ☎ *0224/327–7400* 💲 *Roundtrip teleferik
ride: weekdays 10 TL, weekends 15 TL (prices subject to change)*
☉ *Daily 8:30–8.*

Uluumay Müzesi (*Uluumay Ottoman Folk Costume and Jewelry
Museum*). A fine, albeit small, collection of traditional Ottoman costumes, some dating back to the 15th century, along with gorgeous silver
jewelry, is on display in this museum opposite the Murat II Mosque and

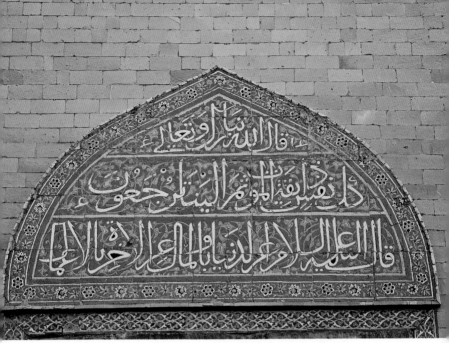

Inside Bursa's Yeşil Cami (Green Mosque), the array of green and blue tiles is mesmerizing.

the ⇨ *Muradiye Tombs*. Mannequins dressed in the costumes revolve to afford a thorough study of the colorful embroidery. The building is a *medrese* (theological school), built in 1475 by Şair Ahmet Pasha, whose tomb is in its garden. A teahouse opposite the tomb in the garden overlooks the city. ⊠ *Muradiye Mahallesi, Murat Cad.* ☎ *0224/222–7575* 🖂 *5 TL* ⊙ *May–Oct., Tues.–Sun. 9–7; Nov.–Apr., Tues.–Sun. 9–5.*

Yeşil Türbe (*Green Tomb*). The "Green Tomb," built in 1421, is the resting place of Mehmet I Çelebi. It's actually covered in blue tiles, added after an earthquake damaged the originals in the 1800s, but inside are incredible original İznik tiles, including those sheathing Mehmet's immense sarcophagus—and these are indeed green. The surrounding tombs belong to Mehmet's children. ⊠ *Yeşil Cad.* ⊙ *Daily dawn–dusk.*

NEED A BREAK?

Tea Gardens. Several tea gardens behind the Yeşil Cami and Yeşil Türbe are pleasant places to have a sandwich or a pastry while taking in views of the city. On the street leading up to the mosque complex from Heykel you'll find some colorful, restored Bursa houses whose ground floors have been turned into gift shops. ⊠ *Yeşil Cad. area.*

WHERE TO EAT

$$$$

TURKISH

✕ **Arap Şükrü Çetin.** The place to be on a busy Bursa weekend evening, this irrepressible *meyhane* offers a delectable selection of fresh fish from the open-air market on the corner. It's said that an Arab named Şükrü once opened a fish restaurant here on Sakarya Caddesi, a narrow side street between Heykel and Çekirge. Now the whole area carries his name, and his sons have filled the street with similar restaurants, sometimes adding their own names to their father's—in this case Çetin. The

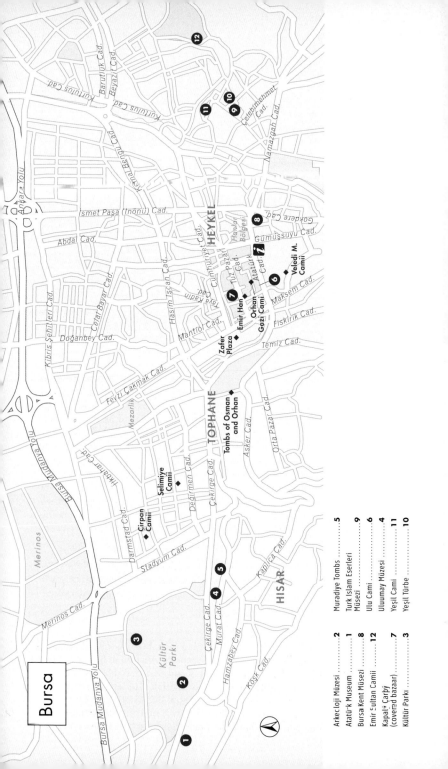

Bursa

Arkecloji Müzesi	**2**	Muradiye Tombs	**5**
Atatürk Museum	**1**	Turk Islam Eserleri Müsezi	**9**
Bursa Kent Müsezi	**8**	Ulu Camii	**6**
Emir Sultan Camii	**12**	Uluumay Müzesi	**4**
Kapalı Çarpy (covered bazaar)	**7**	Yeşil Cami	**11**
Kültür Parkı	**3**	Yeşil Türbe	**10**

LOCAL FLAVORS OF THE AEGEAN SEA

Most cities in Turkey claim some kind of fame for their *köfte* (meatballs), but *İnegöl köfte*—traditionally cooked over charcoal—are especially delicious and said to have been invented in Bursa. Another popular dish that has origins in Bursa is *İskender kebap*, tender beef on *pide* (soft flatbread), which is soaked in tomato sauce, drizzled with hot melted butter, and served with yogurt on the side. Even if you haven't liked

İskender elsewhere in Turkey, try it in Bursa, where it's far superior.

The Aegean region is known for mezes made with wild herbs collected in the area and cooked or dressed in olive oil. Cunda Island in Ayvalık is particularly famous for its amazing range of seafood and fish mezes and main dishes, enriched by lesser-known Greek specialties and the restaurants' own creations.

entire street is a lively and popular dining spot, with affable musicians wandering around the many tables. $ *Average main: 30 TL* ⊠ *Sakarya Cad. 6, Arap Şükrü* ☎ *0224/221–1453* ⊘ *No lunch.*

$$
MIDDLE EASTERN
Fodor's Choice
★

✗ **Darüzziyafe.** Across from the Muradiye Tombs, this kitchen house built by Sultan Murat II in the 15th century to help feed the poor now serves Ottoman and Turkish cuisine in wonderfully atmospheric surroundings. *Hünkar beğendi* (tender lamb on a bed of grilled-eggplant purée) literally means "the sultan liked it," and it's hard not to. The place is also known for its *köfte* (meatballs), made with lamb, beef, chicken, and pistachios, and for its Ottoman desserts. The terrace is pleasant, but dine indoors and you'll feel like you're eating in the sultan's quarters. No alcohol is served. $ *Average main: 15 TL* ⊠ *Murad Cad. 36, Muradiye* ☎ *0224/224–6439* ⊕ *www.daruzziyafebursa.com* ⌕ *Reservations essential.*

$$$
TURKISH

✗ **Kebapcý İskender (Oðlu Cevat).** Eager patrons line up outside this little white-and-blue house near the bazaar to enjoy heaping servings of meat, dished up by a grandson of the inventor of İskender kebap, Mehmet İskenderoðlu. (He's pictured on the wall, opposite Atatürk.) The kebab is tender, the portions large, and the photograph-lined dining rooms quaint. The kitchen closes by 6:30 during the week and 8 on weekends, so go early. $ *Average main: 20 TL* ⊠ *Atatürk Cad. 60, at Orhan Sok., Heykel* ☎ *0224/221–1076* ⊕ *www.iskender.com.tr.*

$$$
TURKISH

✗ **Konak 18.** This old house in the Çekirge section of town, opposite the Çelik Palas Hotel, is a local favorite, with a ground-floor terrace overlooking Kültür Parký, live Turkish music on Saturday nights, and attentively prepared cuisine. Topping the menu are the grilled meats and fish and a tasty *avcı böreği* (hunter's pie), pastry filled with meat or cheese that's served as a starter. $ *Average main: 20 TL* ⊠ *Çekirge Cad. 18, Çelik Palas Oteli Karşısı* ☎ *0224/235–3707* ⊕ *www.konak18. com.tr* ⊘ *No lunch.*

$
TURKISH

✗ **Ömür Köftecisi.** The location is charming, in the covered market by the Ulu Cami, and *köfte* (meatballs) is the thing to order, served with grilled peppers and tomatoes. Among the salad options, *piyaz* (bean salad with vinegar) accompanies *köfte* best. The soup is delicious, too. The restaurant has the same architectural features as the *hans*, with brick and stone walls, and two domes in the ceilings painted in floral patterns. $ *Average main: 10 TL* ✉ *Ulu Cami Cad. 7* ☎ *0224/221–4524* ⏲ *Closed Mon.*

WHERE TO STAY

The main decision for travelers staying in Bursa overnight is whether to lay their heads in Çekirge or downtown (Heykel). Accommodations in Çekirge are typically more upscale (and expensive) but most have thermal baths. Hotels downtown are closer to the sights but tend to be unremarkable.

$$$ HOTEL Fodor's Choice ★ 🏨 **Hotel Çelik Palas.** The most venerable of the Çekirge spa hotels has gone glam with contemporary-style rooms, Las Vegas–worthy lounge areas, and an outdoor pool deck with a stunning view of the city. **Pros:** excellent service; big rooms; luxurious spa area; views. **Cons:** pricey; not easy walking distance to most sights. $ *Rooms from: $160* ✉ *Çekirge Cad. 79* ☎ *0224/233–3800* 🌐 *www.celikpalasotel.com* 🛏 *164 rooms* 🍴 *Breakfast.*

$$ HOTEL Fodor's Choice ★ 🏨 **Hotel Gönlüferah.** Claiming to have the city's best thermal baths, this is the place to enjoy sumptuous Ottoman style, complete with high beds, velvet curtains, and ornamental hanging lamps. **Pros:** big, well-decorated, light-filled rooms; attentive service. **Cons:** extra charge for the thermal baths; far from sights; some bathrooms fairly small. $ *Rooms from: $120* ✉ *1 Murat Cad. 22, Çekirge* ☎ *0224/233–9210* 🌐 *www.gonluferah.com* 🛏 *70 rooms* 🍴 *Breakfast.*

$ HOTEL 🏨 **Safran Otel.** The comfortable accommodations, decorated partly in Ottoman tradition, are within walking distance of the center and most sights, but on a quiet hilltop opposite the tombs of Sultans Osman and Orhan. **Pros:** peaceful; close to the city center. **Cons:** no restaurant. $ *Rooms from: $76* ✉ *Tophane Mahallesi, Ortapazar Cad. 9, Ara Sok. 3* ☎ *224/224–7216* 🌐 *www.safranotel.com* 🛏 *10 rooms* 🍴 *Breakfast.*

NIGHTLIFE

Nightlife in Bursa is liveliest in winter, and the best place is out of town at the ski resort Uludağ, where Istanbul's elite fill the hotels on weekends and holidays. There's popular Turkish and Western music, and lots of dancing. The rest of the year, nightlife in Bursa either imitates the Uludağ scene or sticks to Ottoman tradition with Turkish *fasıl* music, which can be found in restaurants such as Konak 18 or Darüzziyafe during weekend dinners. For nightclubs, try one of the places at the Kültür Parký such as **Altýn Ceylan.**

Club Chyna (formerly **Vici**), 7 km (4 miles) out of town on the way to Mudanya, or **Jazz Bar,** on the way to Uludağ, are other clubbing options; both are liveliest in winter. Near the center, Sakarya Caddesi (aka Arap Şükrü) is a popular spot year-round for meyhane-style dining accompanied by roaming musicians; past the restaurants is **M Pub (Kafe Müsadenizle)**. It doesn't look much like a pub, but its shiny lounge and large terrace are among the nicer places in town to have a few drinks, if you're not averse to Turkish pop music.

SHOPPING

Bursa's **Kapalý Çarþý** is the place to go if you want to shop in the traditional way but the city also has many modern stores. The Zafer Plaza mall at the east end of Atatürk Caddesi has many international brands, and instead of the tea gardens of the old bazaars you'll find a large Starbucks housed underneath a glass pyramid and a food court offering American and Turkish fast food.

Kapalý Çarþý (*covered bazaar*). As is traditional, each section of the Kapalý Çarþý, behind the Ulu Cami, is dominated by a particular trade: jewelers, silk weavers, antique dealers. The Koza Han (Cocoon Caravansary) section next to the Orhan Gazi Mosque by the east entrance is the center of the silk trade. It has a lovely courtyard with a tiny *mescit* (prayer room) and a 150-year-old linden tree under which you can sip your tea. The Emir Han, behind the Ulu Cami, in the southwest section, is an interesting combination of jewelers and a religious books market, and also has a fountain and a courtyard tea garden. Antiques and souvenirs can be found in the small Eski Aynalý Çarþý section of the bazaar, between Koza Han and Emir Han. Try *Karagöz* for traditional shadow puppets and other interesting items. ⊠ *Merkez, Ozmangazi Mh.* ⊗ *Mon.–Sat. 8–8.*

GALLIPOLI AND THE DARDANELLES

Most visitors come to this peaceful and scenic part of the country to pay their respects to the victims of the crucial World War I battle, in which ANZAC (Australian and New Zealand Army Corps), British, and French troops clashed with Turkish forces, with massive losses on both sides. Battles have been fought over the Dardanelles, the commercially and militarily strategic strait separating Europe from Asia and connecting the Aegean Sea to the Marmara Sea, since the 13th-century BC war between the Achaeans and Trojans.

Today, you can visit the region year-round if your intent is sightseeing but spring may be the best time, when it's cool enough to walk comfortably around the sights, and when the area is at its most colorful, with wildflowers dotting the cemeteries and hillsides. Turks commemorate the World War I battle on March 18, and British, Australians, and New Zealanders on April 25. The second date, in particular, brings many travelers to the region for the emotional memorial services, but the mass influx requires that you make reservations for hotels and guided tours well in advance. It's probably best to avoid Gallipoli this time of year unless you wish to join the memorial.

The battlefields are spread along a 35-km (22-mile) stretch of the Gallipoli Peninsula. Most visitors base themselves in Çanakkale, on the south side of the straits, rather than in Eceabat on the European side of the Dardanelles. Even though the latter is actually closer to the battlefields, Çanakkale is livelier, has more options for accommodations and dining, and is where many of the guided tours start. Regular ferries make the short crossing in both directions.

CLOSE UP

War and Peace

The Dardanelles have provided the world with many myths and heroes, romances and tragedies. The most recent, and the main reason that the region draws visitors today, was the Gallipoli campaign in World War I. In this offensive, Britain (with soldiers from Australia and New Zealand, then still British colonies) and France tried to breach Çanakkale's defenses in a campaign devised by the young Winston Churchill, at the time First Lord of the Admiralty. The goal was to capture Istanbul, control the entire waterway from the Aegean to the Black Sea, open up a supply channel to Russia, and pave the way for an attack on Germany from the south. After nine months of bloody fighting that left more than 50,000 Allied and perhaps twice as many Turks dead, the Allies admitted defeat and evacuated, beaten by the superior strategy of Lieutenant-Colonel Mustafa Kemal—later called Atatürk.

Churchill lost his job as a result of the failure in the Dardanelles, and his career suffered until the next world war, two decades later. Mustafa Kemal, on the other hand, became a national hero. He had been an insignificant lieutenant, unpopular among the ruling Committee of Union and Progress, but the fame he earned in this war helped him start and lead the war of independence against the occupying Allies. Soon his enemies were overthrown, and so were the Ottoman

sultanate and caliphate. A few years after the Gallipoli campaign, the modern, secular republic of Turkey emerged with Atatürk as president.

For Australians and New Zealanders, World War I was their first real experience of war overseas, and the shocking losses they sustained left an indelible mark. For the Turks, it was an unexpected defensive victory. It was a war of pride, but also one that left behind many stories of kindness between soldiers on opposing sides. The Anzacs and the Turks came from opposite ends of the earth: there was no history of hostility, or even familiarity, between them, until they were told to kill one another, but in some ways the war marked the start of a friendship and thousands of Anzac pilgrims come to visit the battlefields every spring. Atatürk's speech, engraved on a Turkish monument in Anzac Cove, seemed to foresee this:

"Those heroes that shed their blood and lost their lives! You are now lying in the soil of a friendly country, therefore rest in peace. There is no difference between the Johnnies and the Mehmets to us, where they lie side by side here in this country of ours. You, the mothers who sent their sons from far-away countries, wipe away your tears. Your sons are now lying in our bosom, and are at peace. After having lost their lives on this land, they have become our sons as well."

GALLIPOLI

310 km (192 miles) southwest of Istanbul.

Fodor's Choice The Gallipoli Peninsula lies to the north of the Dardanelles. Turks call it
★ Gelibolu—there's also a town of the same name about 40 km (25 miles) northeast of Eceabat. Thirty-one beautifully tended military cemeteries of the Allied dead from World War I line the Gallipoli battlefields.

LONE PINE

The major battles were in two main areas—along the coast between Kabatepe and Suvla Bay, and at Cape Helles, where the main Turkish memorial is located.

GETTING HERE AND AROUND

From Çanakkale, take the car ferry to Eceabat and then head north along the coast from the ferry terminal, following Route D550/E87 as it turns westward to cut across the peninsula, where fruit stands and sunflower fields line the well-maintained road. It takes about 20–30 minutes to drive from Eceabat to the site entrance, where a well-signed loop road passes the main sights in the Kabatepe/Suvla Bay area, most of which have English-language explanatory texts. For a richer self-guided experience, the Australian Government Department of Veterans' Affairs (⊕ *www.anzacsite.gov.au*) offers detailed instructions for an "Anzac Walk" and other tours, including historical information and free audio commentaries to download. The Commonwealth War Graves Commission (⊕ *www.cwgc.org*) publishes a free pamphlet, "The Gallipoli Campaign, 1915," that can be picked up at hotels in Çanakkale or Eceabat or downloaded from the website. It contains a map of the battlefields, a basic history of the campaign, and short descriptions of key points of interest.

EXPLORING

Cape Helles. On the southernmost tip of the Gallipoli Peninsula, the cape has a massive, four-pillared memorial to Turkey's World War I dead. No one knows how many fell in battle; estimates vary from 60,000 to 250,000. If you take the ferry from Gallipoli to Çanakkale, look for the memorials to the campaign carved into the cliffs. The large one at Kilitbahýr reads: "Stop, O passerby. This earth you tread unawares is where an age was lost. Bow and listen, for this quiet place is where the heart of a nation throbs." ⊠ *Off D550 near Seddülbahir.*

Chunuk Bair (*Çanak Bayırı*). The goal of the Allies was to occupy this strategic location overlooking the Gallipoli Peninsula. They failed, and Mustafa Kemal (Atatürk) became a hero and went on to establish the secular republic of Turkey. It was here that he told his soldiers, "I order you not just to fight, but to die." All the men of one of his regiments were wiped out, and he himself was saved miraculously when a bullet hit the pocket watch that was over his heart, but the line held. The hilltop holds Turkish trenches, a cemetery, and the New Zealand national memorial and offers good views of the peninsula and the Dardanelles strait. ⊠ *Gelibolu Tarihi Milli Parkı, Eceabat.*

Kabatepe Museum and Information Center. Letters from soldiers on both sides of the Gallipoli tragedy are among the most moving of the objects on display at this newly opened interpretive center. Uniforms, weapons, and other findings from the World War I battlefield, along with a 13-part exhibition, complete the experience. The desk at the entrance has plenty of information and maps for self-guided tours of the region, and tea, coffee, and snacks are available upstairs. ⊠ *Gelibolu Tarihi Milli Parkı, Kabatepe Mevkii, Eceabat* ☎ *0286/862–0082* 🎫 *13 TL.*

Fodor's Choice
★

Lone Pine Cemetery. The memorial here bears the names of some 5,000 Australian and New Zealand soldiers with unknown graves killed

The Dardanelles
and the North
Aegean

at Gallipoli during a grueling eight-month World War I campaign to defeat the Ottoman forces. Savage hand-to-hand fighting took place on the battefield where the cemetery was established, and seven Victoria crosses, the highest award given by the British government for bravery and usually quite sparingly distributed, were awarded after the battle. This is the most affecting of all the ANZAC cemeteries, and the epitaphs on the tombstones are very moving. ⊠ *Gelibolu Tarihi Milli Parkı, Eceabat.*

ÇANAKKALE

340 km (211 miles) southwest of Istanbul; 270 km (168 miles) from Bursa.

West of Bursa, on the southern shore of the Dardanelles, Çanakkale is the largest city on the North Aegean coast and makes a good base for visiting the memorials and battlefields of Gallipoli, a half-hour ferry journey across the straits.

The heart of Çanakkale is in the docks area, and you really don't need to go inland. An Ottoman clock tower is between the two halves of the dock. Head toward the sea from this tower and you'll find the ferry that departs for historic Gallipoli. Hotels and restaurants are spread on either side of the docks, along the seafront. Most of the budget hotels, cheap dining options, and bars are in the streets behind the seafront to the left of the tower if you're facing the sea.

GETTING HERE AND AROUND

Flights arrive at Çanakkale Airport (⊕ *www.canakkale.dhmi.gov.tr*), just south of the city center.

By car from Bursa, Route 200 (which becomes E90) runs west toward Çanakkale; the trip is 270 km (168 miles) and takes about four hours. If you're heading for Çanakkale from Istanbul, take E80 west to Tekirdağ and then the E84, turning onto the E87 in Keşan to continue on to Eceabat's car ferry terminal. From Çanakkale, the E87 goes through Troy, Ezine, Ayvacık, Edremit, and Ayvalık. Ezine is 50 km (31 miles) from Çanakkale, and from there you can take the coast road west to Geyikli, where ferries run to Bozcaada, or to Alexandria Troas, Babakale, and Assos, all farther south. This is a coastal road that runs through small villages; it's a bit rough and winding, but quite scenic and enjoyable.

The bus trip from Istanbul to Çanakkale is about six hours and costs about 50 TL. From Bursa to Çanakkale is around five hours and costs about 35 TL. If the ride ends at the new bus terminal outside town, you can take the city bus to the port area in about 20 minutes for a fare of 1.75 TL.

ESSENTIALS

Visitor Information. This small office by the ferry terminal provides maps, lists of local rent-a-car companies, and other useful information. ⊠ *İskele Meydanı 65, Çanakkale* ☎ *0286/217–1187* ☉ *Weekdays 8:30–5:30, weekends 10–12:30 and 1:30–4:30.*

EXPLORING

Arkeoloji Müzesi (*Archaeology Museum*). A number of finds from Troy, including gravestones, jewelry, and kitchenware, have made their way to this quiet and somewhat cavernous museum on the southern end of town, along with artifacts from Assos, Bozcaada, Apollo Smintheon, and other parts of the region. A massive sarcophagus is carved with funeral and sacrificial scenes, and another is painted with images of boar and stag hunts. Labels are in English and Turkish, and you'll probably have the entire place, along with its gazebo-filled garden, to yourself. ⊠ *Barbaros Mahallesi, 100. Yıl Cad. 49, Çanakkale* ☎ *0286/217–6740* 🖭 *5 TL* ☉ *Daily 8–5.*

Çimenlik Fortress. The main reason to come here is for the sweeping view of the mouth of the Dardanelles and the Aegean, but the long history and exhibits come a close second. Built on the orders of Mehmet the Conqueror in 1462, after he successfully stormed Istanbul, the impressive waterfront fortress now includes the **Deniz Müzesi** (Navy Museum). The high walls contain all kinds of weaponry, including dozens of cannons, ancient and modern. There's also a replica of the World War I-era **minelayer ship** *Nusret* docked offshore. Inside the fortress a Turkish-language live-action reenactment of life in the trenches accompanies exhibits in English. ⊠ *İsmetpaşa Mh., Çimenlik Sok. and Hanım Sok., Çanakkale* 🖭 *5 TL.* ☉ *Grounds: daily 9–dusk. Museum and ship: Tues., Wed., and Fri.–Sun. 9–5 (with break for lunch).*

WHERE TO EAT

There are plenty of cheap places to grab a bite to eat in Çanakkale, with numerous bakeries and kebab shops clustered around Fetvane Street near the clock tower and the Yalý Cami.

$ TURKISH 🍴 **Gülen Pide & Kebap Salonu.** Cheery and bright, this casual two-floor eatery near the ferry dock serves delicious *pide* (Turkish pizza), topped with minced meat, sausage, cheese, or any combination. There's also a wide variety of kebabs, *döner*, and other grilled meats, as well as the thin flatbread *lahmacun,* topped with minced meat, and a small selection of traditional desserts. [$] *Average main: 10 TL* ✉ *Cumhuriyet Meydanı 27/A, Çanakkale* ☎ *0286/212–8800.*

$$$$ TURKISH 🍴 **Yalova Restaurant.** Take in views across the Dardanelles as you enjoy such seafood *meze* as grilled octopus in vinegar and sardines wrapped in vine leaves, as well as grilled fish and meat. Fish prices are per kilogram and not listed on the menu, so be sure to ask before ordering, and the same goes for *meze*, fruit plates, and other dishes that might show up on the table without your asking. [$] *Average main: 30 TL* ✉ *Yalı Cad., Gümrük Sok. 7, Çanakkale* ☎ *0286/217–1045* ⏲ *No lunch.*

WHERE TO STAY

$ HOTEL 🏨 **Hotel Helen.** Friendly, helpful service, good-size rooms and bathrooms, views of the Dardanelles, and a good location near the ferry terminal make this an excellent choice for touring the region. **Pros:** good service; pleasant interior; reasonable prices; central location. **Cons:** somewhat lacking in character. [$] *Rooms from: $56* ✉ *Kemalpaşa Mahallesi, Cumhuriyet Meydanı 57, Çanakkale* ☎ *0286/212–1818* 🌐 *www.helenhotel.com* 🛏 *42 rooms* 🍽 *Multiple meal plans.*

$ HOTEL 🏨 **Kervansaray Hotel.** An old Ottoman house near the clock tower is set ahead of the competition by its delicious breakfast and complimentary refreshments. **Pros:** nice character; good location in the heart of the city; reasonable prices; helpful staff. **Cons:** small bathrooms, especially in the single rooms; somewhat dated facilities. [$] *Rooms from: $61* ✉ *Kemalpaşa Mahallesi, Fetvane Sok. 13, Çanakkale* ☎ *0286/217–8192* 🌐 *www.otelkervansaray.com* 🛏 *20 rooms* 🍽 *Breakfast.*

NIGHTLIFE

Fetvane Sokak, on the left of the clock tower if you're facing the sea, is the main bar street. You can choose from spacious open-air bars dominated by pop music, or small, dark dives. Narrow Matbaa Sokak between Fetvane and Rýhtým Caddesi has been converted into a mini version of Istanbul's Nevizade, with bars and restaurants packed in side by side. **Tarihi Yalý Hany,** the historic *han* (inn) near the end of Fetvane, has a leafy, cobbled courtyard for smoking a *nargile* (water pipe) or having a drink, with a smooth selection of blues and jazz in the background. Additional seating is available upstairs. On the other side of the ferry terminal, **Telefone Café** (✉ *Cevatpaşa Caddesi 24/A*) is popular with locals for coffee or a drink. Some of the waterfront tea gardens north of the ferry terminal also serve beer.

SHOPPING

The Fetvane and Yalı streets in the old city are packed with attractive old stone buildings, and many have been converted into bookshops or markets, selling everything from fine Bozcaada wines to white Ezine cheese and olive oil from Ayvacık. Follow Çarþý Caddesi southeast to see more and eventually come across **Aynalý Çarþý**, the Mirrored Bazaar.

Aynalý Çarþý. The Mirrored Bazaar remained unused for much of the last century, but has been renovated and about a dozen souvenir and pottery shops are based in its small but historic hall. Its design is based on Istanbul's Mýsýr Çarþý, and it was completed in the late 1800s, only to be seriously damaged during shelling in the Gallipoli campaign. It features in a celebrated folk song about the conflict, the "Ballad of Çanakkale." ✉ *Çarşı Cad., Aynalı Çarşı, Kemalpaşa Mh., Çanakkale.*

ECEABAT

335 km (208 miles) southwest of Istanbul.

Eceabat, on the Gallipoli Peninsula, is the closest town to the most-visited battlefields and cemeteries. The town is small and most of the restaurants and hotels are along the waterfront. So is the Tarihe Saygý Parký (Respect for History Park), created in 2010, which has maps, murals, and dioramas related to the Gallipoli battle, with text in both English and Turkish.

GETTING HERE AND AROUND

The Eceabat ferry puts you right in the middle of town. Car ferries make the 30-minute crossing from Çanakkale to Eceabat every half hour (hourly late at night) from 7 am to midnight in both directions.

WHERE TO EAT

$$$ TURKISH 🍴 **Liman Balýk Restaurant.** Newer and shinier options on the peninsula have failed to tempt the Liman's loyal clientele away from this decades-old favorite, where large windows overlook a small park next to the sea. The fare is fish, meat, and *meze*, served as set menus or à la carte; all are fresh and tasty. The prawn casserole is especially good. Reservations are essential during war anniversaries. [$] *Average main: 20 TL* ✉ *İsmet Paşa Mahallesi, İstiklal Cad. 67* ☎ *0286/814–2755* 🌐 *www.limanrestaurant.net.*

$$$ SEAFOOD 🍴 **Maydos Restaurant.** A few minutes' walk from the ferry port, the Maydos specializes in seafood and *meze*—including a few unusual selections, such as anchovies with chopped olives. If the weather is good, ask for a table outside on the terrace, which has fine views across the Dardanelles. Connected with Hassle Free Travel Agency, the restaurant offers a free boat transfer from Çanakkale. [$] *Average main: 20 TL* ✉ *İsmetpaşa Mahallesi (on shore road south of ferry port), İstiklal Cad.* ☎ *0286/814–1454* 🌐 *www.maydos.com.tr/restaurant* 🕘 *No lunch.*

WHERE TO STAY

$ HOTEL 🏨 **Crowded House Hotel.** Don't let the grimy concrete exterior put you off; the interior is quite colorful, with a lobby decorated to make visitors from Australasia feel at home, along with bright, clean guest quarters. **Pros:** reasonable prices; pleasant common areas. **Cons:** rooms are

basic. $ *Rooms from: $40* ✉ *İsmetpaşa Mahallesi, Hüseyin Avni Sok.
5* ☎ *0286/814–1565* ⊕ *www.crowdedhousegallipoli.com* ⇄ *26 rooms*
†◯† *Breakfast.*

$$
B&B/INN
☷ **The Gallipoli Houses.** Located in a small farming village between Eceabat and Kabatepe, Gallipoli Houses offers a relaxed, intimate getaway with large rooms that are rustic but comfortable, each with a terrace or balcony, and home-cooking that includes a hearty breakfast and (for an extra charge) a delicious dinner. **Pros:** quiet, peaceful location; lots of atmosphere; close to battlefields; discounted prices are available for longer stays. **Cons:** getting around can be difficult without a car; closed in winter. $ *Rooms from: $76* ✉ *Kocadere Village* ☎ *0286/814-2650* ⊕ *www.gallipoli.com.tr* ⇄ *10 rooms* ⊙ *Closed late Nov.–early Mar.*
†◯† *Breakfast.*

$
HOTEL
☷ **Grand Eceabat Hotel.** Just steps from the ferry terminal, this hotel has enviable views of the Dardanelles from some rooms, and the stylish rooftop bar-restaurant is great for watching the sunrise and sunset. **Pros:** modern hotel with nice views; central location; friendly staff. **Cons:** rooms facing ferry terminal can be noisy $ *Rooms from: $31* ✉ *Cumhuriyet Cad. 2/D* ☎ *0286/814-2458* ⊕ *www.grandeceabathotel.com* ⇄ *33 rooms* †◯† *Breakfast.*

NORTH AEGEAN

The ancient ruins at Pergamum, Troy, and Assos draw most travelers to this relaxed, rural region, but those who linger will find the North Aegean to be one of the loveliest parts of the coastline, with unspoiled natural landscapes, sleepy fishing villages, and outdoor activities all year round. The whole area, so close to Greece, is also where you can see what life was like when the area was Greek, while experiencing its rural Turkish present. Ayvalık is the only large town in the region that can't fairly be called unspoiled, but even it has its own rewards.

TROY (TRUVA)

32 km (20 miles) south of Çanakkale.

Troy, known as Truva to the Turks and Ilion to the Greeks, is one of the most evocative place names in literature.

GETTING HERE AND AROUND

Most tours to Troy operate out of Çanakkale, where independent travelers can also hop a minibus to the site, about a half-hour ride from town. If you're driving, the turnoff for Troy is about 30 km (19 miles) from the Çanakkale city center on Route E87 toward İzmir; the ruins are another 5 km (3 miles) farther south. Though it's easy enough to get to Troy on your own, with or without a car, a good guide will significantly enhance your visiting experience, as the ruins are, frankly, not much to look at without some knowledge of the city's history, both real and legendary.

In addition to the tours from Çanakkale or Istanbul, Mustafa Aþkin of the Hisarlýk Hotel & Cafe & Restaurant near the site gives one- to two-hour tours of Troy; he grew up in the area, speaks excellent English, and has written books about the fabled city. His narrative will illuminate easily overlooked features of the ruins (☎ 286/283–0026 ⊕ *www.thetroyguide.com*).

Fodor'sChoice
★

Troy (Truva). The wooden horse that stands outside the site is a modern addition, there to remind us of Homer's epics, but the city walls, layer upon layer of them, date back several millennia. Long thought to be a figment of the Greek poet Homer's imagination and written about in his epic *The Iliad*, Troy was excavated in the 1870s by Heinrich Schliemann, a German businessman who had struck it rich in California's gold rush. While scholars scoffed, he poured his wealth into the excavations and had the last laugh: He found the remains not only of fabled Troy but of nine successive civilizations, one on top of the other, dating back 5,000 years (and now known among archaeologists as Troy I–IX). Subsequent excavations during the 1930s revealed 38 additional layers of settlements.

Schliemann found a hoard of jewels that he believed were those of King Priam, but have more recently been dated to a much earlier era. Adding to the controversy that surrounded his discoveries, Schliemann smuggled the jewels out of the country, and his wife was seen wearing them at fashionable social events. Schliemann later donated them to Berlin's Pergamon Museum, but they disappeared during the Red Army's sack of Berlin in World War II. They reappeared in 1993, when Moscow announced that its State Pushkin Museum of Fine Arts housed what they called the lost "Treasure of Priam." Though Germany, Greece, and Turkey have all claimed the treasures, recent custom dictates that archaeological finds belong to the country in which they were originally found; unfortunately, these have yet to make their way back to Turkey.

What you see of Troy today depends on your imagination or the knowledge and linguistic abilities of your guide. You may find the site highly suggestive, with its remnants of massive, rough-hewn walls, a paved **chariot ramp**, and strategic views over the coastal plains to the sea. Or you may consider it an unimpressive row of trenches with piles of earth and stone. Considering Troy's fame (and the difficulties involved in conquering it), the city is surprisingly small. The best-preserved features are from the Roman city, with its *bouleuterion* (council chamber), the site's most complete structure, and small theater. A site plan shows the general layout and marks the beginning of a sign-posted path leading to key features from several historical civilizations. ⊠ *Follow signs from Rte. E87, Tevfikiye Köyü* ☎ *0286/283–0536* 🖼 *15 TL; parking: 3 TL* ☉ *Daily 8–4:30 (to 7 pm Apr.–Oct.).*

WHERE TO STAY

$
HOTEL

🖬 **Hisarlýk Hotel & Cafe & Restaurant.** Run by three brothers, this is the only lodging in the immediate vicinity of the Troy ruins and is very basic, but it has a decent restaurant. **Pros:** great location for touring Troy. **Cons:** basic rooms; prices somewhat high for what you get. Ⓢ *Rooms from: $55* ⊠ *Tevfikiye Köyü* ☎ *0286/283–0026* ⊕ *troyhisarlik.com* 🛏 *11 rooms* ❏ *Breakfast.*

**OFF THE
BEATEN
PATH**

Bozcaada. Heading south from Troy, you'll pass through Ezine or Geyikli. In either case you'll see a signpost for Bozcaada, one of the two Aegean islands that belong to Turkey. If you have time, spare a day for this island (though you'll probably then want to spare another) with its unspoiled harbor town, beautiful old houses, pristine sandy beaches, and lovely countryside covered with vineyards. The local wine may be the best you'll taste in Turkey without having to spend a fortune.

BEHRAMKALE (ASSOS)

25 km (16 miles) southeast of Gülpınar; 65 km (40 miles) south of Troy; 17 km (11 miles) south of Ayvacık.

Fodor's Choice
★

The port is a marvel, pressed against the sheer cliff walls. It's crammed with small hotels that were built of volcanic rock, a fleet of fishing boats, and a small rocky beach at each end. Behramkale village is home to the lofty ruins of ancient Assos—the Acropolis—which provide a panoramic view over the Aegean. It has blossomed in recent years and now surpasses the port area in terms of prices—and perhaps in charm as well. Nowadays the name "Behramkale" is used for the village at the top and "Assos" for the port area.

Outside of June, July, August, and weekends the rest of the year, the area is less crowded and prices are likely to come down a bit, especially in the port. For more spacious and sandier beaches try Kadırga, on the way to Küçükkuyu.

GETTING HERE AND AROUND

Buses from Çanakkale in the north and Ayvalık or İzmir in the south stop at Ayvacık, which is the closest (17 km/11 miles) town to Behramkale. From there, minibuses make the 20- to 30-minute trip to Behramkale about every hour for 4.5 TL, though less frequently out of high season. Make sure you get one that goes down to the port, if that's your final destination.

To take the minibus between the port and the village is a five-minute ride, costing 2 TL. The minibus also goes to Kadırga beach, a 15-minute ride, for 8 TL. If driving, as you approach, the road forks, with one route leading to the ancient, pretty village atop the hill and the other twisting precariously down to the tiny, charming harbor.

EXPLORING

Acropolis. The hilltop Acropolis measures about five square city blocks. Founded about 1000 BC by Aeolian Greeks, the city was successively ruled by Lydians, Persians, Pergamenes, Romans, and Byzantines, until Sultan Orhan Gazi (ruled 1324–62) took it over for the Ottomans in 1330. Aristotle is said to have spent time here in the 4th century BC, and St. Paul stopped en route to Miletus in about AD 55. The textile and trinket sellers along both sides of the road will show you the way from the village. You're best off leaving your car on one of the wider streets and making your way on foot up the steep, cobbled lanes to the top of the summit, where you'll be rewarded with a sensational view of the coastline and, in the distance, the Greek island of Lesbos, whose citizens were the original settlers of Assos.

HOMER'S STORY

Because *The Iliad* was written 500 years after the war—traditionally believed to have taken place around 1184 BC—it's hard to say how much of it is history and how much is invention. Nonetheless, it makes for a romantic tale: Paris, the son of King Priam, abducted the beautiful Helen, wife of King Menelaus of Sparta, and fled with her to Troy. Menelaus enlisted the aid of his brother, King Agamemnon, and launched a thousand ships to get her back. His siege lasted 10 years and involved such ancient notables as Achilles, Hector, and the crafty

Odysseus, king of Ithaca. It was Odysseus who ended the war, after ordering a huge wooden horse to be built and left outside Troy's gates. Then the Greeks retreated to their ships and pretended to sail away. The Trojans hauled the trophy into their walled city and celebrated their victory. Under cover of darkness, the Greek ships returned, the soldiers hidden inside the horse crept out and opened the city's gates, and the attackers at last gained entry to Troy. Hence the saying: "Beware of Greeks bearing gifts."

At the summit is the site of the **Temple of Athena** (circa 530 BC), which has splendid sea views but has been somewhat clumsily restored. A more modern addition, right before the entrance to the ruins, is the **Murad Hüdavendigâr Camii,** a mosque built in the late 14th century. The mosque is simple—a dome atop a square, with little decoration. The Greek crosses carved into the lintel over the door indicate the Ottomans used building material from an earlier church, possibly one on the same site. Back down the slope, on the road to the port, is a parking area for the **necropolis** and city walls stretching 3 km (2 miles), as well as the ruins of a gymnasium, **theater,** and *agora* (marketplace). Assos was known for its sarcophagi, made of local limestone, which were shipped throughout the Greek world. Unfortunately, most of the tombs are in pieces. ⊠ *At the top of Behramkale village, Behramkale* ☎ *0286/721–7218* ⊕ *assosarchproject.com* ⊠ *8 TL* ⊗⊠ *Apr.–Oct., daily 8–7; Nov.–Mar., daily 8–5.*

WHERE TO EAT

The fish restaurants are not cheap, but the fish will be fresh, the mezes tasty, and the setting beautiful. Evening dining options in Behramkale are fairly slim, but many *pansiyons* (guesthouses) serve good homemade local dishes to guests for an additional charge.

$$$$
TURKISH

✕ **Assos Köyüm Restaurant.** There's no menu at this friendly, family-run spot in Behramkale's tiny main square: Just pick from the selection of *meze* on display (don't miss the crunchy, garlicky greens called *deniz börülcesi*) and let one of the young waiters tell you what meat dishes are on offer that day, perhaps *köfte* (meatballs), chicken *şiş,* or *saç kavurma,* a sizzling plate of diced lamb and vegetables. The covered terrace looks over the village and down to the sea while a few seats out front allow diners to watch the comings and goings on the square. Alcohol is served. Ⓢ *Average main: 40 TL* ⊠ *Behramkale village square, by çay bahçesi, Behramkale* ☎ *0286/721–7424.*

The ruins at Troy are not as well preserved as others in Turkey, but are still atmospheric.

$$$ TURKISH 🍴 **Kale Restaurant.** A few minutes' walk from the ⇨ *Acropolis*, this casual eatery with stone tables and colorful flower pots is a welcome stop on the way back from a visit to the ruins, especially on a hot day. The *ayran* (a salty yogurt drink) is thirst-quenching and a great restorative. Try the *mantı* (Turkish ravioli in garlicky yogurt sauce), the *tavuk şiş* (chicken kebab), or the *gözleme,* thin Turkish pastry filled with minced meat, mashed potato, or cheese and cooked on a flat stone. [$] *Average main: 22 TL* ✉ *Acropolis road, Behramkale* ☎ *0543/317–4969* 💳 *No credit cards.*

WHERE TO STAY

Most hotels in Assos port include breakfast and dinner, though some will agree on deals for breakfast only.

$$ B&B/INN Fodor's Choice ★ 🏨 **Assos Alarga.** In a gorgeous old stone house centered on a shady courtyard, this guesthouse offers a serene and intimate stay in the quiet end of Behramkale village, and its pool and garden ensure an idyllic getaway atmosphere. **Pros:** beautiful house and rooms; serene location; friendly owner and staff. **Cons:** bathrooms on the small side. [$] *Rooms from: $135* ✉ *Behramkale 88, Behramkale* ☎ *0537/721–7260* 🌐 *www.assosalarga.com* 🛏 *3 rooms* 🍽 *Breakfast.*

$$ HOTEL 🏨 **Assos Kervansaray Otel.** The best located of the waterside hotels, at the far end of the harbor, offers rooms in a variety of sizes and styles, many of which have a terrific view of the Aegean. **Pros:** romantic setting near the Aegean; swimming in pools and sea. **Cons:** the half-board arrangement may not be desirable; slightly impersonal atmosphere. [$] *Rooms from: $140* ✉ *Assos Liman (Assos Harbor), Behramkale*

☎ 286/721–7093, 286/721–7198 🌐 *www.assoskervansaray.com* 🛏 *80 rooms* 🍴 *Some meals.*

$$ B&B/INN Fodor's Choice ★ 🏨 **Biber Evi.** Beautiful rooms and the warmest of welcomes make this sublimely tranquil boutique hotel a top choice for a peaceful getaway. **Pros:** great atmosphere and location; good breakfast; attractively decorated rooms. **Cons:** bathrooms are basic and showers are not enclosed. [$] *Rooms from: $150* ✉ *Behramkale Köyü 46, Behramkale* ☎ *0286/721–7410* 🌐 *www.biberevi.com* 🛏 *6 rooms* 🍴 *Breakfast.*

$$ B&B/INN 🏨 **Eris Pansiyon.** You'll feel more like a friend than a paying guest in the 250-year old stone house that American retiree Emily Vickers operates as a *pansiyon*. **Pros:** quiet and intimate; nice garden; good food; on the edge of Behramkale, about 10 minutes' walk from the Acropolis. **Cons:** easier to reach with own transportation. [$] *Rooms from: $120* ✉ *Behramkale Köyü 6, Kadirga Çıkışı, Behramkale* ☎ *0286/721–7080* 🌐 *www.assos.de/eris* 🛏 *3 rooms* 💳 *No credit cards* 🍴 *No meals.*

NIGHTLIFE

Uzun Ev Bar (*Long House Bar*). You can have drinks at any of the hotel bar-restaurants or check out the only actual bar in the Assos Harbor, the Uzun Ev, which also serves a full menu of fish and *meze*, including a variety of Aegean greens. The whitewashed stone walls with antique bread-making equipment hanging from them give the interior some character and there are eight tables outside by the harbor. The music is good, too: soft jazz during the day, a live guitarist playing Turkish and foreign music on weekend nights during the summer and holidays. It's open until 2 or 3 am on summer weekends if there are still customers. ✉ *Behramkale Köyü Sahili, Behramkale* ☎ *0286/721–7007.*

AYVALIK

48 km (30 miles) from Edremit; 117 km (73 miles) from Çanakkale.

Fodor's Choice ★ Ayvalık is beautiful, stretching onto a peninsula and surrounded by islands, with many bays swirling in and out of its coastline. The bustling harbor town and Cunda Island across the way retain strong evidence of the Greek community that flourished here and prospered in the olive oil trade until being deported in the population exchange of 1923. Atmospheric back streets are full of crumbling old Greek houses. A long, sandy beach is just a short minibus ride away and various pleasure boats stand ready to take visitors on swimming and snorkeling excursions.

Ayvalık has some of the finest 19th-century Greek-style architecture in Turkey, and recent restoration has begun to reverse decades of neglect. Unlike typical Ottoman houses (tall, narrow, and built of wood, with an overhanging bay window), Greek buildings are stone, with classic triangular pediments above a square box. The best way to explore is to turn your back to the Aegean and wander the tiny side streets leading up the hill into the heart of the old residential quarter (try Talatpaşa Caddesi or Gümrük Caddesi). The artsy Tarlakuşu café on Cumhuriyet Caddesi has some useful maps to get you started.

Several historic churches in town have been converted into mosques. St. John's is now the **Saatli Cami** (Clock Mosque). St. George's is now the

Çýnarlý Cami (Plane Tree Mosque). There are many mosques converted from churches in Turkey, but these are among the most striking—the elaborate style of Orthodox churches does not suit the plain minimalist style of mosques, and the unimpressive minaret erected later at the Çınarlı Mosque looks almost absurd. The pictures of the saints inside are painted over but can still be seen if you look carefully. The now-shuttered **Taxiarchis Church** holds a remarkable series of paintings done on fish skin depicting the life of Christ. Barbaros Caddesi on the south end of the pier will take you to **Phaneromeni Church** (Ayazma Kılisesi), displaying beautiful stone craftwork, and to the **Hayrettin Paşa Camii,** also converted from a church.

In summer, Sarımsaklı Plajı, the 10-km (6-mile) stretch of sandy beach 7 km (4½ miles) from the center of town, is popular, and easily and cheaply reached by minibuses that stop near the harbor. It's a crowded resort with a mess of concrete hotels right behind the seafront, and traffic and parking can be a problem, but the beach and sea are lovely.

Day or evening cruises to the bays and islands of Ayvalık are enjoyable, and range from party-boat trips to lower-key swimming excursions to the Patriça Nature Reserve on the far side of Cunda Island. Hucksters on the docks will try to sell you a trip as you walk by the boats, and competition makes prices very reasonable—about 30 TL for a day trip including a fish meal. Diving trips are also available at a higher cost. The tours are offered from May until the end of October.

Şeytan Sofrası ("the devil's dinner table"), a hilltop 9 km (5½ miles) from town, on a right turn on the road from Ayvalık to Sarımsaklı, is the place to get a panoramic view of the islands and the bays and enjoy a cup of tea or a snack at one of the cafés. It's particularly lovely at sunset, when minibuses make the return trip from town for about 5 TL.

GETTING HERE AND AROUND

There's a regular bus service from Çanakkale, a journey of about three hours; tickets cost about 43 TL one way. By road, it's just off E87.

ESSENTIALS

Visitor Information. ✉ *In front of Tansaş supermarket, opposite harbor* ☎ *0266/312–4494* 🕑 *May–Sept., daily 8–7 (subject to change); Oct.–Apr., daily 8–5.*

WHERE TO EAT

Waterfront restaurants tend to be expensive, but the two *çay bahçe* (tea gardens) at the south end of the harbor are pleasant spots to enjoy a cheap plate of fried fish, mussels, or calamari (7 to 12 TL) along with a beer.

$$$ TURKISH ✕ **Fýrat Lokantasý.** In the heart of Ayvalık, just north of Saatli Cami, this eatery serves up hearty lunches to hardworking street traders; it's tiny but almost always full, so you may have to share one of the dozen or so tables. An old-fashioned telephone adds some character. The Turkish home cooking—rice, beans, eggplant with minced meat, and lamb stew—is delicious and this is the perfect place for lunch when wandering the historic part of the town. [$] *Average main: 16 TL* ✉ *Cumhuriyet Cad. 25/A* ☎ *0266/312–1380* 🕑 *Closed Sun. No dinner.*

$$ TURKISH 🍴 **Girit Mutfaðý.** This tiny restaurant, run by an all-female team, offers a daily selection of home-cooked dishes along the lines of sautéed chard, oven-cooked chicken, *köfte* (meatballs), soup, and chickpeas. If visiting in summer, don't miss the stuffed squash blossoms (*kabak çiçeği*). The *lor tatlısı* (ricotta cheese dessert) is delicious. Beer is available. [$] *Average main: 12 TL* ✉ *Talatpaşa Cad. 15/A* ☎ *0266/312–2128* 💳 *No credit cards* 🕐 *Closed Sun.*

$$$$ TURKISH 🍴 **Hüsnü Baba'nýn Yeri.** Tucked away from the water on a vine-covered cobblestone backstreet in Ayvalık's market area, "Father Hüsnü's Place" has friendly service, cheap prices, and tasty food. The rice-stuffed mussels, zucchini fritters, lightly fried *papalina* (a small local fish), potatoes croquette, calamari, and *deniz börülcesi* (samphire) in olive oil all go well with a glass of *rakı* or beer. Plan on a late dinner (it doesn't open until 9 pm, at least in summer), and get a seat outside for the best atmosphere. [$] *Average main: 30 TL* ✉ *Tenekeciler Sok. 16* ☎ *0266/312–8714* 🕐 *No lunch.*

A QUICK TRIP TO GREECE

A trip to the Greek island of Lesbos will allow you to see another country and culture with a sea journey of little more than an hour, though the timing of trips can be a challenge. Ferries depart from Ayvalık pier for Lesbos daily, but only the Wednesday, Friday, Saturday, and Sunday sailings at 9 am allow for a same-day return. The other days the boats don't sail from Ayvalık until early evening, with a morning return from Lesbos, so a tourist from Ayvalık would need to stay at least two nights. Fares are about 80 TL for the round trip. Offices next to the port compete to sell tickets.

WHERE TO STAY

$$ HOTEL 🏨 **Butik Sýzma Han.** The unrivaled setting on Ayvalık's serene waterfront will allow you to enjoy a fortifying glass of wine by the glistening sea without even having to leave the property. **Pros:** good location; full amenities; easy access to sea. **Cons:** downstairs rooms by lobby can be noisy; some interior areas a bit musty. [$] *Rooms from: $150* ✉ *Gümrük Caddesi, 2. Sok. 49* ☎ *0266/312–7700* 🌐 *www.butiksizmahan.com* 🛏 *10 rooms* 🍽 *Breakfast.*

$$ B&B/INN 🏨 **Günebakan Taliani Hotel.** Perched on a hillside above Ayvalık's harbor, just below the main road out of town toward İzmir, the "Sunflower" has bright and airy rooms dotted around a rambling old house belonging to the family of the charming owner. **Pros:** relaxed atmosphere; good hospitality; comfortable rooms. **Cons:** a bit of a hike from town; facilities are a bit outdated. [$] *Rooms from: $150* ✉ *13 Nisan Cad. 163* ☎ *0266/312–8484* 🌐 *www.talianihotel.com* 🛏 *17 rooms* 🍽 *Breakfast.*

CUNDA ISLAND (ALI BEY ADASI)

Just off the coast of Ayvalık (connected by a causeway to mainland).

Like Ayvalık, Cunda Island was once predominantly Greek, and some Greek is still spoken here. The island has a mix of the two cultures in its food, music, and nightlife, and lately has been deliberately cultivating this, having realized the tourism potential. There's a growing number of cafés, bars, bakeries, and small restaurants in the charming cobbled backstreets away from the water, which are full of old Greek buildings in various states of repair. At the top of the hill, the "Nostaljik Café" at the small Sevim and Necdet Kent Library (look for the stone windmill) is open 9:30 to 9:30 daily and has great views.

GETTING HERE

There are regular buses to Cunda from Ayvalık, but the best way to travel is by boat (3 TL one way); they run every hour each way from 10 am to midnight in summer (June 15–September 15), and dock at the quay right in the middle of the restaurant area in Cunda. In winter, buses and dolmuşes are the only option (2.5 TL).

EXPLORING

St. Nicholas Church. Many of the island's varied Greek houses are well-preserved, and the 19th-century Greek church of St. Nicholas (better known as Taksiyarhis, or Taxiarchis, to the locals) in the middle of town is a landmark. With large cracks in the facade, caused by an earthquake in 1944, and the presence of birds flying around the airy domes, the place has a ghostly air. If restoration is complete by 2014, you can see some of the frescoes, several of which have been defaced (the eyes of the apostles were gouged out). On the left side of the church's quiet courtyard is a small café and *pansiyon*, ⇨ *Zehra Teyze'nin Evi*. The surrounding neighborhood rewards leisurely exploration with views of similarly ruined houses and shops, and an attractive old windmill farther up the hill. ✉ *Namik Kemal Mh., Seref Sok. 7, Ayvalık.*

WHERE TO EAT AND STAY

Cunda has become a popular place for accommodations and nightlife as well as dining. Unlike mainland Ayvalık, Cunda is purely a tourist resort and also attracts weekend escapers all year around, though it doesn't (not yet, at least) attract big tour groups. Most of the hotels on Cunda are quite expensive for what they offer, but the restaurants lining the waterfront, although also expensive, are among the best in Turkey. They're noted for their grilled *çipura* (a local fish) and for an amazing variety of other Turkish and Greek seafood dishes served grilled, fried, baked, or in cold salads. For casual eats, try Pizza Uno (not the American chain) in the center of town, a popular spot for kebabs, pasta, and *pide* (soft flatbread) as well as pizza.

$$$$ SEAFOOD 🍴 **Bay Nihat** (*Lale Restaurant*). The most popular and probably most expensive of the waterfront restaurants on Cunda offers a meze selection that is a feast for the eyes as well as the stomach. Many options are original creations based on Greek and Turkish cuisine—cockles, octopus in mastic sauce, calamari in saffron sauce, and cured fish *pastırma* are among the unusual specialties. [$] *Average main: 79 TL* ✉ *Sahil Boyu 21, Cunda Adası, Ayvalık* ☎ *0266/327–1777* 🌐 *www.baynihat.com.tr* ✍ *Reservations essential.*

$$$ B&B/INN 🏨 **Zehra Teyze'nin Evi.** This small *pansiyon*, with cozy, traditionally furnished rooms and a small garden, is hidden among the trees in the courtyard of the St. Nicholas Church. **Pros:** wonderful location; casual and warm atmosphere. **Cons:** standard rooms are quite small; pricey for what you get. [$] *Rooms from: $250* ✉ *Namik Kemal Mh., Seref*

Sok. 7, Alibey Adası, Ayvalık ☎ *0266/327–2285* ⊕ *www.cundaevi.com*
➟ *8 rooms* ⊺○⊺ *Breakfast.*

NIGHTLIFE

In Sarımsaklı, the beach area in Ayvalık, you'll find discos and clubs that play pop and electronic techno; Cunda has bars that play Turkish and Greek pop music. The island also hosts a short series of outdoor concerts in July; look for posters reading "Cunda Müzik Günleri" (Cunda Music Days) for dates and times. Muhabbet Sokak, between Atatürk Boulevard and the sea, has a selection of busy bars, with live blues, jazz, and rock on weekends.

PERGAMUM (BERGAMA)

62 km (39 miles) from Ayvalık.

Fodor'sChoice
★

The windswept ruins of Pergamum, which surround the modern town of Bergama, are among the most spectacular in Turkey. Pergamum was one of the world's major powers, though it had only a relatively brief moment of glory, notably under the rule of Eumenes II (197 BC–159 BC), who built the city's famous library. Of more lasting influence perhaps was the city's Asklepion, an ancient medical center that had its heyday under the renowned early physician, writer, and philosopher Galen (131 AD–210 AD). By then Pergamum was capital of the Roman province of Asia, which for centuries supplied the empire with great wealth. Bergama has not been heavily influenced by tourism, except perhaps for the carpet shops at the base of the Acropolis road. People still ride tractors, lead donkeys, and drive vegetable trucks through town, and a bus inching along behind a herd of sheep is not an uncommon sight.

GETTING HERE AND AROUND

If you're coming from Ayvalık, drive 51 km (32 miles) south on E87, then turn off following the signs to Bergama on Rte. 240 for another 11 km (7 miles). The bus from Ayvalık takes about an hour and a half and costs 10 TL. Frequent buses travel onward from Bergama to İzmir.

The Bergama bus terminal is 8 km (5 miles) out of the city center, but there's a free municipal shuttle service at least once an hour that stops near the post office and Red Basilica in the center of the old town. There's also minibus service for 1.5 TL. If a taxi driver tells you there's no bus service and tries to charge you 25 TL for the short trip, know that there are other options—or bargain with him. Be sure to check times for buses back to Ayvalık, as they stop running at 6 pm. If you find yourself stuck, take a minibus to nearby Dikili and change for Ayvalık.

There's no useful minibus service to the area's attractions, but in part thanks to the *teleferik* (gondola lift) to the Acropolis, the town's three main sights are reachable by foot. If you want to hire a taxi to take you around, expect to pay 50 TL to 60 TL for the driver to shuttle you from site to site for a few hours. Some hotels have bicycles for guest use but local roads can be narrow and rocky and both the Acropolis and the Asklepion are uphill from town.

ESSENTIALS

Visitor Information ⊠ *Hükümet Konağı, B Blok, ground fl.* ☎ *0232/631–2852* ⊙ *Daily 8:30–noon and 1–5:30.*

EXPLORING

Acropolis. The most dramatic of the remains of Pergamum are at the Acropolis. Take a smooth, 15-minute ride on the *teleferik* (gondola lift; TL 10 for round trip), which offers sweeping views on its way up the hill, or follow signs pointing the way to the 6-km (4-mile) road to the top, where you can park. The parking lot is across from the row of souvenir stands, which sell drinks and reasonably good picture books containing site maps. Buy your ticket at the gate. Broken but still mighty triple ramparts enclose the **upper town,** with its temples, palaces, private houses, and gymnasia (schools). In later Roman times, the town spread out and down to the plain, where the Byzantines subsequently settled for good.

After entering the site through the Royal Gate, there are several different paths. To start at the top, pick the path to the far right, which takes you past the partially restored **Temple of Trajan,** at the summit. This is the very picture of an ancient ruin, with burnished white-marble pillars high above the valley of the Bergama Çayý (Selinus River). The vaulted foundations of the temple, later used as cisterns, are also impressive. On the terraces just below, you can see the scant remains of the **Temple of Athena** and the **Altar of Zeus.** Once among the grandest monuments in the Greek world, the Altar of Zeus was excavated by German archaeologists who sent Berlin's Pergamon Museum every stone they found, including the frieze, 400 feet long, that vividly depicts the battle of the gods against the giants. Now all that's left is the altar's flat stone foundation. There's much more to see of the **Great Theater,** carved into the steep slope west of the terrace that holds the Temple of Athena: It could seat some 10,000 spectators and retains its astounding acoustics.

Nearby are the ruins of the famous library, built by Eumenes II (197 BC–159 BC) and containing 200,000 scrolls. As the Pergamum library came to rival the great library in Alexandria, Egypt, the Egyptians banned the sale of papyrus to Pergamum, which responded by developing a new paper—parchment—made from animal skins instead of reeds. This *charta pergamena* was more expensive but could be used on both sides; because it was difficult to roll, it was cut into pieces and sewn together, much like today's books. The library of Pergamum was transported in 41 BC to Alexandria by Mark Antony as a gift for Cleopatra. It survived there until the 7th century AD, when it was destroyed by the fanatical Caliph Omar, who considered the books un-Islamic.

Farther down the hill, following signs to the lower agora, the excavated living quarters of **Building Z** hold well-restored 2nd-century AD mosaics. ⊠ *Akropol Cad.* ☎ *0232/631–0778* 🖃 *20 TL; parking 3 TL* ⊙ *Apr.–Oct., daily 8:30–7; Nov.–Mar., daily 9–5.*

Arkeoloji Müzesi (*Archaeology Museum*). Though not terribly well-lighted or inviting, this small museum houses a substantial collection of statues, coins, and other artifacts excavated from the ancient city as well as an ethnography section. A relief from the Kýzýl Avlu (Red

Basilica) showing gladiators fighting bulls and bears and some elaborate sarcophagi and gravestones from the region are particularly noteworthy. The well-preserved statue of Nymphe comes from the site of Allianoi, a Roman spa town now submerged under the waters of a dam completed in 2010. ⊠ *Cumhuriyet Cad. 10* ☎ *0232/631–2884* 🎫 *5 TL* ☉ *Tues.–Sun. 8:30–5:30 (to 6:30 Apr.–Oct.).*

Asklepion. This is believed to have been one of the world's first full-service health clinics. The name is a reference to Asklepios, god of medicine and recovery, whose snake and staff are now the symbol of modern medicine. In the center's heyday in the 2nd century AD, patients were prescribed such treatments as fasting, colonic irrigation, and running barefoot in cold weather. Roman emperors Hadrian, Marcus Aurelius, and Caracalla sought treatments at the Asklepion, and Galen, the physician and philosopher who was more or less a resident medic for the Roman Empire's star gladiators, was born in Pergamum and trained here.

The entrance to the complex is at the column-lined **Sacred Way,** once the main street connecting the Asklepion to Pergamum's Acropolis. Follow it for about a city block into a small square and through what was once the main gate to the temple precinct. Immediately to the right is the **library,** a branch of the one at the Acropolis. Patients also received therapy accompanied by music during rites held in the intimate theater, which is now used each May for performances of the Bergama Arts Festival. Nearby are pools that were used for mud and sacred water baths. A subterranean passageway leads down to the sacred cellar of the **Temple of Telesphorus,** where the devout would pray themselves into a trance and record their dreams upon waking; later, a resident priest would interpret the dreams to determine the nature of the treatment the patient required. ⊠ *Bahçelievler Mh., Asklepion Cad.* ✛ *Follow Cumhuriyet Cad. west to Rte. E87; near tourist information office, follow sign pointing off to right 1.5 km (1 mile)* ☎ *0232/631–2886* 🎫 *15 TL; parking 3 TL* ☉ *Apr.–Oct., daily 8:30–7; Nov.–Mar., daily 9–5.*

Kýzýl Avlu *(Red Basilica).* The Red Basilica in Bergama is named for the red bricks from which it's constructed. You'll pass it on the road to and from the Acropolis—it's right at the bottom of the hill, in the old part of the city. This was the last pagan temple constructed in Pergamum before Christianity was declared the state religion in the 4th century, when it was converted into a basilica dedicated to St. John. The walls remain, but not the roof. Most interesting are the underground passages, where it is easy to imagine how concealed pagan priests supplied the voices of "spirits" in mystic ceremonies. The main building is fenced off for ongoing restoration, but one of the two towers has been restored and has some displays inside; the other tower is used as a mosque. ⊠ *Kurtuluş Mh., Kınık Cad.* ☎ *0232/631–2885* 🎫 *5 TL* ☉ *Apr.–Oct., daily 8:30–7; Nov.–Mar., daily 8–5.*

WHERE TO EAT

$

TURKISH

✕ **Arzu Pide and Çorba Salon.** In the heart of town, Arzu has inexpensive, simple, and satisfying Turkish fare and is popular with the locals, especially at lunchtime. The *pide, lahmacun,* and lentil soup are particularly tasty and the staff is friendly. The restaurant's interior is a bit cramped, but there are more tables on the sidewalk outside. $ *Average main: 10 TL* ⊠ *Istiklal Meydanı 35* ☎ *0232/631–1187.*

$$
TURKISH

✕ **Bergama Sofrasý.** Tucked alongside a 16th-century hammam in downtown Bergama, this casual room offers around 20 dishes—stews, casseroles, grilled meats, and soups (fewer options are available at dinnertime). Try the *kadın budu köfte* (ground meat mixed with rice and parsley and lightly fried in egg batter) and the *kemalpaşa*, a traditional sweet served with *kaymak* (clotted cream) and tahini, for dessert. No alcohol is served. Restrooms are outside. $ *Average main: 15 TL* ⊠ *Bankalar Cad. 44* ☎ *0232/631–5131* ⊙ *Closed Oct.–Apr.*

WHERE TO STAY

The run-down but charming old quarter, on the way to the Acropolis, is the best place to stay, with several clean, inexpensive hotels.

$
HOTEL
FAMILY

⌂ **Akropolis Guest House.** This is a quiet hotel at the edge of town, near the Kýzýl Avlu (Red Basilica), and is a good choice for its good value and pleasant atmosphere. **Pros:** near Red Basilica and Acropolis. **Cons:** downstairs rooms may get noise from pool and common areas. $ *Rooms from: $55* ⊠ *Kurtuluş Mahallesi, Kayalık Sok. 3* ☎ *0232/631–2621* ⊕ *www.akropolisguesthouse.com* ⤳ *12 rooms* ⦿*Breakfast.*

$$
HOTEL
Fodor's Choice
★

⌂ **Hera Hotel.** Bergama's most attractive lodging is a favorite with couples on romantic retreats as well as visiting archaeologists, and all are made equally welome by the multilingual owner—a mine of local information. **Pros:** serene location; beautiful rooms; good hospitality. **Cons:** no restaurant. $ *Rooms from: $110* ⊠ *Talatpaşa Mahallesi, Tabak Köprü Cad. 21* ☎ *0232/631–0634* ⊕ *www.hotelhera.com* ⤳ *10 rooms* ⦿*Breakfast.*

$
B&B/INN

⌂ **Odyssey Guest House.** The best budget deal in Bergama occupies two restored 19th-century Greek houses in the heart of the old town, with a view of the Red Basilica from the rooftop dining terrace. **Pros:** excellent value; friendly owners; central location. **Cons:** breakfast extra; cash only; some rooms have shared bathrooms. $ *Rooms from: $40* ⊠ *Talatpaşa Mahallesi, Abacıhan Sok. 13* ☎ *0232/631–3501* ⊕ *www.odysseyguesthouse.com* ⤳ *11 rooms* ▭ *No credit cards* ⦿*No meals.*

THE CENTRAL AND SOUTHERN AEGEAN COAST

WELCOME TO THE CENTRAL AND SOUTHERN AEGEAN COAST

TOP REASONS TO GO

★ **Feast on local seafood and fresh mezes:** Enjoy a relaxing meal at one of the many seafood restaurants.

★ **Swim, windsurf, and scuba dive:** Some of the brightest and bluest waters in the Aegean region surround the sophisticated coastal towns of Çeşme and Bodrum.

★ **Take a Blue Cruise:** A *gulet,* or wooden boat, is the perfect vehicle for exploring the Aegean coast, visiting secluded coves sprinkled along pristine clear waters.

★ **Visit Ephesus:** For a glimpse into the Hellenistic, Roman, and Byzantine periods, take a walk through the ruins of Ephesus, lined with the remains of temples, houses, shops, and the famed Library of Celsus.

★ **Wander through Şirince:** This picturesque winemaking village is surrounded by lovely restored houses; the hills are great for hiking.

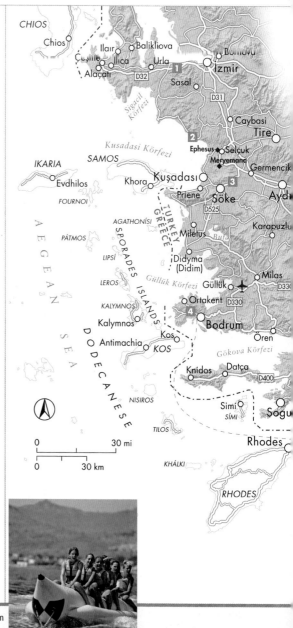

Bodrum

Ephesus

1 İzmir and Çeşme. The port city of İzmir (ancient Smyrna) is the third largest city in Turkey, with enough sights and glimpses into everyday Turkish life to keep you well occupied for a day or two. Nearby Çeşme, a dry peninsula at the western tip of the region, has some of the region's most pristine waters. Some of the best beaches are located in Altınkum and Pırlanta, southwest of Çeşme—the names literally mean "golden sand" and "sparkling." For the trendy beach clubs, head to Ayayorgi Bay and for nightlife, head to Alaçatı.

2 Selçuk, Ephesus, and Şirince. Selçuk is the town nearest to the archaeological ruins at Ephesus and a charmer; it's also well worth the extra 15-minute drive to see the hill village of Şirince.

3 Kuşadası and Environs. These days, Kuşadası's claim to fame is as a cruise port, with passengers disembarking for day trips to Ephesus; unless you like bland and overdeveloped ports, give it a miss. Within driving distance, however, are several sites worth visiting: the ancient Roman city of Aphrodisias, the layered limestone-travertine terraces and hot springs of Pamukkale, and the ruins of Didyma, Miletus, and Priene are worthwhile stops as you work your way south toward Bodrum.

4 Bodrum Peninsula. Throbbing resort life has descended upon the coves and bays of this stylish peninsula on the southern Aegean coast over the years, but each town still has its own charms: some have excellent water sports, some are great for relaxation, and others are all about the nightlife.

GETTING ORIENTED

In addition to gorgeous white-sand and pebble beaches, crystal clear waters, and a variety of water sports and nightlife, the central and southeast Aegean regions of Turkey have some of the most captivating historical sites, including the ruins of Ephesus, Aphrodisias, and the travertine cliffs of Pamukkale. You'll never lack for delicious local food; the soil yields bumper crops of figs, peaches, olives, vegetables, and citrus fruits.

Fishing boat on the Aegean Sea

St. John's Basilica, Selçuk

Updated by
August Siena
Thomas

The Aegean is one of Turkey's most visited and most developed regions, for good reason: the area is home to some of Turkey's most captivating treasures, from gorgeous white-sand beaches to the ancient ruins of Ephesus.

The Roman city of Ephesus is the big draw for sightseers, and rightfully so. Bodrum and its surrounding beach towns attract sun seekers from around the world and spoil them with sophisticated hotels, a buzzing nightlife scene, and remarkably unspoiled historic sites. Even İzmir, Turkey's third-largest city and no stranger to concrete sprawl, will surprise travelers with a nice collection of museums, bustling bazaars, and lively seaside promenades. Then there are the many places in between these major stops: charming hill towns like Şirince; the otherworldly white cliffs and thermal springs at Pamukkale; the seaside charms of sleepy Gümüşlük village, near snazzy Bodrum; the ancient cities of Priene, Miletus, Didyma, and Laodicea; and long, sandy beaches at Altinkum and elsewhere along the coast.

PLANNING

WHEN TO GO

July and August are the high season, and Ephesus gets lots of tourists, especially those coming in from the cruise ship port at Ku adası. In June and September you'll have the beaches pretty much to yourself, though the water is cooler. If you want to visit the historical sights in mild weather, plan your trip between October and May—traveling at this time also guarantees fewer crowds and more affordable accommodations. The winter months can be rainy, but if you don't mind a chill in the air, it's an off-season treat to stroll through windy, deserted ancient monuments, then duck into a toasty kebab restaurant for lunch. Some hotels and restaurants close for the winter, but almost all sites and museums stay open.

PLANNING YOUR TIME

If you have extremely limited time, you could fly to İzmir and overnight in Şirince or Selçuk, then visit Ephesus and other nearby attractions in one day, leaving again the next morning. With a little more time, you could spend several hours visiting Aphrodisias on the way to Pamukkale, make a relatively quick visit there, overnight in Pamukkale town, then fly out early the next morning from Denizli. To explore the region in depth, allow about 10 days, working your way south from İzmir to Bodrum, stopping at sights and beaches along the way.

GETTING HERE AND AROUND

AIR TRAVEL

The quickest way to get to the Central and Southern Aegean coast is by plane. Daily flights connect Istanbul with airports in İzmir and Bodrum. Depending on the season, there are direct flights to İzmir and Bodrum from Ankara, Adana, and Antalya as well.

Contacts Bodrum Airport Taksi (Milas-Bodrum Airport) ⊠ *Bodrum, Turkey* ☎ *0252/523–0024* ⊕ *www.bodrumairporttaxi.com.* **Bodrum Tour** ⊠ *Bodrum, Turkey* ☎ *252/524–5050* ⊕ *www.bodrumtour.com.* **Havalimanı Taksi (İzmir airport taxi)** ☎ *232/274–2075.* **Havaş** ☎ *252/523–0040 Bodrum, 212/444–0487 toll free (from Turkish phones), 232/274–2276 İzmir* ⊕ *www.havas.net.* **Proper Car Rental & Airport Transfers** ☎ *252/316–9540* ⊕ *www.propercar.com/bodrum-airport-transfer.htm.*

BUS TRAVEL

A number of bus lines serve the Aegean coast—Varan, Ulusoy, and Kamil Koç are the bigger ones, with a range of perks such as air-conditioning, free snacks, and reserved seats. However, bus travel is not always time efficient, and can be tiring, especially with kids. Websites have online booking in English, but telephone reservations are in Turkish only. The ride from Istanbul to İzmir takes around 9 hours, and from Istanbul to Bodrum about 12. There are bus lines linking İzmir, Selçuk, Kuşadası, Didyma, and Bodrum, too. Typical travel times are: İzmir to Bodrum, 3½ hours; İzmir to Çeşme, 1 hour; İzmir to Selçuk, 1½ hours; İzmir to Kuşadası, 1¼ hours; and Çeşme to Bodrum, 4½ hours.

Contacts Kamil Koç ☎ *0212/444–0562 reservations; press 1 to buy tickets* ⊕ *www.kamilkoc.com.tr.***Ulusoy** ☎ *212/444–1888 reservations; press 1 to buy tickets* ⊕ *www.ulusoy.com.tr.* **Varan** ☎ *212/444–8999 reservations; press 1 to buy tickets* ⊕ *www.varan.com.tr.*

CAR TRAVEL

A car will give you more freedom to explore this region, especially off the beaten path. Major roads and modern highways are in good condition and clearly marked, so driving from İzmir to Ephesus (in Selçuk) is quite easy; navigating the small winding roads around the towns of the Bodrum Peninsula can be tricky, so make sure you have a good local map (not just a smartphone). Portions of the highway that run along the Aegean coast are quite beautiful, especially as you approach Çeşme and Bodrum. For an idea of distances: İzmir to Ephesus, 79 km (49 miles); İzmir to Çeşme, 85 km (53 miles); İzmir to Selçuk, 46 km (29 miles); İzmir to Kuşadası, 100 km (62 miles); İzmir to Bodrum, 243 km (155 miles); and Ephesus to Bodrum, 172 km (107 miles).

TAXI AND DOLMUŞ TRAVEL

In resort towns like Çeşme, Bodrum, and Kuşadası, taxis have day and night rates: from midnight until 6 am, prices are substantially higher, but there is no charge for luggage. You can hail a cab on the street, or go to a taxi stand (usually the most reliable choice). There are flat rates for traveling between towns, but bargaining is appropriate. Traveling by *dolmuşes* (shared minibuses) is a more economical way to travel in and around the resort towns. To get dropped off along the driver's route, use the phrase *"inecek var,"* (Ee-neh-jeck var), which means "I want to get off." Be sure to speak loudly and clearly—drop one syllable by accident and you'll find yourself announcing, "inek var," which is Turkish for "there is a cow!"

Contacts Alsancak Camii Taksi ✉ *Alsancak, İzmir, Turkey* ☎ *252/422–6754.* **Park Taksi** ✉ *Konak, İzmir, Turkey* ☎ *0232/445–6618.*

RESTAURANTS

Dining out along the Aegean coast is a pleasure, especially if you enjoy seafood and fresh produce. There are countless seafood restaurants at all price ranges. A typical meal includes an assortment of hot and cold *mezes* (appetizers), a mixed salad, and the catch of the day, capped off with a Turkish dessert. To make it authentic, accompany your meal with *rakı* (a spirit similar in taste to oúzo). Some of the more common fish you'll find along the Aegean coast are *levrek* (sea bass), *çipura* (sea bream), *barbunya* (red mullet), and *lahos* (grouper), as well as tasty smaller fish like sardalya (sardines). Of course, there are plenty of meat and kebab restaurants around, too, if that's what you're craving.

For dessert, try local *dondurma* (Turkish ice cream, often thickened with orchid root), as well as milk puddings and baklava.It's often better to avoid hotel restaurants at lunch and dinner—you can frequently find better and less expensive food a short walk away—but luxury and boutique hotels are an exception as they are often firm favorites on the local restaurant scene.And don't forget street snacks! In season, you can grab fat local Smyrna figs, a cup of icy, dark berry *şerbet* (think of it as Ottoman Gatorade), or a sesame-studded feta-and-tomato sandwich, each for less than a dollar in central İzmir. *Simit,* the classic Turkish bagel-like street snack, is called *gevrek* in the İzmir region

Prices in the reviews are the average cost of a main course or if dinner is not served, at lunch.

⇨ *For more about the fish you'll find on the menu in Turkey, see the "Seafood on the Turkish Coast" food spotlight in Chapter 5.*

HOTELS

Hotels along the Aegean coast range from international-standard luxury properties and city-center corporate options to artsy or historic boutique hotels, and from rather stark lodgings for local business travelers to family-run bed-and-breakfasts or *pansiyons* (guesthouses). Almost everywhere offers free Wi-Fi and air conditioning (but check before booking), and most include breakfast in the price—a basic spread usually consisting of cucumbers and tomatoes, tea, instant coffee, eggs, feta cheese, bread with jam and butter, and watermelon in summer. The Bodrum and Çeşme peninsulas are infamous for A-list hotel prices to match their swanky clientele, with world-class resorts frequented by international glitterati, especially around Bodrum. İzmir has luxury options, too, mostly a bit more sedate. If you don't care about certain amenities (pool, spa, interior design), decent and reasonably central budget options are almost always available, even in the fanciest destinations.

Lodging in small towns like Selçuk and Gümüşlük tends to be less expensive, and often has more local flavor. To get the best deal, check prices on the hotel's website or a third-party booking site, then call the hotel in advance to see if they'll quote you a better rate. Hotels listed here are generally honest, helpful, and hospitable, and many will gladly offer advice on visiting local sites. Always ensure that a hotel's location suits your requirements: central for walkable sightseeing or remote for pure relaxation. If you're arriving by public transportation, ask in advance how best to travel from the bus station to the hotel. You'll need your passport to check in, so if you think a daytrip might turn into an overnight stay, take it along.

Prices in the reviews are the lowest cost of a standard double room in high season. For expanded reviews, visit Fodors.com.

BLUE CRUISES

Blue Cruises started in the 1970s as inexpensive boat tours catering to Turkish intellectuals, and they're still an enjoyable and relaxing way to explore the secluded coves of the Aegean coastline. Of course, nothing is inexpensive anymore, and there are plenty of luxury options. A typical Blue Voyage cruise lasts about seven days, but can be shorter or longer—there's not much to do other than reading, swimming, and relaxing, so many find that three or four days is optimal. April through October is the best time for a cruise; prices vary according to the month, the type of boat, and whether you opt for full board. You can arrange your trip before you leave home, or when you get to the docks. On the Aegean coast, Bodrum marina is the best place to hire a boat, with the most options. ⇨ *See the "Blue Cruising" box in Chapter 5 for more information.*

Contacts Era Yachting ☎ 252/316–2310 ⊕ www.erayachting.com. . **Motif Yachting** ☎ 252/316–2309 ⊕ www.motifyachting.com. **Neyzen Tours** ☎ 252/316–7204 ⊕ www.neyzen.com.tr.

VISITOR INFORMATION

Visitor Information offices are generally open daily between 8:30–12:30 and 1:30–5. ⇨ *See city listings below for contact information.*

İZMIR AND ÇEŞME

İzmir, with its large, modern airport and national and international flight connections, is a major jumping-off point for visits to the South Aegean, and many make it a base for visits to Ephesus. Don't rush through İzmir, though; the city has some fascinating sights and a vibrant cosmopolitan edge. It has a less-than-lovely concrete hinterland, but a lovely waterfront, interesting history, and an irresistibly bustling bazaar.

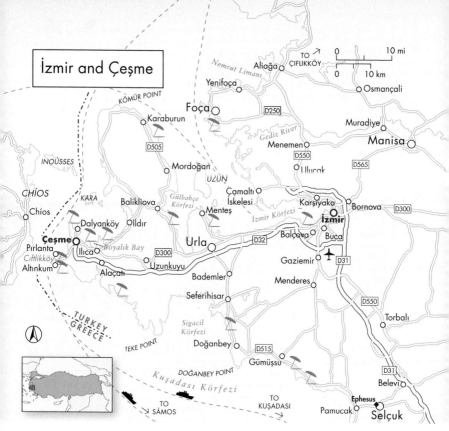

Çeşme, at the westernmost end of the peninsula, is a coastal resort town with a shoreline of sandy beaches, crystal clear waters, several state-of-the-art marinas, and a dining and nightlife scene that competes with the major metropolitan cities in Turkey. Çeşme has long been popular with Turkish vacationers but somewhat off the foreign travel route, though this might change with a six-lane highway that connects Çeşme with İzmir in only about 45 minutes.

İZMİR

565 km (351 miles) south of Istanbul.

At first glance, Turkey's third-largest city (formerly known as Smyrna) may seem modern and harsh—even the beautiful setting, between the Gulf of İzmir and the mountains, doesn't soften some of the starkness of industrial districts and sprawling concrete suburbs. Spend a few days here, though, either on your way to other parts of the South Aegean, or as a base for visiting Ephesus and the surrounding area, and you'll find an extremely pleasant, progressive city with 7,000 years of history, and much to occupy the modern traveler. The key is to make a beeline for the waterfront. An attractively refurbished promenade known as the Kordon follows the Gulf of Smyrna for almost 3 km (2 miles), chocka-block with cafés and restaurants its entire length. A short walk inland, a refreshing wealth of landmarks include the Kemeraltı outdoor bazaar and a collection of fine museums, while the ancient Kadifekale fortress crowns a hill of the same name.

The waterside Konak district is at the heart of İzmir life, with shops, restaurants, and clubs that are continually moving farther afield along the waterfront into the narrow lanes of the old Alsancak and Pasaport neighborhoods. You can take in the scene on a walk along Pasaport pier, past arestored customs house originally built by Gustave Eiffel or on the Asansör (elevator), an early-20th-century relic-turned-gourmet-restaurant (also called Asansör) that connects the slopes of Karataş, a Jewish enclave that is one more piece of this cosmopolitan city that will delight you with its richness. The relaxed, largely residential neighborhood of Karşıyaka is a delightful ferry ride across the harbor.

GETTING AROUND
While in İzmir, you can travel around by bus (you can buy tickets on board; credit cards not accepted), the expanding metro system, *dolmuş*, or taxi. From the İzmir airport, the most comfortable and economical way to get downtown is via Havaş shuttle bus (about 10 TL one way). If you're arriving by intercity bus at the main İzmir bus station (otogar), most major bus companies offer a free shuttle service to the city center.

ESSENTIALS
Taxi Information26 Ağustos Taksi ⊠ *Alsancak, İzmir* ☏ *232/422–1958.*
Üçkuyular Terminal Taksi ⊠ *İzmir* ☏ *232/278–1538.*

TOURS
If time is tight, you can tour Ephesus, Bergama, and other major archaeological sites from İzmir, though it's not the ideal base for these excursions.

Ephesus Tours. This company is based in Kuşadası but also offers tours of Ephesus (day tour about TL 215) starting from İzmir. ⊠ *İzmir* ☏ *0256/613–0500* ⊕ *www.ephesustours.com.* **Tourist Information Office** ⊠ *Next to the Chamber of Commerce (Ticaret Odası), 1344 Sok. 2, Pasaport, İzmir* ☏ *232/483–8086* ☉ *Weekdays 8:30–5:30.*

EXPLORING
TOP ATTRACTIONS
Fodor's Choice ★ **Kemeraltı.** Konak Meydanı marks the start of this energetic marketplace that spills into a maze of tiny streets, filled with shops and covered stalls. Wide, unbeautiful Anafartalar Caddesi runs around the outside of the bazaar, and there are lots of cafés and restaurants along Fevzipaşa Bulvarı. You'll have more fun exploring the smaller side streets, where you'll find tiny districts dedicated to musical instruments, leather, costume jewelry, and accessories, among other things. Begin at a restored Ottoman *kervansaray,* the **Kızlarağası Hanı,** completed around 1745 (*kızlarağası* translates as "lord of the girls" and was the title of the powerful eunuch in charge of the palace harem). It houses many vaulted shops selling quality Turkish goods, such as jewelry, miniatures, and prayer rugs for the Hajj pilgrimage, as well as cheesy souvenirs. The nearby, late 16th-century **Hisar Mosque** (one of the largest and oldest in İzmir) is worth a peek, and surrounded by tasty kebab joints. Go farther into Kemeraltı and you'll wind up at the **Kestane Pazarı** (Chestnut

CLOSE UP

History of İzmir

Turkey's third-largest city, with a population of approximately 3.4 million, was called Smyrna until the founding of the Republic of Turkey in 1923. A vital trading port, though often ravaged by wars and earthquakes, the city had its share of glory, too. Homer, the legendary Greek poet, is said by some to have been born in Old Smyrna sometime around 850 BC. Alexander the Great ousted the Persians and rebuilt the city at the foothills of what is today called Kadifekale in 333 BC.

İzmir fell into assorted hands after the Romans. It was an important religious center during the Byzantine Empire and was a battlefield during the Crusades, passing back and forth between Muslim and Christian powers. Destroyed and restored successively by the Byzantines and the Seljuks, Smyrna was held by the Knights of Rhodes in 1402 when the Mongol raider Tamerlane came along, sacked the city yet again, and slaughtered the inhabitants. The city came under the Ottoman Empire during the reign of Sultan Mehmet I Çelebi in 1426. Toward the end of the 15th century, Jews driven from Spain settled in Smyrna, creating a lasting Sephardic community. By the 18th and 19th

centuries, Smyrna had become a successful, sophisticated commercial port with an international flavor and a sizable number of Italians, Greeks, Armenians, British, and French. This era came to an end with World War I, when Ottoman Turkey allied itself with Germany. In 1918 the Greek army, encouraged by the British and French, landed at the harbor and claimed the city. The occupation lasted until 1922, when Turkish troops under Mustafa Kemal Atatürk (the founder of the Turkish Republic) defeated the Greek forces and forced them to evacuate the city. On September 9, 1922, Atatürk made a triumphant entry into the port. The joy was short-lived—shortly thereafter a fire destroyed three-fourths of the city. Fanned by the wind, it burned wooden houses like matches and hidden stores of munitions exploded.

The city was quickly rebuilt to a modern urban plan prepared by brothers Rene and Raymond Danger, French urban designers, and was renamed İzmir. Like its name, much of the city center dates from the 1920s, with wide boulevards lined with palm trees, office buildings, and apartment houses painted in bright white or soft pastels.

Bazaar), a smaller, outdoor version of Istanbul's Spice Bazaar, where you'll find a good selection of spices, fruits, tea, coffee, fabric, and a vast number of confectioners. ⚠ The bazaar can be crowded, so mind your wallet. If you're a lone female traveler, Kemeraltı should be fine, but it's probably not the best place to try out that new pink miniskirt. ✉ *Konak, İzmir.*

NEED A BREAK?

Ömer Usta Kahveci. Making your way through Kemeraltı can be exhausting. Stop by Ömer Usta Kahveci, near the back entrance of the Hisar Cami, for a shot of Turkish coffee brewed in the cup (beware the scalding hot cups!), or exemplary homemade lemonade. The atmosphere is pleasant and lively, with low, carpeted tables and a local crowd. If you're traveling in

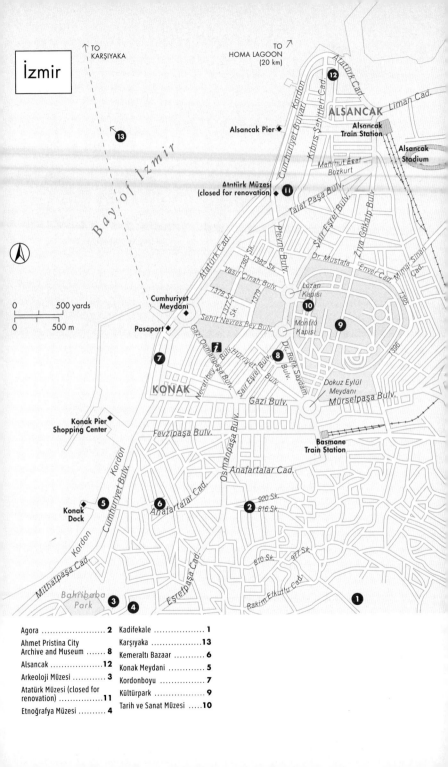

İzmir

↑ TO
KARŞIYAKA

TO ↗
HOMA LAGOON
(20 km)

Bay of İzmir

ALSANCAK

Alsancak Pier ◆

Alsancak
Train Station

Alsancak
Stadium

Atatürk Müzesi
(closed for renovation) ◆ ⓫

Cumhuriyet
Meydanı

Pasaport ◆

⓭

Lozan
Kapısı

⓰

Montrö
Kapısı

❽

KONAK

❼

Konak Pier
Shopping Center

Gazi Bulv.

Dokuz Eylül
Meydanı

Mürselpaşa Bulv.

Fevzipaşa Bulv.

Basmane
Train Station

Anafartalar Cad.

Konak
Dock

❺

❻

❷ 920 Sk.
816 Sk.

Bahribaba
Park

❸

❹

810 Sk.   977 Sk.

❶

0   500 yards
0   500 m

Agora 2	Kadifekale 1
Ahmet Pristina City Archive and Museum 8	Karşıyaka 13
	Kemeraltı Bazaar 6
Alsancak 12	Konak Meydanı 5
Arkeoloji Müzesi 3	Kordonboyu 7
Atatürk Müzesi (closed for renovation) 11	Kültürpark 9
Etnoğrafya Müzesi 4	Tarih ve Sanat Müzesi 10

Take a horse-drawn carriage ride along İzmir's Kordon, the waterfront promenade. —photo by eerkun, Fodors. com member

summer, there are plenty of shaded areas to keep you cool. ⊠ *905 Sok. 15, İzmir* ☎ *232/425–4706.*

Konak Meydanı (*Konak Square*). At the water's edge, this vast space is one of the city's two main squares (the other, Cumhuriyet Meydanı, or Republic Square, is to the north along Atatürk Caddesi), and is a good place to pick up a cheap street snack from roving vendors. The **Saat Kulesi** (clock tower), the city's icon, stands out at the center of the plaza, with its ornate, late-Ottoman design. The tower was built in 1901, in honor of Sultan Abdulhamid's 25th year on the imperial throne, and the clock itself was sent as a gift from Kaiser Wilhelm II. The small, 18th-century single-domed **Yalı Mosque** (sometimes known as Konak Mosque), set back from the clock tower, is decorated with colorful tiles and was originally built by Mehmet Paşa's daughter, Ayşe. Just to the north is ⇨ *Konak Pier.* ⊠ *İzmir.*

Konak Pier. On the waterfront an easy stroll north from Konak Meydanı (turn right if you're facing the water), the 19th-century pier is now an updated shopping mall with several restaurants, a movie theater and bookstore with some English-language options, and fabulous views. It was originally designed as a customs house by the famous French architect Gustave Eiffel. ⊠ *Waterfront, İzmir.*

FAMILY
Fodor's Choice
★
Kordon. The delightful waterfront promenade is the most fashionable section of town and is perfect for a summer stroll; many locals use the sea breeze to fly kites. It starts at the museum complex in Bahribaba Parkı, in Alsancak, and stretches north along the busy harbor, past Konak Meydanı. Along the grassy, waterfront strip are several excellent

seafood restaurants and cafés, all with outdoor seating overlooking the Aegean Sea. It's fun to tour the area by *fayton* (horse-drawn carriage); they are stationed in the Cumhuriyet Meydanı, steps from the beginning of Kordon (be sure to agree a fair price in advance). ⊠ *İzmir.*

WORTH NOTING

The Agora. Near the foot of Kadifekale Hill, just off 920 Sokak (920 Street), this was the Roman city's market. The present site is a large, dusty open space surrounded by ancient columns and brick foundations, with decent signage in English. Alas, a substantial part has been closed off for excavations, though there are still some ruins to satisfy classical history buffs, and an interesting collection of Ottoman gravestones heaped near the entrance. (You can also walk down the hill to the Agora from Kadifekale, though it's not a very picturesque stroll.) If you want gobsmacking ancient grandeur, head for Ephesus, but if you're in İzmir, the Agora makes for an interesting excursion. ■ TIP→ Ask for a brochure at the entrance. ⊠ *Off E refpa a Cad., 920 Sok., İzmir* ☎ *5 TL* ⊗ *Daily 9–6:30 in summer; daily 8–5 in winter (changeover dates vary).*

Ahmet Piristina City Archive and Museum. Just south of the Kültür Parkı (Culture Park), the archive and museum chronicles 7,000 years of the city's history through colorful posters with informative descriptions in English and Turkish. The museum doubles as a library dedicated to İzmir's history, and is located in the city's old fire station, with a special section dedicated to the history of İzmir's multiple fires and its fire brigade. ⊠ *Şair Eşref Bul. 1/A, İzmir* ☎ *232/441–6178* ⊕ *www.apikam.org.tr* ☎ *Free* ⊗ *Mon.–Sat. 8:30–5:30 in summer; Mon.–Sat. 8–5 in winter (dates vary).*

Alsancak. Stretching inland from the breezy Kordon waterfront, the trendy, upscale neighborhood now known as Alsancak ("red banner", a reference to the Turkish flag) was called Punta in the Ottoman era, when many Christians and Jews lived here. Look closely, and you'll notice there are still a number of synagogues and churches in the area. Though Alsancak is mostly slick and modern, pretty two- and three-story Levantine houses with bay windows are tucked away along some of the back streets, which perk up at night with an influx of young İzmirians drawn to the quaint cafés, bars, and restaurants. ⊠ *İzmir.*

Arkeoloji Müzesi (*Archaeology Museum*). Look over the railing in the lobby, down at a spectacular classical mosaic of lions, peacocks, and other brightly colored creatures, then wander down haunting (but pitiably lit) halls of statuary, which include a front-row Hellenistic theater seat carved with griffins, a Hellenistic bronze of a running athlete, and evocative Roman faces. Upstairs you'll find unusual painted ceramic sarcophagi (including the heart-breaking skeleton of a Byzantine new born), and a modest collection of jewelry and coins—and there's a neat view of the city. An English-language audioguide is included in the price of admission, and is highly recommended. ⊠ *Cumhuriyet Bul., Bahribaba Parkı, İzmir* ☎ *232/489–0796* ☎ *8 TL* ⊗ *Tues.–Sun. 8:30–5:30.*

Etnoğrafya Müzesi (*Ethnography Museum*). This delightfully hokey museum, across the street from the Archaeology Museum, focuses on folk art and daily life. The collection includes everything from a reconstructed Ottoman bridal chamber (the mannequin groom looks like he's had second thoughts) to camel-wrestling gear, 19th-century embroidery, and a reconstruction of an old İzmir pharmacy. ■ TIP→ **Because of a major roadworks project, it's trickier than usual to find your way from the waterfront up the hill to the museums.** If you need directions, ask, *Arkeologi Müzesi nerede?* ("Where's the Archaeology Museum?")—it's easier to say in Turkish and is just across the street. ⊠ *Cumhuriyet Bul., Bahribaba Parkı, Konak, İzmir* ☎ *232/489–0796* 🖃 *Free* ☉ *Tues.–Sun. 8:30–6:30.*

Kadifekale (*Velvet Fortress*). Climb the windy, restored ramparts of the Kadifekale (Turkish for "velvet castle"), built soon after Alexander the Great swept through Smyrna, for sweeping views of the city and its harbor. Perched on Mount Pagos, the castle was frequently rebuilt after various mishaps, and was enlarged and strengthened by successive conquerors. The structure looks like a childhood fantasy of a medieval castle, with solid stone blocks (some dating from Alexander's day), Byzantine cisterns, and Ottoman buttresses jutting out to support the walls. ⚠ **Locals will warn solo visitors (especially women) not to visit the Kadifekale alone for fear of being hassled or harassed, particularly by people who inhabit the shanty-like area around the site. Consider asking a taxi to wait for you.** ⊠ *İzmir.*

Karşıyaka. On a hot summer day, the 20-minute ferry ride from Konak to Karşıyaka is a great way to cool off, and on arrival, you can walk along the commercial strip, İzmir's version of Istanbul's İstiklâl Caddesi. Karşıyaka, which means the "opposite side/shore" in Turkish, is one of several purported birthplaces of the poet Homer, and was the residence of one of Turkey's most famous contemporary poets, Attila Ilhan. For years, it was a tranquil summer resort for İzmir's upperclass, but the area has been expanded and developed to accommodate İzmir's growing population. Try some *lokma* (sweet doughnut holes), for which the district is famous, or delicious hot *pide* (a Turkish cross between a pizza and a calzone, with cheese, meat, and/or vegetables). Depending on where you are on the Kordon, you can catch the ferry (about 4 TL) from the pier in Konak or Pasaport. ⊠ *İzmir.*

Kültür Parkı. İzmir's vast, central park has approximately 8,000 trees to stroll under, as well as 14 exhibition halls, an open-air theater, a culture center, the History and Arts Museum, a sports arena, a swimming pool, tennis courts, and more. ⊠ *İzmir.*

Tarih ve Sanat Müzesi (*History and Art Museum*). On the grounds of Kültür Parkı, this museum compound is made up of three buildings, which showcase statuary, ancient ceramic finds. The museum is rarely crowded, and the the Hellenistic and Roman-era statues are delightfully evocative—look out for the tiny statue of a hermaphrodite, as well as monumental carved gods and goddesses recovered from Izmir's Agora and nearby sites. With better lighting than the Archaeology Museum, if you're picking just one museum in Izmir to see with kids, this museum's manageable size, interesting contents, and park location make it a strong contender. ⊠ *East of Lozan and Montrö squares, Kültür Parkı, İzmir* ☎ *232/445–6818* 🖃 *3 TL* ☉ *Tues.–Sun. 8:30–6:30*

WHERE TO EAT

Many of İzmir's most delightful restaurants crowd the Kordon waterfront; others are tucked away on back streets.

$$ ✕ **100% Cafe & Restaurant.** Enthusiastically professing 100% commitment to the quality of the food and service, this popular spot (the name is "Yüzdeyüz" in Turkish) is a favorite for upscale İzmirian business and social meals. It perches right at the far tip of the Konak pier shopping area, with spectacular views over the harbor from the elegantly decorated indoor and outdoor dining areas. The international menu includes a bit of everything, from pizza and pasta to kebabs and even rather pricey sushi, plus superb Turkish tea. Reservations are recommended at peak hours. $ *Average main: 20 TL* ⊠ *Konak Pier AVM, off Attaturk Cad., Konak, İzmir* ☎ *232/441–5593* ⊕ *www.yuzdeyuz.info.*

INTERNATIONAL
FAMILY

$ ✕ **Ankara Lokantası Osman Usta.** If you're catching a train at Basmane station, carefully cross the perilous intersection for hearty Turkish home cooking from Ramazan Usta, who's been serving up roast chicken, stuffed peppers with yogurt, fried eggplant, and other homey favorites at this no-frills eatery for more than 30 years. The menu changes daily, and you can point to what looks best at the counter. $ *Average main: 10 TL* ⊠ *Akıncı Mh., Basmane, Konak, İzmir* ☎ *232/445–3607.*

TURKISH

$$ ✕ **Balıkçı Hasan.** There are many popular seafood restaurants along the Kordon waterfront in Alsancak but this one, with indoor and outdoor seating areas, is especially busy. Originally located on the Çeşme peninsula, Balıkçı Hasan has brought its excellent menu to the city. It features a good selection of appetizers, including the decadent *sütlü karides* (shrimp sautéed in butter, then topped with béchamel and mozzarella), as well as the usual seasonal seafood choices. The restaurant has a more relaxed feel than many on the Kordon dining scene. ■TIP→ Balıkçı Hasan means "Hasan the fisherman", and the sign simply shows a picture of a fish (balık), followed by "çı Hasan." $ *Average main: 25 TL* ⊠ *Atatürk Cad. 186/A Kordon, Alsancak* ☎ *232/464–1354* ⊕ *www.balikcihasan.com.tr.*

SEAFOOD

$$ ✕ **Balık Pişiricisi Veli Usta.** On the waterfront in the popular Kordonboyu area, this seafood restaurant has been open since 1970 and is especially popular with families. The specialty of the house is fillet of sole, and the atmosphere is friendly and fun. There is outside seating, as well as indoor tables. This is the most pleasant of several branches around the city. $ *Average main: 25 TL* ⊠ *Atatürk Cad. 212A, İzmir* ☎ *232/464–2705* ⊕ *www.izmirbalikpisirici.com.*

SEAFOOD

$ ✕ **Can Döner.** Not far from the clock tower at the entrance of Kemeraltı, this small local favorite has served traditional *Iskender döner* from the city of Bursa since 1981. The döner is sliced thin and topped with melted butter and tomato sauce. A glass of homemade *ayran* (plain yogurt drink) is the traditional accompaniment to the meal. Alcohol is not served. Come for lunch or an early dinner, as they're only open until the meat runs out, usually around 6:30 pm. $ *Average main: 15 TL* ⊠ *Milli Kütüphane Cad. 9, İzmir* ☎ *232/484–1313* ⊕ *www.candoner.com* ⊙ *Closed Sun.*

TURKISH

$$ ✕ **Deniz.** Deniz means "sea" in Turkish, an appropriate name for this popular, pricey seafood eatery on the waterfront in Kordonboyu, whose

SEAFOOD

tables spill out the ground floor of the İzmir Palas Hotel. It's buzzing with local notables, travelers, and a swanky business crowd, who come to splurge on exceptional fish and *mezes*, including samphire with garlicky yogurt. And it can easily turn into a splurge in terms of price, depending on the number of courses chosen. Tourists also flock here to try the *sütlü balık*, a hot appetizer prepared with sea bass, grouper, or a similar fish, and béchamel sauce—order this heavy, slow-cooked dish when making a reservation or soon after arriving, or plump for the faster, equally good sea bass in creamy basil sauce. $ *Average main; 25 TL* ✉ *İzmir Palace Hotel, Atatürk Cad. 188/B, Alsancak, İzmir* ☎ *232/464–4499* ⊕ *www.denizrestaurant.com.tr.*

$$ ✕**Köşebaşı.** The Kordon waterfront outpost of this popular, upscale,
TURKISH　and now international Istanbul-based meat and kebab restaurant offers sizzling specialties from the cities of Adana and Tarsus in the Southern Anatolia region. The menu includes a tempting array of appetizers, such as mini *lahmacun* (thin Turkish-style pizza prepared with minced meat and spices), as well as excellent kebabs and meat dishes—all with a sea view. $ *Average main: 20 TL* ✉ *1. Kordon, Atatürk Cad. 174/B, Alsancak, İzmir* ☎ *232/463–5350* ⊕ *www.kosebasi.com.tr.*

$$ ✕**Mandolin.** Popular with families, young people, and "ladies who
INTERNATIONAL　lunch," this café is in the swanky Konak Pier shopping mall. It offers free Wi-Fi, a casual outdoor seating area with sweeping views of the bay, and an international menu with a variety of salads, meat dishes, pastas, quesadillas, and sweets, including cheesecake and a banana split. Cocktails are available, too, as well as the nonalcoholic "Mandolin Ayran," a unique and refreshing concoction of basil, mint, dill, lemon juice, and *ayran*, a Turkish yogurt drink. $ *Average main: 30 TL* ✉ *Konak Pier AVM, off Atatürk Cad., Konak, İzmir* ☎ *232/483–3902.*

$ ✕**Reyhan Patisserie.** With baked goods like strawberry cheesecake, intri-
CAFÉ　cate confections, house-made ice cream and chocolates, along with
FAMILY　Turkish classics like creamy rice pudding (*sütlaç*), this pastry shop has been popular for decades. This branch of the legendary patisserie, in the heart of trendy Alsancak, is also a sit-down café serving coffee and Turkish-style breakfast. $ *Average main: 10 TL* ✉ *Mustafa Bey Cad. 24, Alsancak, İzmir* ☎ *232/422–2802* ⊕ *www.reyhan.com.tr.*

$ ✕**Tarihi Kemeraltı Lokantası.** Established in 1939, this traditional Turkish
TURKISH　restaurant near the Kemeraltı Bazaar is the place for typical home-style
FAMILY　Turkish meals in modest surroundings. The menu changes, but usually includes a range of hearty stews, Turkish meatballs, and vegetable dishes. You can select your meal from the open display showcasing the specials of the day; prices are reasonable. It opens early for breakfast but closes at 8:30 in the evening. Alcohol is not served. $ *Average main: 15 TL* ✉ *Veysel Çıkmaz Kemeraltı, Anafartalar Cad. 47/A, Kemeraltı, İzmir* ☎ *232/425–5393* ⊕ *tarihikemeraltilokantasi.org.*

WHERE TO STAY

$$ ▦ **Key Hotel.** If James Bond came to İzmir, he'd stay here—the city's
HOTEL　sleekest, chicest hotel, where scrupulous attention to detail paired with
Fodor'sChoice　up-to-the-minute technology draws a grown-up crowd, from major
★　politicians to honeymooners. **Pros:** superlative service; excellent location on the Kordon, near Konak Square; slick amenities; excellent bar

and restaurant. **Cons:** very modern feel; small exercise area; not all rooms have sea views. $ *Rooms from: 300 TL* ⊠ *1 Mimar Kemalettin Cad., Konak, İzmir* ⊕ *www.keyhotel.com* ⊷ *31 rooms* ⦿ *Multiple meal plans.*

$$ ⊡ **Kilim Otel.** A central location on the fashionable Kordonboyu water-
HOTEL front, bright interiors, helpful staff, and harbor views from many rooms compensate for the lack of local color, and make this a comfy value alternative to much pricier options nearby. **Pros:** sea views; prime location; very good value; nice breakfast. **Cons:** street views in some rooms, no real on-site recreation options; some fixtures a bit dingy. $ *Rooms from: 190 TL* ⊠ *Atatürk Bul., Kazim Dirik Cad. 1, Alsancak, İzmir* ☎ *232/484–5340* ⊕ *www.kilimotel.com.tr* ⊷ *75 rooms* ⦿ *Breakfast.*

$$ ⊡ **Karaca.** In an appealing location, this good-value, central option
HOTEL caters to a mostly business and family clientele—and includes free tickets to the next-door movie theater. **Pros:** good value; five minutes from the Kordonboyu waterfront on a palm-lined street; more intimate than many luxury hotels. **Cons:** rooms could use an update; bland restaurant with oblivious waitstaff; small spa area. $ *Rooms from: 196 TL* ⊠ *Necatibey Bulvarı 1379 Sok. 55, Alsancak, İzmir* ☎ *232/489–1940* ⊕ *www.otelkaraca.com.tr* ⊷ *73 rooms* ⦿ *Breakfast.*

$$$ ⊡ **Mövenpick Hotel İzmir.** Steps from the Kordonboyu promenade, this
HOTEL posh outpost of the Swiss hotel chain is in an excellent location and some rooms have striking views of İzmir Bay. **Pros:** reasonably priced for its excellent location; a short walk to many fine-dining options; indoor pool; the famous Mövenpick ice cream available in the lobby. **Cons:** small health and fitness center; central air can make rooms stuffy in summer. $ *Rooms from: 360 TL* ⊠ *Cumhuriyet Bul. 138, Pasaport, Alsancak, İzmir* ☎ *232/488–1480* ⊕ *www.moevenpick-hotels.com* ⊷ *185 rooms* ⦿ *Breakfast.*

$$ ⊡ **Otel İzmir Palas.** The fancier older sister of the Kilim Otel farther
HOTEL down the Kordon waterfront, this recently revamped hotel has full sea views from half the relaxing, attractive rooms. ⇨ **Pros:** many rooms have sea views; nice buffet breakfast with a view; upscale restaurant; great location. **Cons:** rather nondescript rooms; some rooms are small; no pool. $ *Rooms from: 230 TL* ⊠ *Atatürk Cad., Vasıf Çınar Bul. 2, Alsancak, İzmir* ☎ *232/465–0030* ⊕ *www.izmirpalas.com.tr* ⊷ *148 rooms* ⦿ *Breakfast.*

$$$ ⊡ **Swissôtel Grand Efes İzmir.** An İzmir institution since the '60s, now
HOTEL under clockwork Swiss management, this swish business hotel is a
FAMILY serene place to recharge, with most rooms overlooking the Aegean or the lush gardens and outdoor pool. **Pros:** state-of-the-art spa and wellness center; centrally located steps from the Kordonboyu waterfront promenade; kid-friendly resort feel. **Cons:** in its own world apart from the neighborhood; often hosts large trade conventions; pricey restaurants. $ *Rooms from: 492 TL* ⊠ *Gaziosmanpaşa Bul. 1, Alsancak, İzmir* ☎ *232/414–0000* ⊕ *www.swissotel.com/hotels/izmir* ⊷ *402 rooms, 55 suites* ⦿ *Multiple meal plans.*

$$ ⊡ **Wyndham İzmir Özdilek.** Off the beaten path in the neighborhood of
HOTEL Balçova, 23 km (14 miles) from the airport, this posh property overlooks İzmir Bay. **Pros:** free shuttle service to/from airport and the center

of the city; state-of-the-art thermal spa and health center; pet-friendly; two in-house restaurants. **Cons:** far from the city center. $ *Rooms from: 300 TL* ✉ *Inciraltı Cad. 67, Balçova, İzmir* ☎ *232/292–1300* ⊕ *www. wyndhamizmir.com* ⟿ *219 rooms* ⦿ *Breakfast.*

NIGHTLIFE AND THE ARTS
NIGHTLIFE
The Alsancak neighborhood has a lively nightlife scene with an assortment of bars, especially along Gazi Kadınlar Sokaği, which is a great street to check out in general for its cafés and attractive Levantine homes.

Café del Mundo. Decorated with colorful souvenirs of the owners' global wanderings, this hip "travelers' café" and bar in Alsancak has made a name for itself with a keenly priced international menu (from Turkish breakfast to pad thai to steak with oyster sauce) and a merry round of theme nights, quiz nights, and happy hours, with a wide range of cocktails on offer. ✉ *Kibris Sehitleri Cad. 13, Muzaffer Izgü Sok., Alsancak, İzmir* ☎ *232/421–0584* ⊕ *www.delmundocafe.com.*

Eko Pub. By day a restaurant, open from 7 am, and by night a pub, open until 2 am, that's popular with expats and a mixed crowd of buisinesspeople and students. ✉ *Plevne Bul. 1, Alsancak, İzmir* ☎ *232/421–4459.*

Mavi Bar. For rock music—sometimes live—this newly freshened-up bar is your best bet. It's open until 4 am. ✉ *2. Kordon, Cumhuriyet Bul. 206, Alsancak, İzmir* ☎ *232/463–0194.*

Sardunya Bar. A semi-alternative crowd hangs out at the main branch of this bar on one of Alsancak's popular streets, with live jazz and alternative music events, and an international menu at their family-friendly café. ✉ *Kıbrıs Şehitleri Cad. 1482 No. 11, İzmir* ☎ *232/464–4665* ⊕ *www.sardunyabar.com.*

THE ARTS
Kültür Parkı. For outdoor concerts of classical and Turkish music, check out the open-air theater here. ✉ *İzmir.*

State Opera and Ballet House. Ballet performances, classical music concerts and opera (generally in the original language) are staged here, and tickets can often be purchased at the theater on the day of the performance. ✉ *Milli Kütüphane Cad., İzmir* ☎ *232/484–6445* ⊕ *www. dobgm.gov.tr.*

SPORTS AND THE OUTDOORS
BIRD-WATCHING
FAMILY **Homa Dalyani** (*İzmir Kuş Cenneti or Homa Lagoon*). Also called *Kuş Cenneti* (Bird Heaven), this is a natural reserve on the Gediz Delta, on the north shore of İzmir Bay near Çamaltı. It's an excellent day trip out of the city. The delta's lagoons, mudflats, salt marshes, reed beds, and farmland provide diverse habitats to more than 230 species of birds, mammals, reptiles, and fish. Tours of the lagoon can be taken by car or on foot: all tours start at the visitor center and are free. Only a few staff members speak English. You'll need a car to get here, or you can hire a taxi for the trip; it's 18 km (11 miles) from Karşıyaka neighborhood in İzmir. ✉ *İzmir* ☎ *232/482–1218* ⊕ *www.izmirkuscenneti.gov.tr* ⊠ *Free.*

HIKING

The most popular region for hiking (and skiing) near İzmir is the 120-km (75-mile) stretch between the Gediz and Küçük Menderes rivers.

Trails on the slopes of **Mount Bozdağ,** 110 km (68 miles) from İzmir, are also a welcome refuge from the city's sometimes suffocating heat. At Gölcük, trails climb gentle hills that cradle a lake, which is ideal for a picnic. Several tour companies organize daily trips to the area from İzmir.

SHOPPING

For high-end, brand-name, and designer clothing, the Alsancak neighborhood has it all. Konak Pier shopping center is also full of glossy global brands, in addition to restaurants, a movie theater, and **Remzi Kitabevi,** a bookstore with English-language titles and maps. Head to Kemeraltı bazaar or Karşıyaka for local color and edible souvenirs.

Bostanlı pazar (*Bostali bazaar*). The open-air bazaar held on Wednesday, in the Bostanlı neighborhood of Karşıyaka, is known for its good-quality, inexpensive apparel: the earlier you go, the better the selection. ⊠ *Karşıyaka, İzmir.*

Dösim. Under the auspices of the Ministry of Culture and Tourism, the Dösim shops around the country sell top quality Turkish handicrafts, books, and souvenirs. Prices are moderate to expensive. ⊠ *Cumhuriyet Bul. 115, Alsancak, İzmir* ☎ *232/483–0789.*

ÇEŞME

85 km (53 miles) west of İzmir.

Known for its hot springs and beaches, Çeşme has always been a summer resort for İzmirians, but in recent years the gorgeous sands have been luring Istanbullus and an international crowd, too. Despite rapid and often unsightly development, the town retains its provincial charm, and it's still more off the beaten path than the resorts of the Bodrum Peninsula. The real lures, understandably, are the beaches that span 29 km (18 miles) of coastline.

Çeşme has a large marina, but for sandy beaches and crystal clear waters, head to one of the nearby seaside villages (frequent public transportation available by *dolmuş*). Ilıca, with its deluxe hotels, is closest and the most popular, with a long sandy beach. Dalyanköy is on the northern tip of the bay and is quite quiet and peaceful, known more for its fish restaurants than its swimming. The most beautiful beaches, Altınkum and Pırlanta, are in Çiftlikköy. Alaçatı, with its almost constant wind, is a windsurfer's paradise and is known for its restaurants and hotels. Boyalık Bay and Ayayorgi attract a hip crowd. The villages are close enough that you can move around by car or public transportation quite easily.

Public beaches are generally crowded and don't have amenities, so if you're planning more than a quick dip, you'll do well to spend 20 TL or so to secure a spot with chaise longues, umbrellas, towel service, and often a restaurant and bar. The swimming season starts in April and continues until mid-November—high season is July and August.

GETTING HERE AND AROUND

The villages are quite close together so getting around by taxi, *dolmuş,* or rental car is quite easy. Bus service is limited. From Çeşme proper, Alaçatı is 12 km (7½ miles), Dalyanköy is 4 km (2½ miles), Ilıca is 6 km (nearly 4 miles), and Çiftlikköy is 10 km (6 miles).

Çeşme Seyahat Bus Company provides the only bus service between İzmir and Çeşme. In summer, buses shuttle between Çeşme's main bus station (*otogar*) and İzmir's main bus terminal, or smaller Üçkuyular station, every 15 minutes, between 7 am and 8 pm. Reservations are highly recommended. The cost is around 15 TL per passenger.

For a quick hop to a Greek Island, head to Chios (or Sakız Adası, literally "gum mastic island," in Turkish), about a 45-minute boat ride away. Several ferry companies at the Çeşme docks offer excursions; fares are typically quoted in euros and are about €15 to €25 (40 to 70 TL) per person. Chios town has nice waterfront dining options; rent a car or join a tour to see the picturesque medieval villages where mastic is produced, and the island's UNESCO-listed Nea Moni monastery can be found.

ESSENTIALS

Bus Information Çeşme Seyahat Bus Company ✉ *Çeşme terminal, İzmir/ Üçkuyular bus station* ☎ *232/712–6499, 232/259–3415 bus station.*

EXPLORING

Alaçatı. Known for its windmills, trendy cafés, boutiques, and startlingly good restaurants, this pretty village lies 2 km (1 mile) south of Ilıca. On summer evenings, the main strip of Alaçatı bustles with hip crowds; to avoid the hubbub come in the afternoon, when the crowd is mostly locals and storeowners, although it can get very hot. Wander the back streets to see picturesque Greek houses and the Greek church-turned-mosque (*Pazaryeri Camii*), where a curtain hides 19th-century Orthodox icons at prayer times. ✉ *Alaçatı.*

Ayios Haralambos. Named for St. Charalampus, a local bishop martyred at the age of 113, and whose skull is still venerated in Greece, this large, mid-19th-century Greek basilica church is a relic of Çeşme's former Greek Orthodox inhabitants, and was restored by the municipality in 2012. It's worth taking a look inside you stroll down the main street of Çeşme's shopping district. The space is now used as a cultural center that hosts art exhibitions and handicrafts bazaars; look up to see painted saints peering down at you from the ceiling. ✉ *Inkilap Cad.*

FAMILY
Fodor'sChoice
★
Çeşme Kalesi. Constructed during the reign of Sultan Bayezid II (ruled 1481–1512) to defend the port, this castle is very picturesque, with its stone walls often lined with sun-basking lizards and tortoises. The keep is often deep in wildflowers. The castle houses a small Archaeology Museum, displaying weaponry from the glory days of the Ottoman Empire, cannons from 18th-century sea skirmishes with the Russians, and a modest collection of ancient artifacts. Clamber around the towers for sweeping views of the sea and the city; keep close watch on kids around the less-than-sturdy railings. ⊕ *5 TL* ☉ *Tues.–Sun. 9–6:30.*

BEACHES

Alaçatı Beach. The sandy beach at Alaçatı, about 2 km (1 mile) south of town, is ideal for windsurfing, with strong winds and few waves. Unfortunately, there is only a small, public beach here, but many of the comfortable private beach clubs and hotels with private beaches allow nonguests for a day rate. The water is cooler at Alaçatı than it is at other beaches, and stunningly blue over the pale, fine sand. Water sports like water-skiing, banana boat rides, and windsurfing are available here. **Amenities:** food and drink; toilets; water sports. **Best for:** windsurfing. ⊠ *Alaçatı Plajı, Alaçatı.*

FAMILY **Altınkum.** The name is Turkish for "golden sand," and this beach has crystal clear and calm water lapping the silky sand. The area has yet to undergo a huge development boom and there are many private and public beaches to choose from, most with shallow waters. You can rent a beach chair and umbrella at many points along the beach. **Amenities:** food and drink; parking; toilets; showers; water sports. **Best for:** swimming; walking. ⊠ *About 10 km (6 miles) east of Çeşme off Hulusi Ozten Cad., Sht. Mehmet Cad. 18 Sok.*

Ayayorgi Bay *(Ayayorgi Koyu).* The most sheltered water and trendiest spot for a dip is at this dazzling turquoise bay named after St. George, Turkey's legendary dragon-slayer. A quick drive from Çeşme center, near Boyalık Bay, Ayayorgi Bay's beach clubs and restaurants are ever-popular with hip İzmirians and Istanbullus. There's no public beach, so plan to hang out at one of the swanky beach clubs (snazzy favorites are Babylon Aya Yorgi and Paparazzi), which metamorphose into beach bars as the sun goes down, often with live music. **Amenities:** food and drink; parking (fee); showers; toilets; water sports. **Best for:** partiers; swimming. ⊠ *Off Ayayorgi Yolu, Boyalık Bay.*

Boyalık Bay. Just west of Ilıca, Boyalık Bay has a 5-km (3-mile) beach-front of warm turquoise waters and pale, smooth sand. Boyalık Bay has many private and public beaches and hotels, including cheery but slightly down-at-the-heel Altınyunus Tatil Köyü (Golden Dolphin Holiday Village), as well as a campground. You may have to walk between summer residences to reach the sea. But once you reach the shore, you will find clear, relatively calm waters over smooth, almost milky-colored sand, with umbrellas and beach chairs available to rent. Boyalık Bay is getting better known, but its relaxing waters are not yet as crowded as Ilıca beach. **Amenities:** food and drink; toilets. **Best for:** swimming. ⊠ *Off Altinyunus Cad., Çeşme.*

Dalyanköy. This small fishing village is known for the excellent seafood restaurants that line the small harbor. The beaches are not that note-worthy, so save your trip out here for the evening, when you can wine and dine by the water. ⊠ *About 5 km (3 miles) north of Çeşme.*

FAMILY **Ilıca.** Still a summer retreat for İzmir's wealthy, Ilıca fronts one of the peninsula's most popular beaches, with many hotels lined up along the seafront and unusually warm, crystal clear water and white sand—the name means "hot spring" or "spa" in Turkish. The public beach here is large but gets crowded on weekends. There are lots of waves, but few amenities like lounge chairs or umbrellas. The town has plenty of shops and eateries and is particularly known for its *kumru* (literally translated as "dove"), a Turkish-style panini sandwich prepared with *kaşar* cheese (similar to mild cheddar), *sucuk* (a spicy, Turkish beef sausage), salami, sliced tomatoes, and pickles stuffed inside sesame-seed bread and served piping hot. There's no kitesurfing in summer, but it's allowed in winter if you bring your own gear. Jet skis and banana boats are available. **Amenities:** food and drink; showers; toilets; water sports. **Best for:** swimming, walking. ⊠ *Ilıca Plajı, Ilıca.*

> **MASTIC: A TASTE OF THE TREES**
>
> New Englanders have maple syrup; the inhabitants of Çeşme have their own iconic tree sap: mastic resin, or *sakız* in Turkish. This piney, aromatic resin of the small evergreen, *Pistacia lentiscus,* is imported from nearby Chios island (known by Turks as *Sakız Adası*), and used to flavor *sakızlı* ice cream, milk pudding, Turkish delight, and other dishes.

FAMILY
Fodor's Choice
★

Pırlanta Beach. The name means "brilliant" or "diamond" and this beach outside Çiftlikköy certainly has seawater that's as clear as glass, gentle and shallow (you can sit in the water and read a book!). The waters are warmer here than at nearby beaches such as Altınkum, and mercifully free of seaweed or sea urchins. The pale, fine sand is usually clean, the beach peaceful, and there are changing rooms. You can snorkel, but kitesurfing is prohibited. If you want shade, you'll have to rent a beach chair and umbrella from the snack shack. There are many motels and *pansiyons* near this area, as well as a campground. **Amenities:** food and drink; parking; toilets. **Best for:** swimming; walking. ⊠ *About 10 km (6 miles from Çesme, Pırlanta Plajı, Çiftlikköy.*

WHERE TO EAT

$$
ITALIAN
Fodor's Choice
★

✕ **Agrilia Restaurant.** This Italian-Argentinian restaurant in the garden courtyard of an old Greek house, now the TashMahal Hotel, (⇨ *see Where to Stay*) was around long before the rest of Alaçatı's trendy restaurants came on the scene, and remains one of the best and most stylish in town. The candlelit, leafy courtyard, deliciously inventive food, and romantic atmosphere make Agrilia a local favorite—worth the stroll down one of Alaçatı's quieter back streets. The homemade tagliatelle with shrimp in a light, garlic sauce is excellent. You can also get creative fresh fruit juice concoctions here. $ *Average main: 23 TL* ⊠ *Kemal Paşa Cad. 75, Tokoğlu Mh., Alaçatı* ☎ *232/716–8594* ⊕ *www.agriliarestaurant.com* ⌕ *Reservations essential* ☯ *Closed Oct.–Apr.*

$$$
SEAFOOD
Fodor's Choice
★

✕ **Dalyan Restaurant "Cevat'ın Yeri".** This outdoor terrace overlooking the waterfront is an ideal spot in Dalyanköy for a splurgy seafood dinner. Everything here is prepared with great attention to taste and presentation, and the service is impeccably gracious. After mezes of stuffed zucchini flowers (*kabak çiçeği dolması*) and samphire (*deniz börülcesi*), and a main of fish baked in salt (*tuzda balık*) or grilled, try to find room for *sakızlı muhallebi*, creamy traditional milk pudding flavored with gum mastic. $ *Average main: 40 TL* ⊠ *Dalyan Mah., 4226 Sok. 45/A, Dalyanköy* ☎ *232/724–7045* ⊕ *www.dalyanrestaurant.com* ⌕ *Reservations essential.*

$$ TURKISH FAMILY 🍴 **Dost Pide & Pizza.** Stopping here for *pide* (Turkish-style pizza or *calzones,* piled with a variety of ingredients that can include cheese, spinach, meat, or egg) is a highlight of a trip to Ilıca and a great choice for a quick lunch, or even breakfast. The menu also includes kebabs, soup, döner, pizza, and traditional Turkish desserts. It's open 24 hours in peak season, and from breakfast time until late the rest of the year. [$] *Average main: 28 TL* ✉ *5152 Sok. 27, Ilıca* ☎ *232/723–2059* 🌐 *www.dostpidepizza.com.*

$ BAKERY FAMILY 🍴 **Furun Café & Patisserie.** A group of siblings has turned this 100-year-old bakery into a clever, hip patisserie, with jasmine-flavored cheesecake and blueberry meringue on offer, alongside traditional favorites like rice pudding. Surrounded by busy restaurants in Alaçatı's picturesque historic center, it's perfect for an after-dinner treat or a teatime sugar rush. [$] *Average main: 10 TL* ✉ *Tokoğlu Mh., 1005 Sok. 9, Alaçatı* ☎ *232/716–6644* 🌐 *www.furun.com.tr.*

4

$ TURKISH FAMILY 🍴 **Kumrucu Şevki.** Ilıca is known for *kumru*—Turkish-style panini prepared with special homemade rolls and stuffed with salami, *sucuk* (beef spicy sausage), cheese, and tomatoes and pickles—and this place serves the best in town. Pair your sandwich with a glass of *ayran,* a refreshing yogurt drink. There are branches of this popular local chain in Çeşme as well. It's open 24 hours. [$] *Average main: 8 TL* ✉ *Yıldızburnu Mevki 2, Ilıca* ☎ *232/723–2392.*

$$ ECLECTIC 🍴 **Kydonia.** In this spacious and casual waterfront dining room, the emphasis is on splendid hot and cold *meze* (appetizers)—more than 70 types are on offer and include traditional favorites from Çeşme and the Greek island of Crete. Many are based on seafood, and there are various vegetarian choices as well. You can accompany your meal with a selection from the nice wine list. **TIP→ Travelers dining alone may want to ask for a mixed meze tasting plate.** [$] *Average main: 20 TL* ✉ *Port Alaçatı Marina 63, Alaçatı* ☎ *232/716–0765* 🌐 *www.kydonia.com.tr* ✍ *Reservations essential* 🕒 *Daily 7 pm–midnight* 🕒 *Closed Oct.–Apr.*

$$$ INTERNATIONAL 🍴 **Mi Casa Trattoria.** Although not far removed from the hub of the nightlife in Alaçatı, this comfortable bar and romantic dining room is tucked away on a secluded side street. The excellent menu features international cuisine, including house-made Italian pastas, and a legendary pumpkin and shrimp risotto, and is accompanied by a good, fairly international wine list. There are some very special desserts, including a warm fig soufflé. [$] *Average main: 50 TL* ✉ *Tokoğlu Mh., 1052 Sok. 3, Alaçatı* ☎ *232/716–6075* 🌐 *www.micasa-restaurant.com* ✍ *Reservations essential* 🕒 *Closed mid-Sept.–mid-May.*

$$$ TURKISH 🍴 **Tuval Cafe Restaurant & Bar.** Opened in 2010, this seafood and grill restaurant at Çeşme Marina is a branch of one of Alaçatı's most beloved restaurants (also called Tuval), with a menu of international and Turkish dishes. These include both classic (mezes, pizza, fajitas, grilled lamb chops) and inventive (calamari with milk thistle, slow-cooked veal ribs, baked peaches with hazelnut-amaretto biscuits). They have a respectable, if pricey, selection of wines and cocktails, and a lovely waterside location with views of the castle; the winking lights far across the water are from the Greek island of Chios. [$] *Average main: 35 TL* ✉ *Çeşme Marina, Musalla Mah., Kemalpaşa Cad. 83, Çeşme* ✣ *From the castle*

or kervansaray, walk to the sea's edge, then left along the waterfront toward the harbor ☎ 232/716–1444 ⊕ *www.tuvalcafe.com* ⚔ *Reservations essential.*

WHERE TO STAY

ALAÇATI

$$$$ 🎴 **Alaçatı Beach Resort.** Right on the beach and built of attractive Alaçatı

RESORT   stone, this resort is a fabulous getaway, with extremely attractive rooms,

FAMILY   most of which open to sea-facing balconies. **Pros:** lots of nearby water sports, and the hotel has its own surf and kiteboarding school; large seawater pool. **Cons:** 10 to 15 minutes by car or *dolmuş* to Alaçatı center. Ⓢ *Rooms from: 860 TL* ⊠ *Çark Plajı, Liman Mevkii, Alaçatı* ☎ *232/716–6161* ⊕ *www.alacati.com* ⛵ *55 rooms* ⦿❘ *Breakfast.*

$$$ 🎴 **Alaçatı Marina Palace.** Rustic stone walls and stylish interiors offer

HOTEL   comfortable and atmospheric surroundings at this peaceful boutique hotel, only a short drive from antiquing, dining, and nightlife in picturesque Alaçatı. **Pros:** close to the nightlife at Port Alaçatı Marina; near the beach; especially relaxing surroundings and traditional local interior design; free tea and cookies; on-site restaurant. **Cons:** need private tranportation or *dolmuş* to reach downtown Alaçatı; 10-minute stroll to beach. Ⓢ *Rooms from: 400 TL* ⊠ *Liman Mevkii, Alaçatı* ☎ *232/716–0740* ⊕ *www.alacatimarina.com* ⛵ *14 rooms* ⦿❘ *Breakfast.*

$$$ 🎴 **Sakızlı Han.** Kids and pets are welcome in this country-style bed-

B&B/INN   and-breakfast, formed from two lovely restored stone houses in the

FAMILY   heart of picturesque Alaçatı. **Pros:** free shuttle service to nearest beach; family-friendly feel; pleasant area. **Cons:** not walking distance to the sea, though there's a free shuttle to the nearest beach. Ⓢ *Rooms from: 350 TL* ⊠ *Kemalpaşa Cad. 114, Alaçatı* ☎ *232/716–6108* ⊕ *boutiquehotel7.com* ⛵ *14 rooms* ⦿❘ *Breakfast.*

$$$ 🎴 **TashMahal.** This cozy and charismatic old building and its lush gar-

B&B/INN   den provide a perfect retreat from busy Alaçatı, but it's just a five-

Fodor'sChoice   minute stroll to the town's restaurants and antique shops. **Pros:** a short

★   walk to village center; lovely garden, shared at night with chichi Agrilia Restaurant (⇨ *see Where to Eat*); surrounding neighborhood is atmospheric; delicious breakfast. **Cons:** not walking distance to a beach; more romantic than family-friendly in high season. Ⓢ *Rooms from: 374 TL* ⊠ *Tokoğlu Mahallesi, 1005 Sok. 68, Alaçatı* ☎ *232/716–0122* ⊕ *www.tashmahalotel.com* ⛵ *8 rooms* ⦿❘ *Breakfast.*

ÇEŞME

$$$ 🎴 **Kanuni Kervansaray Historical Hotel.** This atmospheric former *kervan-*

HOTEL   *saray*, next to Çeşme's medieval castle, is encased in stone walls and

FAMILY   decorated in Ottoman-inspired style, with a palm-shaded courtyard and a rooftop terrace with sweeping views of the town and harbor. **Pros:** historic setting; authentic look and feel; nice courtyard swimming pool and terrace; Turkish bath on premises. **Cons:** some distance from a beach; basic interior style and amenities for this price range; uneven service; spotty Wi-Fi because of the ancient walls. Ⓢ *Rooms from: 343 TL* ⊠ *Çarşı Mevkii Kale Yanı 5* ☎ *232/712–0630* ⊕ *www.cesmekervansaray.com.tr* ⛵ *28 rooms, 1 suite* ⊘ *Closed Nov.–Mar.* ⦿❘ *Multiple meal plans.*

$$ ⊡ **Pasifik.** A good option for families, this waterfront hotel is closer to
HOTEL the beach than any other Çeşme center hotel and is just a ten-minute
FAMILY walk from the main square—though far enough away to ensure peace
and quiet at nighttime. **Pros:** no charge for kids up to age four; nice
quiet location. **Cons:** adjacent beaches get crowded during the day and
you'll need transportation to reach nicer alternatives; no pets allowed;
no pool. $ *Rooms from: 277 TL* ⊠ *3264 Sok. Tekke Plajı Mevkii
16* ☎ *232/712–2700* ⊕ *www.pasifikotel.com* ⬭ *16 rooms* ⦿*Multiple
meal plans.*

ILICA

$$$$ ⊡ **Ilıca Spa & Wellness Thermal Resort.** Lots of on-site amenities make
RESORT this luxurious beachside resort a great place for families and the bun-
FAMILY galow option offers greater privacy. **Pros:** kid-friendly; private beach;
spa. **Cons:** long walk to Ilıca's nightlife and shopping area; no pets
allowed. $ *Rooms from: 600 TL* ⊠ *Boyalık Mevkii, Ilıca* ☎ *232/723–
3131* ⊕ *www.ilicahotel.com* ⬭ *248 rooms, 12 suites, 3 bungalows*
⦿*Some meals.*

$$$$ ⊡ **Sheraton Çeşme Hotel, Resort & Spa.** Spacious, well-appointed rooms,
RESORT a private beach, a sundeck extending into the sea, a spa, and no end
FAMILY of water sports are among the many amenities at this deluxe seaside
resort in Ilıca. **Pros:** extremely comfortable accommodations; exten-
sive resort amenities. **Cons:** expensive; meal-inclusive rates compulsory
in high season; need private transportation; international-style resort
lacks local flavor; charge for Internet. $ *Rooms from: 1,386 TL* ⊠ *Şifne
Cad., 5152 Sok. 43, Ilıca* ☎ *232/723–1240* ⊕ *www.sheratoncesme.com*
⬭ *398 rooms* ⦿*Some meals.*

NIGHTLIFE

Çeşme has a happening nightlife scene, especially around the marinas.
There are all sorts of restaurants, bars, and clubs with DJs or live music.

Outside Çeşme, the various beach towns have a more laid-back night-
life. **Yıldız Burnu,** the trendy waterfront in Ilıca, is lined with bars and
lounges that cater to a young crowd. The beach clubs and bars in
Ayayorgi Bay and Boyalık Bay are popular with the late-night crowd.

Açık Hava Tiyatrosu. Çeşme's open-air theater hosts a series of Turkish
concerts in summer. ⊠ *Adnan Menderes Cad., 2053 Sok.*

Babylon Ayayorgi. This popular Istanbul jazz club spends its summer
seaside at the Ayayorgi Bay and doubles as a beach club and restau-
rant by day. Evenings bring live music—Turkiish and internationally
recognized jazz, pop, and rock artists. ⊠ *Ayayorgi Bay, Boyalık Bay*
☎ *232/712–6339* ⊕ *www.babylon.com.tr.*

Paparazzi. The DJs at this popular place spin music from the 1970s
through the '90s, which is appropriate because the club has been around
for almost 30 years. Partying goes till the wee hours of the morning. The
food isn't bad, either. ⊠ *Ayayorgi Bay, Boyalık Bay* ☎ *232/712–6767*
⊕ *www.paparazzi.com.tr.*

SPORTS AND THE OUTDOORS
BOAT TOURS

During high season, daily boat tours to coves along the coastline leave from the main harbors in Çeşme and Ilıca. The cost varies, depending on whether lunch and beverages are served. One of the most popular stops is Donkey Island (Eşek Adası). Be warned that in high season the boats tend to be crowded and play loud music, so consider renting a boat privately.

SHOPPING

The main street in Çeşme has many gift shops selling trinkets and souvenirs, beachwear, carpets, and leather items. There are also many jewelry stores selling silver and gold; bargaining is acceptable and expected. Çeşme Marina also has many high-end shops. Downtown Alaçatı is also great for shopping, and high-end retailers and jewelry stores occupy stone houses along the narrow lanes. The antique shops are treasure troves of interesting trinkets, and sometimes more.

SELÇUK, EPHESUS, AND ŞIRINCE

The ruins of Ephesus bring most visitors to Selçuk and the picturesque village of Şirince. You will need approximately one full day to explore Ephesus and visit some of the surrounding early Christian sites. If you have time, plan another day for more sightseeing, and to soak in the area's bucolic charms. Staying in Selçuk is convenient, while the hilltop village of Şirince offers a rural getaway that is within easy reach of what you will want to see. Try to time your stay to coincide with Selçuk's Saturday market, when villagers descend from the hills with local produce and dry goods, alongside purveyors of cowbells and scythes, antique bric-a-brac, and cheap shoes.

SELÇUK

79 km (49 miles) south of İzmir.

Selçuk, the closest city to Ephesus, lies beneath the ancient **Fortress of Ayasuluk** and is unfortunately often overlooked. The former farming village has interesting sights of its own to offer—St. John the Evangelist is said to have been buried here, just below the medieval fortress, and the city has one of the oldest mosques in western Turkey, the lovely **İsa Bey Camii**. On her visit over half a century ago, the renowned explorer Freya Stark rhapsodized over the historical treasures of the small city of Selçuk: "All are tightly clustered together," Stark wrote in her book *Ionia: A Quest*, "like the landscape in a medieval book of hours. And that is indeed what it is, though the hours are centuries, and the book written on the transformations of earth." Selçuk is easy to navigate on foot (keep an eye out for small gems of Seljuk and Ottoman architecture scattered across town), and there are many excellent casual restaurants along the main square and along side streets where you can eat outside. Rather pricey shops selling carpets and jewelry cater to souvenir seekers. The town hosts an annual camel-wrestling festival every third weekend in January.

GETTING HERE AND AROUND

By car, Selçuk is about 30 minutes from İzmir on Rte. E87, following the well-marked *otoyol* (toll highway) toward Aydın. The Selçuk exit is well marked. If driving from Selçuk to Ephesus, look for brown signs with its Turkish name, Efes.

Alternatively, if you do not want to rent a car, you can take a train to Selçuk from İzmir. Direct trains depart from the Basmane Station in central İzmir and travel time is about two hours; for schedules and online tickets, visit ⊕ *www.tcdd.gov.tr*. Local bus companies also offer minibus service to Selçuk, with departures from the main bus terminal in İzmir.

Bus Information Kamil Koç ⊠ *Selçuk Bus Terminal* ☎ *444–0562 (no area code needed), 232/892–6263* ⊕ *www.kamilkoc.com.tr.* **Metro Turizm** ⊠ *Selçuk Otogar* ☎ *444–3455 no area code needed* ⊕ *www.metroturizm.com.tr.*

ESSENTIALS

Tourist Information Office. ⊠ *Across the street from the museum, 37 Uğur Mumcu Sevgi Yolu Sok.* ☎ *232/483–5117* ⊗ *Weekdays 8:30–noon, 1–5:30; weekends 9–noon, 1–5.*

EXPLORING

FodorśChoice **Ephesus Archaeological Site.** ⇨ *See the highlighted Ephesus feature in this*
★ *chapter.*

Ephesus Müzesi. Slated to re-open in 2014 after major renovations, this small museum has one of the best collections of Roman and Greek artifacts found anywhere in Turkey. Along with some fine frescoes and mosaics are two white statues of Artemis. In each, the goddess is portrayed with several rows of what are alternatively described as breasts, or a belt of eggs, or sacrificed bull testicles; in any case, they symbolize fertility. Check with your hotel or the tourist office to see if the museum is still under a dusty cloud of construction. ⊠ *Atatürk Mah., opposite the Selçuk Tourist Information Center, Uğur Mumcu Sevgi Yolu* ☎ *232/892–6010* ⊗ *Currently closed for construction work.*

İsa Bey Camii (*İsa Bey Mosque*). Lovely and evocative, this is one of the most ancient mosques in western Turkey, dating from 1375. The jumble of architectural styles suggests a transition between Seljuk and Ottoman design: like later-day Ottoman mosques, this one has a large courtyard, though the interior is plain (in the 19th century, it doubled as a *kervansaray*). The structure is built out of *spolia*, or "borrowed" stone: marble blocks with Latin inscriptions, Corinthian columns, black-granite columns from the baths at Ephesus, and pieces from the altar of the Temple of Artemis. Don't miss it if you're visiting the St. John Basilica—it's a three-minute walk downhill as you turn out of the gate. ⊠ *Corner of St. Jean Cad. and 2040 Sok.* ⊗ *Daily 9–6.*

Meryem Ana Evi (*Virgin Mary's House*) ⇨ *See the highlighted Ephesus feature in this chapter.*

FodorśChoice **St. John Basilica.** Step through the impressive, pre-Justinianic marble
★ portal (its huge blocks likely plundered from the nearby Temple of Artemis) to approach the basilica. In the 6th century AD, after earthquakes

destroyed the modest church believed to mark the grave of St. John the Evangelist, Byzantine Emperor Justinian and his wife Theodora commanded that a grand marble basilica be erected over the site on Ayasuluk Hill, its eleven domes grand enough to rival the imperial pair's other legendary building project, Hagia Sophia. The basilica's barrel-vaulted roof collapsed after another long-ago earthquake, but the ruined church is still an incredibly evocative sight, with its labyrinth of halls and marble courtyards, and occasional mosaic fragments. It provides stunning views of Selçuk's castle, the Plain of Ephesus, the Isa Bey Mosque, and of towering Ayasuluk Castle (still closed after almost two decades of restoration work, but expected to reopen in 2014). **TIP→ Come by in the late afternoon when there are rarely crowds, pick up a brochure at the ticket office, and ramble around the site. ⚠ Unscrupulous dealers in dubious "antiquities" cluster around the gates; they should be ignored.** ✉ *Off St. Jean Cad., just east of Isa Bey Cami* 🎫 *10 TL* ⏲ *Daily 8–6:30.*

WHERE TO EAT

$ TURKISH FAMILY Fodor's Choice ★

🍴 **Ejder Restaurant.** This popular spot overlooking the Selçuk aqueduct is run by a family team—husband, wife, and son—and offers a menu that includes such traditional vegetarian dishes as exemplary stuffed peppers and fried eggplant. It may sometimes take a while for the generous, juicy lamb and chicken kebabs to cook in the small hearth, but it's worth the wait. The family takes pride in the guestbook filled with customers' comments and drawings, so make sure to add your own alongside the likes of the late Steve Irwin! [$] *Average main: 15 TL* ✉ *Cengiz Topel Cad. 9/E* ☎ *232/892–3296.*

$$$ TURKISH

🍴 **Eski Ev.** The Ottoman motifs seem a bit touristy, but the place is done up nicely, in the peaceful, open-air courtyard of an old house, shaded by a towering grapefruit tree. Eski Ev ("old house" in Turkish) serves a wide selection of Turkish *meze* (appetizers) and main dishes, including the Old House special, a delicious concoction of lamb, vegetables, and pilaf, served on a copper dish with its own tiny flame beneath. They also have nice choices for vegetarians. [$] *Average main: 40 TL* ✉ *1005 Sok. 1/A* ☎ *232/892–9357.*

$$ TURKISH

🍴 **Tat Restaurant & Cafe.** Hearty kebabs and *pide*, tasty soups and mezes at reasonable prices, a central location, free Wi-Fi at outdoor tables, cheery staff speaking fluent English, and a multilingual bookshelf make this casual restaurant a longstanding traveler favorite. It can get a little rowdy later in the evening, depending on the clientele. [$] *Average main: 18 TL* ✉ *Atatürk Mh., Cengiz Topel Cad. 19* ☎ *232/892–1916.*

WHERE TO STAY

$ B&B/INN FAMILY

🏨 **Alihan Guesthouse.** A great option for budget travelers and families, this cosy, old-fashioned guesthouse has zero frills, but accommodations are comfortable and it's handy for city center sights and the bus station. **Pros:** very central location behind the museum; many rooms have balconies; great value and affordable family rooms. **Cons:** basic amenities, including functional, but rather flimsy showers; rooms are quite close together and some are small. [$] *Rooms from: 99 TL* ✉ *Ataturk Mh., 1045 Sok. 34* ☎ *232/892–9496* 🌐 *www.alihanguesthouse.com* 🛏 *9 rooms* 💳 *No credit cards* 🍽 *No meals.*

$$ HOTEL FAMILY 🏨 **Hotel Akay.** Steps from the enchanting Isa Bey Mosque and a five-minute walk to St. John Basilica, this family-run hotel offers a peaceful respite. **Pros:** good location; one of the owners speaks excellent English; free pickup from bus or train station; pool. **Cons:** rooms can be stuffy; decor uninspired; bathroom fixures in some rooms show signs of age. [$] *Rooms from: 190 TL* ✉ *Atatürk Mahallesi, 1054 Sok. 3* ☎ *232/892–3172* 🌐 *www.hotelakay.com* 🛏 *25 rooms* 🍴 *Breakfast.*

$$ HOTEL Fodor's Choice ★ 🏨 **Hotel Bella.** A fabulous location near sights and restaurants, free shuttle service to Ephesus, and charming boutique style make this hotel an excellent choice. **Pros:** basilica views; large and inviting outdoor terrace; small library on-site. **Cons:** some rooms are a bit small, and not all overlook the basilica; not the best place for kids; breakfast is served plated, not buffet style. [$] *Rooms from: 156 TL* ✉ *Atatürk Mahallesi, St. Jean Cad. 7* ☎ *232/892–3944* 🌐 *www.hotelbella.com* 🛏 *10 rooms* 🍴 *Multiple meal plans.*

$$ B&B/INN 🏨 **Kalehan.** After a day of sightseeing, the large landscaped garden with a pool is very welcome. **Pros:** refreshing pool and garden. **Cons:** some rooms can feel a bit stuffy; inconvenient location outside the center of town. [$] *Rooms from: 248 TL* ✉ *Atatürk Cad. 49* ☎ *232/892–6154* 🌐 *www.kalehan.com* 🛏 *46 rooms* 🍴 *No meals.*

$ HOTEL Fodor's Choice ★ 🏨 **Wallabies Aqueduct Hotel.** The casual, welcoming feel brings guests of all ages and nationalities to this cheerful place in the heart of town, just a one-minute walk to the train station. **Pros:** good value; views; great restaurant right at the foot of the aqueduct; remarkably friendly and helpful staff. **Cons:** rooms are simple and some are a bit small; no pool. [$] *Rooms from: 50 TL* ✉ *Cengiz Topel Cad. 4* ☎ *232/892–3204* 🌐 *www.wallabieshostel.com* 🛏 *24 rooms* 💳 *No credit cards* 🍴 *Breakfast.*

SHOPPING

Selçuk's weekly bazaar is held on Saturday in the main square from 9 to 6. There's also a daily market by the İsa Bey Camii that sells souvenirs and Turkish-themed touristy gifts.

4

ŞIRINCE

8 km (5 miles) east of Selçuk; 12 km (7½ miles) from Ephesus.

Once upon a time, villagers of this picturesque little hilltop aerie christened their town Çirkince (Turkish for "rather ugly"), allegedly to keep outsiders from discovering its charms. Now renamed Şirince (appropriately, the name means"cute" or "quaint"), this lovely cluster of shops, traditional Greek houses, and restaurants is set on a lush hill; the rows of houses have decorative eaves with nature motifs. A former Greek enclave, Şirince has a 19th-century church and a stone basilica, also 19th-century, which has been restored and turned into an art gallery. In the past few years, the village has become popular with travelers visiting the nearby historical sites. Village shops cater to them with quality handicrafts, including beautiful felt, or keçe at Kırkınca Keçe in the village center, as well as the famous locally produced fruit wines (the villagers also grow olives, peaches, figs, apples, and walnuts and the approach road is lined with tempting farm stands). In December 2012, believing Şirince's "positive energy" would shield the village from

Continued on page 236

EPHESUS
CITY OF THE GODS

One might naturally think that the greatest Roman ruins are to be found in Italy. Not so fast! With an ancient arena that dwarfs the one in Pompeii, and a lofty library that rivals any structure in the Roman Forum, Ephesus—once the most important Greco-Roman city of the Eastern Mediterranean—is among the best-preserved ancient sites in the world. Set on a strategic trade route, it first won fame as a cultural and religious crossroads. Here, shrines honored Artemis, the ancient goddess of fertility, St. Paul did some serious soul-searching, and—legend has it—the Virgin Mary lived out her last days. Today, modern travelers can trace the fault lines of ancient civilizations in Ephesus's spectacular landscape of ruined temples, theaters, and colonnaded streets.

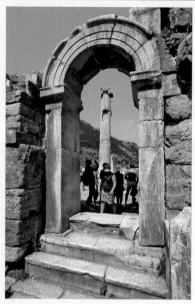

THE AWESTRUCK ADMIRERS who disembark from cruise ships and tour buses to wander through the largest Roman ruins of the Eastern Mediterranean are not really out of sync with ancient times, since Ephesus was a bustling port of call in the pre-Christian era. Home to upwards of 500,000 people at its height, Efes drew visitors from near and far with its promise of urbane and sybaritic pleasures, including baths, brothels, theaters, temples, public latrines, and one of the world's largest libraries. Even then, visitors approaching from the harbor (which has since silted up) could wander under the marble porticos of the Arcadian Way—the ancient world's Rodeo Drive—and visit shops laden with goods from throughout the Mediterranean world.

✉ Efes (Ephesus), 4 km (2.5 mi) west of Selçuk on Selçuk-Ephesus Rd.

☎ 0232/892-6010 (this is the museum's number; ask to be connected to the site. no official Web site)

💳 25TL; terraced houses, 15TL; parking: 7.50TL

🕐 Apr.–Oct., daily 8–6:30; Nov.–Mar., daily 8–5:30.

SPIRIT & THE FLESH

Ephesus in pre-Hellenic times was the cult center of Cybele, the Anatolian goddess of fertility. When seafaring Ionians arrived in the 10th century BC they promptly recast her as Artemis, maiden goddess of the hunt. With her three tiers of breasts, this symbol of mother nature was, in turn, both fruitful and barren, according to the season; as such, she was also worshipped by thousands as the goddess of chastity. The riches of her shrines, however, awoke greed; in the 6th century BC, Croesus, king of Lydia, captured Ephesus, but was himself defeated by Persia's Cyrus. The wily Ephesians managed to keep on good terms with everyone by playing up to both sides of any conflict but by the 2nd century BC, Ephesus had become capital of the Roman province of Asia and Artemis had been renamed Diana. Today, the virgin reverenced here is called Mary.

THE GOSPEL TRUTH?

As with other Roman cities, Ephesus eventually became Christian, though not without a struggle. The Gospel of Luke recounts how the city's silversmiths drove St. Paul out of Ephesus for fear that his pronouncements—"there are no gods made with hands"—would lessen the sale of their silver statues. After Paul addressed a gathering of townsfolk in the amphitheater, the craftsmen rioted, but he succeeded in founding an early congregation here thanks to his celebrated "Epistle to the Ephesians." Another tourist to the city was St. John, who visited between 37 and 48 AD (he died here in AD 95 shortly after completing his Gospel); tradition has it he was accompanied by Mary, whom he brought to fulfill a pledge he had made to Jesus to protect her. Whether or not this is true, Ephesus's House of the Virgin Mary—where Mary is reputed to have breathed her last—draws pilgrims from across the world.

Top, Gateway to Odeon; Right, The Arcadian Way

DID YOU KNOW?

When Ephesus became a Roman capital in the 2nd century B.C., numerous shrines were erected to the ancient gods, including Hercules (figure at left). But by the 4th century, the early Christians had plundered Ephesus's classical temples for the building of numerous churches.

PRECIOUS STONES: WHAT'S WHERE

"Is there a greater city than Ephesus?" asked St. Paul. "Is there a more beautiful city?" Those who dig ruins can only agree with the saint. Ephesus is the best preserved Greco–Roman city of the Eastern Mediterranean.

1 Temple of Domitian. One of the largest temples in the city was dedicated to the first-century Roman emperor.

2 Odeon. At this intimate theater, an audience of about 1,500 sat on a semicircle of stone seats to enjoy theatricals and music recitals.

3 Prytaneion. One of the most important buildings in town was dedicated to Hestia, goddess of hearth and home. Priests kept vigil to ensure her sacred flame was never extinguished.

4 Curetes Street. One of the main thoroughfares cuts a diagonal swath through the ancient city and was a processional route leading to the Temple of Artemis; "curetes" are priests of Artemis.

5 Temple of Hadrian. Elegant friezes and graceful columns surround the porch and main chamber of this monument to the 2nd-century Roman emperor. A frieze, probably Medusa, guards the entrance to ward off evil spirits; in another, the Christian

Emperor Theodosius is surrounded by classical gods—a sign that worldly Ephesus was a tolerant place.

6 Terrace Houses. The luxurious homes of well-to-do Ephesians of the 1st to 7th centuries climb the slopes of Mount Koressos. Liberally decorated with frescoes and mosaics, this enclave is evocative of life in the ancient town.

7 Library of Celsus. One of the most spectacular extant ruins of antiquity, this remarkable two-storied building was commissioned in the 2nd century and was destined for double duty—as a mausoleum for Julius Celsus, Roman governor of the province of Asia minor and as a reading room stocked with more than 12,000 scrolls.

8 Brothel. Footsteps etched into the marble paving stones along Curetes Street led the way to one of the busiest businesses in town.

9 Theater. St. Paul preached to the Ephesians in this magnificent space. One of the largest

outdoor theaters of the ancient world was carved out of the flanks of Mount Pion over the course of 60 years and seats as many as 40,000 spectators.

10 Arcadian Way (Harbour Street). The grandest street in town was flanked by mosaic-floored porticos that were lined with elegant shops and—a luxury afforded by few ancient cities—torch-lit at night. This is where Cleopatra paraded in triumph.

11 Stadium. This 1st-century BC structure accommodated more than 70,000 spectators, who enjoyed such entertainments as chariot races and gladiatorial spectacles.

12 Temple of Artemis. A lone column rising from a swamp is all that remains of one of the Seven Wonders of the Ancient World. The largest building in the ancient Mediterranean, once surrounded by 127 columns, was a shrine to the goddess of fertility, abundance, and womanly concerns.

Top Left, Temple of Hadrian; Center, Library of Celsus; Top Right, Odeon

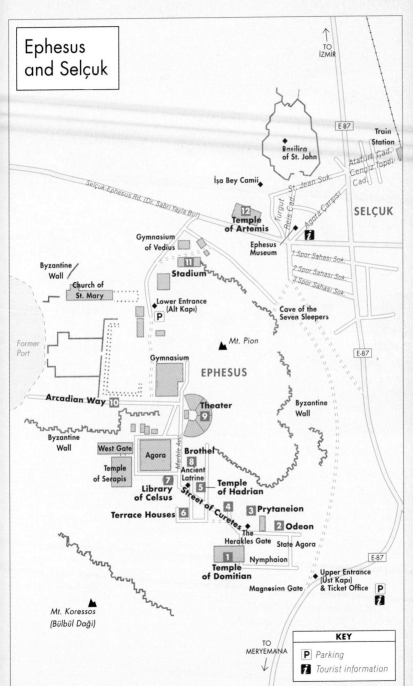

Ephesus and Selçuk

TO İZMİR

E 87

Train Station

Basilica of St. John

İşa Bey Camii

Selçuk-Ephesus Rd. (Dr. Sabri Yayla But)

12 Temple of Artemis

St. Jean Sok.

Turgut Reis Cad.

Agora Çarşısı

Atatürk Cad. Cengiz Topel Cad.

SELÇUK

Ephesus Museum

1 Spor Sahası Sok.
2 Spor Sahası Sok.
3 Spor Sahası Sok.

Gymnasium of Vedius

11 Stadium

Byzantine Wall

Church of St. Mary

Lower Entrance (Alt Kapı)

Cave of the Seven Sleepers

E-87

Former Port

Mt. Pion

Gymnasium

EPHESUS

Arcadian Way **10**

Theater **9**

Byzantine Wall

Byzantine Wall

West Gate

Agora

Marble Ave.

Brothel **8**
Ancient Latrine **5**
Temple of Hadrian

Temple of Serapis

Library of Celsus **7**

Street of Curetes

4

3 **Prytaneion**

2 **Odeon**

Terrace Houses **6**

The Herakles Gate State Agora

1 Nymphaion

Temple of Domitian

Magnesian Gate

Upper Entrance (Üst Kapı) & Ticket Office

E-87

P

Mt. Koressos (Bülbül Daği)

TO MERYEMANA

KEY	
P	Parking
i	Tourist information

4

IN FOCUS EPHESUS: CITY OF THE GODS

PLANNING YOUR VISIT

Most people who tour Ephesus (Efes) base themselves in nearby Selçuk, a much nicer choice than Kuşadası. If arriving by car, take the road from Selçuk toward Kuşadası, turning left and following the signs to the archaeological site. There are two public parking lots, at the top and bottom of the site near the two main gates. Note that if you arrive by car you'll have to backtrack the hill one way or the other after walking the site (or opt for an cab ride back). It may be best to forgo your car and take taxis to and from Selçuk. There is also a *dolmuş* (shared taxi) that connects the lower gate with Selçuk.

TIPS FOR TOURING

The main entrance (Lower Gate) is near the turnoff to Selçuk; this is where you'll arrive by *dolmuş*. For the upper Magnesian Gate, follow the signs for the Cave of the Seven Sleepers and House of the Virgin Mary (Meryemana). Since Ephesus is laid out on the slopes of Mounts Pion and Koressos, many opt to begin their tour at the upper Magnesian Gate, visiting the state and religious buildings on the higher reaches before descending to where most of the public arenas and agoras are located.

The main avenue runs about a mile downhill but there are any number of side streets with intriguing detours. Con-

EPHESUS GUIDES

Perhaps the easiest way to see all the sights is to take a guided bus tour, which allows you to travel between the Ephesus site, the Ephesus Museum, the House of the Virgin Mary, and the Basilica of St. John stress-free. The day trip (lunch included) usually costs $75–$90. Tour agencies can be found in Izmir and Kuşadası, although the most convenient are located in Selçuk. Here are two recommended outfitters:

■ No Frills Ephesus. (✉ Atatürk Mah. St. Jean Caddesi 3/A, Selçuk ☎ 232/892-8828 ⊕ www.nofrillsephesustours.com).

■ Apasa Travel. (✉ Atatürk Mah. 1006 Sokak 4, Selçuk ☎ 232/892-9547 ⊕ www.apasastravel.com).

The guides who flock around the entrance gates to the main site are not particularly knowledgeable, and they usually charge around $50 for a two-hour tour. The best option—in addition to consulting one of the handy site guidebooks—is to rent the excellent one-hour audio guides (15TL).

sequently, a minimum visit of two hours can easily stretch to four, not including an hour in the museum and an hour or two at nearby sites like the Cave of the Seven Sleepers and Meryemana.

You'll better appreciate the treasures of Ephesus Museum if you tour the ancient city first—knowing where the statuary, mosaics, and other artifacts were located raises them from the dust to life when you visit the museum. As for timing, a visit in early morning or late afternoon might help you skirt the heaviest of the cruise ship crowds from Kuşadası. In summer you'll want to avoid the midday heat and sun. Be sure to bring water and a light snack—there are no concessions beyond the gate.

Above, Library of Celsus

WHO'S WHO IN ANCIENT EPHESUS

ALEXANDER THE GREAT

Upon entering Ephesus in triumph after defeating the Persians in 333 BC, Alexander saw the reconstruction efforts of the temple to Artemis underway and offered to pay for the new edifice with the proviso that his name be inscribed over the entrance. The Ephesians, not wanting to offend their goddess, diplomatically informed the noble warrior and mighty king that it would not be right for one divine being to so honor another.

ANDROKLOS

Banished from Athens upon the death of his father, King Kadros, in the 10th century BC, Androklos arrived at the shores of Asia Minor. The oracle at Delphi had told the prince that a fish and a boar would guide him on his way. A fish that Androklos was roasting on the beach leapt from the flames into the bush, and the commotion routed out a wild boar who led him to a fertile valley: the future Ephesus. Androklos went on to unite the twelve cities of Asia Minor as the Ionian League.

HEROSTRATUS

Stories of all great cities include at least one villain, and in Ephesus the most infamous is Herostratus. One night in 356 BC, the deranged young man burned the most important building in town, the Temple to Artemis. As fate would have it, Alexander the Great was born the same night. The Roman historian Plutarch later observed that the goddess was "too busy taking care of the birth of Alexander to send help to her threatened temple." Ephesian authorities executed Herostratus and tried to condemn him to obscurity by forbidding the mention of his name, but this obviously didn't work.

ST. PAUL

The well-traveled missionary stopped twice in Ephesus, of which he wrote in 1 Corinthians 16, "a great door and effectual is opened unto me, and there are many adversaries." Among them were local merchants, who were infuriated by Paul's proclamation that they should stop selling images of Artemis, lest the practice encourage the worship of pagan idols. Paul may have written his "Epistle to the Ephesians" while being held prisoner in Rome, before his execution in AD 67.

ST. JOHN

Legend has it that the author of the Fourth Gospel arrived in Ephesus with the Virgin Mary and died at age 98. He had his followers dig a square grave, proclaimed "You have called me to your feast," and expired, or so people thought: dust could be seen moving above his grave as if he still drew breath. Emperor Justinian's cathedral—it would be the seventh-largest in the world if reconstructed—was built directly over St. John's grave.

Center, Silver tetradrachm issued by Erythrai ca. 200–180 BC, obverse: Alexander the Great as Herakles wearing the lion skin. Above, Tomb of St John in Mezrai, St. John's basilica in Selçuk

BEYOND THE RUINS: OTHER SIGHTS

House of the Virgin Mary

Cave of the Seven Sleepers

THE HOUSE OF THE VIRGIN MARY (MERYEMANA)

Legend has it that the Virgin Mary traveled to Ephesus with St. John and spent her last days in this modest stone dwelling. Such claims were given a boost of credulity in the 19th century when a bedridden German nun had a vision that enabled her to describe the house in precise detail. A hallowed place of pilgrimage, the house and adjoining sacred spring have been visited by three popes. John is allegedly buried nearby beneath the now-ruined Basilica of St. John in Selçuk. Surrounded by a national park, Mary's house is 7 km (4 mi) southwest of Selçuk, near the entrance to ancient Ephesus. There are regular religious services. ✉ *Off Rte. E87* ☎ *232/894–1012* 💲 *15TL/ person, 8TL/car* 🕐 *Daily 8–6 (Closes earlier in winter.)*

EPHESUS MUSEUM

While many of the finds from Ephesus were carted off to the British Museum in London and the Ephesus Museum in Vienna, some treasures remain in Selçuk. Among the mosaics, coins, and other artifacts are dozens of images of Artemis, including the famous statue of the fertility goddess with several rows of egg-shaped breasts. ✉ *Agora Çarşısı opposite visitor center in Selçuk* ☎ *232/892–6010* 💲 *5TL* ⚠ *Closed for renovations as of presstime.*

CAVE OF THE SEVEN SLEEPERS

Ephesus is awash in legend, but the story associated with this hillside cavern takes the prize. It's said that during persecutions ordered by the Roman Emperor Decius in the 2nd century, seven young Christian men were sealed into a cave and left to die. Two centuries later, when Christianity had become the state religion, a farmer happened to unseal the cave and found the men, now aged, in deep slumber. On awakening, they wandered into Ephesus, as shocked at the affixed to churches as the townsfolk were confused by the sight of these archaically clothed characters who offered two-centuries-old coinage to buy food. After their deaths, a church was erected in their honor. The story has found its way into works as diverse as the Koran and the *Golden Legend*, the chronicle of the lives of the saints. ✉ *South of Sor Sahası Sok. 3* 💲 *Free.*

Fertility Goddess, Ephesus Museum

the impending Mayan Apocalypse, would-be refugees flocked to the mountaintop. Canny villagers produced a commemorative wine, presumably some comfort to the "survivors." Hiking around Şirince is quite pleasant, as the hills are a bit cooler than the lowlands. In winter, Turkish visitors come for local wine by a roaring fireplace, as the cold rain readies the valley for spring.

GETTING HERE AND AROUND

A narrow but well-marked road connects Selçuk and Şirince. The road is narrow and windy, so it is best to travel during daylight hours, and with strong nerves. You can also take the *dolmuşes* (shared minibuses) that depart periodically from the central Selçuk bus depot (*otogar*) between 8:30 and 5 (until around 7 in the summer). The last minibus usually leaves Şirince around 6, somewhat later in the summer months.

WHERE TO EAT AND STAY

$
TURKISH
FAMILY
Fodor's Choice
★

✕ **Arşipel Restaurant.** Summer and winter, the dining room at the Kırkınca Houses Boutique Hotel is the best in town, overlooking the lovely landscape and serving delicious and authentic dishes prepared with oil produced from olives harvested in the garden. Among the delicacies are creamy eggplant soup; *şevketi bostanı*, a root vegetable cooked with tender pieces of lamb; and delicious homemade pasta, *erişte*, served in a light cream and almond sauce. You can accompany your meal with wines produced in Şirince. There is sometimes live music. $ *Average main: 15 TL* ⊠ *Şirince Köyü* 🕾 *232/898–3133* ⊕ *www.kirkinca.com/arsipel_.html.*

$$
TURKISH

✕ **Artemis Restaurant & Wine House.** The terrace and a dining room decorated in traditional style afford a superb view of the valley. Grilled lamb chops and other regional specialties are delicious, and a good selection of local wines is available. $ *Average main: 20 TL* ⊠ *Şirince Köyü* 🕾 *232/898–3240* ⊕ *www.artemisrestaurant.com.*

$$
B&B/INN
FAMILY
Fodor's Choice
★

🕎 **Kayserkaya Dağ Evleri** (*Kayserkaya Mountain Cottages*). Hotel rooms here are in the form of rustically furnished little cottages, with working fireplaces and private pools, and the mountainside setting near Şirince makes it an excellent getaway for couples or families. **Pros:** peaceful and bucolic setting; lovely green views; free shuttle service into town; privacy. **Cons:** need transportation to Şirince village dining options; cottage cooking facilities minimal; not wheelchair accessible. $ *Rooms from: 297 TL* ⊠ *Kayserkaya* 🕾 *232/898–3133* ⊕ *www.kayserkaya.com* 🛏 *7 cottages* ⏐⊘⏐ *Breakfast.*

$$
B&B/INN

🕎 **Kırkınca Houses Boutique Hotel.** Peaceful in summer, cosy in winter, and always atmospheric, these two historic Greek houses in the village center are individually decorated in rustic style. **Pros:** friendly owners; delicious food; family-friendly; cosy fireplaces. **Cons:** slightly on the pricey side for Şirince; some rooms quite small and not all have views, and those without can be dark. $ *Rooms from: 277 TL* ⊠ *Şirince Köyü* 🕾 *232/898–3133* ⊕ *www.kirkinca.com* 🛏 *7 rooms* ⏐⊘⏐ *Breakfast.*

$$
B&B/INN

🕎 **Markiz Konakları.** The rooms and suites of these two historic houses are prettily embellished with tradtional furnishings, stone and whitewashed walls, rich textiles, and working fireplaces. **Pros:** attractive and comfortable accommodations; in village center; complimentary homemade lemonade. **Cons:** theme-scented rooms can be a bit overbearing;

Camel Wrestling

CLOSE UP

While Americans are busy stuffing turkeys and stocking up on Christmas trees, Turkish camels and their owners prepare for an intense season of travel, confrontation, and competition. Every year, around 100 male camels and their owners tour the Marmara, Mediterranean, and the Aegean regions to compete in more than 30 camel-wrestling festivals.

There are different theories about camel wrestling's origins, although many argue it was a nomadic practice and part of a competition between caravan owners. Nomadic or not, these festivals have become a deep-rooted cultural pastime in Turkey. Their primary motivation: get the girl. Camels will wrestle only during their mating season, which lasts from November to March, and a female camel is paraded around to provoke them into these contests. The camels' mouths are tied during the match so that they can't do real harm to each other, and among the judges, separators (*urgancı*), and commentators (*cazgirs*), are 21 officials (not including the camel owners) moderating the events.

The camels begin their wrestling "career" at age four, when many are purchased from Iran. They train for the next four years and spend years 8 through 10 coming of age and developing their own strategies. Their rite of passage, much like that of Turkish boys, occurs at this age, when the camels receive *havuts*, decorative cloths with their name and the word *maşallah* (may God protect him) sewn on the inside. According to camel owners and those familiar with the sport, wrestling is not a foreign, inhumane practice being imposed on the camels. On the contrary, these

dayluk (as they're called until age seven, when they become *tüylü* or hairy) begin wrestling naturally in the wild during their first years out of the womb, and if trained, can continue until age 25.

Celebratory events actually begin the day before the match, during *halı gecesi*, or carpet night, when camels are flaunted around to percussive music, their bells jingling as they amble along. The camel owners, who often get to know one another during the prefestivities, are also dolled up in cornered caps, traditional neck scarves, and accordion-like boots.

To prevent wearing out the camels, the matches last no more than 10 minutes, and camels compete only once a day. The victor, the camel who gets the most points for outsmarting his rival by swiftly maneuvering and having the most control over the match (which might simply mean not running away), can win anywhere from 5,000 TL to 50,000 TL depending on the competition. There's usually a wrestling World Cup of sorts at the culmination of the festivals, in which the top camels compete.

The exact dates, times, and locations of the festivals change from year to year, but competitions are always held every Sunday between December and March. The central and southern Aegean cities of Selçuk, İzmir, Bodrum, and Kuşadası host camel-wrestling festivals. Local tourism offices will have specific information about that year's festivals. Tickets cost around 15 TL per match and can be purchased on-site.

—Evin Dogul

some rooms are rather dark. $ *Rooms from: 248 TL* ✉ *6 Sok. 20/1* ☎ *232/898–3282* ⊕ *www.markizkonaklari.com* ⤶ *6 rooms, 2 suites* ❏ *Breakfast.*

KUŞADASI AND ENVIRONS

These days Kuşadası is primarily known as a cruise port. It's a brash, highly touristy place crammed with pubs, fish-and-chips restaurants, and tacky souvenir shops. On a positive note, Kuşadası is within easy reach of Ephesus and is also close to one of Turkey's most beautiful national parks, as well as Pamukkale and Aphrodisias.

KUŞADASI

15 km (9 miles) southwest of Selçuk on Rte. 515.

Kuşadası long ago lost its local charm to invasive, sterile buildings and overpopulation, and these days it's often overrun with cruise ship passengers disembarking to make a mad dash to Ephesus. So, what was a small fishing village up until the 1970s is now a sprawling, hyperactive town packed with curio shops and a year-round population of around 65,000, rising to about half a million in season with the influx of tourists and Turks with vacation homes.

GETTING HERE AND AROUND

Kuşadası is 85 km (53 miles) from Adnan Menderes Airport in İzmir and 15 km (9 miles) from Selçuk. Several local bus companies provide service between İzmir and Kuşadası, while you can travel between Selçuk and Kuşadası by taxi or dolmuş. You can also travel around Kuşadası town and reach the nearest beach, Kadınlar Plajı, by dolmuş.

ESSENTIALS

Visitor Information. ✉ *Near cruise ship dock, Mahmut Esat Bozkurt Cad. 7* ☎ *256/614–1103* ⊙ *Weekdays 8–noon; 1:30–5:30; open on weekends only when big cruise ships dock.*

EXPLORING

Kervansaray. Kuşadası's 300-year-old *kervansaray*, a short stroll from the cruise ship dock, is now the Hotel Club Kervansaray. It's loaded with Ottoman atmosphere and its (rather over-restored) public areas are worth a peek even if you're not staying here. ✉ *Atatürk Bulvarı 1.*

FAMILY

Fodor's Choice

★

Dilek Peninsual National Park (*Dilek Yarimadası Milli Parki; Milli Park*). If you're looking for beaches, either head north from Kuşadası to Pamucak or travel 33 km (20 miles) south to this lovely national park, which has good hiking trails and several quiet stretches of sandy beach. The İçmeler beach, closest to the entrance, is also the most crowded. Travel 15 minutes to Karaburun for a more low-key atmosphere. To get to the park, take the coast road, marked Güzelçamlı or Davutlar, for about 10 km (6 miles) south of Kuşadası. The park also contains the so-called Cave of Zeus, and an archaeological site from when the peninsula was known as Mycale. ✉ *Güzelçamlı* 🎫 *6 TL* ⊙ *Daily 8–7 (closes at 5 in winter).*

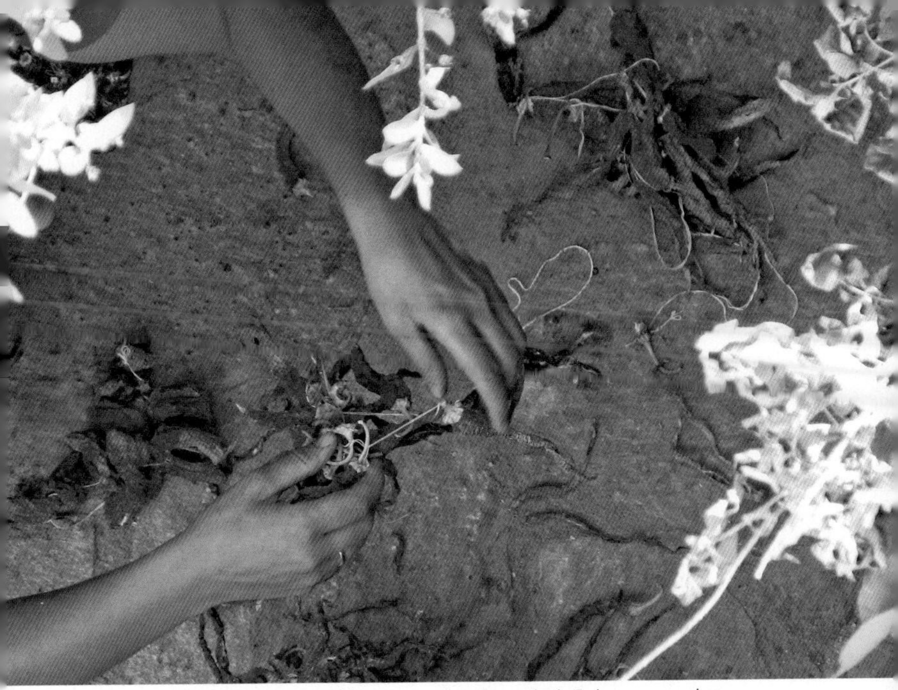

Dried peppers are strung together in an artful manner. —photo by sarabeth, Fodors.com member

WHERE TO EAT

$$ SEAFOOD 🍴 **Ali Baba Restaurant.** An appetizing and colorful display of the catch of the day greets you at the entrance to this waterside eatery, where the interior is simple, the view over the bay soothing, and the food good. *Meze* (appetizers) include cold black-eyed pea salad, marinated octopus salad, and several meat dishes are available for those not inclined toward seafood. Their batter can be a bit heavy, so the grilled options are usually best. [$] *Average main: 25 TL* ✉ *Belediye Turistik Çarşısı 5* ☎ *256/614–1551* ✍ *Reservations essential.*

$$ SEAFOOD 🍴 **Ferah.** Since it opened in 2009, this laid-back, upscale waterfront seafood restaurant has become a favorite with locals, who spill out from the stone walls and onto the terrace. The menu features excellent meze, including fried calamari and grilled eggplant with a punchy white sauce, and fish either simply grilled or cooked with béchamel or tomatoes. Oven-baked halvah with ice cream is a good choice for dessert. Alcoholic drinks are available. [$] *Average main: 25 TL* ✉ *Güvercinada Cad.10* ☎ *256/614–1281* ✍ *Reservations essential.*

$$ TURKISH 🍴 **Öz Urfa.** The name means "pure Urfa" (Urfa is a city famed for its sizzling grilled meats), and the focus at this causal, 50-year-old spot is on kebabs and other meaty Turkish dishes, at slightly high but still reasonable prices. The comfortable surroundings, including a pleasant terrace, are just off Barbaros Hayrettin Caddesi, the main thoroughfare (though there are no views). Alcohol is not served. [$] *Average main: 20 TL* ✉ *Cephane Sok. 7/A* ☎ *256/612–9881* 🌐 *www.ozurfakebabs.com.*

$ TURKISH FAMILY 🍴 **Yuvam.** A five-minute walk from the *kervansaray*, "My Nest/Home" truly lives up to its name, offering the kind of food you'd find in a Turkish home. At lunchtime, items sell out quickly, so get there early to enjoy

Genoese Castle . . . 1
Kervansaray 2

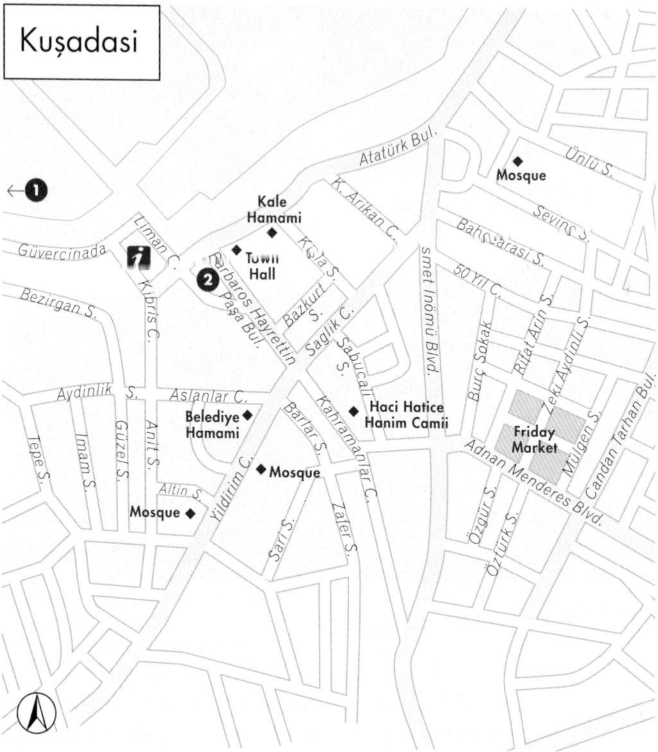

mantı (Turkish style ravioli with plain yogurt and tomato/butter sauce), *bamya* (okra) in a tomato-olive oil sauce, meat stew, and baked chicken with rice. The menu also includes soups, grilled meats, and vegetarian dishes. Alcohol is not served. $ *Average main: 15 TL* ✉ *Camikebir Mh., Kaleiçi Yedieylül Sok. 4* ☎ *256/614–9460.*

WHERE TO STAY

$$ HOTEL **Club Caravanserail.** A real sense of history awaits at this refurbished 300-year-old stone inn right across from the port—it was once a way station for camel caravans and retains an Ottomanesque style. **Pros:** atmospheric building fun for history buffs; historic Turkish style; central location. **Cons:** live-music nights can be loud; touristy feel; you'll need transport (car or dolmuş) to reach a beach. $ *Rooms from: 228 TL* ✉ *Atatürk Bul. 2* ☎ *256/614–4115* 🌐 *www.caravanserailhotel.com* *26 rooms* 🍽 *Multiple meal plans.*

$$ HOTEL FAMILY **Hotel Carina.** A good choice for families, this hotel, surrounded by beautifully landscaped gardens, is just a short walk from the city center. **Pros:** close to shops, restaurants, and nightlife; rates including some meals are available; refurbished in late 2013; kids welcome. **Cons:** a good beach is a 10-minute walk away. $ *Rooms from: 188 TL* ✉ *Yılancıburnu Bay 1* ☎ *256/612–4023* 🌐 *www.hotelcarina.com.tr* *59 rooms* ⏲ *Closed Nov. –Apr.* 🍽 *Multiple meal plans.*

$$$ HOTEL FAMILY **Kısmet.** This boutique hotel is one of Turkey's classic getaways, set on a private peninsula with its own beach and overlooking the marina on one side and the Aegean on the other. **Pros:** view of harbor and sea; central location near town and sights; gracious restaurants and bars; beautiful gardens; spacious rooms. **Cons:** could use some updating; need transportation to reach town center. [$] *Rooms from: 446 TL* ✉ *Akyar Mevkii, Türkmen Mahallesi* ☎ *256/618–1290* 🌐 *www.kismet.com.tr* 🛏 *82 rooms* 🍴 *Multiple meal plans.*

$ HOTEL **Mr. Happy's Liman Hotel.** This good-value, homey, family-run hotel near the cruise ship dock is cheerful, basic, and clean, with gorgeous views from the rooftop terrace. **Pros:** remarkably helpful owners; very central location with great views; rooftop restaurant. **Cons:** no pool or fitness area; basic amenities; need transportation to reach the beach. [$] *Rooms from: 148 TL* ✉ *Kıbrıs Cad. Buyral Sok. 4* ☎ *256/614–7770* 🌐 *www.limanhotel.com* 🛏 *14 rooms* 🍴 *Breakfast.*

NIGHTLIFE

Barlar Sokak. There are several Irish- and British-style pubs along Barlar Sokak, not far from the harbor.

Club Kervansaray. In addition to dining, this place hosts a rather cheesy "Turkish night" on Tuesday and Friday evenings. ✉ *Atatürk Bul. 2* ☎ *256/614–4115.*

PAMUKKALE (HIERAPOLIS)

170 km (105 miles) from Selçuk; 191 km (119 miles) from Kuşadası.

Pamukkale (pronounced pam-ook-ka-lay), which means "cotton castle" in Turkish, first appears as an enormous, chalky white cliff rising 330 feet from the plains. Mineral-rich volcanic spring water cascades over basins and natural terraces, crystallizing into travertines—white curtains of what looks like solidified white water, seemingly suspended in air. The hot springs at Pamukkale are believed to cure rheumatism and other ailments and have attracted visitors for millennia, as illustrated by the ruins of the Roman spa city of Hierapolis, whose well-preserved theater and necropolis lie within sight of Pamukkale.

In the mid-1990s, the diversion of water from the springs to fill thermal pools in nearby luxury hotels in the adjacent spa village of Karahayıt reduced the volume of water reaching Pamukkale. This, combined with a huge increase in the number of visitors, discolored the water's once-pristine whiteness. As a result, wearing shoes in the water is prohibited to protect the deposits. Although Pamukkale is not quite as dramatic as it once was, for first-time visitors the white cliffs are still an impressive sight. Parts of the site are now blocked off, as the authorities strive to conserve and restore a striking natural wonder to its former magnificence. However, you can still venture down the white cliffs and soak in the water: the rock can be prickly and slippery by turns, so remember to watch your step, no matter how enthralled you are.

If you have time, spend the night in Pamukkale, as the one-day bus tours from the coast are exhausting and limiting: you'll end up spending more time on the bus than you do at the actual site. A full day at

Pamukkale will give you enough time to enjoy the water and the ruins. The site is large, but you can easily navigate it without a guide, if you want the freedom to swim, wade, and explore at your own pace. If you have more time, the area around Pamukkale is dotted with interesting geological formations and archaeological sites, including the nearby ruins of Laodicea and the springs of Karahayıt.

GETTING HERE AND AROUND

Pamukkale is approximately a three- to four-hour drive from İzmir, Selçuk, Kuşadası, or Bodrum on Rte. E87 (follow road signs after Sarayköy) There are daily bus tours from all of these towns to Pamukkale during the high season. You can also fly into Denizli airport, about an hour's drive away.

If you don't have your own car, a local travel agency can be very helpful.

TOURS

Hermosa Tours. Run by the same family as the Artemis Yörük Hotel, this agency arranges tours of the Pamukkale region, Laodicea, Aphrodisias, and beyond. ⊠ *Kale Mh., Atatürk Cad. 5/A* ☎ *258/272–2666.*

Tours 4 Turkey Travel (T4T). This agency has offices in both Pamukkale and Kuşadası, and offers tours of Pamukkale, Aphrodisias, and other places. ⊠ *Kale Mh., Cumhuriyet Meydanı 7* ☎ *258/272–2820* ⊕ *www. tours4turkey.com.*

EXPLORING

Hierapolis. The well-maintained site of Hierapolis is lovely proof of how long the magical springs of Pamukkale have drawn eager travelers and pilgrims to partake of the waters' supposed healing powers. The ruins that can be seen today date from the time of the Roman Empire, but there are references to a settlement here as far back as the 5th century BC. Because the sights are spread over about ½ km (¼ mile), prepare for some walking—or hop on the open-air shuttle (3 TL). Near the North Gate is a macabre indication of the former popularity of the healing springs, a vast and beautiful **necropolis** (cemetery) with more than 1,000 cut-stone sarcophagi spilling all the way down to the base of the hill. Continue on to reach a well-preserved gate, public bath complex, and the market street. Near the high **theater** stand the ruins of a **Temple of Apollo** and a bulky **Byzantine church.** The monumental fountain known as the **Nymphaion,** just north of the Apollo Temple, dates from the 4th century AD. Especially intriguing is the **Ploutonion,** built over a cave that leaks poisonous fumes from the bowels of the earth, so deadly that the Romans revered and feared it as a portal to the underworld. Unfortunate birds still occasionally suffocate in the fumes. Below the theater, near the **Sacred Pool,** the stone building that enclosed Hierapolis' public baths is now the **Pamukkale Müzesi** (museum) with a fine display of marble carvings found at the site.

If you have no interest in the ruins, you can put your bathing suit on under your clothes, and enter at the site's **South Gate (Güney Kapı)** on Mehmet Akif Ersoy Bulvar and wade your way up through the travertine pools, and over the crest of the cliff to the **Sacred Pool.** The South Gate is easy walking distance from Pamukkale town. If, however, you want to see the ruins before getting wet, get a lift to the **North**

Gate (**Kuzey Kapı**) of the site (open 8 am to 10 pm), walk through the site, then go downhill through the travertine pools to Pamukkale town. ☎ *258/272–2077 visitor center (for information), 258/272–2034 museum* ⤳ *20 TL.*

Karahayıt. Only 6½ km (4 miles) from Pamukkale, this down-to-earth village attracts visitors for its "red springs," where the warm mineral water and gooey mud are popular for their supposed health-giving properties. The springs are open to the public and flanked by inexpensive restaurants—mud baths and dead-skin-nibbling "doctor fish" pools are also available for a fee. Locals will tell you that drinking the springwater is good for digestion, and those with a strong stomach may want to put this to the test. ⊠ *Karahayıt.*

Laodicea (*Laodikeia*). On a hill overlooking the white travertines of Pamukkale about 10 km (6 miles) to the north, the relatively little-visited ruins of the ancient city of Laodicea on the Lycus are perfect for an atmospheric ramble down collonaded streets, or (with care) down the crumbling slopes of two unrestored, yet poetically lovely ancient theaters. Founded in the 3rd century BC, Laodicea passed into Pergamene, then Roman hands, and was a prosperous trading city, known for its black wool. Luxurious public buildings, including baths and a temple to an unknown divinity testify to its wealth. Roman Laodicea's relatively large Jewish population (in the thousands) likely contributed to the early adoption of Christianity in the city, and the basilica (currently under restoration) was one of the "Seven Churches of Asia" in the Book of Revelation; try to catch a glimpse of its extensive geometric mosaics. ◧TIP➜ **You can join a tour from Pamukkale center. If driving, be sure to check with your hotel that the site is not closed for excavations.** ⊠ *Goncali.*

FAMILY
Fodor'sChoice
★

Sacred Pool. There are several reasons visitors flock to the thermal waters of the Sacred Pool at Hierapolis: the bathtub-warm water (a relatively constant 95 degrees Fahrenheit), the reputed therapeutic properties of the mineral-rich water (Cleopatra supposedly used it as toner), and the atmospheric marble columns and ancient stone carvings scattered about. The lushly landscaped complex has changing rooms, lock boxes (5 TL) to store your stuff, and a snack bar. Entry to the pools is expensive (you need to pay to get into Hierapolis as well) but floating over ancient ruins in hot, faintly effervescent mineral water is more fun than it sounds. If you don't want to spend the time/money, you can relax at the snack bar with a beverage instead. The pool gets crowded in the summer months so plan your visit for early morning or after the tour buses depart. The pool closes earlier in winter months but it's also much less crowded during the day. Consider bringing your own towel. ⊠ *Hierapolis* ⤳ *35 TL* ☉ *Daily 8–7.*

WHERE TO EAT AND STAY

$$
TURKISH

✕**Ünal Restaurant.** There are no views here, but this helps to give the restaurant a less touristy vibe than is usual in Pamukkale. The good menu features simple village food and grills, including delicious *kuzu pirzola* (lamb chops), at city prices. Mains are on the small side, but their generous helpings of delicious vegetable mezes would make a

Turkish granny proud—get the roasted eggplant in garlicky yogurt, or a mixed plate for the hungry and indecisive. Meals are served on a patio during the summer months. [$] *Average main: 17 TL* ✉ *Cumhuriyet Meydanı* ☎ *258/272–2451.*

$ HOTEL FAMILY Fodor's Choice ★ 🏨 **Artemis Yörük Hotel.** Though the accommodations are basic, outstanding customer service from super-helpful staff makes this budget hotel a top choice in Pamukkale—and it's just a two-minute walk from the travertines and five minutes from the ruins. **Pros:** large pool and free sauna; comfy public spaces; creditable buffet breakfast, great value; knowledgeable staff, restaurant also serves dinner. **Cons:** some rooms are a bit run-down; down-to-earth feel; no views of travertines. [$] *Rooms from: 69 TL* ✉ *Atatürk Cad. 48* ☎ *258/272–2674* 🌐 *www.artemisyorukhotel.com* 🛏 *40 rooms* 🍴 *Breakfast.*

$$ HOTEL 🏨 **Ayapam Boutique Hotel.** The many resort-like amenities here include a hammam (Turkish bath), sauna, and Jacuzzi, and rooms have views of the travertines. **Pros:** fresh, bright, tastefully decorated surroundings; lovely terrace; restaurant with panoramic view; elevator; large outdoor pool. **Cons:** dinner-inclusive rates required; 10-minute walk through town to the travertines. [$] *Rooms from: 227 TL* ✉ *Kale Mahallesi, Bahçe Sok. 2/1* ☎ *258/272–2203* 🌐 *www.ayapamboutiquehotel.com* 🛏 *20 rooms* 🍴 *Some meals.*

$$ HOTEL 🏨 **Hal-Tur Hotel.** Most of the clean, fresh rooms at this distinctive palestone hotel have balconies overlooking the white travertines, and one large family room has its own Jacuzzi and vast terrace. **Pros:** staff are knowledgeable about Pamukkale and the surrounding area; full view of the travertines from breakfast area and many rooms; midsize, kid-friendly pool. **Cons:** a bit expensive given the fairly basic comforts; no elevator; four-minute walk to village center. [$] *Rooms from: 200 TL* ✉ *Mehmet Akif Ersoy Bul. 71* ☎ *258/272–2723* 🌐 *www.haltur.net* 🛏 *11 rooms* 🍴 *Breakfast.*

SPORTS AND THE OUTDOORS

FAMILY Fodor's Choice ★ **Pamukkale Natural Park.** At the very foot of the white travertines, this delightful park with grassy lawns entertains local families and visitors alike, with fantastically shaped pedalo boats on the pond, ducks to feed, private swimming pools, a cheery open-air café that stays open into the night, and ice cream stands. It's free to enter; the pools and boats cost extra. Nowhere in town has better views. ✉ *Mehmet Akif Ersoy Bul.* ☎ *258/272–2244* 🌐 *www.pamukkalenaturalpark.net.*

APHRODISIAS

80 km (50 miles) from Pamukkale.

Aphrodisias, the city of Aphrodite, goddess of love, is one of the largest and best-preserved archaeological sites in Turkey. It's interesting to compare this site to Ephesus, so although it's a bit of a detour, it's quite rewarding. You'll need a few hours to get a true taste of the site. It was home to a magnificent school of sculpture, and a number of surviving masterworks are on display in the Aphrodisias Museum.

GETTING HERE AND AROUND

Aphrodisias is off the E87—turn south on Rte. 585 and head for the town of Geyre. If you'll be driving from Pamukkale to Selçuk, İzmir, or Kuşadası, or vice versa, it is most convenient to follow the example of most bus tours and visit Aphrodisias en route. You will save much time and energy if you rent a car and visit this and the other nearby ancient sites on your own because a private tour can eliminate backtracking.

EXPLORING

FAMILY
Fodor'sChoice
★

Aphrodisias. The city of Aphrodite, goddess of love, is one of the largest and best-preserved archaeological sites in Turkey. Though most of what you see today dates from the 1st and 2nd centuries AD, archaeological evidence indicates that the local dedication to Aphrodite follows a long history of veneration of pre-Hellenic goddesses, such as the Anatolian mother goddess and the Babylonian god Ishtar. Only about half of the site has been excavated. It's much less crowded than Ephesus, and enough remains to conjure the ancient city.

Granted autonomy by the Roman Empire in the late 1st century BC, the city prospered as a significant center for religion, literature, and arts (especially sculpture) in the early 1st century AD. Imposing Christianity on the citizens later proved difficult, however, because of Aphrodite's large following. One method used to eradicate remnants of polytheism was to rename the city, first Stavropolis (City of the Cross), then simply Caria—archaeologists believe this is the origin of the name of the present-day village of Geyre, which contains Aphrodisias in its borders.

The excavations here have led archaeologists to surmise that Aphrodisias was a thriving sculpture center, with patrons beyond the borders of the city—statues and fragments with signatures of Aphrodisian artists have shown up as far away as Greece and Italy. The towering Babadağ range of mountains, east of the city, offered ancient sculptors a copious supply of white and delicately veined blue-gray marble, which has been used to stunning effect in statuary, in spiral and fluted columns, and in the delicate reliefs of gods and men, vines, and acanthus leaves on decorative friezes.

You'll take a short, bumpy ride on an open-air shuttle from the parking area to the main gate. Past the site museum, follow the footpath to the right, which makes a circuit around the site and ends up back at the museum. The lovely **Tetrapylon** is a monumental gateway with four rows of columns and some of the better remaining friezes. Notice the touching memorial to an archaeologist who devoted his life to Aphrodisias. Behind it, the vast **Temple of Aphrodite** was built in the 1st century BC on the model of the great temples at Ephesus, and later transformed into a basilica church. Its gate and many of its columns are still standing; some bear inscriptions naming the donor of the column. Follow the footpath across a field to the **stadium,** which once was the scene of foot races, boxing and wrestling matches, and other competitions. One of the best preserved of its kind anywhere, the stadium could seat up to 30,000 spectators. Back near the Temple of Aphrodite cluster a magnificent ruined residence, the fine **Odeon,** an intimate, semicircular concert hall and public meeting room, towering **public baths** (currently under excavation), and the sprawling **agora**, which once included a wide pool. The 5,000 white-marble seats of the city's **theater**, built into the side of a small hill, are simply dazzling on a bright day. The adjacent **School of Philosophy** has a colonnaded courtyard with chambers lining both sides, where teachers worked with small groups of students.

After a ramble around the ruins, head back to the beauties of the **site museum**, just before the ticket booth, where Aphrodisias bursts back into life in vivid freizes and sculptures that seem almost about to draw breath. The museum's collection includes several impressive statues from the site, including Aphrodite herself. Be sure to pick up an audioguide (10 TL) and a map—you'll need them, as the signage is poor.

⚠ Aphrodisias may make you feel like Indiana Jones, but don't venture beyond marked areas; ancient walls have been known to cave in beneath the feet of unwary tourists. ✉ *Geyre* 🎫 *10 TL* ☉ *Daily 8–7 in summer; 8:30–4:30 in winter. Museum closed Mon.*

PRIENE, MILETUS, AND DIDYMA

Priene is 38 km (24 miles) from Kuşadası; from Priene it's 22 km (14 miles) to Miletus; from Miletus it's 22 km (14 miles) to Didyma; Didyma is 139 km (86 miles) from Bodrum.

The three towns of Priene, Miletus, and Didyma make up part of Ancient Ionia, homeland of many of the ancient world's greatest artistic and scientific minds, and each endowed with haunting ruins. They're all within 40 km (25 miles) of each another, and if you get an early enough start, you can visit them all in one day, either with a car or on a PDM (Priene, Miletus, Didyma) tour with a local agency. If you decide to spend a night in the area, you'll find the most hotels in and around Didyma, where the modern town has developed into a lively seaside resort, populated largely by foreigners.

GETTING HERE AND AROUND

Tours to these towns can be arranged from İzmir, Selçuk, Kuşadası, and Bodrum. The Pamukkale Bus Company offers service from İzmir to Didyma (Didim), and minibuses departing Didyma stop at Priene and Miletus. You can also go to Didyma from Bodrum via the Bodrum Express Lines Hydrofoil and Ferryboat Services. To reach Miletus by public transportation, take a dolmuş to Söke, and another from Söke to Akköy, 5 km (3 miles) from the site. Take a taxi or dolmuş from Akköy to the ruins. For Priene, you can travel by dolmuş from Kuşadası or Selçuk to Söke, and from Söke to Güllübahçe, the small town at the foot of the ruins, and hike up to the site. For all these destinations, a car or tour will be much more efficient, especially if you are visiting two or more of the towns.

EXPLORING

Didyma. Didyma (Didim in Turkish), a resort town quickly becoming overcrowded, was an important sacred site connected to Miletus by a sacred road lined with statues (currently under excavation). The temple of Apollo is here, as well as some beaches, which are increasingly frequented by Brits who have bought real estate in the area.

Didyma is famous for its magnificent **Temple of Apollo.** As grand in scale as the Parthenon—measuring 623 feet by 167 feet—the temple has 124 well-preserved columns, some still supporting their archıtravés. Started in 300 BC and under construction for nearly five centuries, the temple was never completed, and some of the columns remain unfluted. The oracle here rivaled the one at Delphi, and beneath the courtyard is a network of underground corridors used by temple priests for their oracular consultations. The corridor walls would throw the oracle's voice into deep and ghostly echoes, which the priests would interpret. The tradition of seeking advice from a sacred oracle here probably started long before the arrival of the Greeks, who in all likelihood converted an older Anatolian cult based at the site into their own religion. The Greek oracle had a good track record, and at the birth of Alexander the Great (356 BC) predicted that he would be victorious over the Persians, that his general Seleucus would later become king, and that Trajan would become an emperor.

Around AD 385, the popularity of the oracle dwindled with the rise of Christianity. The temple was later excavated by French and German archaeologists, and its statues are long gone, hauled back to England by Sir Charles Newton in 1858. Fragments of bas-reliefs on display by the entrance to the site include a gigantic head of Medusa (twin of the one in Istanbul's Underground cistern, across from Hagia Sophia) and a small statue of Poseidon and his wife, Amphitrite. ⊠ *22 km (14 miles) south of Priene on Rte. 09–55, Didyma* ⊞ *5 TL; audioguide 10 TL* ☉ *Daily 8:30–6.*

Miletus. Before the harbor silted over, Miletus was one of the greatest commercial centers of the Greek world, and the Milesians renowned for their quick wits and courage. The first settlers were Minoan Greeks from Crete who arrived between 1400 BC and 1200 BC. The Ionians, who arrived 200 years later, slaughtered the male population and married the widows. The philosopher Thales was born here in the early 6th century BC. He calculated the height of the pyramids at Giza, suggested that the universe was actually a rational place despite its apparent disorder, and coined the phrase *"Know thyself."* Miletus was also home to the mathematicians Anaximenes and Anaximander—the former contended that air was the single element behind the diversity of nature; the latter's ideas anticipated the theory of evolution and the concept of the indestructibility of matter—and one of the architects of Hagia Sophia. Like the other Ionian cities, Miletus was passed from one ruling empire to another and was successively governed by Alexander's generals Antigonus and Lysimachus and Pergamum's Attalids, among others. Under the Romans the town finally regained some control over its own affairs and shared in the prosperity of the region. St. Paul preached here at least twice in the 1st century.

The archaeological site is sprawled out along a desolate plain, and laced with well-marked trails. The parking lot is right outside the city's most magnificent building—the **Great Theater,** a remarkably intact 25,000-seat, freestanding amphitheater built by the Ionians and maintained by the Romans. Along the third to sixth rows some inscriptions reserving seats for notables are still visible. The fabulous *vomitoria,* huge vaulted passages leading to the seats, have the feel of a modern sporting arena. Climb to the top of the theater for a look at the walls of the defensive fortress built atop it by the Byzantines, and a view across the ancient city. Try to picture the busy harbor and the waves that once lapped what is now the edge of the parking lot.

To see the rest of the ruins, follow the dirt track down from the right of the theater. A row of buildings marks what was once a broad processional avenue. The series begins with the **Delphinion,** a sanctuary of Apollo; a **stoa** (colonnaded porch) with several re-erected Ionic columns; the foundations of a **Roman bath** and **gymnasium;** and the first story of the **Nymphaion,** all that remains of the once highly ornate three-story structure, resembling the Library of Celsus at Ephesus, that once distributed water to the rest of the city.

To the south, the dirt track becomes a tree-lined lane that leads to the **Ilyas Bey Camii,** a mosque built in 1404 in celebration of its builder and namesake's escape from Tamerlane, the Mongol terror. The mosque has been rather over-restored, but still retains some charm. Nearby stands a **Seljuk hammam** (public bath) added to the site in the 15th century, with pipes for hot and cold water still visible. Parts of the site are sometimes overgrown, and snakes have been spotted here, so wear close-toed shoes if planning to explore beyond the main path.

A three-minute drive outside the gates of the site, the small, newly opened **Milet Müzesi** presents interesting artifacts from the site and the surrounding area with panache. Their bright displays will help you conjure a vision of ancient Miletus and its world. Ask your tour guide in advance if you can make at least a short stop here. If driving, ask the guards to point you in the right direction as you exit the Miletus archaeological site. ⊠ *22 km (14 miles) south of Priene on Rte. 09–55* ☎ *256/875–5206 museum* ⛁ *5 TL; audioguide 10 TL; museum 3 TL* ⊙ *Daily 8–7 (closes around 5 in winter); museum Tues.–Sun. 8–7 (closes around 4 in winter).*

Priene. Spectacularly sited, these remains top a steep hill above the flat valley of the Büyük Menderes Nehri (Maeander River, whose twisting course gave us the verb *meander.* Dating from about 350 BC, the present-day remnants of the city were still under construction in 334, when Alexander the Great liberated the Ionian settlements from Persian rule. At that time, Priene was a thriving port, but as in Ephesus, the harbor silted over, so commerce moved to neighboring Miletus, and the city's prosperity waned. As a result, the Romans never rebuilt Priene and the simpler Greek style predominates as in few other ancient cities in Turkey. First excavated by British archaeologists in 1868–69, the site is smaller than Ephesus and far quieter and less grandiose.

From the parking area, the walk up to the Priene ruins is fairly steep. Routes through the ruins are fairly well marked. After passing through the old city walls, follow the city's original main thoroughfare and notice the drainage gutters and the grooves worn into the marble paving stones by the wheels of 4th-century BC chariots. Continuing west, you come to the well-preserved *bouleterion* (council chamber) on the left. The 10 rows of seats flank an orchestra pit with a little altar, decorated with bulls' heads and laurel leaves at the center. Passing through the doors on the opposite side of the council chamber takes you to the Sacred Stoa, a colonnaded civic center, and the edge of the **agora** (marketplace). Farther west along the broad promenade are the remains of a row of **private houses,** each of which typically has two or three rooms on two floors: of the upper floors, only traces of a few stairwells remain. In the largest house a statue of Alexander was found.

A block or so farther along the main street is the **Temple of Athena,** the work of Pytheos, architect of the Mausoleum of Halicarnassus (one of the Seven Wonders of the Ancient World) and the design was repeatedly copied at other sites in the Greek empire. Alexander apparently chipped in on construction costs for the temple, a dwelling for the goddess Athena rather than a place for worshippers to gather—only priests could enter. Between the columns, look on the marble floor for a small circle, criss-crossed with lines like a pizza—a secret symbol of Ionia's ancient Christians. Walk north and then east along the track that leads to the well-preserved little **theater,** sheltered on all sides by pine trees. Enter through the stage door into the orchestra section and note the five front-row VIP seats, carved thrones with lions' feet. If you scramble up a huge rock known as Samsun Dağı (behind the theater and to your left as you face the seats) you will find the sparse remains of the **Sanctuary of Demeter,** goddess of the harvest; only a few remnants of the columns and walls remain, as well as a big hole through which blood of sacrificial victims was poured as a gift to the deities of the underworld. Since few people make it up here, it is an incredibly peaceful spot with a terrific view over Priene and the plains. Beyond are the remnants of a Hellenistic fortress. (⚠ Check safety conditions before you climb.)

▰TIP➔ Bring bottled water; the stand at the foot of the hill is very overpriced. ✉ *37 km (23 miles) from Kuşadası, southeast on Rte. 515, south on Rte. 525, west on Rte. 09–55 (follow signs), Güllübahçe* 🖧 *5 TL* ☉ *Daily 8–7 (closes at 5 in winter).*

WHERE TO EAT AND STAY

$$
TURKISH
FAMILY
✕ **Didim Şehir Lokantası.** The quality and price of the offerings make the trip out to this residential neighborhood (sometimes still known by its old name "Yenihisar Mahallesi") well worth the effort. The *İskender kebab,* thin strips of döner served on a bed of pita bread with tomato sauce and plain yogurt, is especially good, as are the grills, *pide,* and home-style meat and vegetable dishes; they also serve soup all day long. Alcohol is served, despite the new mosque across the street. ▰TIP➔ Call ahead (they speak English) and they'll give you a free ride to the restaurant from Didyma center. $ *Average main: 17 TL* ✉ *Çarşı İçi 830, Didyma* ☎ *256/811–4488* ⊕ *www.didimsehirlokantasi.com.*

$$$ SEAFOOD 🍴 **Kamacı 2.** One of the best (and pricier) restaurants in Altınkum is right on the water at the end of the pier, with a beautiful view of the sea and fresh, locally sourced seafood. Prawns, seasoned and cooked to perfection, are a great appetizer to share. The atmosphere is peaceful, and evenings here can be romantic, especially when the moon is in view. [$] *Average main: 35 TL* ✉ *Iskele Karşısı, Yali Cad., Altınkum, Didyma* ☎ *256/813–2349* ✍ *Reservations essential.*

$$ HOTEL 🏨 **Orion Beach Hotel.** On its own beach in Altınkum, this resortlike getaway is also close to the town's restaurants and shops. **Pros:** good value, pleasant interior style, on the beach; 15-minute walk to the Temple of Apollo; pool. **Cons:** some distance to Miletus and other ancient sights; nearby bars can be a bit noisy; dinner-inclusive room rates required. [$] *Rooms from: 236 TL* ✉ *Yalı Cad. 73, Altınkum, Didyma* ☎ *256/813–2041* 🌐 *www.orionhoteldidim.com* 🛏 *78 rooms* 🕒 *Closed Oct.–Apr.* 🍽 *Some meals.*

SPORTS AND THE OUTDOORS

FAMILY **Altınkum.** For a break after all the history, continue another 5 km (3 miles) from Didyma south to Altınkum, popular for its pale-sand beach. The sand stretches for a bit less than 1 km (½ mile) and is bordered by a row of decent seafood restaurants, all facing the water, and some small modest hotels. At peak times, a lifeguard watches over the 500-meter public, Blue Flag–designated beach (*halk plajı*), which quickly gets crowded in summertime. **Amenities:** food and drink; lifeguards; showers; toilets. **Best for:** swimming. ✉ *At the end of Atatürk Bul., Didyma.*

THE BODRUM PENINSULA

Until the mid-20th century, the Bodrum Peninsula was little known, and its gorgeous coastline was home to fishermen and sponge divers. Then a bohemian set (artists, writers, and painters) discovered Bodrum and put the place on the map. Today, Bodrum is booming—a year-round getaway for Turks and foreigners alike. You'll be in the center of the action in Bodrum town, the busiest spot on the peninsula, but a stay in one of the smaller villages nearby will reveal the region's quieter charms and its landscape of tangerine orchards and stone windmills. The lovely, mysterious stone domes that dot the landscape are old water cisterns.

BODRUM

789 km (490 miles) from Istanbul; 242 km (150 miles) from İzmir; 161 km (100 miles) from Kuşadası; 125 km (78 miles) from Didyma.

On the southern shores of a broad peninsula that stretches along two crescent-shape bays, Bodrum has for years been the favorite haunt of the Turkish upper classes. Today, thousands of foreign visitors come here, too. The town is throbbing with cafés, restaurants, and discos. Bodrum is decidedly not the quaint village it once was, but it's still beautiful, with gleaming whitewashed buildings covered in bougainvillea and unfettered vistas of sparkling bays.

Bodrum Peninsula

Küçük Tavsan Island

Güllük Korfezi

Türkbükü

Gündoğan **Göl-Türkbükü)**

İkiz Island

Yalıkavak

Geriş

Pazar Mournuni ▲

Torba Bay

Torba

390

B O D R U M   P E N I N S U L A

Karakaya

Ortakent

Yahşi

Agacli

Bodrum

Gümüşlük

Bitez

Gümbet

Kadikalesi

Yalıçiftlik

Kargi Bay

Turgutreis

Bagla Bay

İc Ada Island

Karaincir

Bodrum Korfezi

Akyarlar

Karaincir Bay

Kara Ada Island

Koca Point

Akyar Point

TO KOS, GREECE   TO DATÇA   TO KORMEN

0 _____ 2 mi

0 _____ 2 km

GETTING HERE AND AROUND

The Bodrum Ferryboat Association has ferry service from Bodrum to Kos, Symi, Rhodes and Kalymnos, in Greece, and in Turkey, Turgutreis and Datça, a beachy peninsula between the Mediterranean and Aegean seas. The Bodrum Express Lines Hydrofoil and Ferryboat Services has ferry and hydrofoil service from Bodrum to Sedir (Cleopatra Island), Datça, Marmaris, Dalyan, and Didymain in Turkey, as well as to the islands of Kos, Kalymnos, Symi, and Rhodes in Greece. Thanks to millennia of shared history, these Greek islands retain striking harmonies with the Turkish mainland, but are different enough to merit an excursion, if you have time. Make sure you bring your passport if traveling to Greece, and brace yourself for less-than-efficient passport control lines at the border.

Contacts Bodrum Express Lines ☎ 252/316–1087 ⊕ www. bodrumexpresslines.com. **Bodrum Ferryboat Association** ☎ 252/316–0882 ⊕ www.bodrumferryboat.com.

Travel Agencies/Tour Operators Akustik Tourism Center ✉ Neyzen Tevfik Cad. 146, Marina, Bodrum ☎ 252/313–4523 ⊕ www.akustik.tc. **Neyzen Tours** ✉ Kibris Şehitleri Cad. 34, Bodrum ☎ 252/316–7204 ⊕ www.neyzen.com.tr.

EXPLORING

Ancient Theater (*Antik Tiyatro*). Consruction of the magnificent, 5,000-seat ancient theater began during the 4th century BC reign of King Mausolus *(⇨ See Mausoleum, below)*, back when Bodrum was known as Halicarnassus of Caria. The Hellenistic theater was used and updated through the Roman era, and remains one of the ancient city's best-preserved monuments; it is still used for concerts and other performances. The view of Bodrum and the Aegean Sea is breathaking from this high, hillside vantage point. ⊠ *Kıbrıs Şehitleri Cad., Yeniköy Mh., Bodrum* ⊡ *Free* ⊙ *Tues.– Sun. 8–5.*

> ### GETTING AROUND BODRUM
>
> Renting a car is a good idea if you wish to venture beyond Bodrum proper. Taxis are widely available, though pricey, and *dolmuşes* (inexpensive shared-ride minibuses) ply the route up and down the peninsula, departing from Bodrum's central *otogar* (bus station). Look for the name of your destination in the window of the dolmuş.

Mausoleum. Little remains of the extravagant white-marble tomb of Mausolus of Halicarnassus, one of the Seven Wonders of the Ancient World—and the source of the word *mausoleum*. During the 4th century, Bodrum (then called Halicarnassus) was governed by King Mausolos. Upon his death in 353 BC, Queen Artemisia, his wife and sister, ordered the construction of the great white-marble tomb. At almost 150 feet in height, the **Mausoleum at Halicarnassus** must have been quite a sight—a towering rectangular base topped by Ionic columns and freizes of spectacular relief sculpture, surmounted by a pyramidal roof, and crowned with a massive statue of Mausolus and Artemisia, riding a chariot into eternity. The Mausoleum stood for over a millennium, but the 15th-century Knights of St. John plundered its stones to build the **Petronion**, while 19th-century Brits carted many of the surviving sculptures off to the British Museum. Admission price is relatively high for what little you'll see, but it does offer s a rare opportunity to reflect on how a Wonder of the World has been reduced to fallen masonry and broken columns. The site also contains a bare but interesting earlier underground burial chamber. ⊠ *Tepecik, Gerence Sok., Bodrum* ⊡ *8 TL* ⊙ *Tues.–Sun. 8–7 (closes at 5 in the off-season).*

FAMILY

Fodor's Choice

★

Petronion and Museum of Underwater Archaeology (*Bodrum Castle*). Built in the early 15th century by the Knights Hospitaller (Knights of St. John), the **Petronion,** also known as Bodrum Castle or the Castle of St. Peter, rises between Bodrum's twin harbors like an illustration from a fairy tale. With German knight-architect Heinrich Schlegelholt at the helm, the knightly builders plundered the **Mausoleum at Halicarnassus** for green volcanic stone, marble columns, and reliefs to create this showpiece of late-medieval architecture, whose walls are studded with 249 coats of arms, including the crests of the Plantagenets and d'Aubussons. The castle's towers and gardens are visible from many parts of town, and the name "Bodrum" itself likely derives from the word *Petronion*. The castle's five towers are named after the home-lands of the knights who built them: France, Germany, Italy, Spain and

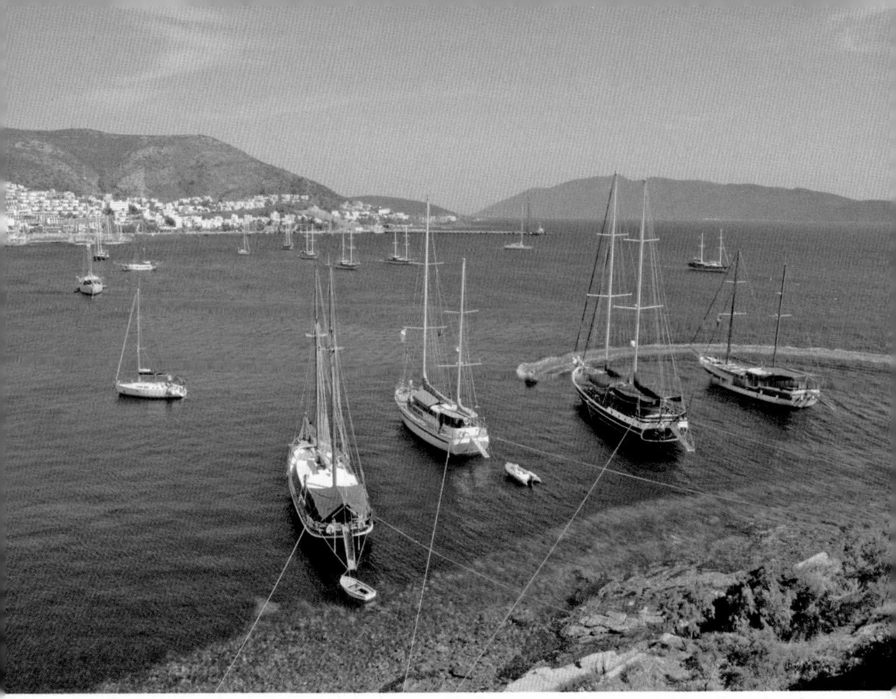

Daily boat cruises from the marina in Bodrum's city center will take you to nearby coves and bays for a day of swimming and sunbathing.

England (the English Tower, embellished with a relief of a lion, is known as the Lion Tower, and houses a medieval hall).

The castle now houses the delightful **Museum of Underwater Archaeology,** where displays include the world's oldest excavated shipwreck (Uluburun), the tomb of the so-called "Carian Princess," and the sunken cargos of many ancient and medieval ships that sank off the treacherous Aegean coast. ✉ *Kale Cad., Bodrum* ☎ *252/316–2516* 🌐 *www.bodrum-museum.com* 🎫 *20 TL, audioguide 10 TL* 🕒 *Tues.–Sun. 8:30–4:30 (closes 6:30 mid-Apr.–mid-Oct.).*

WHERE TO EAT

$$ TURKISH FAMILY 🍴 **Denizhan Et Lokantası.** The best meats and kebabs in Bodrum are served in outlying Konacık, about 3 km (2 miles) from the center. Appetziers, including *lahmacun* (Turkish-style whisper-thin flatbread topped with spices and minced meat) and vegetable dishes are also very good; in season, they use figs and lemons from their own garden. In warm weather, seating is on a terrace in front or a spacious back garden with views of the mountains and valley. The wine list is extensive. [$] *Average main: 26 TL* ✉ *Atatürk Bul. 277, Konacık, Bodrum* ☎ *252/363–7674* 🌐 *www.denizhan.com* ✍ *Reservations essential.*

$$ TURKISH 🍴 **Gemibaşı.** For almost half a centurty, this popular presence near the marina has been serving the freshest seafood in town, in no-frills indoor and outdoor surroundings that are always packed during the season, often with locals. House specialties include fish soup and octopus with pilaf, and their fried calamari has been voted one of the best versions in Turkey. [$] *Average main: $30* ✉ *Neyzen Teyvfik Cad. 176, Bodrum* ☎ *252/316–1220* 🌐 *www.gemibasi.com* ✍ *Reservations essential.*

$$$
SEAFOOD
Fodor'sChoice
★

✕**Kalamare.** Down a discreet, historic alley, this restaurant is an authentic and affordable new star on the Bodrum seafood scene, and its white, candlelit tables quickly fill with hungry locals. Accompany a heaping plate of fried local calamari (probably the most generous in town) with an inexpensive tasting plate of up to four vegetable mezes with toasted bread, and, if you're still hungry, order grilled fish and rakı. Its sister establishment, a wine bar called Modrum, is a few steps down the street; the waterfront is a two-minute stroll in the opposite direction. $ *Average main: 39 TL* ✉ *Çarşı Mh., Sanat Okulu Cad. 9, Bodrum* 🕾 *252/316-7076.*

$$$
MEDITERRANEAN
Fodor'sChoice
★

✕**Kocadon.** The owners have transformed the palm and mulberry tree-filled courtyard of their 200-year-old family home into a romantic haven, where candlelit peacefulness and exquisite Mediterranean cuisine provide one of the loveliest dining experiences in Bodrum. À la carte and tasting menus are available (including a three-hour gourmet option). $ *Average main: 40 TL* ✉ *Neyzen Tevfik Cad., Saray Sok. 1, Bodrum* 🕾 *0252/316-3705* ⊕ *www.kocadon.com* ⌕ *Reservations essential* ⊘ *Closed Nov.–mid-Apr.*

$$$$
TURKISH

✕**Körfez.** This long-standing, family-run fish house overlooks the harbor and is especially noted for a wide selection of Cretan dishes and seafood appetizers that include delectable shrimp cooked in butter, garlic, and seaweed. Some meat dishes are also served, as is brunch. It's a local institution, with correspondingly high prices. $ *Average main: 118 TL* ✉ *Neyzen Tevfik Cad. 2, Bodrum* 🕾 *252/313-8248* ⊕ *www. korfezrestaurant.com.tr* ⌕ *Reservations essential.*

$
TURKISH
FAMILY

✕**Liman Köftecisi.** *Köfte* (Turkish-style meatballs), in all their sizzling variety, are the specialty at this casual and charming blue-and-white eatery in the heart of the waterfront promenade, where the prices are modest and the home-style cooking is excellent (it's run by the same group as the swanky Marina Yacht Club). If you're not in a meatball mood, they have good local vegetable mezes and desserts. Breakfast is also served. $ *Average main: 15 TL* ✉ *Neyzen Tevfik Cad. 172, Bodrum* 🕾 *252/316-5060.*

$$
ITALIAN
FAMILY

✕**Sünger Pizza.** With no view, but a large and cheery summer terrace 30 yards from the waterfront, Sünger Pizza offers up Italian-inspired pastas, salads, and calzones, alongside traditional Turkish chicken and beef dishes, and breakfast until 2 pm. Local families and tourists sit back at wooden tables groaning under enormous calzones—try the Sünger, which oozes calamari, shrimp, garlic, tomatoes, and cheese. Alcohol is served, and not at a ludicrous mark-up. $ *Average main: 20 TL* ✉ *Neyzen Tevfik Cad. 160, Bodrum* 🕾 *252/316-0854* ⊕ *www. sungerpizza.com.*

$$
TURKISH
FAMILY

✕**Tadım Pide.** Just off Neyzen Tevfik Caddesi, Bodrum's main harbor road, this no-frills, bright little *pide* joint fires made-to-order *pide* and the fabulous, classic *lahmacun* (crisp, thin Turkish "pizza" topped with diced meat and spices, wrapped around piles of fresh-chopped parsley and greens) at unbeatable prices. Wash it down with *ayran*, a slightly salty yogurt drink. $ *Average main: 16 TL* ✉ *Tepecik Mh., Hamam Sok. 9/A, Bodrum* 🕾 *252/313-5180* ⊟ *No credit cards.*

WHERE TO STAY

$$$$
RESORT
FAMILY
Fodor's Choice
★

⊞ **Kempinski Hotel Barbaros Bay.** This is by far one of the most beautiful deluxe hotel properties in all of Bodrum, and its location on a private bay in secluded Yalıçiftlik makes it a preferred choice for international clientele seeking to avoid the paparazzi in luxurious comfort. **Pros:** luxurious splendor; four fine dining restaurants (also open to nonguests); world-class infinity pool and spa. **Cons:** on-site restaurants predictably pricey; 20-minute ride to Bodrum city center, 14 km (9 miles) distant (bus and private transfers available). $ *Rooms from: 1,078 TL* ⊠ *Kırağaç Koyu, Gerenkuyu Mevkii, Yalıçiftlik, Bodrum* ☎ *252/311–0303* ⊕ *www.kempinski.com/bodrum* ⌧ *149 rooms, 24 suites* ⊙| *Some meals.*

$$$
HOTEL
Fodor's Choice
★

⊞ **Manastır Hotel & Suites.** No other hotel in Bodrum can match the serene surroundings and sublime views of this former monastery (*manastır* in Turkish), on a glorious perch overlooking Bodrum Bay. **Pros:** Beautifully maintained; lovely surroundings; exquisite sea views; peaceful. **Cons:** A bit of a trek from town. $ *Rooms from: 354 TL* ⊠ *Kumbahçe Mh., Mustafa Kemal Cad. 37, Bodrum* ☎ *252/316–2854* ⊕ *www.manastirhotel.com* ⌧ *73 rooms, 13 suites* ⊙| *Breakfast.*

$$$
HOTEL

⊞ **Marina Vista.** A great location across from the marina and sea or pool views from most of the bright, stylish rooms make this convenient in-town lodging, popular with couples, seem like a resort. **Pros:** close to all restaurants and nightlife; serene atmosphere; buffet breakfast. **Cons:** 15-minute walk to reach a beach; most rooms don't face the sea; no organized activities, though concierge can help; not best for lively kids. $ *Rooms from: 393 TL* ⊠ *Neyzen Tevfik Cad. 168, Bodrum* ☎ *252/313–0356* ⊕ *www.hotelmarinavista.com* ⌧ *87 rooms, 11 suites* ⊙| *Breakfast.*

$$$$
HOTEL

⊞ **The Marmara Bodrum.** Most of the elegant rooms at this hilltop aerie enjoy views of Bodrum and the sea from balconies and terraces, while a free shuttle to a private beach club puts the seaside within easy reach. **Pros:** nicely decorated and appointed rooms; beautiful surroundings; special promotional rates and packages offered from time to time; pets welcome. **Cons:** a bit of a distance from the city center. $ *Rooms from: 747 TL* ⊠ *Yokuşbaşı Mahallesi 18, Bodrum* ☎ *252/313–8130* ⊕ *www. themarmarahotels.com* ⌧ *97 rooms* ⊙| *Multiple meal plans.*

NIGHTLIFE

The nightlife scene in Bodrum is quite diverse. Bars and clubs with DJs or live music on Cumhuriyet, simply called Barlar Sokağı ("street with bars"), attract the young and restless. Trendier and more chichi bars and clubs are by the water on Neyzen Tevfik.

Less than 4 km (2 miles) from Bodrum center, the adjoining bay of Gümbet is known for its restaurants and lively bars, where beachside revelers (many foreign) party 'til dawn. It's more noisy than it is glamorous. Dolmuş services keep shuttling from here to Bodrum well into the night.

Halikarnas ("The Club"). Across the curve of the harbor from the castle, this place bills itself as "probably the most amazing nightclub in the world." It is probably the best known in Bodrum, but is, in fact, rather like discos more commonly found in western Mediterranean resorts, complete with a huge dance floor, fog machines, laser lights, and theme nights. Reservations are recommended, drinks can be pricey, and in summer there is an admission charge. ⊠ *Cumhuriyet Cad. 178, Bodrum* ☎ *252/316–8000* ⊕ *www.halikarnas.com.tr.*

Küba Restaurant & Lounge Bar. With topnotch food and music, Küba is always crowded, especially on weekends. ⊠ *Neyzen Tevfik Cad. 62, Bodrum* ☎ *252/313–4450* ⊕ *www.kubabar.com.*

Fodor's Choice ★ **Marina Yacht Club.** Surrounded by a forest of sailboat masts, this is the first place both Bodrum locals and Turkish tourists will recommend for a night out. The good live music (jazz, classical, etc.) is as diverse as the age groups that come to listen. The dining area on the second floor has a long bar with a terrific view of the marina; the club restaurant is open to children as well, with a menu that ranges from cheap Turkish dishes like *menemen* (eggs scrambled with minced tomatoes, peppers and spices) to seafood dishes with three-figure prices. ⊠ *Milta Bodrum Marina, Bodrum* ☎ *252/316–1228.*

Mavi Bar. A Bodrum institution, the small and quaint Mavi Bar (Blue Bar) occupies century-old premises and features live Turkish music—some of Turkey's most prominent rock stars have appeared here. ⊠ *Cumhuriyet Cad. 175, Bodrum* ☎ *252/316–3932* ⊕ *www.bodrummavibar.com.*

NewOld Club. A two-story open-air space has elegantly decorated lounges in which to drink and socialize, and DJs spin dance, house, pop, R&B, and especially Latin and salsa music for the late-night dancing crowd—mostly 29 and up. In the wee hours, a boat ferries tireless partiers from the Marina Yacht Club (under the same management) to this still-lively club. ⊠ *Eski Han, Kale Cad. 29, Bodrum* ☎ *252/316–9454* ⊕ *www.newold.com.tr* ☼ *Daily 11 pm–5 am.*

SPORTS AND THE OUTDOORS

The Bodrum Peninsula offers plenty of outdoor activities, including scuba diving, sponge diving, horseback riding, hiking, waterskiing, and windsurfing.

DIVING

The sea around Bodrum provides some of the best diving in the Aegean. There are 16 dive spots. At least 10 schools are registered with PADI, the worldwide diving organization.

Aegean Pro Dive Centre. In Bodrum city center, this is one of the most reliable PADI-certified dive operators in Bodrum. ⊠ *Eski Çesme Mah., Kavaklısarnıç Sok., Asarlık Sitesi 30, Bodrum* ☎ *252/316–0737* ⊕ *www.aegeanprodive.com.*

Erman Dive Center. This PADI-certified outfitter has three locations in Bodrum: this one at the Bodrum Karada Marina; another at the Hapimag Resort Sea Garden; and the third at the Kempinski Hotel Barbaros Bay in Yalıçiftlik. ⊠ *Karada Marina, Neyzen Tevfik Cad., Bodrum* ☎ *252/368–9594* ⊕ *www.ermandive.com* ☼ *Closed Nov.–Apr.*

Motif Diving. With PADI-certified and multilingual instructors, this company offers departures from Gümbet. ⊠ *Caferpasa Cad. 15/A, Bodrum* ☎ *252/316–6252* ⊕ *www.motifdiving.com.*

HORSEBACK RIDING

Gündoğan is the best place for horseback riding, with nice forest trails; Ortakent and Turgutreis are good alternatives.

Country Ranch Horse Riding Club. The stables here offer tuition for all ages, pony-trekking for children, and horseback safaris for adults. ⊠ *Akcaalan Mevkii Islamhaneleri, Piren Cad. 30, Turgutreis* ☎ *252/382-5654, 533/654-9586 cellphone, for English* ⊕ *www.countryranch.net.*

Farilya Horse Ranch. This horseback riding establishment is on the Turkbuku-Gundogan road. ⊠ *Yukarı Göl Mevkii, Gündoğan* ☎ *252/357-7977.*

Yahşi Horseback Riding. Various packages are offered here. ⊠ *Yeşil Vadi Yolu, Ortakent* ☎ *252/358-6382.*

WINDSURFING

Bitez, Yalıkavak, and Fener, near Turgutreis, are ideal for windsurfing.

Windsurfing Schools. If you would like to try your hand at windsurfing, try Fener Windsurf Club, on Fener Beach, about 20 km (12 miles) from the Bodrum city center. Instructors speak English. ⊠ *Fener Plaji* ☎ *252/393-8414* ⊕ *www.fenerwindsurf.com* ☉ *Mid-Apr.–mid–Nov.*

SHOPPING

There is an open-air bazaar every day of the week in Bodrum and in the surrounding towns. You will find fruits and vegetables and other foodstuffs; household goods; clothing, shoes, handbags; souvenirs; and at some, high-quality jewelry and rugs. The schedule of the bazaars is: Türkbükü on Monday; Bodrum (no food) and Gölköy on Tuesday; Ortakent, Gümüşlük, and Gündoğan on Wednesday; Yalıkavak on Thursday (probably the best of all of them for quality goods); Bodrum (fruits, vegetables, and other foodstuffs, on the second floor of the otogar) on Friday; Turgutreis on Saturday; and Gümbet and Mumcular on Sunday.

Ali Güven Sandalet. Bodrum's handmade leather sandals are renowned. The late Ali Güven, who once made sandals for Mick Jagger, was the most trusted and well-established of the cobblers; his workshop continues to put out lightweight designs that are made from specially worked leather, very comfortable for the Mediterranean summer, and aesthetically pleasing as well. ⊠ *Bodrum Sq., Bodrum.*

Hammam. If you'd rather just sit back and relax, the luxurious neo-Ottoman marble **hammam** (Turkish bath) and **spa** at the Kempinski Hotel Barbaros Bay, an easy 20-minute ride from Bodrum, offers everthing from a traditional Turkish scrub to Californian *watsu* (shiatsu massage in a warm pool), with special programs for expectant mothers. If you've never tried a hammam before, this is a good, though decidedly pricey, place to start. There are separate facilities for men and women, and staff speak English. ■ TIP➔ **To reach the hotel by public transport, take one of the minibuses at the Bodrum bus station marked "Kempinski."** ⊠ *Kempinski Hotel Barbaros Bay, Kızılağaç Koyu, Gerenkuyu Mevkii, Yalıçiftlik* ☎ *252/311-0303* ⊕ *www.kempinski.com.*

Tarihi Yunuslar Karadeniz Unlu Mamüller. Stop by this incredibly popular bakery on Bodrum's main pedestrian shopping street for classic puddings, cheesecakes, pastries, and luxurious fruit-and-cream parfaits. ✉ *Çarşı Mh., Cumhuriyet Cad. 13, Bodrum* ☎ *252/316–4137* 🌐 *www.yunuslarkaradeniz.com.*

THE BODRUM PENINSULA'S OTHER TOWNS

Visitors flock to the Bodrum Peninsula and its environs for its numerous coves, bays, and crystal-clear waters, as well as its lively, often glitzy, wining, dining, and nightlife scenes. Each municipality and its surrounding villages have their own style, charm, and ambience, so where you decide to stay will be based on your personal preferences. You can catch a *dolmuş* (minibus) to almost any town in the peninsula from the central Bodrum bus station (*otogar*) for 5 TL or less per person. You may have to return to Bodrum to transfer between other towns.

BITEZ

The inland village of Bitez lies 8 km (5 miles) west of Bodrum, and its beach, the longest on the peninsula, is a 2-km (1-mile) drive to the south. The stone houses in the village were built right on the road to make room for mandarin trees in the backyard. Until several decades ago, residents picked and packed the mandarins onto camels, which then carried them to the nearby ports. Walk along the back roads of Bitez to take in the fresh, citric scent of the mandarins, intermingled with 500-year-old olive trees. The village also has a *kahve* (traditionally, a Turkish café where only men socialize and play backgammon) for women, opened up by the Bitez municipality. The kahve is on Atatürk Caddesi. Most of the sand in this semicircle cove is covered by chaises or plush pillows set up in little, enclosed enclaves. A pedestrian walkway leads through the 2-km (1-mile) stretch of beach, dividing the cafés and hotels from the shore.

WHERE TO EAT AND STAY

$$ TURKISH 🍴 **Bağarası.** Tables are tucked into a lovely hidden garden in summer and in cooler weather service is in a quaint, Bodrum-style one-story house. The Mediterranean cuisine includes some local favorites, such as *lokum pilav* (rice prepared with local herbs and spices) and *girit köfte* (Crete-style meatballs). Alcohol is served. [$] *Average main: 29 TL* ✉ *Pınarlı Cad. 59* ☎ *252/363–7693* ✍ *Reservations essential* ⏲ *Closed Mon. in winter.*

$ TURKISH FAMILY 🍴 **Bitez Pidesi.** The *pide* (pizza- or calzone-like oven-fired dough stuffed with meat, cheese, spinach, and other fillings) sold here is renowned locally, and little wonder. The crusts are crispy, the fillings delicious, and the prices at this no-frills eatery are unbeatable. You'll need transportation if coming from Bitez beach. They also have a branch in Ortakent. In summer, they stay open into the wee hours. [$] *Average main: 10 TL* ✉ *Atatürk Cad. 98, Bitez* ☎ *252/363–7925* 💳 *No credit cards.*

$$ INTERNATIONAL 🍴 **Sarnıç Beach Club & Restaurant.** Though the beach scene and loud music makes this spot a bit too much to handle during the day, things quiet down in the evening, when the seaside setting is serene and outstanding homemade *mantı* (Turkish-style ravioli, topped with buttery tomato sauce and plain yogurt), stuffed vine leaves, and other traditional favorites provide a casual alfresco meal. If you crave adrenaline

after a long lounge on the pillows of their wooden dock, the (unaffiliated) windsurfing school next door offers lessons. $ *Average main: 25 TL* ✉ *Bitez Mah., Aktur Sitesi-Çokertme Cad. 23* ☎ *252/343–1433* ⊕ *www.cafesarnic.com* ✆ *Closed Oct.–May.*

$$$$ ⊟ **Doria Hotel Bodrum.** This modern hilltop haven overlooking Bitez Bay
RESORT may not be right on the beach, but there's a complimentary shuttle to
FAMILY the hotel's hedonistic private beach club nearby. **Pros:** spacious rooms; glorious views; glamorous bar and restaurant. **Cons:** not on the beachfront. $ *Rooms from: 689 TL* ✉ *Gündönümü Mevkii, Adnan Menderes Cad.* ☎ *252/311–1020* ⊕ *www.doriahotelbodrum.com* ✒ *92 rooms, 11 suites* ❑⦾ *Multiple meal plans.*

GÖL-TÜRKBÜKÜ

The two adjacent coastal towns Gölköy and Türkbükü, 20 km (12 miles) north of Bodrum, merged a decade ago to become Göl-Türkbükü, the most glamorous part of the Bodrum Peninsula. Türkbükü, which has been aptly called the "St. Tropez of Turkey," is the summer playground of jet-setting, high-society Turks and foreigners, and its coastline is pleasantly packed with bars, cafés, restaurants, and boutiques. Gölköy has a slower pace and more stretches of undeveloped waterfront; Türkbükü is the see-and-be-seen hot spot for socializing, partying, and dining. Note that there's not much more to do in Gölköy besides sunbathe. Neither of its two beaches has sand, but the water is accessible from wooden decks. Private motorboats splash between the two bays; the local dolmuş is more prosaic, but a lot cheaper.

WHERE TO EAT

$$$ ✕ **Garo's.** The peripatetic Turkish-Armenian maestro Garo heads the
MEDITERRANEAN kitchen at this stone cottage–turned–waterfront restaurant with a comfy
Fodor's Choice Greek-taverna feel, friendly staff, and an outdoor terrace with blue-
★ and-white checkered tablecloths. Reasonably priced seafood dishes and inventive mezes belie its white-hot trendiness amongst the international cognoscenti. Not in the mood for fish? Order spicy Turkish meatballs, as Camilla, Duchess of Cornwall, did on her visit here in 2012. Come for dinner, a more casual morning coffee, or a seaside lunch. $ *Average main: 40 TL* ✉ *Menemene Mh., 83 Sok. 9, Göl-Türkbükü* ☎ *252/377– 6171* ⊕ *www.garosturkbuku.com* ⚭ *Reservations essential* ✆ *Closed late Oct.–mid-Apr.*

$ ✕ **Hoca'nın Yeri.** The specialty of the house at this simple eatery on the
TURKISH boardwalk in Türkbükü is *çiğ böreği*, a Crimean dish brought to Turkey
FAMILY that consists of flat, fried pastry stuffed with ground beef, onion, and spices. Come in the morning for a Turkish breakfast by the restaurant's own little patch of beach, or any time for *mantı* (tiny Turkish "ravioli", stuffed with minced meat—get them fried or baked) or *gözleme* (Turkish savory crepes with various fillings). The eponymous Hoca, who earned his honorific as imam at the mosque you can see from the restaurant, presides with a smile. $ *Average main: 15 TL* ✉ *Yalı Mevkii 78, Göl-Türkbükü* ☎ *252/377–5907* ⊕ *www.hocanin-yeri.com* ✆ *Closed Oct.–Apr.*

$$$$ ✕ **Melengeç.** When you spot dozens of sparkling lanterns carved from
SEAFOOD gourds, clustered around a white trellis that juts into the sea, you have found Melengeç, a brand-new, glamorous addition to the Gümüşlük

seafood scene. Every night in season, dozens of hot and cold mezes—from cool, savory yogurt with vegetables and herbs to stuffed zucchini flowers to sizzling calamari—and fresh, simply prepared local fish draw eager visitors from across the Bodrum peninsula, and beyond. Come at sunset for views of the ancient ruins of Rabbit Island, surrounded by bobbing rowboats. [$] *Average main: 55 TL* ✉ *Yali Mevkii 1, Gümüşlük Koyu, Gümüşlük* ☎ *252/394–4858* 🌐 *www.melengecgumusluk.com* ✍ *Reservations essential* ⏲ *Closed Nov.–Apr.*

$$ SEAFOOD 🍴 **Miam.** Wonderfully prepared seafood (including their popular John Dory) is served with polish, as are the meat and pasta dishes; meals are accompanied by soothing sea views from their terrace on the Türkbükü waterfront in summertime. Breakfast is also served. In wintertime, regulars cluster indoors around a cosy fireplace. [$] *Average main: 30 TL* ✉ *Yalı Mevkii 51, Göl-Türkbükü* ☎ *252/377–5612* ✍ *Reservations essential.*

WHERE TO STAY

$$$$ HOTEL Fodor's Choice ★ 🏨 **Amanruya.** Perched above the Aegean Sea is a 36-room retreat whose name is aptly translated to "peace" and "dream," offering guests the tranquil sense that they are all alone, even when every villa is occupied. **Pros:** on the beach; great service; private pools are large. **Cons:** not all the pools are heated; water in the outdoor showers tends to be tepid. [$] *Rooms from: 2,150 TL* ✉ *Bülent Ecevit Cad., Demir Mevkii, Göl-Türkbükü* ☎ *252/311 12 12* 🌐 *www.amanresorts.com/amanruya/home.aspx* 🛏 *36 cottages* 🍽 *No meals.*

$$$$ HOTEL Fodor's Choice ★ 🏨 **Flamm.** If you think that bombshell lounging on Flamm's wide private beach in Gölköy looks just like Naomi Campbell or Uma Thurman, that's probably because she is. **Pros:** effortlessly glam, without the intensity of the Türkbükü scene; stylish comfort steps from the water; private. **Cons:** for shopping or a change from the hotel's restaurant, you'll need to head over to Türkbükü; not all rooms have sea views; understated übercool style may not be for everyone, or best for young kids. [$] *Rooms from: 590 TL* ✉ *Yalı Mahallesi, 30. Sok. 3, Göl-Türkbükü* ☎ *252/357–7600* 🌐 *www.flammbodrum.com* 🛏 *11 rooms* ⏲ *Closed Oct.–Apr.* 🍽 *Breakfast.*

$$ B&B/INN FAMILY 🏨 **Karianda Boutique Hotel.** Overlooking a large, well-tended beach, and with lovely gardens (and pet chickens) this is a perfect place for families. **Pros:** cozy feel with everything at your fingertips; excellent food. **Cons:** some rooms quite small; four-person family rooms have a double bed for the children. [$] *Rooms from: 295 TL* ✉ *Cumhuriyet Cad. 104–106, Gölköy, Göl-Türkbükü* ☎ *252/357–7303 hotel, 533/357–7819 owner's cell* 🌐 *www.karianda.com* 🛏 *32 rooms* 🍽 *Breakfast.*

$$$$ HOTEL 🏨 **Maça Kızı Boutique Hotel & Restaurant.** You'll be in sophisticated company and away from the crowds at this hotel, the "Queen of Spades," nestled on a hillside in a secluded bay at the tip of Göl-Türkbükü. **Pros:** private pontoon beach; sophisticated surroundings. **Cons:** enthusiastically expensive (1,000% markup on bottled water); pool is lovely but small; meal-inclusive rates required. [$] *Rooms from: 1,378 TL* ✉ *Kesire Mevkii, Narçiçeği Sok., Göltürkbükkü* ☎ *252/377–6272* 🌐 *www.macakizi.com* 🛏 *81 rooms* 🍽 *Some meals.*

NIGHTLIFE

Each beach town around Bodrum has its own nightlife scene. Göl-Türkbükü's is the most renowned, frequented by the Turkish elite and international crowd; the waterfront is lined with bars and clubs.

Ship Ahoy. The first nightclub in Türkbükü, it parties on under a mast and rigging raised over the boardwalk. In high season, it's usually packed to the hilt with clubbers trying to squeeze into very small quarters well into the wee hours. There's no cover charge, but be prepared to pay a premium price for your drinks (and likely be squashed next to Turkish movie stars). During the day, it converts into a well-loved but pricey restaurant, open from breakfast on. ⊠ *Yalı Mevkii, Göl-Türkbükü, Bodrum* ☎ *252/377–5070.*

AKYARLAR AND KARAINCIR

On adjacent bays southwest of Bodrum, Akyarlar and Karaincir are ringed with some of the peninsula's most picturesque beaches. Peaceful, sandy Karaincir was once famous for its black figs, and Akyarlar is only 5 km (3 miles) across the water from the Greek island of Kós.

WHERE TO STAY

$$
HOTEL
Fodor'sChoice
★

🏨 **Castello di Akyarlar.** A beautiful natural setting on a pretty beach and a laid-back feel make this historic boutique hotel a great choice for a restful retreat. **Pros:** beachfront; very attractive and restful surroundings. **Cons:** 40 minutes from Bodrum; meal-inclusive rate required in high season. $ *Rooms from: 256 TL* ⊠ *Yalı Cad. 45, Akyarlar* ☎ *252/393–6025* ⊕ *www.castellobodrum.com* ⤳ *20 rooms* ⦿*Some meals.*

TURGUTREIS

Named for an Ottoman admiral (some say pirate), Turgutreis lies due west on the opposite side of the peninsula. The second-largest town on the peninsula, it has a more developed coast, and a popular and lively bazaar. Its marina attracts the yachting crowd and is more touristy than the other bays. After swimming in the pristine sea at Akyarlar and Karaincir, Turgutreis' 2½ km (1½ miles) of sandy beach may feel a little crowded.

WHERE TO EAT AND STAY

$$
TURKISH

✕**EG Arşipel Cafe & Restaurant.** A clifftop retreat in Şevket Sabancı Park, just outside Turgutreis, offers bird's-eye views of the sea, and a nice selection of Turkish and international dishes. Alcohol is served, as is breakfast. Reservations are advisable in high season. $ *Average main: 20 TL* ⊠ *Gazi Mustafa Kemal Bul.* ☎ *252/382–2608* ⊕ *www. arsipelrestaurant.com.*

$$
HOTEL

🏨 **Hotel Kortan.** A private beach stretches in front of this family-run seaside escape in central Turgutreis, where simple elegance, tasteful furnishings, and beachside quiet are de rigeur. **Pros:** nice seaside terrace with view for sunbathing; private beach; on-site bar and restaurant. **Cons:** on the main stretch, so not totally private. $ *Rooms from: 197 TL* ⊠ *Atatürk Meydanı, Sabancı Cad. 5* ☎ *252/382–2932* ⊕ *www. kortanotel.com* ⤳ *25 rooms* ⦿*Breakfast.*

GÜMÜŞLÜK

Charming Gümüşlük (named for its ancient silver mines) is built on the ancient ruins of Myndos 23 km (14 miles) west of Bodrum. It is one of the peninsula's more authentic, slower-paced, less-developed villages—no high-rises or large hotels are allowed. Much of the Myndos ruins are submerged underwater, but major land excavations are taking place to recover the ancient city, and a drainage system dating to Myndos' Roman civilization period has already been discovered. The bewitching little town is popular for its fish restaurants and "village breakfasts" on the water; it also has a Blue Flag public beach. One of the popular things to do is wade through the shallow water to Tavşan Adası, Rabbit Island (unfortunately, the island's pre-Roman ruins, visible from the water, are off-limits unless you are an archaeologist or a rabbit). Glassmakers and other artists reside and keep shop at the handicrafts bazaar near the harbor, where you can sometimes see them at work; leather sandals are classic souvenirs, as are handmade beach dresses by the talented sisters at the İnci Butik. The restored, hilltop Eklisia Church hosts many cultural and arts events, including a summertime classical music festival. If you have the time, and a car, you can make the trip up to Karakaya, a village of stone houses perched above Gümüşlük and surrounded with cactus and other foliage. In winter, the local population is augmented by writers and artists, drawn by the inspiring serenity and the off-season prices.

WHERE TO EAT AND STAY

$$$ SEAFOOD FAMILY Fodor's Choice ★

🍴 **Aquarium.** At branches on the water in Gümüşlük and Yalıavak, begin a meal with stuffed zucchini flowers, roasted eggplant with *tulum* cheese, and octopus salad—you may want to just keep working your way through the starters—a meal in themselves—or let the owner, Cengiz Bey, help you select the best local fish for the grill. Whatever you choose, don't skip dessert. After years of buying all their *baklava* from Gaziantep, Aquarium finally imported a Gaziantepli baklava-whisperer, who uses only pistachioes from his hometown, and makes a mean *irmik helvası* (traditional warm semolina halvah, served with ice cream) as well. [$] *Average main: 35 TL* ✉ *Yalı Mevkii, Gümüşlük Koyu* ☎ *252/385–4151 Gümüşlük, 252/394–3682 Yalıkavak, 0533/344–8943 Bodrum* 🌐 *www.aquariumgumusluk.com* ✍ *Reservations essential.*

$ TURKISH

🍴 **Dalgıç.** If you're tired of fish, try these homemade, traditional Turkish dishes as a refreshing alternative. They are served in pleasant, friendly surroundings, with a few outdoor tables, and include traditional soups, meze, flatbreads, and grills. [$] *Average main: 15 TL* ✉ *Across from the pier, off 1120 Sok.* ☎ *252/394–4229.*

$$ TURKISH

🍴 **Gümüş Café Fish Restaurant.** Don't let the name fool you—this lovely restaurant on the waterfront in sleepy Gümüşlük specializes not only in fresh fish and an eclectic selection of salads and traditional Turkish fare, but also a princely summer brunch of watermelon, homemade jams (including one made from eggplant, a local specialty), cheeses, eggs, vegetables, and more—a perfect lazy summer feast. Tables are only a few feet from the peaceful waters of the bay, with a truly romantic view of the ancient ruins of Rabbit Island, often with a soft breeze.

The waitstaff are cheery and attentive, and though the kitchen has been refurbished almost beyond recognition, it retains a 300-year-old hearth from when it served as the bakery for the surrounding villages. $ *Average main: 25 TL* ⊠ *Gümüşlük Yalısı, 1120 Sok. 82, Gümüşlük Koyu* ☎ *252/394–4234* ⊕ *www.gumuscafe.com.*

$$ ✕**Limon Cafe.** Settle into a lovely, fig-scented garden about 2 km (1
TURKISH mile) outside town, overlooking citrus trees, the sea, and the ancient city of Myndos and enjoy a meal in these rural surroundings. Lunch or dinner should begin with the excellent fried calamari; the *mantı* (Turkish style ravioli) is homemade. A late-risers' breakfast is served until 3 p.m. daily; better still, come for the sunset while savoring one of the house-specialty cocktails. $ *Average main: 30 TL* ⊠ *Yalı Mevkii 1* ☎ *252/394–4044* ⊕ *www.limongumusluk.com* ⚑ *Reservations essential* ⊙ *Closed Oct.–Apr.*

$$$ ✕**Mimoza.** This seafood restaurant is highly popular with the trendy
SEAFOOD jet-setters from Turkey and abroad. Located on the farthest tip of the Gümüşlük bay, it is secluded and private. The sunset from its elegantly decorated restaurant is amazing. The food and service are excellent and very expensive—but most say it is definitely worth it! $ *Average main: 40 TL* ⊠ *Yalı Mevkii 44/1, Gümüşlük* ☎ *252/394–3139* ⊕ *www. mimozagumusluk.com* ⚑ *Reservations essential.*

$$ ⌂**TaşEv Gümüşlük Otel.** In a beautiful rural setting, this family-run B&B,
B&B/INN just a few minutes from the sea and the excellent restaurants that line
Fodor'sChoice Gümüşlük harbor, is an appealing hillside haven. **Pros:** elegant, simple
★ style; great food; discounts for longer stays in winter. **Cons:** a three-minute walk downhill through the orchard to the Blue Flag public beach; basic amenities. $ *Rooms from: 177 TL* ⊠ *Karakaya Mah., Yalı Mevkii, Atatürk Cad. 81, Gümüşlük Koyu* ☎ *252/394–4395* ⊕ *www. tasevgumusluk.com* ⊅ *5 rooms* ⦿*No meals.*

YALIKAVAK

This town on the northwestern tip of the Bodrum Peninsula, 20 km (12 miles) from Bodrum and 6 km (4 miles) from Gündoğan, is surrounded by tangerine orchards and olive groves and easily identified by the beautiful windmills atop its hill. Once a tiny sponge-divers' village, Yalıkavak is still quiet, with some fine restaurants and a big marina, as well as many fine beaches ringing the surrounding coves. Strong wind makes Yalıkavak ideal for windsurfing. It is known for its fabulous Thursday market, with 1,200 stalls selling local produce, delicacies, handicrafts, and more, which draws locals, tourists, and even visitors from the nearby Greek islands.

WHERE TO EAT AND STAY

$ ✕**Kavaklı Köfteci.** *Köfte* (Turkish style meatballs) is the mainstay of this
TURKISH popular, no-frills eatery, and you can enjoy these delectable morsels with a side of *piyaz salad* (navy bean salad, with or without onions), homemade bread, and *ayran* (plain yogurt drink). Further delicious home-cooking is available at their restaurant across the street. No alcohol served. $ *Average main: 14 TL* ⊠ *Merkez Çarşı İçi* ☎ *252/385–4748* ⊕ *www.kavaklikofteci.com* ▭ *No credit cards.*

$$$$ RESORT FAMILY 🏨 **Palmalife Bodrum Resort & Spa.** Privacy is among the amenities at this lovely getaway, facing its own bay and offering sophisticated accommodations amid lush seaside gardens. **Pros:** beautiful surroundings; private beach, state-of-the art spa and wellness center; welcoming bars and restaurants; kids' club. **Cons:** expensive; need transportation to get around; no pets allowed. [$] *Rooms from: 1,000 TL* ✉ *Gökçebel Mahallesi, Kızılburun Cad. 1* ☎ *252/396–6050* 🌐 *www.palmaliferesort.com* 🛏 *40 rooms* 🍴 *Breakfast.*

$$ TURKISH 🍴 **Köşebaşı.** The Kordon waterfront outpost of this popular, upscale, and now international, Istanbul-based meat-and-kebab restaurant offers sizzling specialties from the cities of Adana and Tarsus in the Southern Anatolia region. The menu includes a tempting array of appetizers, such as mini *lahamcun* (thin Turkish-style pizza prepared with minced meat and spices), as well as excellent kebabs and meat dishes—all with a sea view. [$] *Average main: 20 TL* ✉ *1. Kordon, Atatürk Cad. 174/B, Alsancak, İzmir* ☎ *232/463–5350* 🌐 *www.kosebasi.com.tr.*

THE TURQUOISE COAST

WELCOME TO THE TURQUOISE COAST

TOP REASONS TO GO

★ **Appreciate the landscape:** Pine-covered mountains plunge into a turquoise sea that's broken by romantic coves and remote peninsulas.

★ **Relax on beaches:** Some of the Mediterranean's most blissful beaches are here; lie on your sun bed or dive in from a floating platform.

★ **Sleep in one-of-a-kind lodgings:** Bed down in an Ottoman mansion-turned-hotel on the Datça Peninsula or an old stone house in the winding streets of Antalya's Kaleici.

★ **See spectacular ruins:** Explore remains of ancient cities—from mountaintop Termessos and overgrown Olympos to the extraordinarily intact Roman theater at Aspendos.

★ **Take a Blue Cruise:** Sail away on your own chartered yacht, perhaps dropping anchor en route to take a swim or catch a fish for dinner.

★ **Trek the Lycian Way:** Choose a one-day or multiday hike along the legendary trail that runs parallel to much of the Turquoise Coast.

View from the Acropolis of Simena

1 The Datça Peninsula. Chartering a yacht in Marmaris or Bodrum is the best way to view the craggy hills and sublime coves of one of Turkey's most unspoiled stretches of shoreline.

2 The Lycian Coast. Rent a car from the Dalaman or Antalya airport and slowly explore the charming ports, less crowded beaches, and ancient ruins along this less developed coastal circuit.

3 Antalya and Pamphylia. Vibrant Antalya has everything—an old city, beaches, eateries, nightlife—plus it's a good base for visiting the age-old sites of Aspendos, Perge, Termessos, and Phaselis. The area around Antalya, including Side and Alanya is considered historic Pamphylia.

Gulets harbored in Simena

Apollon Temple, Side

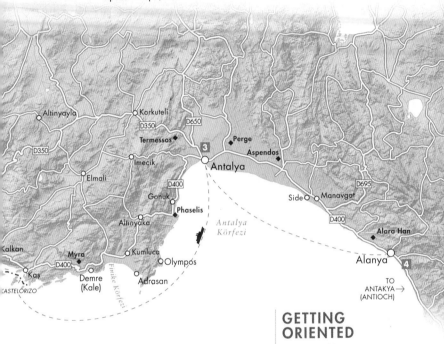

GETTING ORIENTED

The area known as the Turquoise Coast extends along the Mediterranean from the wild Datça Peninsula on Turkey's south-western tip to the resort hotels springing up along the Antalya-Alanya strip. The fir-clad mountains rising behind the water are punctuated by the ruins of splendid ancient cities, through which passed the likes of Alexander the Great, Julius Caesar, and St. Paul.

Olüdeniz Beach

4 East of Alanya. Beyond Alanya, leave the tour buses behind on a road trip that takes in uncrowded towns and off-the-beaten-path ruins all the way to ancient Antioch (Antakya).

SEAFOOD ON THE TURKISH COAST

The kebab might be the first thing that comes to mind when you think about Turkish food, but in Istanbul and along Turkey's Aegean, Mediterranean, and Black seas, fresh seafood is readily available.

Considering the long coastline, it's not surprising that fish is an integral part of Turkish cuisine, and locals eat it at lunch or dinner, usually either grilled or fried, and served with little more than a squeeze of lemon and a side of fresh arugula or slices of raw onion. In winter, hearty fish soups—similar to chowder—are added to many restaurant menus. Varieties might be a bit different from what you're used to, but these are some of the more common ones you'll find.

Fresh fish served in restaurants is usually sold by weight, so be sure to ask the price before ordering.

WILD VS. FARMED

Although many of the fish served in Turkey are seasonal, the growth of aquaculture here has led to a more dependable year-round supply. Many diners, however, still insist on eating the more flavorful (and more expensive) wild variety. If you want the open-sea version, ask for the *deniz* type, which is "from the sea."

BARBUNYA

The tasty small red mullet is a top choice in Turkey. As the name implies, its skin is speckled with glistening reddish spots. Mild-tasting *barbunya*, usually only a few inches long, are typically panfried whole, an order can easily be shared. The prime season for them is spring through early summer.

ÇIPURA

Gilthead bream is the most popular fish caught in the Aegean area. Like *levrek*, it's mild tasting with white, flaky meat, usually grilled whole and served unadorned. Fish farms now supply much of the *çipura* sold in restaurants, but the wild variety, known as *deniz çipurasi* is also available.

HAMSI

Size isn't everything. The finger-length anchovy is often referred to in Turkey as the "little prince" of fishes. In the Black Sea area, where *hamsi* are caught, they are used in numerous dishes and form an important part of the local economy. Hamsi typically comes fried in a light coating of corn meal, but hamsi *pilav*—a rice and anchovy dish infused with an aromatic mix of herbs and spices—is also common. Hamsi season is fall and winter.

LEVREK

Sea bass, one of the most popular types of fish in Turkey, is prized for its delicate, almost sweet taste and firm white

meat. *Levrek* is usually charcoal grilled whole and served with a drizzle of oil and a squeeze of lemon. Or a whole levrek might be encased in sea salt and baked in the oven. Many eateries serve the cheaper, smaller farmed variety. Wild levrek is called *deniz levreği*. Both are available all year.

LÜFER

This is the general name for bluefish, which are generally tastier than the U.S. varieties. Bluefish is common enough that the different sizes have their own names: small bluefish are *çinekop*, large bluefish are *kofana*, and medium bluefish are *sarıkanat*.

PALAMUT

Also known as bonito, *palamut* is related to tuna. Unlike levrek and çipura, it's a strong-tasting, oily fish, similar to mackerel. Palamut fillets are often grilled, but another popular—and perhaps tastier—way they are prepared is baked in the oven with an onion and tomato sauce. Palamut appear in Turkish waters fall through winter.

KARA DENİZ
SÜPER
HAMSİ
KİLO
2.500

Updated by
Scott Newman

The Turquoise Coast is just as stunning as its name suggests. Luminous blue waves in that signature shade (the word "turquoise" actually comes from the French for "Turkish") lap at isolated coves and some of the country's most iconic beaches—including Ölüdeniz, Patara, and İztuzu. Inhabited for millennia, spectacular archaeological ruins of Greek, Roman, and Byzantine origin are never far away. Termessos is said to have defied Alexander the Great because he was daunted by its height, and the antique theater in Apsendos rivals the Colosseum in Rome.

In the west is the Datça Peninsula, a Mediterranean landscape of rolling hills and olive trees looking out on a sea dotted with Greek islands. East of Marmaris, a more-touristy town, you'll find the Lycian coast with its rich mix of ruins and camera-ready beaches. Each Lycian coast destination has a distinct feel: Ölüdeniz, crowded but with a lovely lagoon; laid-back, alternative Kabak; low-key Patara; upscale Kalkan; lively Kaş; and the green and relaxed Olympos area. Antalya, the biggest city on this stretch, has long beaches lined with resorts. The package tourists, though, often skip Old Antalya, which is filled with historic mansions (many now converted into boutique hotels). Antalya also has the coast's best museum and archaeological sites, Aspendos among them. East of the resort towns of Side and Alanya, the region becomes rugged and tourists rare. Ruins, castles, and beaches remain plentiful; however, the taste of "real Turkey" is more pronounced.

PLANNING

WHEN TO GO
The ideal months on the Turquoise Coast are May and June and September and October. Summers can be hot and humid, especially in July and August; that's also when beaches tend to be busiest and waterfront

discos pump out their most egregious levels of noise. Alanya and Side—which stay warmest longest—are best visited before or after the high season, when charter tourists are least likely to be about.

Along the Lycian coast, expect thunderstorms after late October and an average 12 days of rain per month in December and January; otherwise, while not swimsuit weather, it can be sunny enough for T-shirts. Snow graces mountain peaks well into May, a magnificent sight from Antalya and Fethiye. Although not a winter sun destination, it rarely drops below freezing on the coast. Some hotels stay open between mid-December and March, often with limited facilities.

PLANNING YOUR TIME

If you just have a weekend or so to spend on the Turquoise Coast and want to see historic sites, base yourself in Antalya and drive out to nearby Termessos, Olympos, or Aspendos: they're some of the best preserved classical ruins in the country.

The Lycian coast is beautiful and filled with the remains of ancient cities like Xanthos, Patara, and Olympos. Motorists should count on about 10 hours of driving in total, starting in either Antalya or Dalaman. There are many unspoiled towns and lovely hotels en route. You could spend as few as three days here, but five to seven would be more relaxing and allow for some beach time. On a sample six-day tour you could spend the morning in Antalya's Kaleiçi quarter, then drive up to Termessos and cross the mountains to Fethiye, overnighting around Ölüdeniz. On Day 2, visit the gorgeous lagoon at Ölüdeniz, the ghost town of Kaya, or the pine-fringed beach at Kabak, returning to the same hotel as the previous night. On Day 3, visit the Lycian city of Tlos, then explore the Saklıkent canyon, Xanthos, and Letoon; cap the day with a swim in Patara before checking into a hotel in Patara, Kalkan, or Kaş. On Day 4, take an excursion boat from Kaş to Kekova, and return to Kaş for the night. On Day 5, visit St. Nicholas Basilica in Demre, have lunch in Finike, and visit Arycanda in the afternoon, overnighting in Çıralı so that you can see the burning Chimera. On Day 6, visit Olimpos and Phaselis, then return to Antalya.

GETTING HERE AND AROUND

AIR TRAVEL

It makes sense to fly to the Turquoise Coast if you're coming from Istanbul or elsewhere in Turkey. The main airports here are in Dalaman and Antalya. Antalya has one of the country's busiest international airports, serving the coast from Alanya to Kaş, including Side, Olympos, and Finike. Dalaman Airport serves the coast from Kaş to Datça, including Kalkan, Fethiye, Göcek, Dalyan, and Marmaris. There are also airports in Adana and Antakya. Turkish Airlines frequently flies here, as do budget carriers like Pegasus.

Car rental concessions operate at all airports, and all international agencies are represented. Havaş airport buses also link the two largest airports to major towns. Many hotels and travel agencies will arrange airport shuttles as well (usually for a fee). Yellow airport taxis are somewhat expensive for individuals but are usually well regulated, with a clear legal pricing system prominently displayed, and these are a good option if you're sharing.

Taking a bus from Antalya airport into Antalya costs about 12 TL; they're timed to meet all in-coming flights and leave the city center hourly. Buses to the airport leave the Turkish Airlines building on Cumhuriyet Caddesi (on the cliff-top boulevard) once every hour or two. Another bus leaves from nearby **Wing Turizm** (☎ 242/244–2236) at more irregular times. Yet another option if you're leaving from Antalya's main bus station is to take a bus down the highway east of Antalya, get out at the airport intersection, and take one of the taxis waiting there for the last 2 km (1 mile) into the airport itself—it's a bit of a hassle but only costs about 6 TL. A taxi to the airport from the center, by comparison, costs 40 TL.

From Dalaman Airport, airport buses will take airline passengers east via Göcek to Fethiye (24 TL) and west to the Marmaris intercity bus terminal (30 TL). Theoretically, the buses will leave Marmaris three hours before any flight and Fethiye 2½ hours before. For more precise information, call Havaş, the Dalaman operating representative.

Contacts Havaş ☎ 212/465–5656 central Turkey call center ⊕ www.havas.net/en/iletisim/.

BLUE CRUISING

A relaxing yacht charter in a *gulet,* a wooden motorboat or sailing boat, is the quintessential way to explore Turkey's coast. For the full effect, plan at least four days and at best a week, perhaps from Antalya to Fethiye, or along the Datça Peninsula from Marmaris. ⇨ *For more information, see the Blue Cruising Close Up in this chapter.*

BOAT AND FERRY TRAVEL

A car ferry (two hours) links Bodrum with Datça's Körmen port—it is several kilometers on the other side of the peninsula, but a bus meets the ferry. In the June–September season, the Bodrum–Datça boats run from both ports at 9 am and 5 pm. In winter they run just Monday, Wednesday, and Friday, at 9 am from Datça to Bodrum and at 5 pm from Bodrum to Datça. If you're taking a car, reserve in advance. Datça, Marmaris, Fethiye, and Kaş have regular Greek Island departures.

Contacts Yesil Marmaris ☎ 252/412–2290 ⊕ www.yesilmarmaris.com.

BUS AND DOLMUŞ TRAVEL

Inexpensive intercity buses travel between major towns all over Turkey—it's about 80 TL one way for the 12-hour journey from Istanbul to Antalya. These days, though, that's only about half the price of flying.

Buses and minibuses (*dolmuşes*) run regularly between the main Turquoise Coast cities but rarely travel to remote archaeological sites, such as Tlos and Pinara. Every city has a bus terminal, and minibuses to smaller destinations usually set off from there, too. Major routes, such as Marmaris to Fethiye and Fethiye to Antalya, have hourly buses into the early evening; fares are typically about 14 TL per person for every 100 km (62 miles) traveled. Minibus schedules depend on the popularity of the route and these buses generally stop anywhere if asked to.

Most are designed to take people from the villages into the city rather than the other way around.

When the intercity bus terminal is outside the city center (as in Antalya), major companies usually provide minibus service from their downtown locations to the station: ask for a *servis* (minibus transfer service) when you book your ticket—otherwise, finding your own way to the terminal can be difficult and time-consuming. The Varan Bus Company is more expensive than others, but has better service, a better safety record, and its own privately owned and spotlessly clean rest stops.

Contacts Varan Bus Company ☎ 212/444–8999 national ⊕ www.varan.com.tr.

CAR TRAVEL
Once here, you'll find renting a car allows you to get around with the most ease; many of the sights you'll want to see are off the main road, and the area is filled with beautiful coastal drives.

Although the highways between towns are well maintained, smaller roads are often unpaved and rough, and the twisty coastal roads require concentration. To estimate driving times, figure on about 70 km (43 miles) per hour. By car from Istanbul to Marmaris or Antalya is at least a 10-hour, 750-km (470-mile) trek. The speed limit is 90 kph (56 mph) on most country roads—120 kph (75 mph) on real highways—and for your own safety it's best to stick to it. The police have radar devices and they do use them.

All airports have several car rental agencies to choose from; many hotels can also arrange rentals. In general, the smaller and more remote the place, the cheaper the rental, but the more minimal the service.

TAXI TRAVEL
Provincial taxis are somewhat expensive; fares generally work out to about 4 TL for every 1 km (½ mile) traveled. It's best to take a taxi from an established taxi stand, where you see several lined up, since the drivers there will be regulars and if you should have a dispute or lose something, it is much easier to retrace the car. It's normal, however, to hail taxis in the street. For longer journeys, you may wish to settle a price in advance, but within city limits, the taxi driver should automatically switch on the meter when you get in. As elsewhere, if he doesn't, insist upon it.

TRAIN TRAVEL
There is no train service on the Turquoise Coast.

RESTAURANTS
This coast has been serving tourists for a long time, and you will find a rich choice of restaurants. There's no shortage of older, established eateries, which dish out the standard national fare (think mezes, kebabs, assorted grilled meats, and fresh seafood). Simple—but often superb—spots are as popular with vacationing Turks as they are with foreigners. In recent years, the number of fine dining options has also increased, especially in larger cities and tourist centers. The top ones prepare creative dishes, combining high-quality local ingredients with international flair.

Regional specialties along the Turquoise Coast include mussels stuffed with rice, pine nuts, and currants; *ahtopot salatası*, a cold octopus salad, tossed in olive oil, vinegar, and parsley; and grilled fish. Most of Turkey's tomatoes, cucumbers, eggplants, zucchinis, and peppers are grown along the coast, so fresh salads are delicious. In Lycia, a local home-cooking specialty is stewed eggplant with basil—wonderful if you're offered it. *Semiz otu* (cow parsley) is a refreshing appetizer in a garlic yogurt sauce.

Prices in the reviews are the average cost of a main course at dinner or if dinner is not served, at lunch.

⇨ *For more about great seafood, see the "Seafood on the Turkish Coast" feature in this chapter.*

HOTELS

Swaths of this coveted coast have long been dominated by large "could be anywhere" concrete resorts that are inhabited by European package tourists who are often more interested in the beach than the country. Of varying quality, the best of the bunch have excellent facilities; and you can often find good deals if you want to add a few relaxing sun-and-sand days to your itinerary. There's also a tradition of simple family-run *pansiyons*; though basic in terms of amenities, these can provide a more personal experience and a pleasant refuge from mass tourism. In recent years, a number of stylish smaller hotels have also appeared. Century-old houses that have been restored and converted into high-caliber boutique hotels offer the ultimate in character. Most are found in Antalya's Kaleiçi, where they come in a variety of sizes and prices; there are also several in Eski Datça and Alanya as well as farther east.

Prices in the reviews are the lowest cost of a standard double room in high season. For expanded reviews, visit Fodors.com.

TOURS

Trekking opportunities abound in this part of Turkey. For serious walkers, the 530-km (331-mile) Lycian Way is the standing challenge. When you have finished that there's the Carian Trail (opened in 2013, it covers the country's southwest corner, known to the ancients as Caria). Both have helpful websites for DIY types. If you prefer to have a guide, individually or as part of a group, contact Middle Earth Travel—the company can also provide camping equipment. The area is great for rafting trips, too. The three main areas are around Fethiye and Ölüdeniz, in Köprülü National Park near Antalya, and along Alanya's Dimçay River. You'll pass through soaring canyons and under Roman bridges. Trans-Nature and the Alraft Rafting and Riding Club are two reputable operators in Alanya. In Side, Get Wet can arrange rafting, as well as a host of other outdoor activities. If sea kayaking is more your style, try Seven Capes in the Fethiye-Ölüdeniz area or Bougainville Travel in Kaş (the latter also offers scuba diving excursions).

History- and religion-oriented tours are not uncommon around the south coast, particularly due to its association with St. Paul, who evangelized the area. A 400-km (250-mile) trekking route known as the St. Paul Trail takes in some places he is known to have passed through. A guide isn't really necessary and trekkers are usually independent, but

Middle Earth Travel does organize tours. More traditional weeklong bus trips look at Christian sites in the Antalya area before going on to Ephesus, where St. Paul preached in the theater. More information can be obtained from Paul's Place in Antalya.

If you want to book a local tour—anything from boat tours to trekking tours or local special-interest tours—you're best off wandering through the center of whatever town you're in. Choose a local travel agency that looks well kept, and chat with the owner. Don't hesitate to move politely on to another one if you feel hassled or inadequately served. You can also ask at your hotel: they're likely to recommend the agency that gives them the best commission, and they'll probably add a commission from you, too, but it can be worth the cost for convenience and reliability.

Contacts Alraft Rafting and Riding Club ☎ *242/513-9155.* **Bougainville Travel** ☎ *242/836-3737* ⊕ *www.bougainville-turkey.com.* **Carian Trail** ☎ *537/403-3779* ⊕ *www.cariantrail.com.* **Get Wet** ☎ *242/753-4071* ⊕ *www.getwet.com.tr.* **Lycian Way** ☎ *242/243-1148* ⊕ *www.lycianway.com.* **Middle Earth Travel** ☎ *384/271-2559* ⊕ *www.middleearthtravel.com.* **Paul's Place** ☎ *242/247-6857* ⊕ *www.stpaulcc-turkey.com/pauls-place.* **Seven Capes** ☎ *537/403-3779* ⊕ *www.sevencapes.com.* **<TransNature** ☎ *242/324-0011* ⊕ *www.transnature.com.tr/eng/index.html.*

THE DATÇA PENINSULA AND MARMARIS

Modernity confronts antiquity in the westernmost portion of the Mediterranean coast. The beaches are gorgeous and the mood is laid-back if you don't stay in the resort areas of Datça or Marmaris proper. Datça is quieter than Marmaris, but for something even more charming and remote, try Eski Datça and Reshadiye, lovely little villages where you can appreciate a calmer way of life.

DATÇA PENINSULA

76 km (47 miles) west of Marmaris; 167 km (104 miles) west of Dalaman on Rte. 400.

If you make it all the way to the Datça Peninsula, you may never want to leave. It's a landscape of olives tree, pine forests in sheltered hollows, and stunning blue water. Until about 20 years ago, this was one of the most inaccessible parts of Turkey, and driving along the thin neck of land between the Aegean Sea to the north and the Mediterranean to the south feels like entering the gateway to another, older world. This is not somewhere to drop by for a day or two: you need at least three days to savor the uncluttered joys of this unique destination—far from the world of tour buses, it's a place with few pressures, but wide horizons and more than 50 little beaches for inner contemplation. The best time to visit is in spring, when the hills are carpeted in poppies, daisies, and wildflowers, and restaurants offer dishes concocted with wild thyme, rosemary, and other herbs that flourish in the hills and by the sea; in autumn, you can watch the locals harvest olives.

The timeless stone alleys of Eski Datça give a similar sense of being in another, less stressful world. The ancient ruins of Knidos constitute one of the loveliest and most evocative sites along the whole coast.

Datça is a small port with some characteristics of a resort. It's one of the most relaxed towns along the whole coast, but Eski Datça and Reşadiye are older and have more charm. Even if you don't stay here, spend an evening wandering around the harbor and sipping a drink at one of the quayside cafés. The weekly market is on Saturday, which is what attracts Greek islanders from nearby Symi. It's also the best place to arrange a boat trip to Knidos. A lovely day out and a meal at an unspoiled beach can also be had at Kargı Koyu, 3 km (2 miles) south of central Datça.

GETTING HERE AND AROUND

There are two ways to get to Datça: either fly to Dalaman Airport and make the three-hour drive west or, more pleasantly, fly to Bodrum Airport and then take a two-hour car-ferry ride from Bodrum to Datça's Körmen port. In the June–September season, boats run from both ports at 9 am and 5 pm. In winter they run only on Monday, Wednesday, and Friday at 9 am from Datça to Bodrum and at 5 pm from Bodrum to Datça. Regular buses go to Marmaris from the Pamukkale office in town, and in summer *dolmuşes* to Yazıköy continue to Knidos.

WHERE TO EAT

$$$
TURKISH
Fodor'sChoice
★

× **Culinarium.** On a terrace overlooking the harbor, this upscale option blends European style, atmosphere, and creativity with indigenous ingredients and flavors. The result is a refined low-key environment, with excellent food that provides an interesting variation on typical Turkish cuisine. From the meat and seafood to the herbs and vegetables, there is an emphasis on local products. Regulars recommend the steak; the boneless fish in lemon butter or saffron sauce makes a pleasant change from the simple fried fillets that are standard along the coast. $ *Average main: 40 TL* ⊠ *İskele Mah, overlooking the harbor, Datça* ☎ *252/712–9770* ⊕ *www.culinarium-datca.com* ☽ *Closed Dec.–Mar.*

$$
SEAFOOD

× **Emek Restaurant.** Everything is made on the premises of this excellent eatery overlooking Datça Harbor, where the menu includes seafood, Turkish grills, and various curries. The owner and chief chef Seyyar Kantarlı says her secret is all fresh ingredients. Her son Uğur catches most of the fish (the fried squid and octopus are delicious), and wild Datça herbs make menus interesting in spring. The homemade bread is among the best on the coast. ▥**TIP→ Call in the morning to reserve a balcony table.** $ *Average main: 20 TL* ⊠ *Yat Limanı, Datça* ☎ *252/712–3375* ☽ *Closed Nov.–Feb.*

$
TURKISH

× **Yeşim Bar Restaurant.** One of only three buildings on the pleasant beach at Kargı Koyu, Yeşim has sun beds, umbrellas, and showers available all day for customers. A lawn out back, with trees shading a bar, makes a cool respite from the sun. If you can, grab one of the prime tables under a tree on the beach itself. The menu includes pizzas, fish, and assorted meats. The bar is open late, so you can stay for a drink after dinner. $ *Average main: 14 TL* ⊠ *Follow road south 3 km (2 miles) from Datça until you see beach, it's the first building past carpark, Datça* ☎ *252/712–8399* ⊕ *yesimbar.com/contact/?lang=en.*

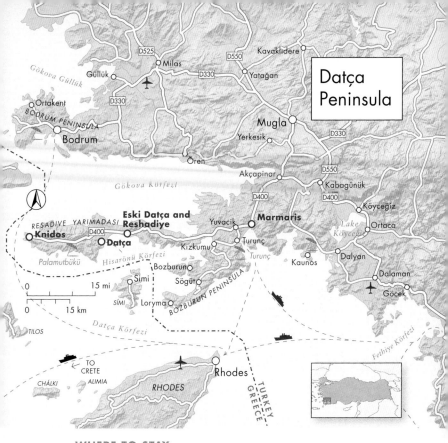

WHERE TO STAY

$$ **Bora Hotel.** If you want to stay in town, this modern hotel right behind
HOTEL   Datça Harbor has clean, bright rooms. **Pros:** central location; free Wi-Fi
and parking. **Cons:** unexceptional furnishings. $ *Rooms from: $103*
✉ *Street behind the yacht harbor, Datça* ☎ *252/712–2040* ⊕ *www.*
borahotel.com.tr ⤵ *18 rooms* ☽ *Closed Nov.–April* ⦿ *Breakfast.*

$$ **Türk Evi.** Built in the style of an Ottoman mansion and set in a pretty
HOTEL   garden just south of the yacht harbor, this small boutique hotel is a
relaxing place to stay. **Pros:** comfortable and unpretentious; all rooms
have balconies. **Cons:** no pool; rooms are on the small side. $ *Rooms*
from: $117 ✉ *Head west from harbor and look for signs, Datça*
☎ *252/712–4081* ⊕ *www.datcaturkevi.com* ⤵ *8 rooms* ⦿ *Breakfast.*

$$ **Villa Aşina.** All rooms have a sea view at this pretty hotel that looks
HOTEL   out over the Greek islands of Symi and Rhodes. **Pros:** lovely rooms;
Fodor's Choice   attentive host. **Cons:** a little out of town; no elevator. $ *Rooms from:*
★   *$137* ✉ *From Datça harbor, head south along coast, following signs*
to Villa Aşina on left after large hill, Datça ☎ *252/712–0443* ⊕ *www.*
villaasina.com ⤵ *20 rooms* ⦿ *Breakfast.*

NIGHTLIFE

There are many bars along the yacht harbor.

Club Gallus. Club Gallus, just west of the port, serves as the main discotheque for Datça; doors don't open until after midnight. ✉ *Kargı Yolu, just south of the center, Datça.*

ESKI DATÇA AND RESHADIYE

3 km (2 miles) inland from Datça harbor on the road to Reshadiye

Turkish satirical poet and polemical left-wing social critic Can Yücel retired to a modest old stone house in Eski Datça, setting an artistic tone for this pretty backwater spot and for nearby Reshadiye. The formerly Greek-populated village is one of the few in Turkey that has survived intact. Fine restoration efforts have produced several lovely small houses, which vacationers can rent. Nobody hurries through the stone-paved alleys.

GETTING HERE AND AROUND

Eski Datça and Reshadiye are both just off the main Datça–Marmaris road, 3 km (2 miles) and 4 km (2½ miles) respectively. There is a regular bus service between Datça and both towns.

WHERE TO EAT

$ TURKISH 🍴 **Datça Sofrası.** This is an ideal lunch spot, with a vine-covered terrace and traditional Turkish braised meats emerging from under a brass-hooded charcoal brazier. The menu is also rich in vegetarian dishes and starters concocted from local wild herbs. The specialty is *bademli köfte* (meatballs with almonds). [$] *Average main: 14 TL* ✉ *Hurma Sok. 16, Eski Datça* ☎ *252/712–4188* 💳 *No credit cards.*

$$$ TURKISH 🍴 **Elaki Restaurant.** Even if you don't stay at the Mehmet Ali Ağa Konağı Mansion, consider soaking up the ambience for an evening at its restaurant. The seating is right beside the hotel, effectively the courtyard, and it's usually possible to have a look around. As you'd expect in such a stellar location, the food is a gourmet's delight and the service five-star. The menu changes regularly, with a focus on Mediterranean and Ottoman dishes that make good use of the area's wild herbs. The mezes are excellent and the mixed platter recommended. There is also a fine wine cellar. [$] *Average main: 40 TL* ✉ *Kavak Meydan, Reshadiye* ☎ *252/712–9257* 🌐 *www.kocaev.com/elaki-restaurant.php.*

$$ INTERNATIONAL 🍴 **Koca Ev 2.** When a pair of art history professors retired to Eski Datça in 2013, they brought with them the best of Istanbul style to their new café-restaurant. Occupying a 170-year old Greek stone house, it has a cool interior and a lovely open garden. The menu—based on the owners' own home cooking—represents a blend of European and Turkish flavors (the traditional köfte cooked in a Neapolitan sauce is a case in point). Fish, pizzas, mezes, and soups are also featured. [$] *Average main: 18 TL* ✉ *Çeşme Sok. 11, opposite the mosque, Eski Datça.*

WHERE TO STAY

$$ B&B/INN 🏨 **Eski Datça Evleri.** Scattered throughout the village, the Eski Datça Evleri (or Old Datça Houses) is a collection of traditional stone homes, each with its own garden. **Pros:** true Turkish charm; good if you want

to be self-sufficient. **Cons:** walk to main house for breakfast; not all houses have Wi-Fi. $ *Rooms from: $101* ⊠ *D1 Sokak 26, on right as you enter village, Eski Datça* ☎ *252/712–2129* ⊕ *www.eskidatcaevleri.com* ↩ *11 rooms* ⦿ *Breakfast.*

$$$$ 🖼 **Mehmet Ali Ağa Konağı.** A stay in this restored mansion offers the
HOTEL   unique chance to experience the lifestyle and surroundings of a 19th-
Fodor'sChoice   century Ottoman noble. **Pros:** absolutely beautiful; delicious food. **Cons:**
★   small "cupboard" bathrooms in the mansion; pricey. $ *Rooms from: $413* ⊠ *Kavak Meydan, Reshadiye* ☎ *252/712–9257* ⊕ *www.kocaev.com* ↩ *15 rooms, 2 suites* ⦿ *Closed Nov.–mid-Apr.* ⦿ *Breakfast.*

$ 🖼 **Yağhane Pansiyon.** If you're eager for inner reflection, this comfort-
B&B/INN   able stone-built hotel with a fine English lawn out front specializes in weeklong courses of yoga, meditation, Ayurvedic treatments, and "the search for your inner snake." **Pros:** peaceful; great meditation facilities. **Cons:** not for everyone. $ *Rooms from: $35* ⊠ *Yağhane Sok. 4, Eski Datça* ☎ *252/712–2287* ⊕ *yaghane.net* ↩ *4 rooms* ▭ *No credit cards* ⦿ *Breakfast.*

KNIDOS

38 km (24 miles) west of Datça.

Windswept Knidos sits on a headland at the very end of the Datça Peninsula, at the point where the Aegean meets the Mediterranean. A primitive archaeological site, its ruins are scattered amid olive groves and a few hints of modern civilization. There is a small restaurant by the jetty where the tour boats arrive.

GETTING HERE AND AROUND

Knidos is most romantic when reached by sea, and in summer boats leave regularly from Datça; the trip takes three hours each way, with swimming stops en route. By car, you can reach Knidos from Datça in 40 minutes over bumpy roads. *Dolmuşes* to Yazıköy go on to the ruins in season.

EXPLORING

Knidos. Knidos was founded in the 7th century BC by Dorian Greeks and prospered because of its excellent location on shipping routes between Egypt, Rhodes, Ephesus, the Greek mainland, and other major ports. The center of the archaeological site is the large agora, or marketplace, down by the water. If you continue up the hill on the ancient main street, with its views over the harbor and the modern lighthouse, you'll pass the temple of Apollo and then reach the circular temple of Aphrodite, which used to house one of classical Greece's most famous statues, a lifelike rendering of the titular goddess.

Around the back of the site is the Corinthian temple with its ancient sundial; back by the harbor is a small **odeon,** or concert hall. On the hill to the east there's a giant platform with a stone **lion,** a remembrance of a victory over Sparta. The original is now on display in the British Museum, along with another famous relic from Knidos, a statue of the goddess Demeter. Her **sanctuary,** however, is up the original stairway that leads to the upper portion of the town on the east side of the ruins. ✉ *38 km (24 miles) west of Datça* 🎫 *8 TL.*

Palamutbükü Beach. Just before Knidos, a road heads south past many fishing villages. The popular Palamutbükü Beach, in a long bay on the south side of the peninsula, is a nice place to stop after visiting the ruins. Behind the beach are a number of restaurants, each serving their own zone of sand. **Amenities:** food and drink; parking (free); showers; toilets. **Best for:** walking; swimming. ✉ *4km (2.5 miles) south of Yakaköy on the Datça-Knidos road.*

MARMARIS

91 km (56 miles) west of Dalaman Airport.

This big, brash resort city has two faces, and they're hard to reconcile. From the sea, a line of hotels stretches around the northern edge of a great bay, the whole encircled by a magical necklace of pine-clad mountains. Behind those same hotels, however, the city has been overwhelmed by boxy concrete development and streets lined with a hundred generically named eateries. An annual horde of European tourists descends on these workaday establishments, but for the international traveler, there is little about Marmaris that can't be savored elsewhere in Turkey. Although it is a pretty spot, there isn't much reason to linger unless you are meeting a yacht, traveling on to the Greek island of Rhodes, or perhaps snapping up an unbeatable deal at one of the top resorts, some of which are spectacular worlds unto themselves.

GETTING HERE AND AROUND

A series of color-coded minibuses run from the center of town for about 2 TL: light green goes to the bus station, orange to İçmeler, and pink to the "yacht marina." A 60-minute catamaran service to the Greek island of **Rhodes** leaves Marmaris harbor every day at 9 am, returning at 4 pm, with a single or day return ticket costing 107 TL. It's worth spending the night in Rhodes, since Greek island life typically grinds to a halt during the midday hours.

ESSENTIALS

Marmaris Tourist Office ✉ *İskele Meyd. 2, by marina* ☎ *252/412–1035* 📠 *252/412–7277.*

EXPLORING

Good day outings from Marmaris include a boat trip from the harbor to **Turunç** on a visit easily arranged by yourself, your hotel, or any of the many travel agencies. Another fine destination is **Sedir Island** (Cedar Island).

This will likely involve a bus ride north to the Gulf of Gökova and then a boat. Sedir harbors one of the most perfect beaches in the world—if only one could have it to oneself. The sand is made up of tiny egg-shape pearls of a luminous white marble, making the water brilliantly clear as you swim before the impressive escarpments of Mt. Kavak over the sea to the north. An hour's bus ride from Marmaris will also take you to the refreshing sulfurous mud baths near Lake Köyeceğiz or, on a long but doable day trip, to the town of **Dalyan** and the ruins of ancient Kaunos.

Marmaris Bay is home to some of Turkey's biggest and busiest marinas, and is one of the main bases from which sailing yachts and wooden gulets can be chartered for Blue Cruises.

Seafront Promenade. The city's best achievement is a 10-km (7 mile) seafront promenade that stretches all the way from the easternmost marina known as Netsel, past the old fortress, along the palm-lined main boulevard of town, and then out between the beach and the fancy hotels that line the coast, all the way west to the outlying resort of İçmeler. Along the way there are any number of cafés at which to pause for refreshment or to take in fine views of sea and mountains.

> **NAKED APHRODITE**
>
> In antiquity Knidos's main claim to fame was its 4th-century BC statue of Aphrodite. It was the first naked statue of a goddess, and when its commissioners, the people of Kos, saw it they were so shocked that they sent it back and asked for something a little more respectable. The citizens of Knidos were looking for a statue of Aphrodite at the time and bought the rejected work, which rapidly became a hit. Knidos turned into an ancient tourist attraction, drawing travelers from afar, among them Cicero and Julius Caesar.

For 10 TL, you can ride back on one of the shared water taxis that run up and down the coast in season (usually April–November).

Citadel. There are few historic sites in what was until a few decades ago a small, sleepy fishing port. One is a modest 16th-century citadel: first built by Süleyman the Magnificent, then shelled to bits by the French in the First World War, and rebuilt in the 1980s. There is a small museum inside (both are closed on Monday).

WHERE TO EAT AND STAY

Some city blocks in Marmaris appear to be made up entirely of restaurants with a pavement-to-pavement profusion of tables and menus that seem like a catalog of world food. The most striking views can be had from cafés where the seafront promenade curves into the bay around the citadel, and these attract the tourists. Locals, however, prefer the slightly better-prepared food in restaurants that look out onto the Netsel yacht marina just to the east.

$$
ECLECTIC
✕ **Pineapple.** This restaurant in the Netsel marina has a lot more style and dignity than you would guess from the name, and it's a great escape from the mass tourism of Marmaris. The house specialty is tender Anatolian oven-cooked lamb; however, the chef also prepares octopus, pasta, pizza, steak, Turkish grills, and divine desserts. Above Pineapple is its sister restaurant, My Marina English, which has quite nice balcony views. $ *Average main: 30 TL* ✉ *Netsel Marina* ☎ *252/412–0976.*

$$
TURKISH
✕ **Yat Marina Restaurant.** Far from Marmaris's madding crowds, this is where to go for a taste of international yachting life. The chefs don't go in for the omnibus menus common in town, preferring to concentrate their considerable talents on getting favorite Turkish dishes just right. Dishes include pasta, steak, and, not surprisingly, a lot of seafood. It's fun to walk around the busy marina where huge rigs pull millionaires' luxury motor cruisers from the water as European pensioners scrub

CLOSE UP

Blue Cruising

The most charming way to visit the Turquoise Coast, or the Aegean coast, is by taking a Blue Cruise aboard a *gulet*—a wooden motor yacht or sailboat. Since time has done remarkably little to spoil the crystal clear waters, wooded inlets and limpid lagoons, this will be one of the most unforgettable holidays you've ever had. Some organization is, however, necessary.

How much will it cost? Gulets come in all shapes and sizes, the majority with between 4 and 12 two-person cabins. To hire your own boat, prices work out to between 160 TL to 300 TL per person per day in July and August, about half that in April or October. Most charter on terms that cover everything but food and drink. After a discussion with the boat's cook, you and a member of the crew go to the local supermarket and load up. Cabin charters—when you join a group of strangers—are generally on an all-inclusive basis, and start at about 600 TL per week.

When to go? May is pretty, uncrowded, and charters are cheap, but the water is cooler. June is warm and still not too busy. July and August are hotter, busier, and more expensive. September and early October are often perfect at sea, but the mountainsides are less green.

Other things to consider are how long you have and which port is closest to the sites you want to see. Fethiye is a major jumping-off point, as are Bodrum, Marmaris, and Göcek. Ideally, two weeks are needed to see the whole coast from Bodrum to Antalya, but most travelers only have one.

Look for a boat with a large area for relaxing in the stern and a good flat space on the foredeck for sleeping outside in hot weather. Don't accept anything too squashed: eight cabins in a boat under 80 feet are too many. If you're out in July and August, look for air-conditioning—and enough power-generation capacity for it. Ask about extras like windsurfers or kayaks.

The captain is important, too. Make sure you can communicate, and if you're arranging the cruise from abroad, insist on a telephone conversation before sending your deposit. Look for someone who listens to your wishes, and be wary if you are met with a patronizing "leave-it-all-to-me" attitude. If you want to sail rather than motor, you need to be doubly sure you have the right vessel. When you get to the boat, check the captain's license, insist on seeing life vests, and test emergency equipment like radios.

If you're hiring a boat after you've arrived in Turkey, you can walk down the quayside and haggle, but this can be risky in high season. Most people book months ahead. Look for operators registered with both the Turkish Association of Travel Agencies (TURSAB) and the Chamber of Shipping.

There are websites for individual boats and large agencies operating from major ports. For Marmaris, try ⊕ *www. yesilmarmaris.com*. Fethiye is popular, with ⊕ *www.albatrosyachting.com*, ⊕ *www.bethereyachting.com*, ⊕ *www. compassyachting.com*, ⊕ *www. fethiyeyachting.com*, or ⊕ *www. alestayachting.com*. Antalya is served by ⊕ *www.olymposyachting.com*.

the hulls of their much smaller "pocket" yachts. ∎**TIP**→ Patrons can use the pool beside the restaurant. $ *Average main: 20 TL* ⊠ *Follow coast road 8 km (5 miles) east out of Marmaris and park outside marina gate* ☎ *252/422–0022.*

$$$ | 🏨 **D-Resort Grand Azur.** This international resort is one of the few places
RESORT | with any real architectural style in Marmaris and its sleek, curving profile overlooks lush tropical gardens. **Pros:** nice private beach area. **Cons:** average rooms for the money. $ *Rooms from: $152* ⊠ *Kenan Evren Bul. 13* ☎ *252/417–4050* ⊕ *www.hotelgrandazur.com* ⇆ *257 rooms, 30 suites* ⊙*Some meals.*

> **FRANKINCENSE**
>
> The area around Marmaris is known for its frankincense forests, and on the water's edge is a lovely national park. In Marmaris market you can buy the frankincense, which is the dried sap of the trees. As incense it's known to be quite soothing.

NIGHTLIFE

Marmaris comes alive at night with a wide selection of bars and dance clubs. European charter tourists practice the art of serious drinking on **Bar Street** in the old town and its four solid blocks of drinking establishments. The major clubs here offer seething dance floors, and it's generally an opportunity for excess.

Back Street Garden Bar. The largest open-air club on Bar Street is Back Street Garden Bar. ⊠ *Old Town* ☎ *252/412–4048.*

Malibu Beach. The party goes on farther west, toward İçmeler, at the restaurant-bar Malibu Beach. ⊠ *Uzunyalı 248 Sok. 9* ☎ *252/412–6778.*

At İçmeler Beach itself are dance clubs and karaoke bars with raucous crowds partying into the night.

THE LYCIAN COAST

Lycia is the heart of the Turquoise Coast. The rugged landscape dotted with pine forests and olive groves contrasts with stunning blue sea. While it's certainly not undiscovered territory, the lack of airports has limited development, so you can expect charming port towns, unique hotels, and uncrowded beaches. The ancient Lycians had their own distinct culture and the coast holds some of Turkey's most fascinating ancient ruins: Xanthos, Pinara, Patara, Olympos, and Phaselis. This is also wonderful trekking terrain and home to the 530-km (331-mile) Lycian Way, a trail that includes many good day hikes. There are other adventures to be found in the region, too—paragliding from Ölüdeniz's 6,800-foot high Babadağ, kayaking around the sunken city of Kekova, and diving off Kaş. And seafood lovers will find plenty of fresh-off-the-boat treats.

DALYAN

25 km (16 miles) west of Dalaman Airport on Rte. 400 and local roads.

Dalyan is a lovely place for a three-day break, especially if you prefer a quiet destination that's been developed in a way that is sensitive to

The Lycian Coast

Güney

Karamanlı

Abbas

Tefenni

D 585

D 400 Köyceğiz

D 650

Ortaca

Söğüt

D 350

Korkuteli

Kavnos

Altınyayla

Karain Cave

Dalyan

Termessos

Dalaman

Göcek

Kadyanda

D 350

Antalya
see detail
map

İztuzu
Beach

Kargi

İmecik

D 400

Günlükla
Beach

Lycae

Fethiye

Elmalı

Mt. Olympos

Gemiler Island

Kaya

Ölüdeniz

L Y K I A

Göynük

Kabak

D 400

Tlos

Pınara

Saklıkent

Arycanda

Xanthos

Altınyaka

Phaselis

Letoön

D 400

Çıralı

Kalkan

Myra

Kumluca

Olympos

Patara

D 400

Finike

Kaş

Simena

Üçağız

Demre
(Kale)

Adrasan

KASTELORIZO

Aperlai

KEKOVA

Apollonia

Mediterranean Sea

0   15 mi
0   15 km

KEY

Beaches

Ferry Lines

the natural surroundings and the native flora and fauna. The town
sits on the winding Dalyan River, between the great expanse of Lake
Köyeceğiz and the lovely beach of İstuzu. Its Carian tombs, which are
carved into the cliff that rises behind the 15-foot-high reeds fringing the
undeveloped west bank, make an especially fine sight when floodlit at
night. Boats lined up along the quayside in the center of town will take
you on expeditions to the beach, to sulfur baths, to the ruins of ancient
Kaunos, and to the pretty bay of Ekincik. If your hotel is on the river,
the boatmen will pick you up there, too. (Note that all boats are part
of the Dalyan Kooperatifi; fares are regulated, so there is no bargaining
unless many are idle.) Trekking and footpaths are developing fast, and
include walks to Ekincik and elsewhere. Bird-watchers love the lake,
where 180 species of bird have been logged. Local markets are also
colorful: there's one in Dalyan on Saturday and one at the local center
of Ortaca on Friday.

GETTING HERE AND AROUND
Dalyan is about 6 km (10 miles) southwest of the highway, and there
are regular minibuses to the nearby town of Ortaca.

EXPLORING

FAMILY **İztuzu Beach.** Unspoiled İztuzu Beach stretches for 8 km (5 miles), with the Mediterranean on one side and a freshwater lagoon on the other. In June and July *Caretta caretta* sea turtles lay their eggs here. This is a conservation area (signs along the beach mark possible nesting places and warn you not to stick umbrellas in the sand or behave in other ways that could disturb them); there's even a turtle hospital you can visit. Regular boats and minibuses from Dalyan cost about 10 TL return. **Amenities:** food and drink; toilets; showers; parking. **Best for:** swimming; walking. ✉ *12 km (8 miles) south of Dalyan.*

Kaunos. The ancient ruins at Kaunos can be reached in 15 to 30 minutes by boat from Dalyan; alternately, you can find the *geçit* (a rowboat crossing), and then walk south for 30 minutes. Up from the port is the agora, which has a restored fountain house and a ruined portico dotted with the foundation of statues. An old Roman street takes you up the hill, past the nice temple terrace, to a crumbling Byzantine basilica, a massive Roman bath, and a well-preserved semicircular theater that is cut into the hillside in the Greek style. Most of the remains date from the 4th century BC, and reflect a blend of Carian and Lycian influences. From the ruins there is a pretty cliff-top walk to Ekincik, which takes three to four hours with the possibility of returning by boat. ✉ *About 1 km (0.6 miles) southwest of Dalyan* 🎫 *8 TL.*

5

WHERE TO EAT AND STAY

$$ TURKISH 🍴 **Dalyan La Vie.** This pleasant open-air restaurant, which occupies a prime spot on the river, opposite the tombs, is the most upmarket in town. There's a wide selection of appetizers and the usual array of mains, with lots of seafood as well as steak, chicken, and pasta. Though not as gourmet as it aspires to be, the food is a definite step up from the kebab places that line the main street. Pity about the noisy bar next door. [$] *Average main: 25 TL* ✉ *Sağlık Cad., Maraş District. Follow Dalyan River bankside walkway 500 m south from main square* ☎ *252/284–3166* 🌐 *www.dalyanlavie.com.*

$$ HOTEL 🏨 **Asur Hotel.** With a large swimming pool and gardens overlooking the Dalyan River, this one-story property is a smart choice. **Pros:** friendly service; good value; complimentary bikes for guest use. **Cons:** 1 km (½ mile) from center of town. [$] *Rooms from: $95* ✉ *South edge of town* ☎ *252/284–3232* 🌐 *www.asurotel.com* 🛏 *34 rooms, 10 suites* 🕓 *Closed Oct.–May* 🍽 *Breakfast.*

$$ B&B/INN FAMILY 🏨 **Beyaz Gül.** On the riverfront, south of the town center, this curious hotel is run by an old-fashioned Turkish lady, and staying here is like living in a fairy-tale cottage. **Pros:** not your average hotel; feels like a little oasis. **Cons:** grounds dominated by restaurant; may be too quirky for some tastes. [$] *Rooms from: $82* ✉ *Balikhane Cad. 92/93, Maraş* ☎ *252/284–2304* 🌐 *www.beyazgul.info* 🛏 *4 rooms* 💳 *No credit cards* 🍽 *Multiple meal plans.*

$$ RESORT 🏨 **Dalyan Resort.** This beautiful spot opened in 2005 on a bend in the Dalyan River. **Pros:** nice pool area; free Wi-Fi and shuttle boat to beach. **Cons:** upscale but not a lot of character; on the very edge of town. [$] *Rooms from: $97* ✉ *Kaunos Cad. 50* ☎ *252/284–5499* 🌐 *www.dalyanresort.com* 🛏 *42 rooms, 2 suites* 🍽 *Breakfast.*

$$ 🖼 **Happy Caretta.** This small hotel is in a shady garden on the banks
HOTEL   of the Dalyan River, opposite the Kaunos tombs. **Pros:** gorgeous riv-
Fodor's Choice   erside gardens; friendly service; altogether lovely. **Cons:** a bit hard to
★   find. **$** *Rooms from: $91* ✉ *Kaunos Cad. 26, Maraş District; drive
south down Dalyan River and look for signs to right* ☎ *252/284–2109*
⊕ *www.happycaretta.com* ⤷ *10 rooms, 4 suites* ⦿ *Breakfast.*

GÖCEK

22 km (11 miles) east of Dalaman Airport on Rte. 400.

A 20-minute drive over the mountains from Dalaman Airport, Göcek is
perfect for visitors who want to sample the grandeur of the Turquoise
Coast but have little time to spare. This tranquil resort town offers
gorgeous vistas of sea and mountains, easy access to the water, plus
upmarket places to eat, sleep, and shop. Having avoided the excesses of
package tourism and overdevelopment, it is focused on a pleasant, car-
less waterfront. Three marinas and an annual regatta make this a major
center for Turkey's yachting world, and weekends see it awash with
Istanbul *sosyete* (essentially the rich, frequently spoiled, and occasion-
ally glamorous children of the upper classes). From Göcek, an hour's
drive reaches the natural beauties of Dalyan, the sights around Fethiye/
Ölüdeniz, or great Lycian sites like Tlos and Xanthos. There is only
one private beach in Göcek itself, so hop on one of the several wooden
tour boats that head out each morning to explore elsewhere. The best
swimming and snorkeling are around the beaches or in the coves of the
Twelve Islands, strung out like a necklace across the mouth of the bay.

Göcek is in prime Blue Cruise territory, so you can join a day cruise
or rent a yacht or a *gulet* for as much time and money as you have
to spare. The most popular anchorages include Tersane, Kapı Creek,
Cleopatra's Bay, the obscure ruins at Lydae, Tomb Bay, or the lovely
island of Katrancı.

GETTING HERE AND AROUND
The main highway passes immediately behind the town with exits to
the east and west.

EXPLORING
Sundowner Beach. Run privately by the D-Resort Göcek, Sundowner
Beach, at the eastern end of the Port Göcek marina, is one of the most
spectacular—and expensive—on the Turquoise Coast. It costs 40 TL
for nonguests. Some will feel that this is a small price to pay for an
excellently maintained beach and bar establishment, and a completely
unspoiled, wraparound view of the bay and mountains. The beach is
open 10 am to 6 pm (later if anyone wants to stay); the bar is open
in the evening, and dinner is served after 7 pm. **Amenities:** food and
drink; showers, toilets. **Best for:** swimming. ✉ *On the D-Resort property*
☎ *252/645–2760.*

WHERE TO EAT
$$ ✗ **Can.** This busy harborside fish restaurant is popular with Göcek
SEAFOOD   natives because the large interior space is open year-round—and Wi-Fi
access is free. Though it moved into a new building in 2011, Can has

Sea kayaking around the Göcek Islands

been around for more than 15 years and is a town institution. In summer, the seating extends out toward the waterfront, under broad tropical trees. Specialties (like fish baked in salt) are typical, but the pride of the menu is its selection of 30 starters, including tuna with onion sauce and cheese, served with arugula salad. The homemade bread is delicious, and wild mountain mushrooms are served as a side dish in spring and fall. [$] *Average main: 28 TL* ✉ *Western edge of municipal harbor* ☎ *252/645–1507.*

$$ SEAFOOD 🍴 **Özcan.** Cushioned bamboo chairs, attentive waitstaff, and possibly the best grilled octopus you've ever tasted await you at Özcan, a fish restaurant on the wide esplanade that makes up Göcek's main public harborside. The wide range of starters includes unusual mushrooms from the mountains out back, fresh seaweed dishes, and squid in garlic, oil, and lemon. The menu is predominantly seafood but there are also excellent kebabs and local lamb dishes. [$] *Average main: 30 TL* ✉ *Middle of municipal yacht harbor* ☎ *252/645–2593.*

WHERE TO STAY

$$$ RESORT FAMILY 🏨 **The Bay Beach Club.** This pretty resort, made up of wooden cabins under the chestnut trees, opened in 2008. **Pros:** gorgeous waterfront cabins. **Cons:** isolated setting. [$] *Rooms from: $202* ✉ *At Gunlüklü Beach, take the right-hand road* ☎ *252/633–6310* 🌐 *www.thebaybeachclub.com* 🛏 *47 cabins* ⏲ *Closed Nov.–Mar* 🍽 *All meals.*

$$$$ RESORT 🏨 **D-Resort Göcek.** This D-Resort outpost has all the luxury and excellent service you'd expect from an international chain. ⇨ **Pros:** central but separate; stylish beach area. **Cons:** pricey; rooms are pleasant but unexceptional. [$] *Rooms from: $275* ✉ *Cumhuriyet District*

☎ 252/661–0900 ⊕ *www.dresortgocek.com.tr* ⋗ *57 rooms* ☉ *Closed Nov.–mid-Apr.* ¶◎¶ *Breakfast.*

$$ ⬚ **Hotel Forest Gate.** This quiet cluster of white two-story villas sur-
HOTEL rounded by pines has generous rooms organized around a pool that's shaded by a great carob tree. **Pros:** friendly atmosphere; nice pool area. **Cons:** out of the way; some rooms are just average. ⓢ *Rooms from: $110* ✉ *From main road, turn into Göcek at gas station at entrance of town and follow signs east* ☎ 252/645–2629 ⊕ *www.hotelforestgate. com* ⋗ *14 rooms, 9 suites* ¶◎¶ *Breakfast.*

$$ ⬚ **Villa Danlin.** On Göcek's main shopping street, this is a good small
HOTEL hotel with rooms shielded from most noise. **Pros:** central location. **Cons:** rooms are nothing special. ⓢ *Rooms from: $80* ✉ *Çarşı İçi* ☎ 252/645–1521 ⊕ *www.villadanlin.com* ⋗ *13 rooms* ☉ *Closed Nov. –Apr.* ¶◎¶ *Breakfast.*

$$ ⬚ **Yonca Resort.** This small, friendly place is not really a resort—despite
B&B/INN the name it's more like a family-run *pansiyon.* **Pros:** friendly; attention to detail. **Cons:** tricky to find. ⓢ *Rooms from: $110* ✉ *Gonca Sok. 7* ☎ 252/645-2255 ⋗ *6 rooms, 2 suites* ¶◎¶ *Breakfast.*

EN
ROUTE **Gunlüklü Beach.** If you get overheated on the main road between Göcek and Fethiye—or just need an antidote to the relentless fashionability of the former—follow the brown sign south to Gunlüklü Beach. It's a good place to stop for a picnic in a forest of small chestnut trees or to take a swim in the unspoiled bay from a dark sand beach. Be forewarned, though: this spot tends to get crowded on weekends with Turkish day-trippers from Fethiye, and the facilities can be a bit rough and ready. **Amenities:** food and drink; toilets; showers; parking (fee). **Best for:** swimming. ✉ *About 10 km (6 miles) from Göcek, 17 km (11 miles) from Fethiye* 🖾 *8 TL per car.*

FETHIYE

50 km (31 miles) east of Dalaman Airport on Rte. 400.

This busy port city is a good base for exploring the ruins of ancient Lycia in the mountains that rise to the east. Fethiye was known in antiquity as Telmessus (not to be confused with Termessos, near Antalya) and was the principal port of Lycia from the Roman period onward. In front of the town hall is one of the finest of several tombs found throughout the city: it represents a two-story Lycian house, with reliefs of warriors on both sides of its lid.

The small original town was called Mekri and populated mainly by Greeks before the 1923 Greek-Turkish population exchange. It was renamed in 1934 for Fethi Bey, a famous Ottoman pilot. He was killed on the eve of the First World War when he crashed in the mountains of Lebanon while attempting a historic flight that was to link all the Middle Eastern provinces of the Ottoman Empire. Today's town is quite modern, having been substantially rebuilt after a 1957 earthquake. Strolling along the seafront promenade is pleasant, and scuba enthusiasts can choose between half a dozen dive boats that collect in the harbor. The harbor also has many yachts available for Blue Cruis-

Continued on page 293

MEZE: MOUTHWATERING MORSELS

Prepare your taste buds for a Turkish culinary experience: tangy yogurt, pungent garlic, fresh herbs, smoky eggplant, marinated salads, and roasted vegetables await.

Whether you're sitting down for dinner along Turkey's coast, in one of Istanbul's historic neighborhoods, or somewhere in the untouristed southeast, your meal will almost certainly begin with meze—the assortment of small dishes that are the heart and soul of Turkish cuisine. Similar to the idea of tapas, meze are more than just a quick snack or an appetizer. For Turks, eating meze is often a meal in itself—a languorous repast made up of countless small plates and an ample supply of rakı, the anise-flavored liquor that is Turkey's national drink and the preferred accompaniment to meze.

Dolma

Eating meze is a centuries-old national tradition, influenced by Persian, Arab, and Greek cooking, and you'll find regional differences in what's offered. Dishes in the country's southeast have more of a Middle Eastern influence, while those in Istanbul and the Aegean area have more of a Greek flavor. What they have in common, though, is the Turkish belief that the meze experience is about more than eating and drinking—free-wheeling conversation is an essential component. As one famous Turkish saying goes: "The best meze is good table talk."

WHAT'S ON THE MEZE MENU

A typical meze menu includes dozens of mostly meatless dishes, hot and cold, emphasizing freshness and seasonality. In Istanbul's *meyhanes*—rollicking, tavern-like restaurants that specialize in meze—servers arrive at your table with large trays piled high with small dishes. You choose whatever catches your eye.

Left: Octopus salad. Right: A variety of Turkish salads.

TASTES TO EXPECT

When it comes to meze, Turks tend to have a conservative palate. Meze meals, for example, often start with the simplest but most traditional dish of all—a piece of tangy feta cheese accompanied by a slice of sweet honeydew melon and a glass of rakı. Meze restaurants (with some notable exceptions) are not trying to outdo one another by inventing ever more creative dishes. Rather, they stick with tried and true meze that have become the classics of Turkish cooking. Here are some of the traditional meze you should be on the lookout for:

COLD (SOĞUK) MEZE

BAKLA EZMESİ—Dried fava beans that are cooked, mashed with garlic, olive oil, dill, and lemon juice, and turned into an earthy pâté.

BARBUNYA PİLAKİ—*Barbunya* beans (Roman or red beans), usually fresh from the pod, stewed in a garlicky tomato sauce.

ÇERKEZ TAVUĞU—A highlight of classical Turkish cooking, this dish consists of poached chicken that is ground with garlic and walnuts to make a deliciously enticing and flavorful dip.

DENİZ BÖRÜLCESİ—A wonderfully fresh-tasting dish made of samphire, a crunchy green that grows by the sea. It's cooked in olive oil and flavored with lemon juice.

ENGİNAR—Artichoke hearts stewed in olive oil with onion and carrot, served cold.

EZME—A salad of finely chopped tomatoes and onion, sometimes flavored with pleasantly astringent pomegranate molasses.

HAYDARİ—A dip made of thick and creamy strained yogurt, flavored with garlic and dill.

İMAM BAYILDI—Literally meaning "the imam swooned," this dish is one of Turkey's most famous: an eggplant is stuffed with onion, garlic, parsley, and tomato and stewed in olive oil.

KISIR—The Turkish version of tabbouleh, this is a tangy and somewhat spicy salad made out of bulgur wheat and red pepper paste.

LAKERDA—Turkey's take on lox, this is cured mackerel, sliced thick.

MİDYE DOLMASI—An Istanbul favorite sold by street vendors: mussels cooked with rice, pine nuts, currants, herbs, and spices and stuffed back into their shell.

PATLICAN SALATASI—An eggplant salad or dip, of which there are many variations (see the "Ubiquitous Eggplant" sidebar).

SEMİZOTU—When in season, purslane (a variety of green similar to watercress that's rich in vitamins and Omega-3 fatty acids) is mixed with yogurt to make a tangy salad.

YAPRAK SARMA—Grape leaves stuffed with rice, currants, and pine nuts.

ZEYTİNYAĞLI—Vegetables such as green beans and artichoke hearts that are stewed in olive oil and served cool or at room temperature. (*Zeytinyağı*, pronounced "zey-teen-yah," is the Turkish name for the oil.)

Kabaklı börek (filo pastries with zucchini).

THE UBIQUITOUS EGGPLANT

According to Turkish culinary lore, there are more than a thousand ways to cook eggplant (*patlican* in Turkish, pronounced "pat-li-jahn"). That may be an exaggeration, but you could certainly lose count of how many dishes feature the humble nightshade—it's even made into a jam! The vegetable certainly plays a starring role on the meze tray: cubes of fried eggplant come covered in a yogurt and tomato sauce; charcoal-roasted eggplant is turned into a smoky puree; and sun-dried eggplants are served stuffed with rice and herbs.

HOT (SICAK) MEZE

ARNAVUT CİĞERİ—Cubes of lamb's liver, fried with red pepper flakes.

BÖREK—Filo pastries, sometimes rolled up like cigars and stuffed with cheese, or layered over *pastırma*, which is spicy cured beef.

DOLMA OR SARMA—Stuffed grape leaves and other vegetables, such as peppers or cabbage, that are filled with a combination of rice, herbs, spices, and sometimes ground meat.

KALAMAR—Calamari rings batter-fried and served with an addictive sauce made of ground walnuts and garlic known as *tarator*.

KARİDES—Shrimp in a butter or tomato sauce, usually baked in a terra-cotta dish.

MÜCVER—Zucchini and herb fritters.

PAZI SARMA—Swiss chard stuffed with ground meat and rice, with yogurt on the side.

HELPFUL WORDS TO KNOW

Eating out in Istanbul is often a festive experience.

Being confronted with a tray filled with dozens of little dishes can be daunting, but knowing a few key words will help you navigate the meze maze. Of course, there's nothing wrong with pointing at any mysterious meze and giving your waiter an inquisitive look—most will know a few words in English to help you along. Also remember, there is no need to order everything at once. You can order a few, then call your waiter back when you're ready for more.

ACILI—means "spicy."

ACISIZ–literally "not spicy."

DOMATES–tomato.

ET–meat: *kuzu* is lamb, *dana* is beef, *tavuk* is chicken; you'll rarely see pork, *domuz*, on menus.

IZGARA–grilled.

KIZARTMA–fried.

PEYNİR–cheese; *beyaz peynir* is feta cheese, *kaşar peynir* is a semi-soft yellow cheese.

SALATALIK–cucumber.

SARIMSAK–garlic; a dish with garlic in it is called *sarımsaklı.*

SOĞAN–onion; a dish with on-ions on top is called *soğanlı.*

Kısır

AND TO DRINK?

Although wine and beer are gaining in popularity, anise-flavored rakı (similar to Greek ouzo or French pastis) is still the undisputed top choice for a drink to accompany meze. For years, the dependable Yeni Rakı brand was pretty much the only choice available, although new brands are now becoming popular. Rakı made by the brand Efe is worth seeking out.

Drinking rakı, like eating meze, has its own rituals. It's rarely drunk straight because it's so potent: 80 proof or higher. Typically, a shot of rakı is mixed with water, turning the drink a milky white. Most rakı drinkers also add ice. Even when diluted, rakı can be pretty strong, though fans say it goes down smooth with a slight sweetness. They also maintain that a good rakı buzz is conducive to entertaining conversation.

ing. Fethiye is most fun on Tuesdays, when village folk flock in for the weekly market.

GETTING HERE AND AROUND

Fethiye's modern bus station is 1 km (½ mile) east of the center. Buses running east and west along the coast depart regularly, and several a day cross the mountains for Denizli and Pamukkale. Minibuses to Ölüdeniz, Göcek, and other nearby destinations leave from Akdeniz Caddesi, a few blocks west of the center.

ESSENTIALS

Official Tourist Office Fethiye ⊠ *İskele Karşısı 1* ☎☎ *252/614–1527.*

EXPLORING

Castle. Along the crest of the hill overlooking the old town are the battlements of a castle; the foundations, which date back to antiquity, were later built up by the crusading 12th-century crusader Knights of St. John. ⊠ *Kaya Cad.*

Fethiye Müzesi (*Fethiye Müzesi*). Fethiye has a relatively small but modern museum with an excellent collection of artifacts from nearby sites. There is some good sculpture, mostly from Tlos and the Fethiye theater. You'll also see the Letoon trilingual stele (a stone slab with Greek, Lycian, and Aramaic inscriptions), the mosaic from the Temple of Apollo, and a series of altars and stelae dedicated to the gods in thanks. Other displays include an interesting golden bowl with figures of bulls and a 19th-century Greek ship's figurehead. ⊠ *Off Atatürk Cad.* ☎ *252/614–1150* ☜ *3 TL* ☉ *Daily 8:30–7.*

Hammam. The 16th-century hammam is still in use. Though a bit touristy, it is full of atmosphere, with 14 domes and 6 arches. It's not the country's greatest Turkish bath but can be a fine way to scrub off the barnacles after a long voyage. ⊠ *Hamam Cad., close to main harbor square* ☎ *252/614–9318* ⊕ *www.oldturkishbath.com* ☜ *35 TL.*

Rock tombs. Impressive ancient Lycian rock tombs are carved into the cliff that looms above town. These can be admired from a distance. But if you're keen to get an up-close look, follow the signs to Kaya Caddesi, near the local bus station, and then climb the many steps leading up. Your effort will be well rewarded—particularly at dusk, when the cliffs take on a reddish glow. The largest is the **Tomb of Amyntas,** presumably the burial place of a 4th-century-BC ruler or nobleman. Inside are the slabs where corpses were laid out. ⊠ *Follow the steps from Kaya Cad.* ☜ *3 TL.*

Theater. The main road around Fethiye's central harbor square also runs past the stage of the antique theater of Telmessus, a recent chance rediscovery that gives a sense of history to the modern buildings all around. The rest of the ancient town remains under its urban tomb. ⊠ *Fevzi Çakmak Cad., opposite the Yacht Habor.*

OFF THE
BEATEN
PATH

Kadyanda. The ruins of ancient Kadyanda, a short drive north of Fethiye, are a pleasant day-trip destination in the heat of summer. You enter past some tombs to a large agora, or marketplace, behind which is a well-preserved running track and a collapsed temple. Heading back down the trail, you'll pass a large Roman theater. ■TIP→ Watch

out for the frequent large holes left by treasure hunters. Poised on a remote shady ridge at more than 3,000 feet, the site is uphill from the mountain village of Üzümlü, which has some interesting old houses. ✉ *From Fethiye, take road north toward Göcek and look for turnoff for Üzümlü, continue through village looking for signs for Kadyanda* 🎟 *10 TL.*

WHERE TO EAT

$$ SEAFOOD 🍴 **Fethiye Fish Market.** Those who are tempted by Turkey's fish markets but have nowhere to cook can head to Fethiye's lively local market area. For a small cover charge, several casual restaurants will cook your purchase, adding mezes and salads. Non-fish eaters can buy steak instead on the same system. Everyone has their favorite: **Recep's Place** and **Hilmi** are both reliable choices. [$] *Average main: 25 TL* ✉ *Just west of main market area, between Hükümet, Belediye, 96, and 97 streets.*

$$ TURKISH 🍴 **Meğri Lokanta.** The Meğris pretty much rule the restaurant market in Fethiye, but it's a well-deserved hierarchy because their food is quite consistently the best in town. This excellent, straightforward Turkish meat restaurant is on the western edge of the bazaar and much favored by locals. [$] *Average main: 20 TL* ✉ *Western edge of the bazaar* ☎ *252/614–4047.*

$$ ECLECTIC 🍴 **Meğri Restaurant.** In the center of the bazaar, the permanent part of this upscale restaurant has stone walls, high wood ceilings, and decorative kilims. In summer, most of the tables spill out into a large courtyard in the middle of the bazaar. A vast menu mixes dishes from Asia, France, Turkey, and the Mediterranean. Portions are large and the food is quite good. [$] *Average main: 30 TL* ✉ *Eski Cami Geçidi Likya Sok. 8–9* ☎ *252/614–4046* 📠 *252/612–0446.*

$$ INTERNATIONAL 🍴 **MOD Yacht Lounge.** This glass-fronted, pleasingly modern café-restaurant on the harborfront walkway has a chill nautical vibe and an unimpeded water view. In summer, dishes from its international menu can be enjoyed on the deck at tree-shaded tables. TIP→ **With a wide range of cocktails, this is also a great place to stop in for an evening drink.** [$] *Average main: 30 TL* ✉ *Ece Marina, Karagözler* ☎ *252/614–3970.*

$$ TURKISH 🍴 **Mozaik Restaurant.** This restaurant in a backstreet garden, a stone's throw from the gauntlet of Fethiye's bazaar area, has been earning fans with its good food and tranquil atmosphere. Mains include *belen tava* (a cheese-topped meat-and-vegetable casserole) and the Mozaik kebab with grilled chicken and lamb in a yogurt sauce. The chef himself sometimes anonymously leaves the kitchen to proudly place his creation on your table. TIP→ **Booking advisable in high season.** [$] *Average main: 20 TL* ✉ *Sokak 90/91* ☎ *252/614–4653.*

WHERE TO STAY

$$$ HOTEL 🏨 **Ece Saray.** Modeled on the grand hotels of the French Riviera, this luxury option has a lovely location on the harborfront. **Pros:** quality accommodations with lots of extras. **Cons:** sea but no beach; in need of some modernization. [$] *Rooms from: $234* ✉ *Ece Marina, Karagözler* ☎ *252/612–5005* 🌐 *www.ecesaray.net* 🛏 *34 rooms, 14 suites* 🍽 *Breakfast.*

$$ **Villa Daffodil Hotel.** If you're looking for a midsize, midprice hotel,
HOTEL Villa Daffodil—on the quieter west end of Fethiye's waterfront—works
well. **Pros:** good value. **Cons:** a little out of town; some rooms are
dark. $ *Rooms from: $81* ⊠ *Fevzi Cakmak Cad. 139* ☎ *252/614–9595*
⊕ *www.villadaffodil.com* ⤴ *45 rooms* ⭘ *Breakfast.*

$$$ **Yacht Classic.** Probably the best hotel east of the harbor, the medium-
HOTEL size Yacht Classic has been slowly moving upmarket: it underwent
a major face-lift in 2010 and in 2013 added five gorgeous Greek-
inspired "'water villas" that share a common infinity pool. **Pros:** nice
waterfront pool area, incredible design-oriented villas. **Cons:** back
rooms have no view and are subject to traffic noise. $ *Rooms from:*
$165 ⊠ *Karagözler 24, just east of Ece Marinapro* ☎ *252/612–5067*
⊕ *www.yachtclassichotel.com* ⤴ *35 rooms, 5 villas* ⊟ *No credit cards*
⭘ *Breakfast.*

NIGHTLIFE
On weekends there are clubs off Hamam Caddesi in the center of
Fethiye.

Mango Bar. This small indoor dance club with live Turkish music some
nights is a reliable favorite. ⊠ *45 Sok.* ☎ *252/614–4681.*

Outside town there is a strip of cheaper, less appealing hotels along Çaliş
Beach that stretches west of town—this is where the package tours from
northern Europe tend to stay and there are plenty of bars. It's a long
way to go for a drink if you're staying in town, but the scene has an
appeal for the younger crowd. During the week, nightclubs are busiest
in Hisarönü, between Fethiye and Ölüdeniz.

SPORTS AND THE OUTDOORS
Boat tours. Boats and water taxis operating out of Fethiye offer a variety of tours to Göcek, the Twelve Islands, or Ölüdeniz. Itineraries are
posted, and there are people on hand to answer questions. Be sure to
shop around, though, as packages vary widely and some are essentially
booze cruises. Standard boats, which charge about 30 TL per person
with lunch, are large; smaller ones are generally worth the extra cost.
If Ölüdeniz is your destination, be aware that windy weather can make
for heavy waves. Most tours leave about 10 am, returning about 6 pm.
⊠ *Harborfront.*

KAYA

10 km (7 miles) south of Fethiye; 6 km (4 miles) west of Ölüdeniz.

The valley behind Fethiye promises a cooler climate and evocative
ruins that are decidedly different from their ancient counterparts on
the Mediterranean coast. Kaya was a thriving Greek community until
1923, when the villagers were moved out in a compulsory population
exchange that saw Greek Orthodox Christians living in Turkey evicted
from their homes. Nowadays it's essentially an overgrown ghost town,
with some charming settlement on the edges. Several hotels and open-
air restaurants are scattered among the olive trees.

GETTING HERE AND AROUND

A dramatic, though potentially dangerous, route signposted from Fethiye runs directly over the hills, close to the Lycian tombs. An easier way to reach the village is to take the Ölüdeniz road as far as Hisarönü, and then make a right turn marked 3 km (2 miles) for Kaya.

EXPLORING

Kaya. Spread across three hills, the old Greek town of Levissi—called Kaya by the Turks—is atmospheric and eerily quiet. It had a population of about 2,000 before residents of Greek origin were "sent home" to a motherland they had never known in 1923. Novelist Louis de Bernières offers a fictionalized account of the mass exodus in *Birds Without Wings* (his follow-up to *Captain Corelli's Mandolin*). Today you can wander through crumbling cube houses reminiscent of those in the Greek Islands, some with a touch of bright Mediterranean blue or red still visible on the walls. There are two large churches, many chapels, plus schools and a fountain house. **TIP→ From the chapel on the hill at the southwest corner, a path leads down to the remote beach of Cold Water Bay, a 30-minute walk away.** ✉ *Kaya* 🎫 *12 TL* 🕒 *Daily 9–6:30.*

WHERE TO EAT AND STAY

$$ INTERNATIONAL 🍴 **Izela.** Part of the Gunay's Garden villa complex, this tranquil spot in the far corner of Kaya village blends the best of Turkish and European cuisine, using homegrown ingredients as much as possible. There is a good range of largely organic starters; try the mixed meze plate. Mains include excellent fish, steak, pizzas, and a lovely oven-cooked lamb. [$] *Average main: 30 TL* ✉ *Gumruk Sokak, Kaya* ☎ *252/618–0033* 🌐 *www.gunaysgarden.com/izelaRestaurant.asp.*

$$$ ECLECTIC 🍴 **Levissi Garden Wine House and Restaurant.** What was once the house of a prosperous Greek merchant is now a fine restaurant specializing in steak and an ultra-tender *lamb kleftiko* (the latter is marinated in wine and slowed cooked in a 400-year-old oven). The wine cellar has more than 10,000 bottles, including a good selection of Turkish wines. On hot summer days, you can take refuge in the cool basement; at night, the restaurant floodlights the abandoned buildings all around, creating an atmosphere that is romantic or spooky, depending on your take. **TIP→ Free transportation is available to/from hotels in the Fethiye-Ölüdeniz area.** [$] *Average main: 35 TL* ✉ *Kayaköy, near western ticket office, Kaya* ☎ *252/618–0173.*

$$$ RENTAL FAMILY 🏨 **Gunay's Garden.** Half a dozen attractive stone villas are clustered around a pretty garden and pool at this self-catering property; spacious two- and three-bedroom options have full kitchens, multiple bathrooms, and comfortable terraces. **Pros:** well-equipped villas arranged to maximize privacy; good on-site restaurant (Izela). **Cons:** popular with young families, which may not be best for others; one-week stays preferred. [$] *Rooms from: $160* ✉ *Gumruk Sokak, Kaya* ☎ *252/618–0033* 🌐 *www.gunaysgarden.com* 🛏 *6 villas* 🍽 *No meals.*

ÖLÜDENIZ

60 km (38 miles) east of Dalaman Airport; 8 km (5 miles) southeast of Fethiye.

Little wonder Ölüdeniz appears on so many Turkish promotional posters. With a photogenic mountain and a fringe of fragrant evergreens behind it, this oh-so-blue, beach-rimmed lagoon really is picture-perfect. The same, unfortunately, cannot be said of the bland package-tourist town that serves it.

GETTING HERE AND AROUND

Ölüdeniz can be reached by day cruise from Fethiye as well as by dolmuş or car. If you're driving, one inland route is through Ovacık (it's the shorter option when coming from outside Fethiye); a prettier one leads past the ruined town of Kaya, climbing steeply from a point 1 km (½ mile) west of the harbor.

EXPLORING

The water of Ölüdeniz is warm and the setting delightful, despite the crowds. The view is even more splendid from the air (this is one of Turkey's premier locations for paragliding). Travel agencies in town will organize Jeep safaris into the surrounding high mountain pastures and villages for about 80 TL a day, lunch included.

Ölüdeniz Natural Park. If you want to bathe at the iconic sandbar that lies across the mouth of the lagoon, then you must first enter Ölüdeniz Natural Park. To do so, go down to the seafront, turn west, then left at the fork where you can see the toll booth; the charge is 10 TL per car or 5 TL per person on foot. There's a capacious car park but, even from here, it can be a hot trek of several hundred yards. The setting is absolutely beautiful, and the crowds love it. Pretty much the entire pebbly beach is taken up by densely packed lounge chairs and umbrellas, either of which can be rented for 5 TL. Just around the corner a concession rents out pedalos and kayaks for 20 TL per hour. The sea gets deep quickly and there are several diving platforms anchored a short swim out. **Amenities:** food and drink; parking; showers, toilets; water sports. **Best for:** swimming. ⊠ *Ölüdeniz.*

Another sand beach can be found behind the park in the shallow, warm waters of the lagoon; this one is popular with families. Although theoretically public property, in practice this beach is run by the campsites and restaurants that line the shore. Use of their facilities, however, is unlikely to be much more expensive than those in the park itself.

The Lycian Way starts in the hills above Ölüdeniz, and one of its most pleasant sections is the three- to five-day walk to Patara.

WHERE TO EAT AND STAY

$$
INTERNATIONAL
✕ **Oyster Mediterranean Restaurant.** This restaurant in the Oyster Residences, at the western edge of the strip of bars and eateries along the beach, probably has the best food in town. Putting a contemporary spin on Mediterranean staples, its menu features lots of seafood (including swordfish kebabs), as well as steaks and beautiful baked lamb. The restaurant is set in a small garden terrace, which is cozy and tranquil despite its proximity to the busy waterfront area. $ *Average main: 30 TL*

✉ *On water, one block east of main intersection, Belcekiz Mevkii 1 Sok., Ölüdeniz* ☎ *252/617–0765* ⊕ *www.oysterresidences.com/Oyster.aspx#.*

$$$$
HOTEL
✉ **Meri Hotel.** Built in 1975, this hotel was the first—and last—to be allowed by the government to set up shop on the famed Ölüdeniz lagoon. **Pros:** location, location, location. **Cons:** average rooms; daunting stairs. $ *Rooms from: $262* ✉ *On the lagoon, Ölüdeniz* ☎ *252/617–0001* ⊕ *www.hotelmeri.com* ⤳ *70 standard rooms, 24 family rooms* ⦿ *All meals.*

$$
RESORT
✉ **Montana Pine Resort.** It's not Montana, but this resort—located uphill from Ölüdeniz in neighboring Hisarönü—does have a splendid mountain setting and temperatures that seem refreshingly cool compared to the coast. **Pros:** daily shuttle service to Ölüdeniz beach; professionally run; many guests return every year. **Cons:** you'll have to walk the last 100 yards because outside vehicles aren't permitted. $ *Rooms from: $138* ✉ *Asagi Yasdam Cad., Hisarönü, Ölüdeniz* ☎ *252/616–7108, 252/616–6366* ⊕ *www.montanapine.com* ⤳ *149 rooms, 5 suites* ☾ *Closed Nov.–May* ⦿ *Breakfast.*

$$
RESORT
✉ **Ocakköy Holiday Village.** A quiet, shady cluster of restored or reconstructed stone cottages give this 6-acre spread a real village vibe. **Pros:** good for families; lots of extras; helpful staff will arrange boat excursions. **Cons:** can seem overly resort-ish. $ *Rooms from: $115* ✉ *4 km (3 mi) from Fethiye on the Ölüdeniz road, a sign points the way at the first turning on the right. Keep right and head uphill* ☎ *252/616–6156, 252/616–6157* ⊕ *www.ocak-koy.com* ⤳ *41 cottages* ⦿ *Breakfast.*

$$$
HOTEL
Fodor's Choice
★
✉ **Oyster Residences.** Nestled among olive trees just off the beach, this elegant boutique hotel is a happy misfit in package-tourist dominated Ölüdeniz. **Pros:** nice décor; larger rooms have Jacuzzis. **Cons:** some evening noise from nearby bars. $ *Rooms from: $207* ✉ *Belcekiz Mevkii 1. Sok., one block east of main intersection, Ölüdeniz* ☎ *252/617–0765* ⊕ *www.oysterresidences.com* ⤳ *26 rooms* ⦿ *No meals.*

NIGHTLIFE

Most bars operate only between May and October; after a history of keeping the town awake, they are now supposed to close at 1 am.

Buzz Beach Bar. The Buzz Beach Bar lets you cool down with frozen cocktails and other frosty drinks. ✉ *Oludeniz Beach, Ölüdeniz* ☎ *252/617–0526* ⊕ *www.buzzbeachbar.com.*

Help Beach Bar. At the funky—and friendly—Help Beach Bar, drinks are often accompanied by live music and surprisingly good food. ✉ *Waterfront promenade, Ölüdeniz* ☎ *252/617–0650.*

Whether you're looking for a British-style expat pub or something more raucous, you'll find further options in nearby Hisarönü.

SPORTS AND THE OUTDOORS
BOATING

Ölüdeniz Kooperatif. A good day out on a boat can be arranged by the skippers of Ölüdeniz Kooperatif, who work from a kiosk halfway between the main body of hotels and the beach. May through November, their 15 boats will take groups to locales with catchy names like Blue Cave, Butterfly Valley, Aquarium Bay, St. Nicholas Island, Cold Water Spring, Camel Beach, and Turquoise Bay. Trips usually run from

11 am to 6 pm and cost about 25 TL per person with lunch included (cold drinks extra). It's a great way to see the area, though some fellow passengers may be more interested in beer than sightseeing. ✉ *Ölüdeniz.*

PARAGLIDING

The first thing you'll notice in Ölüdeniz is people soaring through the sky; paragliding is a busy industry here and a major spectator sport. The launch point is about 1,700 yards up Mt. Baba, some 20 km (13 miles) by forest tracks from Ölüdeniz—tour operators will drive you up from town. Tourists flying tandem with a pilot (around 200 TL) generally stay up for 30 to 40 minutes before landing gently on the beach. Full training and internationally recognized certificates in solo piloting are also available. Most travel agencies can arrange a flight.

KABAK

16 km (10 miles) south of Ölüdeniz; 29 km (18 miles) south of Fethiye.

If you like your beaches in deep coves, framed by towering cliffs and pine forests, without a deck chair or beach umbrella in sight, then you'll love Kabak. For years it was one of Turkey's best-kept secrets, attracting hippies and alternative types. These days, accommodations are multiplying, but it's still one of the quieter places along the coast.

GETTING HERE AND AROUND

Just before the Fethiye road reaches Ölüdeniz, there's a turn to the left—from here it's 25 km (15 miles) to Kabak. Regular dolmuş service is available from Fethiye and Ölüdeniz via the village of Faralya. The main road does not continue to the beach itself. A section of the Lycian Way starts behind Mama's Restaurant and drops to the beach in about 30 minutes—the less intrepid may find the path rough and steep in patches. Alternatively there is a Jeep dolmuş called "Last Stop" (☎ *531/345–7164*) that takes passengers down a rough road to the beach.

WHERE TO STAY

$$ B&B/INN Fodor's Choice ★ 🏨 **Olive Garden.** Perched on a terrace just down from the main road, this friendly, family-run place has a million-dollar view. **Pros:** views; fresh and tasty food; nice people. **Cons:** no a/c means cabins can get hot during day; steep walk to beach. [$] *Rooms from: $91* ✉ *Look for signs, the turn is beside Mama's Restaurant, Kabak* ☎ *252/642–1083* 🌐 *www.olivegardenkabak.com* 🛏 *10 cabins* 🍴 *Some meals.*

$$ RESORT 🏨 **Turan Hill Lodge.** Surrounded by gardens, Kabak's original place to stay has several sleeping options; accommodations range from luxury tents to full cabins with bathrooms and fans (but not a/c). **Pros:** lush garden. **Cons:** difficult to access; tiny pool. [$] *Rooms from: $126* ✉ *Take path down to beach, follow signs left/up as you reach bottom, Kabak* ☎ *252/642–1227* 🌐 *www.turanhilllounge.com* 🛏 *22 rooms* 🍴 *Some meals.*

TLOS

22 km (14 miles) east of Fethiye.

A day expedition to Tlos, a spectacular ancient Lycian city high above the valley of the Xanthos River, can be arranged from any town on the coast from Göcek to Kaş.

GETTING HERE AND AROUND

Head east from Fethiye on D90/E400. After 20 km (12 miles), follow signs for Antalya via Korkuteli. Drive another 1.2 km (¾ mile). Just after the bridge, there is a right turn for Tlos and Saklıkent. After 8 km (5 miles) there is a left turn for Tlos, 2.2 km (1½ miles).

EXPLORING

Tlos. From the **acropolis** of Tlos a fine view can be had to the west of the Xanthos Valley—then as now a rich agricultural area—and to the east of the mountains that cradle Tlos's Roman theater. The fortress at the summit is Turkish from the 18th century and was a popular haunt of the pirate Kanlı ("Bloody") Ali Ağa. Below the fortress, off a narrow path, is a cluster of rock tombs. Note the relief here of Bellerophon, son of King Glaucus of Corinth, mounted on Pegasus, his winged steed. The monster he faces is the dreaded Chimera—a fire-breathing creature with a lion's head, goat's body, and serpent's tail. (Famously, Bellerophon had been sent to the King of Lycia with a sealed message saying that he should be put to his death on arrival. Unwilling to kill this noble figure outright, the Lycians sent him on apparently fatal tasks like fighting the Chimera. He survived them all with the aid of Pegasus and won half a kingdom. The Chimera's fire can still be seen coming up from the ground near Çirali/Olimpo.) Beside the acropolis is a large flat agora, with seats on one side from which spectators watched foot races. ☒ *From Fethiye take exit to Rte. 400 and follow local road east to Antalya where a yellow sign marks right turn that leads southwest for 15 km (9 miles)* ☜ *5 TL* ☼ *Daily 8:30–sunset.*

Yaka Park Restaurant. Continue up the hill beyond Tlos to the nearby village of Yaka Köyü (it's signposted) and you'll reach the vast but peaceful Yaka Park Restaurant, which has become an attraction in its own right. On the site of a now-demolished windmill, it has its own trout farm, guaranteeing the fish will always be fresh. The chilly water is everywhere, gurgling around traditional Turkish wooden platforms where diners sit, and there is even a little channel in the bar where fish can swim around your chilled beer. ☒ *Yaka Köyü* ☎ *252/634–0036.*

**EN
ROUTE**

Saklıkent Gorge. Continue south from Tlos to reach this spectacular gorge. It's a popular spot for picnicking and a wonderful place to cool off on a hot summer's day; children especially love wading up through the icy stream at the bottom of a deep rock crevasse. The first section goes over a walkway above the torrent to a pleasant leafy tea garden, beyond which the adventurous can cross the glacial water and carry on up the canyon. The first 30 minutes are straightforward; then the wading gets deeper and the rock scrambles more difficult, so know your limits—and expect to get wet. The road here heads south to Çavdir, which is just across the highway from Xanthos. ☒ *15 km (9 miles) south of Tlos* ☜ *5 TL* ☼ *Daily 8:30–sunset.*

CLOSE UP

Ancient Cultures of Lycia and Its Neighbors

Turkey's Mediterranean coast is steeped in 5,000 years of history—so much so that in Side the hotels, restaurants, and nightclubs are literally built into the ruins of the Greco-Roman city.

Broadly speaking, the geographic divisions of ancient times survive today. The westernmost area from Datça to Dalyan was part of Caria, an ancient Hellenistic kingdom based in nearby Bodrum/Halicarnassus. Caria reached the height of its power in the 4th century BC, and the tomb of its most famous ruler, Mausolus, was such a wonder of the world that it coined the word *mausoleum*. From Dalyan to Phaselis the coast is thought of as Lycia, after a people of very ancient but uncertain origin, some of whom possibly colonized this section of Anatolia from Crete. It now hosts small-scale hotels and harmonious yachting ports. From Antalya to Alanya is the area called Pamphilia, thought to mean "the land of all the tribes," much of which is now quite built up and commercial.

Caria, Lycia, and Pamphilia share much the same rather obscure history, and museums (the best is in Antalya) exhibit relics from Bronze Age settlements that date back to 3000 BC. Our knowledge of indigenous cultures is patchy, but notable in many ways. In Homer's epic, Lycia's Sarpedon memorably declaims that the privileges of the elite must be earned through a readiness to fight for their people; and, although not a matriarchal society, Lycians are thought to have been matrilineal and gave women a more equal place than, say, ancient Greeks. Some locals were fiercely independent. The people of Xanthos, for example, committed mass suicide rather than submit to the first Persian conquest; later they burned their city (again) rather than pay extra taxes to Rome's Brutus. In addition, the democratic, federal basis of the Lycian League is acknowledged as one source of the U.S. constitution.

Overall, the population of this whole area has long been a mixture of waves of new arrivals—whether Greek colonists, Persian administrators, retired Roman legionaries, Turkic shepherds, or today's sun seekers. Despite wars, plagues, and population exchanges, however, there is some degree of continuity: genetic tests discovered that all two dozen of the local workers on a site north of Antalya were distantly related to the bones that they had just dug out from 1,300-year-old graves.

PINARA

40 km (24 miles) southeast of Fethiye; 40 km (25 miles) northwest of Kalkan.

Pınara (meaning "something round" in Lycian) is a romantic ruin around a great circular outcrop backed by high cliffs, reachable from most holiday spots in western Lycia.

GETTING HERE AND AROUND

From Fethiye take E90/D400 toward Kalkan for 47 km (30 miles), and then take the right turn marked for Pınara. From there it's a further 6 km (4 miles) via the village of Minara.

EXPLORING

Pınara. Pınara was probably founded as early as the 5th century BC, and it eventually became one of Lycia's most important cities. You need time and determination to explore, though, as it's widely scattered, largely unexcavated, and overgrown with plane, fig, and olive trees. You can park in the village of **Minare** and make the half-hour hike up the clearly marked trail. At the top of a steep dirt track, the site steward will collect your admission and point you in the right direction—there are no descriptive signs or good maps.

The spectacular **Greek theater,** which has overlooked these peaceful hills and fields for thousands of years, is one of the country's finest. It's perfectly proportioned, and unlike that of most other theaters in Turkey, its stage building is still standing. The site also contains groups of rock **tombs** with unusual reliefs (one shows a cityscape) and a cliff wall honeycombed with hundreds of crude rectangular "pigeonholes," which are believed to have been either tombs or food storage receptacles. Nearby villagers volunteer to show tourists around; it's not a bad idea to accept the offer as they know the highlights. A tip is customary. ⊠ *40 km (25 miles) north of Kalkan, look for sign on Rte. 400.* 🖾 *10 TL* ☉ *Daily 8:30–sunset.*

LETOON

63 km (39 miles) southeast of Fethiye; 17 km (11 miles) northwest of Kalkan.

This site was not a city but rather a religious center and political meeting point for the Lycian League: the world's first democratic federation. It's quite rural and can be reached on a day trip from western Lycia's main centers—Fethiye, Ölüdeniz, Kaş, or Kalkan. Plan to visit in the late afternoon, perhaps after a stop in nearby Xanthos, which administered the temples in ancient times.

GETTING HERE AND AROUND

There are several signposted routes including one from across the Xanthos bridge, 5 km (3 miles) away. You can continue past Letoon to the western end of the Patara beach. Occasional buses run to Kumluova from Fethiye.

EXPLORING

Letoon. Excavations have revealed three temples in Letoon. The first, closest to the parking area, dates from the 2nd century BC and was dedicated to Leto, the mother of Apollo and Artemis (hence the name); she was believed to have given birth to the twins here, while hiding from Zeus' jealous wife, Hera. The middle temple, the oldest, is dedicated to Artemis and dates from the 5th or 4th century BC. The last, dating from the 1st century BC, belongs to Apollo and contains a copy of a mosaic depicting a bow and arrow (a symbol of Artemis) and a sun and lyre (Apollo's emblems). These are the three Gods most closely associated with Lycia. Compare the first and last temples. The former is Ionic, topped by a simple, triangular pediment and columns with scroll-shape capitals. The latter is Doric, with scenic friezes and detailing on the ornate pediment and undecorated capitals on its columns. Re-erecting some columns of the Temple of Leto has made the site more photogenic. There is also a well-preserved Roman theater here—look for the carvings of theatrical masks on the northern wall. The once-sacred pool, now filled with ducks and chirping frogs, lends atmosphere. About 10 km (6 miles) south of Letoön, the road continues to a beach. Across a rickety bridge at the river mouth are the ruins of an early Lycian fort called Pydnai. ⊠ *17 km (11 miles) north of Kalkan on Rte. 400, just beyond Kumluova* 🖼 *6 TL* ☯ *Daily 8:30–sunset.*

XANTHOS

61 km (48 miles) southeast of Fethiye; 17 km (10 miles) northwest of Kalkan on Rte. 400.

Xanthos, perhaps the greatest city of ancient Lycia, is famed for tombs rising on high, thick, rectangular pillars. It also earned the region a reputation for fierceness in battle. Determined not to be subjugated by superior forces, the men of Xanthos twice set fire to their own city—with their women and children inside—and fought to the death. The first occasion was against the Persians in 542 BC, the second against Brutus and the Romans in the 1st century BC. The site was excavated and stripped by the British in 1838, and most finds are now in London's British Museum; the remains, however, are worth inspecting. Allow at least three hours and expect some company. Unlike other Lycian cities, Xanthos is on the main tour-bus route.

GETTING HERE AND AROUND
Xanthos is a short distance off Route 400. Buses along the highway will stop at the adjacent town of Kınık. In summer there are frequent minibuses from Xanthos to Patara, Kalkan, and Kaş.

EXPLORING
Xanthos. Start your exploration across from the parking area at the Roman-style **theater**: Inscriptions indicate that its restoration was funded by a wealthy Lycian named Opromoas of Rhodiapolis after the great earthquake of 141 AD. Alongside the theater are two much-photographed pillar **tombs**. The more famous of the pair is called the Harpy Tomb—not after what's inside, but because of the half-bird, half-woman figures carved onto the north and south sides. Other reliefs show a seated figure receiving various gifts, including a bird, a pomegranate, and a helmet. This tomb has been dated to 470 BC; the reliefs are plaster casts of originals in the British Museum. The other tomb consists of a sarcophagus atop a pillar—a rather unusual arrangement. The pillar section is probably as old as the Harpy Tomb, the sarcophagus added later. On the side of the theater, opposite the Harpy Tomb and past the agora, is the Inscribed Pillar of Xanthos. Dating from about 400 BC, it is etched with 250 lines (written in both Greek and Lycian) that recount the heroic deeds of a champion wrestler and celebrated soldier named Kerei. Check out the large Byzantine **basilica** with its abstract mosaics before following the path uphill, where you'll find several sarcophagi, a good collection of rock-cut house tombs, and a welcome spot of shade. Xanthos's center was up on the acropolis behind the theater, accessible by a trail. ⊠ *17 km (10 miles) north of Kalkan* 🖼 *5 TL* ☯ *Daily 9–sunset.*

PATARA

70 km (44 miles) southeast of Fethiye; 20 km (13 miles) northwest of Kalkan off Rte. 400.

Patara was once Lycia's principal port. Cosmopolitan in its heyday—Hannibal, St. Paul, and the emperor Hadrian all visited, and St. Nicholas, the man who would be Santa Claus, is said to have been born here—the port eventually silted up. Dunes at the edge of the village are now part of one of Turkey's longest and completely unspoiled sand beaches. From here, too, runs one of the best sections of the Lycian Way, a three- to five-day walk to Olüdeniz. Thanks to the ruins and the turtles that nest on the beach, new development was banned in the modern village, making it a quiet alternative to the bustle of nearby Kalkan.

GETTING HERE AND AROUND

The village is 3 km (2 miles) south of the highway; the ruins and beach are a further 3 km (2 miles) along the same road. Main buses will drop you at the highway, and frequent minibuses run between the beach, village, and Kınık (Xanthos), Kalkan, and Kaş, spring through fall.

EXPLORING

Patara Beach. Beyond the ruins is a superb 11-km (7-mile) sweep of sand dunes. Popular with Turkish families and tourists from Kalkan, it's never so crowded that you need to walk far to find solitude. Note that umbrellas should only be planted within 20 yards of the sea to prevent disturbing the nests of *Caretta caretta* turtles. **Amenities:** food and drink; parking (free); showers, toilets. **Best for:** walking; swimming.

Ruins. The ancient city of Patara, now being excavated by Antalya's Akdeniz University, is slowly emerging from the sands. The heavy stones that make up the front of the monumental **bathhouse** are impressive, and a **triple arch** built by a Roman governor in AD 100 seems a tenth of its age. Beyond are two theaters, several churches, and an impressive section of a colonnaded street. Follow the path west and you'll see the recently discovered Roman lighthouse. Still waiting to be found is the Temple of Apollo: Herodotus wrote that its oracle worked only part-time, as Apollo spent summers away in Delos (probably to escape the heat!). 🎟 *5 TL.*

WHERE TO EAT AND STAY

$$ TURKISH 🍴 **Tlos Restaurant.** This simple little restaurant just off the main intersection is keenly kept by a chef from the town of Bolu, legendarily the hometown of Turkey's best cooks. Individual attention is assured. There is an extensive menu with many hot and cold starters, seafood, and grilled meat. [$] *Average main: 20 TL* ✉ *On the right just off the main street leading to the ruins* ☎ *242/843–5135* 🕒 *Closed Nov.–Apr.*

$ HOTEL 🏨 **Dardanos.** Finally one of the older hotels in "no new development" Patara has benefited from a good refit. **Pros:** modern perks include air-conditioning and free Wi-Fi. **Cons:** no pool; limited English spoken. [$] *Rooms from: $70* ✉ *On the main side street in the middle of the village towards the river* ☎ *242/843–5151* 🌐 *www.pataradardanoshotel.com* 🛏 *18 rooms* 🍽 *Breakfast.*

CLOSE UP

The Lycian Way

Until the 1950s, the only way to reach the Lycian coast was by boat or via bone-rattling trips through the mountains in antiquated motor vehicles. Even the main roads today date only from the 1970s, which is why this was the perfect place to establish Turkey's first and most famous long-distance trekking route, the Lycian Way.

The footpath, marked by red-and-white painted blazes, runs along the sea for 530 km (331miles), following ancient Roman roads, and sometimes clambering up barely visible goat tracks to peaks that rise nearly 6,500 feet at Mt. Tahtalı (one of the many high mountains known in antiquity as Mt. Olympos). Upsides include breathtaking views, innumerable ancient ruins, and a chance to accept hospitality in villages little touched by tourism or time. The downside is that backpacks can be heavy and hills steep; and while most of the path is well marked, finding the trail can occasionally be difficult. If you lose it, go back to the last marker you saw—they're positioned 45 to 90 meters (50 to 100 yards) apart—and try again. Despite government support, the track has no legal status and is subject to adjustments due to road building, landslides, and fencing by landowners.

It would take a month to walk the Lycian Way from end to end, but there's a lot you can do without a tent. Because the trail crosses many towns and highways, it's easy to break up into day hikes, and you can cover about half of it while staying in *pansiyons* that have sprung up along the way. Kate Clow, the Englishwoman who first designed and mapped the Lycian Way in 2000, recommends several popular walks near Olympos in her book *The Lycian Way* (the route's only guide and a source of good maps). The website ⊕ *www.lycianway.com* provides updates and satellite grid references.

Middle Earth Travel. As a trekking agent and mule organizer, Clow recommends Middle Earth Travel. The company runs excursions on the Lycian Way and St. Paul's Way, as well as Cappadocia, the Kaçkars, and Mt. Ararat. ✉ *Gaferli Mah., Cevizler Sokak 20, Göreme, Nevşehir* ☎ *384/271–2559* ⊕ *www.middleearthtravel.com.*

The best times to walk are spring, when days are long and wildflowers are out, and autumn, when the seawater is warm and the weather cooler. Summer is too hot; in winter there may be some perfect days, but the weather is not reliable enough to make advanced plans.

$ View Point. One of the larger hotels in Patara, the View Point sits up
HOTEL on the hill west of town. **Pros:** friendly, knowledgeable hosts; well run. **Cons:** the walk up the hill. $ *Rooms from: $73* ✉ *Up hill to left as you come into town* ☎ *242/843–5110* ⊕ *www.pataraviewpoint.com* ⌂ *27 rooms* ☉ *Closed Nov.–Apr* ❖ *Breakfast.*

KALKAN

80 km (50 miles) southeast of Fethiye; 27 km (17 miles) west of Kaş, on Rte. 400.

> **WORD OF MOUTH**
>
> "I think one of the nicest options on the Turquoise Coast is Kalkan—which I much preferred to Kaş or Bodrum. If you prefer somewhere quiet, consider Patara—about 30 minutes away—which has the longest beach in the Mediterranean, I believe. You should definitely visit Ölüdeniz if you're nearby. It's visually stunning—though it will certainly be crowded." —Steve_James

Kalkan has two distinct sides: on one hand it has fine restaurants and excellent hotels to match its superb, steep views of the Mediterranean Sea. But it's also a bit overpriced, and regulars complain that the recent explosion of foreign-owned vacation villas, which are often rented out online, has changed the town's character for the worse. With only a small, rocky beach, a few narrow blocks of whitewashed stone houses, and not much archaeology of its own, Kalkan is trying hard to develop its tourism offerings. Despite its growing overexposure, it's still a decent base for touring the area and the surrounding sites.

GETTING HERE AND AROUND

The highway is immediately behind town, so getting here is straightforward.

WHERE TO EAT

$$$ TURKISH 🍴 **Aubergine.** This restaurant proves an exception to the general rule about avoiding harborfront eateries. The menu is adventurous and includes excellent pasta, salmon *en croute,* stuffed sea bass with bacon, extra large steaks, and occasionally wild boar shot in the mountains. All the desserts are homemade. [$] *Average main: 40 TL* ✉ *On the harborfront* ☎ *242/844–3332.*

$$$ MEDITERRANEAN 🍴 **Gironda.** This gourmet restaurant evokes an elegant villa, complete with sumptuous sofas and plaster-of-Paris statuary. The food—which alone merits a stay in Kalkan—is outstandingly fresh and the dishes are well thought out. Specialties include fillet of lamb in phyllo pastry, pan-seared sole in Champagne sauce, fish baked in parchment, and a wide variety of pastas. **TIP→ Tables on the terrace upstairs offer great views of Kalkan Bay.** [$] *Average main: 35 TL* ✉ *Two streets up from harbor in old town* ☎ *242/844–3136* ✍ *Reservations essential* ⊗ *Closed Nov.–Apr.*

WHERE TO STAY

$$ HOTEL 🏨 **Happy Hotel.** Despite the unimaginative concrete-block architecture, this well-run hotel overlooking Kalamar Bay is a good value. **Pros:** sizable suites; good facilities; free Wi-Fi. **Cons:** hilly walk into town takes 20 minutes. [$] *Rooms from: $100* ✉ *Head west of Kalkan to Kalamar Bay, follow road left as you come over ridge and follow signs down hill* ☎ *242/844–1133* 🌐 *www.happyhotel.com.tr* 🛏 *32 standard rooms, 18 suites* 🍽 *Breakfast.*

$$ HOTEL 🏨 **Hotel Pirat.** This 1986 concrete construction lacks personality, but the location is great: It's right on the harbor, and the three pools have superb

DID YOU KNOW?

Kapıtaş Beach, between Kaş and Kalkan, is dramatically set between the cliffs.

views of the bay. **Pros:** central location; excursions can be arranged. **Cons:** feels dated; no elevator. $ *Rooms from: $115* ✉ *Kalkan harbor* ☎ *242/844–3178* ⊕ *www.hotelpirat.net* ↩ *126 rooms, 10 suites* ⦿| *Breakfast.*

$$$$
HOTEL
Fodor's Choice
★

☷ **Hotel Villa Mahal.** Clinging to a cliff face with a wraparound view of Kalkan Bay, this immaculate establishment is one of Turkey's most spectacular hotels. **Pros:** posh rooms and public areas; stunning location. **Cons:** isolated; a long way trek down to the beach. $ *Rooms from: $415* ✉ *Patara Evler Yani, about 2 km (1 mile) east of Kalkan. Down and around signposted road. Take care on precipitous last approach* ☎ *242/844–3268* ⊕ *www.villamahal.com* ↩ *12 rooms, 1 suite* ⊗ *Nov.–Apr.* ⦿| *Breakfast.*

EN ROUTE

Kapıtaş Beach. Since neither Kaş nor Kalkan have proper beaches, this pretty spot between the two is quite popular. Set in a narrow, steep-sided inlet, there are 186 stairs leading down to it. The position between dramatic cliffs is picturesque, though the beach itself is small and can get crowded in summer. **Amenities:** food and drink; parking (free). **Best for**: swimming. ✉ *On the highway, 6 km (4 miles) from Kalkan.*

KAŞ

27 km (17 miles) southeast of Kalkan on Rte. 400; 180 km (112 miles) from Antalya via Korkuteli mountain road.

In the 1980s, Kaş, with its beautiful wide, island-filled bay, was the main tourist destination on the Lycian coast. But it fell by the wayside because it lacked a real beach and A-list attractions. This has, fortunately, kept away the worst overdevelopment; now Kaş is being rediscovered, with regular visitors migrating from Kalkan. There are excellent hotels and restaurants, the location is relatively central, and the size is about right, making it a good stop on your way along the coast. Like Kalkan, Kaş is also a good base for sightseeing in the area.

GETTING HERE AND AROUND

Route 400 runs immediately above the town, and there are two turns with large "Şehir Merkezi" (city center) signs and tiny signs for "Kaş." As you enter, there are marked turns—right for the Çukurbağ Peninsula, left for the seafront hotels.

Official Tourist Office Kaş ✉ *Cumhuriyet Meyd. 5* ☎☎ *242/836–1238.*

EXPLORING

Kastellorizon. The hour-long boat ride to the Greek island of Kastellorizon (called Meis in Turkey) gives you a taste of Greece and lets you imagine what Kaş must have been like before the 1923 population exchange, when most residents were of Greek origin.

Isolated from the rest of its country, Kastellorizon has escaped major tourist development and maintains the charm of an island that time forgot. Attractions include a small 12th- to 16th-century crusader castle, notable for its crenellated gray-stone walls; a large cave with fine stalactites; and the 1835 church of St. Konstantine and Eleni, which reused granite columns taken from the Temple of Apollo at Letoon in Lycia (usually locked).

Meis Express (⊕ *www.meisexpress.com* ☎ *242/836–1725*) has an office on Kaş's waterfront, with ferry departures at 10:20 am daily; afternoon trips, returning in the evening, are sometimes available. In either case, expect to pay about 55 TL for a return ticket. Since the typical day trip only enables you to see Kastellorizon when most Greeks are having their midday siesta, it's worth overnighting at one of the island's hotels or *pansiyons*; try Hotel Kastellorizo (⊕ *www.kastellorizohotel.gr* ☎ *224/604–9044*) on the harborfront. ⊠ *Kastellorizon, Greece.*

Ruins. Kaş—Antiphellus in ancient times—has a few ruins, including a monumental **sarcophagus** under a massive plane tree, up the sloping street that rises behind the main square. The tomb has four regal lion's heads carved onto the lid. In 1842, a British naval officer counted more than 100 sarcophagi in Kaş; however, most have been destroyed over the years as locals nabbed the flat side pieces to use in new construction.

A few hundred yards west of the main square, along Hastane Caddesi, a small, well-preserved antique **theater** sits amid the olive trees; superb ocean views make it particularly lovely at sunset. Next to the district prefect's office, east of the harbor, is an old wooden barn of the type once universally used as granaries in Lycian villages—and still clearly modeled on old Lycian architectural forms. If you really want to immerse yourself in history, Kaş is also a good base for scuba excursions. A profusion of dive boats shows the growing demand for the area's rich underwater sights, though a lot of the water is Greek and off limits. For details on diving opportunities, contact Bougainville Travel (⊕ *www.bougainville-turkey.com* ☎ *242 836–3737*).

Other excursion options include Simena and Kekova Sound; Demre, site of the old church of St. Nicholas; or Patara and Patara Beach. Be aware that high winds can make for a very rough boat ride, particularly round the cape to Kekova.

WHERE TO EAT

$$
TURKISH
✕ **Bahçe & Bahçe Balik.** Bahçe is a courtyard restaurant serving delightful Turkish dishes in a quiet garden setting, just opposite Kaş's 4th-century-BC King's Tomb. The waitstaff is one large family—each taking part in the preparation and serving of food. The starters are famous in Kaş. Especially tasty options are grated carrot with yogurt, mashed walnut, cold spinach, fish balls, and *arnavut ciğeri* (fried liver prepared with chopped nuts). The same family runs a fish restaurant opposite, Bahçe Balik, which has the town's best seafood. $ *Average main: 25 TL* ⊠ *Anıt Mezar Karşisi 31* ☎ *242/836-2370.*

$$$
INTERNATIONAL
✕ **Chez Evy.** No place in Kaş has more character than this delightful restaurant. Prices might be high, but that's because portions are usually double the size of anywhere else. The short but varied menu includes wild boar from the mountains. Dining is in an intimate garden around the back in summer. $ *Average main: 40 TL* ⊠ *Terzi Sok. 2* ☎ *242/836–1253.*

$$
TURKISH
Fodor's Choice
★
✕ **Ikbal.** This addition to the cluster of restaurants near the Lycian tomb has earned a reputation for the quality of its food. Run by a German-Turkish couple, it offers a mix of Turkish and Mediterranean dishes. Warm starters—such as the delicious *paçanga börek* (a pastry filled

with cheese and dried meat) or *emücver* (deep-fried eggplant)—are a house specialty; all are cooked fresh rather than reheated as at most other restaurants. For main courses there's the usual range of fish, köfte, lamb, chicken, and steak; and the tempting dessert menu includes their popular apple pancakes. $ *Average main: 28 TL* ⊠ *Süleyman Sandıkçı Sok. 6* ☎ *242/836–3193.*

WHERE TO STAY

$$$
HOTEL

🏨 **Gardenia.** The first thing you notice here is the art, acquired by the owner on his off-season trips to Asia and South America; it fills the lobby, expands up the stairs, and overflows into the rooms, setting the tone for this boutique hotel. **Pros:** stylish. **Cons:** some rooms are small; no elevator and lots of stairs. $ *Rooms from: $180* ⊠ *Hükmet Cad. 41* ☎ *242/836–2368* ⊕ *www.gardeniahotel-kas.com* ↴ *10 rooms, 1 suite* ⊙ *Closed mid-Nov.–Apr* ⫼ *Breakfast.*

$$$
HOTEL
Fodor'sChoice
★

🏨 **Hadrian Hotel.** This is a beautifully designed and immaculately kept waterfront hotel on the peninsula outside Kaş. **Pros:** gorgeous location; romantic. **Cons:** hotel is 500 yards down a steep hill from the main road, so a rental car is vital if you plan to do much sightseeing in the area. $ *Rooms from: $207* ⊠ *Doğan Kaşaroğlu Cad. 10, south side of Çukurbağ Peninsula* ☎ *242/836–2856* ⊕ *www.hotel-hadrian.de* ↴ *10 rooms, 4 suites* ⊙ *Closed Nov. 15–Apr. 15* ⫼ *Some meals.*

$$
HOTEL

🏨 **Kayahan.** Set a little uphill from the waterfront hotels, this mid-ange option offers wonderful views from its terrace, and (a rare treat in Kaş) it has an elevator to take you up there. **Pros:** elevator; terrific roof terrace; comfy rooms. **Cons:** not on coast; small pool. $ *Rooms from: $83* ⊠ *Koza Sok. 9* ☎ *242/836–1313* ⊕ *www.hotelkayahan.com* ↴ *33 rooms* ⫼ *Breakfast.*

$$
HOTEL

🏨 **Medusa Hotel.** This is probably the best run of the hotels that line the seafront road east of the harbor. **Pros:** friendly and helpful. **Cons:** small rooms; lots of stairs. $ *Rooms from: $110* ⊠ *Küçük Çakıl 62* ☎ *242/836–1440* ⊕ *www.medusahotels.com* ↴ *36 rooms, 1 suite* ⊙ *Closed Nov.–Apr.* ⫼ *Breakfast.*

NIGHTLIFE

Echo Café & Bar. Echo Café & Bar is both a disco and a live-jazz venue. It's probably also the only club in the world to boast a 3rd-century-BC basement cistern carved out of solid rock (now laid out with tables, and quieter than upstairs). The cistern was discovered by chance a few decades ago when the building—originally a stable for camels— was being extended. ⊠ *Uzun Çarsi Cad., on eastern edge of harbor* ☎ *242/836–2047* ⊕ *www.echocafebar.com.*

SIMENA-KALEKÖY AND KEKOVA SOUND

30 km (19 miles) east of Kaş.

Simena (known in Turkish as Kaleköy), Kekova Island, and its surrounding coastline are among the most enchanting spots in Turkey— especially when the reflection of the full moon slowly traces its way across Kekova Sound. Kekova Island stands slightly off a shore notched with little bays, whose many inlets create a series of lagoons. This area is famed for its "sunken city" and although swimming around the fragments of the partly submerged buildings is now banned, it is still an interesting place to explore.

The village of Üçağız, which has small *pansiyons* and waterside restaurants, is the base for boat trips across the bay to the island. Simena-Kaleköy, a 10-minute boat ride or half-hour walk away, is a concrete-free village that resembles a Greek island before development. It's a pleasing jumble of boxy houses built up a steep rocky crag alongside layers of history: Lycian tombs, a tiny Greek theater, and the medieval ruins of Simena Castle atop the rocky hill. You'll enjoy the place even more once the day-trippers have departed. There are now numerous basic *pansiyons*, which, while rather expensive for the quality of the rooms, have balconies with sublime views. All offer boat pickup from Üçağız. Reserve well in advance, in season.

GETTING HERE AND AROUND

Kekova Sound is a beautiful patch of water that begs to be explored by boat. Day trips leave from Kaş and Üçağız. Some boats come directly from Kaş while others bus their customers into Üçağız. Expect to pay around 80 TL. If driving, look for a turnoff from Route 400 signposted "Üçağız," 14 km (9 miles) east of Kaş. After 16 km (10 miles) you'll reach Çevreli, where there is a turn to Üçağız, a further 3 km (2 miles) onward.

EXPLORING

Aperlai & Apollonia. West of Kekova are two small, infrequently visited ruins, linked together by a section of the Lycian Way; they make a good day trip or overnight excursion for those who want to get off the beaten track. Apollonia is minor site on a small hill just southwest of the village of Sahil Kılınçlı on the Kaş–Üçağız road 7 km (4½ miles) south of the highway. Take the branch road through the village, then head west when you get to the top of the rise. First you'll see a good range of ancient Lycian tombs, scattered east and north of the walled acropolis hill. Continue west for the city proper; there's a small theater and a well-preserved church with views west over the coast toward Kaş. Back on the side road, look for the signed turnoff to the right, then walk two hours down the hill to the ruins of Aperlai on a pretty little inlet. The city walls are impressively intact. Buildings inside them include a well-preserved church, houses, and a bath by the water, as well the sunken remains of the ancient port—which you can explore with a mask and snorkel from the nearby Purple House *pansiyon*. If all that activity makes you hungry, the Purple House has a restaurant; from Aperlai a 20-minute walk takes you to an alternate eatery on the Kekova inlets. Another three hours, first inland, and then along the water, will take you to Üçağız. Some boats will drop you at the inlet, and give you time to walk to Aperlai and back.

WHERE TO STAY

$$ **Ankh Pansiyon.** This simple family establishment is the place to
B&B/INN choose if you want to escape from the world and soak up the otherworldliness of Kekova Sound. **Pros:** more private than other places around. **Cons:** rooms lack character. $ *Rooms from: $110* ⊠ *Eastern*

side of village, follow signs through maze of streets ☎242/874–2171 ⊕ *www.ankhpansion.com* ⛵8 *rooms* ⊘ *Closed Nov. 10–Apr.* ❑*Breakfast.*

$$ \text{\$\$} $$

$$ ❑ Kale Pansiyon. This intimate

B&B/INN family-run lodging is in a pretty stone building on the eastern side of the waterfront. **Pros:** central yet separate; lovely old wooden ceil-ings. **Cons:** ground-floor rooms have less of a view. $ *Rooms from: $110* ⊠ *Just east of the Sahil Pansiyon, follow the signs* ☎242/874–2111 ⊕ *www.kalepansiyon.com* ⛵11 *rooms* ⊘ *Closed Nov.–Apr* ❑*Breakfast.*

$ ❑ **Purple House.** This little *pansiyon* on an idyllic inlet is the ultimate

B&B/INN escape from the mass tourism of the Turkish coast. **Pros:** "away from it all" ambience. **Cons:** very basic. $ *Rooms from: $40* ⊠ *Aperlai* ☎0539/859–9196 ⛵6 *rooms* ▬ *No credit cards* ❑*No meals.*

$$ ❑ **Sahil Pansiyon.** You'll find this pint-size place above a restaurant and

B&B/INN general store in the center of the Kaleköy waterfront. **Pros:** central loca-tion; great views; excursions can be arranged. **Cons:** less private; sparse décor. $ *Rooms from: $76* ⊠ *Kaleköy waterfront, look for the shop* ☎242/874–2263 ⊕ *www.sahilpension.com* ⛵4 *rooms* ❑*Breakfast.*

DEMRE (KALE)

37 km (23 miles) east of Kaş; 140 km (87 miles) southwest of Antalya on Rte. 400.

Demre is where Saint Nicholas, who later became known as Father Christmas, made his reputation as bishop of the Greco-Roman diocese of Myra in the first half of the 4th century. Among his good deeds, St. Nicholas is said to have carried out nocturnal visits to the houses of local children to leave gifts, including gold coins as dowries for poor village girls; if a window was closed, said the storytellers, he would drop the gifts down the chimney.

Demre was once one of the most important cities along the coast. An ancient theater and some rock-cut tombs offer proof, but its remains lie mostly under the concrete of the modern urban center and the large greenhouses that dominate the hillside to the north. Now primarily an agricultural region (it's known as the tomato capital of Turkey), tourists typically view Demre as a quick stopover on their trip along the coast.

GETTING HERE AND AROUND

Demre is right along Route 400. St. Nicholas Basilica is a few blocks off the highway, signposted "Noel Baba." The theater is about 1½ km (1 mile) further north.

EXPLORING

Andriake. Andriake, the port of ancient Myra, was a major stopover on the Egypt-to-Rome route that supplied most of Rome's wheat. St. Paul changed ships here on his journey to Rome in 60 AD, and Hadrian built a huge granary on the site (it's hidden in the bushes south of the road just before you get to the modern port of Demre, and is also clearly visible from the Kaş-Demre road, just west of Demre, as you come around the last bend). Recent excavations found a synagogue in the same area. If you're willing to ford the waist-deep water of the creek, Üçağız is about a seven-hour walk on the Lycian Way with several pretty costal sections. ⊠ *West edge of Demre on the road leading to the Yacht Harbor (Yat liman)*.

Myra. The monuments of ancient Myra—a large, well-preserved Roman theater and a cliff face full of Lycian rock tombs—sit just north of Demre. The theater dates from the 2nd century AD and for a time hosted gladiator spectacles and wild animal hunts. In the cliffs above it are some good reliefs (ascend the stairs to the raised viewing platform for a closer look). Up a stone ramp east of the theater, a section of Lycian Way leads to the acropolis, offering nice views over the theater and town. There are more tombs farther east. ⊠ *2 km (1 mile) north of Demre* ⌨ *15 TL* ☉ *Daily 8:30–5 or 5:30*.

St. Nicholas Basilica. The grave of Myra's famous 4th-century bishop—St. Nicholas (aka Santa Claus)—quickly became a pilgrimage site. A church was built around his tomb in the 6th century but later destroyed in an Arab raid. In 1043, St. Nicholas Basilica was rebuilt with the aid of the Byzantine emperor Constantine IX and the empress Zoë; it was, in turn, heavily restored in the 19th century courtesy of Russian noblemen. It's difficult to distinguish between parts of original church and the restorations, although the bell tower and upper story are clearly late additions. The reputed sarcophagus of St Nicholas is in the southernmost aisle; however, his remains were stolen and taken to Bari, Italy, in 1087, where the church of San Nicola di Bari was built to house them. A few bones remained, so the story goes, and these can be seen in the Antalya Museum. A service is (theoretically, at least) held in the church every year on December 6, the feast day of St. Nicholas. ⊠ *Near the center of Demre, a few blocks from the main square* ⌨ *15 TL* ☉ *Daily 9–7 (winter 8:30–5:30)*.

Sura. This was ancient Myra's most important pre-Christian holy site. (Priests of Apollo would release fish into the sacred pool here, and then "read" the future from the movements.) It still has Lycian tombs and a small acropolis, from which the temple of Apollo is visible in the overgrown valley below. ⊠ *Beside the turnoff to Kekova, a few hundred meters north of Andriake*.

WHERE TO EAT

$
TURKISH
✕ **Ipek Restaurant.** One of the best of the group of traditional Turkish *lokantas* around the church of St. Nicholas, Ipek doesn't look like much and the waiters can be surly, but excellent meat dishes make this the restaurant of choice for many. ⓢ *Average main: 10 TL* ⊠ *As you exit the church, turn left along the pedestrian street. Ipek is 100 yds down, on the left* ☎ *242/871–5150*.

$
TURKISH
✕ **Nur Pastaneleri.** After paying your respects to St. Nick, repair here to enjoy arctic air-conditioning and a cold drink or tea accompanied by some of Turkey's freshest *baklava*, the diamond-cut honeyed pastry with nuts. Until early afternoon the café also serves *su böreği*, a salty

pastry flavored with feta cheese or mincemeat. $ *Average main: 5 TL* ⊠ *As you exit St. Nicholas Basilica, walk south to the square; on your right is a modern shopping center; Nur Pastaneleri is on the corner* ☎ *242/871–6310.*

FINIKE AND ARYCANDA

30 km (18 miles) east of Demre; 111 km (70 miles) southwest of Antalya on Rte. 400.

Finike is a good lunch stop or jumping-off point for Arycanda and the series of less glamorous Lycian sites that dot the citrus- and vegetable-growing coastal plain. This small port town is less touristy than other coastal communities—and more friendly, helpful, and inexpensive. It's not the most exciting place to stay, but if you just want a decent bed for a night, it's the best option between Olympos and Kekova. Although a yacht marina harbors many European boats, Finike, which makes most of its money from its acres of orange trees, seems to take their presence unfussily in its stride. A colorful town market is held every Sunday.

GETTING HERE AND AROUND
Finike is right on the highway. The old road for Arycanda goes north from the major bend at the center of town, and soon crosses the river, where you can then join the new road. Drive 35 km (22 miles) toward Elmalı, and then watch for the Arycanda sign to the right, at a popular roadside market.

EXPLORING
Arycanda. The well-preserved walls and lovely location of Arycanda, high in a mountain valley above Finike, make this ancient Lycian town one of the most beautiful and least crowded archaeological sites on the Turquoise Coast. A parking area and easy-to-follow trail lead up to the acropolis, first passing a church and the monumental **Roman baths** (perhaps Turkey's best-preserved), with intact mosaic floors, standing walls, and windows framing the valley. The tombs, farther east along the trail, are more properly Roman rather than Lycian—it's worth the hike to see the carved gateway on the last one. At the top of the hills sit a sunken agora, or market, with arcades on three sides and an intimate odeon, or small concert hall, topped by a Greek-style theater that offers a breathtaking view of the valley and mountains often capped with snow. Even higher up is the town's stadium or running track. Farther north is a second, long thin agora, with a small temple above it. From here the official trail scrambles down to some Roman villas, but you may find it easier to backtrack. Back toward the car park is a temple of Trajan with an ancient Roman toilet underneath. ⊠ *30km (19 m) north of Finike on the Elmalı road* ☎ *535/856–6059* 🖺 *3 TL* ☉ *Daily 9–7:30.*

Elmalı. North of Arykanda, the mountain town of Elmalı is the center of the country's apple (elma) industry. Although a glimpse of traditional Turkey and the cool mountain air are the main draws, Elmalı is also known for its traditional, half-timber houses and the Ömer Pasha mosque (1602), which is one of the best Ottoman mosques in southern Turkey. Several important preclassical sites have been excavated in the area, and a hoard of nearly 2000 coins from the 5th century BC, called

The mythical Chimaera (for which the flame at Olympos is named) was a fire-breathing monster with the body of a goat, the head of a lion, and the tail of a serpent.

the "Treasure of the Century" was unearthed near here. Most finds are now in the Antalya Museum, but a small museum, Elmalı Müzesi, opened here in 2011 (9–2, closed Monday). ✉ *60 km (37 miles) north of Arykanda.*

WHERE TO EAT AND STAY

$ TURKISH 🍴 **Altın Sofra.** This restaurant in the marina is famed for lamb and lambs' liver, but it serves a full menu. There is a pleasant garden shaded by plane trees and acacias. Everything here is so fresh that the chef refuses to add anything but olive oil and salt to flavor his meats. [$] *Average main: 10 TL* ✉ *Inside the yacht marina, 100 yds past the entrance* ☎ *242/855–1281.*

$$ SEAFOOD 🍴 **Anfora Balık Restaurant.** A large fishing fleet gives Finike one of the coast's most reliable supplies of fresh seafood—and you can taste the results at this unassuming-looking eatery. In a cool basement cavern set into the hillside, it offers fine seafood and excellent value. Specialties include pots of cooked squid, octopus, and shrimp. [$] *Average main: 20 TL* ✉ *100 yds past the marina entrance on Kordon Cad. (Rte. 400)* ☎ *242/855–3888.*

$ HOTEL 🏨 **Hotel Grand Finike.** This large, bright, older hotel opposite the yacht harbor is a comfortable yet inexpensive place to stay. **Pros:** good value. **Cons:** Finike isn't much of a destination in its own right. [$] *Rooms from: $74* ✉ *Center of town on main road* ☎ *242/855–5805* 🌐 *www.grandfinikehotel.com* 🛏 *52 rooms, 4 suites* 🍽 *Breakfast.*

OLYMPOS AND ÇIRALI

Olympos is 49 km (30 miles) west of Finike; 89 km (55 miles) southwest of Antalya from Rte. 400.

Olympos and its "sister" towns, Çiralı and Adrasan, are places unique on the Turquoise Coast for their natural beauty, ancient ruins, low-rise development, and easygoing culture that embraces international backpackers, Turkish students, and European families. The trio is also next to some of the best day walks on the Lycian Way, though the Olympos ruins and beach are the main area attractions. All three towns are accessed via a secondary road, parallel to the highway. Olympos has the most character but can be noisy and crowded in summer and offers limited accommodations. The area above the valley has better places to stay, but you'll have a short drive to the beach. Çiralı shares the beach with Olympos and is much quieter, with the best range of hotels and a more family-friendly atmosphere. Little Adrasan feels like the beach town the world forgot—peaceful and a little scruffy.

GETTING HERE AND AROUND

Olympos is off Route 400, between Kumlucu and Tekirova. There are signposted turns to Adrasan (9 km/6 miles), Olmpos (12 km/7½ miles), and Çiralı (7 km/4½ miles). From Upper Olympos a second road connects to Adrasan. There is no direct road between Olympos and Çiralı, but it's a short walk along the beach.

EXPLORING

The ancient city of Olympos is named after a nearby peak that towers above the mountain range behind the beach. A lovely 500-yard walk through the overgrown site gives access to one end of the long sand-and-pebble strand, still unspoiled and backed by an amazing amphitheater of pine-clad mountains. The sights can be seen in a day, but the natural beauty and laid-back atmosphere may prove addictive. One of the hotels has a slogan: "Come for a day, stay for a week," and it's surprising how often that happens. Olympos is, perhaps, a little too beautiful for its own good: popular with backpackers and younger Turks, it can get crowded and noisy in summer. Out of season, it returns to bucolic tranquility. There is a no-concrete rule for development in the region, so accommodations consist mostly of wooden cabins—even Olympos's famous "tree houses" can best be described as basic cabins on stilts. A few miles inland, out of the gorge, is a collection of other *pansiyons,* which can be quieter and more upmarket. The nearby town of Çiralı shares the long gorgeous beach and caters mainly to families and those looking for something more sophisticated. There are few restaurants and most lodgings include an evening meal.

Olympos. The ruins of the ancient city of Olympos, enshrouded in dense vegetation, have received little excavation and, as a result, are wonderfully atmospheric. Being next to a river and shaded by tall firs, flowering oleander bushes, and a mountain gorge, they are also delightfully cool in summer, the perfect time to explore.

Olympos was once a top-voting member of the 2nd-century-BC Lycian League, but most of the buildings viewable today date from Roman times. Roman-era construction started in earnest after officers—including the young Julius Caesar—crushed a two-year-long occupation of the city by pirates in about 70 BC. Many tombs are scattered around the ancient city, which is reached by two parallel paths that continue down to the beach. In the center of the northern half of the site is the large cathedral complex, once the main temple, which includes a much-photographed 18-foot-high gate, dedicated to Marcus Aurelius in AD 171 and mistakenly referred to by signs as a temple. Note how some walls around the site have clearly been rebuilt in later centuries with narrow arrow slits in the windows as if the city suddenly had to fortify itself. A second side path leads along a water channel to some interesting tombs and a large building, probably a grand mansion. At the beach exit is a poetic inscription on a sarcophagus in memory of an ancient ship's captain, along with a carving of his beached boat—not that different from today's gulets. From here you can also climb to a small acropolis and some medieval fortifications where ancients would keep a lookout for ships and pirates.

The southern side of the ancient city is best reached by crossing the riverbed (dry in summer) by the land-side ticket office and heading east toward the beach along a well-beaten path that starts with a remarkable row of tombs. Farther along are shipping quays, warehouses, a gorgeously overgrown theater, a bathhouse, and a church whose two great rows of granite columns have collapsed inward toward each other and now lie half-buried in what feels like the floor of a tropical jungle. Excavations by the river on what was probably the agora, or marketplace, began in 2011. Farther south along the beach are the walls of a medieval castle and church variously occupied and improved by Crusaders and also used as an outpost of Italian city-states. ⊠ *89 km (55 miles) southwest of Antalya* 🎫 *5 TL for 1 visit or 10 TL for 10 visits.*

Olympos Beach. This 5-km (3-mile) sweep of beach, with a line of fir trees behind it and a surrounding amphitheater of mountains that includes the 8,000-foot peak of Mt. Olympos, is one of the wonders of Turkey. Although it has managed to escape the ravages of industrial tourism, there are several good beachfront restaurants where you can eat during the day or while away an evening. Note that Olympos and Çıralı are only separated by a short walk along the beach, but it's a long drive around the mountain. ■**TIP➔** The surface here consists mostly of smooth white and multicolor pebbles mixed with some light gray sand, so prepare to recline on a lounger rather than a beach towel. **Amenities:** food and drink; parking (free); toilets. **Best for:** walking; swimming. ⊠ *Between Olympos and Çıralı.*

Chimaera. At the far end of Çıralı, an evening scramble up a sometimes-steep path will bring you to the Chimaera, named after the ferocious fire-breathing beast of legend. Flames can still be seen rising from cracks in the rock, apparently also burning the gas deep below, since they reignite even if covered. In times past, the flames were apparently more vigorous, even visible by sailors offshore. The Chimaera is inland from the far southern end of of Çıralı; take either of the main roads to the end, and then head inland. If you're staying in Olympos it's a 7-km (5-mile) 90-minute walk, so you may want to drive to the bottom of the hill or take a tour. From the parking lot it's a half-hour walk up a lot of stairs. Most hotels in the area will arrange a tour. You can see the flames in the day, but they're best at night. ■TIP→ **Bring a flashlight for all those stairs, since there's no lighting, and in peak season go as late as possible to avoid the crowds.** ⊠ *In from Çıralı; 7 km (5 miles) outside Olympos* ⊠ *5 TL* ⊙ *24 hrs daily.*

OFF THE BEATEN PATH About 16 km (10 miles) from Olympos, **Adrasan** is a relaxed little town on a long beach. It's a world away from the flashy resort areas, so don't expect five-star hotels, gourmet restaurants, tour buses, or touts—just a great stretch of rarely crowded beach and some decent family-run *pansiyons*. Boat tours that take you to swim in local coves set off each morning at about 10 and cost about 50 TL, including lunch. A wonderful, mostly shaded day's walk along the Lycian Way will take you through forests over Mt. Musa to Olympos; another leads to the lighthouse at the point of the Tekke Peninsula; a third, more difficult route goes around the peninsula to the wonderful lighthouse at Cape Gelidonya and to the small beach town of Karaöz. Bring along the official Lycian Way guidebook (it comes with a map), adequate water, and preferably a guide for the often-lonely pathways. Note that there is limited public transport to Adrasan, so you're best off if you have a car.

WHERE TO EAT AND STAY

IN THE OLYMPOS VALLEY

$
B&B/INN
Şaban. One of the older lodgings in the gorge, Şaban is popular among foreigners of all ages. **Pros:** friendly and comfortable; not just for backpackers. **Cons:** Olympos can be noisy and crowded in summer. $ *Rooms from: $50* ⊠ *Near Adrasan where the road crosses the dry stream, opposite the large, ugly "Turkomens"* ☎ *242/892–1265* ⇌ *50 bungalows, 10 treehouses, 1 dorm* ⟍◯⟋ *No meals.*

ÇIRALI

$$$
HOTEL
Fodor's Choice
★
Arcadia. This spot has the prettiest bungalows in the area; at present five occupy a perfect position between the road and the beach, while five more sit across the road. **Pros:** well-equipped cabins with air-conditioning and Wi-Fi; friendly staff. **Cons:** comparatively pricey. $ *Rooms from: $193* ⊠ *At the far, southern end of main beachfront road, Çıralı* ☎ *242/825–7340* ⊕ *www.arcadiaholiday.com* ⇌ *10 cabins* ⊙ *Closed mid-Nov.–Mar.* ⟍◯⟋ *No meals.*

$$
HOTEL
Canada Hotel. Run by a Turkish-Canadian couple, this hotel near Çıralı is one of the friendliest and most popular in town. **Pros:** family-friendly; nice pool. **Cons:** not on the water. $ *Rooms from: $83* ⊠ *On main road into Çıralı, on right before you cross bridge, Çıralı* ☎ *242/825–7233* ⊕ *www.canadahotel.net* ⇌ *26 rooms, 14 bungalows* ⟍◯⟋ *Multiple meal plans.*

$$
HOTEL
Myland Nature Hotel. This relaxed and friendly *pansiyon* is across from the water, about halfway along the beach road. **Pros:** good food; rental bikes available. **Cons:** cabins are nice but not exceptional. $ *Rooms from: $120* ⊠ *Çıralı, halfway along main beachfront road, on left* ☎ *242/825–7044* ⊕ *www.mylandnature.com* ⇌ *13 cabins* ⟍◯⟋ *Breakfast.*

These Lycian rock tombs have been carved into the cliffside of the ancient city of Myra.

ABOVE THE OLYMPOS VALLEY

$$
B&B/INN
[i] **Daphne House.** This pleasant stone hotel is on the edge of a pine forest. **Pros:** friendly vibe; tranquil environment. **Cons:** some rooms are small, and accessed by a spiral staircase. [$] *Rooms from: $149* ✉ *50 yds after last turning to Olympos, just past forest fire station with a very small sign* ☎ *242/892–1133* ⊕ *www.daphneevi.com* 🛏 *6 rooms* ⊗ *Closed Nov.–Apr.* ¶⊙¶ *Breakfast.*

$$$
HOTEL
[i] **Olimpos Mitos.** This low-key but high-end hotel complex is one of the nicest places to stay in the neighborhood. **Pros:** emphasizes sustainability and "soft" tourism; relaxing. **Cons:** out of the way. [$] *Rooms from: $165* ✉ *As you descend from Rte. 400, look for sign down a dirt track about 500 yds before you reach a river ford and final turn for Olympos itself* ☎ *242/892–1158* ⊕ *www.olymposmitos.com* 🛏 *16 rooms, 6 suites* ⊗ *Closed Oct. 15–May 15* ¶⊙¶ *Some meals.*

IN ADRASAN

$
MEDITERRANEAN
✕ **Chill House Lounge.** "Chill" is the perfect word to describe this relaxed spot. Popular with locals, its tables are mostly set out in the prime open area, toward the southern end of the beach. The food ranges from snacks to grilled meat, seafood, and pasta. In the evening, Chill evolves into a bar and the closest thing Adrasan has to a disco. [$] *Average main: 10 TL* ✉ *Adrasan, main beach road* ☎ *532/775–2626.*

$$
HOTEL
[i] **Ceneviz Hotel and Restaurant.** This hotel set back from the beach has modest, clean rooms, some with a sea view. **Pros:** central location. **Cons:** rooms are quite basic. [$] *Rooms from: $101* ✉ *Deniz Mahallesi, Adrasan (halfway along Adrasan Beach)* ☎ *242/883–1030* ⊕ *www.cenevizhotel.com* 🛏 *18 rooms* ⊗ *Closed Nov.–Apr.* ¶⊙¶ *Breakfast.*

$$
HOTEL

Ford Hotel. This Adrasan hotel sits between the sea and a mountain on a prime spot at the southern end of the beach. **Pros:** near the beach. **Cons:** at the far end of town. $ *Rooms from: $126 ⊠ Sahil Cad. 220, far end of the beach, Adrasan* ☎ *242/883–1044* ⊕ *www. fordhotel.net* ⤳ *27 rooms, 2 suites* ❙❖❙ *Some meals*

$$
B&B/INN
FAMILY

Ottoman Palace. This hotel, just inland from the beach, makes a friendly base in Adrasan. **Pros:** nice modern building; good for trekkers and divers. **Cons:** not on the beach. $ *Rooms from: $152 ⊠ Adrasan, a few hundred yds in from the beach.* ☎ *242/883–1462* ⊕ *www. jonnyturk.com* ⤳ *12 rooms* ❙❖❙ *Some meals.*

> ### BEYOND OLYMPOS
>
> Why go to Adrasan if you've seen Olympos, you might ask. It's one of Turkey's last quiet, basic, and locally run beachfront holiday spots. Hotels are also up to a third cheaper than those in Çıralı.

NEED A
BREAK?

✕ **Tropik.** Not far from Olympos and Çirali, Rte. 400 passes by the great high spring of Ulupinar, which supplies water to much of this part of the Tekke peninsula. In the heat of summer, it's lovely to stop and eat under the cool high trees, with water gurgling all around you. The speciality is fish, which come from the fish farms at the bottom of the hill. One of the best of the restaurants here is the Tropik, where you can dine on a platform over the river or even at a table with your feet right in the cold spring. The menu includes delicious oven-roasted lamb. A section of the Lycian Way goes from here across the valley to Çıralı, via the Chimaera; it's about a four- or five-hour trek. $ *Average main: 20 TL ⊠ Midway between Kumluca and Kemer on Rte. 400* ☎ *242/825–0098.*

SPORTS AND THE OUTDOORS

Olympos. Towering Mt. Olympos is one of Turkey's premier rock climbing destinations. Kadirs, a few hundred yards up from the main cluster of buildings in the valley, has a climbing center which provides support for new and experienced climbers. ⊠ *Adrasan* ☎ *242/892–1316* ⊕ *www.olymposrockclimbing.com.*

PHASELIS

31 km (19 miles) north of Olympos; 60 km (37 miles) southwest of Antalya on Rte. 400.

Majestically located at the edge of three small bays, the ruins of the ancient port city of Phaselis make an atmospheric stop along the Lycian coast.

GETTING HERE AND AROUND

The well-marked turnoff is a short distance north of Tekirova; from there to the ruins and beach is about 2 km (1¼ miles). A bus regularly runs from Tekirova as far as the ticket office, about halfway along this road.

EXPLORING

Phaselis. The ruins of Phaselis, the ancient port city majestically located at the edge of three smalls bays, are as romantic as the reputation of its ancient inhabitants was appalling: Demosthenes the Greek called them unsavory, and Roman statesman Cicero called them rapacious pirates. Since the first Greek colonists from Rhodes bought the land from a local shepherd in the 7th century BC for a load of dried fish, classical literature is replete with the expression "a present from the Phaselians," meaning a cheap gift. Still, the setting is beautiful and Alexander the Great spent a whole winter here before marching on to conquer the East. A broad main street, flanked by some remarkably well-preserved buildings, cuts through the half-standing walls of the Roman **agora.** At each end of this main street is a different bay, both with translucent water ideal for swimming. A third bay, to the north, has great harbor stones carved by the ancients, and is less likely to be disturbed by tour boats.

A small **theater** with trees growing among the seats has a divine view of Mt. Olympos, and fine **sarcophagi** are scattered throughout a necropolis in the pine woods that surround the three bays. The ruins are poetic and impressive, ideal for a picnic or a day at the beach, but weekends and high season days can be crowded and downright depressing when tour yachts from Antalya arrive with loudspeakers blaring. **TIP→ For some reason the refreshment stands at Phaselis are in a legal limbo; today's pirates of Phaselis are the men selling overpriced drinks under the trees, so bring your own.** ✉ *2 km (1.2 mile) north of Tekirova* 🎫 *8 TL* 🕒 *June–Sept., daily 8:30–7, Oct.–May, daily 8:30–5.*

5

WHERE TO STAY

$$ B&B/INN 🏨 **Sundance Camp.** This is a popular green-minded stopover for Lycian way trekkers and arty types taking a break from Istanbul. **Pros:** good food; private beach. **Cons:** no pool, TV, or disco. [$] *Rooms from: $125* ✉ *Between Phaselis and Tekirova, follow the signs to the "Ecopark" and keep going, Phaselis* ☎ *242/821–4165* 🌐 *www.sundancecamp.com/en* 🛏 *14 bungalows, 3 lodges, 10 treehouses* 🍴 *Breakfast.*

ANTALYA AND PAMPHYLIA

When the Greeks migrated from central Turkey to the Mediterranean coast, around the 12th century BC, the area east of Antalya became known as Pamphylia, "the land of all the tribes," reflecting the mixed origins of the new inhabitants. Today the bustling city of Antalya is easily the biggest along the coast, with all the services and facilities you'd expect. Worth seeing in its own right, it also makes a good base for exploring the region's major archaeological sites: Termessos, Perge, Aspendos, Side, and even Olympos and Phasilis. East from Antalya, a long beach continues through Belek to Side and Alanya, with many (perhaps too many) resorts along the way. If an all-inclusive beach holiday isn't what you have in mind, consider staying in one of Old Antalya's wonderful *pansiyon*s, which are in restored Ottoman houses.

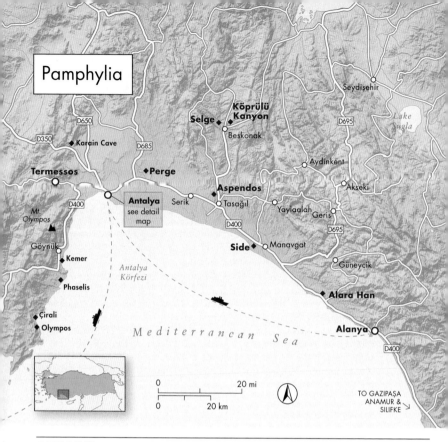

ANTALYA

298 km (185 miles) northeast of Fethiye.

Sophisticated Antalya is a definite tourist hub, and with a population approaching the 1-million mark, it's among Turkey's fastest growing cities. These days the international terminals of Antalya airport are busier even than those in Istanbul. Most visitors are on package tours, but Antalya is a popular destination among Turks, too. Enormous hotels east of the city help accommodate them; however, you can bed down in one of the restored mansions or *pansiyon*s found in the atmospheric Kaleiçi quarter and hardly notice the big urban conglomeration all around. On the hilltop above the harbor are tea gardens and bars with views that extend south to the Bey Mountains and north to the Taurus Mountains.

GETTING HERE AND AROUND

The main bus station is north of the city, and there's a new tramline from there to the center (4 TL). Buses going to Phaselis, Olympos, and the Lycian coast stop at a makeshift terminal opposite the Hotel Su, which is a much shorter taxi ride from the old city than the main station.

A ring road bypasses the inner city and joins with the roads southwest to Olympos and the Lycian coast or east to Side and Alanya. Another road heads north, signposted "Istanbul," and from this there is a left turn for Termessos and the mountain road to Fethiye. Signs and buses to the city center are marked "Kalekapısı." An older tram along the Antalya seafront, between Lara and the Antalya Museum, runs every half-hour (2 TL).

ESSENTIALS

Tourist Office Antalya ⊠ *Head west from Saat Kulesi, and turn right onto Ana-fartlar Cad., the first major road, Anafartlar Cad. 31* ☎ *242/241–1747.*

EXPLORING

Antalya Müzesi (*Antalya Museum*). The province of Antalya has a rich collection of archaeological sites and their assembled finds means a first-rate collection at the Antalya Müzesi. The star is Perge, statues from which fill gallery after gallery, including one just for the gods, from Aphrodite to Zeus. There are also Turkish crafts, costumes, prehistoric artifacts from the Carian Cave, and preclassical statues from Elmalı, with bits of Byzantine iconography and some prehistoric fossils thrown in. One gallery has several fine Roman sarcophagi from the 2nd century AD, including a wonderful one illustrating the labors of a steadily aging Hercules. Upstairs are several coin hordes; the large one from Elmalı was recently returned to the museum after being smuggled to the United States. On-site, you'll also find a good, reasonably priced cafeteria and gift shop. ■ TIP➜ If you have the time, walk to the museum from the center of town along the cliff-top promenade, which has a fine sea view. ⊠ *Konyaalti Cad. 88* ☎ *242/238–5689* ⊕ *www.antalyamuzesi. gov.tr* 🖺 *15 TL* ☉ *Tues.–Sun. 9–6.*

Karaalioğlan Parkı. Shady Karaalioğlan Parkı is a traditional green space with trees, grass, and benches, as well as a view of the Mediterranean. At the northwest end is a stone tower, called Hıdırlık Külesi, which dates from the 2nd century AD. At sunset, sip a drink at the Castle Café and Bar next door and enjoy an unforgettable panorama of the Bey Mountains. ⊠ *Agustos Cad. at Atatürk Cad.*

INSIDE THE KALEIÇI (OLD TOWN)

The old town of Antalya lies within the fortified city wall; it's an excellent example of a traditional Ottoman neighborhood. A restoration project launched in the 1980s saved hundreds of houses, dating mostly from the 19th century. Most of these were converted into *pansiyons,* rug shops, restaurants, and art galleries.

Hadrian's Gate. One way to enter the old town is via Hadrian's Gate, a short walk from the main Saat Kulesi intersection along pleasant palm-lined Atatürk Caddesi. The gate was constructed in honor of a visit by the Roman emperor in AD 130 and has three arches, each with coffered ceilings decorated with rosettes. Ruts in the marble road show where carts once trundled through. From here a straight Roman road leads through town past Kesik Minare Camii to the Hıdırlık Külesi and the sea. ⊠ *Eastern edge of old town walls.*

Kesik Minare Camii. The "Mosque of the Truncated Minaret" on Hıdarlık Sokak, a few blocks east of Hadrian's Gate, was once the city's cathedral and dedicated to the Virgin. It was probably built in the 5th century AD

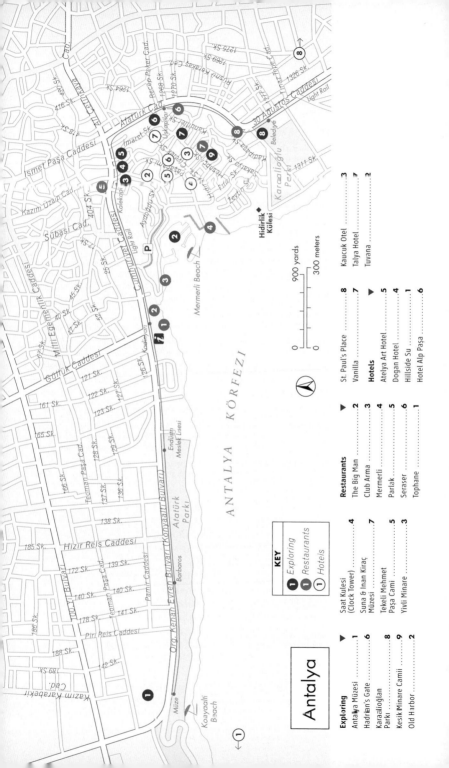

Antalya

KEY

- 🔘 Exploring
- 🔘 Restaurants
- ⑴ Hotels

Exploring

▶	
Antalya Müzesi	1
Hadrian's Gate	6
Karaalioğlan Parkı	8
Kesik Minare Camii	9
Old Harbor	2
Saat Kulesi (Clock Tower)	4
Suna & İnan Kıraç Müzesi	7
Tekeli Mehmet Paşa Camii	5
Yivli Minare	3

Restaurants

▶	
The Big Man	2
Club Arma	3
Mermerli	4
Parlak	5
Seraser	6
Tophane	1
St. Paul's Place	8
Vanilla	7

Hotels

Atelya Art Hotel	5
Doğan Hotel	4
Hillside Su	1
Hotel Alp Paşa	6
Kaucuk Otel	3
Talya Hotel	7
Tuvana	2

ANTALYA KÖRFEZİ

| 0 | 900 yards |
| 0 | 300 meters |

and later converted to a mosque. It's usually locked, but you can get a good look from the outside. ✉ *Hesapçı Sok.*

Old Harbor. Another way to enter the old city is via the Old Harbor, now filled with yachts, fishing vessels, and tourist-excursion boats. If you're in a car, follow the signs to the *yat limanı* (harbor) and you'll find a convenient, free parking lot behind the quaysides. From here you can head up any of the lanes leading north and east out of the harbor to get to the heart of the old town. Alternatively wander down from Saat Kulesi, forking to the right past the T-shirt and perfume shops, until you reach the bottom. ✉ *İskele Cad.*

Saat Kulesi (*Clock Tower*). At some point one of the city's Roman towers gained a clock and was dubbed the Saat Kulesi (Clock Tower). Several of the old town's cobbled lanes pass through the wall here. The area, also known as Kalekapısı (Castle Gate), serves as one of the interfaces between the old town and the new. ✉ *Cumhuriyet Cad.* ☎ *242/242–4333.*

Suna & Inan Kiraç Müzesi. Fifty yards inside Hadrian's Gate, turn left for the Suna & Inan Kiraç Museum: a little oasis in a group of restored buildings with an unusual painted exterior that experts say reflects the way most Antalya houses looked in Ottoman times. The museum is part of a privately funded research institute and has an excellent library (accessible with special permission), plus a shop that sells a good range of guidebooks. The main display area has interesting pictures of Old Antalya and a couple of rooms with waxworks that re-create Ottoman wedding scenes. The best part of the museum is the restored church in the garden, where there is a delightful display of historical kitsch. ✉ *Kocatepe Sok. 25* ☎ *242/243–4274* ⊕ *www.akmed.org.tr* 💰 *3 TL* ⊙ *Thurs.–Tues. 9–noon and 1–6.*

Tekeli Mehmet Paşa Cami. Behind the clock tower, this mosque was built around 1600 and heavily restored in the 19th century. Commissioned by a wealthy official who was Grand Vizier for only 10 days, it is one of the finest surviving Ottoman mosques in the region. ✉ *Uzunçarşı Sok., beside Kale Kapısı.*

Yivli Minare (*Fluted Minaret*). Dark blue and turquoise tiles decorate the Yivli Minare, a graceful 13th-century cylinder erected by the Seljuk sultan Alaaddin Keykubat I. The adjoining mosque, named for the sultan, was built on the site of a Byzantine church. Within the complex are two attractive *türbes* (tombs) and an 18th-century *tekke* (monastery), which once housed a community of whirling dervishes. The monastery is now used as an unremarkable art gallery. The Nigar Hatun Türbe (Tomb of Lady Nigar), next to the monastery, is a 15th-century copy built in Seljuk style. The *medrese* (theological school) adjacent to the Fluted Minaret has now been glassed in under a bus-station-style roof and is a tourist-oriented shopping center. It sells standard Turkish fare (think pottery, copperwork, carpets, and tiles) but prices are better than at most other resorts along the coast. ✉ *Cumhuriyet Cad., south side of Kalekapısı Mey.*

WHERE TO EAT

$$$ INTERNATIONAL
🍴 **The Bigman.** Almost opposite the Antalya Museum but hidden a little down the hill towards the sea, this restaurant may well have the best view in town. Owned by an Antalyan former basketball player (aka the Big Man), it's a popular place for locals to come for a special meal. The menu focuses on meat, pasta, pizza, and kebabs. The quality can be hit or miss, but regulars praise the steak and the portions are, well, big. [$] *Average main: 31 TL* ✉ *Konyaaltı Cad., inside Atatürk Parkı* ☎ *242/244–4636.*

$$$ INTERNATIONAL
🍴 **Club Arma.** You can't miss this restaurant—it has a spectacular location halfway up the main road from the old harbor with a panoramic view of the old city and the sea. Inside, airy stone arches give it elegant style despite the fact that this was once the port's petroleum depot. Club Arma is Antalya's most luxurious restaurant, serving octopus carpaccio, lobster, duck, chocolate soufflé, chestnut parfait, and fresh cheesecake, along with a full range of foreign spirits and cigars from a humidor. At 11 pm, the dance club alongside swings into action. [$] *Average main: 45 TL* ✉ *Kaleiçi Yatlimanı 42* ☎ *242/244–9710* 🌐 *www.clubarma.com.tr.*

$$ TURKISH
🍴 **Mermerli Restaurant.** At the eastern end of the harbor, the Mermerli has good prices and a broad menu that includes fish, steak, Turkish grills, and all-day breakfasts. But the location is its best asset. A breezy terrace offers excellent views. **TIP→ It's a good place to eat if you want to relax on Mermerli Beach—the bathing spot is just down the steps, and the restaurant controls access.** [$] *Average main: 20 TL* ✉ *Banyo Cad. 25* ☎ *242/248–5484.*

$ TURKISH
🍴 **Parlak Restaurant.** If shopping in the jewelry bazaar opposite the clock tower has tired you out, try this long-time Antalya favorite. The specialty is chicken roasted over charcoal, but there's also a full range of fish, meat, and mezes to choose from. In summer, tables are spread out in front of the restaurant. [$] *Average main: 14 TL* ✉ *Zincirli Han, Kazım Özalp Cad. 7, just past the statue of Attalos* ☎ *242/241–9160.*

$$$ INTERNATIONAL
🍴 **Seraser Fine Dining Restaurant.** With fine food and excellent service, the stylish Seraser aspires to be the best restaurant in all of Turkey. Part of the Tuvana Hotel (⇨ *Where to Stay*), it is set in the leafy courtyard of a historic house, with indoor and outdoor dining areas. The menu is conservative European, so don't expect anything Turkish other than the quality ingredients—90% of which are organic. Starters include goat cheese and aubergine soufflé; grouper and chargrilled lamb are popular mains, but do save room for dessert (try the sugarless, flourless truffle cake). With over 300 options, the wine list is equally impressive. [$] *Average main: 45 TL* ✉ *Karanlık Sok. 18* ☎ *242/247–6015* 🌐 *www.seraserrestaurant.com.*

$ AMERICAN
🍴 **St. Paul's Place.** A friendly, clubby retreat on the southern edge of the old city, St. Paul's Place is run by expats and serves great coffee, American cakes, and home-cooked lunches. It also has a library of exchange books and a nice garden. Warm and welcoming to all, this Christian religious center sometimes organizes religion-oriented tours and can give helpful advice on faith-based tourism. [$] *Average main: 10 TL* ✉ *Yenikapı Cad.* ☎ *242/247–6857* 🌐 *www.stpaulcc-turkey.com* 💳 *No credit cards* 🕐 *Closed the last week of Aug.*

$ ✕**Tophane.** Sitting in this tea garden, looking out to the harbor, sea, and
CAFÉ mountains beyond, is one of Antalya's great pleasures. The drinks and
snacks are inexpensive, but the views are priceless. It's a good stop on
the way to the museum—you can walk or catch the old tram, which
leaves from here every half hour. $ *Average main: 5 TL* ✉ *Cumhuriyet
Alanı* ⊟ *No credit cards.*

$$$ ✕**Vanilla.** If you are kebabed out, this old city restaurant has some of the
MODERN best contemporary cuisine on the coast and serves it in an appropriately
EUROPEAN stylish setting. The menu changes regularly, though it's basically modern
Fodor'sChoice European with a touch of Asia and includes items like pork that you
★ don't see too often in Turkey. The owners, English chef Wayne and his
Turkish wife Emel, also operate a very cool lounge next door where you
can order coffee during the day or cocktails at night. $ *Average main:
48 TL* ✉ *Hesapçı Sok. 33* ☎ *242/247–6013* ⊕ *www.vanillaantalya.com.*

WHERE TO STAY

$$ ▥**Atelya Art Hotel.** Inexpensive and friendly, this hotel has larger than
HOTEL usual lodgings and a good location in the old town. **Pros:** good value;
spacious rooms; lots of character. **Cons:** some street noise. $ *Rooms
from: $83* ✉ *Kaleiçi Civelek Sokak 21, near Kesik Minare Mosque*
☎ *242/241–6416* ⊕ *www.atelyahotel.com* ⌁ *25 rooms, 2 suites* ⊟ *No
credit cards* ◎ *No meals.*

$$ ▥**Doğan Hotel.** Every room is unique and tastefully decorated in this
HOTEL family-run establishment, made up of three restored houses, with a
pretty garden and pool. **Pros:** updated décor with traditional touches;
a short walk from the old harbor and Mermerli Beach. **Cons:** some
rooms are a little dark. $ *Rooms from: $104* ✉ *Mermerli Banyo Sok.
5* ☎ *242/247–4654* ⊕ *www.doganhotel.com* ⌁ *41 rooms* ◎ *No meals.*

$$ ▥**Hotel Alp Paşa.** This hotel—a mansion restored with a contemporary
HOTEL aesthetic—might be the most atmospheric place to stay in the old city.
Pros: stylish rooms. **Cons:** small pool; mediocre food. $ *Rooms from:
$126* ✉ *Hesapçı Sok.* ☎ *242/247–5676* ⊕ *www.alppasa.com* ⌁ *106
rooms* ◎ *Breakfast.*

$$$$ ▥**Hotel Su.** Notable for its all-white color scheme, the Su is popular with
HOTEL the weekend crowd from Istanbul. **Pros:** funky, eclectic atmosphere.
Cons: maybe too weird to be completely comfortable. $ *Rooms from:
$252* ✉ *Dumlupınar Cad., Konyaaltı* ☎ *242/249–0700* ⊕ *www.hotelsu.
com.tr* ⌁ *294 rooms* ◎ *Breakfast.*

$$ ▥**Kauçuk Otel.** This small boutique hotel is made up of two houses
B&B/INN that have been authentically restored with an eye to contemporary
design. **Pros:** pleasant oasis in bustling Kaleiçi. **Cons:** some street noise.
$ *Rooms from: $138* ✉ *Paşa Camii Sok. 22* ☎ *242/244–2377* ⊕ *www.
kaucukotel.com* ⌁ *8 rooms, 3 suites* ◎ *Breakfast.*

$$$ ▥**Talya Hotel.** This prime property rises over the cliffs just to the east of
HOTEL Karaalioğlan Parkı, commanding spectacular views of the Bey Moun-
tains. **Pros:** modern, professional luxury hotel. **Cons:** rather character-
less. $ *Rooms from: $171* ✉ *Fevzi Cakmak Cad. 30* ☎ *242/248–6800*
⊕ *www.divan.com* ⌁ *204 rooms* ◎ *No meals.*

$$ ▥**Tuvana Hotel.** One of the classier options in Kaleici, this hotel is
HOTEL made up of four old houses and has comfortable lodgings, excel-
lent service, and a wide range of facilities. **Pros:** great restaurant;

traditional ambience. **Cons**: room sizes vary widely. $ *Rooms from:* *$138* ⊠ *Karanlık Sok. 18* ☎ *242/244–4054* ⊕ *www.tuvanahotel.com* ⤴ *45 rooms* ⫶◎⫶ *Breakfast.*

NIGHTLIFE AND THE ARTS

Atatürk Kulture Merkezi. Also known as AKM, the Atatürk Kulture Merkezi is a cultural complex with an exhibition space and several theaters located in a cliff-top park about 3 km (2 miles) west of the city center. It hosts concerts year-round—look for fliers posted around the city—as well as an annual film festival. ⊠ *Atatürk Kültür Parkı, 100 Yıl Bulvarı* ☎ *242/238–5444.*

Castle Café and Bar. The perfect start to any evening out in Antalya starts by watching the sun set from the cliff-top Castle Café and Bar, next to Hıdırlık Kulesi—you can accompany your drink with some of their sesame-and-garlic dip, known as *hibeş*. ⊠ *Hıdırlık Cad. 48/1* ☎ *242/242–3188.*

Other than the cliff-top Castle Café and Bar, Antalya's bars are centered on three main areas: in Kaleiçi; in the new part of town, on Barlar Caddesi (Bar Street), running off Cumhuriyet Caddesi; and in Atatürk Park. Most visitors prefer Kaleiçi, where a profusion of bars competes for your attention.

SPORTS AND THE OUTDOORS

BEACHES

Konyaaltı Beach. For many Turks, Antalya is synonymous with the thick crowds of holiday-makers on Konyaaltı Beach, and the packed pebble strand is a hot, somewhat off-putting sight in high season. The city has worked hard to improve the quality of the beach experience, though, with especially impressive results on the 1-km (½-mile) section starting after the museum and ending under the Su Hotel. The beach is largely divided up by concessions, each with its own restaurant, deck chairs, umbrellas, and showers. **Amenities**: food and drink; parking (no fee); showers; toilets; water sports. **Best for**: partiers; walking; swimming.

Mermerli Beach. If you didn't know that Mermerli Beach was there, you'd never guess it. This small strip of sand and pebbles outside the harbor wall is reached via the Mermerli Restaurant, halfway up the hill east of the harbor. The 11 TL admission price to this quiet oasis in the heart of town includes loungers and umbrellas. **Amenities**: food and drink; showers; toilets; water sports. **Best for**: swimming. ⊠ *Below Banyo Cad. 25* ☎ *242/248–5484.*

RAFTING

Rafting has become a major activity, with several agencies offering trips to various canyons; most will pick you up at your hotel. Another option is to drive your own vehicle to Köprülü Canyon. To avoid the crowds, get up to the water in the early morning before the package tourists are out of bed.

TransNature ☎ *242/324-0011* ⊕ *www.transnature.com.tr/eng/index.html.*

SHOPPING

The shopping streets here have more variety than anywhere else on the Turquoise Coast, although the merchandise, in general, is the same sort of stuff you find all over Turkey. The less expensive clothing shops and jewelry arcades are concentrated east and north of the old town walls, while the old town itself has more decorative souvenirs. Kenan Evren Boulevard, along the seafront cliffs toward the museum, has the most upmarket clothing shops. A short taxi ride to the west of town is Antalya's fanciest mall, the Migros Shopping Center. Set behind the Su Hotel, it has a large supermarket, eight cinemas, and a large food court, as well as 100 shops that represent both international brands (like Swatch, Lacoste, and Tommy Hilfiger) and Turkey's big clothing chains (including Mavi Jeans, LCW for children's clothes, Derimod for upmarket leathers, Bisse and Abbate for shirts, and Vakkorama and Boyner for general clothing).

TERMESSOS

37 km (23 miles) northwest of Antalya.

Writers in antiquity referred to Termessos as the Eagle's Nest, and when you visit the 4,500-foot high site, you'll understand why. Seemingly impregnable, Termessos remained autonomous for much of its history and was quite wealthy by the 2nd century AD. Most of the remains date from that period. A visit takes at least four hours, and there is no restaurant on-site, so pack water and lunch, and wear sturdy shoes.

GETTING HERE AND AROUND

Termessos is best reached by car. Alternately, tours can be arranged by agencies in Antalya, or you can catch any bus from the bus station to Korkuteli and get off at the Termessos intersection where taxis usually wait; one way is around 30 TL.

EXPLORING

Termessos. The attractions in Termessos start right by the parking area, with a monumental **gate,** part of an ancient temple dedicated to Hadrian. The steepness of the path that leads up to the craggy remains of the city walls soon makes it clear just why Alexander the Great declined to attack. Next, on your left, are a **gymnasium,** a **colonnaded street,** a **bath** complex built of dark gray stone blocks, and then, up and around, a 5,000-seat **theater** perched at the edge of a sheer cliff, which has one of the most spectacular settings in Turkey. From this staggering height you can see the sea, the Pamphylian plain, Mt. Solymus, and the occasional mountain goat or ibex. Farther around is the well-preserved *bouleterion,* where the city council met, surrounded by several temples, the very overgrown market, and some huge underground cisterns. Termessos has one more wonder: several vast **necropolises,** with nearly 1,000 tombs scattered willy-nilly on a rocky hill. A signposted alternate route back to the parking lot takes you past several rock-cut tombs; another large collection of tombs can be accessed via a path from the ticket office. ✉ *Take E87 north toward Burdur, bear left at fork onto Rte. 350 toward Korkuteli and follow signs to Termessos* 🎫 *5 TL* ☉ *Daily 8:30–7.*

PERGE

22 km (14 miles) east of Antalya on Rte. 400.

Perge's biggest problem is that it suffers from comparison with its neighbors. It is, however, one of Turkey's best examples of a Roman city.

GETTING HERE AND AROUND

The ruins are well signposted 2 km (1½ miles) north of the small town of Aksu, 22 km (14 miles) east of Antalya on Route 400. There are frequent buses from Antalya Otogar to Aksu.

EXPLORING

Perge. Although **Perge** isn't beautifully situated like Termessos or an A-list attraction like Aspendos, it is an ideal place to get an overall impression of a Roman city. The first thing you'll see is a splendid theater, which has unfortunately been closed for repairs for years. The stadium next door is open and is one of the best preserved in the ancient world. The vaulted chambers under the stadium bleachers held shops (marble inscriptions record the proprietors' names and businesses).

The rest of the site is about 1 km (½ mile) north. After parking just outside the old city walls, you'll enter near sturdy 3rd-century-BC garrison towers. Directly ahead is a fine, long-colonnaded avenue, unique for the water channel that ran down its center, starting at a fountain at the far end. This street was trodden by St. Paul as he passed by on his way to Psidian Antioch in the mountains. Beside the entrance is the old agora or marketplace; the slender, sun-bleached columns lining the street once supported a covered porch filled with shops. Look for a backgammon-like board game cut into a block of marble. Opposite is the well-preserved bath house. Follow the main street to the end, and then climb the hill for a literal overview of the site. The rest of Perge is rather overgrown, but the keen-eyed can hunt down several churches and a gymnasium. ⊠ *2 km (1½ mile) north of Aksu, Perge* 🖃 *15 TL* ⊙ *Daily 8–7.*

WHERE TO EAT

$ ✕ **Öz Şimşek.** This is one of a few humble eateries in a town where fresh
TURKISH   local ingredients result in good incarnations of standard Turkish dishes. Try the nice cumin-flavored köfte meatballs with baked garlic and mild peppers, along with a plate of the local speciality *piyaz* (white beans in a sauce with sesame paste, tomato, parsley, egg, and olive oil). 💲 *Average main: 15 TL* ⊠ *In Aksu, on the Mersin-Antalya road, 2 km (1¼ miles) south of Perge, Perge* 🕾 *242/426–3920.*

ASPENDOS

49 km (31 miles) east of Antalya on Rte. 400.

Most experts agree that the theater in Aspendos is one of the best preserved in the world. A splendid Roman aqueduct that traverses the valley (another superior example of classical engineering) utilized the pressure of the water flowing from the mountains to supply the summit of the acropolis. The water tower dates from the 2nd century AD, and its stairway is still intact.

GETTING HERE AND AROUND

From Antalya, take Route 400 east and follow the yellow signs. There are frequent buses to the nearby town of Serik, but minibuses to Aspendos are rare.

EXPLORING

Fodor's Choice
★

Aspendos. Pay your admission to the main site at what was once the actors' entrance to the theater. Although there are many Roman theaters none are quite as perfect as this one built by a local architect called Xenon during the reign of Emperor Marcus Aurelius (AD 161–180). Much of its preservation owe to it being reused by Seljuk Turks as a royal palace in the 13th century; traces of the distinctive Seljuk red-and-yellow paint work are still visible. The theater is striking for the broad curve of seats, perfectly proportioned porticoes, and rich decoration. The Greeks liked open vistas behind their stages, but the Romans preferred enclosed spaces. The stage building you see today was once covered by an elaborate screen of marble columns, and its niches were filled with statues. The only extant relief on-site depicts Dionysus (Bacchus) watching over the theater. The acoustics are fine, and the theater continues to be used—for concerts and for the Antalya International Opera and Ballet Festival, held every June and July, rather than for wild-animal and gladiator spectacles as in Roman times. Note the stone brackets on the outside, these once held a vast awning that shaded the audience.

Aspendos was a city, dating back to the Hittite times, but most visitors just see the theater. The rest is up a short zigzagging trail behind it. The rewards are a tall **Nymphaion** (a sanctuary to the nymphs built around a fountain decorated with a marble dolphin) and the remains of a Byzantine **basilica** and **market hall**. You can also see, below in the plain, the **stadium** and the **aqueduct** which used an ingenious syphon system. ⊠ *49 km (31 miles) east of Antalya* 🖃 *15 TL* ⏱ *Daily 9–7.*

Selge and Köprülü Kanyon. Just east of Aspendos, a turnoff leads north to the ruins of Selge and Köprülü Kanyon, a popular spot for white-water rafting. Just before Beşkonak (30 km/18 miles) the road splits and one branch crosses the river, passing the pleasant riverside Selge and Perge restaurants. After 10 km (6 miles) the two roads meet again at the start of the canyon proper—you'll drive over a very well-preserved Roman bridge. There are dozens of raft operators on the river. One of the largest is **TransNature** (⊕ *www.transnature.com.tr* ☎ *242/247–8688*); the Selge and Perge restaurants have local rafting guides as well. The rapids are rated fairly easy. From here you head another 15 km (9 miles) up a steep road through rock formations to the town of Zelve, the site of the Roman city of Selge. Just before you reach town, take the left turn and the impressive Roman theater will soon come into view. Most visitors are happy to clamber over the theater, but from the top you can see the ruins of the city itself on the hill opposite. The area is part of the Saint Paul Trail hike. If you'd like to explore with a local guide, call Adem Bahar (☎ *535/762–8116*). ⊠ *Aspendos.*

SIDE

75 km (47 miles) east of Antalya on Rte. 400.

Charter-tour hotels crowded along this stretch of coast threaten to over-shadow Side, but the city remains a delightful mix of ancient ruins and modern amenities. Sandy beaches border it on each side, with the ruins in the middle. Side, like Antalya or Alanya, offers all sorts of activities, from shopping and late-night dancing to kayaking in mountain canyons. It's also close to the major sites of Aspendos and Perge, and less than an hour from Antalya Airport. Like its bigger Pamphylian sisters, Side is best visited out of the heat of high season (July and August). Even at peak times, though, most tourists stay in all-inclusive resorts and head home for dinner. This means that at night it's still possible to experience how Side felt in the 1960s, when the city was off the beaten track, and the likes of dancer Rudolph Nureyev and French intellectual Simone de Beauvoir were visitors.

GETTING HERE AND AROUND

Take the turnoff just west of Manavgat on Route 400—it's another 11 km (7 miles) into town. There's a large parking lot just outside the walls of ancient Side. Frequent buses come from Antalya and Alanya to Manavgat, and minibuses from Manavgat Otogar to Side run every few minutes, stopping at the same parking lot.

Official Tourist Office Side ⊠ *1 mile north of the center on the main road* ☎ *242/753-1265* 🖷 *242/753-2657.*

EXPLORING

Resist any sense of disappointment as you follow the "Antik Side" signs in from Route 400—it will dissipate when you suddenly find yourself driving onto the little peninsula through the delightful ruins of a Greco-Roman city. Founded by early Greeks, who minted coins from 500 BC, ancient Side only began to expand when Pompey cleared out the slave-trading pirates in 67 BC. Most of the ruins, laid bare by one of the only systematic excavations of a whole city, date from the prosperous Roman period. These include a lovely theater and a 2nd-century temple dedicated to Apollo.

Side Müzesi (*Side Museum*). Across the street from the agora, the Side Müzesi is housed in a restored Roman bath. The collection of Roman statues is small but interesting: a gorgeous group of marble torsos includes the Three Graces, various cherubs, a brilliant satyr, and a bust of Emperor Hadrian. The sculpture garden behind the museum is larger than the museum itself and overlooks the Mediterranean. You may find the admission steep for the size of the museum. ⊠ *Beside the theater* ☎ *242/753-1006* 🖃 *10 TL.*

Temple of Apollo. If you follow the main street full of shops selling jewelry and cheap clothes till you reach the water, and then turn left, you reach Side's picture-postcard Temple of Apollo, built of gleaming white marble that's set off beautifully by the blue ocean behind. 🖃 *5 TL.*

Theater. Opposite the Side museum is the city's large theater. It was rebuilt in the 2nd century, though the design is more Greek than Roman. There are views out over the agora, which is closed for excavations. 🖃 *10 TL.*

WHERE TO EAT

$$$ INTERNATIONAL
🍴 **Orfoz.** If you want to eat in the harbor area, many would say this is the best restaurant to choose. The tables are well spaced, the trees are shady, the service is good, and the food is excellent. Fresh seafood is the specialty, including melt-in-the-mouth garlic prawns, but there's something for everyone on the international menu. **TIP→ The view over the western beach is just right at sunset; if there's a chill in spring or autumn, attentive waiters will even bring out blankets.** [$] *Average main: 35 TL ✉ Liman Cad. 58/C ☎ 242/753–1362.*

$$ TURKISH
🍴 **Paşaköy Bar and Restaurant.** What differentiates this pleasant restaurant from the rest is its weird and wonderfully kitsch garden, decked out with garden gnomes, mock-classical statuary, and stuffed animals. The grilled meat dishes are good, a kids' menu is available, and the waitstaff is friendly. The bartender can make a cocktail with a kick, too. [$] *Average main: 29 TL ✉ Liman Cad. 98 ☎ 242/753–3622 ⏲ Closed Dec.–May.*

$$ MEDITERRANEAN
🍴 **Soundwaves Restaurant.** This open-air restaurant on a pedestrian walk overlooking the sea has a long and reliable reputation; it's run by the same management as the nearby Beach House Hotel. Specialties include fish baked in salt, garlic prawns, and (thanks to an Australian half-owner), a deep-fried seafood dish called Tasmanian Squid. [$] *Average main: 16 TL ✉ Barbaros Cad. ☎ 242/753–1607 ⏲ Closed Dec.–Apr.*

WHERE TO STAY

$$$ RESORT
🏨 **Barut Hotel Acanthus.** This older four-story hotel is done in Mediterranean style, with whitewashed walls, dark-wood trim and terraces, a red-tile roof, and direct access to a fine sand beach. **Pros:** good beach location not too far from town; well run. **Cons:** typical international package tourist resort. [$] *Rooms from: $207 ✉ Turgut Ozal Cad. ☎ 242/753–3050 🛏 104 rooms 🍽 Some meals.*

$ HOTEL FAMILY
🏨 **Beach House Hotel.** If you want a few charmed days on the Side seafront, the Beach House is great place to book. **Pros:** friendly and helpful staff; great value. **Cons:** opposite, rather than on, the beach; may be past its prime. [$] *Rooms from: $60 ✉ Barbaros Sok. ☎ 242/753–1607 🌐 www.beachhouse-hotel.com 🛏 23 rooms 🍽 Breakfast.*

$ B&B/INN
🏨 **Doğa.** This pleasant *pansiyon* is in an old stone house a block from the beach. **Pros:** intimate; full of character; good organic food. **Cons:** not right on the beach. [$] *Rooms from: $61 ✉ Lale Sok. 8 ☎ 242/753–6246 🌐 www.sidedoga.com 🛏 7 rooms 🍽 No meals.*

$$ HOTEL
🏨 **Kamer Motel.** This modest, clean option in a quiet part of town has a great location on eastern shore, with views of the sea and a private though rocky beach area. **Pros:** nice views; good value. **Cons:** uninspired architecture and décor. [$] *Rooms from: $97 ✉ Barabaros Cad. 47 ☎ 242/753–1007 📠 242/753–2660 🌐 www.kamermotel.net 🛏 16 rooms 🍽 Breakfast.*

NIGHTLIFE

Lighthouse. Down by the harbor is the open-air Lighthouse discotheque and bar. *✉ Liman Cad. 1 ☎ 242/256–9987.*

Pegasus Bar. On the shore west of the theater, almost behind the museum, Pegasus Bar is a good place to sit with a drink while watching the sunset over the ocean; it has a vast range of cocktails and 15 types of coffee, plus live music at night. ✉ *Yasemin Sok.*

Royal Castle Bar. The action begins after sunset at places like the Royal Castle Bar. Just in from the water on the southwest corner, its pub-like atmosphere and televised soccer games keep British patrons happy. There is also live music most evenings in season. ✉ *Turgut Reis Cad. 62* ☎ *242/753–4373.*

SPORTS AND THE OUTDOORS
BOAT TRIPS
Boat trips along the Manavgat River can be arranged either from Side or from Manavgat (on Rte. 400). Prices vary widely depending on the length of the trip and whether food is provided. You should definitely bargain. Times often change, but a boat also usually leaves each morning about 9 am for Alanya: check the evening before at the sales desk in the middle of the Side harborfront. Boats stop to let you swim, and some arrange for activities such as Jet Skiing, waterskiing, or parasailing; be warned, however, that not all operators are properly licensed or insured, and serious accidents have occurred.

JEEP SAFARIS
Jeep safaris are also popular and can be arranged from one of several travel agencies in Side.

Unser Tour. One good option is Unser Tour. ☎ *532/413–8431 mobile, 242/453–5583 office* ⊕ *unserreisen.com.*

ALARA HAN

118 km (73 miles) east of Antalya; 43 km (26 miles) east of Side.

The Seljuk Turks fostered the prosperity of their 11th- to 13th-century domains with trade protected by a network of *kervansarays*, or inns—also called *hans* in Turkish. Alara Han is one of the best surviving examples.

GETTING HERE AND AROUND
Turn north off Route 400 near the town of Okurcular onto a local road signposted "Alara Han." The site is 9 km (6 miles) inland via the village of Ulugüney. There is no public transport.

EXPLORING
Alara Han. With its majestic vaulted interior, Alara Han is among the most romantic *kervansarays* (inns) in Turkey. Built in the early 13th century and now beautifully restored, it has a fountain, prayer room, unusual lamp stands carved into stone, and lions' heads at the bases of the arches. In summer, the inland countryside location also provides welcome relief from the sweltering coast. If you're feeling energetic, an unusual hand-carved tunnel leads up to the Seljuk fortress built on the crags above the inn. To get here, follow the road to the **Alara Cennet Piknik** restaurant *(544/260–5520).* ■TIP→ **A flashlight is essential to make the climb—if you don't have your own, ask to borrow one at the restaurant.** Afterwards, you can return there to dine on fresh-caught trout or just relax with a cold drink on the riverbank, enjoying a cool

breeze from the crystal clear snow-fed river. ⊠ *43 km (26 miles) east of Side, Alara, Side.*

ALANYA

135 km (84 miles) east of Side on Rte. 400.

Alanya is Turkey's hottest resort town—literally. Temperatures here are higher than almost anywhere else in Turkey, averaging 106°F (27°C) in July and August; the waves lapping the long Mediterranean beaches that sweep toward Alanya's great rock citadel are only a degree or two cooler. This makes high summer in Alanya heaven for sun-starved, disco-loving, hard-drinking northern Europeans but rather hellish for anyone seeking a quiet holiday surrounded by nature. That said, Alanya is home to one of Turkey's biggest year-round expatriate communities, and in spring and autumn it's a pleasantly warm and inexpensive place to indulge in a few days of easily accessible swimming, historic sites, and good food.

Foreign influence has encouraged this city to clean up its act. Former wastelands of concrete-block apartments are now colorfully painted; Ottoman districts around the harbor are well on the way to being restored; and the eclectic jumble of houses inside the magnificent red-walled citadel contains an increasing number of handsome boutique hotels. Other improvements include the opening of a microbrewery (Red Tower, which serves what may be the best beer in Turkey) and the debut of touch-screen bike rentals around the city center.

Alanya is famed for its sandy beaches, within walking distance of most hotels. The best swimming place is known as Cleopatra's Beach—yet another accretion to the fables surrounding Mark Antony's courtship of the Egyptian queen—and its yellow sands extend northwest from the citadel. Boats can be hired from the harbor for relaxing day tours to caves around the citadel and a view of the only surviving Seljuk naval arsenal. Alanya, called Kalanaoros by the Byzantines, was captured by the sultan Alaaddin Keykubad in 1221 and became the Turkish Seljuks' first Mediterranean stronghold in their centuries-long migration westward. Several amusing stories explain the Seljuk sultan's conquest: one says he married the commander's daughter, another that he tied torches to the horns of thousands of goats and drove them up the hill in the dark of night, suggesting a great army was attacking. Most likely, he simply cut a deal. Once settled, he modestly renamed the place Alaiya, after himself, and built defensive walls to ensure he would never be dislodged. The Ottomans arrived in 1471, and gave it its current name, Alanya.

GETTING HERE AND AROUND

The highway passes around the city's northern outskirts. The castle marks the center of town, and there are two distinct clusters of hotels, shops, and restaurants on either side of it. There are frequent buses from Antalya and Side, and less frequent ones to Anamur and Adana.

Official Tourist Office Alanya ⊠ *Damlataş Cad. 1* ☎ *242/513–1240* 🖷 *242/513–5436.*

EXPLORING

Alanya Müzesi (*Alanya Museum*). It's worth dropping by the small, recently renovated small Alanya Müzesi just to see the perfectly preserved Roman bronze statue of a gleaming, muscular Hercules from the 2nd century AD. There are also two nice mosaics, some interesting stone altars, and limestone ossuaries. Note the Ottoman Greek inscriptions in Karamanli—Turkish written with the Greek alphabet. ⊠ *Azaklar Sok., south of Atatürk Cad.* ☎ *242/513–1228* 💷 *3 TL* ⊙ *Tues.–Sun. 9–7.*

Kale (*citadel*). Views of the splendid castle or *kale*, on a mighty crag surrounded on three sides by the sea, dominate all roads into Alanya. The crenellated outer walls are 7

THE SELJUK TURKS AND THE MEDITERRANEAN

The empire of the Roman Seljuks was the first Muslim empire to extend into Anatolia, long before the Ottomans arrived. It reached its height in the 13th century, when the Seljuks established full control of Turkey's Mediterranean and Black Sea coasts. Their capital was at Konya (Iconium), in central Anatolia, where winters were bitterly cold. As a consequence, the Seljuks established Alanya, the nearest point on the coast, as a secondary winter capital, and there are many Seljuk remains in the area, including the Alara Han.

km (4 miles) long and include 146 towers. The road pierces these outer walls through a modern break, dividing as it heads up the summit. One section leads to the **İç Kale** (inner fortress), the other to the **Ehmediye**; both have places to park. If you don't have a car, there is a bus to the summit, which allows you to walk up or down through the old city's residential area, starting or ending at the Kızıl Kule—it's a hot trek in summer, though.

In the center of the castle are the remains of the original *bedestan* (bazaar); the erstwhile old shops are now rooms in the lackluster Bedestan Hotel. Along a road to the top of the promontory, a third wall and a ticket office defend the **İç Kale (Keep)**. Inside are the ruins of a Byzantine church, with some 6th-century frescoes of the evangelists. Keykubad probably also had a palace here, although discoveries by the McGhee Center of Georgetown University—itself housed in a beautiful Ottoman mansion perched on the cliff face between the first and second ring of walls—indicates that in times of peace the Seljuk elite probably preferred their pleasure gardens and their hunting and equestrian sports on the well-watered plain below. Steps ascend to the battlement on the summit. A viewing platform is built on the spot where condemned prisoners and women convicted of adultery were once cast to their deaths. The ticket is also valid for the **Ehmediye** area, past the 17th-century Suleymaniye Camii, where a small citadel is built on the foundations of classical walls. Admire the ruined monastery down below but do not attempt to descend toward it—the mountainside is very treacherous. ☎ *242/512–3304* 💷 *10 TL for İç Kale and Ehmediye* ⊙ *Tues.–Sun. 9–7.*

Kızıl Kule (*Red Tower*). A minor masterpiece of Mediterranean military architecture, the 100-foot-high Kızıl Kule was built by the Seljuks in 1225 to defend Alanya's harbor and the nearby shipyard known as the **tersane** (arsenal). Sophisticated technology for the time was imported in the form of an architect from Aleppo who was familiar with Crusader castle building. The octagonal redbrick structure includes finely judged angles of fire for archers manning the loopholes, cleverly designed stairs to cut attackers off, and a series of troughs to convey boiling tar and melted lead onto besieging forces. Nowadays the Red Tower's cool passages house temporary exhibits, usually less captivating than the view from the roof. A short walk south along the water—or along the castle walls, if you prefer—is the **tersane**, which is made up of five workshops, all under an arched roof. Ships could be pulled up under the vaulted stone arches for building or repairs, and the cover was likely also useful for storing war supplies. ✉ *Eastern harbor at south end of İskele Cad.* 🎫 *4 TL (6 TL with tersane).*

WHERE TO EAT

$$ MEDITERRANEAN 🍴 **Filika Restaurant.** This fine restaurant is poised on a pretty terrace right on Cleopatra's Beach, and it looks up to the citadel towering overhead, with enough foliage to make modern Alanya disappear. The dinner menu is heavy on meat (try the lamb with rosemary), but there is also a more basic snack menu at lunch. [$] *Average main: 30 TL* ✉ *Güzelyalıı Cad., diagonally opposite the museum* ☎ *242/519–3227.*

$$ TURKISH 🍴 **Flash.** A few blocks north of the fray, Flash attracts more locals than tourists and survives on word of mouth. It's known for soups, steaks, kebabs, and *kiremit* stew cooked in clay bowls. [$] *Average main: 25 TL* ✉ *Hacet Cad.* ☎ *242/511–4220* 🌐 *www.flashrestaurant.com.tr.*

$$$ TURKISH 🍴 **Güverte Restaurant.** This long-standing favorite promises a delightful view of the harbor and excellent traditional Turkish fare that's focused on fresh seafood. If you're lucky, they'll have *grida* (grouper) as a daily special; if not, try the fried squid with local *tarator* sauce—a mixture of yogurt, garlic, lemon, walnuts, olive oil, and bread. [$] *Average main: 35 TL* ✉ *Çarşı Mahallesi, İskele Cad. 70* ☎ *242/513–4100.*

$ CAFÉ 🍴 **Özsüt Alanya.** This modern, air-conditioned cake shop is the best place in town for restoring lagging caffeine or blood sugar levels—perhaps before an assault on the citadel above. It's part of a modern chain that has expanded rapidly through Turkish cities thanks to the excellent cakes, pastries, and sweets. **TIP→ The upstairs area has a nice harbor view.** [$] *Average main: 8 TL* ✉ *Çarşıı Mah., Iskele Cad., Kamburoğlu Apt. No. 84, just before Red Tower* ☎ *242/512–2202.*

$$$ TURKISH 🍴 **Red Tower Brewery Restaurant.** This is one of Turkey's first microbreweries, and the beer here is some of the best you'll find in the country. Choices include a traditional pilsner and dark Marzen ale. Different eateries on each floor serve everything from kebabs to sushi; all overlook the Alanya harbor and Red Tower fortifications. In summer you can dine on the terrace across the road. On the roof is an open-air Skylounge Bar. [$] *Average main: 32 TL* ✉ *Iskele Cad. 80* ☎ *242/513–6664* 🌐 *www.redtowerbrewery.com.*

WHERE TO STAY

$$ HOTEL 🏨 **Elysée Beach Hotel.** This relatively quiet, clean, and modest hotel is right on Alanya's Cleopatra Beach, a short walk from the center of town. **Pros:** prime beach location. **Cons:** few rooms have real sea views. [$] *Rooms from: $119* ✉ *Saray Mah., Atatürk Cad. 145*

☎ *242/512–8791* 🌐 *www.elyseehotels.com* 🛏 *60 rooms* 🕘 *Closed mid-Dec.–Mar.* 🍴 *Some meals.*

$$ HOTEL **Grand Okan.** The four-star Grand Okan is the slickest hotel on Cleopatra's Beach. **Pros:** fresh; some sea views; relatively central. **Cons:** large, impersonal resort hotel. [$] *Rooms from: $120* ✉ *Atatürk Cad., west of center where main road meets beach road* ☎ *242/519–1637* 🌐 *www.grandokan.com* 🛏 *155* 🍴 *No meals.*

$$ B&B/INN Fodor's Choice ★ **Lemon Villa.** An Ottoman building, just up from the Red Tower, was transformed into this intriguing boutique hotel in 2013. **Pros:** beautiful rooms; lots of personal touches; top floor has a wonderful view; close to center. **Cons:** no views from garden. [$] *Rooms from: $100* ✉ *Tophane Cad. 20* ☎ *242/513–4461* 🌐 *www.lemonvilla.com* 🛏 *9 rooms* 🍴 *Breakfast.*

$$ B&B/INN **Villa Turca.** Opened in 2011, this restored mansion boasts a gorgeous shady terrace with an unbeatable view, plus some beautiful, refined rooms. **Pros:** wonderful terrace; unique rooms. **Cons:** a little far from the center. [$] *Rooms from: $110* ✉ *Kargi Sok. 7* ☎ *530/547–4641* 🌐 *www.hotelvillaturka.com* 🛏 *9 rooms, 1 suite* 🍴 *Breakfast.*

NIGHTLIFE

Alanya's nightlife centers around its harbor and the explosive beat on İskele Caddesi—although there are also a few large dance clubs in Dimçay, about 5 km (3 miles) outside town. Bars often have extensive menus, and restaurants frequently have live music or turn into impromptu discos after dinner.

James Dean Bar. The James Dean Bar is popular and less expensive than some of the other haunts on the strip. ✉ *İskele Cad.* ☎ *242/512–3195.*

Robin Hood Bar. The Sherwood Forest–themed, three-floor Robin Hood Bar is the biggest on the block; it's open year-round and tries to cater to all tastes. ✉ *İskele Cad. 24* ☎ *242/511–7692.*

Summer Garden. Near the seafront on the road to Antalya, this hugely popular club and its sister restaurant **Fresco** are part of the same sprawling complex. Two large bars among the palm trees have a dance floor cooled with outdoor air-conditioning (really!). Drinks start flowing at 6 pm, and the music doesn't stop until about 4 am. **TIP→ Free transport to/from Alanya is available for groups of five or more.** ✉ *Konaklıı Kasabasi, 10 km (6 miles) from downtown Alanya* ☎ *242/565–0059, 535/768–1326* 🌐 *www.summer-garden.com* 🕘 *Closed mid-Nov.–mid-May.*

SPORTS AND THE OUTDOORS

Alanya's main strand, Cleopatra's Beach, remains relatively uncrowded except in the height of summer. It's also easy to reach other nearby beaches, coves, and caves by boat. Legend has it that buccaneers kept their most fetching maidens at **Korsanlar Mağarası** (Pirates' Cave) and **Aşıklar Mağarası** (Lovers' Cave), two favorite destinations. Tour boats usually charge from 20 TL to 40 TL per person; hiring a private boat, which you can do at the dock near the Red Tower, should cost less than 15 TL an hour—don't be afraid to bargain.

Alanya International Triathlon. Organized sporting events are new for sweltering, nightlife-oriented Alanya, but the past few years have seen the advent of the Alanya International Triathlon in late spring. There is also beach volleyball, basketball, handball, and other sporting events, especially in summer. ⊕ *www.alanya.bel.tr/Triathlon/index.htm.*

EAST OF ALANYA

Although few tourists continue east of Alanya, it can be a scenic route to Cappadocia or onward to Antioch and eastern Turkey, with some interesting stops along the way. Mountains rise up from the sea and the road winds tortuously along the coast, which is very pretty in spots (one long stretch is reminiscent of the Amalfi Coast or the French Riviera). Beyond the growing resort town of Gazipaşa the communities are mostly agricultural, with the occasional cluster of Turkish holiday homes, until the plain opens out again around Adana, Turkey's fourth-largest city. As you head east, food and accommodation become cheaper, and you're more likely to have the sights to yourself.

ANAMUR

130 km (80 miles) southeast of Alanya on Rte. 400.

Anamur is an uninspiring agricultural town, known throughout Turkey for its bananas. The ruins of ancient Anemurium and the dramatic Marmure Castle, however, give you a reason to stop. The roads both east and west of here are some of the windiest in Turkey. If you want to break up the journey, try one of the low-key waterfront resorts.

GETTING HERE AND AROUND

There are regular buses to Anamur, but they are much less frequent than on other stretches of coast. The highway passes through the center of town, where there is a turn to Anamur's seaside suburb of İskele. Anemurium and Marmure Kalesi, to the east and west respectively, are well signed.

EXPLORING

Anamur Müzesi (*Anamur Museum*). A small museum in the waterfront district of İskele displays finds from Anemurium and other area sites. The most interesting are the tomb mosaics and a bronze head of Athena. ✉ *İskele Mah.* ☎ *324/814–1677* 🎫 *Free* ⊙ *Daily 8–5.*

Anemurium. Five kilometers (3 miles) before Anamur is the marked turn-off to ancient Anemurium. The extensive ruins here—mostly dating from the late Roman/early Byzantine period—are built out of durable Roman concrete, which makes them better preserved but less picturesque than the average stone ruins. Beside the entrance is a **bath building**, once part of a gymnasium. Beyond this is a small, well-preserved theater, or **odeon**, opposite which sit the scant remains of a large **theater**. A second Roman **bath building** is easily the best preserved in the country, with even its great vaulted roof standing. Beside the road there are also numerous **tombs**, some with frescoes and mosaics. ▥ TIP→ At the end of the road there's a pebbly beach, where you can take a dip when you've finished, but with no showers or other facilities.

Mamure Kalesi (*Mamure Castle, also known as Mamuriye*). On the southeast edge of town the highway goes right past Mamure Kalesi—a castle constructed in Roman times to protect the city from seaborne raiders. It was expanded by the Seljuks, who captured it in the 13th century, and later rebuilt by the Karamanoğulları, who controlled this part of Anatolia after the Seljuk Empire collapsed. Note the inscription to the Karamanoğulları prince, İbrahim Bey II, dating from 1450. The place is so impressively preserved you'd think it was a modern reconstruction. ⛏ 3 TL.

WHERE TO STAY

$$ 🛏 **Ünlüselek Hotel.** In Anamur's beachfront suburb of İskele, this older,
HOTEL renovated hotel has spacious guest rooms; all have sea-view balconies and most have been recently decorated, perhaps with excessive enthusiasm. **Pros:** waterfront location. **Cons:** décor verging on kitsch; waterfront lounge/breakfast area a bit basic. $ *Rooms from: $100* ✉ *Fahri Görgülü Cad., Hurma Sokak İskele* ☎ *324/814–2121* ⊕ *www. unluselekhotelanamur.com* ↝ *25* rooms ⦿ *Some meals.*

SILIFKE

120 km (74 miles) east of Anamur on Rte. 400.

Lively, non-touristy Silifke is a small agricultural town beside the Göksu River that's dominated by a Byzantine castle. Traces of its long history are evident in the cave-church home of St. Thecla, one of St. Paul's most prominent disciples.

GETTING HERE AND AROUND

There are occasionally buses between Silifke and Anamur.

EXPLORING

Seleuceia Trachea. In the vicinity of the castle, remains have been found indicating there was a settlement here as far back as the Bronze Age, though most of what can be seen today is from the Roman city known as Seleuceia Trachea, or Calycadnos Seleuceia. The ruins include a theater, a stadium, and the Corinthian columns of the 2nd-century-AD Temple of Zeus. Also left are a basilica and tomb dedicated to St. Thecla, St. Paul's first convert and the first female Christian martyr. Most interesting is the cave church where Thecla lived—the Patriarchate in Istanbul now organizes services here sometimes. ⛏ 3 TL.

Silifke Müzesi (*Silifke Museum*). Local finds are displayed in the small Silifke Müzesi, just out of the city center towards Anamur. ⛏ 3 TL ⊙ *Daily 8–5.*

Uzuncaburç. The small village of Uzuncaburç, in the mountains north of Silifke, makes a nice day trip. It's dotted with the ruins of Diocaesaria, a town run by the priests of Zeus Olbios. Along the ancient main street you'll see a theater, a curious columned structure that once marked the main crossroads, a fountain, a temple of Tyche, and another temple dedicated to Zeus. The last of these is one of the earliest surviving Corinthian-style buildings. North of the temples is the impressive North Gate; to the northeast is a well-preserved five-story watchtower. The most straightforward road here is signposted from Silifke; after 6 km (4 miles) you'll pass ancient Imbriogon (Demircili), where there are four temple tombs. ⊠ *30 km (19 miles) north of Silifke.*

Heaven and Hell. Between Silifke and Kız Kalesi, you can turn north off Route 400 onto a local road signposted "Cennet ve Cehennem Derisi." About 3 km (2 miles) inland is an intriguing attraction that has been drawing visitors since before Roman times. Looking beyond a small café and ticket booth you'll see a completely enclosed valley that was created by an ancient subsidence, sort of a sinkhole. This is called the **Valley of Heaven,** "Cennet Derisi." A five-minute walk takes you down to the peaceful valley floor and the well-preserved 5th-century AD Byzantine Church of the Virgin Mary. The path then descends into a huge, aircraft-hanger-like natural cavern, which may have been the site of a spring known among the ancients as the fountain of knowledge.

Back up the stairs a short walk leads to the **Valley of Hell,** "Cehennem Derisi," which is narrower, with walls too steep to enter, and deep enough for little sunlight to reach the bottom. A dark and gloomy place, pagan, Christian, and Muslim sources all identify it as an entrance to hell. The road continues to a third cavern, the **Cave of Wishes,** "Dilek Mağarası": Romans picked crocuses here, and even today you may be met by villagers selling bunches of the little flowers.

Down the hill from the highway, the village of Narlıkuyu is a picturesque inlet dotted with fish restaurants. The site of ancient Corycos, it now has a small museum with an excellent mosaic depicting the "Three Graces." ⊠ *17 km (10 miles) east of Silifke, turn north at Narlıkuyu* 💰 *3 TL entry to Heaven and Hell; museum is free.*

KIZ KALESI

22 km (14 miles) east of Silifke on Rte. 400.

This small town is easily the best place to stop on the long drive east of Alanya. Although a bit scruffy, it has a nice stretch of beach and a picture-perfect castle sitting just off the shore.

GETTING HERE AND AROUND

The town itself, between the highway and sea, is small and most hotels have frequent signs.

EXPLORING

Kız Kalesi (*Maiden's Castle*). Just off the coast, an island—known to have been settled as early as the 4th century BC—is home to an evocative castle called Kız Kalesi. Several offshore castles in Turkey bear the same name, which is derived from a legend about a king, a princess, and a snake: the beautiful princess, apple of her father's eye, had her fortune read by a wandering soothsayer who declared she would die of a snakebite. The king therefore sent her to a castle on a snake-free island. Destiny, however, can never be avoided, and the offending serpent was accidently delivered in a basket of grapes sent as a gift from her father's palace. More prosaically, this particular castle was an important part of the row of defenses built and rebuilt over the centuries to stop invaders from Syria entering Anatolia via the coast route to Antalya. What you see dates mostly from the 11th-century and was constructed by Byzantines to keep out

The three Graces, or Charities, depicted in this mosaic are said to have linked arms to show that one kindness should lead to another.

Antioch-based Crusaders. Boatmen will offer to take you out, but hiring a paddle boat is the most popular way to explore.

WHERE TO STAY

$$ HOTEL 🏨 **Club Barbarossa Hotel.** This hotel boasts great views of the castle, its own section of beach, and attractive accommodations; guest rooms have tasteful contemporary furnishings, private balconies (most with sea views) plus up-to-date perks like LCD TVs and Wi-Fi. **Pros:** modern well-equipped rooms; great location. **Cons:** hotel building itself is rather dated. [$] *Rooms from: $100* ✉ *Head down the peninsula and look for signs on your left* ☎ *324/523–2364* 🌐 *www.barbarossahotel.com* 🛏 *79 rooms* 🍴 *Some meals.*

$ HOTEL 🏨 **Yaka Hotel.** This is easily the most popular budget option in Kizkalesi and archaeologists working on nearby sites often stay here. **Pros:** popular; friendly. **Cons:** not right on the beach. [$] *Rooms from: $60* ✉ *On your left as you head down the pensinula* ☎ *324/523–2444* 🌐 *www.yakahotel.com.tr* 🛏 *16 rooms* 🍴 *Breakfast.*

TARSUS

105 km (65 miles) northeast of Kızkalesi; 28 km (17 miles) east of Mersin.

The dusty, provincial town of Tarsus is known as the place where St. Paul was born some 2,000 years ago. It has a broad range of Roman, Byzantine, and Turkish remains, and effort is now being put into restoration. No individual site is exceptional, but taken collectively, they make Tarsus the most interesting stop between Kız Kalesi and Adana.

GETTING HERE AND AROUND

Route E90 passes along the southern edge of the city, so you need to take the old Adana Bulavarı into the center. Most of the frequent buses between Mersin and Adana stop here, but there is no actual bus station or luggage storage; buses stop just east of the Makam-ı Şerif Mosque.

EXPLORING

Near the center of town, beside the tourist office, is an excavated section of Roman Road. North of here is a well in a small garden; it's traditionally identified as connected to the house of St. Paul, though the less pious may doubt it is worth the 4-TL entry fee. South of the well are some of Tarsus's best-preserved old houses, many of which are being restored. Head east on the main road and you'll find Eski Cami (now a mosque, it was built as a church by the Armenians in 1102). Opposite Eski Cami is the 19th-century Makam-ı Şerif, which is said to have been erected over the grave of the Prophet Daniel. Nearby are the 16th-century Ulu Cami, or Great Mosque, and a covered bazaar dubbed **Kırkkaşık,** or "40 Spoons," dating from the same period. To the south is the Church of St. Paul, a Greek-style edifice from the 19th century, now a museum (4 TL). West of here is the Tarsus American College, established by Presbyterian missionaries in 1888 and still in operation. Back toward the main street is the **Gate of Cleopatra.**

WHERE TO STAY

$$ B&B/INN 🏨 **Konak Efsus.** This boutique hotel is as good a reason as any to stop in Tarsus; opened in 2009, it occupies two restored mansions and has lots of character (picture wooden floors, Turkish carpets, and antique-style furnishings). **Pros:** nice rooms; spacious bathrooms. **Cons:** since you can tick off the sites in a few hours, do you really want to stay in Tarsus? [$] *Rooms from: $80* ✉ *Tarihi Evler Sokak 31–33, Tarsus* ☎ *324/614–0807* 🌐 *www.konakefsus.com* 🛏 *9 rooms* 🍴 *Breakfast.*

ADANA

53 km (33 miles) northeast of Tarsus.

Adana is Turkey's fourth-largest city after Istanbul, Ankara, and İzmir. Being a commercial and industrial center, it is the least known to tourists; however, there are a few worthwhile attractions.

GETTING HERE AND AROUND

The main east–west road in Adana, Turhan Cemal Beriker Boulevard, divides the old and new city. There are frequent buses to Osmaniye and İskenderun.

Both Yılan Kalesi and Toprakkale are beside Route E90, but there is no exit from the newer O50 tollway. Toprakkale guards the route south to İskenderun and Antakya. Karatepe is 30 km (19 miles) north of Osmaniye, which is 94 km (58 miles) east of Adana on the E90. Pass through Osmaniye, following signs for Kadirli, then the large signs for Karatepe. Alternately, from Kozan, there is a road, via Kadirli, to Karatepe.

EXPLORING

Adana's archaeology museum has a small but good collection; next door is the city's most prominent building and the largest mosque in Turkey, the Sabancı Merkez Camii. Completed in 1998, it is largely a copy of the 16th-century Selimiye Mosque of Edirne. Heading south along the river is another civic symbol, the impressively long **Taş Küprü**, or "stone bridge," built by the Emperor Hadrian in 125 AD and restored by later rulers. Inland is the **Ulu Camii**, more Arabic in style than Turkish. One of the prettiest mosques in the country, its patterned stonework has been well restored. Behind the mosque is Adana's lively market area, with several old mosques, including the Yağ Camii (Oil Mosque) on Alimunif Caddesi, built in 1501 incorporating a Byzantine church.

East of Adana, across the Çukurova Plain, there are many ancient remains, including several castles, mostly dating back to Armenian rulers of the 12th to 14th centuries AD. The easiest to reach, **Yılan Kalesi**, the "Castle of the Snake," sits conspicuously beside the old highway, 40 km (25 miles) east of town: take the marked turn off and drive up to the parking lot, beside the small restaurant and ticket booth. There isn't a lot to see, but the walls are well preserved and the views of the fertile Çukurova Plain from the top are impressive. Farther east, just before Osmaniye and the turnoff to İskenderun, is a second Armenian Castle, Toprakkale; 70 km (45 miles) north of Yılan Kalesi, Kozan is another fine castle that was an important residence of the Armenian rulers of Cilicia.

About 130 km (81 miles) northeast of Adana, **Karatepe** makes a (long) day trip from Adana or a worthwhile detour if you're heading to Antakya. Karatepe was a fortress founded in the 8th century by Asatiwatas, the ruler of the post-Hittite state of Adana. A short walk from the parking lot are two ancient gateways, where dozens of well-preserved carved stones (once the foundation of mudbrick walls) have been left in place as an open-air museum. There is also a small indoor museum behind the ticket office. The area around the site is a beautiful national park, and you can picnic here or swim in the adjacent dam. It's best visited from Osmaniye, passing ancient Heiropolis-Kastabala, but a secondary road leads from Kozan past Kadirli, which has a well-preserved Byzantine church.

WHERE TO EAT AND STAY

$$
INTERNATIONAL
✕**North Shield.** Part English pub, part restaurant, the North Shield is popular with local expats. It has tasty steaks and pasta, plus a wide selection of wine, beer, and other beverages. $ *Average main: 25 TL* ✉ *Ziya Paşa Blv. 10/a* ☎ *322/458–6262.*

$$
TURKISH
✕**Yüzevler.** For most Turks Adana means the Adana kebab, minced lamb slow charcoal-grilled on a long, wide, metal skewer. Everyone in town has an opinion on where to find the best one, but the traditional favorite is Yüzevler. Obviously, Adana kebabs are the star of the show, but the *pide* (Turkish pizza) is good, too. This is probably also one of the safest places to try the famous raw ground meat *Çiğ Köfte*, literally "raw köfte" that's "cooked" with spices. $ *Average main: 25 TL* ✉ *64018 Sok. 25/A, just off Ziyapaşa Bulvarı* ☎ *322/454–7513.*

$$ **Akkoc Butik Otel.** This well-run midsize hotel isn't quite boutique;
HOTEL   however, it does a nice job of filling the gap between the city's two- and
five-star accommodations. **Pros:** in the cool part of town. **Cons:** more
of a business hotel. $ *Rooms from: $115* ⊠ *63005 Sok. 22* ☎ *322/459–
1000* ⊕ *www.akkocotel.com.tr* ⟿ *30 rooms* ¶◯¶ *No meals.*

$$ **Hotel Bosnali.** Adana finally has a true boutique hotel—an intimate,
B&B/INN   well-run option occupying a restored, 19th-century mansion in the
heart of the old city. **Pros:** central location on the west bank of the
Seyhan River; Wi-Fi and valet parking are welcome amenities. **Cons:**
often booked out by tour groups. $ *Rooms from: $104* ⊠ *Seyhan Cad.
29* ☎ *322/359–8000* ⊕ *www.hotelbosnali.com* ⟿ *10 rooms, 2 suites*
¶◯¶ *No meals.*

ANTAKYA (ANTIOCH)

191 km (118 miles) southeast of Adana.

Antakya—perhaps better known by its old name, Antioch—was
founded in about 300 BC and quickly grew, thanks to its strategic location on the trade routes. Under the Romans, it became the empire's third
most important city, surpassed only by Rome and Alexandria. Famed
for its luxury and notorious for its depravity, Antioch was chosen by
St. Paul as the objective of his first mission. The cave church in which
he preached remains a pilgrimage site today, while stunning displays in
the Hatay Müzesi testify to the artistic achievements of the Roman era.

After enduring earthquakes and assorted raids, the city fell to Crusaders in 1098; then was nearly leveled by the Egyptians in 1268. A late
addition to the Turkish Republic, Antakya was occupied by France after
1920 as part of its mandate over Syria, which still has an outstanding
territorial claim on it. Though the city reverted to Turkey just before
World War II, it still maintains a distinctive character. The people here
are mostly bilingual, speaking both Turkish and a local dialect of Arabic. In the cobbled streets of the old quarter you can also hear Syriac
(Aramaic), the language spoken by many of Turkey's Christians.

GETTING HERE AND AROUND

The old city, on the east bank of the River Orontes, is relatively compact. Senpiyer Kilisesi, north of the old city, is far enough to drive.
There are frequent buses to Adana, Osmaniye, and Gaziantep, though
sometimes you need to change in İskenderun.

EXPLORING

Habib Neccar Cami. The River Orontes (Asi in Turkish) divides Antioch in
two. In the old town you will find the Habib Neccar Cami, a mosque on
Kurtuluş Caddesi, just south of St. Peter's. It's popularly dated from the
7th century and called Turkey's oldest mosque. More likely, a church of
John the Baptist originally stood here, replacing a temple, and this was
converted to a mosque, converted back to a church by the Crusaders,
then destroyed in 1268 by the Mamluk Sultan Baybars. He then had
the current building constructed. It has since been much restored. A side
chamber contains two sarcophagi, labeled as the prophet Jonah and
John the Baptist, while downstairs are the tombs of "Habib-i Neccar,"

an otherwise unidentified early Christian martyr mentioned in the Koran, and "Sham'un al-Safa" (Simon the Loyal), perhaps the Apostle Simon Peter. All presumably survive from the Byzantine Church, and with that pedigree could even be genuine. Between here and the river is the bazaar quarter, a real change of pace: the feel is more Syrian and Arab than Turkish. ⊠ *Corner of Kurtuluş and Kemalpaşa Cad.*

Harbiye. Most mosaics at the Hatay Museum come from villas in Harbiye. Originally called Daphne, this beautiful gorge of laurel trees and tumbling waterfalls was said to have been chosen by the gods for the Judgment of Paris and contained one of the ancient world's most important shrines to the god Apollo. Mark Antony chose it as the venue for his ill-fated marriage to Cleopatra in 40 BC. Daphne was also a favorite resort for wealthy Antiochenes and developed such a reputation for licentiousness that it was put off-limits to the Roman army. Nothing ancient survives but it's still a popular escape and there are many open-air cafés and restaurants, all fairly similar, overlooking the river. ⊠ *7 km (4 miles) south of Antakya on Rte. E91.*

Hatay Müzesi (*Hatay Museum*). Although little survives of old Antioch, the large collection of mosaics here hints at the city's glorious past. Experts consider the dozens of Roman mosaics in the Hatay Müzesi— portraying scenes from mythology and replete with figures such as Dionysus, Orpheus, Oceanus, and Thetis—to rank among the highest achievements of Roman art. There is also a beautiful marble sarcophagus and a giant statue of the Roman Emperor Lucius Verus. The area's preclassical past is well represented, too—check out the 3,000-year-old lion, discovered in 2011. As of this writing, the entire collection is slated to move into a new, larger facility on the edge of the city, past the Church of St. Peter, although the timing of the move is not known yet. ⊠ *Gündüz Cad. 1* ☎ *326/214–6167* ⊕ *www.muze.gov.tr/hatay* ☷ *3 TL* ☉ *Tues.–Sun. 9–6:30.*

Latin Church. The Catholic Church maintains its presence with a small sanctuary run by Capuchin monks. It is set in a garden on Kutlu Sokak, several winding blocks in from the Sermaye Mosque. Enter its small courtyard from the side street. You may recognize the image of the church bell, with the mosque minaret behind—it's on tourist office brochures as a symbol of religious harmony. Services are held Monday to Saturday at 8:30 am and 6:30 pm, Sunday at 6 pm (5 pm in winter). ⊠ *Kutlu Sok. 6, just off Kurtuluş Cad.* ⊕ *www.anadolukatolikkilisesi.org.*

Senpiyer Kilisesi (*Church of St. Peter*). On the northern edge of town is Senpiyer Kilisesi, or Saint Peter Church—a tiny cave high up on a cliff, blackened by centuries of candle smoke and dripping with water seeping out of the rock. According to tradition this is where the apostle secretly preached to his converts and where they first came to be called Christians. It may well be the oldest of all churches; the facade you see, however, was added by the Crusaders in the 11th-12th centuries. Closed for renovations since 2012, the church will hopefully be open when you arrive. The area around it was a cemetery in classical times, and there are numerous rock-cut tombs and tunnels. A path leads up to giant carved face of Charon, the legendary boatman who took the dead across the river Styx. Adventurous visitors can follow the valley just south to view a large section of the Byzantine walls, which also served as a bridge and dam. ✉ *Off Kurtuluş Cad., well signposted* 🎫 *10 TL* ⏲ *Daily 9–noon and 1–6.*

OFF THE BEATEN PATH

Samandag and Seleuceia ad Pieria. South of the city, you'll find a beach at Samandag (also known as Çevlik Beach), as well as tasty but inexpensive fish restaurants. You'll also find the scant remains of Antioch's old port, Seleuceia ad Pieria. The real attraction here is a large underground water channel, 1,400 meters (1,526 yards) long, which was built entirely by hand in the 1st century AD to prevent flooding. Nearby there are some large rock tombs. ✉ *28 km (17 miles) south of Antakya.*

WHERE TO EAT

$$ TURKISH

🍴 **Anadolu Restaurant.** Although service can be a little slow and the modern roof over the garden is unattractive, locals still flock here to dine on savory mezes, popular regional dishes such as *et sato* (minced meat with cheese) or *kağıt kebabi* (meat and vegetables wrapped in thin bread), and, for dessert, *künefe* (a pastry made with cheese and nuts). [$] *Average main: 16 TL* ✉ *Hürriyet Cad. 30/A* ☎ *326/215–3335* 🌐 *www.anadolurestaurant.com.tr.*

$ TURKISH

🍴 **Antik Han.** Welcome to the Hummus Zone. The mezes are particularly good at this restaurant, which has both a rooftop terrace and a pleasant courtyard where you can relax and eat. It serves a good range of kebabs and other dishes. Alcohol is available. [$] *Average main: 14 TL* ✉ *Hurriyet Cad.* 💳 *No credit cards.*

$ TURKISH

🍴 **Hatay Sultan Sofrası.** Tour groups often fill this restaurant at dinner for good reason: the food is both delicious and inexpensive. That combination also makes it popular with locals at lunch. Expect all the usual Turkish dishes plus local specialties including soups, stews, and *börek* pastries. [$] *Average main: 12 TL* ✉ *İstiklal Cad. 20* ☎ *326/213–8759.*

WHERE TO STAY

$$ HOTEL Fodor's Choice ★

🏨 **The Liwan Hotel.** This stylish hotel in a restored 1920s mansion is easily the best of the new crop of boutique hotels in town. **Pros:** excellent quality. **Cons:** some noise from the bar, particularly on weekends. [$] *Rooms from: $131* ✉ *Silahlı Kuvvetler Cad. 5* ☎ *326/215–7777* 🌐 *www.theliwanhotel.com* 🛏 *24 rooms* 🍽 *No meals.*

$ HOTEL

🏨 **Saadet Grand Hotel.** Opened in 2013, the Saadet Grand is a solid mid-range choice on the southern side of town. **Pros:** tasteful and new; good value; better-than-average English spoken. **Cons:** rooms lack character. [$] *Rooms from: $66* ✉ *Harbiye Cad.101* ☎ *326/444–3308* 🌐 *www.saadetgrandhotel.com* 🛏 *42 rooms* 🍽 *No meals.*

6

CAPPADOCIA AND CENTRAL TURKEY

with Ankara and Konya

Visit Fodors.com for advice, updates, and bookings

WELCOME TO CAPPADOCIA AND CENTRAL TURKEY

TOP REASONS TO GO

★ **Balloon over Cappadocia:** Dangling high above the spectacular terrain in a basket, you will sail past ethereal rock cones and photogenic fairy chimneys.

★ **Explore underground cities:** Kaymaklı, Derinkuyu, and other vast, multistoried subterranean complexes once housed tens of thousands of inhabitants.

★ **Hike the valleys of Cappadocia:** Trails lead past fantastical rock formations and deposit you at cave entrances that open on ornately decorated churches.

★ **Luxuriate in a cave:** Some of Cappadocia's finest hotels are tucked into elaborately appointed caves, where soft lighting, plush beds, antique accents, and even Jacuzzis are common amenities.

★ **Peer into the past:** From the displays at Ankara's Museum of Anatolian Civilizations to Konya's Seljuk-era mosques, Central Turkey bears traces of the numerous cultures that have occupied it.

1 Cappadocia. The extraordinary landscape here is like a giant outdoor sculpture garden filled with elaborate pillars, needles, and cones. As if these natural phenomena weren't enticing enough, hundreds of caves conceal frescoed churches from the early days of Christianity.

2 Konya. A popular pilgrimage site, Konya contains the tomb of the 13th-century philosopher Rumi and is the spiritual home of whirling dervishes. Medieval mosques enhance the city's holy feel. Nearby, Çatalhöyük ranks among the oldest known human settlements.

3 Ankara. Turkey's capital is the best place to witness the enduring legacy of Mustafa Kemal Atatürk, founding father of the secular Turkish Republic. Museums and historical sites are a stone's throw from the ancient citadel, which offers panoramic views of the city.

GETTING ORIENTED

Central Turkey stretches across a vast, arid plateau, littered with the ruins of ancient civilizations, slashed by ravines in places and rising to the peaks of extinct volcanoes in others. Think of the region as a triangle, with Ankara, Turkey's sprawling capital, to the northwest; Cappadocia, the land of surrealistic geological formations, to the east; and Konya, the city where the dervishes whirl, to the southwest, en route to Antalya and the Mediterranean coast.

6

Aritsans at work, Avanos.

Updated by Vanessa H. Larson

Some of the world's oldest known human habitations were established in the hills and valleys of Central Anatolia, but today the main attraction here is the magical landscape of Cappadocia, where wind and rain have shaped the area's soft volcanic rock into a kind of fairytale landscape.

In Cappadocia you'll discover incredible rock formations, spectacular valleys, ancient cave churches, and underground cities that reach many stories beneath the surface. The small towns of Ürgüp, Göreme, Uçhisar, Ortahisar, and Avanos are good bases for exploring the region's otherworldly landscape. Whether hiking through the amazing terrain on foot, exploring underground passageways, or floating over the incredible landscape in a hot-air balloon, you'll find Cappadocia to be unlike any place you've ever been before.

Southwest of Cappadocia is Konya, home to the tomb of Rumi—the 13th-century founder of the whirling dervishes—and to a fascinating museum dedicated to him. Known as Turkey's most religiously conservative city, Konya is not a place for those looking for nightlife (alcohol can be difficult to find) or a sophisticated dining scene. But centuries-old mosques and religious seminaries lend historic character to Turkey's seventh-largest city.

The region's other major city is Ankara, Turkey's capital and second-largest metropolis. Though lacking the mystique of Cappadocia or Konya, this modern urban center has one of the best archaeological museums in the country and a handful of interesting historical sites, including a citadel that surrounds an evocative neighborhood. Also in Ankara, the imposing mausoleum of Atatürk, founder of the Turkish Republic, offers visitors a great deal of insight into the modern Turkish psyche.

As you travel through the Turkish heartland, you'll see mostly agricultural regions—the province of Konya, with its vast plains where grains and other crops are grown, is known as the country's breadbasket—and encounter a slice of provincial life.

PLANNING

WHEN TO GO

Much of Central Anatolia is blazing hot in summer and freezing cold in winter. The best time to visit is in the spring (May) before the crowds and heat arrive or early fall (September), when the crowds are gone and winter hasn't yet descended.

PLANNING YOUR TIME

In Cappadocia, you can tick off the open-air museums, major valleys, an underground city, and perhaps a balloon ride in two to three days, but you may want to spend several more just soaking up the enchanting landscapes and enjoying the region's comfortable lodgings. Outdoor enthusiasts who like hiking, biking, or horseback riding will certainly want to allow extra time.

Though Ankara is not considered much of a vacation destination, it is home to some significant sights and monuments. You could spend a day seeing the highly regarded Museum of Anatolian Civilizations and the Anıtkabir, Atatürk's mausoleum, saving some time to explore the historic citadel area as well.

GETTING HERE AND AROUND

AIR TRAVEL

Air travel isn't much more expensive than bus travel, and flying to Central Anatolia saves a lot of time. Ankara's Esenboğa Airport is served by frequent flights from numerous Turkish cities, as well as direct flights from several European cities; Konya is served by frequent flights from Istanbul. The Cappadocia region has two airports—Kayseri and Nevşehir—with the majority of flights coming from Istanbul, though some arrive from İzmir and, in summer, from Antalya.

BUS TRAVEL

Cappadocia and Central Anatolia are well served by intercity buses, but the distances from other places you are likely to be visiting are long. The 10- to 12-hour trip from Istanbul to Cappadocia costs about 70 TL, while fares from Ankara (four to five hours) or Konya (three and a half to four hours) are around 35 TL–40 TL. In Cappadocia there are local minibuses connecting the towns, making it relatively easy to get around, at least in summer; service is less frequent in winter.

CAR TRAVEL

Once you're here, renting a car is a good idea because you'll probably be traveling around a lot. Highways in Central Anatolia are generally well maintained and lead to all the major sights. Minor roads, however, may be rough and full of potholes. On narrow, winding roads, look out for oncoming trucks whose drivers often don't stay on their own side, and be especially careful at night, when farm vehicles without proper running lights and animals may be on rural roads.

There are good roads between Istanbul and the main cities of Anatolia: Ankara, Konya, and Kayseri. However, truck traffic on the main highway from Istanbul to Ankara, a distance of 454 km (281 miles), can be heavy. Two long stretches of toll road (*ücretli geçiş*) linking Istanbul and

Ankara—E80 to beyond Düzce and E89 south from Gerede—provide some relief from the rigors of the other highways.

From Ankara, Konya is 261 km (162 miles) to the south, while Kayseri—the gateway to Cappadocia—is 312 km (194 miles) to the southeast.

You can also travel from Central Anatolia on major highways to the Mediterranean and Black Sea coasts: from Ankara, E90 (also known as Route 200) leads southwest toward Sivrihisar; continue southwest on E96 to Afyon, where you can pick up highways going south to Antalya or west to İzmir. Route E88/200 leads east out of Ankara and eventually connects with highways to the Black Sea coast.

TRAIN TRAVEL

The 2014 launch of a long-awaited high-speed train connecting Istanbul with Ankara and Konya should make getting to Central Anatolia by rail much faster and easier. The expected travel time is about three hours to Ankara and about five to Konya (train journeys on these routes were previously overnight). High-speed trains already run regularly between Ankara and Konya. A few regular-speed trains also operate in the region, including an overnight train linking Ankara and İzmir. The trip between Ankara and Kayseri takes about seven hours—considerably slower than traveling by bus. There is little to no train service between small towns in Central Anatolia.

RESTAURANTS

Central Anatolia is the one region in Turkey that does not touch water, so fish has to be trucked or flown in. Be prepared for a lot of meat served in various permutations, including kebabs and stews. In Cappadocia, popular specialties include lamb roasted in a tandır, or underground pit, and meat cooked in a testi, a type of earthenware vessel. In Konya you'll see *etli ekmek* (flatbread topped with ground lamb and sometimes cheese) as well as local dishes, such as okra soup. Main courses in the region are often preceded by a delicious array of mezes—most notably warm hummus served with *pastırma* (Turkish pastrami), the local specialty.

In Cappadocia and Ankara, restaurants that cater to tourists serve beer, wine, and liquor, including rakı. In Konya and other conservative towns, however, alcohol can be quite difficult to find. The inhabitants of Cappadocia have been making wine for thousands of years, though the modern revival of the industry is still somewhat in its fledgling stages. Of the local varietals, whites like the Emir tend to be better than reds, which include the Kalecik Karası. Vintners are also producing increasingly successful wines with grapes from other regions of Turkey, as well as with foreign ones like Syrah and Cabernet Sauvignon. Whatever you eat and drink, you'll likely dine in atmospheric surroundings—restored caravansaries, caves, Ottoman mansions, garden patios. In some traditional restaurants you'll sit on cushions on the floor, and your meal might be accompanied by live music.

Prices in the reviews are the average cost of a main course at dinner or if dinner is not served, at lunch.

HOTELS

Cappadocia is rightly famous for its cave hotels—indeed, staying in one is a quintessential experience here. Carved out of soft tufa rock, they range from homey inns decorated in traditional style to high-end boutique properties with contemporary design and large hotels with luxurious furnishings. Some have been occupied for hundreds or even thousands of years, and original architectural details add authenticity. Most visitors find troglodyte lodgings absolutely charming, but bear in mind that they really are caves; some may have little natural light, low ceilings, and occasional falling dust. Cave hotels can also involve numerous interconnecting levels with nary an elevator in sight—that's part of the fun but does require climbing. (Travelers with mobility issues are advised to contact a hotel before booking.) For those not wanting to stay in a cave, some hotels also offer "stone rooms" built using traditional masonry techniques, often with beautiful vaulted ceilings and decorative carvings.

For the most part, hotels in Konya and Ankara don't come close to matching the atmosphere of Cappadocia's unique accommodations, but there are a few interesting boutique hotels to be found among the large international chains.

Prices in the reviews the lowest cost of a standard double room in high season. For expanded reviews, visit Fodors.com.

TOURS

In Cappadocia, consider joining a tour or hiring a private guide for at least one day. Guides know the terrain and can lead you to places you might not otherwise find (such as hidden rock churches), filling you in on fascinating details about the geology of the region and its early inhabitants. Most daily tours follow one of several broad itineraries, with slight variations: Göreme Open-Air Museum, Uçhisar castle, and nearby valleys; Ihlara Valley, Derinkuyu underground city, and scenic viewpoints; or the Soğanlı Valleys and nearby points of interest. A number of companies also offer half- or full-day hikes through scenic spots like Rose Valley. With the exception of very high-end agencies, expect to pay about 120 TL–160 TL per person for a daylong group tour. Prices for private tours are about twice as much, running about 550 TL–600 TL for two people (there is usually a single supplement for one person). Hotels can make recommendations, or contact one of these companies directly.

Argeus. One of Cappadocia's best-regarded—and priciest—agencies, Argeus has 20 years of experience. It specializes in customized private tours but also organizes small group day trips (maximum eight people), one- and multiday mountain biking trips, plus airport shuttles. ☎ 384/341–4688 *in Ürgüp* ⊕ *www.argeus.com.tr.*

HtR Travel. With 15 years of experience, HtR Travel offers daily sightseeing tours of Cappadocia (maximum 18 people) at reasonable rates. It also arranges private hiking tours in the region, as well as tailor-made tours, and the guides are excellent. ☎ 384/341–5548 *in Ürgüp* ⊕ *www. htrturkeytours.com.*

Kirkit Voyage. Horseback riding, hiking, mountain biking, boating, camping, and other outdoor activities—offered as day trips or multi-day excursions—are the specialty of this agency, which also organizes sightseeing tours in Cappadocia. ☎ *384/511–3259 in Avanos* ⊕ *www.kirkit.com.*

Rock Valley Travel. Friendly, family-run Rock Valley Travel organizes private and small group day tours (maximum 12 people) as well as three-day trips to Mt. Nemrut and Urfa. The tours are good value and the guides are professional. ☎ *384/341–5819 in Ürgüp* ⊕ *www.rockvalleytravel.com.*

Fodor'sChoice ★ **Turkish Heritage Travel.** This well-regarded company organizes photo safaris, cooking classes, grape-harvesting excursions, and other unique outings aimed at introducing guests to authentic Turkish culture. Their knowledgeable, personal guides also lead more traditional group and private tours of Cappadocia— and there are no shopping stops. ☎ *384/271–2687 in Göreme* ⊕ *www.goreme.com.*

Ürgüp Travel. The knowledgeable, professional team at Ürgüp Travel runs good-quality outings around Cappadocia and beyond. Private tours, guided hikes, and cooking classes are also available. ☎ *384/341–5015 in Ürgüp* ⊕ *www.urguptravel.com.*

VISITOR INFORMATION

There are three government-run tourism information offices in the Cappadocia region. In the provincial capital of Nevşehir, you'll find one inside the former governor's mansion (✉ *Atatürk Bul.* ☎ *384/213–3659*); the others are in Ürgüp and Avanos (⇨ *see individual sections for details*). Ankara also has three tourism offices—at the airport, the train station, and in Gençlik Parkı—the first of which keeps longer hours. Konya's visitor office is located behind the Mevlâna Museum; the multilingual staff is knowledgeable and helpful regarding all sorts of inquiries.

CAPPADOCIA

Cappadocia comprises the triangle of land formed by the towns of Nevşehir to the west, Ürgüp to the east, and Avanos to the north. Inside this triangle is one of the most unusual natural landscapes you'll ever encounter. More than 10 million years ago, three volcanoes erupted, dropping lava, mud, and ash on the region. Over eons, the explosive products of Mt. Erciyes, Mt. Hasan, and Mt. Melendiz cooled and compressed to form tufa—a soft, porous rock easily worn by erosion. Water poured down, carving and separating giant ridges of this rock into gorgeous valleys. Wind whipped around the formations, further shaping them into elaborate pinnacles, cones, pillars, and mounds. Harder layers of rocklike basalt resisted erosion longer and often ended up perfectly balanced, like hats, on top of a tall cone. Oxidation gave the formations color, and then humans began to do their own carving and shaping.

Today, the region is full of so-called "fairy chimneys"—odd, unforgettable rock formations that collectively create a landscape so otherworldly that you'd be forgiven for thinking you were wandering around on

another planet. Hiking amidst these geological marvels can be a mystical experience for many people. Indeed, Cappadocia has an undeniable spiritual side, and its natural endowment is only part of the attraction.

The region is thought to have been first occupied by the Hatti and then by the Hittites (⇨ *see the boxed text in the Ankara section of this chapter*), who ruled much of Anatolia between about 1800 and 1200 BC and worshipped a pantheon of anthropomorphic gods. The area was later occupied by a series of regional states before Tiberius claimed Cappadocia as a province of Rome in AD 17. Early Christians, who more than anyone else left a human mark on Cappadocia, began settling in the region not long afterward.

The Christians who established secluded communities here apparently found the landscape suitable both to their aesthetic tastes and to their need to hide from persecution. They sat on Cappadocia's rock pillars for long periods of time in prayer and carved hundreds of churches into the soft rocks, decorating them with beautiful frescoes. You can still explore these churches, and by the end of a trip you won't be surprised when you duck into a nondescript cave entrance and find carved columns, a domed ceiling, and vivid scenes painted on the stone walls.

Arab raiders also came into the region sporadically between the 7th and 10th centuries, forcing inhabitants underground, where they renovated and expanded subterranean cities left by earlier peoples. It's believed that many underground complexes have yet to be discovered, and the true extent of some of the 40-odd ones that have been found to date is still unknown.

Cappadocia remains an unfamiliar place in other ways, too. Some local residents still travel between farms and shops in horse-drawn carts. Women dry strings of apricots and paprika by draping them on their houses and, during harvest season, boil enormous cauldrons of grape molasses over open fires. In the distance, minarets pierce the sky, silhouetted against distant mountains. Even the hotels—many of them inside caves—are decidedly exotic.

GETTING HERE AND AROUND

Several airlines operate direct flights from Istanbul to the city of Kayseri, about an hour's drive from the heart of Cappadocia. SunExpress flies there direct from İzmir multiple times a week; and, in summer, SunExpress and Pegasus Airlines generally operate one or two weekly flights each from Antalya. Flying into the Nevşehir airport gets you closer to Cappadocian towns; however, it only has direct service from Istanbul on Turkish Airlines and Pegasus Airlines, and the winter schedule is limited. Travel agencies can arrange a shuttle to take you from either airport to any hotel in the main towns for 20 TL–40 TL; most hotels will also arrange pickups for guests.

With the exception of Metro and Süha, most long-distance bus companies don't serve small towns here directly, so if you choose that mode of transport you may need to buy a ticket to Nevşehir and then transfer to a local bus. If you don't rent a car during your stay, you may end up passing through Nevşehir repeatedly as it is the hub for a number of local minibuses. Several daily minibuses also run between Avanos and Ürgüp, with a stop along the way in Göreme. Note that local buses tend to operate less frequently and/or keep shorter hours in winter.

Taxis within Cappadocian towns aren't expensive, but fares for travel between them add up. Expect to pay 10 TL–15 TL between Uçhisar and Göreme, around 35 TL from Göreme or Uçhisar to Ürgüp, and 40 TL or more from Uçhisar or Nevşehir to Avanos. All taxis have meters, but you or the driver may prefer to negotiate a flat rate for longer trips.

MUSEUM PASS CAPPADOCIA

The recently launched Museum Pass Cappadocia allows single entry over a 72-hour period into many of Cappadocia's most popular attractions: Göreme Open-Air Museum and the Dark Church, Zelve Open-Air Museum, Ihlara Valley, Derinkuyu underground city, Kaymaklı underground city, and Özkonak underground city. Priced at 45 TL (versus 77 TL if you pay each entry fee separately), it's a good deal if you plan on visiting most of the sights on your own rather than on guided tours, where entry fees are already included.

ÜRGÜP

300 km (180 miles) south of Ankara; 80 km (48 miles) west of Kayseri airport; 23 km (14 miles) east of Nevşehir.

Ürgüp is especially known these days for its charming small hotels, many of which are in restored cave houses and have views overlooking the town and the nearby cliffs. Some beautiful old mansions that were formerly owned by prominent local families—including Greeks, who were a significant presence in the area until the 1923 Greek-Turkish population exchange—have also been converted into hotels.

Downtown Ürgüp is a somewhat tacky jumble of buildings built up mostly for the tourism industry, but you'll find banks, money exchanges, travel agencies, carpet and trinket shops, and even a Turkish bath, along with a few low-key nightlife venues. During the winter months, certain hotels and restaurants in Ürgüp close, which means somewhat reduced options for travelers but a more tranquil atmosphere.

GETTING HERE AND AROUND

Ürgüp is not quite as close to the sights and scenic valleys as some other Cappadocian towns, so you may want to rent a car. Minibuses run regularly between Ürgüp and other towns in high season, less frequently in low season.

Ürgüp has a larger population than Göreme, Uçhisar, or other nearby villages; and the town itself has several distinct neighborhoods. From the Esbelli neighborhood, where many small hotels are located, it's a pleasant 10-minute downhill stroll to the town center—you may want to take a taxi when returning at night to avoid the steep climb. To reach Kayakapı Cave Suites and the surrounding neighborhood restoration project, on a cliff side overlooking the newer part of town, you will need a car or taxi.

ESSENTIALS

Visitor Information. ⊠ *Kayseri Cad. 37, inside park, Ürgüp* ☎ *384/341–4059.*

EXPLORING

Turasan Winery. Established in 1943, one of the region's largest wine producers offers tastings in the factory store, as well as brief tours of the production facilities and cellars. Turasan, having substantially expanded and improved its range in recent years, makes wines from both local grape varieties (namely the white Emir and red Kalecik Karası) and from foreign ones. Prices here are about 30% less than at a retail store. ⊠ *Çimenli Mevkii, Tevfik Fikret Cad. 6A–B, Ürgüp* ☎ *384/341–4961* ⊕ *www.turasan.com.tr* 🎫 *15 TL for factory/cellar tour and 3 tastings* ⊙ *Daily 8:30–sunset.*

WHERE TO EAT

$$$

TURKISH

Fodor'sChoice

★

✕ **Muti by Prokopia.** Run by a long-time restaurateur from Istanbul, Muti by Prokopia offers a diverse menu influenced by Ottoman cuisine, the cosmopolitan kitchens of Istanbul, and Turkey's Aegean region—all in sophisticated surroundings. Delicious starters include classic *mezes* with a twist, such as *halloumi* cheese wrapped in grilled eggplant. Main courses, like baked lamb shank cooked with quince and red wine, are excellent and portions are generous. The restaurant occupies several interconnected

Ballooning in Cappadocia

One of the best ways to appreciate Cappadocia's expansive, diverse landscape is from above. Hot-air balloon flights take off around sunrise (when the air is calmest) and last about an hour or an hour and a half. A skilled pilot can take you right into a valley, sailing through so that rock cones loom on either side, then climb the edge of a tall fairy chimney. The trip usually ends with a traditional champagne toast. Cappadocia is an ideal place to experience ballooning not only because of its spectacular scenery, but because the region's microclimate—with clement weather and at least 300 flying days per year—makes it one of the world's safest ballooning destinations. Flights are offered year-round, but April through November offer balmier temperatures and a lower probability of cancellation due to weather conditions.

Generally speaking, you should expect to pay about 590 TL for a long flight and about 420 TL for a shorter one; hotel transfers are included, and most companies offer some sort of complimentary refreshments before taking off. Hotels and tour agencies in Cappadocia often make high commissions on bookings. You won't necessarily save anything by making your own arrangements, but many operators do give a small discount if you pay in cash.

Balloon companies have mushroomed here in recent years, and competition is intense. Nonetheless, it's recommended that you choose an outfit based on reputation and safety record rather than going for the cheapest-priced option. The top-quality companies have the most experienced staff and also change their takeoff locations on a daily basis according to wind currents, to ensure passengers see as much as possible on their flight.

Ballooning over Cappadocia at Sunrise." — photo by rward, Fodors.com member

Contacts Butterfly Balloons. Small and personal, Butterfly Balloons has highly qualified pilots with American and European commercial pilot's licenses. Pilots have great rapport with passengers, who also benefit from generous legroom. ☎ 384/271–3010 in Göreme ⊕ www.butterflyballoons.com.

Cappadocia Voyager Balloons. Run by experienced professionals, Cappadocia Voyager Balloons has certified pilots and newer balloons than some competitors. Three flight categories, based on capacity and duration, are available. ⊠ Göreme ☎ 384/271–3030 ⊕ www.voyagerballoons.com.

Kapadokya Balloons. The oldest and largest balloon company in Cappadocia, Kapadokya Balloons has been in business since 1991 and prides itself on its experienced team and professionalism. ☎ 384/271–2442 in Göreme ⊕ www.kapadokyaballoons.com.

Royal Balloon. Working with some of the most experienced Turkish and foreign pilots in Cappadocia, Royal Balloon emphasizes boutique service and offers passengers a hot buffet breakfast. ☎ 384/271–3300 in Göreme ⊕ www.royalballoon.com.

rooms in a 250-year-old *kervan-saray*, with wooden ceilings and stone arches; in the summer, seating is in a pleasant courtyard. $ *Average main: 37 TL* ⊠ *Cumhuriyet Meydanı 26, Ürgüp* ☎ *384/341–5808* ⊕ *www.mutibyprokopia.com* ☞ *Reservations essential* ☾ *Closed Jan. and Feb.*

$$ ✕ **Old Greek House.** In the sleepy vil-
TURKISH lage of Mustafapaşa, about 5 km (3 miles) from Ürgüp, the Old Greek House serves delicious home-cooked specialties, including mezes, meat dishes such as *karnıyarık* (eggplant stuffed with tomatoes and ground meat), and homemade baklava. Portions are generous, and the set menus are a genuine feast. Seating is on cushions on the floor around low, round tables or at regular-height ones in the atmospheric, vine-covered central courtyard. The 250-year-old building—still with original frescoes on the stone walls and original paint on the wooden ceilings—doubles as a simple but comfortable inn. $ *Average main: 30 TL* ⊠ *Davutlu Mah. 12, Mustafapaşa, Ürgüp* ☎ *384/353–5306* ⊕ *www.oldgreekhouse.com* ☞ *Reservations essential.*

$$ ✕ **Şömine.** Right on Ürgüp's main square, this welcoming lair takes its
TURKISH name from the fireplace in the center that warms guests in winter; in summer, you can dine outside on the rooftop terrace. The menu focuses on regional specialties. Appetizers include warm hummus with *pastırma* (Turkish pastrami). For a main, try the *testi kebabı* (a meat and vegetable dish cooked in a clay vessel, which you break open yourself by whacking it with a large knife) or one of the *kiremit* stews baked in a terra-cotta casserole. $ *Average main: 25 TL* ⊠ *Cumhuriyet Meydanı 9, Ürgüp* ☎ *384/341–8442* ⊕ *www.sominerestaurant.com.*

$$$ ✕ **Ziggy Cafe.** The ambience at this Ürgüp favorite is especially inviting—
TURKISH picture attractive table arrangements, richly upholstered armchairs,
Fodor'sChoice wrought-iron lamps, and three open-air terraces with sofa-like seats
★ and stone-topped tables. The contemporary, Mediterranean-inspired menu, moreover, is a refreshing change from the heavy, meat-based fare typical of Central Anatolia. The mezes, such as char-grilled eggplant or cubed feta cheese and olives, are where Ziggy really shines. To sample a variety, try the reasonably priced tasting menu, which includes nine cold mezes, a hot starter, a main dish, and dessert. In a space below the restaurant, owner Nuray Suzan Yüksel sells her handmade jewelry. $ *Average main: 33 TL* ⊠ *Tevfik Fikret Cad. 24, Yunak Mah., Ürgüp* ⊕ *www.ziggycafe.com* ☞ *Reservations essential.*

WHERE TO STAY

$$ ☷ **Esbelli Evi.** Carved into a rocky hillside, one of Cappadocia's lon-
B&B/INN gest-established cave hotels has spacious, comfortable, spotlessly clean
Fodor'sChoice accommodations—often with beautiful natural color banding in the
★ volcanic-stone walls. **Pros:** extremely attentive staff; great for families; excellent value. **Cons:** closed in winter. $ *Rooms from: $150* ⊠ *Dolay Sok. 8, Esbelli Mah., Ürgüp* ☎ *384/341–3395* ⊕ *www.esbelli.com* 🛏 *4 rooms, 11 suites* ☾ *Closed Dec.–Mar.* ☷◯☷ *Breakfast.*

WORD OF MOUTH

"In Cappadocia we stayed at what was probably my favorite hotel of any I have ever been to—The Esbelli Evi. So many people on Fodors.com recommended this place—and we were not disappointed." —Ian

6

$$$ ⊞ **Fresco Cave Suites and Mansions.** Spread over three Ottoman mansions
HOTEL connected by courtyards and terraces, this appealing spot has both
cave and non-cave rooms—a few featuring small original frescoes and
painted floral moldings. **Pros:** elegant rooms; spacious, atmospheric
common areas; close to town center. **Cons:** rooms vary greatly in style
and features; can be warm and stuffy; no elevator. $ *Rooms from:*
$175 ⊠ *Esat Ağa Sok. 15, Musa Efendi Mah., Ürgüp* ☎ *384/341–6660*
⊕ *www.frescomansions.com* ⤴ *12 rooms, 5 suites* ✺ *Breakfast.*

$$$ ⊞ **Kayakapı Premium Caves.** This luxurious rock-cut hotel conveys a
HOTEL sense of the past through wooden floors and furnishings, rich Ana-
tolian textiles, traditional low sofas, and accents like framed caftans.
Pros: extremely spacious lodgings; modern touches like Nespresso
coffee makers; attentive service. **Cons:** hilltop location far from town
center, not reachable on foot; food could be better; limited common
areas and facilities while hotel is in development. $ *Rooms from: $152*
⊠ *Kuşçular Sok. 43, Kayakapı Mah., Ürgüp* ☎ *384/341–8877* ⊕ *www.*
kayakapi.com ⤴ *7 rooms, 22 suites* ✺ *Breakfast.*

$$$ ⊞ **Serinn House.** Sleek wood, designer furniture, sheepskin rugs on
B&B/INN stone floors, and glass-enclosed showers give these cave accommo-
Fodor's Choice dations looking onto a courtyard a true contemporary flair. **Pros:**
★ sophisticated yet unpretentious; highly personal service; outstanding
breakfast. **Cons:** low lighting in bathrooms; closed in winter. $ *Rooms*
from: $160 ⊠ *Esbelli Sok. 36, Esbelli Mah., Ürgüp* ☎ *384/341–6076*
⊕ *www.serinnhouse.com* ⤴ *6 rooms* ☉ *Closed Nov.–Apr.* ✺ *Breakfast.*

$$ ⊞ **Ürgüp Evi.** Poised atop a hill with wonderful views of Ürgüp and
B&B/INN the surrounding scenery, this friendly guesthouse has large, rustic
cave rooms with soft lighting, fireplaces, wooden floors with tribal
rugs, and comfortable beds; many have a cozy outdoor sitting area in
front. **Pros:** relaxed atmosphere; good for families. **Cons:** rather steep
uphill walk to hotel; somewhat limited room amenities (no TVs); bathrooms a bit outdated. $ *Rooms from: $130* ⊠ *Esbelli Mah. 54, Ürgüp*
☎ *384/341–3173* ⊕ *www.urgupevi.com.tr* ⤴ *10 rooms, 2 suites, 1*
house ✺ *Breakfast.*

$$$ ⊞ **Yunak Evleri.** Centered within an old Greek mansion, the stylish cave
HOTEL rooms here have kilim-covered stone floors, wrought-iron beds, and
luxurious modern bathrooms; all have balconies or a shared terrace.
Pros: sophisticated atmosphere; inviting public spaces; alcoholic drinks
available on the honor system. **Cons:** views from rooms vary; lots of
steps to some rooms. $ *Rooms from: $185* ⊠ *Balcı Sok. 22, Yunak*
Mah., Ürgüp ☎ *384/341–6920* ⊕ *www.yunak.com* ⤴ *25 rooms, 14*
suites ✺ *Breakfast.*

GÖREME

10 km (6 miles) northeast of Nevşehir; 9 km (5½ miles) northwest of
Ürgüp.

Bustling Göreme offers the most options for hotels, dining, nightlife,
shopping, and other commercial enterprises. Back in the early days
of tourism in Cappadocia, the town was more or less inundated with
backpackers, who still find inexpensive accommodations and laid-back

bars and cafés. In recent years, though, a number of excellent midrange and higher-end hotels have opened, too. The main reason to be here is to see some of the most spectacular fairy chimney valleys in the region and the nearby Göreme and Zelve open-air museums, both UNESCO World Heritage sites and two must-sees in Cappadocia. The Göreme "museum," which tends to be packed with tourists, is a cluster of fairy chimneys famous for their spectacular cave churches. Somewhat less crowded Zelve is a valley, which provides a glimpse into how people once lived in the rock-cut communities.

GETTING HERE AND AROUND

Small yet centrally located, Göreme is the most convenient base for exploring Cappadocia if you don't have a car. The Göreme Open-Air Museum is a pleasant 1½-km (1-mile) walk from the town; to get to Zelve, another 6 km (4 miles) past the Göreme museum, take a taxi, rent a scooter, or join a day tour.

Some of the area's most beautiful valleys and hiking trails begin just at the outskirts of Göreme. Although the town itself is somewhat hilly (like most of Cappadocia), it's compact and easily navigated on foot.

EXPLORING

Fodor'sChoice **Göreme Open-Air Museum.** *See the highlighted Cappadocia feature in*
★ *this chapter.*

Zelve Open-Air Museum. *See the highlighted Cappadocia feature in this chapter.*

WHERE TO EAT

$$$ ✕ **A'la Turca.** One of Göreme's more upscale restaurants, A'la Turca
TURKISH serves a delicious array of cold *mezes* and warm appetizers, including traditional hummus with Turkish pastrami. Stylishly presented main courses tend to be heavy on meat, whether in classic kebabs, *köfte*, or grilled steaks and chops, but there are also a few seafood items on the menu. For dessert, don't miss the walnut-stuffed dried apricots and figs cooked in grape syrup. The decor—terra-cotta-tile floors with kilims, white-tablecloth service—is elegant but not overdone, and there's a roof terrace open in summer. $ *Average main: 38 TL* ✉ *Müze Cad., Gaferli Mah.* ☎ *384/271–2882* ⊕ *www.alaturca.com.tr* ⌂ *Reservations essential.*

$$ ✕ **Orient Restaurant.** The menu at this longtime Göreme restaurant is
TURKISH extensive and diverse. Typical mezes and grilled kebabs are served, as well as a range of steak and lamb options, chicken with spinach or a saffron sauce, and even pastas. But the best deal is the four-course set menu, with several choices of appetizers, mains, and desserts that provide excellent food at an unbeatable value. The lanterns hanging from the traditional wooden ceilings and the carved stone walls decorated with copper trays create an ambience that's attractive and cozy. $ *Average main: 28 TL* ✉ *Adnan Menderes Cad. 3* ☎ *384/271–2346* ⊕ *www. orientrestaurant.net.*

$$$ ✕ **Seten Restaurant.** Housed in a magnificent old mansion at the top of
TURKISH Göreme's hotel hill, Seten provides a classy setting in which to enjoy a
Fodor'sChoice range of top-notch mezes and delicious mains. Standout dishes include
★ *imam bayıldı* (braised stuffed eggplant), Circassian-style chicken, and

Continued on page 374

ROCK OF AGES
UNEARTHING HOLY CAPPADOCIA

A fantasy come true, Cappadocia's phantasmagorical landscape of rock pinnacles, or "fairy chimneys," is one of Turkey's most otherworldly sights. A natural hideout—thanks to Mother Nature's chiseling tools of wind and water—the region became a sort of promised land for Anatolia's earliest Christians. Over the course of the 6th to 12th centuries, these early Cappadocian inhabitants incised the fantastic escarpments of Göreme and Zelve with a honeycomb of cave churches. Today you can trace the saga of the early Christians' religious faith by exploring this spectacular setting. As the first monks might have proclaimed: You have to believe it to see it!

Opposite: Cappadocia. Top: Göreme National Park

AN EARLY CHRISTIAN WONDERLAND

Remote and inaccessible, Cappadocia seemed custom-made for early Christian communities, whose members erected their churches in hollowed-out caves and expanded vast underground cities to hide from enemies and live reclusive monastic lives.

The story of Cappadocia begins more than ten million years ago, when three volcanoes began a geological symphony that dropped lava, mud, and ash over the region. Over eons, frequent eruptions of Mt. Erciyes, Mt. Hasan, and Mt. Melendiz covered considerable parts of the land with tufa—a porous rock layer formed of volcanic ash—over which lava spread at various stages of hardening.

Erosion by rain, snow, and wind created soaring stone "fairy chimneys," surrealistic shapes of cones, needles, pillars, and pyramids, not unlike the looming pinnacles of Arizona's Monument Valley. As time went on, earthquakes added valleys and rivers (mostly long-vanished) and slashed rifts into the fragile tufa. Depending on the variable consistency of the rock, the changes occurred more or less violently, with utterly fantastic results.

A REAL RUBBLE-ROUSER

Fast forward some millennia. Persecuted by authorities and often on the run from invading armies (Cappadocia was a frontier province), early Christians found the region's cliffs, rock pinnacles, and tufa caves ideal for the construction of their secluded colonies. Within a few hundred years of the death of Jesus, a regional bishopric had been established in nearby Kayseri (then Caesarea).

By the 4th century the number-one industry in the region was prayer, and the early recluses carved dwellings into Cappodocia's malleable stone, using simple tools. The ease of construction set a fashion that quickly led to the formation of anchorite colonies. These early monastic communities deftly combined the individuality of meditation with the communal work favored by St. Basil.

Above: Rock formations (chimneys) in the Göreme Valley

THE WORD MADE ROCK

The worship of God remained of uppermost importance here, and cave chapels and churches proliferated, especially throughout the Göreme Valley. When Arab raiders first swept through the region in the 7th and 8th centuries, large numbers of Christians sought refuge in rocky hide-outs and underground cities like Derinkuyu and Kaymaklı, which grew sufficiently large to house populations of up to 20,000 people.

After the Isaurian dynasty of Byzantine emperors repulsed the Arabs in 740, hollowed-out churches began to appear above ground. Reflecting contemporary Byzantine architectural styles, they were decorated with geometrical paintings. Following Empress Theodora's restoration of the use of holy imagery in the 9th century, churches were given increasingly ambitious frescoes. Many of these were painted in color schemes that rivaled the yellow, pink, and russet hues of their rock surroundings.

WHAT CREATED CAPPADOCIA'S "FAIRY CHIMNEYS"?

The volcanoes that formed Cappadocia are inactive now, but the most recent may have erupted just 8,000 years ago; Neolithic humans depicted the eruption in cave dwellings at Çatalhöyük (near present-day Konya). Nature continues to sculpt the landscape of Cappadocia. In the future, it is likely that some formations now visible will have turned to dust, and other forms will have been separated from the mountains, providing new experiences for tomorrow's travelers.

Top: Göreme Open-Air Museum.
Bottom: Rock homes, Göreme Valley

GÖREME: A ROCKBOUND HEAVEN

A UNESCO World Heritage Site, the Göreme Açık Hava Müzesi (Göreme Open-Air Museum) is a must-see for its amazing landscape and churches. These rock-hewn holy sanctuaries may be *in* the earth but they are not *of* it.

While Cappadocia is sprinkled with hundreds of cave churches—most built between the 10th and 12th centuries, though some as early as the 6th century—the best are found in the open-air museum at Göreme. Many Göreme churches are built in an inscribed Greek cross plan, a common Byzantine design, wherein all four arms of the church are equal in length.

The central dome almost always features a depiction of Christ Pantocrator ("Omnipotent"). Though dictated in part by Cappadocia's landscape, the small size and intimate feel of Göreme's rock-cut churches was also deliberate: the monastic community living here designed them not as houses of worship for the public but as chapels where members of the community could engage in solitary prayer and worship of specific saints.

EARTH AS ART

Most churches were commissioned by local donors who hired teams of professional artists—some local and some brought from as far away as Constantinople—to paint elaborate frescoes of scenes from the Old and New Testaments and the lives of the saints.

Visible in places where frescoes have peeled off, underlying geometric designs, crosses, and other symbols were painted directly onto the rock walls in red ochre. It is thought that these decorations were made when a church was first carved out of the rock, in order to consecrate the space. Sometime later, professional artists then painted their detailed frescoes on top of these designs. Note that the eyes of some of the figures have been scratched out, probably much later by Muslims who believed that visually representing human beings was blasphemous.

Above: Göreme Valley. Photo by yversace, Fodors.com member. Opposite: Elmalı Kilise (Church with the Apple).

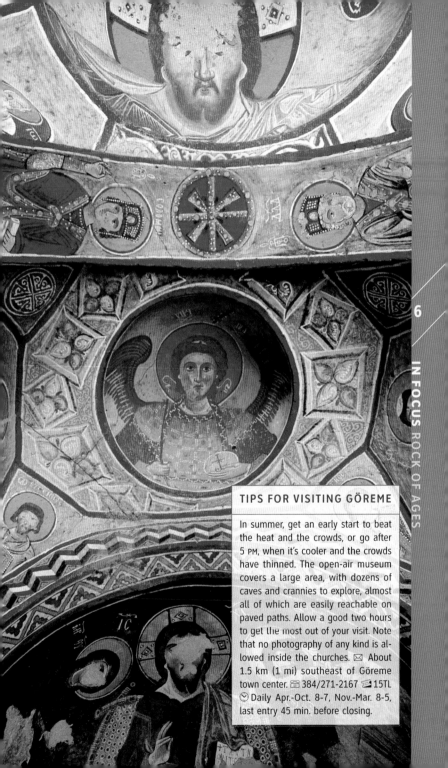

TIPS FOR VISITING GÖREME

In summer, get an early start to beat the heat and the crowds, or go after 5 PM, when it's cooler and the crowds have thinned. The open-air museum covers a large area, with dozens of caves and crannies to explore, almost all of which are easily reachable on paved paths. Allow a good two hours to get the most out of your visit. Note that no photography of any kind is allowed inside the churches. ⊠ About 1.5 km (1 mi) southeast of Göreme town center. ☎ 384/271-2167 🎟15TL ⊙ Daily Apr.-Oct. 8-7, Nov.-Mar. 8-5, last entry 45 min. before closing.

WHAT TO SEE AT THE GÖREME OPEN-AIR MUSEUM

Fresco of St. George and St. Theodorus killing the dragon in Yılanlı Kilise.

1 Convent & Monastery. After you enter the site, you'll see a large chimney to your left: this housed a six-story convent, which had a kitchen and refectory on the lower levels and a chapel on the third; large millstones lay ready to block the narrow passages in times of danger. Opposite is a monastery with the same plan. Unfortunately, these structures were deemed unsafe and are closed to visitors.

2 Elmalı Kilise (Church with the Apple). Accessed through a tunnel, this 11th-century church has wonderfully preserved frescoes of biblical scenes and portraits of saints; red and gray tones predominate. There are an impressive nine domes: eight small and one large; the largest shows Christ Pantocrator "on His heavenly throne." You can see the red-ochre geometric designs and Maltese crosses where the frescoes have peeled off.

Elmalı Kilise (detail of fresco)

3 Barbara Şapeli (Chapel of St. Barbara). Above the Elmalı Kilise, this chapel has only a few frescoes, including Christ Pantocrator and St. Barbara. Far more interestingly, most of the chapel is decorated with red ochre symbols painted on the rock, including geometric designs and some unusual, almost whimsical, creatures.

4 Yılanlı Kilise (Snake Church/Church of St. Onuphrius). Small but intriguing, this church takes its Turkish name from the scene on the left wall depicting St. George slaying the dragon, which here—as in many Cappadocian churches—takes the form of a snake. More unusual is the story of St. Onuphrius, on the right wall of the church: the naked saint is depicted with both a beard and breasts. While the official story says that St. Onuphrius was a pious hermit who lived in Egypt, another version has it that the saint was a loose woman who repented, embraced Christianity, and was given a beard.

5 Refectory/Kitchen. You can still picture the huge rock-carved dining table here packed at mealtimes with priests. The table could seat 40 to 50 people; carved into the opposite wall are niches for wine making. There are several kitchens in Göreme, but this refectory (near the Yılanlı Kilise) is the largest.

6 Karanlık Kilise (Dark Church). Entrance to this church, which was extensively restored by UNESCO, costs an extra 8 TL, because of the exceptional group of frescoes. Vibrant scenes, dominated by deep blue colors, decorate the walls and domed ceiling; the frescoes have retained their brilliant colors due to the structure of the church, which lets in little light (hence the name). The frescoes show scenes from the Old and New Testaments; the Crucifixion scene is particularly intense.

7 Çarıklı Kilise (Church of the Sandal). Climb up a metal ladder to reach this church, named after the footprints (some might say indentations) on the floor below the Ascension fresco; some believe these to be casts of Jesus' own footprints. The beautiful frescoes in this 11th-century church have been restored and portray a similar narrative cycle to those in the Karanlık Kilise. Note also

Karanlık Kilise
(Dark Church)
6

Çarıklı Kilise
(Church of the Sandal) **7**

Yemekhane
(Refectory/Kitchen)
5

Azize Katerina Kilise
(St. Catherine Church)

Kızlar Manastırı
(Convent & Monastery)
1

Yılanlı Kilise
(Snake Church) **4**

Barbara Şapeli
(Chapel of St. Barbara) **3**

Tokalı Kilise
(Church with
the Buckle)
8
↓

Aziz Basil Kilisesi
(St. Basil Church)

Elmalı Kilise
(Church with the Apple)
2

the geometric and floral patterns between the frescoes.

8 Tokalı Kilise (Church with the Buckle). Don't miss this church, across from the main museum area and a short way down the road toward Göreme (use the same entrance ticket). The oldest church in the open-air museum, and one of the largest and most impressive, it has high ceilings and brilliant blue colors. It's made up of an "Old Church" and a "New Church." The former was built in the early 10th century, and less than a century later it became the vaulted atrium of the "New Church," which was dug deeper into the rock; both sections have well-preserved frescoes depicting the life of Christ. This is the only church in Göreme in which the narrative scenes take place in chronological order. The church is to remain open while it undergoes restoration.

Left: Interior of Çarıklı Kilise, Christian frescoes dating from the 11th century AD.
Right: Murals from Tokalı Kilise

GREAT HIKES

One of the most rewarding walks from Göreme is through the **Rose Valley** (Güllüdere), where cave entrances lead to multistory, ornately decorated churches with columns that are two or three stories high. Roman graves, now unreachable, are adorned with Christian crosses and sit high upon eroded fairy chimneys. A hike through the valley often ends up at **Paşabağı**, a great monastic settlement of fairy chimneys. There are also spectacular hikes through **Love Valley** (Aşk Vadisi), perhaps named for the preponderance of phallus-like rock protrusions.

Though farther afield, the lush **Ihlara Valley** (see the section in this chapter) also hosts a wealth of rock-carved churches, which are an interesting contrast to those at Göreme because they were carved and decorated not by professional artists, as in Göreme, but by local monks living in the remote valley. The liturgical cycle depicted in the frescoes is somewhat abridged and the style more improvised. There are occasionally even spelling errors, such as in the Kokar Kilise, where the abbreviation of Jesus' name is misspelled with the Greek letters HC instead of IC.

ZELVE'S CAVE DWELLINGS

In typical Cappadocian fashion, humans improved on Nature's work to create Zelve, a village of rock-hewn houses that even Fred Flintstone would have envied.

While the prizes at Göreme are the fresco-decorated churches, the outdoor Zelve Açık Hava Müzesi (Zelve Open-Air Museum) provides a fascinating look at how people lived in fairy-chimney communities. Zelve was a center of Christian monastic life in the 9th through 13th centuries, and the town was inhabited until the early 1950s, when erosion and cracking began causing slabs of rock to fall and villagers were moved out of the hundreds of cave dwellings.

The site is only about 2,145 feet long, but there's plenty to explore. The valley is made up of several uneven, naturally carved rows of fairy chimneys. These and just about every spare rock face shelter hundreds of dwellings that vary in size—some are just simple cavelike openings and others are multistory houses with rooms on several floors linked by stairs carved deep inside the rocks. There's also a rock-cut mosque and several small churches. Some of the structures have collapsed and giant pieces of carved ceiling lie upside down on the ground.

Be prepared to climb around, and definitely bring a flashlight or you won't be able to explore some of the most interesting and extensive dwellings. You can probably see the whole place in a little over an hour, but you could easily spend more time.

> ✉ 6 km (4 mi) northeast of the Göreme Open-Air Museum, 3 km (2 mi) off the road to Avanos.
>
> ☎ 384/271-3535 💳 8TL
>
> 🕐 Daily, Apr.-Oct. 8-7, Nov.-Mar. 8-5, last entry 45 min. before closing.

stuffed squash blossoms. Cooked to perfection and served in generous portions, the signature "Seten-style kebab"—eggplant and chicken or lamb roasted vertically on a skewer in a traditional brick oven so the juices of the two mix—is also not to be missed. Seating is in small, intimate rooms or outside in summer $ *Average main: 32 TL* ⊠ *Aydınlı Sok. 42, Aydınlı Mah.* ☎ *384/271–3025* ⊕ *www.setenrestaurant.com* ≋ *Reservations essential.*

> **TAKE A FLASHLIGHT**
>
> Take a flashlight, or better yet, a headlamp, to explore many of the rock-cut churches, underground cities, and cave dwellings. Small hotels will often lend you a one; if you hire a guide make sure to ask if they can supply equipment.

WHERE TO STAY

$$$$ **Anatolian Houses.** Beautifully set among the fairy chimneys, this
HOTEL   romantic retreat has junior and multiroom suites that are notable for their plush decor—sometimes with traditional accents, sometimes more contemporary. **Pros:** luxurious, pampering atmosphere. **Cons:** a bit over the top; given the price, service could be better; rooms can be warm and stuffy due to poor ventilation and lack of air-conditioning. $ *Rooms from: $312* ⊠ *Cevizler Sok. 32, Gaferli Mah.* ☎ *384/271–2463* ⊕ *www.anatolianhouses.com.tr* ➳ *33 suites* ⊙ *Breakfast.*

$$ **Aydınlı Cave House.** Mustafa Demirci converted his centuries-old fam-
B&B/INN   ily home into a picturesque guesthouse and has since taken over the place next door, too: both offer simple accommodations with wood and wrought-iron furniture, antique items, and travertine-lined bathrooms. **Pros:** hospitable owner and staff; amazing views from breakfast area; slightly less far up the hill than some lodgings. **Cons:** lots of stairs to upper-level rooms and breakfast area; a few bathrooms small and only separated from room with curtain. $ *Rooms from: $105* ⊠ *Aydınlı Sok. 12, Aydınlı Mah.* ☎ *384/271–2263* ⊕ *www.thecavehotel.com* ➳ *6 rooms, 8 suites* ⊙ *Breakfast.*

$$$ **Cappadocia Cave Suites.** Comfortable, elegantly designed rooms—
HOTEL   many of which are quirkily shaped and carved from rock—combine antiques, old-fashioned wrought-iron beds, and folk-art spreads with modern conveniences like satellite TVs, kettles for making tea or coffee, and (in most cases) Jacuzzis. **Pros:** luxurious feel; inviting public spaces with layout that allows for privacy; attentive staff. **Cons:** lots of steps to reach some rooms and common areas; restaurant/breakfast area feels rather impersonal. $ *Rooms from: $180* ⊠ *Ünlü Sok. 19, Gaferli Mah.* ☎ *384/271–2800* ⊕ *www.cappadociacavesuites.com* ➳ *22 rooms, 14 suites* ⊙ *Breakfast.*

$$ **Kelebek Hotel.** One of Göreme's longest-standing hotels—immensely
HOTEL   popular for both its cozy atmosphere and personal service—Kelebek
Fodor'sChoice   caters to travelers on different budgets, offering accommodations rang-
★   ing from small, somewhat basic cave rooms to spacious, antiques-filled cave and stone-built suites with bathtubs and fireplaces. **Pros:** good value; young, friendly feel; great views from the rooftop bar-restaurant. **Cons:** hotel is a longish uphill walk from town center; some lower-category rooms noisy due to proximity to common areas; poor or non-existent Wi-Fi in some rooms. $ *Rooms from: $90* ⊠ *Yavuz Sok. 1,*

Aydınlı Mah. ☎ *384/271–2531* ⊕ *www.kelebekhotel.com* ⇆ *22 rooms, 14 suites* ❙❀❙ *Breakfast.*

$$ ❏ **Kısmet Cave House.** At this lovely family-run spot in a somewhat qui-
B&B/INN eter part of Göreme, each carefully decorated room is named after a different flower, which features in colorful paintings and wooden fur-niture. **Pros:** extraordinary hospitality; inspired decor; intimate feel; dinner can be served on request. **Cons:** rooms aren't so large; ground-floor ones can be a bit noisy, no views. $ *Rooms from: $98* ✉ *Kağnı Yolu 9* ☎ *384/271–2416* ⊕ *www.kismetcavehouse.com* ⇆ *7 rooms, 1 suite* ❙❀❙ *Breakfast.*

$$ ❏ **Koza Cave Hotel.** Run by an exceptionally friendly local family, Koza
B&B/INN Cave Hotel's charming cave rooms are centered around a small court-yard with amazing views from terraces on several different levels. **Pros:** warm, obliging hosts; character-filled rooms. **Cons:** steep walk up from town; no doors (only curtains or archways) separate some rooms from bathrooms; breakfast a bit basic. $ *Rooms from: $105* ✉ *Çakmaklı Sok. 49, Aydınlı Mah.* ☎ *384/271–2466* ⊕ *www.kozacavehotel.com* ⇆ *7 rooms, 3 suites* ❙❀❙ *Breakfast.*

$$ ❏ **Sultan Cave Suites.** High on one of Göreme's hills, this hotel offers
HOTEL clean, comfortable cave and stone rooms that are simply decorated; wooden or stone floors are covered with kilims, wrought-iron beds are topped with embroidered spreads, and old-fashioned furnishings abound. **Pros:** good value; welcoming, professional staff; some suites have balconies; best breakfast in Cappadocia. **Cons:** steep uphill walk from town center; dim natural and artificial lighting in some cave rooms; limited room amenities. $ *Rooms from: $105* ✉ *Aydınlı Sok. 40, Aydınlı Mah.* ☎ *384/271–3023* ⊕ *www.sultancavesuites.com* ⇆ *21 junior suites, 9 suites* ❙❀❙ *Breakfast.*

UÇHISAR

7 km (4 miles) east of Nevşehir; 3 km (2 miles) southwest of Göreme.

A lovely little town on a hill, built around a huge fairy chimney known as Uçhisar Castle, Uçhisar has some of the nicest places to stay in Cap-padocia. There are carpet shops and trinket stalls near the base of the castle, but the town still feels calmer and a bit more residential than Göreme, with clustered stone houses overlooking the valleys. From here, it's easy to take off for a walk through Pigeon Valley (Güvercin-lik Vadisi), so named for the birds the villagers traditionally raised in distinctive-looking cotes lodged in the walls of the valley.

GETTING HERE AND AROUND
Despite being fairly central, Uçhisar is less well served by minibuses than other nearby destinations; especially during the low season, it can be difficult getting to and from the town without a car. Once you're in Uçhisar, however, restaurants, hotels, and shops are conveniently located within walking distance of one another. The main attraction, Uçhisar Castle, is no more than a stone's throw from any hotel; and some hiking trails can be accessed from the edge of town.

EXPLORING

Uçhisar Kalesi (*Uçhisar Castle*). Uçhisar Kalesi is not so much a "castle," as its Turkish name implies, but the highest fairy chimney in Cappadocia. It was used as a fortress in the late Byzantine and early Ottoman periods, and later inhabited by the locals. The striking formation is riddled with rock-cut dwellings, giving it a Swiss-cheese look, but it was evacuated in the 1960s when erosion put everything in danger of collapse and the structure was declared a disaster zone (residents were moved to safer homes in the shadow of the giant rock). There's a great view of the town and the valleys from the top—though you'll have to do a good bit of climbing to get there—and it's a beautiful spot from which to watch the sunset. ✉ *Near center of town, Uçhisar* 🎫 *5 TL* ⏲ *Summer, daily 6 am–10 pm; winter, daily 8–4:30.*

WHERE TO EAT

$$ TURKISH 🍴 **Center Restaurant.** It's far from fancy, but this unpretentious local favorite on the town square is one of Uçhisar's best places for reliably good food at fairly reasonable prices. Portions are generous, and even staples like *çoban salatası* (shepherd's salad) are above average. The limited menu consists of a few hot starters and salads along with simple mains—mostly grilled meats and variations on spaghetti. In warm weather, seating is in a shady garden; in winter, diners move inside by a fireplace. [$] *Average main: 23 TL* ✉ *Belediye Parkı, Uçhisar* ☎ *384/219–3117.*

$$$ TURKISH 🍴 **Seki Restaurant.** Offering splendid views, this restaurant in Argos in Cappadocia hotel (⇨ *Where to Stay*) features contemporary adaptations of Turkish dishes that bring together local ingredients and international cooking techniques. Creative appetizers include a deconstructed version of traditional *imam bayıldı* (braised stuffed eggplant) served with chunks of lamb, and a delectable chard-wrapped duck confit with stewed apricots and roasted almonds. Tender veal cheek served with white bean stew stands out among the well-executed mains. A vast wine list has an extensive Turkish selection as well as some foreign vintages. With white tablecloths, candlelight, and low music playing, the ambience is upscale yet cozy and romantic. [$] *Average main: 45 TL* ✉ *Argos in Cappadocia, Aşağı Mah. Kayabaşı Sok. 23, Uçhisar* ☎ *384/219–3130* 🌐 *www.seki.com.tr* ✍ *Reservations essential.*

WHERE TO STAY

$$$$ HOTEL Fodor's Choice ★ 🏨 **Argos in Cappadocia.** Exceptional service, a spectacular location, and accommodations that meld sophisticated yet understated contemporary design with lovely local touches make Argos one of Cappadocia's best hotels. ⇨ **Pros:** tranquil atmosphere; inviting public spaces; first-rate service; magnificent views over Pigeon Valley. **Cons:** you won't want to leave; some cave rooms have little natural light or ventilation; hotel layout has many stairs and lots of twists and turns. [$] *Rooms from: $255* ✉ *Aşağı Mah. Kayabaşı Sok. 23, Uçhisar* ☎ *384/219–3130* 🌐 *www.argosincappadocia.com* 🛏 *36 rooms, 17 suites* 🍴 *Breakfast.*

$$ HOTEL 🏨 **Kale Konak Cave Hotel.** Occupying three old houses joined by a courtyard and underground tunnels, the charming Kale Konak promises the intimacy of a small guesthouse and the professional service of a larger hotel. **Pros:** central location just steps from Uçhisar Castle; splendid

terrace views; accommodating owner and staff; an oasis of calm. **Cons:** few rooms have views; little natural light in cave rooms; maze of stairways and passageways require lots of climbing. $ *Rooms from: $145* ✉ *Kale Sok. 9, Uçhisar* 🕾 *384/219–2828* ⊕ *www.kalekonak.com* ⤳ *11 rooms, 3 suites* ⦿| *Breakfast.*

$$$ ⊡ **Les Maisons de Cappadoce.** French architect Jacques Avizou has
RENTAL   restored 16 houses—some carved out of caves, others built from local
Fodor'sChoice   stone—to create one of the most beautiful places to stay in Cappa-
★   docia. **Pros:** lovely atmosphere; magnificent views; houses provide privacy and a less touristy experience; great for families. **Cons:** some studios are smallish; lodgings are far from reception; some bathrooms are a bit basic. $ *Rooms from: $195* ✉ *Belediye Meydanı 6, Uçhisar, Nevşehir* 🕾 *384/219–2813* ⊕ *www.cappadoce.com* ⤳ *5 studios, 11 houses* ⦿| *Breakfast.*

$$$$ ⊡ **Museum Hotel.** This cluster of cave and stone building accommoda-
HOTEL   tions connected by labyrinthine passages is a work of art; befitting the name, it is filled with the owner's impressive collection of antiques, ranging from metalwork to Ottoman caftans to carpets. **Pros:** authentic vintage decor; beautiful public areas and scenery. **Cons:** some cave rooms can be dark; service could be better, given the price; lots of steps and narrow passageways to navigate. $ *Rooms from: $358* ✉ *Tekelli Mah. 1, Uçhisar, Nevşehir* 🕾 *384/219–2220* ⊕ *www.museumhotel.com. tr* ⤳ *7 rooms, 23 suites* ⦿| *Breakfast.*

$$$ ⊡ **Taşkonaklar.** Five houses sharing a grassy courtyard have been care-
HOTEL   fully restored to evoke an authentic sense of place while providing modern amenities; the cave and stone guest rooms inside, most with fireplaces, are elegant but not overdone. **Pros:** spectacular views overlooking Pigeon Valley; attentive, professional service; attractive rooms. **Cons:** hotel somewhat lacking vibrancy; little natural light in cave rooms. $ *Rooms from: $156* ✉ *Gedik Sok. 8, Uçhisar* 🕾 *384/219–3001* ⊕ *www.taskonaklar.com* ⤳ *6 rooms, 14 suites* ⦿| *Breakfast.*

ORTAHISAR

5 km (3 miles) southwest of Nevşehir; 6 km (4 miles) southeast of Ürgüp.

A rather sleepy farming village overlooking scenic Pancarlık Valley, Ortahisar was traditionally famous for its underground caves where fruit was stored. Although it has recently gotten into the tourism business, with the opening of a few small hotels and places to eat, Ortahisar is still a functioning village and retains a more pleasantly authentic atmosphere than most other area towns. Visitors tend to appreciate the off-the-beaten-path vibe but should be aware that dining options and other services for travelers are limited, and the place can feel a bit deserted at night. Ortahisar, meaning "middle fortress," is named after its main landmark, a large rock outcropping/fairy chimney that was once used as a fortress.

GETTING HERE AND AROUND

Aside from a minibus route that links Ortahisar with Ürgüp, transportation options are rather limited, so it's best to have a car here. Most tourist-oriented establishments are in walking distance of the castle.

EXPLORING

Ortahisar Kalesi. Recently reopened after years of restoration, Ortahisar's 86-meter (282-foot) "castle" is Cappadocia's tallest fairy chimney, though it appears lower than Uçhisar's because it is located in a slight depression rather than atop a hill. As in Uçhisar, the castle has been carved out into a honeycomb of rooms and tunnels. Formerly used both as a fortress and for dwellings, it offers splendid views of the surrounding area. ⚠ Getting to the top requires climbing up some extremely steep metal staircases and ladders. ⊠ *Center of town, Ortahisar* ⊠ *2 TL* ☉ *Summer daily 8:30–7; winter, daily 8:30–5.*

Ortahisar Kültür Müzesi (*Ortahisar Culture Museum*). The region's only ethnographic museum showcases the traditional lifestyle and culture of Cappadocian villages. A dozen rooms house dioramas depicting local customs and scenes from daily life, such as a bride's henna party. Although small and funded privately, it has informative, well-written English texts plus an on-site restaurant. ⊠ *Cumhuriyet Meydanı 15, Ortahisar* ☎ *384/343–3344* ⊕ *www.culturemuseum.com* ⊠ *5 TL* ☉ *Summer daily 9–7; winter daily 9–5.*

WHERE TO STAY

$$$
HOTEL
Fodor's Choice
★
🛏 **Hezen Cave Hotel.** This enchanting hotel has wonderful views of Ortahisar castle from several lovely terraces, tasteful cave rooms that are simple yet stylish, and down-to-earth service that makes guests feel right at home. **Pros:** delightful guest rooms and common spaces; welcoming staff; great views; delicious breakfasts. **Cons:** rather far from most sightseeing and dining options. $ *Rooms from: $180* ⊠ *Tahir Bey Sok. 87, Ortahisar* ☎ *384/343–3005* ⊕ *www.hezenhotel.com* ⊅ *8 rooms, 6 suites* ⦿ *Breakfast.*

$$
B&B/INN
🛏 **Queens Cave Cappadocia.** Set amidst a lush garden and flower-accented patio near the bottom of one of Ortahisar's valleys, Queens Cave has an intimate, off-the-beaten path setting. **Pros:** secluded, relaxing setting; stylish rooms; great food. **Cons:** fairly isolated and reached on rough, unpaved roads; minimal storage space in some rooms; limited privacy between some rooms and bathrooms. $ *Rooms from: $118* ⊠ *Dere Sok. 24–26, Ortahisar* ☎ *384/343–3040* ⊕ *www.queenshotelcappadocia.com* ⊅ *10 rooms* ☉ *Closed late Nov.–late Mar.* ⦿ *Breakfast.*

AVANOS

17 km (11 miles) northeast of Nevşehir; 10 km (6 miles) north of Göreme; 12 km (7 miles) northeast of Uçhisar.

Avanos is a fun little town on the Kızılırmak (Red River), so named for the color of the clay that lines its banks. A wobbly suspension footbridge crosses the river near the busy town square and a couple of cafés are located on the waterfront (there are bridges for vehicles a short way up- and downriver). Pottery making vies with tourism as the biggest industry here. Using clay from the river, artisans create designs inspired by Central Anatolian archaeological findings, particularly Hittite-style vessels and motifs; many also produce their own unique pieces, both functional and decorative. Pottery is a family affair, so in shops you'll see younger family members decorating pieces as their fathers and grandfathers operate the kick wheel. Almost all local potters will give free demonstrations that showcase traditional techniques.

GETTING HERE AND AROUND

Though located somewhat farther afield from Cappadocia's main sights, Avanos is easy to reach if you have a car; minibuses also connect Avanos with other nearby towns. Most hotels, restaurants, shops, and businesses are along the northern bank of the river or just a short walk away.

ESSENTIALS

Visitor Information ⊠ *Atatürk Cad., Dr. Hacı Nuri Bey Konağı, Avanos* ☎ *384/511–4360* ⏱ *Daily 8–5; closed weekends in winter.*

WHERE TO EAT AND STAY

$$
TURKISH
✕ **Dayının Yeri.** This friendly, brightly decorated grill house with windows facing the riverfront caters to both locals and visitors with a fairly standard but well-prepared menu of Southeastern Turkish specialties. For a starter, try the *lahmacun*, a thin, round flatbread topped with ground meat and spices. Meat entrées—including spicy Adana kebabs and lamb chops—are prepared on a traditional-style grill near the entrance. $ *Average main: 20 TL* ⊠ *Köprübaşı* ☎ *384/511–6840.*

$
B&B/INN
▢ **Kirkit Pension.** In these five converted Ottoman stone houses, the clean, mainly stone-built accommodations are decorated with carpets and Uzbek blankets; some upper-level rooms have nice views of the river, while others look out over the hotel's interior courtyard or the street. **Pros:** friendly, relaxed atmosphere; affordable rates. **Cons:** limited room amenities (no TVs or minibars); some small rooms. $ *Rooms from: $65* ⊠ *Atatürk Cad. 50, Avanos* ☎ *384/511–3418* ⊕ *www.kirkitpension. com* ⤴ *17 rooms* ⦿*| Breakfast.*

$
HOTEL
▢ **Sofa Hotel.** At this quaint complex of more than a dozen late-Ottoman houses built around a courtyard, sitting areas, winding passages, and shady outdoor spaces abound. **Pros:** good value; unique ambience. **Cons:** cluttered, slightly knickknack-y feel to some rooms; room amenities vary and can be rather basic; lots of steps up to some rooms. $ *Rooms from: $72* ⊠ *Orta Mah. Gedik Sok. 9* ☎ *384/511–5186* ⊕ *www.sofa-hotel.com* ⤴ *31 rooms, 2 suites* ⦿*| Breakfast.*

SHOPPING

The shops are generally open seven days a week during tourist season, from 9 to around sundown, depending on business.

Avanos Çarşı Seramik (*Chez Ferhat*). Run by a small cooperative, Avanos Çarşı Seramik has an excellent array of functional and decorative ceramics, ranging from pieces with Hittite designs to the Kütahya and İznik styles more commonly seen in Western Turkey. Prices are negotiable. ⊠ *Atatürk Cad. 13–19(across from PTT)* ☎ *384/511–4871.*

Chez Ali Baba. This friendly shop, along with sister store Harput Seramik around the corner, offers a broad selection of ceramics, from traditional

Hittite wine pitchers to colorful, rather rustic red-clay pieces in local styles. Prices are fair and negotiable. ⊠ *Fırınbaşı Sok., up and to right from PTT* ☎ *384/511–3166.*

Chez Galip. The oldest, most famous, and by far the funkiest pottery shop in Avanos, Chez Galip is known not just for ceramics but also for having what its owner calls the world's largest collection of human hair— thousands upon thousands of locks are on display. The pottery selection includes both typical styles and interesting freehand sculptural pieces. ⊠ *Across from PTT* ☎ *384/511–4577* ⊕ *www.chezgalip.com.*

Ömürlü Seramık. You can browse the extensive inventory, see artists at work, and even try your hand at the wheel inside this friendly showroom and shop about a 15-minute walk from the center of Avanos. The company makes both decorative and functional pieces featuring Hittite styles, traditional Turkish and Ottoman motifs, and the artisans' own designs. ⊠ *Yeni Mah. 3. Cad. 2. Sok. No. 26* ☎ *384/511–3231* ⊕ *wwww.omurlu.com.*

DERINKUYU AND KAYMAKLI

Kaymaklı is 20 km (12 miles) south of Nevşehir; Derinkuyu is 9 km (6 miles) south of Kaymaklı.

The underground cities of Cappadocia have excited the imaginations of travelers since the Greek mercenary leader/historian Xenophon wrote about them in the 5th century BC. Hittite artifacts discovered in some suggest they may have been initially constructed a millennium before, but no one really knows for sure who dug the cities, or when, or why. The underground networks were certainly modified and probably also significantly expanded later by the early Christians who inhabited them. Some of these complexes are merely passages between different belowground dwellings. Others really deserve the title of "city": The largest, including Kaymaklı and Derinkuyu, have multiple levels and were equipped to house thousands of people for months at a time. The impermeable tufa, or porous rock, kept the insides of the cities dry, while ventilation shafts supplied air and interior wells provided water. Ground-level entrances were cleverly disguised, and in the event that invaders did make their way in, huge, round stones resembling millstones were used to block off different passageways and secure the city.

GETTING HERE AND AROUND

Kaymaklı and Derinkuyu are on Route 765 and can be reached by car or public minibus via Nevşehir. Travel time from Nevşehir is about a half hour for Kaymaklı and an additional 10 minutes or so for Derinkuyu.

An easier and probably more time-efficient option is to join a day tour. These usually include a visit to one of the underground cities, where your guide will help you navigate the labyrinthine passageways and provide background that will bring the place to life.

If you visit the cities on your own, particularly during peak season, it's a good idea to get there as early in the day as possible, before the tour groups arrive.

HACIBEKTAŞ FESTIVAL

The mystic and philosopher Hacı Bektaş Veli founded a Muslim sect in the 13th century that was a synthesis of Shiite, Sufi, and humanist thought. He gained a following of Sufi dervishes, the Bektashis, as well as considerable political influence; the Janıssary corps of warriors of the Ottoman Empire, established a century after Hacı Bektaş' death, made Bektashism their official order and revered him as their spiritual leader. A colorful three-day festival celebrating Hacı Bektaş begins each year on August 16 in Hacıbektaş (40 km/25 miles northwest of Avanos on Rte. D765), the town that both bears his name and contains his tomb. Sufi dancing and music fill the streets, while souvenir shops sell trinkets with pictures of Hacı Bektaş, Atatürk, and the Imam Ali.

EXPLORING

Derinkuyu. Derinkuyu, meaning "deep well," is the deepest of the known underground cities that have been explored—eight floors are open to the public, though there may be many more. The subterranean labyrinth has stables, wineries, a chapel and baptismal pool, a school, scores of other interconnected rooms, and as many as 600 entrances and air ducts. You'll also see a ventilation shaft that plunges 55 meters (180 ft) from ground level. Claustrophobes take note. Spaces here are so tight that you'll have to walk doubled over for a hundred meters (about 330 feet) up and down steps in a sloping cave corridor. ⊠ *Derinkuyu village* ☎ *384/381-3194* 🎫 *15 TL* ⊙ *Apr.–Oct., daily 8–7; Nov.–Mar., daily 8–5; last entry 45 min before closing.*

Kaymaklı. About 9 km (6 miles) north of Derinkuyu, Kaymaklı was discovered in 1950 and is thought to be the largest of Cappadocia's underground cities in square area, though fewer levels can be visited than at Derinkuyu. It's believed that many of the current homes in the area are connected to the tunnels, and the story goes that before parts of the underground city were closed off to the public, unsuspecting homeowners periodically found tourists popping up in their living rooms. The city extends belowground for eight levels, of which only four are currently open. Sloping corridors and steps connect the floors, with different areas used as stables, kitchens, wineries, and a church. The ceilings are low and can be difficult for tall visitors to navigate. ⊠ *Kaymaklı village* ☎ *384/218-2500* 🎫 *15 TL* ⊙ *Apr.–Oct., daily 8–7; Nov.–Mar., daily 8–5; last entry 45 min before closing.*

IHLARA VALLEY

110 km (68 miles) southwest of Nevşehir; 52 km (32 miles) west of Derinkuyu.

A verdant river canyon dotted with rock churches carved into the cliffs above, the Ihlara Valley offers a pleasant change of scenery from the arid terrain typically seen elsewhere in the region and the chance to see more of Cappadocia's rich artistic heritage. The valley, which can be explored with or without a guide, makes an easy day trip from the Avanos-Nevşehir-Ürgüp triangle.

GETTING HERE AND AROUND

If you're coming from Nevşehir, take Route 300 west to Aksaray, then drive 42 km (25 miles) southeast past Selime. If coming from Derinkuyu, head west on the winding road called Gülağaç-Derinkuyu Yolu. Alternatively, join a day tour that takes you to the most noteworthy rock churches and includes a stop for lunch at one of the restaurants inside the canyon—it's a good way to hit the highlights while leaving the driving to someone else.

EXPLORING

Fodor'sChoice **Ihlara Valley.** The landscape changes dramatically when you head south
★ through Cappadocia toward Ihlara: the dusty plains turn rich with vegetation, and the Melendiz River carves a rift into the sheer tufa cliffs, which rise up to 149 meters (490 feet). If you can afford to spend a day here, it can be refreshing to hike through the beautiful, lush valley and explore some of the approximately 100 churches hidden in nooks above the river.

There are four entrances to the 14-km-long (8½-mile-long) valley: from Selime at the north end, from Belisırma or the Ihlara Vadisi Turistik Tesisleri (Ihlara Valley Touristic Facilities) at points along the valley, and from Ihlara village at the south end. Walking the entire valley will take you the better part of a day, but if you just want to get a taste of it, the most interesting part is the middle section. From the Ihlara Vadisi Turistik Tesisleri, you'll have to walk down nearly 400 wooden steps to reach the valley floor. A cluster of fresco-decorated churches are within walking distance of one another, including the Ağaçaltı (Under-a-Tree) church, Kokar (Fragrant) church, Yılanlı (Serpent) church, and the Church of St. George. Belisırma village, about 2 km (1½ miles) north of the Ihlara Vadisi Turistik Tesisleri and roughly a three-hour walk from either end of the valley, has a handful of scenic restaurants, some of which have open-air cabanas built on stilts over the river—an idyllic place for a simple meal, accompanied by the relaxing sound of running water. ⊠ *Ihlara Vadi Turistik Tesisleri, 2 km (1 mile) from Ilhara village* ⊒ *8 TL* ☉ *Summer, daily 8–7; winter, daily 8–5 (last entry 45 minutes before closing).*

SOĞANLI VALLEYS

45 km (28 miles) southeast of Ürgüp.

The swath of Cappadocia between Ürgüp and the Soğanlı Valleys was once considered to be off the beaten path. Though the sights are now well-marked and guided tours are increasingly offered, it is still often blissfully uncrowded, and remains almost totally uncommercialized.

GETTING HERE AND AROUND

About 9 km (6 miles) past the village of Güzelöz on Ürgüp Yolu, turn right onto Soğanlı Köyü Yolu and proceed about 3 km (2 miles) to the entrance to the Soğanlı Valleys.

The underground city of Derinkuyu is believed to have been home to thousands of people.

The Keşlik Monastery and the archaeological site of Sobessos are both on the way from Ürgüp to the Soğanlı Valleys. From Ürgüp, take Ürgüp Yolu about 15 km (9 miles) to the village of Cemil; you will see signs for Keşlik Monastery about 2 km (1¼ miles) past the village on your right (west). Sobessos is about 6 km (4 miles) farther south on Ürgüp Yolu on the left (east), in the village of Şahinefendi.

There is almost no public transport to these areas, so you'll need to take your own car, hire a guide, or join a day tour.

EXPLORING

Keşlik Monastery. This small but interesting monastery complex has two main churches and a refectory carved out of rock. The Archangelos Church, thought to date to the 11th or 12th century, has extensive, but blackened, frescoes (a flashlight is essential), including one on the wall facing the entrance that shows the Archangel Michael fighting Lucifer in a landscape that strongly resembles Cappadocia. The walls and ceiling of the nearby Stefanos Church are covered with colorful, almost contemporary-looking floral and geometric designs dating to the 7th or 8th century. The monastery's ever-present caretaker, Cabir Coşkuner, speaks some English and is happy to guide visitors around. ⊠ *2 km south of Cemil village, off Ürgüp Yolu* 🚗 *5 TL* ☉ *Daily 8:30–sunset.*

Sobessos. Excavations of this 4th-century Roman town have been going on for about a decade. So far, the well-preserved remains of a Roman bathhouse and a meeting hall with an extensive mosaic floor have been uncovered, as well as a Byzantine church that was later built on top of the mosaics. A roof protects part of the site. There are catwalks and some limited explanatory panels for visitors. ⊠ *Şahinefendi village* 🎫 *Free* ⊙ *Daylight hours.*

Soğanlı Valleys. These two scenic wooded valleys that form a V shape were home to a monastic community during Byzantine times, and there are hundreds of rock dwellings and churches cut into the cliffs. The northern, or "upper," valley (on the right-hand side), has most of the churches, while the southern, or "lower," valley is noteworthy for its many dovecotes. In the former, a path follows a little stream past enormous, house-size boulders and comes to churches including the Karabaş Kilisesi ("Church of the Black Head") and Yılanlı (Snake) Church, with extensive frescoes that have been badly damaged by graffiti. The two-story Kubbeli (Domed) Church has an unusual rock-cut cylindrical dome, reminiscent of medieval Armenian churches. If you're lucky enough to come on a day when there are no tour groups, you'll practically be on your own. Climb up the cliff face and you'll be rewarded with incredible views. ⊠ *Soğanlı Köyü Yolu* 🎫 *5 TL* ⊙ *Daily 9–5.*

OFF THE BEATEN PATH

Sultan Sazlığı Bird Sanctuary. One of Turkey's most important bird sanctuaries, Sultan Sazlığı is a national park and Ramsar-protected wetland that's a 32-km (20-mile) drive from the turnoff for the Soğanlı Valleys. A total of 301 species have been observed here, including flamingos, spoonbills, buzzards, gray herons, lapwings, and great white egrets. There's no admission fee for the park but first-timers are encouraged to hire a field guide to take them out by boat, jeep, or foot (depending on the water level in the marshes). ■ TIP➜ Spring is the best time to visit. Contact the guides who run Sultan Pansiyon in Ovaçiftlik village in advance to make arrangements. ⊠ *Off Yahyalı Yolu, Ovaçiftlik* ✛ *From the turnoff for Soğanlı, head east 12 km (7½ miles) on Soğanlı Köyü Yolu to Yeşilhisar, turn south onto D805 (Kayseri-Niğde Yolu), and go about 9 km (5½ miles) before turning left (east) onto Yahyalı Yolu. Continue until you see the left-hand turnoff for Ovaçiftlik village (Ovaçiftlik Köyü Yolu).* ☎ *352/658–5549 for Sultan Pansiyon* ⊕ *www.sultanbirding.com* 🎫 *Free.*

NIĞDE

85 km (53 miles) south of Nevşehir.

The small city of Niğde is primarily an agricultural center and offers little of interest to the modern traveler. In the 13th century, however, the city flourished under the Seljuks, who built the triple-domed Alaaddin Camii and the neighboring fortress. The Ak Medrese, dating to 1409, has stone carvings and a small museum and cultural center. A little ways out of town is Niğde's most important attraction, Eski Gümüşler Monastery.

GETTING HERE AND AROUND
Niğde and the Eski Gümüşler Monastery are best accessed by car via Route 765, but it's also possible to take a local bus from Nevşehir to Niğde and then a minibus to Eski Gümüşler from the terminal in Niğde's town center.

EXPLORING

Eski Gümüşler Manastiri (*Eski Gümüşler Monastery*). Some say the 11th-century Eski Gümüşler church inside this monastery complex has the only picture of a smiling Virgin Mary in the world. Others say that this is due to an error made during the church's restoration. Whatever the case, the frescoes inside, though dark, are beautiful and amazingly preserved. (The "smiling" Virgin is in a rock niche in the back left corner of the church.) Parts of the monastery were carved as early as the 7th century but most frescoes are from around the 11th; they were later painted over by local Turkish Muslims, who considered the depiction of human beings idolatrous. The paintings were cleaned and carefully recovered in the 1960s. In a room above the church are frescoes of animals, thought to be depicting scenes from Aesop's fables—an unusual example of nonreligious art in this region. The monastery also contains a kitchen, rock-carved monks' chambers around the central courtyard, and two levels of underground rooms that may have been used in part as a water reservoir. The sign for the monastery will be one of the first things you'll see as you approach Niğde; it's about 4 km (2.5 miles) down the road from there. ⊠ *9 km (6 miles) northeast of downtown Niğde, east off Rte. 805, in village of Gümüşler, Niğde* ☎ *5 TL* ☀ *Summer, daily 8–12:30 and 1:30–6; winter, 9–12:30 and 1:30–5.*

KONYA

258 km (160 miles) south of Ankara; 188 km (117 miles) southwest of Ihlara.

Famous for being the location of Rumi's tomb, Konya has long attracted both religious pilgrims and travelers drawn to the city's spiritual, even mystical, atmosphere. Its most important site is the Mevlâna complex, at once a secular museum with displays on dervish life and a mausoleum where the religious devotion the renowned Sufi philosopher inspires is immediately palpable. During the annual Mevlâna Festival in December, Konya is transformed by an influx of acolytes—and other curious souls—who come from around the world to observe the anniversary of Rumi's death. The other main event is the International Mystic Music Festival in September.

The rest of the year, Konya is a quiet, rather provincial city; nevertheless, visitors can find evidence of its long and interesting history. Konya, for instance, was the capital of the Seljuk Empire during much of the 12th and 13th centuries, and some notable medieval mosques and theological seminary buildings—now housing museums—showcase the characteristic architectural style of that period. You can probably see most city sights in a day. Going back further in time, the Neolithic archaeological site of Çatalhöyük can be explored on a side trip.

Not surprisingly, Konya is known throughout Turkey as a religious and rather conservative city, where almost all of the restaurants are dry. Until recently, it catered mainly to domestic travelers, who still make up the overwhelming majority of visitors. But the last few years have

The tomb of Mevlâna Celaleddin Rumi, the founder of the Whirling Dervishes, is also a popular museum in Konya.

seen the opening of several hotels and inns aimed more at foreign guests, and the museums typically have good signage in English.

GETTING HERE AND AROUND

Turkish Airlines, its low-cost sub-brand AnadoluJet, and Pegasus Airlines all offer frequent daily flights from Istanbul to Konya. Konya is also served by major bus companies, including Ulusoy, Kamil Koç, and Metro, as well as local firms Kontur and Özkaymak.

Train travel time from Istanbul to Konya should be reduced to about five hours after high-speed trains are launched in 2014. A high-speed rail line already connects Ankara and Konya, with the ride lasting just 1 hour and 50 minutes: trains run eight times daily in each direction and an economy class ticket costs 25 TL.

Modern Konya is extremely spread out, but its tourist attractions are all concentrated in the city center near Alaaddin Tepesi (Alaaddin Hill). From the airport, 18 km (11 miles) to the northeast, Havaş shuttle buses make regular trips to the city center (10 TL). Konya's bus terminal is about 15 km (9 miles) north of the city center; it's a 30-minute tram ride from the terminal to the Alaaddin tram stop downtown. The train station, 3 km (2 miles) southwest of the city center, is only accessible by minibus or taxi. Taxis are relatively inexpensive for short distances downtown but can add up if you are going to the bus terminal or airport.

ESSENTIALS

Bus Information Kontur ☎ 332/265-0080 bus terminal ticket office, 444-4042 call center ⊕ www.kontur.com.tr. **Metro** ☎ 332/265-0040 bus terminal ticket office, 444-3455 call center ⊕ www.metroturizm.com.tr. **Özkaymak**

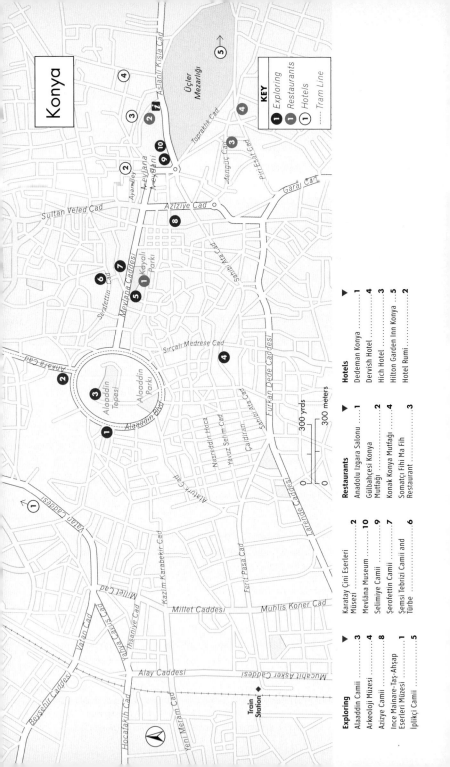

Konya

KEY

- **1** Exploring
- **1** Restaurants
- **①** Hotels
- ----- Tram Line

Exploring ▶

Alaaddin Camii	3
Arkeoloji Müzesi	4
Azizye Camii	8
İnce Mainare-Taş-Ahşap Eserleri Müzesi	1
İplikçi Camii	5
Karatay Çini Eserleri Müzesi	2
Mevlâna Museum	10
Selimiye Camii	9
Şerofettin Camii	7
Şemsi Tebrizi Camii and Türbe	6

Restaurants ▶

Anadolu Izgara Salonu	1
Gülbahçesi Konya Mutfağı	2
Konak Konya Mutfağı	4
Somatçı Fihi Ma Fih Restaurant	3

Hotels ▶

Dedeman Konya	1
Dervish Hotel	4
Hich Hotel	3
Hilton Garden Inn Konya	5
Hotel Rumi	2

0 ____ 300 yds

0 ____ 300 meters

☎ *332/265–0160 bus terminal ticket office, 444–4206 call center* ⊕ *www. ozkaymak.com.tr.*

Tour Information **Selene Tour.** This agency offers tours in Konya and to nearby destinations, such as Çatalhöyük; it can also arrange for visitors to attend the annual Mevlâna festival. Owner Mete Horzum, a dervish himself, is knowledge-able about Konya, Rumi, and Sufism. ✉ *Aziziye Cad. 25, Güneş Apt.* ☎ *332/353–6745* ⊕ *www.selene.com.tr.*

Visitor Information ✉ *Aslanlı Kışla Cad. 5, behind Mevlâna Museum* ☎ *332/351–1074* ⊙ *Mon.–Sat. 8–5.*

EXPLORING
TOP ATTRACTIONS
Karatay Çini Eserleri Müzesi (*Karatay Museum or Ceramics Museum*). The Karatay Medresesi—a seminary founded in 1251 by Celaleddin Kara-tay, a Seljuk emir—is now home to Konya's small ceramics museum. The main attraction is the building itself, which was recently restored and features a stunning dome lined with blue, black, and white tiles representing the starry heavens; in the vaulted corners below are stylized ceramic inscriptions of the names of the prophets. The frieze beneath the dome and the vaulted hall, or *eyvan*, at the end of the building, are just as dazzling. The emir's tomb is to the left of the main hall; other side rooms display smaller tile and ceramic works. Most impressive is a collection of rare figurative tiles from Kubadabad Palace in Beyşehir that show the Persian influence on Seljuk art. These include hunting scenes, people with distinctively Eastern features and clothing, and figurines of animals and mythological creatures, all highlighted in rich shades of cobalt blue and turquoise. ✉ *Ankara Cad. at Alaaddin Bul.* ☎ *332/351–1914* 💰*3 TL* ⊙ *Summer, Tues.–Sun. 9–7; winter, Tues.– Sun. 9–5 (last entry 20 minutes before closing).*

Fodor'sChoice ⭐ **Mevlâna Museum.** When the Sufi mystic philosopher-poet Mevlâna Cela-leddin Rumi died in 1273, he was buried in Konya beside his father and a great shrine was erected above them. As Rumi's mystic teach-ings of love and tolerance, ecstatic joy, and unity with God spread and his poetry gathered a greater following, his mausoleum drew pilgrims from all parts of the Islamic world. In 1926, three years after the estab-lishment of the Turkish Republic, his shrine was declared a museum, though the Sufi order he founded had been officially banned in 1925 as part of the drastic secularization of Turkish society under Atatürk. Today, the museum is one of the most visited sites in Turkey, attract-ing at least 1.5 million people a year, the majority of them Turks. Sufi dervishes have also been assigned special status as "Turkish folk danc-ers," allowing them to perform their mystic whirling without the state overtly recognizing its undeniable religious basis.

The mausoleum building is a holy site and, in line with Muslim tradi-tions, women visiting it must cover their heads; scarves can be bor-rowed at the entrance to the museum. Visitors are also required to put plastic covers over their shoes. Photography is prohibited. The interior of the mausoleum resembles that of a mosque, with its intri-cately painted domes, ornate chandeliers, and Islamic inscriptions on

Continued on page 394

TURKEY'S
WHIRLING DERVISHES

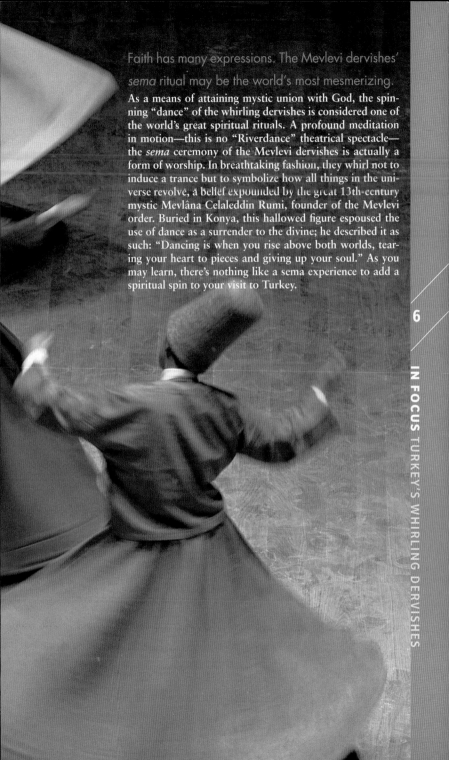

Faith has many expressions. The Mevlevi dervishes' *sema* ritual may be the world's most mesmerizing.

As a means of attaining mystic union with God, the spinning "dance" of the whirling dervishes is considered one of the world's great spiritual rituals. A profound meditation in motion—this is no "Riverdance" theatrical spectacle—the *sema* ceremony of the Mevlevi dervishes is actually a form of worship. In breathtaking fashion, they whirl not to induce a trance but to symbolize how all things in the universe revolve, a belief expounded by the great 13th-century mystic Mevlâna Celaleddin Rumi, founder of the Mevlevi order. Buried in Konya, this hallowed figure espoused the use of dance as a surrender to the divine; he described it as such: "Dancing is when you rise above both worlds, tearing your heart to pieces and giving up your soul." As you may learn, there's nothing like a sema experience to add a spiritual spin to your visit to Turkey.

AROUND THE WHIRL

Extremely detailed and specific directions govern even the slightest pattern and gesture in the ritual dance of the whirling dervishes.

1 To help lift themselves into the spiritual realm, the *semazen* dancers are accompanied by musicians, who play the *ney* (reed flute) and the kettledrum, whose beating signals God's call to "be."

2 First dropping their black cloaks—to signify the shedding of earthly ties—the dervishes stand with their arms crossed over their chests, a posture that represents the number one, a symbol of God's unity. Their costumes are full of symbolism: the conical hat, or *sikke*, represents a tombstone, the jacket is the tomb itself, and the floor-length skirt, or *tennure*, a funerary shroud. The latter is hemmed with chain to allow it to rise with dramatic effect.

3 The dervishes' endless spinning—always right to left, counter-clockwise—symbolizes the rotation of the universe. To receive God's goodness, they keep their right hands extended to the sky; to channel God's beneficence to earth, their left hands point toward the ground.

4 The dervishes usually perform for four *selams*—or salutes—each to a separate musical movement. For the last, they are joined by their Sheikh Efendi—incarnating the figure of Rumi—who stands on a red sheepskin (oriented toward holy Mecca) to represent the channel of divine grace. At the climax, he and the *semazenbaşı* (dance master) join the others and whirl in their midst. At the finale, the dervishes put their cloaks back on—a symbol of return to the material world.

Above: The Sufi mystic, Mevlâna Celaleddin Rumi, inspired the whirl of the dervishes.

WHERE THE DERVISHES WHIRL

Ever since the days of the Ottoman sultans, the Mevlevi dervishes' *semas* have been wildly popular events. In Konya, the Mevlâna Cultural Center hosts free *sema* performances on Saturday evenings, but the best time to see the Mevlevi dervishes whirl is during the annual Mevlâna Festival, which runs every year for the week to 10 days leading up to December 17, the anniversary of Rumi's death. **Konya's Tourism Information Office** (tel. 332/353–4021), as well as local travel agencies, can help you find tickets and make hotel reservations for the festival; it is wise to book tickets as far in advance as possible. The dervishes have been assigned a special status as "Turkish folk dancers," and if you can't get to Konya during the festival or on a Saturday, you stand just as good a chance of seeing them in Istanbul.

Mevlâna Celaleddin Rumi

The Mevlâna Museum in Konya calls Rumi (also known as Jalal al-Din Muhammad Rumi, or simply as "Mevlâna") a "Turkish theosophic philosopher," though in reality he hailed from present-day Afghanistan and wrote his poetry in Persian. Born in the city of Balkh on September 30, 1207, he came to Konya in 1228, when it was a part of the Seljuk Empire. By that time the young Rumi had already been deeply influenced by mystic readings and had made the hajj to Mecca.

Rumi's transformative spiritual moment came in 1248, when his companion, Shams Tabrizi, a dervish who initiated Rumi into Islamic mysticism, mysteriously disappeared. Rumi's grief at his beloved friend's disappearance—suspected to be a murder—sparked a prodigious outpouring of verse, music, dance, and poetry. After years of searching for his friend and teacher, Rumi found himself in Damascus, where he had a revelation that the universe was one and each person could be his own holy universe. He exclaimed:

"Why should I seek? I am the same as he.

His essence speaks through me.

I have been looking for myself!"

For the rest of his life, Rumi attributed much of his own poetry to Shams, and in a way that would become characteristic and controversial, mixed his love with his fellow man with his love for God and God's love for man. Rumi became known for his tolerance, his espousal of love, and his use of dance and song to reach spiritual enlightenment. Toward the end of his life, he spent 12 years dictating his masterwork, the *Masnavi,* to a companion. He died in 1273, and the Mevlevi order of dervishes, famous for their *semas,* or whirling ceremonies, was founded after his death.

The central theme of Rumi's philosophy is a longing for unity—of men, of the universe, with God and with God's spirit. Rumi believed in the use of music, poetry, and dancing as facilitators for reaching God and for focusing on the divine. Through ecstatic dancing, singing, or chanting, Sufi worshippers believed they could negate their bodies and vain selves, becoming empty vessels to be filled with love, the essence of the divine. In Rumi's poetry, he talks of God as one might a lover, and the ecstatic states reached through dancing and singing sometimes border on the erotic. In recent years, Rumi's legacy has been revived, ensuring that his timeless teachings endure. His epitaph suggests he would have been happy with that:

"When we are dead, seek not our tomb in the earth, but find it in the hearts of men."

---

the walls. It is well lighted and there is music playing (unusual for a Muslim holy place, it is a further hint that Rumi was not a proponent of traditional interpretations of Islam). The main hall contains many dervish tombs, all of them with carved stone turbans that serve as headstones. Rumi's tomb, located in its own special section on the right, is the largest, covered with an enormous embroidered gray mantle and with two massive green turbans at its head. In what seems like a bit of a contradiction to the simplicity of dervish life, this vaulted section is incredibly ornate—almost every square inch covered with colorful painted floral designs and gold-embossed calligraphic inscriptions. The place is usually filled with Muslim pilgrims standing with their palms outward in prayer, and it is not uncommon to see men and women crying before Rumi's grave.

Rumi was famous for his inclusiveness and would have welcomed you here, no matter what your beliefs. He said:

"Come, come, whoever you are.

Wanderer, idolater, worshipper of fire,

Come even if you have broken your vows a thousand times.

Come, and come yet again.

Ours is not a caravan of despair."

The two rooms on the left contain beautifully preserved holy books; some dervish clothing, including a cloak that belonged to Rumi; and a mother-of-pearl box containing hair from the prophet Mohammed's beard.

Next to the mausoleum is a courtyard with a large *şadırvan,* or ablutions fountain, around which are rooms that formerly served as dervish cells and kitchens. These have been turned into a museum, with each room illustrating a different aspect of life in the dervish brotherhood. Some house artifacts such as traditional musical instruments, clothing and headgear, manuscripts, and calligraphic tools, while other cells have displays of mannequins dressed as dervishes carrying out various activities. ⊠ *off Mevlâna Meydanı* ☎ *332/351–1215* 🖅 *3 TL* ⊙ *May–Sept., Tues.–Sun. 9–7, Mon. 10–7; Oct.–Apr., Tues.–Sun. 9–5, Mon. 10–5.*

WORTH NOTING

Alaaddin Camii (*Alâeddin Mosque*). Completed in 1220 and restored in the 1990s, this graceful mosque crowning Alaaddin Tepesi (Alaaddin Hill) was one of the most important for Seljuk sultans, many of whom are entombed within the complex. The oblong layout shows the influence of Arab architecture, while the timber ceiling is supported by a forest of marble columns and arches reused from Roman temples. An ebony *minbar* (pulpit), dating back to 1155, is beautifully carved with Seljuk motifs and inscriptions. The municipality has done much to improve the appearance of **Alaaddin Tepesi** in recent years. There are cafés near street level and the hill itself is a park, with landscaped flower gardens at the top. On the northern side are the scanty remains of a Seljuk palace—two venerable stumps of walls, which the city has for some reason thrown an unsightly concrete shelter over. ⊠ *Alaaddin Parkı* ⊙ *Daily 8:30–5:30.*

Arkeoloji Müzesi (*Archaeology Museum*). A magnificent **portal** marks the entrance to what was formerly the Sahip Ata complex, a group of structures dating from the late 13th century. A bit to the right is the small but interesting **Arkeoloji Müzesi** (Archaeology Museum), showcasing artifacts from a number of different periods. The most significant room has finds from the 7000 BC Neolithic site of ⇨ **Çatalhöyük,** including pottery, jewelry, weapons and tools, and the remains of an infant burial; these are accompanied by quite informative explanations. There are also artifacts from the Bronze Age and Greek and Roman periods; the 3rd-century AD marble sarcophagus depicting the Twelve Labors of Hercules is outstanding.

Around the left-hand corner from the Sahip Ata portal is the **Sahip Ata Müzesi** (Sahip Ata Museum), housed in the beautifully (but perhaps not that sensitively) restored dervish lodge of the mosque complex. Items on display include carved wooden doors from as early as the 13th century, ceramic fragments, calligraphic works and old Korans, and dervish accoutrements. It's free to visitors. ⊠ *Larende Cad.* ☎ *332/351–3207* ⬚ *3 TL* ☉ *Summer, Tues.–Sun. 9–12:30 and 1:30–5; winter, Tues.–Sun. 9–12 and 1–5.*

İnce Minare–Taş-Ahşap Eserleri Müzesi (*Museum of Stone and Woodwork*). The minaret of the 13th-century İnce Minare Medresesi, or "Seminary of the Slender Minaret," is bejeweled with glazed turquoise tiles. Unfortunately, due to a 1901 lightning strike, it is only half its original height. Also worth noting is the especially ornate Seljuk-style decoration of the beautiful stone entry portal. The building itself houses the small but well-done Museum of Stone and Woodwork, which displays a fine collection of tombstones and other inscribed stone fragments as well as elaborate wooden carvings dating from the 13th century. Highlights are the fascinating Persian-influenced Seljuk stone reliefs, which include double-headed eagles, winged angels, and strange creatures that are part human and part bird or beast. ⊠ *Alaaddin Bul., west side of Alâeddin Tepesi* ☎ *332/351–3204* ⬚ *3 TL* ☉ *Summer, Tues.–Sun. 8:30–7; winter, Tues.–Sun. 9–5.*

Other mosques. A few mosques are located on or just off Mevlâna Caddesi between Konya's ancient acropolis, the Alaaddin Tepesi, and Mevlâna Meydanı. The construction of **Şerafettin Camii** was started by the Seljuks in the 13th century and completed by the Ottomans in 1636. The **Şemsi Tebrizi Camii and Türbe,** north of Şerefettin Camii, off Hükümet Alanı, is dedicated to Mevlâna's mentor and friend and contains his mausoleum. Nearby is Konya's oldest mosque, the **İplikçi Camii** (Thread-Dealer's Mosque), dating from 1202. **Aziziye Camii** (Sultan Abdül Aziz Mosque), which dates from 1676 and was rebuilt in 1875, flanks the bazaar area. The mosque displays a combination of Ottoman and baroque styles and is known for having windows that are larger than its doors.

WHERE TO EAT

$ ✕ **Anadolu Izgara Salonu.** Though decidedly no-frills, this lunch-only
TURKISH   eatery on a backstreet behind Konya's main post office serves well-prepared home-style food—including perhaps the best *kuru fasulye*, or baked beans, anywhere in the area. The reasonable menu changes daily but always includes one or two soups, a few vegetable or meat specials, and the signature beans. Run by the same family for more than 30 years, the cafeteria-style venue has linoleum tables covered with butcher paper, livened up by a handful of potted plants. $ *Average main: 12 TL* ⊠ *A Varışlı İşhanı 24 (inside arcade), Kurşuncular Sok., Karatay* ☎ *332/350–2874* ▭ *No credit cards* ☉ *No dinner. Closed Sun.*

$$ ✕ **Gülbahçesi Konya Mutfağı.** The
TURKISH terrace of this restored mansion
has one of the best views of the
adjacent Mevlâna tomb complex.
Though the food isn't much above
what you'll get elsewhere, the loca-
tion goes a long way. So does the
atmosphere—in upstairs rooms,
guests sit traditional Turkish style,
crossed-legged on cushions around
low tables. Specialties include the
tasty but heavy *tirit*, a layered con-
coction of cubed flatbread, yogurt,
onions, and chopped lamb, drizzled
with melted butter and sprinkled
with parsley and ground sumac.
There are also several versions of
Konya's famous *etli ekmek*, flat-
bread covered with ground meat
and other toppings. $ *Average
main: 22 TL* ✉ *Eflaki Dede Sok. 3,
Karatay* ☎ *332/353–0768* ⊕ *www.
gulbahcesikonyamutfagi.com*
⊜ *Reservations essential.*

> ## THE SELJUKS
>
> Some of Konya's most important
> historical sites were built by the
> Seljuks, members of a nomadic
> Turkic tribe that originated in
> Central Asia. The Seljuk Turks
> converted to Islam in the 10th
> century and began to push west-
> ward. They ruled a great swath
> of Anatolia from the late 11th
> through the beginning of the 14th
> centuries, making Konya their
> capital for much of that period.
> Seljuk architecture is similar to the
> Gothic architecture that was flour-
> ishing in Europe at the same time.
> Many of the mosques, fortresses,
> and caravansaries that brood over
> Turkish villages in the region were
> built in this style.

$$ ✕ **Konak Konya Mutfağı.** A mansion down the road from Mevlâna's tomb
TURKISH is a lovely setting in which to enjoy local specialties. The baby okra
soup is said to be among the best in Konya, and meat dishes (including
kebabs and lamb casseroles), are excellent. Be sure to save room for
the *hoşmerim*, an intensely rich dessert made of panfried clotted cream,
flour, milk, and sugar, sprinkled with ground pistachio nuts and served
warm. In winter, guests eat in small, simple dining rooms; in summer,
seating is in the pleasant, leafy garden. $ *Average main: 16 TL* ✉ *Pi-
riesat Cad. 5, Karatay* ☎ *332/352–8547* ⊕ *www.konakkonyamutfagi.
com* ⊜ *Reservations essential.*

$$ ✕ **Somatçı Fihi Ma Fih Restaurant.** By far the most unique restaurant in
TURKISH Konya (and perhaps the region), Somatçı is the project of a passion-
ate local chef who spent several years recreating dervish cuisine from
Rumi's time through historical and ethnographic research and a bit of
improvisation. The menu features combinations not typically seen in
modern Turkish cuisine, such as almond-spiked meatballs served in
a tangy herb sauce, or beef with quince. Some dishes are downright
unusual, but all are worth trying. Somatçı's delicious signature dessert,
bademli helva, is a thick, melt-in-your mouth almond paste accented
with rose oil. The interior design, melding traditional decor with rather
whimsical wall paintings, seems slightly incongruous. $ *Average main:
20 TL* ✉ *Mengüç Cad. 36, Karatay* ☎ *332/351–6696* ⊕ *www.somatci.
com* ⊜ *Reservations essential.*

6

WHERE TO STAY

$$ | **Dedeman Konya.** The lobby of this 18-story tower in a busy commercial and residential area of Konya exudes opulence (though some may find it a bit overdone); rooms are spacious and nicely furnished, with all the amenities of a first-rate business hotel. **Pros:** high-class service; multiple dining options; extensive fitness center. **Cons:** hotel is about 4 km (2.5 miles) from Konya's tourist attractions; some guests complain of poor a/c. *$ Rooms from: $130 ⊠ Özalan Mah., Yeni Sille Cad., Selçuklu ☎ 332/221–6600 ⊕ www.dedeman.com ➷ 186 rooms, 20 suites ⊚| Breakfast.*

HOTEL

$$ | **Dervish Hotel.** This family-run bed-and-breakfast is in a restored 200-year-old house on a quiet street, a short walk from the Mevlâna Museum. **Pros:** good value; warm, friendly owners. **Cons:** no views of sights; rooms are a bit basic (no TVs, minibars, or safes) and bathrooms a bit tight; guests are asked to remove shoes and wear slippers throughout premises. *$ Rooms from: $78 ⊠ Güngör Sok. 7, Karatay ☎ 332/350–0842 ⊕ www.dervishotel.com ➷ 7 rooms ⊚| Breakfast.*

B&B/INN

$$ | **Hich Hotel.** Konya's first true boutique hotel occupies a pair of nicely restored 19th-century houses across from the Mevlâna Museum. **Pros:** great value; refreshing design; exceptional service. **Cons:** limited indoor public spaces; ground floor rooms can be noisy. *$ Rooms from: $110 ⊠ Celal Sok. 6, Karatay ☎ 332/353–4424 ⊕ www.hichhotel.com ➷ 13 rooms ⊚| Breakfast.*

HOTEL
Fodor's Choice
★

$$ | **Hilton Garden Inn Konya.** Less than a 15-minute walk from the Mevlâna tomb complex, the only international chain hotel in Konya's touristic center has large, comfortable, well-lit rooms with contemporary style—think dark leather headboards, plum-colored velvet armchairs, and silk screen prints of tulips. **Pros:** next to Mevlâna Cultural Center and close to sights; maintains reliable American-style hotel standards. **Cons:** dull views from rooms; hotel set amidst somewhat deserted empty lots and a cemetery; lacks local flavor. *$ Rooms from: $145 ⊠ Kışlaönü Sok. 4, Karatay ☎ 332/221–6000 ⊕ www.konya.hgi.com ➷ 210 rooms, 18 suites ⊚| Breakfast.*

HOTEL

$$ | **Hotel Rumi.** The fifth-floor roof terrace has excellent views overlooking Mevlâna's mausoleum (which is just around the corner), making these clean, well-maintained rooms with contemporary furnishings and modern bathrooms, a good option for sightseers. **Pros:** central location; professional service. **Cons:** some rooms smell strongly of smoke; rooms can be small; not as charming as other small hotels in area. *$ Rooms from: $110 ⊠ Durakfakih Sok. 3, Karatay ☎ 332/353–1121 ⊕ www. rumihotel.com ➷ 30 rooms, 3 suites ⊚| Breakfast.*

HOTEL

THE ARTS

Konya International Mystic Music Festival. Held annually from September 22 to 30, the Konya International Mystic Music Festival hosts free nightly performances of mystical music and dance. Performers come from as far away as Tibet, Korea, and Zimbabwe, and have included big names on the world music scene, such as Zakir Hussain. ⊕ www. mysticmusicfest.com.

Mevlâna Festival. Each December, thousands of pilgrims from around the world descend on Konya for the Mevlâna Festival, which includes sema performances and other events commemorating Mevlâna Celaleddin Rumi. The program, which usually lasts about 10 days, culminates with an intense finale on the night of December 17—the anniversary of Rumi's death, considered his "wedding night" with God. There is no website for the festival, so contact Konya's Tourism Office or a local travel agency such as ⇨ *Selene Tour* for details and tickets. Be sure also to make hotel reservations well in advance, as accommodations are limited and fill up quickly, ☎ *332/353–4021 Konya tourism office.*

Mevlâna Kültür Merkezi (*Mevlâna Cultural Center*). The huge, rather grandiose Mevlâna Cultural Center has a performance hall that seats a few thousand; it hosts free *sema* (whirling dervish) performances every Saturday night, at 8 pm in winter and 9 pm in summer. The center is also the venue for many of the events in the Mystical Music Festival in September (free) and the Mevlâna Festival in December (admission charged). Tickets for semas and festival events can be arranged through travel agencies or the Konya tourism office. ✉ *Aslanlı Kışla Cad., Selimiye, Karatay* ☎ *332/352–8111* ⊕ *www.mkm.gov.tr.*

SHOPPING

Karavan Kilim Shop. This six-floor store, on a street behind Mevlâna Caddesi, is a veritable treasure trove of collector-worthy rugs and antiques. The enormous stock includes pile upon pile of kilims and carpets—many of them vintage—plus an extensive collection of antique carved doors and architectural fragments sourced from across Anatolia. There are also copper items, some glassware and ceramics, traditional Turkish musical instruments, handicrafts, and other funky finds. ✉ *Ayanbey Sok. 6/A* ☎ *332/351–0425.*

Konya's Bazaar. Konya's traditional bazaar quarter isn't as evocative as it once was, but the area just south of Mevlâna Caddesi and west of Aziziye Caddesi is still home to a few shops selling carpets, antiques, and handicrafts, as well as merchants offering an array of ordinary goods of interest mainly to locals. ✉ *Market district, between Mevlâna Cad. and Selimiye Cad. near Aziziye Cad.* ☉ *Closed Sun.*

OFF THE BEATEN PATH

Sille and Horozlu Han. The village of Sille, 9 km (5½ miles) northwest of downtown Konya, can be visited as a day trip or as a detour on your way out of the city. In AD 327, St. Helena, mother of Constantine the Great, built a small church here; it was extensively restored in the 19th century, and again in recent years. Nearby, frescoed rock chapels overlook the shores of a tiny artificial lake. To get to Sille by car, follow Yeni Sille Caddesi out of the city from where it begins near the Dedeman Hotel; or board city bus 64 in front of Selimiye Camii. If you're heading out of Konya in the direction of Ankara, look for the fabulous Seljuk portal at the entrance to the Horozlu Han, a former *kervansaray* (now housing a restaurant) near the four-lane beginning of Route 715.

ÇATALHÖYÜK

48 km (30 miles) southeast of Konya to Çumra, then 20 km (12 miles) north.

Dating to about 7400 BC, Çatalhöyük is the site of one of the oldest human settlements ever found. It was added to the UNESCO World Heritage list in 2012.

GETTING HERE AND AROUND

A round-trip taxi from Konya to Çatalhöyük will cost between 80 TL and 150 TL, depending on your bargaining skills. Alternatively, you can take a public minibus from Konya's downtown Eski Garaj to the town of Çumra and then a taxi to the site, for around 60 TL total. From the same terminal, minibuses labeled Küçükköy/Karkın go directly to the village where the site is located (about 5 TL each way). These typically depart Konya weekdays at noon and return from Küçükköy/Karkın at 3 pm, but it's wise to confirm times with Konya's tourism office so you don't get stranded in the village.

EXPLORING

Çatalhöyük. The significance of this Neolithic archaeological site lies not just in its age but in the wealth of art and artifacts found here, which shed light on humankind's transition to a sedentary, agricultural lifestyle. Thought to have been home to as many as 8,000 people at one time, Çatalhöyük was inhabited for some 1,400 years; and a series of mounds eventually built up as successive generations of residents erected new mud-brick houses atop the old ones. The name Çatalhöyük actually means "forked mound," likely a reference to a pair of distinctive ones—up to 20 meters (66 feet) high and separated by an indentation—which you can clearly see as you approach the site.

British archaeologist James Mellaart discovered and initially excavated about 160 buildings in the early 1960s, uncovering ancient wall murals, some of the earliest known pottery, human burials, and countless artifacts. He theorized that female figurines and other finds pointed to the worship of a mother goddess by the site's prehistoric inhabitants. Although alternate theories have since been presented, the iconic figurines—many of which are displayed in the ⇨ *Museum of Anatolian Civilizations* in Ankara—remain symbolic of Çatalhöyük.

The excavations of the East Mound are protected by two open-air hangarlike structures. This is the older of the two mounds, and 18 settlement levels have been identified here; you can get a good sense of the different layers from the visitor areas at the top. The South Shelter covers the deepest excavations, begun by Mellaart and restarted in 1993 by Ian Hodder of Stanford University, while the North Shelter houses several excavation areas. Illustrated explanatory panels explain what's what.

The "Experimental House," near the entrance, is a re-creation of a prehistoric Çatalhöyük adobe home. With reed mats on the floor and murals on the walls, it has been made to look as realistic as possible. The small museum is modern and informative; however, almost all the artifacts inside are re-creations, the originals having been taken to either Ankara or the ⇨ *Archaeology Museum* in Konya.

Excavations are expected to continue for several years, and in summer you can watch an international team of archaeologists at work. ✉ *Çatalhöyük, Küçükköy, near Çumra* ☎ *332/452–5217 summer only* ⊕ *www.catalhoyuk.com* 💲 *Free* ☉ *Daily 8–5.*

ANKARA

258 km (160 miles) north of Konya; 454 km (281 miles) southeast of Istanbul.

In 1923, right after the War of Independence, Ankara was made the fledgling Turkish Republic's new capital—in part because it was a barren, dusty steppe city more or less in the middle of nowhere, and therefore considered to be secure. The city still feels that way somewhat, despite being the center of national political activity and home to more than 4 million residents. It doesn't come close to having the historical richness or vibrancy of Istanbul, yet Ankara does offer a sweeping overview of the history of this land, both ancient and modern. For proof, visit the Museum of Anatolian Civilizations, repository of the best archaeological treasures found in Turkey, and the Anıtkabir, Mustafa Kemal Atatürk's colossal mausoleum. Atatürk's larger-than-life persona and the impact he had on the country can be sensed more powerfully at the Anıtkabir than anywhere else in Turkey. Indeed, the capital city as a whole is permeated by the great man's fascinating and enduring legacy, and is nothing less than a monument to his overpowering will.

Though largely modern in appearance, Ankara is in fact an ancient settlement that was occupied successively by the Hittites and other Anatolian kingdoms, the Greeks, Romans, Byzantines, Seljuks, and the Ottomans. Glimpses of these layers of history can be seen in the Citadel and Ulus areas, where a few Roman ruins are haphazardly juxtaposed with Seljuk-era mosques, centuries-old Ottoman caravansaries, and nondescript modern buildings. The top of the ancient citadel offers excellent views of the city, and within the walls is a fascinating neighborhood.

Ankara is also a pleasantly green and easily navigable city, with restaurants, clubs, and hotels that are increasingly diverse and cosmopolitan. This is at heart a government and college town, so you'll also find more relaxed attitudes here than in many other parts of Anatolia.

GETTING HERE AND AROUND
Staying at a hotel inside the citadel or in the surrounding neighborhood of Ulus gives you close proximity to almost all of Ankara's sights, and the citadel hotels, especially, are full of historic charm. Aside from a few restaurants, however, the old part of the city has little to offer in the way of nightlife and can feel somewhat deserted at night. The downtown neighborhoods of Kavaklıdere and Çankaya are bustling, with many fine restaurants, shops, and clubs—but you'll need to take a taxi or bus to reach the city's main attractions from these districts.

Ankara is served by all major bus companies, but flying from Istanbul saves a lot of time and is not much more expensive. From the airport, you can get downtown via the Havaş shuttle (10 TL). It picks up passengers in front of the terminal near flight arrivals and makes several stops, including the Havaş office in Ulus (⊠ *19 Mayıs Stadium, B Gate*) and, later, the AŞTİ bus station; passengers can board shuttles going to the airport at the same locations. Shuttles going in both directions generally leave every half hour between 4 am and 9 pm and less frequently at night.

With the opening of a high-speed rail line connecting Istanbul and Ankara in 2014, train travel time between the two cities should be reduced to about three hours. High-speed trains already run between Ankara and Konya in just under two hours, costing 25 TL each way. If you're traveling from the Mediterranean coast to Ankara by rail, the best option is the (slow) İzmir Mavi, or Blue Train, which departs İzmir at 6:30 pm, arriving in Ankara at 9:53 am; it departs Ankara at 6:20 pm and arrives in İzmir at 9:30 am. The cost is 112 TL per person in a double compartment or 174 TL for one person in a single compartment.

Ankara is a big city with chaotic traffic, and you'll save yourself a lot of grief if you use public transportation rather than renting a car to get around. The main neighborhood encompassing the old part of the city is called Ulus; this is where most of the tourist attractions are, and it's quite compact and walkable.

Taxis are more expensive in Ankara than in Istanbul: a taxi from the airport, approximately 35 km (20 miles) from the city center, can cost you about 70 TL to the Ulus area, and 80 TL or more to Kızılay or Kavaklıdere, while a taxi from the Çankaya area to the citadel can cost as much as 25 TL. You can easily hail a cab in the city, or ask your hotel to call one.

There are two subway lines in Ankara: the metro, which runs north from Kızılay; and the Ankaray, which goes east–west from the AŞTİ bus station in the western suburbs, through Kızılay and on to Dikimevi in the east. It's easy to get downtown from Ankara's *otogar* (AŞTİ), which connects directly to the Ankaray. Take the Ankaray to the Kızılay stop and then transfer to the metro (using the same ticket) if you want to continue north to Ulus. The fare is 1.75 TL and you can purchase 2, 5, or 10 tickets at a time; trains run between approximately 6 am and midnight.

ESSENTIALS

Airport Shuttle Information Havaş ☎ *312/398–0376 for airport office*
⊕ *www.havas.com.tr.*

Train Information Ankara train station ⊠ *Talatpaşa Bul. at Cumhuriyet Cad.*
☎ *312/311–0620 for info and reservations, 444-8233 national call center.*

Visitor Information ⊠ *Main office, Gençlik Parkı İçi 10, Ulus* ☎ *312/324–0101.*

From Tamerlane to Ataturk

Tamerlane, the fearsome inheritor of the legacy of Genghis Khan, laid siege to Ankara in 1402 and wrested control of the city away from Beyazıt, the Ottoman sultan. Then, perhaps bored with the landscape or seeking greater riches in China, Tamerlane and his Mongol horde quickly gave the city back to the Ottomans, turned around, and headed back east toward the Central Asian plains. Tamerlane died just three years after the Battle of Ankara.

His brief victory in Ankara was but a later scene in the city's long history. Local legend attributes Ankara's foundation to the Amazons, the mythical female warriors, but many archaeologists have factually identified it with Ankuwash, thought to have been founded around 1200 BC by the Hittites and then taken over by the Phrygians around 700 BC. The city was known to the Greeks and Romans as Ancyra or Ankyra, and later as Angora, famed for its wool. Alexander the Great conquered Ankara centuries before Augustus Caesar annexed the city to Rome in 25 BC.

Over the coming millennia Ankara was attacked and worn down by Persian, Arab, Seljuk, Mongol, and Ottoman invaders. By the early 20th century, it was little more than a provincial town with nice goats and an illustrious past. In 1919, as World War I and the Turkish War of Independence raged, Mustafa Kemal Atatürk made Ankara the headquarters of his secular resistance movement.

When Turkey was declared a republic four years later, Ankara was declared its capital. Atatürk mobilized the young nation's resources to make the city a symbol of a modern and secular Turkish city built on European lines. Tens of thousands of workers streamed in on foot to help build it, with designers intentionally abandoning Ottoman architecture in favor of a symbolic, stark modernism influenced by the Vienna cubist and German Bauhaus schools.

As with most planned cities, Ankara today is mostly pretty lacking in character. Despite Atatürk's dreams, it never made a serious bid to overtake Istanbul as the country's cultural capital.

EXPLORING

TOP ATTRACTIONS

Fodor's Choice ★ **Anadolu Medeniyetleri Müzesi** (*Museum of Anatolian Civilizations*). The Museum of Anatolian Civilizations is a real gem, showcasing many of Turkey's best ancient treasures and providing excellent insight into the incredible amount of history that has played out here. Housed in a 15th-century *bedesten* (similar to a *kervansaray*), the museum covers every major civilization that has had a presence in Anatolia, going back nearly 10 millennia. Highlights of the vast collection include finds dating back to 7500 BC (famous mother goddess figurines among them) from the Neolithic site of Çatalhöyük, one of the oldest human settlements ever discovered; Hatti and Hittite artifacts, such as stylized stag and bull sculptures and drawings; and clay cuneiform tablets (the earliest written records found in Anatolia) from the Assyrian trade colonies period. Another renowned piece is a clay tablet recording a copy of

Ankara

TO İSTANBUL

TO AIRPORT

19th of May Stadium

Ulus Mey.

Ulus

Alaaddin Cami

Ahi Elvan Cami

Samanpazarı

Train Station

Opera House

Gevher Nesibe Yolu

Cemal Gürsel C.

Kurtuluş Parkı

Lozan Mey.

Kızılay Mey.

Kızılay

Mesrutiyet C.

Bakanlıklar

TO BUS STATION (AŞTİ)

İsmet İnönü Bul.

Turkish Grand National Assembly

Kavaklıdere

U.S. Embassy

Ömür S.

Mesnevi S.

KEY

● Exploring

● Restaurants

① Hotels

0   500 yards

0   500 meters

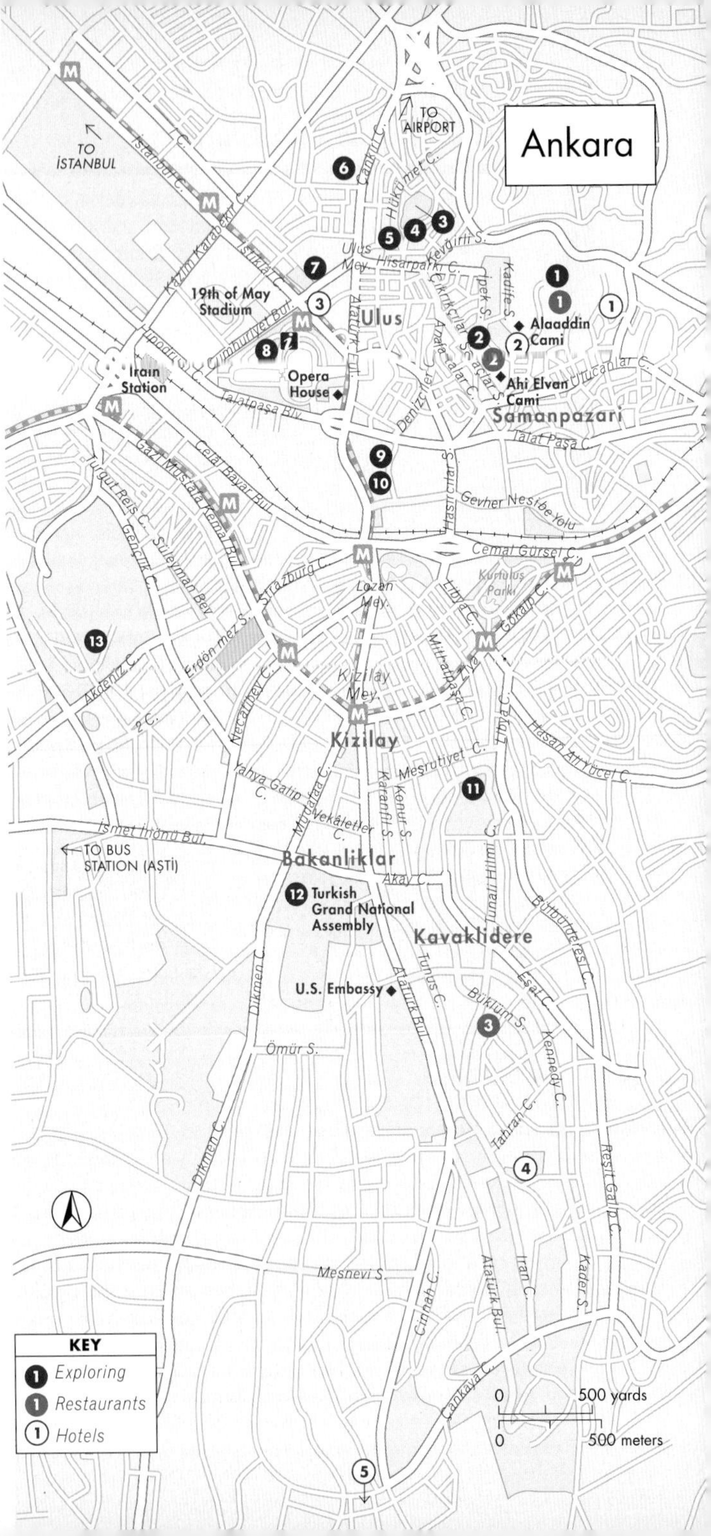

the 13th-century BC Treaty of Kadesh, the world's first known peace treaty (the original was etched in silver), found at the ancient Hittite capital Hattuşa. A significant collection of monumental stonework from around Anatolia, including well-preserved neo-Hittite reliefs depicting the epic of Gilgamesh, from the archaeological site of Karkamış in Gaziantep, is also on display. Note that the museum has been undergoing a major restoration since 2011, and, as of this writing, only a small representative section is open to visitors. The museum is expected to reopen in full by mid-2014. ✉ *Gözcü Sokak 2* ☎ *312/324–3160* 🌐 *www.anadolumedeniyetlerimuzesi.gov.tr* 💰 *15 TL* ⊙ *May–Sept., Tues.–Sun. 8:30–7; Oct.–Apr., Tues.–Sun. 8:30–5.*

Ankara Kalesi (*Ankara Citadel*). Ankara's main historic sites are clustered around its ancient citadel (known as the Hisar or Kale in Turkish), high on a hill overlooking the city. Though the citadel's precise origins are not known, the inner and outer walls standing today are thought to have been built between the 7th and 9th centuries, during the Byzantine period. At that time, Arab armies were repeatedly staging invasions of Central Anatolia, and so the citadel appears to have been somewhat hastily cobbled together—notice the even older architectural fragments, including bits of stonework with Greek and Roman inscriptions, that were haphazardly incorporated into the fortifications. Although the modern city has grown up around the citadel, the area inside the walls has retained an almost villagelike atmosphere, an entire neighborhood with winding, cobblestoned streets and old houses built with timber and plaster.

The easiest place to enter the citadel is from Parmak Kapısı (Finger Gate), also known as Saat Kapısı (Clock Gate), across from the Divan Çukurhan. Head toward the center, where you'll see the recently restored Şark Kulesi (Eastern Tower). Climb up the stone steps to the tower's upper ramparts for excellent panoramic views of the city.

The citadel is also home to Ankara's oldest mosque, Alaaddin Camii, built in 1178 and located just opposite the Şark Kulesi. Unfortunately, it is rarely open and little can be seen from the outside. More interesting are the13th-century Arslanhane Camii (or Ahi Şerafettin Camii) and 14th-century Ahi Elvan Camii, just outside the walls and tucked along the winding streets that slope down from the citadel to Ulucanlar Caddesi, the main street that forms the southern boundary of the Citadel neighborhood. These mosques are remarkable for their original wooden ceilings, columns made from whole tree trunks, and Seljuk-style tiled prayer niches. ✉ *Uphill from Museum of Anatolian Civilizations, Ulus.*

Fodor's Choice
★

Anıtkabir (*Atatürk's Mausoleum*). Atatürk's picture is on every single piece of Turkish currency, his visage hangs in just about every office and official building in the country, and his principles and ideas are the foundations of modern Turkish political thought. So his vast mausoleum, perched on a hilltop overlooking the capital city he built, is on a scale suitable to his stature in Turkey. A marble promenade flanked with Hittite-style lions leads to the imposing mausoleum, where a huge sarcophagus lies beyond a colonnade with inscriptions from his speeches and below a ceiling of brilliant gold mosaics. Soldiers march endlessly around the site, and nearly every important foreign dignitary who visits the capital goes to lay a wreath here in tribute to the man who, it is not an exaggeration to say, created modern Turkey. After Atatürk died in 1938, his body was laid to rest in the building that now houses Ankara's Ethnography Museum. The construction of the Anıtkabir took nine years, from 1944 to 1953. Exactly 15 years after his death, Atatürk's remains were interred under the huge sarcophagus here.

An adjoining museum contains personal belongings from the revered man's life, including his clothes, automobiles, and personal library. The corridors underneath the tomb house an in-depth exhibit on the 1919–1922 War of Independence. The focal points are three enormous dioramas, each more than 35 meters (100 feet) in length, depicting the three major theaters of war: Çanakkale (1915), Sakarya (1921), and the Great Attack (1922). These are accompanied by rather intense sound effects—explosions, gunfire—to further dramatize the events. A map at the end of the Çanakkale hall shows Turkey and the territorial claims various other nations were making on it at the time, which gives some insight into why the Turks felt so besieged. Other exhibits explain major developments during the early republican period, particularly Atatürk's reforms and legacy. There is also a gift shop with every kind of Atatürk souvenir imaginable.

To reach the mausoleum, you can take the metro to Tandoğan and walk up the long road that ascends from the main entrance at the northern end of the grounds. A quicker way is to take a taxi to the alternate entrance on Akdeniz Caddesi, on the southeast side. ⊠ *Anıt Cad. (main entry) or Akdeniz Cad. (alternate entry)* ☏ *312/231–7975* ⊕ *www.tsk. tr/12_anitkabir/sanal_muze/index.html* 🖾 *Free* ☉ *Dec.–Mar., daily 9–4:30; Apr.–Nov., daily 9–5.*

WORTH NOTING

Bakanlıklar. Ankara's government district takes up the area west of Atatürk Bulvarı from Kızılay Meydanı at the northern tip to the Türkiye Büyük Millet Meclisi (Turkish Grand National Assembly), the parliament building, at the intersection with İsmet İnönü Bulvarı on the southern end. Within walking distance, in the Kavaklıdere neighborhood, is Embassy Row, with its gardens, fine restaurants, and world-class hotels.

Cumhuriyet Müzesi (*Museum of the Republic*). In Turkey's first parliament building, which now houses the Museum of the Republic, politicians debated principles and policies that would shape the Turkish Republic as a modern secular nation. The great hall where parliament convened from 1924 to 1960 is decorated in Seljuk and Ottoman styles, with an ornately inlaid wooden ceiling, enormous crystal chandelier, and a loggia-like gallery from which dignitaries addressed the assembly. The museum comprises a small exhibit on the early years of the Republic; although signs are only in Turkish, a free—and very informative— English audio guide is available. ⊠ *Cumhuriyet Cad. 22, off Ulus Meyd., Ulus* ☏ *312/310–5361* ⊕ *www.cumhuriyetmuzesi.gov.tr* 🖾 *3 TL* ☉ *Summer, Tues.–Sun. 8:45–6:45; winter, Tues. –Sun. 8:45–5.*

Etnoğrafya Müzesi (*Ethnography Museum*). Atatürk used this Ottoman Revival–style building as an office, and his body lay here for 15 years after his death while his enormous mausoleum was being built. The small but interesting museum houses a rich collection of Turkish carpets, folk costumes, weapons, Islamic calligraphy, and ceramics. The display of woodwork, which includes intricately carved doors, portals, *minbars* (mosque pulpits), and Seljuk thrones—some pieces dating as far back as the 13th century—is especially impressive. ⊠ *Talatpaşa Cad. and Türkocağı Sok., Ulus* ☎ *312/311–3007* 🎫 *5 TL* ☀ *Summer, Tues.– Sun. 8:30–7; winter, Tues.–Sun. 8:30–5.*

Gençlik Parkı. The pleasant Gençlik Parkı ("Youth Park") has been recently refurbished and, though not large enough to make you forget you're in the middle of the city, is a nice place for a stroll. Plantings are manicured and a small man-made lake is surrounded by a trellised walkway. Ankara's main tourist information office is also in the park. ⊠ *Cumhuriyet Cad. and İstiklal Cad., Ulus.*

Hacı Bayram Camii (*Hacı Bayram Mosque*). Dating to 1427, Hacı Bayram Camii is one of Ankara's most important mosques. Built of yellow stone and brick, it is named after the revered founder of the Bayrami order of dervishes, Hacı Bayram, whose tomb is next to the minaret. The location of the mosque and minaret, close to the ancient Temple of Augustus and Rome, indicates that this area has been a sacred site through the ages. The mosque reopened in 2011 after a major restoration and the construction of a showily decorated new wing that takes away from the site's historic character. ⊠ *Hacı Bayram Veli Cad., north of Hisarparkı Cad., Ulus* ☀ *Daily sunrise to sunset except during prayer times.*

Jülyanüs Sütunu (*Column of Julian*). A stone's throw from the Temple of Augustus and Rome, in a small traffic circle surrounded by government buildings, is the Column of Julian. It commemorates a visit by Julian the Apostate (Rome's last pagan emperor), who passed through town in 362 en route to his death in battle with the Persians. The column, usually topped by a stork's nest, has 15 fluted drums and a Corinthian capital. ⊠ *off Hükümet Cad., Ulus.*

Kocatepe Camii (*Kocatepe Mosque*). It took 20 years to build this gigantic neo-Ottoman mosque in the center of Turkey's secular capital. Officially opened in 1987, the illuminated edifice dominates the Ankara skyline at night and is one of the city's most prominent landmarks. The prestigious mosque is the site of most military and official funerals. The Kocatepe complex also includes shopping venues on the lower floors. ⊠ *On Mithat Paşa Cad., Kızılay* ☀ *Daily, sunrise to sunset.*

Resim ve Heykel Müzesi (*Painting and Sculpture Museum*). These galleries, in an ornate marble building next door to the Ethnography Museum, display a vast number of works by late Ottoman and modern Turkish artists. With a few exceptions, most of the latter haven't earned international recognition, yet this collection provides an interesting glimpse into the way Turkey's artists have been influenced by Western trends over the last century and a half. Schools of art such as impressionism and abstract expressionism are represented among the portraits, landscape paintings, sculptures, and other works on display. ⊠ *Talatpaşa Cad. and Türkocağı Sok., Ulus* ☎ *312/310–2094* 🎫 *Free* ☀ *Tues.–Sun. 9–noon and 1–5.*

6

MEET THE HITTITES

Around 1800 BC a people called the Hittites, who like the Persians spoke an Indo-European language (unlike the Turks, whose language is Ural-Altaic), apparently entered Anatolia after crossing the Caucasus steppes beyond the Black Sea. They claimed the city of Hattuşa—with a fortress, temples, large adminis- trative buildings, houses, cemeter- ies, and decorated gateways and courtyards—as their capital and soon began to build an empire. They worshipped a storm god and a sun goddess, and had a well-ordered society with written laws. At their height, they conquered Babylon and battled the Egyptian pharaohs. One of the most famous finds in Hattuşa is a copy of the Treaty of Kadesh (c. 1259 BC), signed between the Hittite and Egyptian empires after what might have been the largest chariot battle ever fought, involving some 5,000 chariots. The Hittites' reign came to an end after some 600 years, when tribes from the north sacked and burned Hattuşa in 1200

BC. The Phrygians then became the dominant people in the region.

What you can see today at Boğazkale (the modern-day Turkish name for Hattuşa) is mainly the foun- dations of buildings. Yazılıkaya, about 3 km (2 miles) to the east, is far more interesting. Yazılıkaya (meaning "inscribed rock" in Turkish) is thought to have served as Hattuşa's religious sanctuary. The walls here are cov- ered with drawings of Hittite gods, goddesses, and kings from about 1200 BC. On the main shrine, 42 gods march from the left to meet 21 goddesses coming from the right. In the middle is the weather god Tes- hub with horns in his cap, and the sun goddess Hepatu riding a leopard. It's thought that funeral rights for kings were performed here.

The Hittite cities are about 200 km (124 miles) northeast of Ankara, a two-hour drive. A guided trip from Ankara, however, will shed a great deal of light on what are often oth- erwise unintelligible piles of rocks arranged in squares.

Roma Hamamları (*Roman Baths*). You can't bathe at this 3rd-century complex just north of Ulus Square, but you can see how the Romans did. The large bath system featured a frigidarium, tepidarium, and caldarium (cold, warm, and hot rooms), as well as steam rooms that had raised floors. An illustration near the entrance shows the layout of the Roman city superimposed over a map of the modern area, indicat- ing just how little of ancient Ancyra has been excavated. Also scattered around the open-air site are various stone fragments, some of which appear to be ancient gravestones, with Latin and Hebrew inscriptions. ⊠ *Çankırı Cad. 54, Ulus* ☎ *312/310–7280* ≊ *3 TL* ⊙ *Daily 8–5:30.*

Temple of Augustus and Rome. Though it's in a rather sad state today, the Temple of Augustus and Rome, built 25–20 BC, is of great historical significance—inscribed in marble on its walls is the most complete Latin and Greek text of the *Res Gestae Divi Augusti*, in which the Emperor Augustus lists his deeds. The temple is now largely supported by metal scaffolding and the site can only be viewed from a walkway put up around it. ⊠ *Next to Hacı Bayram Camii, Ulus.*

WHERE TO EAT

$$$ ✕ **Çengelhan Brasserie.** The glass-roofed courtyard of the Rahmi M.
TURKISH Koç Museum (the Ankara counterpart of the Istanbul museum, which
focuses on the history of transport, industry, and communications),
next to the Divan Çukurhan hotel, provides a relaxed and stylish din-
ing experience, accented with the soothing splashing of a fountain and
classical music playing in the background. Service is excellent, special
attention is paid to presentation, and the menu offers a blend of Turkish
and contemporary cuisine. Expect starters like shrimp casserole with
porcini mushrooms and mains such as grilled chicken with thyme and
traditional *firik* pilaf. The restaurant stays open in the evening after
the museum closes. $ *Average main: 36 TL* ✉ *Necatibey Mah., Depo
Sok. 1, Ulus* ☎ *312/309–6800* ⊕ *www.divan.com.tr* ☖ *Reservations
essential* ☽ *Closed Mon.*

$$ ✕ **Ege Restaurant.** This charming spot just off fashionable Tunalı Hilmi
SEAFOOD Caddesi specializes in Aegean-style fish dishes (Ege is the Turkish name
for the Aegean Sea) and the décor—painted wood chairs and blue-and-
white walls with seashore motifs—transports you straight to the Aegean
islands. To top it off, a map of the region is painted on the ceiling. The
seafood-based mezes are excellent. $ *Average main: 27 TL* ✉ *Büklüm
Sok. 54/B, Kavaklıdere* ☎ *312/428–2717* ⊕ *www.egerestaurant.com*
☖ *Reservations essential* ☽ *Closed Sun.*

$$ ✕ **Zenger Paşa Konağı.** Several levels of this restored 18th-century Otto-
TURKISH man mansion in the citadel offer panoramic city views. The décor
throughout is rustic and the selection of mezes and kebabs broad. One
highlight is the *saç kavurma,* a meat dish cooked over an alcohol flame
as you watch. The restaurant also makes a tasty village-style flatbread
called *bazlama.* There is live Turkish music every night but Sunday, and
although the place has an undeniably touristy side, it's also popular
with locals. $ *Average main: 25 TL* ✉ *Doyran Sok. 13, Kaleiçi, Ulus*
☎ *312/311–7070* ⊕ *www.zengerpasa.com* ☖ *Reservations essential.*

WHERE TO STAY

$$ ☗ **Angora House Hotel.** A beautifully restored 19th-century Ottoman
B&B/INN house inside the walls of Ankara's ancient citadel has the feel of a pri-
vate home—six charming rooms have original wood floors and ceilings,
antique chandeliers, and comfortable beds. **Pros:** good-size rooms; historic area; property has lots of character; friendly staff. **Cons:** neighborhood can be noisy; somewhat difficult for vehicles to reach and for
taxis to find; no elevator. $ *Rooms from: $130* ✉ *Kale Kapısı Sok. 16,
Hisar, Ulus* ☎ *312/309–8380* ⊕ *www.angorahouse.com.tr* ⮑ *6 rooms*
☒ *Breakfast.*

$$$ ☗ **Divan Çukurhan.** Elegant rooms in a restored 16th-century *kervan-*
HOTEL *saray* at the edge of Ankara's citadel are decorated in different styles,
Fodor's Choice such as Indochinese, Venetian, Tibetan, and Ottoman; some have cita-
★ del or city views, and all feature antique furniture and original works
of art. **Pros:** unique historical atmosphere; personalized service; quiet,
oasis-like rooms. **Cons:** atop a steep hill; no in-room minibar or fridge;
poor Wi-Fi and cell phone reception in rooms. $ *Rooms from: $220*
✉ *Necatibey Mah., Depo Sok. 3, Ulus* ☎ *312/306–6400* ⊕ *www.divan.
com.tr* ⮑ *16 rooms, 3 suites* ☒ *Breakfast.*

$$ **Radisson Blu Hotel, Ankara.** The only international chain hotel in
HOTEL Ankara's historic Ulus district is somewhat lacking in flair but has
comfortable rooms, with light-color woods and colorfully patterned,
contemporary carpets and curtains. **Pros:** convenient location near
major tourist attractions; next to metro station. **Cons:** overlooks a loud,
busy expressway (to avoid street noise, request a back-facing room);
decor feels rather dated; hotel doesn't quite live up to Radisson Blu stan-
dards. $ *Rooms from: $130* ⊠ *İstiklal Cad. 20, Ulus* ☎ *312/310–4848*
⊕ *www.radissonblu.com* ➷ *183 rooms, 19 suites* ❏ *Breakfast.*

$$$$ **Sheraton Ankara.** Unlike many large international chain hotels, the
HOTEL Sheraton Ankara has personality. **Pros:** located in bustling nightlife
and shopping district; professional service; excellent fitness facili-
ties. **Cons:** large complex can feel somewhat impersonal; expensive
food and drinks. $ *Rooms from: $305* ⊠ *Noktalı Sok., Kavaklıdere*
☎ *312/457–6000* ⊕ *www.sheratonankara.com* ➷ *292 rooms, 19 suites*
❏ *No meals.*

$$$ **Swissôtel Ankara.** A setting in the posh Çankaya district is part of the
HOTEL allure here, as are style and sophistication—rooms have elegant décor
in soothing colors; large bathrooms have deep tubs and separate rain
showers; and an extensive wellness center includes a half-Olympic-
size indoor pool, a beautiful hammam, sauna, full spa, and large fitness room. **Pros:** upscale yet relaxed; excellent service, dining options,
and fitness facilities. **Cons:** hotel is in a residential neighborhood far
from major sights and a short drive from nightlife; expensive food and
drinks; extra charge for Internet, which can be slow. $ *Rooms from:
$220* ⊠ *Yıldızlıevler Mah. Jose Marti Cad. 2, Çankaya* ☎ *312/409–3000*
⊕ *www.swissotel.com* ➷ *145 rooms, 5 suites* ❏ *No meals.*

SHOPPING

Kavaklıdere. The upscale district of Kavaklıdere—and in particular, the
main drag, Tunalı Hilmi Caddesi—is home to a range of Turkish and
international brands and designer labels. Karum shopping mall, next
door to the Sheraton, has more of the same.

Kızılay. The pedestrian area of Kızılay, especially Konur Sokak, is a good
place to find books and Turkish music.

Samanpazarı. The area from Atpazarı Sokak down the hill from the citadel towards Ulucanlar Caddesi has narrow, winding streets with shops
selling antiques, handicrafts, carpets, metalwork, and other items. There
are also a few such shops inside the citadel, aimed mostly at tourists
but with some interesting wares.

EXCURSIONS TO THE FAR EAST AND BLACK SEA COAST

WELCOME TO THE FAR EAST AND THE BLACK SEA COAST

TOP REASONS TO GO

★ **Explore the ruins of Ani:** This ancient city was once the seat of a small Armenian kingdom.

★ **Float in Lake Van:** As in Israel's Dead Sea, the water is rich in minerals and very alkaline; you'll be remarkably buoyant in the startlingly blue water.

★ **Take the ferry to Akdamar:** The uninhabited island and its monastery are worth the trek.

★ **Journey up Mt. Nemrut:** The massive stone heads looking out over the horizon are an impressive sight to behold.

★ **Visit the cliff-side monastery of Sümela:** The climb is fairly strenuous, but just seeing this remarkable sight is unforgettable.

★ **Wander through the bustling bazaars of Urfa and Gaziantep:** Craftsmen in these ancient cities still work the same way they have for centuries.

1 **The Black Sea Coast, Trabzon, and the Sümela Monastery.** This region is like no other part of Turkey. With lush green valleys, snowcapped peaks, and small villages with chalet-like homes, it looks like a little piece of Switzerland.

2 **Between Kars and Van.** This is Turkey's eastern frontier, filled with wide-open vistas, high mountain plateaus, and natural and man-made wonders, all offering a wonderful mix of adventure and history. Here you can see the haunting ancient city of Ani, the majestic Mt. Ararat, and various sites around Lake Van, especially the island church of Akdamar.

3 **Around Diyarbakır and Mardin.** This area, part of ancient Mesopotamia, is steeped in history. The old cities are filled with honey-color stone homes and small hillside villages surrounded by vineyards, and look something like a Turkish Tuscany.

4 **Gaziantep and Urfa.** Traveling around these cities will give you a flavor of the Middle East, from bustling bazaars where coppersmiths bang away with hammers to spicy local cuisine. This is also the best spot to begin a journey to the huge stone heads atop Mt. Nemrut.

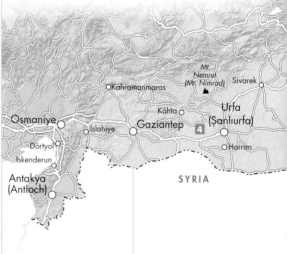

Mt. Nemrut

Climbing Mount Ararat, Doğubeyazit

GETTING ORIENTED

For the visitor who makes it to Turkey's eastern regions, the rewards are plentiful: beautiful scenery, wild nature, and countless historic sites, where tourists are rare and life hasn't changed much over the centuries. Turkey's eastern half is so vast that it's necessary to divide it into separate regions, each offering something different for travelers.

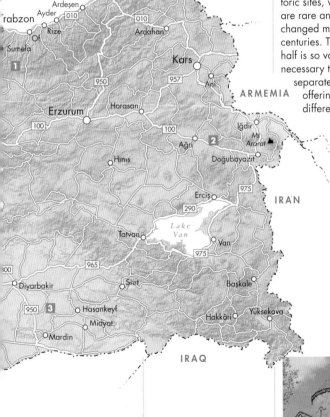

Akdamar Island

Updated by
Scott Newman

Eastern Turkey may not have the resorts, luxury hotels, and chic restaurants found in the more-visited parts of the country, but the rewards of travel here—impressive sites, both natural and man-made—are many.

Wherever you decide to visit in eastern Turkey, you'll find much to see and do. The landscape begins with the rocky beaches of the Black Sea and rises through lush, almost subtropical foothills up to the snow-capped Kaçkar Mountains, then through the stark highlands toward vast Lake Van and the arid semidesert borderlands of the Middle East. This region shows Turkey at its most Middle Eastern, where the call to prayer comes from intricately carved stone minarets and bazaars are filled with locals buying daily necessities rather than tourists buying souvenirs. Ancient history is everywhere, and you're sure to see several churches and living monasteries that have been around for over a thousand years. Some believe this is also the place Abraham himself called home, as well as the final resting place of Noah's Ark.

PLANNING

WHEN TO GO

Spring and fall are generally the best times to visit these areas, with the exception of cities like Kars and Van, where summers are quite cool compared to the rest of Turkey. Cities like Gaziantep, Urfa, and Mardin are best avoided in July and August, when the heat can be sweltering.

GETTING HERE AND AROUND

Getting to eastern Turkey once meant grueling bus rides that sometimes took more than a day. The arrival of budget air travel has changed this dramatically, and several domestic airlines now crisscross Turkey. Many of the major cities in the region, including Trabzon, Van, Mardin, and Gaziantep, have airports.

Most flights come from Istanbul or Ankara, but if you want to travel throughout the region and avoid backtracking, Sun Express Airlines has flights from several eastern cities to İzmir or Antalya.

You'll probably find that a rental car is the easiest way to take in the sights of eastern Turkey, allowing you to reach some of the more remote spots and explore at your leisure. Cars are readily available in most larger towns. You can also travel between major cities by bus, taking tours to sites like Sumela and Ani, but transport is usually by minibus rather than the larger, more comfortable buses found in western Turkey.

RESTAURANTS

You won't find any fancy sit-down restaurants in this region, but eastern Turkey is the place for smaller eateries offering flavorful local cuisine and welcoming patrons. Food in the Black Sea area relies on dishes made with dairy, corn flour, and seafood, especially *hamsi,* which are locally caught anchovies. Although meat kebabs rule the rest of the east, most restaurants will also offer a variety of delicious vegetable dishes cooked in olive oil, along with stews and other ready-made hot dishes, which are usually meat-based.

Prices in the reviews are the average cost of a main course at dinner or if dinner is not served, at lunch.

HOTELS

With some notable exceptions, the hotels in the east are basic, with little in the way of the luxuries you might find along Turkey's Mediterranean coastline. A few boutique hotels are beginning to pop up though, particularly in Mardin, and most cities have at least one decent modern hotel catering to Turkish business travelers. Be sure to book these well in advance.

Prices in the reviews are the lowest cost of a standard double room in high season. For expanded reviews, visit Fodors.com.

TOURS

Tourism here is rather underdeveloped compared to the rest of the country, which makes options for organized tours limited. The main exceptions are tours from Sumela to Trabzon and Kars to Ani, where tours operate daily in season. Several companies can organize hiking expeditions in the Kaçkar Mountains. Usually you can find at least one tour guide in most major towns, but places like Midran, Midyat, and Urfa are fine for exploring on your own.

BEING CAREFUL

During the 1980s and '90s, large parts of Turkey's east and southeast (but not the Black Sea area) were the scene of bitter fighting between the separatists of the Kurdistan Workers' Party (PKK) and Turkish security forces. The fighting has largely stopped, which has allowed tourism in the region to get off the ground again. Cities you're likely to visit are now safe and have been for over a decade. There are still incidents, particularly near the Turkey–Iraq border and in such places like Hakkari and Şirnak. But these are remote areas where few tourists, let alone Turks, go, and the Turkish army will actively stop you from visiting any troubled areas. Recent conflicts in Syria may give visitors to places like Antakya and Gaziantep some alarm, but the border is a whole hour away from these cities, and even if you do venture closer, a lot of barbed wire and Turkish soldiers stand between you and the conflict.

DO YOU SPEAK TURKISH?

These areas are less touristy and finding English speakers can sometimes be a challenge, though tourist offices and most hotels will usually have someone on staff who speaks at least some basic English. In a pinch, try a combination of hand gestures and key English words that nonspeakers are likely to know, but it's a great idea to take a Turkish phrasebook with you on visits to this region.

TRABZON AND THE BLACK SEA COAST

Of all of Turkey's regions, the Black Sea coast least fits the bill of what most visitors imagine to be "Turkish." Instead of long, sandy beaches lined with resorts, the Black Sea's shores are rocky and backed by steep, lush mountains. And instead of sunny days, the area is often shrouded in mist. Culturally, the area has had as many Greek, Georgian, and Armenian influences as it has Ottoman and Turkish. Although less visited than other parts of Turkey, the region is also one of the most rewarding, with interesting destinations like the historic seaside town of Trabzon, the nearby monastery complex of Sümela that clings dramatically to the side of a cliff in a deep valley, and the Kaçkar Mountains with 15,000-foot peaks towering over the area.

Trabzon, wedged between the Black Sea and the green mountains that rise behind it, is a city with a long historic pedigree that stretches back to Byzantine times, though today it's quite modern and, like many other cities in the region, is cursed with an overabundance of ugly concrete buildings. Trabzon is also a good base for visiting the fascinating (though defunct) Orthodox monastery complex of Sümela, breathtakingly hidden in a narrow valley and clinging to the side of a steep cliff. Although the monastery, which was functioning until the 1920s, and its beautiful frescoes have been victims to vandalism over the years, an extensive restoration project is under way.

As you head east from Trabzon, toward the Georgian border, you will pass through Rize, Turkey's tea-growing capital, where hills are carpeted with carefully laid-out rows of dark green tea plants. From there you'll soon approach several valleys that lead up into the majestic Kaçkar Mountains, dotted with small villages and wooden homes that evoke the Alps. Up in the Fırtına valley is Ayder, a mountain village that serves as a wonderful base for hiking and exploring the area's mountain trails and *yaylas*, the high-pasture summer villages where the rhythms of life seem to have changed little over the centuries.

TRABZON

Trabzon has a dramatic location, perched on a hill overlooking the sea, with lush green mountains behind. Once the capital of the empire founded in 1204 by Alexius Comnenus, grandson of a Byzantine emperor, the city was famed for its golden towers and glittering mosaics. Today's Trabzon seems far removed from that imperial past: the city is bustling and modern, with a busy port, crowded streets, and seemingly little to distinguish it from many other provincial Turkish towns.

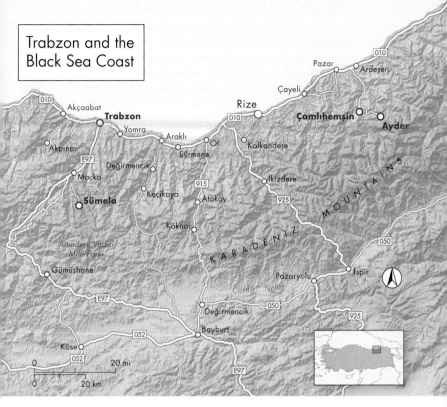

Trabzon and the
Black Sea Coast

It only takes a little digging, though, to get under the modern surface. Byzantine-era churches, such as the lovely Aya Sofya, a smaller version of the similarly named church in Istanbul, can be found not far from modern apartment buildings. Meanwhile, the city's old town with its Ottoman-era houses, pedestrian-only streets, and lively bazaar are a nice break from the concrete and crowds.

GETTING HERE AND AROUND
There are several daily flights to Trabzon from Istanbul, and at least one a day from Ankara, İzmir, and Antalya. Fares are competitive, so check with the different airlines to see who has the best.

You can drive or take a bus to Trabzon, but it's a long way from other Turkish cities you may be visiting—1,071 km (665 miles) from Istanbul, 744 km (462 miles) from Ankara, and 591 km (367 miles) from Kayseri. You're better off flying and renting a car when you arrive.

Bus service between towns runs frequently and is inexpensive. The company with the most reliable and frequent service is Ulusoy, which has an office just off Trabzon's main square, Atatürk Alanı. They also have daily tours to Sumela.

Renting a car, though, is the most convenient way of getting around the Black Sea region, and allows you to explore the mountains more easily.

TURKISH NUTS AND TEA

Economic life on the Black Sea is dominated by two crops: hazelnuts and tea. Near Rize, the hills are covered in row after row of tea plants, tended to by villagers who harvest the leaves in late spring. Every year, more than 200,000 tons of tea are harvested in the area, most of it for domestic consumption. Turkey is also the globe's leading producer of hazelnuts, responsible for more than 80% of the world's supply. Hazelnuts, often fresh off the tree and still in their shell, are easy to find in shops and on the streets throughout Turkey, especially in late summer and early fall.

Avis has an office in downtown Trabzon, as well as one at the airport. There are also several local companies around Trabzon's Atatürk Alanı.

TOURS

Eyce Tours can help with arranging tours to Sümela and the region around Trabzon.

Contacts Eyce ☎ 462/326–7174 ⊕ www.eycetours.com. **Visitor Information.** ⊠ Atatürk Alanı 47, near Atatürk Alanı ☎ 462/326–4760.

EXPLORING

TOP ATTRACTIONS

Atatürk Alanı (*Taksim Meydanı*). The heart of Trabzon's social activity is its pleasing central square, Atatürk Alanı, also known simply as Meydan, up İskele Caddesi from the port. In Byzantine and Ottoman time the camel caravans assembled here before heading across the mountains. Today the square is full of shady tea gardens and surrounded by most of the city's hotels and restaurants. ⊠ *Atatürk Alanı.*

Aya Sofya (*Church of the Holy Wisdom, or St. Sophia*). Trabzon's best-known Byzantine monument is this well preserved 13th-century church sitting on a bluff overlooking the Black Sea that was converted into a mosque in Ottoman times. The highlights are the wonderful Byzantine frescoes housed in the west porch: technicolor angels on the ceiling, Christ preaching in the temple, the Annunciation, and the wedding at Cana—all executed in a style that shows strong Italian influences. Often overlooked are the graffiti of ships, carved into the outside of the apse by sailors for good luck. A shaded tea garden near the entrance is a popular place for breakfast. It was officially reopened as a mosque in 2013, though most of the frescoes are only visible behind large sheets of cloth. ⊠ *Kayakmeydan Cad.* ☎ 462/223–3043 ⊇ *Free* ☉ *Sunrise–sunset.*

Bazaar. The pedestrian-only Kunduracılar Caddesi leads into the maze of the covered bazaar, which includes a 16th-century *bedestan,* or market, that has been restored and now houses several cafés and some gift shops selling unremarkable trinkets. The bazaar largely sells cheap clothes to locals, but does have a small but appealing section of coppersmiths, who make a variety of bowls, trays, and pots. The city's largest mosque, the **Çarşi Cami,** was built in 1839 and is joined to the market by an archway. ⊠ *Just past Cumhuriyet Cad.*

Citadel. Trabzon's Byzantine-era citadel was built on part of a hill formed by two ravines, and while not much is left of the building's former glory, the soaring outside walls and massive columns are still impressive (restored after the Ottoman conquest in 1461) and a testament to the fact that no army ever took Trabzon by force, though many tried. The only remaining part of the interior is the 10th-century church of **Panaghia Chrysokephalos** (the Virgin of the Golden Head), which was the city's cathedral and where many of its rulers were married, crowned, and buried. The Ottomans converted it into a mosque, the **Ortahisar Cami,** in the 15th century. ⊠ *Kale Cad.; from Hükümet Cad. (off Maraş Cad.), follow Tabakhane Bridge over gorge, turn left.*

> **BLACK SEA SPECIALTIES**
>
> Size isn't everything, as the miniscule *hamsi* (Black Sea anchovy) proves. Though usually not much longer than your finger, the hamsi is often called the "Prince of the Black Sea" fish, and it's found in an almost endless variety of dishes: fried in a coating of cornmeal, served in a fragrant pilaf, baked into bread, or thrown into an omelet (there have even been some attempts at making hamsi ice cream). Also try *muhallema* (a type of Black Sea cheese fondue) and honey made in the high mountain villages of the Kaçkars.

WORTH NOTING

Atatürk Köşkü. Trabzon's weathy citizens once retreated to villas in the hills above town. Greek banker Konstantin Kabayanidis built this attractive white gingerbread house, set in a small forest with nice views of the city below, and Atatürk stayed here in 1924, 1930, and 1937. Much of the original furniture remains in place. ⊠ *Soğuksu Cad., 7 km (4 miles) southwest of Trabzon's central square* ☎ *462/231–0028* 🖃 *2 TL* ☉ *May–Sept., daily 8–7; Oct.–Apr., daily 9–5.*

Sekiz Direk Hammam. Turkey's oldest, still-functioning hammam is thought to be Byzantine, from the 12th or 13th centuries. The name comes from the eight (*sekiz*) columns (*direk*) that support the dome of the hot room in the men's section. ⊠ *Sok. 1* ☎ *462/322–1012* 🖃 *20 TL.*

Trabzon Museum. The main attraction of the Trabzon Museum is the building itself, a 1910 mansion built for a local Greek banker. The ornate rooms of the main floor have been restored and filled with period furniture. The basement holds a small collection of archaeological finds from the Trabzon region, while upstairs you'll find a collection devoted to local people and their culture. ⊠ *Zeytinlik Cad. 10* ☎ *462/322–3822* 🖃 *3 TL* ☉ *Tues.–Sun. 9–5.*

WHERE TO EAT

$

SEAFOOD

✕ **Cemil Usta.** In an old stone building on the north side of Atatürk Alanı, you'll find this place serving a mix of seafood and local dishes like *akçaabat köfte* (meatballs) and *kuymak* fondue (made of cheese and flour). Grab a seat streetside or on the long balcony, which is a great spot for dinner on a summer evening. The free baklava dessert is a delight. 🖫 *Average main: 15 TL* ⊠ *Atatürk Alanı 6* ☎ *462/321–6161.*

$$ SEAFOOD 🍴 **Fevzi Hoca.** There's no menu here at Trabzon's most serious seafood restaurant; you'll simply be shown the fish available (this usually includes Trabzon's local obsession, *hamsi,* or anchovies) and you get to choose what you want. The restaurant is decorated with photos of famous Turks dining on the premises, a hint of just how popular it is. Non-fish eaters can order the delicious *akçaabat köfte* (meatballs). [$] *Average main: 25 TL* ✉ *Maraş Cad. İpekyolu İş Merkezi* ☎ *462/326–5444.*

$ TURKISH 🍴 **Kebabci Ahmet Usta.** This sleek modern dining room on lively pedestrian Uzun Sokak is a busy local favorite. It offers all the standard kebabs and pides, plus a few rarer dishes such as *talaş kebabı* (sawdust kebab), lamb wrapped in pastry, and *orman kebabı* (forest kebab), lamb on the bone with vegetables. There are also local specialties such as *kuymak,* a thick syrup of cornmeal, and several dishes with *lahana,* the local cabbage. [$] *Average main: 15 TL* ✉ *Uzun Sok. 56* ☎ *462/326–5666.*

WHERE TO STAY

$$ HOTEL 🏨 **Horon Hotel.** The best thing about these spacious rooms one block off the main square is the helpful service and rooftop restaurant that offers a good-value prix-fixe menu and views over the sea. **Pros:** central location; helpful English-speaking staff; parking and valet service are a blessing. **Cons:** some noise from bar, especially on weekends; a little pricey for what you get. [$] *Rooms from: 270 TL* ✉ *Sıramağazalar Cad. 125* ☎ *462/326–6455* 🌐 *www.otelhoron.com* 🛏 *44 rooms* 🍽 *Breakfast.*

$ B&B/INN 🏨 **Hotel Nur.** At Trabzon's best budget option, rooms are spotless (though small and painted bright green), some overlook the main square, and those in front on the higher floors even have a sea view. **Pros:** overlooks the town square; helpful English-speaking staff. **Cons:** call to prayer from the mosque next door may disturb you in the morning. [$] *Rooms from: 150 TL* ✉ *Cami Sok. 15* ☎ *462/323–0445* 🛏 *20 rooms* 🍽 *Breakfast.*

$$$ HOTEL 🏨 **Novotel Trabzon.** Half of the large, modern rooms face the sea, and all are just footsteps from the beach. **Pros:** beautiful beach location; quality rooms and service. **Cons:** out of town; somewhat generic. [$] *Rooms from: 370 TL* ✉ *Yumra, turn toward sea from lights opposite the Dunya Ticaret Merkezi (World Trade Center) and Cevahir Mall* ☎ *462/455–9000* 🛏 *200 rooms* 🍽 *No meals.*

$$ HOTEL 🏨 **Taş Konak.** This former mansion just east of the city center is the closest thing to a boutique hotel in the region, with many of the stone building's original features still in place, such as carved wooden doors and ceilings. **Pros:** historic building; good service. **Cons:** major busy road out front means noise; not the nicest walk into city center. [$] *Rooms from: 250 TL* ✉ *Yavuz Selim Blvd. 89* ☎ *462/325–7717* 🛏 *15 rooms* 🍽 *Breakfast.*

$$$$ HOTEL 🏨 **Zorlu Grand Hotel.** Trabzon's fanciest hotel offers large, elegant, and comfortably furnished rooms; a marble-lined, atrium-like lobby topped by a stained-glass dome and done up in an art deco–meets-Moorish style; and a courteous and professional staff. **Pros:** central location; extensive facilities; helpful staff. **Cons:** expensive spa services; some rooms overlook busy streets while others face interior courtyard.

The hike up to the breathtaking Sümela Monastery makes for a worthy day trip.

[$] *Rooms from: 450 TL* ✉ *Maraş Cad. 9* ☎ *462/326–8400* 🌐 *www.zorlugrand.com* 🛏 *143 rooms, 14 suites* 🍴 *Breakfast.*

SÜMELA/MEREYEMANA

47 km (29 miles) south of Trabzon.

The Sümela Monastery (also known as the Monastery of the Virgin, and *Mereyemana* in Turkish) is a spectacular and unforgettable sight, perched some 820 feet above the valley floor and often lost in the clouds.

GETTING HERE AND AROUND

Many companies in Trabazon offer day trips to Sümela, usually for about 30 TL; one reliable choice is Ulusoy, on Taksin Caddesi. If you are driving, take Route 885 to Maçka, then head east on the road to Altındere National Park.

Contacts Ulusoy ✉ *Taksim Cad., Trabzon* ☎ *462/321–1281.*

EXPLORING

Fodor's Choice ★ **Monastery of the Virgin.** Set in a dramatic valley and clinging to the side of a sheer cliff, the Sümela monastery is stunnıng to behold. Orthodox monks founded the retreat in the 5th century, living in cliff-top caves surrounding a shrine housing a miraculous icon of the Virgin painted by St. Luke. The labyrinth of courtyards, corridors, and chapels date from the time of Emperor Alexius III of Trebizond, who was crowned here in 1340—the monastery continued under the sultans, remaining until the Greeks were expelled from Turkey in 1922. Although the icon and other treasures have been removed, extensive frescoes done between the 14th and 18th centuries remain. They are not as well preserved as those at Trabzon's Aya Sofya, and sections have been chipped away or scribbled over by graffiti artists, but they are impressive nonetheless in their depictions of Old and New Testament images—look for an Arab-looking Jesus, an almost African virgin, and a scene of Adam and Eve, expelled from Eden, taking up a plough. The first, lower parking lot is beside the river and Sümela Restaurant. From there a well-worn trail to the monastery is a rigorous 40-minute hike. Farther on is a second, upper parking lot, at the level of the monastery, a 15-minute walk away on a level path. Most organized day excursions from Trabzon drop you at the upper lot and collect you from the lower one. ✉ *Altındere National Park* 🎟 *8 TL, 12 TL for parking* ⏲ *Apr.–Oct., daily 9–6; Nov.–Mar., daily 9–4.*

WHERE TO EAT

$ TURKISH 🍴 **Sümela Sosyal Tesisleri.** Just below the Sümela monastery, a series of open-air wood patios spread out along a thunderous rushing stream makes wonderful use of the stunning location. You can order fresh trout or choose from a few regional dishes, such as *kuymak,* the Black Sea version of cheese fondue. Alcohol is available. [$] *Average main: 10 TL* ✉ *Sümela Manastiri* ☎ *462/531–1207.*

$ TURKISH 🍴 **Sümer Restaurant.** These wooden gazebos set on the edge of a small river are a fine spot to have lunch or dinner after visiting Sümela, a 15-minute drive away. There is a wide selection of mezes, along with regional specialties such as *canlı alabalık,* trout baked in butter, and *kaygana,* an omelet made with Black Sea anchovies. On the weekends, the place is filled with families from Trabzon on country outings. [$] *Average main: 10 TL* ✉ *Maçka Sümela Manastırı Yolu Km 2* ☎ *462/512–1581.*

EN ROUTE

Northeast of Rize, several forested valleys lead from the Black Sea into the towering and beautiful Kaçkar Mountains. Dotted with small villages, the cool mountains are a great place for hiking or just kicking back and checking out the alpine views. The mountains are also home to several *yaylas,* high-pasture villages that are inhabited only during the summer and are accessible only by footpath.

Morina Balık Lokantası. This unassuming restaurant on the coastal road halfway between Trabzon and Rize serves some of the best fish in the area and is worth a stop if you're driving through. There's always a varied selection of freshly caught options—including meaty salmon steaks—cooked over hot coals or fried in a dusting of corn flour. The tomato-based fish chowder is also tasty. A pleasant garden is shaded by creeping vines. ✉ *35 km (22 miles) out of Trabzon in direction of Rize, Çamburn/Sürmene, Sürmene* ☎ *462/752–2023.*

Zıraat Parkı. Rize, 75 km (47 miles) east of Trabzon and the capital of the Black Sea's tea-growing region, sits above a small bay below the foothills of the lush Pontic Mountains. There's not much to do here, though you can stop for a glass of the local brew in the hilltop Zıraat Parkı, a botanical garden near the town's western entrance. There's a small kiosk in the parking lot that sells gift packs of tea. ✉ *Rize.*

ÇAMLIHEMŞIN

124 km (77 miles) northeast of Trabzon; 22 km (14 miles) south of Ardeşen.

The small village of Çamlıhemşin, at the junction of two rushing rivers, serves mainly as a gateway to mountain valleys above, particularly to the village of Ayder. Yet this is a pleasant and quiet overnight stop before heading up into the Kaçkars. There's not much to do here other than look out on the green mountains and listen to the river flowing by.

GETTING HERE AND AROUND

You will probably want to make the excursion to Çamlıhemşin by car, the only real way to explore the villages and valleys. Follow the coast east from Trabzon to Ardeşen, then head inland to Çamlıhemşin on a well-marked road. If traveling by bus you have to change in Pazar.

WHERE TO STAY

$$ **Fırtına Pansiyon.** This *pansiyon* in a converted schoolhouse, with six rooms and three bungalows, is set amid green mountains in a completely solitary spot and is the most inviting of the few places to stay in Fırtına Valley. **Pros:** beautiful environs and a quirky style; cabins are good for families. **Cons:** quite remote; intermittent hot water; shared bathrooms. $ *Rooms from: 150 TL* ⊠ *Şenyuva Köyü, Çamlıhemşin* ☎ *464/653–3111* ⊕ *www.firtinavadisi.com* ↝ *6 rooms, 3 cabins* ▭ *No credit cards* ⊘ *Closed Oct.–Mar.* ❖ *Some meals.*

$$
B&B/INN
Fodor's Choice
★
Moyy Minotel. Earthy and arty, traditional and modern, with lots of exposed timber, this beautiful 80-year-old chestnut building beside the river brings a different experience to the area, with six surprisingly stylish rooms with touches like cute wooden bathroom cabinets and funky stone bowl basins; try to get one of the three river-view rooms. **Pros:** cool and intimate; good for visiting both the Fırtına Valley and Ayder. **Cons:** traffic noise in some rooms; small bathrooms. $ *Rooms from: 200 TL* ⊠ *İnönü Cad. 35, Çamlıhemşin* ↝ *6 rooms* ❖ *Breakfast.*

OFF THE BEATEN PATH Most people take a left out of Çamlıhemşin and continue up to the mountain village of Ayder, but continuing straight on the road takes you into the Fırtına Valley, an often mist-shrouded place that sees few visitors and seems forgotten by time. Waterfalls and streams tumble out of the mountains, which are covered by thick stands of green pines. Small villages with peak-roofed two-story wooden houses cling to the mountainsides. As you drive along the road, you'll pass several examples of the elegant Ottoman-era humpback bridges spanning the rivers. Zil Kalesi is a small but spectacular castle along the road some 20 km (12 miles) outside Çamlıhemşin.

AYDER

90 km (56 miles) northeast of Rize; 17 km (11 miles) southeast of Çamlıhemşin on a well-marked road.

At 4,000 feet and surrounded by snowcapped mountains and tumbling waterfalls, the mountain village of Ayder, with its wooden chalets and wandering cows, can seem like a piece of Switzerland transported to Turkey. Once a sleepy *yayla,* a high-pasture village where locals live in the summer, Ayder has become a popular destination for Turkish tourists and, increasingly, foreign ones. Although a few years ago the village's bucolic nature was threatened by overdevelopment, local laws have now ordered all building to be done in the local style, with wooden exteriors and peaked roofs. Summer weekend crowds can fill the small village to capacity, but the setting is still beautiful. The village is also an excellent base for day hikes or extended treks in the Kaçkars and for visiting some of the less accessible yaylas in the region to see a way of life that has changed little over the centuries.

The easiest yayla to visit from Ayder is Yukarı Kavron, about 10 km (6 miles) from the village along a dirt road. A collection of squat stone houses, it's set on a high plateau surrounded by gorgeous mountains. There are several nice hikes leading out of the village. There is regular minivan service in the morning out of Ayder to the yayla, although it's best to check with your hotel or *pansiyon* about the exact schedule.

Ayder has a grassy main square that during the summer frequently plays host to festivals celebrating local Hemşin culture. Locals play music on a version of the bagpipe (known as the *bağlama*) and men and women dance together in a big circle, known as *horon* dancing.

EXPLORING

Hot Springs. Ayder is also known for its hot springs, reputed to cure all types of ailments. True or not, the springs, housed in a modern, marble-lined building near the village's mosque, are good for a relaxing soak after a day of hiking. There are separate facilities for men and women, as well as private rooms for couples that want to bathe together. ☎ *464/657–2100* 🎫 *9TL; 40TL for a private room* 🕐 *Daily 7:30 am–11 pm.*

WHERE TO EAT AND STAY

$ TURKISH 🍴 **Ayder Sofrası.** In good weather, the place to sit is the stone-lined terrace with wooden picnic tables that look over the mountains and the waterfall. The kitchen turns out trout and local dishes such as stuffed cabbage and *muhallama,* the local cheese fondue, as well as meat options, and serves an open buffet breakfast every day. [$] *Average main: 13 TL* ✉ *Ayder Kapalıcaları* ☎ *464/657–2037.*

$ B&B/INN 🏨 **Kuşpuni Dinlenme Evi.** Set on the edge of a green field, this wooden chalet has large, comfortable rooms, and colorful rugs and kilims in the hallways add a homey feel. **Pros:** beautiful terrace with wonderful views; owners are helpful in arranging excursions; more peaceful than other *pansiyons.* **Cons:** small shower cabinets. [$] *Rooms from: 130 TL* ✉ *Yukarı Ambarlik* ☎ *464/657–2052* 🛏 *15 rooms* 🕐 *Closed Oct.–Apr.* 🍽 *Breakfast.*

$$ B&B/INN 🏨 **Natura Lodge.** Some of the front rooms at this basic inn have wonderful views, and the staff is extremely knowledgeable about outdoor activities in the area; an on-premises agency arranges water rafting and guided hikes. **Pros:** beautiful views from some rooms; trekking advice available; alcohol served. **Cons:** lacks personal family-*pansiyon* style of other places; showers are not enclosed. [$] *Rooms from: 200 TL* ✉ *On left, just past springs* ☎ *464/657–2035* 🌐 *www.naturaotel.com* 🛏 *21 rooms* 🍽 *Breakfast.*

$$ HOTEL 🏨 **Otel Ayder Haşimoğlu.** Ayder's only full-service hotel is a large wood-sheathed building near the hot springs. *pansiyon***Pros:** close to the springs, the city center, and restaurants; can organize heli-skiing in winter. **Cons:** a bit pricey for so few amenities; only basic TV stations; hotel only serves breakfast. [$] *Rooms from: 180 TL* ✉ *Ayder Kaplıcaları* ☎ *464/657–2037* 🌐 *www.hasimogluotel.com* 🛏 *58 rooms, 7 cottages* 🍴 *Breakfast.*

$ B&B/INN 🏨 **Serender Pansiyon.** Some of the simple rooms are quite small, but they have wonderful views of the mountains and waterfalls, and breakfast is served on a lovely terrace overlooking the pastures; there's even the occasional sound of a cowbell in the distance. **Pros:** peaceful surroundings. **Cons:** some rooms are small; showers are not enclosed. [$] *Rooms from: 140 TL* ✉ *Yukarı Ambarlik, on your right, at end of second cluster* ☎ *464/657–2201* 🛏 *19 rooms* 🍴 *Breakfast.*

SPORTS AND OUTDOORS

There are lots of hiking opportunities in the area, but most involve serious uphill sections. Well signposted from Ayder is the route to Hazindak, a collection of pretty wooden chalets on a ridge, which is a strenuous climb of around three hours. Much easier is the walk from Yukarı Kavron, a village just south of Ayder, up a valley to a series of lakes. The hike to the first, Adsız Göl (Nameless Lake), should take 1–2 hours. You can continue up the ridge to see a second lake down below.

KARS, MT. ARARAT, AND LAKE VAN

Turkey's east is a region filled with stark contrasts: dusty plains and soaring mountains, simple villages and bustling cities. Near Turkey's border with Armenia and Iran, this remote region is also filled with natural and man-made wonders and offers visitors the chance to see a part of Turkey that has yet to be invaded by the tourist hordes. Although this means that you may not find all the amenities and services available in western Turkey, the friendliness and hospitality of the area's predominantly Kurdish locals will very likely make up for it.

KARS

The setting for Turkish novelist Orhan Pamuk's somber novel *Snow,* Kars is a rustic, forbidding, and grayish city set on a 5,740-foot plateau and forever at the mercy of the winds. Not far from Turkey's border with Armenia and Georgia, it looks like the frontier town it is; since 1064, Kars has been besieged over and over, by various sundry invaders from the Akkoyunlu to the Mongol warriors of Tamerlane. In the 19th century alone, it was attacked three times by Czarist armies from Russia who remained in power until 1920. The Russian influence is still obvious in many buildings.

With its tree-lined streets and low European-style buildings Kars feels different from other Turkish cities. It can be surprisingly relaxed, has a reputation as a liberal and secular-minded outpost, and certainly has more bars and licensed restaurants than other towns in the conservative

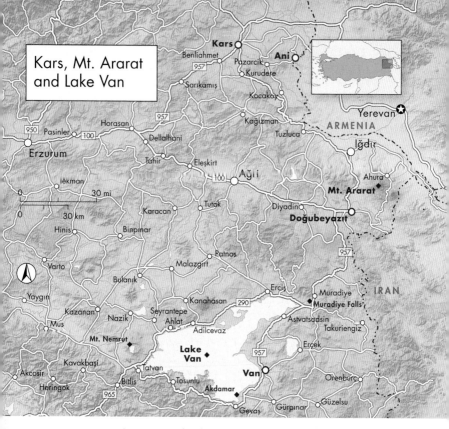

Kars, Mt. Ararat
and Lake Van

east. Attempts to develop a ski industry and lifting restrictions on visiting the ancient city of Ani—previously a closed military zone—has
meant that more tourists are coming through the area, giving locals the
incentive to upgrade what Kars has to offer.

GETTING HERE AND AROUND

The Kars airport is 6 km (4 miles) outside town. Turkish Airlines, Atlas
Jet, and Pegasus have regular flights from Istanbul to Kars and SunExpress flies from İzmir to Kars.

There are daily buses from Istanbul and Ankara to cities in the east,
but it's a long trip (22 hours from Istanbul, 18 from Ankara) and not
much cheaper than flying. Kars is the end of the line for Turkey's train
network, but while the scenery from Sivas is spectacular, the trip is
brutally slow, taking 38 hours or more from Istanbul via Ankara. If
you are planning on limiting your explorations outside Kars to Ani,
you can arrange a tour. Otherwise, you will want to rent a car to visit
other outlying sights.

ESSENTIALS

The English-speaking guide Celil Ersözoğlu is a good option in Kars.
He arranges transport to Ani most days in the summer and can organize
private trips to some of the Armenian and Georgian monuments in the

Spotlight on the Armenians

CLOSE UP

Historically, Armenians have been an integral part of the ethnic mix in Turkey's east, although today very few remain in the region. What happened to them is a topic of sensitive debate in Turkey.

There were various Armenian kingdoms in the region starting in the 3rd century BC and lasting until almost the 11th century AD. After that, the Armenians—who adopted Christianity in AD 301—became the subjects of a succession of rulers, from the Byzantines, to the Persians, and finally the Ottomans. Armenians became the bankers and traders of the Ottoman Empire and ended up living throughout the Ottoman world, with Istanbul eventually becoming one of their main cultural centers. Armenians were legendary builders and many fine examples of their buildings survive, while their influence can also be seen in Seljuk architecture. The great Ottoman architect Sinan was born to an Armenian family and in the 19th century the Armenian Balyan family were the sultan's official architects, designing Istanbul's Dolmabahçe Palace among many other important buildings.

During World War I, when the Ottomans came under attack by Russia and the other Allied powers, some Armenians in the east saw this as a chance for independence and rose up in revolt. The Ottoman Turks, afraid of how much land would be left to them in an empire filled with Greeks, Armenians, and Arabs, deported the entire Armenian population of Anatolia on foot across the mountains into the deserts of Syria and Iraq, a process that led to significant deaths and suffering. Many did not arrive, and Armenian survivors and U.S. consular staff reported massacres. The Armenians claim that hundreds of thousands (some claim even 1.5 million) perished and have been trying to have the events of the time recognized as genocide. The Turks, while admitting that large numbers of Armenians died at the time, say this was the result of war and disease, which also cost the lives of many others living in the region—the deaths of Turkish and Kurdish villagers in revenge attacks are often cited as examples. It remains a highly sensitive topic, but Armenian culture has sprouted in the region in recent years, with an annual Armenian service in the Akdamar Church and the restoration of Diyarbakır's abandoned Armenian cathedral.

area. He often knows when visitors are in the area, and will probably find you before you find him.

Tour Contacts Celil Ersözoğlu ☎ 532/226–3966 ✉ celilani@hotmail.com.
Visitor Information. ✉ Hakim Ali Riza Aslan Cad. 15, one block south of the Grand Hotel Ani ☎ 474/223–6817.

EXPLORING

İç Kale (*Kars Castle*). The town's castle looms over the area from its high, rocky vantage point. Though it dates from the 10th century, in 1386 Tamerlane swept violently through the region and razed the original structure, and most surviving fortifications were commissioned by Lala Mustafa Paşa in 1579. The castle has gone through some restoration

A typical traffic jam in eastern Turkey —photo by BrendaE, Fodors.com member

in recent years and the panoramic views of Kars merit the 10-minute walk uphill. ⊠ *Kale Cad.* 📻 *2 TL* ⊙ *Daily 9–sunset.*

Kars Museum (*Kars Müzesi*). This museum has a lot of preclassical pottery, as well as the beautiful doors of an Armenian church. Located near the train station on the eastern edge of town, it's a long walk from the center and a little difficult to find—you may want to taxi. Easily missed outside is the railway carriage where Ottoman General Kazım Karabekir signed the treaty of Kars with the Soviet Union, settling today's border. ⊠ *485 Cumhuriyet Cad.* ☎ *474/212–2387* 📻 *Free* ⊙ *Daily 8:30–5:30.*

Kümbet Cami (*Drum-Dome Mosque*). Located at the foot of the hill by Kars River, this was originally built in the 10th century as the Armenian Church of the Twelve Apostles. You can still make out the Apostles on the exterior of the drum-shape cupola. The building now serves as a mosque, with the entrance on the far side. ⊠ *Kale Cad., at foot of İç Kale.*

Taşköprü. The area between the castle and the Apostles Church was the heart of Kars prior to its Russian occupation, but only a few early constructions survive. The most notable is the Taşköprü, also known as "the Stone Bridge," of Seljuk origin, dating from the 1400s and built of volcanic rock. On either side of the bridge are several largely abandoned hammams and timber and stone houses; the 300-year-old home of famed poet Nemik Kemal has been restored and is now a cultural center. The rest of the area is somewhat neglected, though local authorities occasionally attempt to rejuvenate the area.

WHERE TO EAT

$ TURKISH 🍴 **Ani Ocakbaşı.** As the name implies—Ocakbaşı means "hearth"—the emphasis here is on grilled meats: the usual kebabs plus the Black Sea meatball specialty, *Akçaabat köfte*. The kitchen also prepares some local stews, but usually only at lunchtime. *[$] Average main: 15 TL ✉ Kazım Paşa Cad. 28 ☎ 474/212–0423.*

$ INTERNATIONAL 🍴 **Kadın Eli Yöresel Yemekleri.** "Women's hands local home cooking" is a rough translation of the name, and it pretty well sums up the way things work in this old Russian building, where old tile blends with modern fittings, and an open kitchen fills one end. The menu changes regularly, but there is a mix of Western, Turkish, and local dishes. Signs with their new motto "El Dante" are more prominent than their actual name. *[$] Average main: 10 TL ✉ Halitpaşa Cad. 41 ☎ 543/617–6611.*

$ TURKISH 🍴 **Ocakbaşı Restoran.** The kebabs are simple and tasty, and embroidered curtains, rust-color tablecloths, and waiters in shiny vests add a bit of atmosphere—though the cave effect is a bit weird. Try the *Ali Nazik kebab* or the *Eyder kababi,* pieces of grilled meat, cheese, parsley, sesame, and egg yoke in a calzone-like wrapping. Kars goose, a local specialty, is also served. *[$] Average main: 13 TL ✉ Atatürk Cad. 276 ☎ 474/212–0056.*

LOCAL FOOD

Along Halitpaşa Caddesi are a number of inviting shops that sell Kars's specialty, an aged *kaşar* cheese that tastes much like Italian pecorino. Many shops also sell local honey, and you can also do as the locals do and stop by in the morning for a takeout breakfast of delicious "*bal* and *kaymak*"—honey with clotted cream.

WHERE TO STAY

$$ HOTEL 🏨 **Grand Hotel Ani.** Some of the large, modern rooms enjoy views of the mountains, and amenities abound—from "foot" spas in the bathrooms to a gym and a large indoor pool. **Pros:** among the better lodgings in town; central location; pleasant restaurant and bar. **Cons:** mountain views, but only from upper floors; usually filled with business travelers midweek. *[$] Rooms from: 250 TL ✉ Ordu Cad. 15 ☎ 474/223–7500 🌐 www.grandani.com.tr 🛏 68 rooms, 4 suites 🍽 No meals.*

$ HOTEL 🏨 **Güngören Oteli.** After a 2011 renovation, this former budget hotel is now the best mid-range option in town. **Pros:** friendly service; quiet street. **Cons:** already starting to show some wear and tear; no great views. *[$] Rooms from: 140 TL ✉ Halit Paşa Cad. 2, corner of Millet Sok. ☎ 474/212–6767 🌐 www.gungorenhotel.com 🛏 34 rooms 🍽 Breakfast.*

$$$ HOTEL 🏨 **Kar's Otel.** A wonderfully restored late 19th-century Russian-built mansion is extremely stylish, with a cool, minimalist white-and-gray color scheme, original art on the walls depicting monuments in Kars, and comfortable rooms furnished with contemporary flair. **Pros:** plush and modern rooms; a warm welcome after a day of skiing or sightseeing. **Cons:** rooms starting to show wear; top-floor rooms can get hot; you'd expect more for this price. *[$] Rooms from: 375 TL ✉ Halitpaşa Cad. 79 ☎ 474/212–1616 🌐 www.karsotel.com 🛏 6 rooms, 2 suites 🍽 Breakfast.*

NIGHTLIFE

Barış Club. Kars is not a party town, and there's not much alcohol to be had. If you want a drink, Barış Club is one of your better options, and there's often live music. The place is popular with students, so it's busy during term and dead in summer. ⊠ *Kale Yolu Atatürk Cad. 33* ☎ *473/233–0702.*

ANI

42 km (26 miles) east of Kars

Most visitors to this remote area of Turkey come to pay a visit to the haunting Ani, one of the country's most important historical sites. Once the capital of an Armenian kingdom that ruled the area more than a thousand years ago and that filled the city with stunning churches, Ani is today more like a ghost town, filled with ruins that still manage to evoke the city's former glory. Its location, at the edge of a windswept gorge with snowcapped mountains in the background and grassy fields stretching out to the horizon, only adds to Ani's mystique. Today a small village called Ocaklı occupies the site.

GETTING HERE AND AROUND

Take Route 36–07 from Kars.

EXPLORING

Fodor'sChoice ★ **Ruins of Ani.** Scarcely a half-dozen churches remain of the medieval Armenian capital of Ani, all in various states of disrepair, but even so, the sprawling site is breathtaking—crumbling majesty amid stark, sweeping countryside, tiny Kurdish settlements, and fields of wildflowers. There is a haunted, yet strangely meditative, feeling at the site, with an open-air museum holding what are considered some of the finest examples of religious architecture of its period.

Ani has little shade and can get quite hot in summer, so be sure to bring a hat and water. You should plan on spending two or three hours at the site if you want to see the highlights, although you could spend an entire day exploring the ruins. The city was built on an easily fortified triangular promontory bounded on two sides by steep river gorges; the third side is closed by the mighty walls, which stretch for more than 8,200 feet and are 32-feet tall, raised in AD 972 by the Armenian king.

Enter through the Aslan Kapısı (Lion's Gate), one of three principal portals. Take the path on the left to the Church of the Redeemer. This circular church was built in 1035 but hit by lightning in the 1950s, slicing it neatly in half, leaving a surrealistic representation of an Armenian church with the rubble of its former half in the foreground. Next to it is the *bezirhane*, a former oil press. Beside the walls is the best preserved of three churches in Ani dedicated to St. Gregory, the Armenian prince who converted his people to Christianity. Built in 1215 by a wealthy Armenian merchant, it is the most impressive ruin in Ani, not least because it's at the foot of a ravine with a view over the Arpaçay River. Inside, note the remarkable cycle of murals depicting the lives of Christ and St. Gregory. If you follow the path into the gorge, you will come to the striking Kusanatz (Convent of the Three Virgins), on a rocky outcrop.

At the center of the site is the former Cathedral, built in 1001 by the architect Trdat. It was once topped by a large dome that fell in an earthquake in 1319. During periods of Muslim rule the structure served as the Fethiye (Victory) mosque. A short distance away is the Menüçehir Cami, which clings to the heights overlooking the Arpaçay River and was originally an Armenian building, perhaps a palace; the minaret, added in 1072, is thought to be the first Turkish building within the country's modern borders.

Return to the walls along the excavated main street, past the shattered ruins of another minaret. Soon you will reach the Church of the Holy Apostles. The church itself is in ruins, but its large Narthex, erroneously called a Seljuk Caravansary, is well preserved with impressive stone work. From here head west toward the second gorge, and find a path backtracking to another small but well-preserved church dedicated to St. Gregory. Continuing back beside the gorge to the walls, you will pass the foundations of the massive round Church of King Gagik. ⊠ *Anı* 🖂 *5 TL* ⊙ *Daily 9–6.*

DOĞUBEYAZIT AND MT. ARARAT

192 km (119 miles) southeast of Kars.

The scrappy frontier town of Doğubeyazıt (doh-*oo*-bay-yah-zuht) is a good base from which to enjoy views of Turkey's highest and most famous mountain, the majestic Mt. Ararat (Ağrı Dağı). Not far from the Iranian border, the place seems neglected, if not downright forgotten, with dusty streets and crumbling buildings. But the pace here is laid-back and the locals are friendly. You'll share the town with sheep and travelers bringing in contraband cigarettes and other cheap goods from Iran. There aren't many carpet and kilim shops here compared to tourist spots in western Turkey, so you can wander the main street, Çarşı Caddesi, without being bothered too much. A day is probably enough time to spend here, catching an early visit to the sites around Mt. Ararat and then the İshak Paşa Saray at sunset.

ESSENTIALS

Tour offices in Doğubeyazıt tend to go in and out of business every week, so if you need a guide, you're best off asking at your hotel and/or getting recommendations from other travelers.

EXPLORING

İshak Paşa Saray (*İshak Paşa Palace*). Doğubeyazıt's only sight, the enchanting İshak Paşa Saray, is in the mountains southeast of town. The fortified palace was built in the late 18th century by local potentate Çolak Abdi Paşa and his son İshak. The interior of the building features ornate stonework, a fantastic mixture of Armenian, Persian, and classical Ottoman styles, but the gold-plated doors were carted off by Russian troops in 1917 and are in St. Petersburg's Hermitage Museum. Like Istanbul's Topkapı, the palace is divided into three areas: the first courtyard, open to all; the second courtyard, which holds the mosque and meeting rooms once used by the pasha and other important personages; and the third courtyard, an inner sanctum housing the massive kitchen and the harem. Note how most rooms are small and equipped with their own hearths for the long cold winters.

Visit in the morning or late afternoon, when the sun casts a deep orange glow over the palace. The palace was the center of the original Doğubeyazıt and across the valley is a mosque built by a 15th-century Ottoman sultan, as well as the ruins of an older and more traditional fortress—whose foundations are Urartian but was rebuilt several times through the centuries. (You can clamber up to the fortress on a rough trail that starts next to the mosque; look for the two Uratian figures carved in the rock.) There is a restaurant and teahouse above the palace, as well as a few Kurdish mud-brick houses. ⌧ *6 km (4 miles) southeast of town on road to Göller, Doğubeyazıt* ⌧ *5 TL* ☉ *Daily 9–5.*

Mt. Ararat (*Ağrı Dağı*). The region's most famous mountain is actually an extinct volcano covered with snow even in summer, soaring dramatically 16,850 feet above the arid plateau and dominating the landscape. According to Genesis, after the Great Flood, "the waters were dried up from off the earth; and Noah removed the covering of the ark, and looked, and behold, the face of the ground was dry." The survivors, as the story goes, had just landed on top of Mt. Ararat. Many other ancient sources—Chaldean, Babylonian, Chinese, Assyrian—also tell of an all-destroying flood and of one man who heroically escaped its consequences. The mountain can be easily viewed from Doğubeyazıt, although actually climbing it requires a permit that can only be obtained by a licensed agency and usually takes a few days to acquire it. Be prepared for a lot of walking on gravel, and be forewarned that the summit is often shrouded in clouds. Local tour offices will take you on a day trip that includes a visit to a village at the base of the mountain, which is the closest you can get to Ararat without a permit. ⌧ *Mt. Ararat, Doğubeyazıt.*

WHERE TO EAT AND STAY

$ ╳ **Murat Camping.** Despite the rustic name (there is a small campground
TURKISH on the premises), this large space with an outdoor terrace on a hillside just below the Ishakpaşa Sarayı, is Doğubeyazıt's only option for a big night out. It might not be the best meal of your life, but the views of Doğubeyazıt and the surrounding mountains are commanding. You'll find the usual selection of mezes and kebabs, as well as live Turkish music most evenings along with wine, beer, and rakı. 🖸 *Average main: 15 TL* ⌧ *Ishakpaşa Sarayı, on road up to Palace, and just before it, Doğubeyazıt* ☎ *472/312–0367* ▭ *No credit cards.*

$ ╳ **Öz Urfa Kebap.** Looking something like a 1960s hunting lodge, with
TURKISH retro furniture and walls of rough wood boards, this kebab house has more atmosphere than most other places in town and works a bit harder at providing good service. On offer are several kinds of well-made kebabs, as well as an assortment of *pides* cooked the traditional way in the wood-burning oven. 🖸 *Average main: 8 TL* ⌧ *Ismail Beşikçi Cad. 34, Doğubeyazıt* ☎ *544/218–0418.*

$ ╳ **Safir Cağ Kebab.** This restaurant serves the specialty of nearby
TURKISH Erzurum: thin tender slices of lamb cooked on a horizontal spit, then served on individual spatulas. Large, clean, and modern, it's about a five-minute walk from the center of town, opposite where the Turkish

HARK! THE ARK!

Mt. Ararat is where, according to biblical accounts, Noah's Ark may have come to rest during the great flood. Sellers have peddled old planks reputedly from Noah's Ark since medieval times, and ark-hunting expeditions have searched the mountain trying to prove the biblical version of history. A few fragments of ancient timber embedded in the ice have been brought back over the years—though radiocarbon-dating tests have been inconclusive.

Satellite photos showed something embedded in a glacier at 12,500 feet, but further examination proved it to be nothing more than a freak formation in the strata.

Nevertheless, expeditions by Christian groups constantly make new claims, and a second Noah's Ark was "discovered" in the 1980s on a hillside 20 km (12 miles) southeast of Ararat—though to most eyes, this "ark" is nothing more than a pile of rocks. The local Kurds believe the ark ended up on a different mountain down by the Iraqi border, and will even show you Noah's grave.

Army parks its tanks. $ *Average main: 12 TL* ⊠ *Ishak Paşa Sarayının Yolu, Doğubeyazıt* ☎ *472/312–5356.*

$ · **Ararat Hotel.** This hotel, popular with Mt. Ararat climbers, is geared
B&B/INN towards backpackers, but tries harder than most places in town, making it your best option in the area. **Pros:** family-run; owner's adult children speak English; can organize tours. **Cons:** basic accommodations; rooms are a bit run-down. $ *Rooms from: 70 TL* ⊠ *Belediye Cad. 16, Doğubeyazıt* ☎ *472/312–4988* ⊕ *www.hotelararatturkey.com* ⬦ *48 rooms* ⬦ *No meals.*

$ · **Hotel Nuh.** The relatively large rooms are on the basic side, though
HOTEL the hotel's greatest asset is its views of Mt. Ararat—enjoyed from most rooms and the large rooftop restaurant. **Pros:** great views of Mt. Ararat; good English is spoken; within walking distance of city center and markets. **Cons:** decor leans toward drab. $ *Rooms from: 150 TL* ⊠ *Büyük Ağrı Cad. 65, Doğubeyazıt* ☎ *472/312–7232* ⬦ *65 rooms* ⬦ *Breakfast.*

NEED A BREAK? If you're driving from Doğubeyazıt to Van, there's not much to see along the way. So the lovely Muradiye waterfalls, some 83 km (51 miles) southwest of Doğubeyazıt, come as a welcome relief. From a small parking lot, a bouncy suspension bridge crosses a swiftly flowing stream and gives you a good view of the 20-foot falls. The area is filled with green poplar trees and local families who come here to picnic. A simple teahouse has a lovely view of the tumbling falls and is the perfect spot for taking a rest.

VAN, LAKE VAN, AND ENVIRONS

Lake Van is 171 km (106 miles) from Doğubeyazıt, continuing past Muradiye to the town of Van.

Van is the commercial center of Eastern Anatolia, and modern streets are lined with shops both modern and traditional and choked with traffic. There's a definite sense of bustle to the town, with restaurants and cafés filled with young people, many of them students from the local university. With its collection of rather uniform-looking and ugly cement buildings, what Van really lacks is a sense of history, which should not be surprising. The Van of today dates back to the early 20th century, when it was rebuilt some 5 km (3 miles) farther inland from Lake Van after being destroyed in battles with the Armenians and Russians during World War I. Old Van first appears in history 3,000 years ago, when it was the site of the Urartian capital of Tushpa, whose formidable fortress—built on a steep cliff rising from the lakeshore—dominated the countryside. What remains of Old Van, in a grassy area near the lake, is a melancholy jumble of foundations that cannot be sorted out; only two vaguely restored mosques, one 13th-century, the other 16th-century, rise from the marshland.

GETTING HERE AND AROUND

Turkish Airlines, Pegasus, and Atlas Jet have regular flights from Istanbul and SunExpress flies to Van from İzmir and Antalya. The airport is on the south of the city, on the road to Akdamar and Tatvan. The airport and city center are just off the main highway that skirts the southern portion of Lake Van. If you're traveling by car, Van is 176 km (110 miles) south of Doğubeyazıt on D975.

ESSENTIALS

The Ayanis travel agency in Van can help with travel arrangements and with organizing tours in the Lake Van area.

Contacts Ayanis ☎ *432/210–1515.* **Visitor Information.** ✉ *Cumhuriyet Cad 223, just south of Fevzi Çakmak Cad.* ☎ *432/216–2018.*

EXPLORING

Fodor'sChoice
★
Akdamar. On the tranquil, uninhabited islet of Akdamar, among the wild olive and almond trees, stand the scant remains of a monastery that include the truly splendid **Church of the Holy Cross.** Built in AD 921 by an Armenian king, Gagik Artzruni of Vaspurakan, the compound was originally part of a palace, but was later converted to a monastery. Incredible high-relief carvings on the exterior make the church one of the most enchanted spots in Turkey. Much of the Old Testament is told here: Look for Adam and Eve, David and Goliath, and Jonah and the whale. Along the top is a frieze of running animals; another frieze shows a vineyard where laborers work the fields and women dance with bears; and, of course, King Gagik, almost hidden above the entrance, is depicted, offering his church to Christ. The wall paintings in the interior of the church underwent an extensive restoration in 2006 and after much controversy a cross was placed on the dome in 2010. The monastery operated until WWI, and since 2010 annual religious services have been allowed, usually in early September. To reach Akdamar from Van, follow Route 300 to Gevaş, which is about 20 miles away. Just past Gevaş, you'll see ferries waiting at the well-marked landing to collect the required number of passengers—between 10 and 15—for the 20-minute ride. Normally it costs 10 TL per person but if there aren't enough passengers the round-trip is 150 TL. ✉ *Rte. 300, 56 km (35 miles) west of Van* 🛳 *3 TL* ☉ *Daily sunrise–sunset.*

The Armenian Church of Holy Cross, on the uninhabited islet of Akdamar, is a work of art, inside and out.

Çarpanak Island. There are several other small islands on Lake Van, with their own Armenian churches. None are as glorious as Akdamar but if you have the money, time, and interest they can make an interesting excursion and you are likely to have the place to yourself. The most interesting is Çarpanak Island, north of Van, often visited in combination with Adır Island. You need to hire a whole boat to visit, which costs around 150 or 250 TL.

Lake Van (*Van Gölü*). Turkey's largest and most unusual lake consists of 3,738 square km (1,443 square miles) of eerily blue water surrounded by mighty volcanic cones, at an elevation of 1,725 meters (5,659 feet). The lake was formed when a volcano blew its top and blocked the course of a river, leaving the water with no natural outlet; as a result the lake is highly alkaline and full of sulfides and mineral salts, six times saltier than the ocean. Lake Van's only marine life is a small member of the carp family, the *darekh,* which has somehow adapted to the saline environment. Recreational water sports are limited, and beaches along the rocky shores are few and far between. Swimming in the soft water is pleasant, but try not to swallow any—it tastes terrible.

The towns of Adilcevaz and Ahlat, on Lake Van's north shore, are worth visiting only if you're in the area; you'll probably want to head instead to Van and the nearby island of Akdamar, along the lake's south shore. ⊠ *Lake Van.*

Mt. Nemrut. Across the lake from Van is one of Turkey's loveliest natural wonders, the beautiful and rarely visited crater lakes of Mt. Nemrut (Nemrut Krateri, which should not be confused with the more famous Mt. Nemrut farther west). From Tatvan, 146 km (91 miles) west of

Van, a rutted road leads up the mountain to the 10,000-foot-high rim of what was once a mighty volcano. From the rim of the crater, you can see down to the two lakes below—a smaller one fed by hot springs and a larger "cold" one. A loose dirt road leads down to the lakes, where very simple tea stands have been set up. The inside of the crater has an otherworldly feel to it, with its own ecosystem: stands of short, stunted trees and scrubby bushes, birds and turtles, and cool breezes. Few tourists make it to the lakes, and chances are your only company will be local shepherds and their flocks.

Van Kalesı (*Van Castle*). Steps—considerably fewer than the 1,000 claimed in local tourist handouts—ascend to Van Kalesi, the sprawling Urartian fortress on the outskirts of town. A path branches right to Urartian tombs in the sheer south rock face; a cuneiform inscription here honors King Xerxes, whose Persian troops occupied the fortress early in the 5th century BC (look for the red metal fence on the south east side). The crumbling ramparts are still impressive, but as is often true in these parts, it's the view—sweeping across the lake and mountains—that makes the steep climb worthwhile. A taxi from the new town should cost no more than 10 TL one-way. Cheaper *dolmuşes* (shared taxis) depart regularly from the north end of Cumhuriyet Cadessi and are marked "Kalc." ✉ *Van Kalesi* 🎫 *Free* ☉ *Sunrise–sunet.*

Van Müzesi (*Van Museum*). Van's most popular museum aims to highlight local Urartian heritage, especially its famous metalwork; the collection includes rich gold jewelry and belts and plates engraved with lions, bulls, and sphinxes. Other items are carved relief of the god Teshup, for whom the Urartian capital was named, and intriguing humanoid stelae found in Hakkâri, in the mountains to the south. As of this writing, the museum was planning a move to a large new building next to Van Castle. Check in with a Turkish tourist office for the latest updates. ✉ *Cengiz Cad., 1 block east of Cumhuriyet Cad., behind Belediye (Municipality)* ☎ *432/216–1139* 🎫 *3 TL* ☉ *Daily 9–5.*

OFF THE
BEATEN
PATH

Çavuştepe and Hoşap Kalesi. From Van, drive 35 km (22 miles) south on the Hakkari road, where the side road to Çavuştepe is signposted on your right. Here you can clamber around the stone foundations of the ruined 8th-century BC Urartian fortress-city Sardurihinli. Nearby are temple ruins of perfectly cut basalt and the remains of a palace with great underground chambers. If you continue 15 km (9 miles) southeast on the same road, you'll reach Hoşap Kalesi, a dramatic fortress looming over a river chasm. The complex, built in 1643 by the local tribal lord Sari Süleyman Bey, was used as a base to "protect" (i.e., ransack) caravans and included a palace, mosques, baths, and a dungeon. The great gate, with its carved lions and an inscription in Farsi, is quite a show of strength; a passage, partly carved through bedrock, leads into the complex from here. ✉ *Çavuştepe* ☉ *Hoşap Kalesi: Daily 9–5.*

WHERE TO EAT

$ ✕ **Grand Deniz Turizm.** A pebbly lakeside beach set with plastic tables is a
TURKISH   good spot for lunch or dinner after a visit to Akdamar. The food, which includes local dishes such as kebabs and trout baked in a terra-cotta dish, is delicious. You can swim off the rocks here and use one of the

showers afterward, and if you're lucky the restaurant's Van cat, with one yellow eye and one blue, will be around. $ *Average main: 13 TL* ✉ *Van-Tatvan Karayolu Km 40, Gevaş* ☎ *432/612–4038.*

$ | TURKISH ✕ **Kebabistan.** Filled with mustachioed men sipping tea, this basic eatery serves the usual kebabs and hot prepared dishes, as well as good *pide* and *lahmacun*, flatbread topped with ground meat and baked. The main dining room is a hive of activity, but upstairs is comfortable and quieter. $ *Average main: 8 TL* ✉ *Sinemalar Sok.* ☎ *432/214–2273.*

$ | TURKISH ✕ **Kervansaray.** Hidden up some unassuming stairs on the west side of Cumhuriyet Cadessi, this popular kebab place is a little bit more refined than the competition around town and has excellent food to boot. There's a broad range of the typical kebabs, plus a few more unusual choices, such as *Beyti kebab*, meat in pastry, here with cheese and *fıstık* (pistachio). $ *Average main: 12 TL* ✉ *Cumhuriyet Cad.* ☎ *432/215–9482.*

$$ | TURKISH ✕ **Tamara Ocakbaşı.** Half the tables at this popular eatery in the Tamara Hotel are equipped with their own *ocak*, or hearth, and you cook your meat yourself, or you can choose a table on the terrace, where your kebab arrives cooked. There's also a decent range of mezes. $ *Average main: 17 TL* ✉ *Yüzbaşıoğlu Sok. 1* ☎ *432/214–3296.*

WHERE TO STAY

$$ | HOTEL 🛏 **Büyük Urartu.** One of the town's best lodging options makes an attempt at character with reproductions of Urartian art on the walls throughout and gold-embroidered bedspreads and floral wallpaper in the small but pleasant guest rooms. **Pros:** 24-hour room service and information desk; live music three nights a week; pool and sauna. **Cons:** hotel books up quickly; popular with tour groups; a little out of the way. $ *Rooms from: 150 TL* ✉ *Cumhuriyet Cad. 60* ☎ *432/212–0660* ⊕ *www.buyukurartuotel.com* ⤵ *72 rooms, 3 suites* ⦿| *Breakfast.*

$$ | HOTEL 🛏 **Merit Şahmaran.** At this comfortable, well-run hotel 12 km (7½ miles) west of town on Lake Van, ask for one of the lakeside rooms, which have views of the lake and mountains—although all rooms are large, with good beds, nice decor, and modern bathrooms with big cabinet showers. **Pros:** great location; full bar and decent restaurants. **Cons:** well out of town; waterfront disco could be noisy; service only average. $ *Rooms from: 200 TL* ✉ *Edremit Yolu Km 12, Edremit* ☎ *432/312–3060* ⊕ *www.merithotels.com* ⤵ *90 rooms* ⦿| *Breakfast.*

$$ | HOTEL 🛏 **Tamara Hotel.** A good range of facilities, large rooms, and a central location compensate for the rather bland decor; all rooms are nicely furnished with modern pieces, and the choicest are those facing the

---

BREAKFAST IN VAN

Breakfast is special in Van: it's served meze style, with an array of small dishes best shared among several people. There's a variety of locally made cheeses, eggs (fried, alone or with salami, or hard-boiled), and, most important, *kaymak*, a delicious clotted cream that's eaten on bread with honey. The city has many small restaurants that serve breakfast all day, but the best ones are along Kahvaltı Sokak, parallel to Cumhuriyet Caddesi; *kahvaltı* is the Turkish word for breakfast.

7

street in the new wing. **Pros:** good facilities; central location. **Cons:** lacks character; anonymous feel. $ *Rooms from: 245 TL* ⊠ *Yuzbasioglu Sok. 1* ☎ *432/214–3295* ⇔ *65 rooms, 4 suites* ❖*No meals.*

DIYARBAKIR, MARDIN, MIDYAT, AND HASANKEYF

Saying that Turkey's southeast region has a rich history is an understatement. This is, after all, part of the ancient area known as Mesopotamia: the land between the Tigris and the Euphrates rivers, where modern civilization got its start. Venturing into the heart of this historic region takes you to cities that trace their pasts not over centuries, but over millennia, and through landscapes that seem unchanged with time. The area is also the historic home of the Assyrian Christians, one of Christianity's oldest sects, and several fascinating Assyrian churches and monasteries remain active and are open to visitors.

DIYARBAKIR

As the region's commercial, cultural, and political center, Diyarbakır and its ancient basalt walls command a bluff overlooking the Tigris River. Despite past skirmishes that led to an unsafe reputation, relative peace and economic development are finally having an effect and the city is starting to creep back onto tourist itineraries.

In the 1980s and '90s, Diyarbakır was forced to absorb a large number of villagers fleeing the fighting in the countryside between Kurdish militants and Turkish security forces. Many villages were compulsorily evacuated, and this huge influx of mostly poor villagers taxed the already poor city's infrastructure and social services and has left lasting social problems. In more recent years, though, the local municipality has embarked on several restoration and beautification projects, such as renovating historic homes in the old city and opening them up to visitors, which is helping bring the city's charm closer to the surface.

Today visitors will find a fascinating city going through a cultural revival, with its 5½-km (3-mile) stretch of massive impregnable black-basalt walls, built at the orders of Constantine the Great, twisting alleyways, old stone homes, wonderful mosques and churches, and a lively bazaar. Be warned that it can still look a bit rough around the edges, as it's still a poor city, with modern concrete houses (some might call them ugly), grubby backstreets, and pestering children. Locals are generally welcoming to visitors; you may want to stick to the main streets and hire a guide to explore the old city in depth.

GETTING HERE AND AROUND
Turkish Airlines, Onur, and Pegasus Airlines have flights from Istanbul to Diyarbakır. SunExpress operates flights from İzmir and Antalya. There are daily buses from Istanbul to Diyarbakır; the ride takes close to 20 hours and costs about 90 TL. From Diyarbakır, minivans leave the local bus station for the one-hour trip to Mardin.

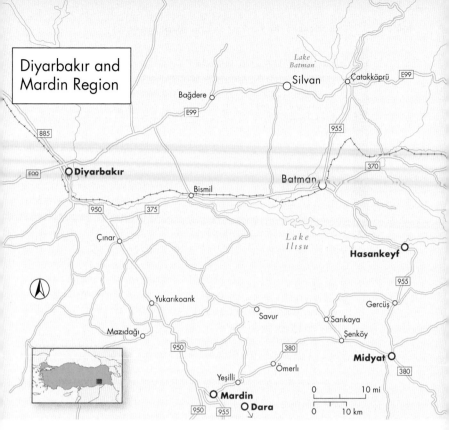

Diyarbakır and Mardin Region

The train ride from Istanbul to Diyarbakır is long—more than 35 hours—but scenic, and inexpensive: about 35 TL (first class) to 70 TL (sleeper bunk).

ESSENTIALS

Visitor Information. ✉ *Outside Dağkapı and opposite the Kervansaray Hotel* ☎ *412/229–2032.*

EXPLORING

Arkeoloji Müzesi (*Archaeological Museum*). The museum has exhibits covering 4,000 years of history, including findings from excavations in the Diyarbakır area, from stone-age tools to Byzantine pottery and coins. It has been closed for several years but is due to reopen in a building (currently under restoration) in Diyarbakır's İç Kale. ✉ *Gazi Cad.* ⊞ *5 TL* ⊙ *Mon.–Sat. 8:30–4:30.*

Bazaar. Diyarbakır's bazaar encompasses the half-dozen streets surrounding Ulu Cami; most stalls are shrines to wrought metal—gates, picks, shovels, plumbing fixtures, plastic shoes, and other things you probably would not want to carry home in your luggage. Across the street from the mosque is the grand 16th-century **Hasan Paşa Hanı**, a photogenic kervansaray, housing a few carpet and souvenir dealers and a tranquil place to stop for a tea. ✉ *Ulu Cami.*

CLOSE UP

Spotlight on the Kurds

An estimated 20 million Kurds live in the mountainous region that covers parts of Iran, Iraq, Syria, and Turkey. Separated by ethnicity and language from their neighbors, the Kurds have for centuries found themselves the subjects of the area's various rulers

Turkey has the region's largest Kurdish population, with an estimated 12 million, most of them living in the country's southeast region. When the new Turkish Republic was founded in 1923, severe restrictions on Kurdish language and culture were put in place, part of a larger effort to unite the country's various ethnic groups under one national identity. During the 1980s, the Kurdistan Workers' Party (PKK), a militant Marxist group, began a bloody separatist war against the Turkish state that ended up

costing the lives of more than 30,000 and causing great damage to social and economic life in the southeast. The PKK called for a ceasefire in 1999 after its leader was captured by Turkey, and fighters retreated to the mountains of northern Iraq. Attacks have continued on a reduced scale since then and wax and wane with the political climate, but violence is usually confined to small areas along the Iraqi border and is nowhere near the level of the 1980s and '90s. At the same time, as part of its efforts to join the European Union, Turkey has over the past few years passed legislation aimed at easing the cultural and political restrictions on the Kurds and has promised to revitalize the local economy, bringing a guarded sense of hope to the battle-scarred region.

Cahit Sıtkı Tarancı Müzesi. Down a narrow alleyway north of the Ulu Cami in the old city, the Cahit Sıtkı Tarancı Müzesi is a historic home dating back to 1734 that has been renovated and turned into an ethnographic museum, with rooms displaying scenes of life as it once was in Diyarbakır. The museum, which has a pleasant courtyard with a fountain, offers probably the best opportunity of seeing what an old Diybarbakır house looked like. ⊠ *Ziya Gökalp Sok. 3* ☎ *412/223–8958* 🖭 *Free* ☉ *Tues.–Sun. 8–12 and 1–5.*

City walls. The Romans left a strong mark on Diyarbakır—not only did they lay the foundations for its famous city walls, but they created the basic layout of the old town: a rough rectangle with two main streets that cross and connect the four gates that are found at each compass point. The walls were constructed by the Byzantine Emperor Constantius in the 4th century and various Arab and Turkish rulers restored and added to them over the centuries, until the local Artakid Turcoman emir al Malik al-Salih Mahmud gave them their current form in 1208. On the whole, the walls remain in good shape along their entire length; indeed, if you feel like a bit of an adventure, the best way to appreciate these great walls is to wander along the top. Of the original 72 towers, 67 are still standing, decorated with myriad inscriptions in the language of every conqueror and with Seljuk reliefs of animals and men; you can also explore their inner chambers and corridors. The easiest and safest section to explore is around **Dağ Kapısı** (Mountain Gate). Alternatively, start at the **Mardin Kapısı** (Mardin Gate), on the south side near the Otel Büyük Kervansaray, where you'll usually find plenty of local tourists. Exercise caution, but you should be able to walk along the wall west as far as **Urfa Kapısı** (Urfa Gate), also called the Bab er-Rum. About halfway you will come to the twin bastions **Evli Beden Burcu** and **Yedi Kardeş Burcu**—the latter is also known as the Tower of Seven Brothers and was added to the fortifications in 1209. From here you can see the old Ottoman bridge over the Tigris, called **Dicle Köprüsü** (Tigris Bridge). Continue clockwise along the city wall, and you'll eventually reach another gate, the **Dağ Kapısı** (Mountain Gate), which divides Diyarbakır's old and new towns. Farther east, inside the ramparts, are the sad remains of the **Artakid Saray** (Artasid Palace), surrounded by a dry, octagonal pool known as the **Lion's Fountain.** Not long ago there were two carved lions here, now there's only one; what happened to the other is a mystery.

Dört Ayaklı Minare. The old town's most recognizable monument is the Dört Ayaklı Minare (Four-Legged Minaret) of the Şeyh Mutahhar Mosque. The minaret balances on four basalt columns, a marvel of medieval engineering. Legend has it that your wish will come true if you circle the minaret seven times. ⊠ *Yenikapı Cad.*

İç Kale (*Inner Fortress*). The inner castle of Diyarbakır's old town is a circular fortress that once held the city's palace and other important buildings. Today the most notable landmark is the 16th-century **Hazreti Süleymaniye Cami**, which contains the grave of the son of Khalid ibn al-Walid, the companion of the prophet Muhammad, who died during the city's capture. It has a tall, graceful minaret and is striped with black basalt and pale sandstone, a favorite design of this city's medieval architects. Its courtyard fountain is fed by an underground spring that has supplied cold, clear water to the city for 5,000 years. The area is the focus of a major restoration and rejuvenation project. ⊠ *İzzet Paşa Cad.* ☉ *Daily sunrise–sunset.*

Meryem Ana Kilisesi. Diybarbakır was once home to a large Christian population—Armenians, Chaldeans, and Assyrians—and several churches remain in the city, although the only one that still holds regular services is the Assyrian Orthodox Meryem Ana Kilisesi, on the western end of the old city. A peaceful oasis in the midst of the bustling city, the church is said to be built on the site of what was a temple used by sun worshippers and has a large courtyard lined with basalt stones. Parts of the church date back to the fourth century—look for the remains of the Roman arch beside the altar—but most of the structure is medieval. Services are held every Sunday at 8 am, although only a few people usually show up. Look for the signs from the Urfa Gate and be aware that this is one of the poorer parts of the old city. ⊠ *Ana Sok. 26* ☉ *Daily 9–5.*

Ulu Cami (*Great Mosque*). In the center of the old city is the Ulu Camı, one of the oldest mosques in Anatolia. Though the present form dates from 1091, its colonnades incorporate elements of the Byzantine Cathedral of St. Thomas that once stood here. Its design follows earlier Arab tradition and closely resembles the great Ummayid Mosque of Damascus. Note the Arabic-style flat roof and almost basilica-like rectangular plan, different from the square-shape and domed mosques common in Turkey. ⊠ *Gazi Cad., opposite Yapı Kredi Bank* ☉ *Daily 10–sunset.*

WHERE TO EAT

$ TURKISH 🍴 **Çarşı Konağı.** You have to pass through a small door off one of Diybarbakır's narrow old city lanes to get to this simple restaurant, in a restored historic stone home with a shaded courtyard—there's a sign but you may need to ask for directions. The small menu includes delicious *sac tava,* chunks of beef sautéed in a wok-like pan with tomatoes and green peppers; it's served in the pan, with a mound of flatbread to soak up the tasty juices. This is also a pleasant spot to enjoy a cup of coffee or tea. [$] *Average main: 15 TL* ✉ *Telegrafhane Sok., off Gazi Cad. Çarşı, across from police station* ☎ *412/228–4673* 💳 *No credit cards.*

$$ TURKISH 🍴 **Camlı Köşk.** Head here if you want to sample authentic local dishes, such as *ciğer* (liver) and spicy *saray saç tava.* The restaurant, part of the modern Greenpark Hotel, is a 14th-century stone mansion with several small dining rooms decked out in rugs and antiques. Live local traditional music is performed every night except Sunday. [$] *Average main: 20 TL* ✉ *In Greenpark Hotel, Gazi Cad. 101* ☎ *412/229–4345.*

$ TURKISH 🍴 **Mustafa'nın Kahvaltı ve yemek Dünyası.** Diyarbakır's best-regarded choice for fine dining is slick and modern, in the new part of town, and offers good food and a diverse menu. Along with regular kebabs are local specialties like *kaburga*, a sheep's ribcage cooked with rice inside, that the waiter dissects for you, and *meftune*, a lamb and eggplant stew. Both come in servings made for two people. [$] *Average main: 15 TL* ✉ *Prof. Selhattin Yazıcıoğlu Cad 24/74, Karakoç Plaza* ☎ *412/223–7676.*

WHERE TO STAY

$$$ HOTEL 🏨 **Greenpark Hotel.** Although the lobby and rooms are somewhat characterless, this is certainly Diyarbakır's fanciest place to stay, with large and comfortable guest quarters, all with desks and some with small couches. **Pros:** quality service; wide range of facilities. **Cons:** for the price, rooms are a bit lacking. [$] *Rooms from: 400 TL* ✉ *Gazi Cad. 101* ☎ *412/229–5000* 🌐 *www.thegreenparkdiyarbakir.com* 🛏 *107 rooms, 7 suites* 🍽 *Breakfast.*

$$ HOTEL 🏨 **Otel Büyük Kervansaray.** At this attractive 16th-century kervansaray with sandstone walls and vaulted ceilings, rooms are on the small side, but you're really paying for the atmosphere and the location. **Pros:** wonderful character; pool and lovely courtyard. **Cons:** rooms and bathrooms are quite small; some furniture is a little dated; popular with weddings so it can get crowded on the weekend. [$] *Rooms from: 200 TL* ✉ *Gazi Cad.* ☎ *412/228–9606* 🛏 *31 rooms, 14 suites* 🍽 *Breakfast.*

$$ HOTEL 🏨 **SV Business Hotel.** As the name implies, these bright, decent-size rooms just inside Dağ Kapısı, Diyarbakır's main city gate, offer comfort and modern amenities rather than character. **Pros:** good location; modern facilities. **Cons:** could be anywhere; hotel is a bit old and decor is lackluster. [$] *Rooms from: 200 TL* ✉ *İnönü Cad. 4 Dağkapı* ☎ *412/228–1295* 🛏 *79 rooms* 🍽 *No meals.*

MARDIN

96 km (60 miles) southeast of Diyarbakır.

With historic stone houses clinging to a citadel-topped mountain that overlooks a vast plain below, Mardin has a magical setting. The city was hit hard by the violence of the 1980s and '90s, and since it's populated largely by Arabs, but on the edge of the Kurdish zone, it slid off Turkey's tourist map. The return of calm to the region has meant that travelers are rediscovering this enchanting city's mazelike old town, intricately decorated homes, and lively bazaars. Mardin has been featured in several popular Turkish TV drama series, and has become popular with tourists from Istanbul and other western Turkish cities. Some nice hotels and restaurants have opened up to serve them—there's even a film festival.

Sitting like a crown that looks down on a wide plain below, Mardin is a wonderful place to wander. The narrow streets are lined with old stone homes, gorgeous mosques, and a bazaar where donkeys still carry most of the goods. Spend the day walking around, then relax in the evening at the terrace of one of the local restaurants and look out at the view of the plains below and the stars above. Although there are some ugly cement homes that have been built in recent years, the local authorities are actively demolishing them and the remaining historic homes give the city a great deal of charm. The stone used to build the old homes is the color of golden sand and looks especially beautiful at sunset. A short distance outside the city is the still active Syriac Monastery of Deyrul Zaferan, parts of which date back to the 5th century.

GETTING HERE AND AROUND

Turkish Airlines, SunExpress, Onur, and Pegasus Airlines have flights from Istanbul to Mardin. There are frequent minivans to Urfa, Diyarbakır, and Midyat. If you are traveling through the region by car, Mardin is 105 km (65 miles) south of Diyarbakır on D950.

EXPLORING

Bazaar. Mardin's lively bazaar runs parallel to the old town's main street, Birinci Caddesi, and is refreshingly free of the stalls selling the usual tourist gifts. This is the place to come if you're looking to buy a new saddle for your donkey or a copper urn—or as is more likely, if you just want to get the feel of an authentic town bazaar. There are also spice shops, fresh fruit and vegetable stands with the produce of the season piled high, and assorted other shops catering to local needs. In the center of the bazaar is the 12th-century Ulu Camii, with its beautifully carved minaret. ⊠ *Birinci Caddesi.*

Kasimiye Madrasa. Follow the signs a short distance west of the city center to Kasimiye Madrasa, which was completed around 1459 by Sultan Kasim of the Akkoyunlu dynasty. The building has two clear halves: To the right is the mosque and to the left, through a beautiful doorway, are cells for the theological students, surrounding a pretty courtyard. ⊠ *Near city center* 🕮 *Free* ☉ *Sunrise–sunset.*

Kirklar Kilisesi (*Church of the 40s*). Mardin was once home to a large Christian community and several churches still remain in the city, although only a few are functioning. The most likely to be open is the Kirklar Kilisesi, an Assyrian Orthodox church. It's on a narrow lane a hundred yards or so west of the Mardin Museum. Parts of the church date back to the year 569, though most of what you see is medieval. There are some beautiful stone carvings and a shady courtyard. Neighborhood children will offer to take you there, which is probably a good idea, since it can be hard to find. ⊠ *217 Sağlik Sok. 8* 🖃 *Free* ☉ *Daily 8–5.*

Mardin Museum. The small museum is on the city's main square, in a grand old stone house that used to be the home of an Assyrian Catholic patriarch. The stone relief carvings on the exterior are quite exquisite, and the small collection includes displays from archaeological digs around Mardin, with pieces from the Roman, Byzantine, Seljuk, and other periods. One floor has an ethnographic exhibit showing life in old Mardin. ⊠ *Cümhurriyet Meydani* 🕾 *482/212–1664* 🖃 *3 TL* ☉ *Mon.– Sat. 8–5:30.*

Post office. One of the best examples of an old Mardin home is the current post office. ⊠ *On Birinci Cad., across street from an open-air teahouse, in the center of town.*

Zinciriye Medrese. Built in 1385 by Artukid Sultan İsa, this medrese sits up just above the rest of the city, and its crenullated dome forms a Mardin landmark. The compound includes a courtyard (now a tea garden), a mosque,and a tomb intended for the sultan. Head up to the upper terrace for one of the best views of the city. ⊠ *Near city center* 🖃 *Free* ☉ *Sunrise–sunset.*

OFF THE
BEATEN
PATH

Orthodox Dayrul Zafran (*Saffron Monastery*). Just 10 km (6 miles) southeast of Mardin is the Syrian Orthodox Dayrul Zafran. Begun in the 5th century and partially restored in the 19th century, the monastery is still in use and sits like a golden jewel in the scrubby hills of a hidden side valley. Highlights include the main church and the burial chapel, which date from the 5th century and are filled with Roman detailing, and an underground chamber, said to be a former sun temple—the heavy stone ceiling is a miracle of Roman engineering. You may catch sight of one of the *rahip* (priests) who still speak and teach Aramaic, the language of Christ. ⊠ *Off road from Mardin to Nusaybin* 🖃 *3 TL* ☉ *Daily 9–11:30 and 1–4:30 (5:30 in summer).*

WHERE TO EAT

$

TURKISH

✕ **Antik Sur.** A restored old vaulted *han*, on the city's main road, is a good place to escape the midday heat. Aside from the range of kebabs typically found in southeastern Turkey, the menu includes a few local dishes, including *kaburga*, rice-stuffed lamb's rib cage. 🖇 *Average main: 10 TL* ⊠ *1 Cad. 8/34* 🕾 *482/212–2425.*

$$

INTERNATIONAL

Fodor'sChoice

★

✕ **Bagdadi.** With excellent food and stylish ambience, this restaurant has won itself a place at the top of Mardin's dining scene. There is a mix of Western dishes such as steak and pasta, with Turkish standards and local specialities like *kaburga* (stuffed lamb) and *kuz tandir* (slow oven-cooked lamb). Local wine is also available. Meals are served on a pleasant outdoor terrace in the evening and the vaulted stone rooms of an old house during the day. $ *Average main: 25 TL* ⊠ *1 Cadde Vali Adil Sok. 2* ☎ *482/212–5555.*

$$ ✕**Cercis Murat Konağı.** One of Mardin's best restaurants and one of the

TURKISH finest in all of Turkey, occupies a restored stone house with several ter-

Fodor's Choice races that provide spectacular views of the plain that unfolds below the

★ town. Dishes served are authentic local ones, such as lamb braised in a tangy green plum sauce and *kitel raha*, layers of mince and chickpea dough. There is also a full spread of tantalizing cold and hot mezes, including tasty chickpea fritters and, owing to the Arab influence on Mardin, hummus and falafel. A locally made red wine is served traditionally, in metal bowls, although you can ask for a glass. $ *Average main: 20 TL* ⊠ *Birinci Cad. 517* ☎ *482/213–6841.*

$ ✕**Kebabçi Yusuf Ustanın Yeri.** This simple outdoor eatery in the heart of

TURKISH town is where locals come for tasty kebabs and frothy village *ayran*, a salted yogurt drink you can find bottled around the country but here is drunk the traditional way: with a ladle from metal bowls. The kebabs are served with fresh flatbread, so you can make your own wrap. $ *Average main: 12 TL* ⊠ *Birinci Cad. Üçyol Mevkii* ☎ *482/212–7985* ▭ *No credit cards.*

WHERE TO STAY

$$ ☷**Artuklu Kervansarayi.** Entering this kervansaray that dates back to

HOTEL 1275 will make you feel like you're taking a trip back in time: The walls are thick stone; the narrow, mazelike corridors seem like something out of a medieval castle; and colorful rugs and antiques accent the decor. **Pros:** wonderful atmosphere; nice public areas **Cons:** a little away from the town center; rooms are small with no view; alcohol is not served. $ *Rooms from: 200 TL* ⊠ *Birinci Cad. 70* ☎ *482/213–7353* ⊕ *www. artuklu.com* ⤳ *40 rooms, 3 suites* ❙⊙❙ *Breakfast.*

$$ ☷**Erdoba Konakları.** These rooms in a series of historic homes with mod-

HOTEL ern additions have stone walls and nice but smallish bathrooms, while suites are especially atmospheric and well worth the extra price. **Pros:** quality rooms and service; good food. **Cons:** standard rooms are small and have no views; the hotel books quickly and is often full. $ *Rooms from: 160 TL* ⊠ *Birinci Cad. 135* ☎ *482/212–7677* ⊕ *www.erdoba. com.tr* ⤳ *45 rooms, 10 suites* ❙⊙❙ *Breakfast.*

$ ☷**Ipekyolu Guesthouse.** This charming small hotel in an old house has a

B&B/INN very friendly and welcoming staff, as well as a pretty, flower-filled court-yard. **Pros:** great staff; beautful building; some proceeds of the hotel go to charity. **Cons:** average bathrooms; some rooms are dark. $ *Rooms from: 140 TL* ⊠ *228 Sokak* ☎ *482/212–1477* ⤳ *9 rooms* ❙⊙❙ *No meals.*

$$ ☷**Reyhani Kasrı.** A modern building made of traditional local stone,

HOTEL the Reyhani has beautiful upscale rooms and three terraces with views that are the envy of all Mardin. **Pros:** quality accommodations; excel-lent views; good service; has elevator, which is rare in this city of stairs. **Cons:** lacks the historic charm of other hotels; views are only from expensive suites. $ *Rooms from: 190 TL* ⊠ *1 Cadde 163* ☎ *482/212–1333* ⊕ *www.reyhanikasri.com.tr* ⤳ *42 rooms* ❙⊙❙ *No meals.*

$ ☷**Tur Abdin Konak.** This tiny hotel near the bazaar provides a well-priced

HOTEL and intimate option. **Pros:** affordable; run by a personable family; nice surroundings. **Cons:** limited services and amenities; family doesn't speak

much English. $Rooms from: 130 TL ⊠ Kültür Sok. 3 ☎ 482/212–
6309 ⊕ www.turabdinkonak.com ⇨ 4 rooms ❑ No meals.

$$ ⊞ **Zinciriye Hotel.** Two adjacent old houses just below Mardin's land-
B&B/INN   mark Zinciriye Medrese are simple, elegant, and filled with character,
with magnificent views from rooms that are comfortable and pleasantly
atmospheric but vary greatly in size. **Pros:** central location; nice views;
excellent public spaces. **Cons:** some rooms are small. $Rooms from:
160 TL ⊠ 1 Cad. ☎ 482/212–4866 ⊕ www.zinciriye.com ⇨ 15 rooms
❑ No meals.

DARA

36 km (22 miles) southeast of Mardin off Route D955.

Dara was one of the most important fortress towns on the Romano-
Byzantine eastern frontier, built by the emperors Anastasius and Justin-
ian in the 5th and 6th centuries. Dara was so important that when the
Persians captured the town in 573–4, Emperor Justin went mad, and
was wheeled around in a cart for the rest of his life, biting those who
came too close. As you arrive you will see a series of huge quarries that
were later reused for tombs. The last in the row is the most interesting,
with an elaborately carved facade. Among the ruins are an enormous
cistern, the excavated main street (labelled "agora"), a Roman bridge,
and what's left of the city's massive walls.

GETTING HERE AND AROUND

Head east from Mardin on the D955 toward Nusaybin, passing the
turnoff for Deyrul Zaferan. After 20km (12 miles), just past Akıncı,
there is a signposted turn left for Dara, a further 9.4 km (6 miles). There
is no public transport on this side road.

MIDYAT

67 km (42 miles) east of Mardin.

Not far from Mardin, the lovely old town of Midyat is an architec-
tural gem that has remained largely untouched by the blight of con-
crete—although the new part of the city is dismal. Formerly almost
an exclusively Assyrian Christian town, old Midyat is filled with an
astonishing number of beautiful homes built of stone the color of honey
or golden sand. Walking through Midyat's narrow streets reveals house
after beautiful house, many of them with gorgeous ornamental carv-
ing work on their exteriors. Many of Midyat's Christians left during
the violence of the 1980s and '90s, and Kurdish has become the domi-
nant language of the old town. The homes and churches remain, and
now that a relative calm has returned to the region, some of them are
even being renovated for use as summer homes by Assyrians who used
to reside here but currently have their primary residences in Western
Europe. Midyat now has some excellent hotels, and you can spend a
quiet day or two exploring the city and visiting some of the nearby
Assyrian churches and monasteries; this is also a good base for visiting
the historical monuments at the nearby riverside town of Hasankeyf.

GETTING HERE AND AROUND

Midyat is 67 km (41 miles) east of Mardin on D380. Regular minibuses make the trip between the two towns.

EXPLORING

Monastery of the Mother of God. In the villages around Midyat are dozens of churches, many still in use and dating back to the 5th through 8th centuries. The area suffered considerably during the Kurdish uprising, and many Christians moved to Germany, Sweden, and Australia, though a small number are beginning to return and many visit in summer. The most extraordinary religious site is the Monastery of the Mother of God at Hah (Anıtlı), probably from the 6th century, which has an elaborately carved classical interior and exterior and is the only Byznatine church, other than the Aya Sofia in Istanbul, to use a dome and two half-domes to create a rectangular space. ⊠ *Dargeçit Cam., Anıtlı* ☎ *Free* ⊙ *Sunrise–sunset.*

Mor Barsaumo Church. With their numbers dwindling, Midyat's Assyrian community rotates services throughout the old town's churches, so it's hard to know which one will be open. Your best bet is the Mor Barsaumo church, open most afternoons. It has a beautiful chapel with distinctive locally made artwork and lovely stonework. ⊠ *Şen Cad. 21, southern end of the old city* ☎ *Free.*

Shiluh. The Syriac Christians have a long tradition of winemaking, but Shiluh is the region's first professional winery. Shiluh has a shop in the center of Midyat, but the winery is 7 km (4 miles) from Midyat on the road to Mor Gabriel, where they plan to eventually open an underground restaurant and a tasting room carved out of the hillside. Note that the unusual, strong flavor of the red wine may not to be to everyone's taste. ⊠ *202 Sokak, Kuyumcular (Silversmiths) Pasajı.*

OFF THE
BEATEN
PATH

Mor Gabriel Monastery. Twenty-five kilometers (15½ miles) southeast of Midyat is the Mor Gabriel monastery, built on the site of a church that dates back to 387. The monastery is on the top of a hill in a desolate area, surrounded by fields and vineyards, a peaceful and tranquil setting. Reopened as a monastery in 1952 after having been closed for some time, the building is a traditionally a nunnery, though barely a dozen women remain; a few monks and the local patriarch, known as a Metropolitan, are also in residence, as are children sent to boarding school here to help preserve the ancient Syriac language. Two churches and a grotto hold the graves of monks who have lived here throughout the centuries. English-speaking guides—young men who live here as students—are usually on hand to show guests around. ⊠ *25 km (15½ miles) southeast of Midyat* ☎ *482/462–1425* ☎ *Free* ⊙ *Daily 9–11:30 and 1–4.30.*

WHERE TO EAT

$

TURKISH

✕ **Cihan Lokantası.** This basic steam-table restaurant serves the usual menu of stews and casseroles but the owners have tried to add some class by hanging white lace curtains and putting pots of plastic yellow flowers on the walls—your call if it's classy or tacky. Either way, the food is tasty, the staff is friendly, and the location, down the street from the Mor Barsaumo church, makes this one of the few decent options near Midyat's old town. $ *Average main: 10 TL* ⊠ *Cizre Yolu Uzeri, Karakol Karş 52* ☎ 482/464–1566 ▭ *No credit cards.*

$

TURKISH

✕ **Tarihi Midyat Gelüşke Hanı.** A beautifully restored han served as an inn for traveling traders for centuries, and you can eat outside by a fountain in the large courtyard or in one of the small private dining rooms, where you sit on rugs and eat from low tables, reclining on pillows when you're done. The kebabs and other grilled meats are tasty and served with a tangy chopped tomato salad and a refreshing cold yogurt soup that has wheat berries in it. If you call a day in advance, they can prepare the Assyrian speciality, *dobo* (lamb stuffed with rice and pistachios). $ *Average main: 15 TL* ⊠ *Eski Midyat Çarşısı* ☎ 482/464–1442.

WHERE TO STAY

$$

B&B/INN

🛏 **Kasr-ı Nehroz.** The owners have converted their family home perched on the city walls into a beautiful retreat, where stone-walled, vaulted-ceiling rooms in the old quarters and a new wing are beautifully decorated in a mix of traditonal and modern styles and surround an airy courtyard. **Pros:** beautiful old mansion; exotic surroundings; good value. **Cons:** some modern rooms lack the character of rooms in the old house. $ *Rooms from: 235 TL* ⊠ *219 Sok. 14* ☎ 482/464–2525 ⊕ *www.hotelnehroz.com* ⬎ *29 rooms* ⦿ *No meals.*

$$

HOTEL

Fodor's Choice

★

🛏 **Shmayaa.** The name of this beautiful old mansion-hotel means "sky" and indeed some of the rooftop rooms open to above; in others, furniture is clustered so nothing touches the extraordinary, well-preserved stonework. **Pros:** beautiful surroudings; lovely outdoor spaces; nice location in old quarter. **Cons:** stairs may pose difficulty for some visitors. $ *Rooms from: 205 TL* ⊠ *126 Sok. 12* ☎ 532/457–5838 ⊕ *www.shmayaa.com* ⬎ *18 rooms.*

$$

HOTEL

🛏 **Turabdin Hotel.** Located in a field on the edge of the east side of the old town, this is the only Syrian-run hotel in Midyat and it's popular with returning former locals. **Pros:** helpful, English-speaking staff; interesting conversations with foreign Syrians returning to their homeland. **Cons:** not much character. $ *Rooms from: 150 TL* ⊠ *Manastır Cad. 17* ☎ 482/464–0104 ⊕ *www.turabdinhotel.com* ⬎ *20 rooms* ⦿ *Breakfast.*

HASANKEYF

43 km (27 miles) north of Midyat.

Just a short drive from Midyat, Hasankeyf makes for a good half-day excursion. This small town has a magical setting, with stone houses on the banks of the Tigris River, lorded over by a cliff topped with the remains of an ancient citadel. One of the only places to cross this section of the Tigris is a now-ruined bridge that was built in 1116 by the Artukid ruler Fahreddin Karaaslan, possibly incorporating parts of a Roman bridge. Above it is a magnificent minaret—all that remains of the Artukid Great Mosque, which collapsed into the waters. Come, explore, have lunch at a string of casual fish restaurants on the banks of the Tigris (at some you can sit in ankle-deep water and enjoy a fish as its smaller relatives nibble at your toes) then return to Midyat, Mardin, Diyarbakır, or even Lake Van.

GETTING HERE AND AROUND

Hasankeyf is 43 km (27 miles) north of Midyat and 135 km (82 miles) north of Diyarbakır on D955. Minibuses make regular runs between Midyat and Hasankeyf.

EXPLORING

Citadel. The citadel, which dates back to Roman times, is at the top of a sheer cliff that rises 328 feet above the river. On the backside of the cliff, the citadel looks over a small canyon where several abandoned cave dwellings have been carved into the rock. Excavations and stablization work is ongoing, hence the "No entry" signs that put some of the site off-limits. The whole site can sometimes be closed for months at a time so be sure to check with locals before you go. ✉ *Edge of town* 🎫 *3 TL* 🕒 *Daily 8:30–5:30.*

Er Rizk Mosque. Just below the citadel, on the way into town, is the Er Rizk Mosque, which dates back to the 14th century and has a beautiful minaret that has intricate stone carvings on its exterior. ✉ *Near town center* 🎫 *Free* 🕒 *Sunrise–sunset.*

Zeynelbey Turbesi. Across the river from the citadel is another spot worth visiting, Zeynelbey Turbesi, a mausoleum built for a prince who died in battle in 1473. The stylized structure has an onion-dome top and is decorated with still-vivid turquoise-color tiles set in calligraphy-like geometric patterns, reminscent of Iran and Central Asia. ✉ *On Batman-Hasankeyf road, near bridge* 🎫 *Free* 🕒 *Sunrise–sunset.*

WHERE TO EAT

$ TURKISH 🍴 **Kasr-i Keyf.** The mix of kebabs is fairly standard, though they are well prepared. The nice setting includes a terrace with a good view out of the town and the Tigris, and there's ice cream for dessert. [$] *Average main: 15 TL* ✉ *Burç Sok, near entrance to the castle.*

THE TIGRIS DAM

For the last several decades a proposed massive dam project along the Tigris has put Hasankeyf in danger of being submerged. A vocal campaign by environmentalists and preservationists succeeded in persuading European financial backers to withdraw, temporarily stopping the project. However, in 2013, work began again with Chinese investors looking to build the dam within the next four or five years, and alas it looks like Hasankeyf's days may be numbered.

GAZIANTEP, MT. NEMRUT, AND URFA

Forget about "George Washington slept here"; in this part of Turkey you're more likely to come across places that claim to have been paid a visit by the biblical patriarch Abraham. Cities and monuments in this part of southeast Turkey trace their roots back to biblical times and beyond. Luckily for the traveler, much of that history hasn't been lost to the sands of time, and the ancient cities and historical sites that are part of this region are remarkably well preserved and visitor-friendly.

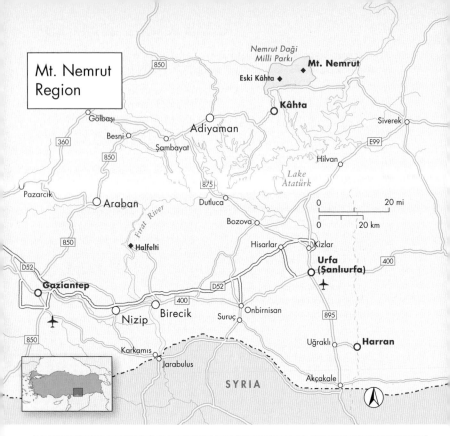

GAZIANTEP

Gaziantep is the last Turkish-speaking city before the Kurdish and Arab areas and somehow manages to mix the modernity of western Turkey with the Middle Eastern flavor of the East. Not long ago it was an average regional city exporting car parts and pistachios, but local authorities have put a huge effort into promoting tourism by developing the old quarter and showing off the tasty food culture as well as the historical mosaics excavated from nearby Zeugma. You can wander the narrow-laned old town, with its graceful stone houses, and venture through the bustling bazaar filled with the sound of hammering coppersmiths. Many old houses and their large interior courtyards survive; some have become museums, cafés, hotels, and inns.

A melting pot of many culinary traditions, Gaziantep is also one of Turkey's most important food capitals, and a collection of restaurants and baklava bakeries are considered among the best in the country. In one day you can see the sights but you could easily spend two days exploring and eating.

GETTING HERE AND AROUND
Turkish Airlines and Onurair fly to Gaziantep from Istanbul and Ankara. SunExpress flies to Gaziantep from İzmir and Antalya.

CLOSE UP

Rediscovering Turkish Food in Gaziantep

Turks can be fiercely proud of the food in their region of the country, but even those from other places will easily admit that Gaziantep has perhaps Turkey's best food. Drawing on culinary influences from Turkish and Arab cooking, the earthy cuisine in Gaziantep is assertively spiced and flavorful. If you've grown tired of kebabs during your time in Turkey, be ready to rediscover them in Gaziantep, where kebab making is seen as both an art and a science. Among some of the best kinds of kebabs you can try here are *sebzeli kebab* (a skewer of lamb, tomato, green peppers, parsley, and garlic minced together) and *Ali Nazik* (cubes of grilled lamb taken off their skewer and served on a heavenly bed of smoky roasted eggplant and garlicky yogurt). Other specialties include *mercimek koftesi* (small ovals made out of red lentils mixed with bulgur wheat, fresh herbs, red pepper paste, and spices) and *yuvalama* (tiny dumplings made out of rice flour and ground meat, served in a yogurt broth).

Most of all, though, Gaziantep is famed for its flaky and buttery baklava, which successfully incorporates one of the area's leading crops, pistachios. It is, without a doubt, the preferred ending to any meal in Gaziantep.

Gaziantep is rightfully known as Turkey's baklava capital and there seems to be a shop on every corner, most incorporating the tongue-twister family name "Güllüoğlu."

There are daily buses from Istanbul to Gaziantep: the ride takes about 18 hours and costs about 70 TL.

ESSENTIALS
The knowledgeable Ayşe Nur Arun at Gaziantep's Arsan travel agency can arrange for tours in Gaziantep, around the region, and to Mt. Nemrut.

Contacts Arsan ☎ *342/220–6464* ⊕ *www.arsan.com.tr.*

EXPLORING
Bazaar. The heart of the bazaar is the **Zincirli Bedestan**, with shops selling copperwork, mother of pearl inlay, saddles, and Ottoman-style leather shoes. Beyond the bedestan is the **Bakırcılar Çarşısı**, the market of the coppersmiths, where an orchestra of craftspeople taps out bowls and coffee cups between customers. From here you emerge at the **Tahmis Coffee House**, one of the most traditional places to try Turkish coffee and where, legend has it, the Sultan Murat IV dropped in for coffee on his way to conquer Baghdad in 1638 (the current shop was built after a fire destroyed the original in the 19th century). The neighboring Sufi lodge, now the **Mevlevihanesi Vakif Museum**, has historic Korans and kilims (along with free admission). ⊘ *Mon.–Sat. 9–6.*

Bey Neighborhood. From the intersection of İstasyon Caddesi and Atatürk Bulvarı, head southwest into the rabbit warren of the **Bey neighborhood**. Many of the old houses have been turned into cafés, like the **Papirus Cafeteria** on Noter Sokak. The Bey neighborhood was

largely Armenian and three old churches survive. The easiest to find is the **Kendirli Church** on Atatürk Caddesi built in 1860 with the support of Napoleon III for Armenian Catholics. The main Armenian Orthodox Cathedral, also built in 19th century, is farther south on Hapişhane Caddesi, now in use as the **Kurtuluş Mosque**. Farther along this street on the far side is another former church, now the **Ömer Ersoy Cultural Centre**. Back on Atatürk Caddesi is the **City Museum** (1 TL). There are very few actual exhibits here; each room has a video screen with an accompanying soundtrack of the free English language audio guide. The most intersting rooms are dedicated to Antep's traditional crafts. ⊠ *Gaziantep*.

Citadel area. The northern exit of the Zincirli Bedestan brings you out beside the 19th-century Alaüddevle Mosque, with its large dome. From here Hamdi Kutlar Caddesi leads past more coppersmiths, several restored 19th-century kervansarays, and the small **Emine Göğüş Culinary Museum** (1 TL) to the prominent *kale* (castle), built over the layers of the pre-Roman city by the Emperor Justinian in the 6th century and remodeled by the Seljuk Turks in the 12th and 13th centuries. It's a steep walk to the top, but the view over the bazaar district is fantastic, if it finally reopens that is. If you need some relaxation after the excursion, on the far side of the castle you'll find the recently restored Naib Hamam, dating from 1640 (25 TL).

Gaziantep Museum. Gaziantep Museum houses a mix of antiquities from throughout the area's long history. The most interesting exhibits are from the Temple of Zeuz Doliche, north of the city, an important shrine until it was destroyed by the Persians in 253. Other finds range from mammoth bones and prehistoric pottery to Hittite statues and Roman surgical equipment. As of this writing, it was undergoing renovations, but planned to reopen by 2014. ⊠ *Kamil Ocak Stat Karşısı 1–2* 🕿 *342/324–8809* 🎫 *5 TL* ⊘ *May–Oct., daily 8:30–noon and 1–6; Nov.–Apr., daily 8:30–noon and 1–4:30.*

Hasan Suzer Ethnographic Museum. While exploring the warren of streets in the Bey neighborhood step into a traditional Gaziantep house, with dressed-up mannequins filling in as residents. The basement carved out of the rock is a common feature of Antep houses, and the shady courtyard is a welcome retreat from the heat and blazing sun. The surprise exhibit is the captured motorcycle of Lawrence of Arabia, who spied against the Ottomans in World War I. ⊠ *Hanifioğlu Sok. 64* 🕿 *342/230–4721* 🎫 *3 TL* ⊘ *Tues.–Sun 8–noon, 1–5:30.*

Fodor'sChoice   **Zeugma Museum and Conference Center.** What claims to be the largest
★   mosaic museum in the world houses a stunning collection of Roman-era mosaics rescued from a nearby archaeological site called Zeugma, which was submerged under the waters of a man-made lake. The intricate mosaics, some portraying scenes from Roman mythology, others more artistic geometric designs, are dazzling to behold. The fragment of a mosaic depicting a young woman with an enigmatic gaze (called "The Gypsy Girl") is quickly earning Mona Lisa–like iconic status across Turkey. Many of the mosaics depict less common myths, such as that of Achilles, hidden by his mother before the Trojan War and disguised

in women's clothing but tricked into showing interest in a sword, and Parthenope and Metiochus, a Romeo and Juliet of the ancient world. Destruction by illegal excavations is also highlighted, and several of the mosaics on display did time in private collections in the United States before being recovered. Unfortunately, the museum is a bit soulless and the lighting is very low and yellow. ✉ *Sani Konukoğlu Bulvarı* 🎫 *8 TL* 🕐 *Tues.–Sun. 9–17.*

WHERE TO EAT

$ TURKISH 🍴 **Baklavacı Güllüoğlu.** This little shop inside a spice bazaar is considered by many Turks nationwide to have the best baklava in the country. Run by a fifth-generation baklava maker, this humble store turns out a delicious version of the classic dessert, as well as other phyllo-and-nut-based sweets. [$] *Average main: 2 TL* ✉ *Elmacı Pazarı 4* ☎ *342/231–2105* 💳 *No credit cards* 🕐 *Closed Sun.*

$$ TURKISH 🍴 **Bayazhane.** A warehouse built in 1909 for a tobacco merchant is now a spot for diners to enjoy their meals in either a large outdoor courtyard or the cool stone-vaulted chambers at the back. There are excellent mezes, quality incarnations of standard kebabs, and a good sampling of local dishes like smoky eggplant kebabs, plus fantastic *yavurma* (meatball and yogurt soup). This is not only one of the nicest places in town, but one of the few that serves alcohol. [$] *Average main: 25 TL* ✉ *Atatürk Bulvarı 119, about 700m (½ mile) west of İstasyon Cad.* ☎ *342/221–0212.*

$ TURKISH 🍴 **Halil Usta.** Two blocks behind the Zeugma, hidden away in a quiet neighborhood, is this Gaziantep institution. While you shouldn't expect a serene dining experience (it can get pretty noisy and crowded), it's surprisingly simple and as the photos on the wall demonstrate, anyone who's anyone in Turkey has eaten here. There's no menu, but the *antep* kebabs are what it's most famous for; you can also try *küşbaşlı* (meat pieces) or *kiyma* (from minced meat), all available as *aci* (spicy) or *sade* (plain). Note that it's only open for lunch. [$] *Average main: 15 TL* ✉ *Tekel Cad. and Öcükoğlu Sokak, two blocks behind Zeugma Museum* 🕐 *No dinner.*

$ TURKISH Fodor's Choice ★ 🍴 **Imam Çağdaş.** Open since 1887, Imam Çağdaş is certainly doing something right, and the crowds pack this restaurant in the bazaar district day and night. There is a small menu of standard kebabs such as *ali nazik,* minced meat kebab served on a purée of roasted eggplant, garlic and yogurt, and the *sebzeli* kebab, a skewer of lamb minced with garlic and parsley. The star at the restaurant is the terrific syrupy baklava, so widely regarded as the best that orders have regularly been received from Turkish presidents and from as far afield as Fidel Castro. [$] *Average main: 15 TL* ✉ *Uzun Çarşı 14, behind the Bedestan* ☎ *342/220–4545* 🌐 *www.imamcagdas.com.*

$ TURKISH 🍴 **Yörem.** Head here for a break from kebabs and get a taste of classic Gaziantep home cooking. A local woman who returned to Gaziantep after living in Europe for several years rotates her menu on a regular basis, but the food is consistently good. Dishes to try include *yuvalama,* a meat-and-dumpling stew. For dessert try the local specialty *zerde sutlaç,* rice pudding with a saffron topping. The restaurant is a bit difficult to find—it's one block east of Fevzi Çakmak Caddesi, which runs north from the Gaziantep Museum. $ *Average main: 12 TL* ✉ *Incilpi-nar Mahallesi 3. Cad. 15, Sokak* ☎ *342/230–5000.*

WHERE TO STAY

$
B&B/INN
✦ **Ali Bey Konağı.** Visitors can stay in this restored 18th-century house that has nice rooms with large bathrooms doubling as Turkish hammams. **Pros:** English spoken; highly praised breakfast. **Cons:** courtyard could be spruced up; location a bit hard to find. $ *Rooms from: 150 TL* ✉ *Tişlaki Mah. Kafadar Sok. 6* ☎ *342/231–4512* ⤴ *6 rooms* ⦿| *Breakfast.*

$$
B&B/INN
Fodor's Choice
★
✦ **Anadolu Evleri.** Down a narrow alleyway and behind a high wall, you'll find four stylish but comfortable historic Gaziantep stone houses, where rooms have been meticulously restored and are charmingly decorated with quirky antiques-like old radios, sewing machines, and antique telephones. **Pros:** central location; friendly staff; owner speaks fluent English. **Cons:** no swimming pool or hammam. $ *Rooms from: 230 TL* ✉ *Şekeroğlu Mahallesi Köroğlu Sok. 6* ☎ *342/220–9525* ⊕ *www.anadoluevleri.com* ⤴ *10 rooms, 3 suites* ⦿| *Breakfast.*

$$
B&B/INN
✦ **Hıdıroğlu Konak Hotel.** In the old Christian Bey neighborhood, this fresh mansion-hotel conversion makes sure you feel like a guest at a real Turkish house (shoes even come off at the door). **Pros:** very homey; great courtyard; everything feels new. **Cons:** a little out of the way; some street noise. $ *Rooms from: 150 TL* ✉ *Hidir Sokak 19 Sahinbey* ☎ *505/501–2260* ⊕ *www.hidiroglukonak.com* ⤴ *6 rooms* ⦿| *No meals.*

HALFETI

20 km (12 miles) northeast of Gaziantep.

Halfeti, a small town of honey-color stone houses on the Euphrates, became half-Halfeti with the flooding of the Birecik Dam in 2000. Enough survives for a pleasant excursion, and there are many small restaurants by the water. The only actual landmark is the town's former mosque, so close to the dam that the water now laps around its door. From Halfeti boats take visitors on excursions on the lake, here more like a wide river, to Rumkale, the "Castle of the Romans." The seat of an Armenian Patriarch from the 12th century, the castle is impressive from the outside, but due to ongoing restoration that's all you see. Beyond Rumkale the boats normally continue to another semisunken village, Savaş, where the minaret pokes out of the water. The trip costs about 80 TL for the smaller boat, which can take around 10 people, and lasts about 90 minutes. If you wait, several other travelers will most likely join you in the boat, so you rarely have to pay the full 80 TL.

KÂHTA

174 km (108 miles) northeast of Gaziantep.

The quiet and dusty little town of Kâhta is nobody's favorite place in Turkey and is really nothing more than a good base for exploring Mt. Nemrut. There are a few good hotels and places to eat, but nothing to see.

The construction of the large Atatürk Dam and the resulting rising waters have meant that Kâhta is now a lakeside town, and a number of restaurants have taken advantage of this, opening up near the water, which makes a pleasant setting for a meal.

GETTING HERE AND AROUND

From Gaziantep follow D850 to Adıyaman, where it becomes D360, and continue on to Kâhta. Regular minivans make the run from Gaziantep to Urfa and from Urfa to Adiyaman, where you can catch a minivan to Kahta. There's an *otogar* (bus station) in each of the main towns.

ESSENTIALS

Contacts **Nemrut Tours** ☎ 416/725–6881.

WHERE TO EAT AND STAY

$ ✕ **Kahta Sofrası.** The pickings might be slim in Kâhta, but this place
TURKISH stands out for its friendly service and well-made food, including freshly baked pide as well as kebabs and prepared dishes like roast chicken and lamb stew. The bright and open restaurant is decorated with colorful rugs. $ *Average main: 10 TL* ✉ *Mustafa Kemal Cad. 15* ☎ *416/726–2055.*

$ ✕ **Neşet'in Yeri.** This lakeside restaurant has an outdoor area shaded
TURKISH by an impressive grape arbor where you can eat trout or kebab while looking at the water. It's a nice spot to unwind after a visit to Nemrut. $ *Average main: 12 TL* ✉ *Baraj Kenari* ☎ *416/725–7675.*

$ 🏨 **Zeus Hotel.** With a pool, quiet garden, and spacious and comfortable
HOTEL rooms, each with a small couch, this well-run hotel is a good base for visiting Mt. Nemrut. **Pros:** pool and nice garden. **Cons:** a little dated. $ *Rooms from: 140 TL* ✉ *Namık Kemal Cad. 20* ☎ *416/725–5694* ⊕ *www.zeushotel.com.tr* ⤳ *58 rooms, 8 suites* ⧉ *Breakfast.*

MT. NEMRUT AND ENVIRONS

228 km (142 miles) northeast of Gaziantep.

Mt. Nemrut, known as Mt. Nimrod in English, rises 7,052 feet above the Anatolian plain, a ruddy outcrop of rock and stunted trees that has become one of Turkey's most iconic historical sites.

EXPLORING

Fodor's Choice **Mt. Nemrut (Nemrut Dağı).** *See the highlighted feature in this chapter.*
★

WHERE TO STAY

$$ 🏨 **Hotel Euphrat.** This low stone building has comfortable, clean rooms
HOTEL and good bathrooms, and is the best of the few places to stay on Mt. Nemrut itself. **Pros:** best rooms on the mountain; nice pool. **Cons:** tour group central; half board required. $ *Rooms from: 190 TL* ✉ *Nemrut Dağı, 54 km (34 miles) from Kâhta, Karadut Köyü, Kâhta* ☎ *416/737–2175* ⤳ *52 rooms* ⧉ *Some meals.*

$ 🏨 **Samos Hotel.** Opened in 2013, this hotel has quickly become the best
HOTEL option in the Nemrut area with its comfortable and nicely furnished midrange rooms and a decent selection of facilities including a pool and sauna. **Pros:** feels luxurious; pool and sauna; great views from rooftop.

Continued on page 464

MEGALOMANIA ON MOUNT NEMRUT

"I, Antiochus, caused this monument to be erected in commemoration of my own glory and of that of the gods."

At the top of remote Mount Nemrut (Nemrut Daği), the monumental tomb of Antiochus (ruled c.69–34 BC), king of the obscure and short-lived kingdom of Commagene on the Euphrates, is one of the world's most extraordinary archaeological sights. Antiochus fancied himself a ruler on par with the gods of antiquity, so he had this grandiose monument to himself erected, to be in the company of his peers.

At 2,150 m (7,053 ft), Mt. Nemrut, not far from the Syrian border, is the highest peak in the area. At the center of the mountaintop site is a huge tumulus, or burial mound of small stones. To the east and west of the burial mound are two great platforms, each with an identical giant statue of Antiochus seated with his fellow gods, overlooking the desertlike landscape and the Euphrates River to the east. Over the years the statues have fallen and now the disembodied stone heads stand separate from their bodies.

Statue heads on West Terrace

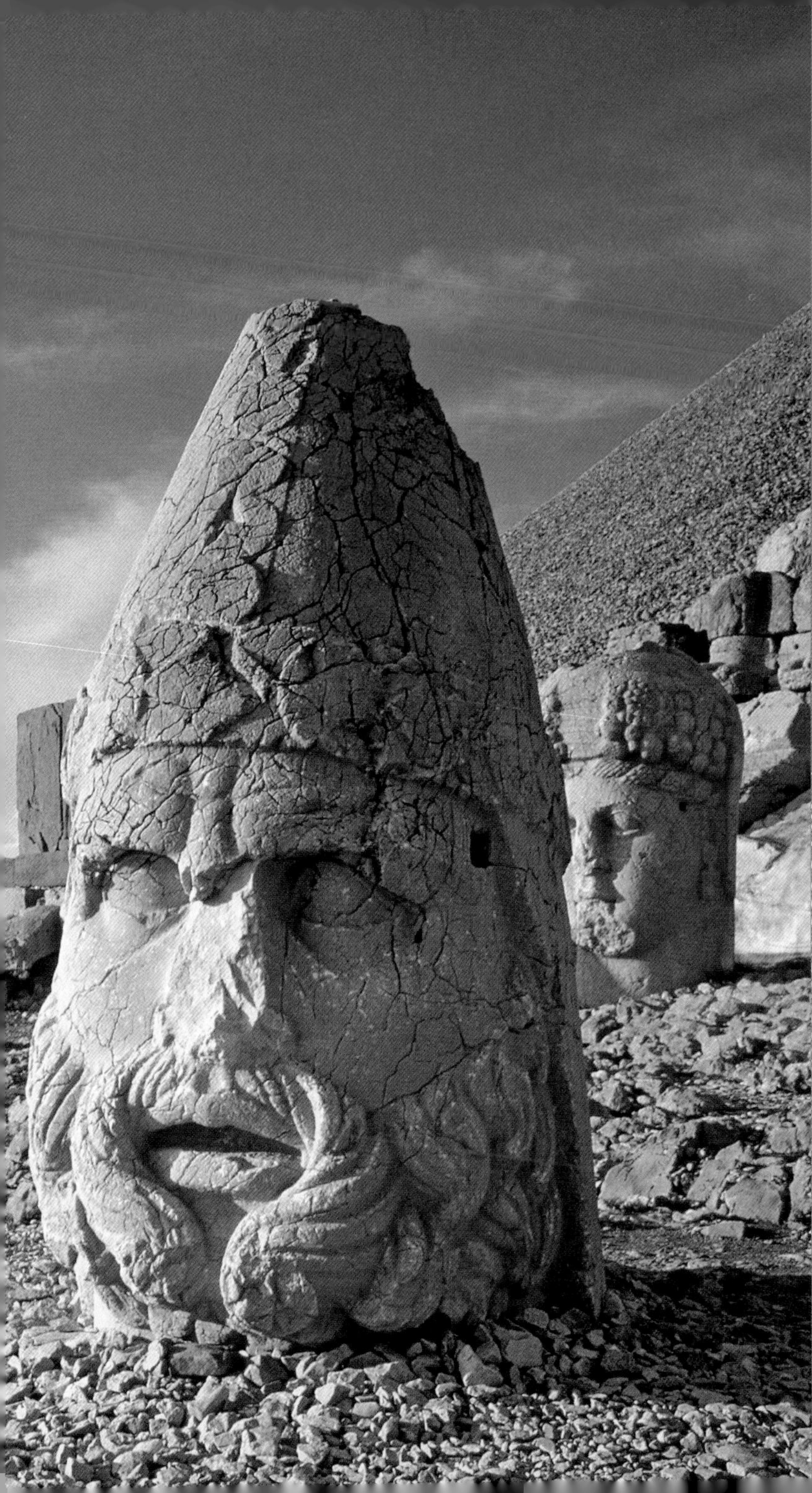

WHAT TO SEE

1 The Tumulus

The center of the site is the giant tumulus, 500 feet in diameter and 150 feet high, made of small pebbles. It's believed that the entrance to King Antiochus's tomb is underneath the rocks, but despite several attempts at tunneling, it has yet to be found.

THE TERRACES

To the east and west of the tumulus, the land was leveled into large terraces where giant statues of Antiochus and the gods were erected. Annual religious ceremonies were performed here.

2 The East Terrace

On the east terrace, the stone bodies of the statues are quite well preserved, giving the best idea of what they originally looked like. The heads are more worn, and are now lined up at the feet of their respective bodies. The head of Tyche is said to have sat on her statue's stone shoulders until as late as the 1960s.

3 The West Terrace

On the west terrace, the statue bodies have crumbled, but the heads, scattered around the area, are well preserved; these are the now classic images of Mount Nemrut.

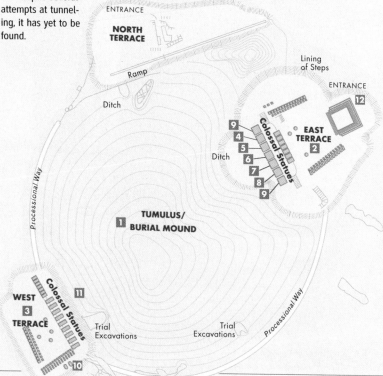

Above: The tumulus

THE GODS

King Antiochus had himself depicted enthroned with his fellow gods in a matching set of 30-ft-tall stone murals on the east and west terraces. The images of the gods are a mix of eastern and western styles, their faces Greek, their clothes Persian.

4 Hercules, Artagnes, and Ares Hercules is bearded, but with a simpler hat than Zeus. Artagnes, or Vahram, was a Persian warrior god, here combined with both the hero Hercules, and Ares, the Greek god of war. On the east terrace, the statue of Hercules bears the symbol of the club.

5 King Antiochus In front of the statues stood a smaller stele of Antiochus posing with his fellow gods. The image of the king was on the left, beardless with a long thin, plume-like hat.

6 Zeus-Oromasdes Zeus, mixed with his Persian equivalent Oromasdes or Ahura Mazda, stood in the center of the site, his stone throne slightly higher than the rest. His bearded face is hard to distinguish from Hercules, but look for the circle and diamond pattern on his conical hat.

7 The Tyche of Commagene Tyche, the goddess of fortune, is the only female figure here and, therefore, the easiest to spot. As an embodiment of fortune and abundance, her headdress is filled with fruit.

Hercules

8 Apollo, Hermes, Helius, and Mithra Apollo is another beardless male, with a simpler, more conical, hat than that of Antiochus. The ancients apparently weren't sure who was the Greek equivalent of the Persian Mithra, spirit of light, so his image is a mix of Apollo (the sun god), Helios (the sun itself), and Hermes (the messenger god).

9 Animal Protectors On either side of the gods stood a giant lion and eagle, which acted as their protectors. The eagles were built of multiple pieces, as were the gods, and their heads sit together on the west terrace.

10 The Ancestors Antiochus had some of the most royal blood in the ancient world. On the back of his throne is carved his royal pedigree: the kings of Persia and Armenia on his father's side, and the Greco-Macedonian kings who ruled the empire of Alexander the Great on his mother's side. Around the great statues are carved reliefs depicting Antiochus with his ancestors. The best preserved are those of him with the great kings of Persia—Darius and Xerxes—on the south side of the west terrace.

11 The Lion Horoscope A relief found on the west terrace has been called the world's oldest horoscope. It depicts a lion (representing the constellation Leo), 19 "stars," including the planets Mars, Mercury, and Jupiter, and the crescent moon. Archaeoastronomers have identified the date of this horoscope as either July 109 BC, perhaps the date of Antiochus's father's coronation, or July 61 BC, believed to be that of Antiochus's own coronation. The relief has been removed for restoration and may be replaced with a replica.

12 The Fire Altar The sacred fire was a central part of the Persian Zoroastrian religion and the east terrace featured a large fire altar—it's hardly noticed today, although the area is the most popular place for tourists to watch the sunrise.

The Lion Horoscope

DID YOU KNOW?

There's no connection
between Mt. Nemrut
and the Biblical Nimrod
(Nemrut in English), creator
of the Tower of Babel.
Somehow the name
got attached and stuck;
Antiochus must be turning
in his monumental grave.

THE ROAD TO NEMRUT AND WHAT TO SEE ON IT

There are several ancient sites along the road from Kâhta to Nemrut that have become standard stops for visitors to the mountain.

King Antiochus and Hercules at Arsameia

THE BURIAL MOUND OF KARAKUŞ

A second royal tumulus—it lacks the grandeur of the more famous mountaintop monument—was built by Antiochus's son, for his sister, wife, and daughter. The name Karakuş, or black bird, comes from the statue of an eagle, set on a large column beside the tomb.

CENDERE BRIDGE

Photos don't do justice to the scale of this huge bridge, a monument to Roman engineering: three large columns once held statues of the Emperor Septimius Severus, his wife Julia Domna, and their son, the future emperor Caracalla. A fourth was probably for the second son, Geta, who was killed by Caracalla, who also tried to erase all trace of his brother's existence.

ARSAMEIA

Partway up the mountain are the few remains of what is left of Arsameia, the summer home of the kings of Commagene: several carved stelai, the most famous picturing King Antiochus in Persian dress with a very naked Hercules. Above is a long inscription in Greek with a deep tunnel disappearing into the mountain.

ESKI KÂHTA

The small traditional village of Eski (old) Kâhta is just off the main road where the mountains start. There is a castle here with a view over a dramatic gorge.

GETTING THERE

Uninspiring Kâhta is the closest town to Mount Nemrut; from here it's a 2-hour drive. The road is good, but steep and bumpy in places, and it can be very windy. You may want to stay in Kâhta and let someone else take the wheel; tours (110-250 TL) also mean the benefit of a guide (there are also multiday tours from Cappadocia). Most tours are timed for sunrise or sunset, when the landscape and its monuments are at their most dramatic—note that in summer, sunrise tours can require a 2 am departure. Dress warmly: even in high summer, nights are chilly atop the mountain. Nemrut can only be visited between about May and October, as snow makes the road to the top impassable in winter. ⛏9 TL ☉ Daily dawn to dusk.

Cons: a bit far from Nemrut. [$] *Rooms from: 130 TL* ✉ *Atatürk Bulvarı 328A, Adiyaman* ☎ *416/214–7373* 🌐 *www.otelsamos.com* 🛏 *56 rooms, 7 suites* 🍴 *Breakfast.*

URFA (ŞANLIURFA)

143 km (89 miles) southeast of Kâhta; 135 km (84 miles) east of Gaziantep.

This is Turkey at its most Middle Eastern, with golden-color stone houses, religious shrines filled with visiting pilgrims, and an authentic bazaar displaying mounds and mounds of the local specialty—crushed red pepper, in various shades and levels of spiciness. Formerly a sleepy and arid frontier town that underwent a huge boom due to GAP (the Güneydoğu Anadolu Projesi, or Southeast Anatolia Project, a large-scale damming and irrigation program undertaken by the Turkish government), Urfa has a long history even by Turkish standards. For Muslims Urfa is most famous as the supposed birthplace of the biblical patriarch Abraham. A half-dozen mosques crowd around the cave where many Muslims believe Abraham was born, and a pool near the cave is filled with what are believed to be sacred carp. Urfa is also the heartland of the unromantically name Pre-Pottery Neolithic Era, a stage of prehistory some 13,500 years ago when humankind was making the first steps toward settlement and agriculture. In the Urfa Museum you can see what is arguably the world's oldest statue and at nearby Göbekli Tepe you can see the oldest monumental construction.

Urfa is sometimes known as Şanlıurfa; *Şanlı,* or "famous," was added by an act of parliament to the city's name in 1984 to commemorate the city's resistance to the French military occupation of the area following World War I. Urfa's old town, at the southern foot of Divan Caddesi, is a remarkable mix of Byzantine, Arab, and Ottoman architecture, albeit heavily eroded over the centuries.

GETTING HERE AND AROUND

Turkish Airlines and Pegasus fly regularly to Urfa from Ankara and Istanbul. By car, Urfa is 135 km (84 miles) east of Gaziantep on E90 and 192 km (120 miles) west of Mardin on E90. Urfa is 143 km (89 miles) southeast of Kâhta on D875. Regular minivans make the run from Gaziantep to Urfa.

ESSENTIALS

Harran-Nemrut tours in Urfa are run by the English-speaking Özcan Aslan, who is friendly and helpful. He can arrange trips to Harran and the surrounding region and also offers one- and two-day tours to Mt. Nemrut from Urfa.

Contacts Şanlıurfa ✉ *Atatürk Bulvarı No 4, Kiosk on corner, Şanlıurfa* ☎ *414/312–5332.*

EXPLORING

Archaeological museum. Urfa's archaeological museum has a good collection covering the area's long history. Especially interesting are sculptures from Göbekli Tepe but the star, unmarked beside the entrance, is a white, alien-looking statue, found in the Gölbaşı Lake in 1993.

The gold-color houses of Urfa

Nearly 13,500 years old, it is the world's oldest full-size man-made human figure. There are also Hittite sculptures from the area, a collection of exquisite carved antique wooden doors, and classical sculpture in the garden. As of this writing, it was due to move to a new building in early 2014. ✉ *11 Nisan Fuar Cad., Şanlıurfa* ☎ *414/313–1588* 💵 *3 TL* 🕐 *Tues.–Sun. 8–5.*

Bazaar. A short walk east from the park leads to Urfa's bazaar, where in summertime merchants wait patiently in the hot sun for the occasional tour group. The bazaar is filled with small *hans*—a collection of stores and workshops built around a central courtyard—that have tailors, coppersmiths, and other artisans working away, using what seem like ancient machines and tools. At the literal heart of the bazaar is the wonderful Bedesten and adjacent Gümrük Han, a large courtyard filled with chatting men playing backgammon or chess and sipping tea. Around the courtyard are the small workshops of tailors sewing inexpensive suits. The bazaar is a good place to shop for spices and copper items and you can usually find bargains, especially on carpets and kilims. ✉ *Şanlıurfa.*

Gölbaşı Parkı. The park is a shady oasis on hot days or summer evenings, and is home to the famed carp pools. According to legend, King Nimrod, angry at Abraham's condemnation of the king's Assyrian polytheism, set about immolating the patriarch. God awakened natural springs, dousing the fire and saving Abraham. The carp, according to the myth, are an incarnation of the wood from Abraham's pyre. Historically the story might not, well, hold water—probably part of a pre-Christian fish shrine, the gorgeous springs remain. The place has a serene and distinctly spiritual feel to it, with groups of visiting pilgrims and families from Turkey and neighboring countries strolling about and feeding what are probably the most pampered fish in the world. Look for the Byzantine era belltower beside the lake. ⊠ *Near center of town, Şanlıurfa* ⊠ *Free* ☉ *Sunrise–sunset.*

Güzel Sanatlar Galerisi. The city's art gallery, right next to the post office, is another restored house that's worth visiting. The art may not be so impressive, but the stone mansion has delightful relief-carving work on its exterior and a lovely indoor courtyard. ⊠ *Sarayönü Cad., Şanlıurfa* ⊠ *Free* ☉ *Weekdays 8:30–5, Sat. noon–4*

The Haleplibahçe Mosaics Museum. A recently discovered Byzantine villa in the Haleplibahçe district, just beyond Gölbaşı, has revealed a wealth of mosaics. You enter via what was a long porch and can check out the mosaics depicting the life of Achilles, including his mother holding him by the heel and dipping him in the waters of the River Styx. Just beyond is a large hall, with damaged mosaics flanked by the remains of two fountains. At the very rear is a magnificent scene of Amazon queens hunting wild beasts. ⊠ *Northwest of the Fish Lake, beyond the Al Ruha Hotel, Şanlıurfa* ☉ *Sunrise–sunset.*

Hazreti İbrahim Doğum Mağarası (*Prophet İbrahim's Birth Cave*). Local legend has it that Abraham was born in the Hazreti İbrahim Doğum Mağarası, a natural cave hidden behind the Hasan Paşa Mosque in the southeast corner of Gölbaşı Parkı. As is usual, men and women enter through separate doorways. Most people huddled inside this small, dark cavern, darkened by 2,000 years of candle smoke, have come to pray, not to snap photos. There's not much to see, but the atmosphere is reverential. Tourists are welcome (many of the visitors inside are themselves from out of town), but remember that this is a shrine. ⊠ *Göl Cad., Şanlıurfa* ⊠ *Free* ☉ *Daily sunrise–sunset.*

Ulu Camii. Urfa's principal mosque was built in the 12th century by Nur al-Din after he captured the city from the Crusaders. It is a relatively simple long vaulted hall, on the southern end of a long grassy courtyard. The town's cathedral once stood here, and you can see the giant octagonal belltower. ⊠ *Just north of bazaar, Şanlıurfa.*

Urfa Kale (*Urfa Fortress*). Apart from the two prominent Roman Columns, Urfa's castle is a motley collection of upturned stones, at the top of a lot of stairs. It's impossible to detect any one architectural intent here, probably because the fortress has been razed and rebuilt at least a dozen times since the 2nd century BC. Climb to the summit for a fantastic view of the city. The stairs down are more fun, as they descend through a tunnel cut from the rock. ⊠ *Kale Cad., Şanlıurfa* ⊠ *4 TL* ☉ *Daily 9–6.*

OFF THE BEATEN PATH

Göbekli Tepe. Erected around 9,000 BC, 6,000 years before Stonehenge, before even the invention of agriculture, this series of stone circles on a hill 15 km (9 miles) northeast of the town of Urfa have been popularly declared the "World's Oldest Temple." The stones' purpose has been subject to wide interpretation: Some believe this was a burial site; others, a place of ritual initiation, or that each circle belonged to a different tribe that gathered here for ritual and trade. What is clear, though, is that no one lived here, and that it would have taken hundreds of people to transport and erect the pillars. The site is formed by a series of circles and ovals formed by large T-shaped pillars of equal height, usually with two larger pillars inside. The pillars are thought to have held a roof. Many of the outer surfaces are carved, some are anthropomorphic, others depict the savage nightmares of a hunter-gatherer's life, such as snakes, foxes, vultures, scorpions, and wild boar. Most curiously of all, the structures were deliberately buried when the site was abandoned. Four structures have been exposed since excavations began in 1995, and another 16 have been identified by geophysicists; excavations continue in spring and fall. The circles themselves are off-limits and enclosed by low fences, but visitors are welcome to follow pathways from which all are clearly visible. Take the old highway the D400 east from Şanlıurfa and look for the marked turning on the left just as you leave the built-up area. This road continues about 15km (10 miles), crossing over the new highway. Shortly after this is a turn, left for the last few miles up the hill to the site. ⚠ **Although the site is open year-round, many of the pillars are covered in winter for protection from the elements.** ✉ *15 km (9 mi.) northeast of Urfa* 🎫 *Free* 🕒 *Sunrise–sunset.*

WHERE TO EAT AND STAY

$ TURKISH 🍴 **Çardaklı Köşk.** An old Urfa stone house looks out over the city's citadel and the fish-pool complex. Sit on the terrace or in one of the several *çardaks,* small private rooms where you can recline on pillows. The food, the usual mix of kebabs and pides, is unexciting, but the location makes up for it and they have live local traditional music most nights. [$] *Average main: 15 TL* ✉ *Balıkgöl Civarı Tünel Çıkışı 1, Şanlıurfa* ☎ *414/217–1080.*

$$ HOTEL 🏨 **Cevahir Konuk Evi.** This grand old stone home with a great view from its terrace, has hallways lined with colorful rugs and antique furniture, while the rooms have high ceilings, stone walls, and white bedspreads embroidered with flowers. **Pros:** rooms are surprisingly modern and spacious for the price; pleasant patio where breakfast and dinner are served. **Cons:** those looking for peace and quiet may not appreciate the live music most nights. [$] *Rooms from: 250 TL* ✉ *Büyükyol Selahattin Eyyubi Cami, Karşısı, Şanlıurfa* ☎ *414/215–9377* 🌐 *www.cevahirkonukevi.com* 🛏 *6 rooms, 1 suite* 🍽 *Breakfast.*

$$$ HOTEL 🏨 **Hilton Garden Inn.** On the northwest edge of the old town and opposite the new museum, Urfa's Hilton offers the style and services you'd expect from a top international chain. **Pros:** oasis of Western comfort in a conservative city; modern facilities; one of the few places in town that serves alcohol. **Cons:** feels disconnected from the city despite central location; no local character. [$] *Rooms from: 378 TL* ✉ *Nisan Fuar Cad. 11, Şanlıurfa* ☎ *414/318–5000* 🛏 *154 rooms, 6 suites* 🍽 *No meals.*

$$ HOTEL 🏨 **Hotel El-Ruha.** Built of local stone, in imitation of area houses, this sprawling hotel tries to mix Urfa character with five-star luxury by offering spacious and comfortable rooms, with large beds, wood furniture, vaulted ceilings, and bathrooms with mosaic-like tiles and baths. **Pros:** modern design with character; pool; central location. **Cons:** large and rather anonymous; not an authentic local building. [$] *Rooms from: 250 TL* ✉ *Balıklıgöl, Şanlıurfa* ☎ *414/215–4411* 🌐 *www.hotelelruha.com* 🛏 *76 rooms, 11 suites* 🍽 *Breakfast.*

7

$ B&B/INN **Urfa Evi.** A series of old houses near the fish ponds, now in the hands of the tourism faculty of the local university, offer an enormous range of rooms, some cut out of the rock à la Cappadocia. **Pros:** good location; nice old building; excellent value. **Cons:** new rooms lack charm. [$] *Rooms from: 95 TL* ✉ *Göl Cad. 44, Şanlıurfa* ☎ *414/215–5995* 🛏 *14 rooms, 2 suites* 🍴 *No meals.*

HARRAN

50 km (31 miles) southeast of Urfa.

A quick ride from Urfa, the ancient city of Harran is well worth a visit. The Urfa region is rife with dubious biblical legends, but there seems to be almost unanimous agreement that this Harran of modern Turkey is quite likely the Harran mentioned in the Old Testament as a place where Abraham spent some time before heading off to the promised land. True or not, today's Harran stands on the spot of a very ancient settlement, with crumbling fortifications surrounding what is now a simple village. The main attraction is the ruins of the 8th-century **Ulu Cami**, called the world's first Islamic university, just below the hill in the center of the town. The ruins' distinctive square minaret can be seen from throughout Harran, although you will probably have to admire it through a fence. In Harran visitors get the sense that not much has changed here over the centuries, and some of the pastoral scenes around Harran, of shepherds driving their flocks of sheep along seem, well, almost biblical.

Harran's main claims to fame, besides playing host to Abraham, are its beehive-shape houses, wondrous structures built of hay and mud, each topped with a conical roof. The small town is filled with them, although many are no longer family dwellings and are now used as stables or are in the process of collapsing.

EXPLORING

The Geleneksel Konik Kubbeli Evi. Just down the road from the Harran Evi is another reconstruction of a beehive house built by a rival local family that's also worth visiting. The family who lives here is especially friendly and rather exuberant, literally running up to the entrance gate with broad smiles to greet visitors. ✉ *Ceşme Sok. 23* ☎ *542/337–8512* 🎟 *Free* 🕐 *Daily 8 am–10 pm.*

UNDERSTANDING TURKEY

Books and Movies

Vocabulary

BOOKS AND MOVIES

Books

Whether Homer's *Iliad* should be classified as fiction or nonfiction is up for debate, but it's still the most evocative reading on the Trojan War and the key players of Turkish antiquity.

Memoirs, Essays and Observations. For keen insight into the ancient ruins that you may encounter on your trip, try George Bean, author of *Aegean Turkey, Turkey Beyond the Meander, Lycian Turkey,* and *Turkey's Southern Shore.* John Julius Norwich's three-volume *Byzantium* chronicles the rise and fall of one of history's great empires, while Caroline Finkel's *Osman's Dream* provides a comprehensive overview of the history of the Ottoman Empire.

Mary Lee Settle provides a vision of Turkey that is both panoramic and personal in *Turkish Reflections.* The book marks Settle's return to the country that was the setting for her novel *Blood Tie,* a 1978 National Book Award winner. Dame Freya Stark chronicles her visits to Turkey in *The Journey's Echo* and *Alexander's Path.* Only a piece of Mark Twain's *Innocents Abroad* is about Turkey, but it offers a witty glimpse of the country as it used to be. Hans Christian Andersen also wrote a memorable travelogue, *A Poet's Bazaar: A Journey to Greece, Turkey and up the Danube. The Letters and Works of Lady Mary Wortley Montagu* is a significant and entertaining book that delightfully documents life in 18th-century Ottoman Turkey—including its much-quoted passages about the harem—through the eyes of the wife of a British consul.

Irfan Orga's exquisite *Portrait of a Turkish Family* is an evocative memoir weaving personal history with modern politics as it addresses the impact of the upheavals of the early 20th century on his own family. Orhan Pamuk's *Istanbul: Memories of a City* interweaves the novelist's memories of his childhood and youth with black-and-white photographs and vignettes from the city's history; many think this nonfiction is much more readable than his fiction.

History. For modern Turkish history and politics, try *Turkey: A Modern History,* by Erik J. Zürcher, or *Turkey Unveiled,* an accessible, journalistic account of Turkish politics by Nicole and Hugh Pope.

More books have been written about Istanbul than about the rest of Turkey. Two of the finest portraits of the city are the excellent *Constantinople: City of the World's Desire 1453–1924,* by Philip Mansel, and *Istanbul: The Imperial City,* by John Freely.

Literature and Fiction. For an introduction to Turkish literature, track down a copy of *An Anthology of Turkish Literature,* by Kemal Silay. If you prefer to plunge into a complete novel, look out for *Anatolian Tales* or *Mehmet, My Hawk,* by Yaşar Kemal, one of the country's most famous modern novelists. Of the younger generation of Turkish writers, the best known is Orhan Pamuk, whose dense melancholy prose means that his work is often more highly regarded than it is enjoyed. His novels include *My Name Is Red* and the acclaimed *Snow.* Louis de Bernieres's novel *Birds Without Wings* offers a portrayal of rural life in Western Anatolia during the final years of the Ottoman Empire.

Agatha Christie's novel *Murder on the Orient Express* provides the proper atmosphere for a trip to Istanbul, and you can still visit Istanbul's Pera Palas Hotel, the terminus of the famous train, where Christie herself stayed. Harold Nicolson's *Sweet Waters* is usually billed as a thriller although it is more of a love story, and the detail draws heavily on the author's years as a junior diplomat in Istanbul in the years leading up to the outbreak of World War I. If you love spy novels, *Istanbul Intrigues,* by Barry Rubin, paints a vivid picture of real cloak-and-dagger intrigues in the city during World War II.

Poetry. *The Penguin Book of Turkish Verse* offers a good selection in English of leading Ottoman and Turkish poets. Nazım Hikmet (1901–63) is generally regarded as Turkey's greatest, if still controversial, poet, and Randy Blasing and Mutlu Konuk have produced excellent English versions of Hikmet's most important poems in *Poems of Nazim Hikmet* and his extraordinary verse epic *Human Landscapes*. (The best English-language biography of Nazım Hikmet is *Romantic Communist,* by Saime Göksu and Edward Timms.)

The poetry of the Sufi mystic Rumi has few rivals in any language, whether for the beauty of his words or for his message of universal love and tolerance. There are several translations of his poetry: the best known include *Rumi: Poet and Mystic,* by Reynold Nicholson, *The Essential Rumi,* by Coleman Barks, and *Rumi: In the Arms of the Beloved,* by Jonathan Star.

Movies

Western movies filmed in Turkey obviously tend to play up Turkey's exotic aspects, for better or worse. Director Joseph L. Mankiewicz's *Five Fingers* (1952), an Ankara-based spy thriller based on the book *Operation Cicero,* by C.L. Moyzisch, is noteworthy both for its action and for its clever dialogue ("Counter espionage is the highest form of gossip"). Peter Ustinov won an Academy Award for best supporting actor for his performance in the Jules Dassin–directed museum-heist film *Topkapi* (1964), which also stars Melina Mercouri and Maximilian Schell.

Alan Parker directed the film version of *Midnight Express* (1978), about Billy Hayes's days in a Turkish prison following a drug conviction. The film's horrific depiction of Hayes's experiences (some of which were not in his memoir) made the Turkish government gun-shy about allowing Western moviemakers into the country. When *Midnight Express* was finally shown on Turkish TV in the mid-1990s, newscasters interviewed people in the street, who wept over the country's portrayal on-screen and the influence they feared the film may have had on perceptions of Turkey in the West.

Peter Weir's *Gallipoli* (1981) follows the exploits of two Australian soldiers preparing for and fighting in the historic battle in the Dardanelles during World War I. Critics generally praise the film, though some have noted a lack of sensitivity to the Turks.

Turkish movies now regularly feature at international film festivals, and an increasing number are available on DVD (although most on sale in Turkey are Region 2, so you will need a multiregion DVD player to be able to play them in the United States). Notable ones include: Nuri Bilge Ceylan's *Uzak* (2000), a hauntingly beautiful depiction of loneliness, set in Istanbul, that manages to be simultaneously melancholic, humorous, and uplifting; Yılmaz Erdoğan and Ömer Faruk Sorak's *Vizontele* (2001), a charming and often hilarious portrayal of the effect of the arrival of electricity on a rural community; and Fatih Akın's *Head-On (Gegen die Wand)* (2004), a stunning, if frequently brutal, love story of a couple who build a relationship out of their shattered lives. Turkey finally took revenge for *Midnight Express* with Serdar Akar and Sadullah Şentürk's *Valley of the Wolves: Iraq* (2006). Poorly scripted, anti-Semitic, and anti-American in tone, the movie nevertheless lays bare some of the many complexes and conspiracy theories that underpin popular Turkish conceptions of current events; it broke all box office records in Turkey on its release.

TURKISH VOCABULARY

ENGLISH	TURKISH	PRONUNCIATION

BASICS

ENGLISH	TURKISH	PRONUNCIATION
Hello	Merhaba	mer-**hab**-a
Yes/no	Evet/hayır	**eh**-vet/**hi**-yer
Please	Lütfen	**lewt**-fen
Thank you	Teşekkür ederim	tay-shake-**kur** eh-day-**reem**
You're welcome	Rica ederim/ Bir şey değil	ree-**jah** eh-day-**reem**/beer shay **day**-eel
Sorry	Özür dilerim	oh-**zewr** deel-air-eem
Sorry	Pardon	**pahr**-dohn
Good morning	Günaydın	goon-eye-**den**
Good day	İyi günler	ee-yee gewn-**lair**
Good evening	İyi akşamlar	ee-yee ahk-shahm-**lar**
Goodbye	Allahaısmarladık/ Güle güle	**allah**-aw-ees-mar-law-deck/ **gew**-leh **gew**-leh
Mr. (Sir)	Bey	by, bay
Mrs./Miss	Hanım	ha-nem
Pleased to meet you	Memnun oldum	**mam**-noon ohl-doom
How are you?	Nasılsınız?	**nah**-suhl-suh-nuhz

NUMBERS

ENGLISH	TURKISH	PRONUNCIATION
one half	buçuk	byoo-**chook**
one	bir	beer
two	iki	ee-**kee**
three	üç	ooch
four	dört	doort
five	beş	besh
six	altı	ahl-tuh
seven	yedi	yed-dee
eight	sekiz	sek-**keez**
nine	dokuz	doh-**kooz**
ten	on	**ohn**
eleven	onbir	**ohn**-beer

ENGLISH	TURKISH	PRONUNCIATION
twelve	oniki	**ohn**-ee-kee
thirteen	onüç	**ohn**-ooch
fourteen	ondört	**ohn**-doort
fifteen	onbeş	**ohn**-besh
sixteen	onaltı	**ohn**-ahl-tuh
seventeen	onyedi	**ohn**-yed-dy
eighteen	onsekiz	**ohn**-sek-**keez**
nineteen	ondokuz	**ohn**-doh-**kooz**
twenty	yirmi	yeer-mee
twenty-one	yirmibir	**yeer**-mee-beer
thirty	otuz	oh-**tooz**
forty	kırk	kerk
fifty	elli	ehl-lee
sixty	altmış	**alt**-muhsh
seventy	yetmiş	**yeht**-meesh
eighty	seksen	sehk-san
ninety	doksan	dohk-**san**
one hundred	yüz	yewz
one thousand	bin	bean
one million	milyon	**mill**-ee-on

COLORS

black	siyah	**see**-yah
blue	mavi	**mah**-vee
brown	kahverengi	**kah**-vay-**rain**-gee
green	yeşil	yay-sheel
orange	portakal rengi	poor-tah-kahl rain-gee
red	kırmızı	ker-muz-uh
white	beyaz	**bay**-ahz
yellow	sarı	sah-**ruh**

ENGLISH	TURKISH	PRONUNCIATION

DAYS OF THE WEEK

Sunday	Pazar	pahz-**ahr**
Monday	Pazartesi	pahz-**ahr**-teh-see
Tuesday	Salı	sa-**luh**
Wednesday	Çarşamba	char-shahm-bah
Thursday	Perşembe	pair-shem-beh
Friday	Cuma	joom-**ah**
Saturday	Cumartesi	joom-**ahr**-teh-see

MONTHS

January	Ocak	oh-**jahk**
February	Şubat	shoo-**baht**
March	Mart	mart
April	Nisan	nee-**sahn**
May	Mayıs	my-us
June	Haziran	hah-zee-**rahn**
July	Temmuz	**tehm**-mooz
August	Ağustos	ah-oos-tohs
September	Eylül	ey-**lewl**
October	Ekim	eh-**keem**
November	Kasım	kah-suhm
December	Aralık	ah-rah-**luhk**

USEFUL PHRASES

Do you speak English?	İngilizce biliyor musunuz?	in-**gee**-**leez**-jay bee-lee-**yohr** moo-soo-nooz
I don't speak Turkish.	Türkçe bilmiyorum.	**tewrk**-cheh **beel**-mee-yohr-um
I don't understand.	Anlamıyorum	ahn-**lah**-muh-yohr-um
I understand.	Anlıyorum	ahn-**luh**-yohr-um
I don't know.	Bilmiyorum	**beel**-meeh-yohr-um
I'm American.	Amerikalıyım	ahm-ay-**ree**-kah-luh-yuhm
I'm British.	İngilizim	**een**-gee-leez-eem

ENGLISH	TURKISH	PRONUNCIATION
What's your name?	İsminiz nedir?	ees-mee-niz nay-deer
My name is . . .	Benim adım . . .	bay-**neem** ah-duhm
What time is it?	Saat kaç?	sah-aht **kahch**
How?	Nasıl?	**nah**-suhl
When?	Ne zaman?	**nay** zah-mahn
Yesterday	Dün	dewn
Today	Bugün	**boo**-goon
Tomorrow	Yarın	**yah**-ruhn
This morning/ afternoon	Bu sabah/öğleden sonra	**boo** sah-bah/**ol-lay**-den sohn-rah
Tonight	Bu gece	**boo** ge-jeh
What?	Efendim?/Ne?	**eh**-fan-deem/neh
What is it?	Nedir?	**neh**-deer
Why?	Neden/Niçin?	**neh**-den/**nee**-chin
Who?	Kim?	keem
Where is . . .	Nerede . . .	**nayr**-deh
. . . the train station?	. . . tren istasyonu?	tee-**rehn** ees-**tah**-syohn-oo
. . . the subway station?	. . . metro duragı?	metro doo-**raw**-uh
. . . the bus stop?	. . . otobüs duragı?	oh-toh-**bewse** doo-**raw**-uh
. . . the terminal? (airport)	. . . hava alanı?	hah-**vah ah**-lah-nuh
. . . the post office?	. . . postane?	post-**ahn**-eh
. . . the bank?	. . . banka?	**bahn**-kah
. . . the hotel?	. . . oteli?	oh-**tel-lee**
. . . the museum?	. . . müzesi?	mew-zay-**see**
. . . the hospital?	. . . hastane?	hahs-**tah**-neh
. . . the elevator?	. . . asansör?	ah-san-**sewr**
. . . the telephone?	. . . telefon?	teh-leh-**fohn**
Where are the restrooms?	Tuvalet nerede?	twah-**let** nayr-deh

ENGLISH	TURKISH	PRONUNCIATION
Here/there	Burası/Orası	**boo**-rah-suh/**ohr**-rah-suh
Left/right	sag/sol	sah-ah/sohl
Is it near/	Yakın mı?/	yah-**kuhn** muh/
far?	Uzak mı?	ooz-**ahk**muh
I'd like	istiyorum	ees-tee yohr ruhm
. . . a room	Bir oda. . .	beer oh-**dah**
. . . the key	Anahtarı. . .	**ahn**-ah-tahr-uh
. . . a newspaper	Bir gazete. . .	beer **gahz**-teh
. . . a stamp	Pul. . .	pool
I'd like to buy . . .	almak istiyorum . . .	ahl-**mahk** ees-tee-your-ruhm
. . . cigarettes	Sigara. . .	**see**-gah-rah
. . . matches	Kibrit. . .	**keeb**-reet
. . . city map	Şehir planı. . .	shay-**heer plah**-nuh
. . . road map	Karayolları haritası. . .	**kah**-rah-yoh-lahr-**uh** hah-ree-tah-**suh**
. . . magazine	Dergi. . .	dair-gee
. . . envelopes	Zarf. . .	zahrf
. . . writing paper	Mektup kagıdı. . .	**make**-toop **kah**-uh-duh
. . . postcard	Kartpostal. . .	cart-poh-stahl
. . . ticket	Bilet. . .	bee-**let**
How much is it?	Fiyatı ne kadar?	fee-yaht-uh **neh** kah-dahr
It's expensive/cheap	pahalı/ucuz	pah-hah-**luh**/oo-**jooz**
A little/a lot	Az/çok	ahz/choke
More/less	daha çok/daha az	da-ha choke/da-ha ahz
Enough/too (much)	Yeter/çok fazla	yay-**tehr/choke** fahz-lah
I am ill/sick	Hastayım	**hahs**-tah-yum
Call a doctor	Doktor çağırın	dohk-toor **chah**-uh-run
Help!	İmdat!	eem-**daht**
Stop!	Durun!	doo-**roon**

ENGLISH	TURKISH	PRONUNCIATION

DINING OUT

A bottle of . . .	bir şişe . . .	**beer** shee-shay
A cup of . . .	bir fincan . . .	beer **feen**-jahn
A glass of . . .	bir bardak . . .	beer **bar**-dahk
Ashtray	kül tablası	kewl tah-blah-**suh**
Beer	bira	**bee**-ra
Bill/check	hesap	heh-**sahp**
Bread	ekmek	ekmek
Breakfast	kahvaltı	kah-**vahl**-tuh
Butter	tereyağı	tay-**reh**-yah-uh
Cocktail/aperitif	kokteyl, içki	cocktail, **each**-key
Coffee	kahve	**kah**-veh
Dinner	akşam yemegi	**ahk**-shahm yee-may-ee
Fixed-price menu	fiks menü	feex menu
Fork	çatal	**chah**-tahl
I am a vegetarian/I don't eat meat	vejeteryenim/et yemem	vegeterian-**eem**/eht yeh-**mem**
I cannot eat . . .	yiyemem . . .	**yee**-yay-mem
I'd like to order . . .	Ismarlamak isterim . . .	us-mahr-lah-**mahk** ee-stair-eem
I'd like . . .	. . . isterim	ee-stair-**em**
I'm hungry/thirsty	acıktım/susadım	ah-**juck**-tum/soo-sah-**dum**
Is service/the tip included?	servis fiyatı dahil mi?	sehr-vees **fee**-yah-tah dah-heel-**mee**
It's good/bad	güzel/güzel degil	gew-**zell**/gew-**zell day**-eel
It's hot/cold	sıcak/soguk	suh-**jack**/soh-**uk**
Knife	bıçak	buh-**chahk**
Lunch	ögle yemegi	**oi**-leh **yeh**-may-ee
Menu	menü	meh-**noo**
Napkin	peçete	**peh**-cheh-teh
Pepper	karabiber	kah-**rah**-bee-behr
Plate	tabak	tah-**bahk**

ENGLISH	TURKISH	PRONUNCIATION
Please give me . . .	lutfen bana . . . verirmisiniz	**loot**-fan bah-nah vair-**eer**-mee-see-niz
Salt	tuz	tooz
Spoon	kaşık	kah-**shuhk**
Tea	çay	chai
Water	su	soo
Wine	şarap	shah-**rahp**

TRAVEL SMART
TURKEY

GETTING HERE AND AROUND

The most common way to get around Turkey, for both Turks and tourists, is by bus, though the rapidly growing number of cheap domestic flights is making air travel an increasingly appealing alternative. If you don't mind the long ride, the extremely popular night buses that connect the major cities inland and on the coast are comfortable and inexpensive. If you are pressed for time or are traveling very long distances—for instance, if you are making an excursion to the eastern part of the country—you may prefer to fly. Once you've arrived at your destination, you can get around by taxi, minibus, *dolmuş* (shared taxi), or rented car. A car gives you more freedom to explore on your own but is more costly and the experience can be a bit stressful at times.

▌ AIR TRAVEL

Flying time to Istanbul is 11 hours from New York or Washington, D.C., 13 hours from Chicago or Houston, and 15 hours from Los Angeles. (Turkish Airlines has announced it will launch additional direct flights from Boston and San Francisco in 2014.) Flights from Toronto to Istanbul take 11½ hours. London to Istanbul is a 4-hour flight. In Turkey, security checks for travelers to the United States mean that you need to be at the airport three hours before takeoff regardless of which airline you are flying, though lines for check-in at Turkish Airlines are generally long in any case.

AIRPORTS

Turkey's major international airport is **Atatürk Airport,** about 18 km (12 miles) from central Istanbul. Sabiha Gökçen Airport serves the Asian part of Istanbul, although it is mainly used by international charters and domestic flights.

Adana, Adıyaman, Ağrı, Amasya, Ankara, Antakya, Antalya, Balıkesir, Batman, Bingöl, Bodrum, Bursa, Çanakkale, Dalaman, Denizli, Diyarbakır, Edremit, Elazığ, Erzincan, Erzurum, Eskişehir, Gaziantep, Iğdır, Isparta, İzmir, Kahramanmaraş, Kars, Kastamonu, Kayseri, Kocaeli, Konya, Kütahya, Malatya, Mardin, Muş, Nevşehir, Samsun, Siirt, Sinop, Sivas, Şanlıurfa, Şırnak, Tekirdağ, Tokat, Trabzon, Uşak, Van, and Zonguldak all have domestic airports.

Airports Atatürk Airport ☎ *212/463–3000* ⊕ *www.ataturkairport.com.* **Sabiha Gökçen Airport** ☎ *216/585–5000* ⊕ *www.sgairport. com.*

GROUND TRANSPORTATION FROM AIRPORTS

In major destinations such as Adana, Ankara, Antalya, Bodrum, Dalaman, Gaziantep, İzmir, Konya, Şanlıurfa, and Trabzon, the Havaş company operates shuttle buses to the airports. (In Istanbul, this service is provided by the similarly named, but separate Havataş.) These run at regular intervals in the major cities and in the provinces are timed to coincide with incoming and outgoing flights.

An alternative is to take a taxi. From the smaller airports, it is sometimes possible to negotiate with a taxi driver for less than the metered fare. Many hotels will arrange for a driver to collect you from the airport and for someone to take you to the airport. In Cappadocia and other popular tourist regions, it is not unusual for hotels to offer this transportation free of charge, although the driver will still appreciate being tipped a couple of TL.

Contacts Havaş ☎ *212/465–5656* ⊕ *www. havas.com.tr.* **Havataş** ☎ *212/444–2656* ⊕ *www.havatas.com.*

FLIGHTS

THY/Turkish Airlines operates nonstop flights from U.S. and European gateways, though an international carrier based in your home country is more likely to have better connections to your hometown. Third-country carriers (foreign carriers based in a country other than your own or Turkey) sometimes offer low fares. Air France, for instance, often has well-priced flights from the United States to Istanbul via Paris. Popular low-cost carriers like SunExpress and Pegasus offer cheap flights throughout Turkey and to/from European cities.

Turkish Airlines operates an extensive domestic network, with nearly two-dozen flights daily on weekdays between Istanbul and Ankara alone. In summer many flights to coastal resorts are added. ■ TIP→ Note that at provincial airports it is often necessary for checked luggage to be identified by boarding passengers before it is put on the plane, and all unidentified luggage is left behind and checked for bombs or firearms. If any luggage has not been identified, an announcement will be made on the plane before departure, based on the name on the luggage label, but attempts at the pronunciation of foreign names can often mean that they are unrecognizable. Airline staff will always announce whether you need to identify your luggage at some point before boarding but the messages may be difficult to hear or understand. If in doubt, ask a member of the airline staff as they are checking your boarding pass.

▌ BOAT AND FERRY TRAVEL

In the greater Istanbul area, ferries can be the most efficient means of getting around. On the Aegean and Mediterranean coasts, boats are used mostly for leisurely sightseeing and yachting.

Şehir Hatları, a subsidiary of Istanbul Metropolitan Municipality, and private companies Dentur Avrasya and Turyol provide regular ferryboat services within Istanbul, while İDO offers boats to Yalova and Bandırma (both in the Marmara region), and to Bursa. From Bodrum and other Aegean resorts, ferries make frequent runs between Turkey and the Greek islands in the summer.

⇨ For information about sailing trips known as "Blue Cruises", see the Blue Cruising box in Chapter 5.

Information Dentur Avrasya ☎ 444-6336 (no area code required) ⊕ www.denturavrasya. com. **İDO (Istanbul sea bus and fast ferry)** ☎ 212/444-4436 ⊕ www.ido.com.tr. **Şehir Hatları (Istanbul local ferries)** ☎ 212/444-1851 ⊕ www.sehirhatlari.com.tr. **Turyol** ☎ 212/251 4421 ⊕ www.turyol.com.

▌ BUS TRAVEL

In Turkey, buses are generally faster than most trains and provide inexpensive service almost around the clock between all cities and towns, and they're usually quite comfortable. Most offer complimentary tea, soda, and biscuits, though with smaller companies you will want to bring your own water in case beverages are not available. All are run by private companies, each of which has its own fixed fares for different routes and, usually more significantly, its own standards of comfort. Most bus companies, such as Varan, Ulusoy, Kamil Koç, Metro, and Pamukkale, which go between major cities and resort areas, can be counted on for comfortable air-conditioned service with snacks. There is often a close correlation between price and comfort, with the more expensive companies such as Varan providing the best amenities. Most of the larger companies have their own terminals and in larger cities run shuttles from locations around the city to the main terminal. ⇨ Contact details for the larger companies are listed below. Note that express buses running between major cities are significantly faster and more comfortable than local buses. By law, all buses are nonsmoking.

FARES AND SCHEDULES
Buses traveling the Istanbul–Ankara route depart either city nearly every 30 minutes, and cost about 45 TL to 55 TL for a one-way trip. The Istanbul–İzmir fare ranges from about 60 TL to 80 TL. All buses make periodic rest stops along the way.

The larger companies have their own sales offices as well as websites and call centers offering e-tickets, though travelers without a Turkish ID number will likely have to purchase their tickets in person. For smaller companies, tickets are sold at stands in a town's *otogar* (central bus terminal); the usual procedure is to go to the bus station and shop around for the best route and price. All seats are reserved. ■ TIP→ When buying your ticket, tell the ticket agent that you would like to sit on the shady side of the bus; even on air-conditioned buses the sun can feel oppressive on a long trip.

Information **Kamil Koç** ☎ 444–0562 no area code required in Turkey ⊕ www.kamilkoc.com. tr. **Metro Turizm** ☎ 444–3455 no area code required in Turkey ⊕ www.metroturizm. tr. **Pamukkale** ☎ 850/444–3535 ⊕ www. pamukkale.com.tr. **Truva Turizm** ☎ 444–0017 no area code required in Turkey ⊕ www. truvaturizm.com. **Ulusoy** ☎ 444–1888 no area code required in Turkey ⊕ www.ulusoy.com.tr. **Varan** ☎ 212/444–8999 ⊕ www.varan.com.tr.

■ CAR TRAVEL

In Turkey a driver's license issued in most foreign countries is acceptable. While Turkey has one of the world's highest car accident rates, driving is an excellent way to explore regions outside the major cities and having a car allows you the freedom that traveling by bus, train, or plane does not. Turkey has 40,000 km (25,000 miles) of paved and generally well-maintained highways, but off the intercity highways, surfaces are often poor and potholes frequent. A system of four-lane toll roads is now in place around Istanbul, Ankara, and İzmir, but most major highways are two lanes, and cars overtake with some frequency. ⚠ Sometimes roads have a third lane meant for passing; although the lane is usually labeled with which direction of traffic is meant to use it, drivers don't always follow this rule, so be extremely careful when passing. In general, always expect the unexpected. Don't,

for example, assume that one-way streets are one-way in practice or that because you wouldn't do something, such as trying to pass in a dangerous situation, the other driver wouldn't either.

In major cities it's possible to hire a driver along with a car. In some remote places, a driver is usually included in the package with the rental car and will either be the owner of the car or an employee of the agency. If you're particularly happy with the service you may wish to give a tip in addition to the price you pay to the agency. Around 20 TL for a day's driving is reasonable.

⚠ Driving in Istanbul and other major cities is best avoided. Urban streets and highways are frequently jammed with vehicles operated by high-speed lunatics as well as otherwise sane drivers who constantly honk their horns. In Istanbul, especially, just because a street is marked one-way, you never know when someone is going to barrel down it in the wrong direction. Parking is also a problem in cities and larger towns. In these places it's best to leave your car in a garage and use public transportation or take taxis.

■ TIP→ If possible, avoid driving on highways after dusk. Drivers often don't use their lights and vehicles may be stopped on the roads in complete darkness. Carts and other farm vehicles are often not equipped with lights.

Highways are numbered or specified by direction (e.g., the route to Antalya). Trans-European highways have a European number as well as a Turkish number (E6 is the European number for Turkish Route D100, for example). ⚠ Note, though, that route numbers may be inconsistent from map to map. Archaeological and historic sites are indicated by brown signposts.

EMERGENCY SERVICES
Road rescue service is available on some highways; before you embark on a journey, ask your car rental agency or hotel for contact numbers to use in case of an

emergency. Most Turkish gas stations have someone with some knowledge of car mechanics who can diagnose problems and provide "first aid" or advice, such as directions to the nearest mechanic. Make sure to take all car-related documents with you if you leave the car in the shop.

GASOLINE

Gas costs about 4.9 TL per liter, making Turkey one of the most expensive places in the world to fuel up. Many of the gas stations on the main highways stay open around the clock, others generally from 6 am to 10 pm. Almost all Turkish gas stations provide full service and have unleaded gas. Many attendants will clean your windows while the car's tank is being filled. Tipping is not obligatory though not uncommon if the attendant has been attentive—1 or 2 TL is usually enough. There may be long distances between gas stations in rural areas, so if you're heading off the beaten track, don't allow the tank to run too low. Most gas stations in towns and major highways take credit cards, though you may need cash in rural areas. Many gas stations also have small shops, or just a cooler, where you can buy snacks and chilled drinks.

RENTING A CAR

In many places, such as Cappadocia and the Turquoise Coast, you may want to rent a car so you can explore on your own. When traveling long distances, however, you may find it easier to take public transportation (either a bus or plane)—unless you plan on sightseeing en route—and renting a car at your destination.

Car rental rates begin at about 120 TL ($60) a day and TL 700 ($350) a week for an economy car with unlimited mileage. The majority of rental cars are equipped with manual transmission, though it's possible to get an automatic (usually for a much higher price). Car seats for children are not compulsory and are often difficult to find, although offices of the multinational firms in larger cities may be able to

provide them. A wide variety of mostly European car makes are available, ranging from the locally manufactured Tofaş (the Turkish licensee to build Fiat models) to Renault and Mercedes.

Check the websites of the major multinational companies to see if they have offices at your destination. Many reliable local agencies also operate throughout Turkey. *Only the contacts for the major companies are listed below. Some local car rental agencies are listed in the relevant chapters of this book.*

Hotels often rent cars or have a relationship with a local agency—the local agency is usually anxious to keep the hotel happy by providing a good service, and it's not unusual for the owner of the agency to be a relative of someone at the hotel. The rates for deals done through the hotel, which will include insurance, etc., are often much lower than rates charged by multinational firms.

The rental agency will usually tell you what to do if you have a breakdown or accident and will provide a contact number—often the personal cell number of someone working at the agency—if they don't, ask for one. It's worth remembering that in the case of an accident, Turkish insurance companies usually refuse to pay until they have seen a police report. It is particularly important to obtain a police report if another vehicle is involved, as the driver will need to submit the report when filing a claim with his or her insurance company or with your rental agency. In such a situation, call the contact number for your rental agency and allow a representative to handle all the procedures.

Most likely, agencies will ask you to contact them before attempting to have any repairs done and will usually bring you a replacement car. Most major car manufacturers in Turkey (for example, Renault, Tofaş, and Opel/General Motors) also have roaming 24-hour services and rental agencies may ask you to contact one of them.

Major Agencies Alamo ☎ *888/222–9075*
⊕ *www.alamo.com.* **Avis** ☎ *800/331–1212 in
U.S.* ⊕ *www.avis.com.* **Budget** ☎ *800/472–
3325 in U.S.* ⊕ *www.budget.com.* **Hertz**
☎ *800/654–3131 in U.S.* ⊕ *www.hertz.com.*
National Car Rental ☎ *877/222–9058*
⊕ *www.nationalcar.com.*

ROAD CONDITIONS

Throughout rural Turkey, roads are often
not well marked, lighting is scarce, and
roads are sometimes rough. City traffic is
generally chaotic. The top speed limit of
120 kph (about 75 mph) is rarely enforced
on major highways, although it is not
unusual for the Turkish police to set speed
traps on other roads. Drive carefully and
relatively slowly. Be prepared for sudden
changes in road conditions and be alert to
the behavior of other drivers.

ROAD MAPS

Road maps can often be found in tourist
areas, and the rental company will usually
provide you with one. Remember, though,
signposting is erratic and maps are often
not very accurate.

RULES OF THE ROAD

Driving is on the right and passing on the
left. Seat belts are required for front-seat
passengers and should be used by those
in back as well. Using a cell phone while
driving is prohibited—but this law is sel-
dom obeyed. Turning right on a red light
is not permitted, but it is legal to proceed
through a flashing red light provided no
traffic is coming the other way. Speed-
ing and other traffic violations are subject to on-the-spot fines. Fines for driving
under the influence of alcohol are steep
and are often accompanied by impris-
onment. Most rental companies do not
allow you to cross international borders
in a rented car.

▌TAXI AND DOLMUŞ TRAVEL

Taxis in Turkey are yellow and easy to
spot. Fares in Istanbul are about 1.80 TL
for 1 km (about ½ mile) with a starting

flat rate of 2.95 TL; the former difference
between the day and night rates has been
abolished. Prices in other large cities are
similar. Be aware that taxi drivers in tourist areas sometimes doctor their meters to
charge more; don't ride in a taxi in which
the meter doesn't work. Before setting
out, ask at your hotel about how much
a ride should cost. Note that saying the
word *direkt* after giving your destination
may help prevent you from getting an
unplanned grand tour of town. In cities
it's fairly easy to flag down a taxi, or you
can go to a taxi stand where drivers wait
for fares. In Istanbul and Ankara many of
the larger hotels will find a cab for you,
usually with drivers or companies they
know and trust. The website *Online Taksi*
lists taxi companies all over Turkey, while
Taksiyle lets you estimate fares for point-
to-point trips in major cities.

As a tip, it's customary to round up to
the next lira. There are no extra charges
for luggage. In Istanbul, if you cross one
of the Bosphorus bridges, you will be
expected to add the 4.25 TL cost of the
toll to the bill regardless of which direction you are going (vehicles only pay
going from west to east—the theory is
that even if he does not have to pay to
take you across, the taxi driver will have
to pay to go back). In Ankara, taxi drivers are allowed to charge "night rates"
(i.e., 50% higher) for trips to the airport
at any hour of the day because it's often
difficult for them to find a fare for the trip
back into town. Particularly in Istanbul
and Ankara, taxi drivers are often recent
arrivals to the country, with a very limited
knowledge of the city and will have to
ask bystanders or other taxi drivers for
directions.

Dolmuşes (shared taxis) are bright yellow minibuses that run along various
routes. You can often hail a dolmuş on the
street, at bus stops, or at dolmuş stands
marked by the signs "D." The destination is shown either on a roof sign or a
card in the front window. The savings
over a private taxi are significant. A trip

by dolmuş is often just as fast as by taxi, and service extends through the wee hours of the morning. Although dolmuşes only run along specific routes, they generally go to tourist destinations, as well as nightlife hot spots. If you're not familiar with your destination, tell the driver where you are going when you get in; he will usually try to drop you as close to your destination as possible.

It is not customary to tip dolmuş drivers, and they will probably be confused if you try to hand them something extra.

Taxi Information Online Taksi ⊕ *www.onlinetaksi.com.* Taksisyle ⊕ *www.taksiyle.com/en.*

▌ TRAIN TRAVEL

Train routes in Turkey tend to meander, meaning that train travel is usually much slower than bus travel—sometimes twice as long. Essentially, the term *express train* is a misnomer in Turkey. The overnight sleeper from Istanbul to Ankara (*Ankara Ekspresi*) is the most comfortable and convenient of the trains, with private compartments, attentive service, and a candlelit dining car. There is also daytime service between Ankara and Istanbul, and a high-speed rail connection will connect the two cities in the coming years. The train trip from Istanbul to Ankara currently takes about 6½ hours nonstop, or roughly 10 hours overnight with stops along the way. High-speed service will reduce the travel time to about 3 hours. Trains also run between Istanbul and Edirne and between Ankara and İzmir. Note that work on the Marmaray underwater rail tube and the high-speed train tracks has heavily disrupted service to and from Istanbul. At the time of this writing, services to Eskişehir, Ankara, and other eastward destinations were expected to resume sometime in 2014, but completion of such targets is often delayed.

Dining cars on trains between the major cities usually have waiter service and offer decent and inexpensive food. Overnight expresses have sleeping cars and bunk beds. The Istanbul–Ankara run costs about 50 TL for a berth in a two-bed room and about 70 TL for a single-bed room, including tips; although advance reservations are a must, cancellations are frequent, so you can often get a space at the last minute.

Fares are generally lower for trains than for buses, and round-trip train fares cost less than two one-way tickets. Student discounts are 10% (30% from December through April). Ticket windows in railroad stations are marked "gişeleri." Some post offices and authorized travel agencies also sell train tickets. It's advisable to book in advance, in person, for seats on the best trains and for sleeping quarters.

Long-distance trains offer a number of accommodation options, such as pullman (first-class type, reclining seats), compartments with six or eight seats, reclining or not, couchette (shared four-bunk compartments), and sleeper (private one- or two-bed compartments). In Turkish, pullman is *pulman,* compartment is *kompartımanlı,* couchette is *kuşetli,* and sleeper is *yataklı.*

Most train stations do not accept credit cards, foreign money, or traveler's checks, so be prepared to pay in Turkish lira.

Turkish State Railways (*Türkiye Cumhuriyeti Devlet Demiryolları*) operates train service throughout the country. The website is helpful and provides information on how to buy tickets at the station or through travel agencies (⇨ *some listed below)* and provides pictures and maps. Seat61.com is another helpful website about train travel in Europe and Turkey. Both Eurail and InterRail passes can be used in Turkey.

ESSENTIALS

▌ ACCOMMODATIONS

Accommodations in Turkey range from international luxury chain hotels to charming inns in historic Ottoman mansions and kervansarays to comfortable but basic family-run *pansiyons* (guesthouses). It's advisable to plan ahead if you'll be traveling in the peak season (April–October), when resort hotels are often booked by tour companies.

Note that reservations should be confirmed more than once, particularly at hotels in popular destinations. Phone reservations are not always honored, so it's a good idea to email the hotel and get written confirmation of your reservation, as well as to confirm again before you arrive.

The lodgings we list are the cream of the crop in each price category. We always list the facilities that are available—but we don't specify whether they cost extra: when pricing accommodations, always ask what's included and what's not. In all but the more luxurious hotels, it's wise to ask to see the room before checking in. It will often be much more basic than the well-decorated reception area. Check for noise, especially if the room faces a street or is anywhere near a nightclub or disco, and in simpler establishments look for such amenities as air-conditioning, as well as basic ones like window screens and mosquito coils—small, flat disks that, when lighted, emit an unscented vapor that keeps biting insects away.

Private bathrooms, air-conditioning, room phones, and a TV are assumed unless otherwise noted. ▌TIP→ **In the low season you should be able to negotiate discounts of at least 20% off the rack rate; it never hurts to try.**

HOTELS

Hotels are officially classified in seven categories in Turkey: one to five stars, "special class," and "boutique hotel." ("Special class" is for hotels that are

unique but don't meet certain requirements of being a "boutique hotel.") There are also many *pansiyons*—guesthouses—outside this system. The star classifications can be misleading, however, as they're based on the number of facilities rather than the quality of the service and interior design, and the lack of a restaurant or lounge automatically relegates the establishment to the bottom of the ratings. In practice, a lower-grade hotel may actually be far more charming and comfortable than one with a higher rating.

Though luxury accommodations can be found in many places in Turkey, the standard Turkish hotel room, which you will encounter throughout the country, has bare walls, low wood-frame beds (usually twin beds, often pushed together in lieu of a double bed), and industrial carpeting or kilims on the floor. Less expensive properties will probably have plumbing and furnishings that leave something to be desired.

These are some Turkish words that will come in handy when you're making reservations: "air-conditioning" is *klima*, "private bath" is *banyo*, "tub" is *banyo küveti*, "shower" is *duş*, "double bed" is *iki kişilik yatak*, and "twin beds" is *iki tane tek kişilik yataklar* ("separate" is *ayrı*; "pushed together" is *beraber*). There is no Turkish word for "queen bed" but they will probably use the English (a direct translation is *kraliçe yatağı*). The same is true for "king bed" (they will probably use the English, though a direct translation is *kral yatağı*). Noise-sensitive travelers should ask for a quiet room, *sessiz bir oda*.

Wherever you stay, keep the following money-saving tips in mind:

High-end chains catering to businesspeople are often busy only on weekdays and drop rates dramatically on weekends to fill up rooms. Ask when rates go down.

Watch out for hidden costs, including resort fees, energy surcharges, and "convenience" fees for such extras as unlimited local phone service you won't use and a free newspaper written in a language you can't read.

Always verify whether local hotel taxes are or are not included in the rates you are quoted, so that you'll know the real price of your stay. In some places, taxes can add 20% or more to your bill.

If you're trying to book a stay right before or after Turkey's high season (April–October), you might save considerably by changing your dates by a week or two. Many properties charge peak-season rates for your entire stay, even if your travel dates straddle peak and nonpeak seasons.

PANSIYONS

Outside the cities and resort areas, these small, family-run establishments are generally the most common option. They range from charming old homes decorated with antiques to tiny, utilitarian rooms done in basic modern style. As a rule, they are inexpensive and scrupulously clean. Private baths are common, though they are rudimentary—stall showers, toilets with sensitive plumbing. A simple breakfast is typically included. A stay in a *pansiyon* is a comfortable money-saver, especially if you plan on spending most of your time out and about.

▮ COMMUNICATIONS

INTERNET

Most hotels, even basic establishments, provide an Internet connection or Wi-Fi, if not in the rooms at least in public areas; ask when you make a reservation. In most cities and tourist destinations, you'll also be able to find Internet cafés or cafés and other establishments with Wi-Fi.

Remember that the Turkish electricity supply runs on 220 volts. Many laptops, tablets, and other devices are equipped with built-in converters, but you will need an adapter that allows you to plug into wall outlets, which take European-type plugs, with two or three round prongs.

PHONES

Telephone numbers in Turkey have seven-digit local numbers preceded by a three-digit city code (toll-free numbers might have fewer or more digits). In Istanbul, European and Asian Istanbul have separate area codes: the code for much of European Istanbul is 212 (making the number look like it's in New York City), and the code for Asian Istanbul (numbers beginning with 3 or 4) is 216. Mobile phone codes vary depending on the carrier but generally start with 5. The country code for Turkey is 90.

CALLING WITHIN TURKEY

Within a city you don't need to dial the code for other numbers with the same code, but in Istanbul you need to dial the code (0212 or 0216) when calling from the European to the Asian side of the city or vice versa. All local cellular calls are classed as long distance, and you need to dial the city code for every number.

To call long-distance within Turkey, dial 131 if you need operator assistance; otherwise dial 0, then dial the city code and number.

With the increase in the use of mobile phones very few people now use pay phones, but it's still possible to find them. Directions in English and other languages are often posted in phone booths, along with other country codes. Directory assistance is not terribly efficient and it can be difficult to find an English-speaking operator; you're best off asking the staff at your hotel to help you find a number.

Public phones use phone cards, which can be purchased at post offices and, for a small markup, at most corner stores, newspaper vendors, and street stalls. They come in denominations of 50 (about 3.75 TL), 100 (about 7.5 TL), 200 (about 15 TL), and 350 (about 19 TL) units; buy a larger card for long-distance calls within Turkey, a smaller one for local use. Make sure to ask for a calling card for a public phone (*ankesörlü telefon*), as calling cards for cellular phones are also available, and you cannot use the two interchangeably. Very few public phones (and only in cities) also take credit cards.

To make a local call, insert your phone card or credit card, wait until the light at the top of the phone goes off, then dial the number.

Some kiosks selling newspapers or small stores have phones that you can use to place calls. The cost is usually approximately the same as it would be for a standard pay phone. If you want to use one, say "telefon" (Turkish for telephone), and the proprietor will usually either produce a phone or show you where you can find one.

CALLING OUTSIDE TURKEY

The country code is 1 for the United States. To make an international call from a public phone in Turkey, dial 00, then dial the country code, area or city code, and the number. If you need international dialing codes and assistance or phone books, you can go to the nearest post office or Internet café. In general, calling from a hotel is almost always expensive, because hotels often add huge surcharges to calls. An inexpensive option is to make international calls from call centers or the post office, and calling cards usually keep costs to a minimum.

Internet cafés typically offer international calling service with prices comparable to a phone card but be sure to ask for rates first.

Access Codes AT&T Direct ☎ *0811/288-0001 in Turkey, followed by the area code and number.* **MCI WorldPhone** ☎ *0/8001-1177 in Turkey, followed by the area code and number.* **Sprint International Access** ☎ *00/800-18488 in Turkey, followed by the area code and number.*

MOBILE PHONES

If you have a multiband phone (some countries use frequencies other than those used in the United States) and your service provider uses the world-standard GSM network (as do T-Mobile, AT&T, and Verizon), you can probably use your phone in Turkey. Roaming fees can be steep, though—99¢ a minute is considered reasonable—and you will probably pay the toll charges for incoming calls. It's almost always cheaper to send a text message than to make a call since text messages have a very low set fee (often less than 5¢).

Renting a phone in Turkey is very expensive, and it's not easy to find shops that rent. The best solution is to buy a SIM card to install in your phone, along with a pay-as-you-go service. Note that if you are staying in Turkey for more than two weeks, you will have to register your foreign phone to use it with a Turkish SIM card or risk having the phone blocked. The bureaucracy and cost (there's a 115 TL tax) involved in this task may make buying a cheap local phone the more pragmatic choice. There are several mobile phone providers in Turkey. The largest is Turkcell, followed by Vodafone and Avea. Each has a network of clearly marked stores, where it is possible to buy SIM cards and pay-as-you-go cards. Most sales people speak enough English to conduct business and answer basic questions. All stores post easy-to-understand signs that indicate unit packages and prices. Expect to pay about 30 TL for 300 minutes (sometimes referred to as units, or *kontör*), regardless of the company. A three-minute conversation within Turkey will generally set you back 4 units, and a three-minute international call will be about 11 units.

▌ CUSTOMS AND DUTIES

Turkish customs officials rarely look through tourists' luggage on arrival. You are allowed to bring in three boxes of cigarettes, 50 cigars, 250 grams of tobacco, 1 kilogram of instant coffee, 1 kilogram of tea, 2 liters of wine or champagne, and 1 liter of hard alcohol. (Note that these limits do change periodically; check the signs in the duty-free shop before heading up to the counter.) Items in the duty-free shops in Turkish airports, for international arrivals, are usually less expensive than they are in European airports or in-flight. Pets are allowed into the country provided that they have all the necessary documentation. Full details can be obtained from the Turkish diplomatic representative in your own country.

⚠ The export of antiquities from Turkey is expressly forbidden, and the ban is rigorously enforced. If you buy a carpet or rug that looks old, make sure to obtain certification that it is not antique. The seller will usually be able to help you. The ban on antiquities extends to historical artifacts, coins, and even pieces of masonry. There have been several recent cases where tourists, some of them children, have tried to take small pieces of stone home as souvenirs and been arrested at the airport on suspicion of trying to export parts of ancient monuments. A genuine mistake is not considered sufficient excuse. Even where the tourists have been ultimately acquitted, they have still had to spend many months either in detention or, more commonly, out on bail but denied permission to leave the country. Turkish antiquities laws apply to every piece of detritus, so don't pick up anything off the ground at archaeological sites.

Visit the Turkish Embassy website in Washington, D.C., and the websites of the U.S. Department of State and the U.S. Embassy in Ankara (⇨ *see Emergencies section*) for more information.

U.S. Information Turkish Embassy
☎ 202/612–6700 ⊕ *www.turkishembassy.org.*
U.S. Department of State ⊕ *www.state.gov.*

▌ EATING OUT

⇨ *For more information about traditional Turkish food and alcohol in Turkey, see the Mezes: Mouthwatering Morsels section in Chapter 5.*

The restaurants we list are the cream of the crop in each price category. A small service or "cover" (*kuver* in Turkish) charge of a few liras per person (a charge just for sitting at the table, the bread, the water, etc.) is often added to the bill, especially in meyhane-style restaurants but you should tip 10% on top of this. If a restaurant's menu has no prices listed, ask before you order—you'll avoid a surprise when the bill comes. ⇨ *For information on food-related health issues, see Health below.*

MEALS AND MEALTIMES

Breakfast, usually eaten at your hotel, typically consists of *beyaz peynir* (soft white cheese, made from cow, sheep, or goat's milk), sliced tomatoes, cucumbers, olives, and yogurt with honey and fresh fruit, with a side order of fresh bread, and tea or Nescafé; the menu varies little, whether you stay in a simple *pansiyon* or an upscale hotel.

Breakfast starts early, typically by 7. Lunch is generally served from noon to 3, dinner from 7 to 10. You can find restaurants or cafés open almost any time of the day or night in cities; in villages getting a meal at odd hours can be a problem. Most Turks fast during daylight hours during the Islamic holy month of Ramadan. If you're visiting during Ramadan, be sensitive to locals and avoid eating on public transportation or other places where you might make mouths water. During Ramadan, many restaurants, particularly smaller ones outside the major cities, close during the day and open at dusk.

Unless otherwise noted, the restaurants listed in this guide are open daily for lunch and dinner.

PAYING

Most relatively upscale restaurants, particularly those in western Turkey, take major credit cards. Smaller eateries will often accept only cash.

⇨ *For guidelines on tipping, see Tipping below.*

RESERVATIONS AND DRESS

It's a good idea to make a reservation at popular restaurants. We mention when reservations are essential (there's no other way you'll ever get a table) or when they are not accepted. We mention dress only when men are required to wear a jacket or a jacket and tie.

▌ ELECTRICITY AND ELECTRONICS

The electrical current in Turkey is 220 volts, 50 cycles alternating current (AC). If you're going to be using U.S. appliances, make sure that you have a voltage converter and an adapter, which allows you to plug into wall outlets; in Turkey these take European-type plugs, with two or three round prongs.

Most laptop, tablet, camera, and mobile phone chargers, and some other small appliances are dual voltage (i.e., they operate equally well on 110 and 220 volts) and so require only an adapter. Always check labels and manufacturer instructions to be sure, though. Don't use 110-volt outlets marked "for shavers only" for high-wattage appliances such as hair dryers.

Contacts Global Electric and Phone Directory. Information on electrical plugs, accessories, and telephones around the world is available here. ⊕ *www.kropla.com.* **Walkabout Travel Gear.** This website has a good

discussion about electricity under "Solving the Riddle of International Electricity" in its Shop Walkabout Travel Gear section. ⊕ *www.walkabouttravelgear.com.*

▌ EMERGENCIES

If your passport is lost or stolen, contact the police and your embassy immediately. If you have an emergency, you're best off asking a Turk to call an emergency number for you because it's unlikely you'll find an English-speaking person at the other end of the telephone, even at the Tourism Police. Bystanders will almost invariably try their utmost to be of assistance and will usually know of nearby hospitals or doctors. The Turkish words for ambulance, doctor, and police—*ambulans, doktor,* and *polis,* respectively—all sound about the same as their English equivalents, as does *telefon* for telephone. Say whichever is appropriate, and you can feel fairly certain that you'll be understood.

Embassies Canadian Consulate (Istanbul) ✉ *Tekfen Tower, 4. Levent, Büyükdere Cad. 209, 16th fl., Istanbul* ☎ *212/385–9700.* **U.S. Consulate (Istanbul)** ✉ *İstinye Mahallesi, Şehitler Sok. 2, İstinye, Istanbul* ☎ *212/335–9000* ⊕ *istanbul.usconsulate.gov.* **U.S. Embassy (Ankara)** ✉ *110 Atatürk Bul., Kavaklıdere, Ankara* ☎ *312/455–5555* ⊕ *turkey.usembassy.gov.*

General Emergency Contacts Ambulance ☎ *112.* **Emergency (police, etc.)** ☎ *155.* **Tourism Police (Istanbul)** ☎ *212/527–4503.*

▌ HEALTH

No serious health risks are associated with travel to Turkey, and no vaccinations are required for entry. However, travelers are advised to have vaccinations for hepatitis A and typhoid and to take precautions against malaria if visiting the far southeast. To avoid problems at customs, diabetics and other persons who carry needles and syringes for medical reasons should have a letter from their physician confirming their need for injections.

LOCAL DO'S AND TABOOS

Turks set great store in politeness. No one will expect you to have mastered the intricacies of polite speech in Turkish, but a respectful attitude and tone of voice, combined with a readiness to smile, will often work wonders.

Although Turks are a very tactile people, particularly with friends of the same sex, this physical contact is like a language, full of pitfalls for the unwary. Be very careful about initiating physical contact, as misunderstandings are easy. Overt public physical displays of affection between the sexes are more common in younger generations in big cities, but are still likely to offend people outside the major cities.

Turks shake hands as a greeting, although this is more common between men than between women. It is quite acceptable, and often very appreciated, if a foreign male initiates a handshake with another male when, for example, leaving a carpet shop. For handshakes between the sexes, unless the Turkish woman is obviously highly Westernized, a foreign male should leave it up to her to initiate any physical contact. It is all right for foreign women to initiate a handshake, but be prepared for a very religious Turkish male to pointedly avoid shaking a woman's hand.

A combination of simultaneously shaking hands and kissing on both cheeks is the usual form of greeting between male friends, while women friends more often kiss without shaking hands; this is usually a cheek-to-cheek "air-kiss," and it's unusual for the lips to make contact with the skin. On occasion, a Turk will actually kiss the cheek, but such a kiss is considered very forward when given to members of the opposite sex, particularly those of little acquaintance, and if you are a recipient, you should draw your conclusions accordingly.

Most Turks consider hospitality both a duty and a source of pride. If you visit Turks in their homes, it is expected that you will take off your shoes on entering. You will not be expected to bring gifts, particularly on a first visit, although a small token, such as fresh nuts or dessert, is always appreciated. Chances are the lady of the house will have gone to considerable trouble to prepare food if she has had prior knowledge of your arrival so you, in turn, should go with an empty stomach and at least try the dishes that are offered to you. In appreciation, it is traditional to say *ellerinize sağlık* ("ell-lair-in-izeh sah-luk"), which translates literally as, "Health to your hands." No offense will be taken if you don't manage to say it, but it will be much appreciated if you do.

BUSINESS ETIQUETTE

Business etiquette is a little different from everyday etiquette. In the major cities, many managers of larger companies will have worked or trained abroad, particularly in the United States, and will be familiar with the ways in which Western companies do business. Punctuality is appreciated, but chronic traffic congestion in Istanbul and Ankara means most businesspeople are used to people arriving a little late for appointments. A telephone call to warn of a late arrival is appreciated.

Business negotiations are usually conducted in a relaxed atmosphere, and the business of the day may be padded with friendly conversation and the ubiquitous cups of tea. Provided you eventually get down to business, it is usually a good idea not to force the pace, as the preliminaries are a way for the parties to assess each other and establish mutual trust.

Rabies can be a problem in Turkey, occasionally even in the large cities. If bitten or scratched by a dog or cat about which you have suspicions, go to the nearest pharmacy and ask for assistance.

Even in areas where there is no malaria, you'll want to use something to ward off mosquitoes. All pharmacies and most corner stores and supermarkets stock a variety of oils and/or tablets to keep mosquitoes at bay, as well as sprays and creams you can apply to exposed skin; it's generally easy to identify these products as the packaging usually includes a picture of a mosquito. If you can't find what you want, try asking using the Turkish word for mosquito: *sivrisinek*. It often seems as though mosquitoes favor foreigners, particularly the fair-skinned, so a Turk's assurances that mosquitoes in a particular place are "not bad" can be both sincere and misleading.

Given the high temperatures in summer, dehydration can be a problem, especially in southern and eastern Turkey. Remember to sip water throughout the day rather than waiting until you are very thirsty.

For minor problems, pharmacists can be helpful. Pharmacists at any *eczane*, or pharmacy, are well versed in common ailments and can prescribe some antibiotics and other medications for common travelers' illnesses. Many of the same over-the-counter remedies available in Western countries can be found in Turkish pharmacies, which are usually well stocked. Even a Turkish pharmacist who doesn't speak English will often be able to recognize a specific remedy—particularly if you write the name down—and be able to find an appropriate alternative if that medication is not available.

Doctors and dentists abound in major cities and can be found in all but the smallest towns; many are women. There are also *hastanes* (hospitals) and *kliniks* (clinics). Road signs marked with an "H" point the way to the nearest hospital. Even if doctors cannot converse fluently in English,

most will have a working knowledge of English and French terminology for medical conditions. Turkish dentists, called diş doktoru or *dişçi*, are highly regarded.

FOOD AND DRINK

Tap water is heavily chlorinated and supposedly safe to drink in cities and resorts. It's okay to wash fruits and vegetables in tap water, but it's best to play it safe and only drink *şişe suyu* (bottled still water) or *maden suyu* (bottled sparkling mineral water, also referred to simply as soda), which are better tasting and inexpensive. ⚠ Do not drink tap water in rural areas or in eastern Turkey. Turkish food is generally safe, though you should still be careful with some types of street food, such as chickpeas and rice (*nohutlu pilav*) and stuffed mussels (*midye dolması*), which can host a number of nasty bacteria.

▎HOLIDAYS

Schools and many offices often close for a full or half day on major Turkish holidays, which are as follows: January 1 (New Year's Day); April 23 (National Independence Day); May 1 (Labor and Solidarity Day); May 19 (Atatürk's Commemoration Day, celebrating his birthday and the day he landed in Samsun, starting the independence movement); August 30 (Zafer Bayramı, or Victory Day, commemorating the final Turkish victory over Greek forces in 1922, during Turkey's War of Independence); and October 29 (Cumhuriyet Bayramı, or Republic Day, celebrating Atatürk's proclamation of the Turkish republic in 1923—many businesses and government offices also close at midday, usually either 12:30 or 1, on the day before Republic Day). November 10, the anniversary of Atatürk's death, is not a full-day public holiday but is commemorated by a nationwide moment of silence at 9:05 am. Many provincial towns also hold celebrations to mark the anniversary of the date that the Greeks were driven out of the area during the Turkish War of Independence.

Turks also celebrate the two main Muslim religious holidays each year: the three-day Şeker Bayramı, marking the end of Ramadan (called "Ramazan" in Turkey) and the four-day Kurban Bayramı, which honors the prophet Ibrahim's (Abraham in the Old Testament) willingness to sacrifice his son to God. Because the Muslim year is based on the lunar calendar, the dates of the two holidays change every year, both moving earlier by 11 to 12 days each year. The precise timing may vary slightly according to the sighting of the moon. Many businesses and government offices close at midday, usually either 12:30 or 1, on the day before the religious *bayrams*. In 2014, Şeker Bayramı is due to begin at midday on July 27 and last until the evening of July 30; in 2015 it will begin on July 16 and end on the 19th. Kurban Bayramı will begin at midday on October 3, 2014, and continue through the evening of October 7; in 2015 it will begin on September 22 and end on the 26th. A word of note: if a religious holiday takes up three or four days of a working week, the government will often declare the rest of the week an official holiday as well. However, such decisions are usually made less than a month before the holiday actually begins.

▌HOURS OF OPERATION

BANKS AND OFFICES
Banks in Turkey are normally open weekdays from 8:30 am until noon or 12:30, and then from 1:30 until 5 pm, but select branches of some Turkish banks, especially those in major cities, now remain open during the middle of the day. Many banks throughout Turkey, even those in small towns, provide 24-hour ATMs with service in English.

GAS STATIONS
Most gas stations are open from early morning until late evening, commonly from 6 am to 10 pm, although there are no fixed rules and there can be considerable variation. In the larger cities and along major highways it is usually possible to find gas stations open 24 hours. Look for the sign "24 saat açık."

MUSEUMS AND SIGHTS
Museums are generally open Tuesday through Sunday from 9:30 am until 5 or 5:30 pm and closed on Monday—this is not a rule, though, so check the times listed in our individual listings. Palaces are open the same hours but are generally closed Monday and Thursday (with the notable except of Topkapı Palace, which is closed Tuesday), while during the summer many popular archaeological sites are open seven days a week and close around sunset. Some museums and palaces may have slightly longer summer hours as well. Many museums and sites stop selling tickets 30 minutes before the actual closing time. Sometimes this is explicitly stated in the official times, but not always. To be on the safe side, try to ensure that you arrive at least 45 minutes before closing time.

PHARMACIES
Most pharmacies (*eczane* in Turkish) are open the same hours as shops, and as with shops, there are variations according to the whim of the pharmacist. Typically, they are open 9:30 am until 7 or 7:30 pm, Monday through Saturday. In larger cities, one pharmacy in each neighborhood is open 24/7 and is called the *nöbetçi eczane*. When a pharmacy is closed, there will be a sign in the window or door with details of the location of the nearest *nöbetçi eczane*, which your hotel will also be able to help you find.

SHOPS
Shops and bazaars are usually open Monday through Saturday from 9:30 to 7 with varying open hours on Sunday. Smaller shops often close for lunch between 1 and 2, although all large stores and even most small shops in the major cities remain open throughout the day. In tourist areas, shops may stay open until 9 pm or even 10 pm and all day Sunday.

▌LANGUAGE

Conversational English, German, and often French are widely spoken in hotels, restaurants, and shops in cities and resorts. In villages and remote areas you may have a hard time finding anyone who speaks anything but Turkish or Kurdish, though rudimentary communications are still usually possible. English is taught in public schools, starting from the primary level, but instruction is often poor, so try to learn a few basic Turkish words; your efforts will be appreciated. ⇨ *See the vocabulary list at the back of this book.*

▌MAIL AND SHIPPING

The Turkish for "post office" is *postane*. Post offices are painted bright yellow and have "PTT" (Post and Telegraph Organization) signs on the front. The central post offices in larger cities are open Monday through Saturday from 8 am to 9 pm, and Sunday from 9 to 7. Smaller ones are open Monday through Saturday between 8:30 and 5. Turks use franking machines in post offices rather than postage stamps. The latter are still available at post offices but are mainly sold to philatelists and nostalgists. Envelopes and boxes are usually sold in kiosks not far from post offices.

Mail sent from Turkey can take from three to 10 days, or more, to reach a destination in Europe or abroad. Be warned that the mail service is erratic and that you may arrive home long before your postcards do.

Postage rates are frequently adjusted to keep pace with inflation. It generally costs about $2 to send a postcard from Turkey to the United States. Shipping a 10-pound rug home via surface mail will cost about $40 and take from three to five months.

If you want to receive mail in Turkey and you're uncertain where you'll be staying, have mail sent to Postrestant, Merkez Postanesi (Central Post Office), in the town of your choice.

OVERNIGHT AND EXPRESS SERVICES

The main couriers (DHL, FedEx, UPS, etc.) have offices in Istanbul, but it will probably take three days for a package to reach the United States or United Kingdom.

SHIPPING PARCELS

Some stores and sellers in bazaars will offer to arrange to ship goods for you but where possible, it's better to carry your purchases home with you—even if you have to pay for excess baggage. Most parcels sent from Turkey through the postal service do eventually arrive at their destination, but be aware there is a risk they may become damaged or lost in transit. (Unscrupulous sellers have also been known to swap out the item actually purchased for a cheaper one of poorer quality.) Other alternatives, such as courier services or shipping companies, are quicker and more reliable but often very expensive.

▌MONEY

Turkey used to be the least expensive of the Mediterranean countries, but prices have risen in recent years. At press time, Istanbul was roughly equivalent to other cities in the Mediterranean in terms of cost, but in the countryside, and particularly away from the main tourist areas, prices are much lower—room and board are not likely to be much more than $50 per person per day.

Coffee can range from about $1.50 to $4.50 a cup, depending on whether it's the less-expensive Turkish coffee or American-style coffee, and whether it's served in a luxury hotel, a café, or an outlet of a multinational chain such as Starbucks or Caffè Nero. Coffee lovers beware: much coffee listed on menus in a restaurant, unless specified otherwise (e.g., as filtre kahve, or "filter coffee"), is likely to be instant coffee (Nescafé). Tea will cost you about 75¢–$1.50 a glass, rising to $2–$3 for a cup (the latter is larger). Local beer will be about $4–$6, depending on the type of establishment; soft drinks, $2–$3; and a lamb shish kebab, $5–$8.

Prices throughout this guide are given for adults. Substantially reduced fees are almost always available for children, students, and senior citizens. ⇨ *For information on taxes, see Taxes.*

ATMS AND BANKS
ATMs can be found even in some of the smallest Turkish towns. Many accept international credit cards or bank cards (a strip of logos is usually displayed above the ATM). Almost all ATMs have a language key that enables you to read the instructions in English. To use your card in Turkey, your PIN must be four digits long.

In Turkey, as elsewhere, using an ATM is one of the easiest ways to get money. Generally the exchange rate is based on the Turkish Central Bank or the exchange rate according to your bank.

CREDIT CARDS
Turkey largely uses the "chip and PIN" system for debit and credit-card payments, a more secure method than swipe-and-sign. (The chip in the card contains identifying information.) The card is inserted in the POS terminal, which reads the chip and sends the information down the line. The user is then asked to enter his/her PIN and this information is also sent down the wire; if everything matches, the transaction is completed. If you don't have a PIN, check with your bank to get one before you leave the United States.

It's a good idea to inform your credit-card company before you travel, especially if you're going abroad and don't travel internationally very often. Otherwise, the credit card company might put a hold on your card owing to unusual activity—not a good thing halfway through your trip. Record all your credit-card numbers—as well as the phone numbers to call if your cards are lost or stolen—in a safe place. American Express, MasterCard, and Visa have numbers you can call (collect if

you're abroad) if your card is lost. If possible, you're better off calling the number of your issuing bank, which is sometimes printed on your card. Note that American Express is not commonly accepted in Turkey.

Although it's usually safer to use a credit card for large purchases (so you can cancel payments or be reimbursed if there's a problem), some credit-card companies and the banks that issue them add substantial percentages to all foreign transactions. Check on these fees before using your card.

Before you charge something, ask the merchant whether or not he or she plans to do a dynamic currency conversion (DCC). In such a transaction the credit-card *processor* (shop, restaurant, or hotel) converts the currency and charges you in dollars. In most cases you'll pay the merchant a 3% fee for this service in addition to any credit-card-company and issuing-bank foreign-transaction surcharges.

DCC programs are becoming increasingly widespread. Merchants who participate in them are supposed to ask whether you want to be charged in dollars or the local currency, but they don't always do so. And even if they do offer you a choice, they may well avoid mentioning the additional surcharges. The good news is that you *do* have a choice.

Credit cards are accepted throughout Turkey, especially in larger cities or towns, but many budget-oriented restaurants or hotels in rural areas do not accept them.

CURRENCY AND EXCHANGE
The Turkish lira is divided into 100 kuruş, and is issued in denominations of 5, 10, 20, 50, and 100 TL notes; 5, 10, 25, 50 kuruş; and 1 TL coins.

Your bank will probably charge a fee for using an ATM abroad, and the Turkish bank may also charge a fee. Even so, you'll get a better rate than you will at currency exchanges or at some banks.

Hotels and banks will change money, as will larger post offices, but in Turkey the rates are usually better at the foreign exchange booths (look for signs saying "foreign exchange" or "döviz"). Most are now connected online to the currency markets and there will be little difference between them.

Exchange bureaus are found only in big cities, usually in the center, so if you are heading to small towns make sure you change your money before leaving.

Bureaus in tourist areas often offer slightly less attractive rates—rarely more than 2%–3% difference—than bureaus in other places. Almost all foreign exchange bureaus are open Monday–Saturday. Hours vary but are typically 9:30 am to 6:30 pm. In tourist areas it is sometimes possible to find bureaus that are open later or on Sunday, but they will usually compensate for the inconvenience by offering a rate 2%–3% worse than during normal working hours.

İş Bankası (İş Bank) is Turkey's largest bank, with many branches in the cities and at least one in each town, usually in the center of town.

∎ PACKING

Although Turkey is an informal country, it is often said that Istanbul isn't Turkey— it's Europe. Expect to see the full spectrum in Istanbul when it comes to style and coverage. You may walk down the street next to a girl in a miniskirt, followed by a woman wearing a head scarf or completely covered from head to toe. Istanbul is a cosmopolitan city, so if you plan on a night out on the town, come prepared to dress accordingly. For men, nice jeans coupled with a clean button-down shirt and decent shoes will usually get you in the door; a jacket and tie are only appropriate for top restaurants in Istanbul, Ankara, and İzmir. Women should feel comfortable wearing fashionable styles but, as in any place, consider what kind of attention you want to attract.

Outside major cities, women would do best to avoid overly revealing outfits and short skirts. The general rule is: the smaller the town, the more casual and, at the same time, conservative the dress.

On the beaches along the Mediterranean, topless sunbathing among foreigners is increasingly common, though not always looked kindly upon by locals. Shorts are acceptable for hiking through ruins, but not for touring mosques. The importance of a sturdy, comfortable pair of shoes cannot be overemphasized. Whether you are in Istanbul, where "everything is uphill," or you're hiking the ruins at Ephesus, you'll be glad you sacrificed style for comfort.

Light cottons are best for summer, particularly along the coast. If you're planning excursions into the interior or north of the country, you'll need sweaters in spring or fall and all-out cold-weather gear in winter. An umbrella is advisable on the Black Sea coast, but as anywhere else in Turkey, as soon as rain begins to fall, people will appear almost magically on the streets to sell cheap umbrellas; so if you don't want to bring one with you, it's almost always possible to find one.

Sunscreen and sunglasses will come in handy. It's a good idea to carry some toilet paper and hand sanitizer with you at all times, especially outside the bigger cities and resort areas. You'll need mosquito repellent from March through October, a flashlight for exploring caves in Cappadocia, and soap if you're staying in inexpensive and moderately priced hotels.

∎ PASSPORTS AND VISAS

All U.S. citizens, even infants, need a valid passport and a visa to enter Turkey for stays of up to 90 days. Visas must be obtained prior to arrival by filling out an application via ⊕ *www.evisa.gov.tr*. The cost is $20.

Even though visas are multiple entry and usually valid for 90 days out of a 180-day period, they cannot be issued for periods longer than the validity of the passport you present. If your passport has less than a month to run, or docs not have enough blank space for entry and exit stamps, you may not be given a visa at all. Check the validity of your passport before applying for the visa. Turkish officials may impose stiff fines for an overstay on your visa.

■■■TIP➜ If your trip includes a stopover to the Greek side of Cyprus before you come to Turkey, make sure you don't get your passport stamped. Instead, ask for a slip of paper indicating your legal entry to Cyprus. Otherwise, you may encounter difficulties getting through passport control in Turkey. This is not an issue if you're coming from Greece proper, however.

▌ RESTROOMS

Public facilities are common in the tourist areas of major cities and resorts and at archeological sites and other attractions; in most, a custodian will ask you to pay a fee (typically ranging from 50 kuruş to 1 TL). In many public facilities, including those in some small restaurants, toilets are Turkish style (squatters) and toilet paper is often not provided (to cleanse themselves, Turks use a pitcher of water set next to the toilet). Sometimes it's possible to purchase toilet paper from the custodian, but you are well advised to carry a supply with you as part of your travel gear. Alas, standards of restroom cleanliness tend to be a bit low compared to those in Western Europe and America.

If you're away from tourist areas, look for a mosque, as many have restrooms as part of the complex of washing facilities for Muslims to perform their ablutions before beginning their prayers. Standards of cleanliness at mosque restrooms are usually higher than at public facilities. Most, but not all, restaurants and cafés have restrooms, but, again, the standard of cleanliness is extremely variable. In general, five-star hotels have the best facilities, and the staff rarely raise any objection if restrooms are used by foreigners not staying at the hotel. Many gas stations have restrooms.

▌ SAFETY

Distribute your cash, credit cards, IDs, and other valuables between a deep front pocket, an inside jacket or vest pocket, and a hidden money pouch. Don't reach for the money pouch once you're in public.

Violent crime against strangers in Turkey has increased in recent years but, when compared with Western Europe or North America, is still relatively rare. You should, nevertheless, watch your valuables, as professional pickpockets do operate in the major cities and tourist areas. Women should be careful of the prospect of bag snatching both when walking and when sitting at open-air cafés and restaurants. Bear in mind that organized gangs often use children to snatch bags.

Though the Kurdistan Workers Party (PKK) has waged an armed campaign in southeastern Turkey, cities and major highways are relatively safe. You should be extremely cautious about visiting more out-of-the-way villages in the region and using unpaved roads or traveling after nightfall. Despite the country's proximity to Syria and Iraq, violence in these countries has had little noticeable impact on security inside Turkey, except in rural areas very close to the border. Many U.S. actions in the Middle East have been deeply unpopular in Turkey, and Turks will often have little hesitation in letting you know how they feel. However, they will invariably distinguish between the actions of the U.S. government and individual Americans. For an up-to-date report on the situation, check with the State Department website.

GOVERNMENT ADVISORIES

As different countries have different worldviews, look at travel advisories from a range of governments to get more of a sense of what's going on out there. And be sure to parse the language carefully. For example, a warning to "avoid all travel" carries more weight than one urging you to "avoid nonessential travel," and both are much stronger than a plea to "exercise caution." A U.S. government travel warning is more permanent (though not necessarily more serious) than a so-called public announcement, which carries an expiration date.

The U.S. Department of State's website has more than just travel warnings and advisories. The consular information sheets issued for every country have general safety tips, entry requirements (though be sure to verify these with the country's embassy), and other useful details.

Consider registering online with the State Department (⊕ step.state.gov/step), so the government will know to look for you should a crisis occur in the country you're visiting.

General Information and Warnings Australian Department of Foreign Affairs and Trade ⊕ www.smartraveller.gov.au. **Foreign Affairs, Trade, and Development Canada** ⊕ travel.gc.ca. **U.K. Foreign & Commonwealth Office** ⊕ www.gov.uk/foreign-travel-advice. **U.S. Department of State** ⊕ www.travel.state.gov.

LOCAL SCAMS

You should keep your credit cards within sight at all times to prevent them from being copied. In many restaurants waiters will swipe your card at the table. If a waiter takes the card away, you should either ensure that it remains within eyesight or ask to accompany the waiter to the POS terminal (you can manufacture an excuse, such as telling the waiter that your bank sometimes asks for a PIN).

There have been a few cases of tourists traveling alone being given drugged drinks and then being robbed. The doctored drinks are usually soft drinks such as sodas. Turks are naturally anxious to ply guests with food and drink, and in the vast majority of cases, there should be no cause for alarm. However, if, for example, you are traveling alone and someone is particularly insistent on you having a cold soft drink and comes back with one already poured into a glass, treat it with extreme caution. If the drink is drugged, the person giving it to you will probably be suspiciously insistent that you drink it. If you have any doubts, do not consume it. Someone who is being genuinely hospitable will probably be confused and maybe a little hurt; but both are better than your being robbed.

In crowded areas be aware of a common scam in which two men stage a fight or similar distraction while an accomplice picks the tourist's pocket. Single male travelers in particular should also be aware of another popular scam that starts with an innocent-seeming conversation on the street (sometimes initiated by being asked the time: "Saat kaç?"), continues with an invitation to go grab a beer, and ends with a preposterously large bill being presented to the unsuspecting foreigner. In extreme cases, the hapless visitor has been brought by force or threat to an ATM to withdraw enough money to pay the tab.

Less intimidating, but annoying, is the "shoeshine trick": An itinerant shoe shiner "accidentally" drops his brush as he walks past a foreigner, who helpfully calls out to him and picks up the brush. The shoeshine man feigns effusive gratitude, and insists on shining the shoes of the visitor—then overcharging, and sometimes refusing to clean the polish off until the price is paid.

Before taking a private taxi, it can be useful to ask the information desk at your hotel what route (i.e., past what landmarks) the driver will likely drive, how many minutes the ride usually is, and what the average cost is: this way you will avoid an unwanted, and often lengthy, tour of the city. Note that Turkish hospitality is such that if you need directions, someone will often insist on accompanying you part or all the way to your destination.

WOMEN IN TURKEY

Turkey is a generally safe destination for women traveling alone, though in heavily touristed areas such as Istanbul's Sultanahmet, Antalya, and Marmaris, women unaccompanied by men are likely to be approached and sometimes followed. In rural towns, where visits from foreigners are less frequent, men are more respectful toward women traveling on their own. In the far east of the country, though, you should be particularly careful; women traveling alone have been known to be harassed in this region. As in any other country in the world, the best course of action is simply to walk on if approached, and avoid potentially troublesome situations, such as walking in deserted neighborhoods at night.

Some Turkish men are genuinely curious about women from other lands and really do want only to "practice their English." Still, be forewarned that the willingness to converse can easily be misconstrued as something more meaningful. If you are uncomfortable, seek assistance from a Turkish woman or move to a place where other women are present; when it comes to harassment by males, there really is safety in female solidarity. If a man is acting inappropriately toward you, it is acceptable to be forward and tell him to go away. The phrase *çok ayıp* ("shame on you") will come in handy, as it will also attract attention from passersby. Another phrase, *defol* ("get lost") is more severe and should dispel any persistent men you may encounter. Women who are pregnant or have small children with them are generally treated with such respect as to be virtually immune from harassment.

Turkey, especially outside tourist areas and major cities, is not the place to sport clothing that is short, tight, or revealing. Longer skirts, and shirts and blouses with sleeves, are less likely to attract unwanted attention. Women are expected to cover their heads with scarves when entering mosques.

Many hotels, restaurants, and other eating spots identify themselves as being for an *aile* (family) clientele, and many restaurants have special sections for women and children. How comfortable you are with being alone will affect whether you like these areas, which are away from the action—and you may prefer to take your chances in the main room (though some establishments will resist seating you there).

When traveling alone by intercity bus, you will almost certainly be seated next to another woman (and often refused a ticket if such a seat is not available). If a man sees that you are traveling alone, he will probably offer his own seat so that you may sit next to a woman.

▌ TAXES

The value-added tax, in Turkey called Katma Değer Vergisi, or KDV, is 18% on most goods and services. Hotels typically combine it with a service charge of 10% to 15%, and restaurants may add a similar charge for service.

Value-added tax is nearly always included in quoted prices. Certain shops are authorized to refund the tax (but you must ask).

When making a purchase, ask for a VAT refund form and find out whether the merchant gives refunds—not all stores do, nor are they required to. Have the form stamped by customs officials when you leave the country. After you're through passport control, take the form to a refund-service counter for an on-the-spot refund (which is usually the quickest and easiest option), or mail it to the address on the form (or the envelope with it) after you arrive home—the processing time can be long, especially if you request a credit card adjustment.

Global Blue is a worldwide service with 270,000 affiliated stores and more than

700 refund counters at major airports and border crossings. Its refund form, called a Tax Free Check, is the most common across the European continent. The service issues refunds in the form of cash, check, or credit card adjustment.

VAT Refunds Global Blue ☎ *866/706–6090 in U.S., 212/232–1121 in Turkey* ⊕ *www.qlobalblue.com.*

▌ TIME

Turkey is 2 hours ahead of London, 7 hours ahead of New York, 10 hours ahead of Los Angeles and Vancouver, 11 hours behind Auckland, and 9 hours behind Sydney and Melbourne. Turkey uses daylight saving time and makes the switch on the European schedule (the last Sunday of March and October, as opposed to the second Sunday in March and the first Sunday in November, when the time changes in the United States).

▌ TIPPING

A 10%–15% charge may be added to the bill in restaurants. In top establishments, waiters expect tips of 10%–15% in addition to the service charge. Although it's acceptable to include the tip with your credit card payment, cash is much appreciated.

In Turkey, taxi drivers are becoming used to foreigners giving them something; round off the fare to the nearest 50 kuruş. Dolmuş drivers do not get tipped. Hotel porters expect about 2 TL. At Turkish baths, staff members who attend to you expect to share a tip of 30%–35% of the bill: don't worry about missing them—they'll be lined up expectantly on your departure.

Tour guides often expect a tip. Offer as much or (as little) as you feel the person deserves, usually 10 TL to 20 TL per day if you were happy with the guide. If you've been with the guide for a number of days, tip more. Crews on chartered boats also expect tips.

Restroom attendants will not expect a tip in addition to the charge for using their facilities.

▌ TOURS

Tours aren't for everyone, but they can be just the thing when making travel arrangements is difficult or too time-consuming. You travel along with a group (sometimes large, sometimes small), stay in prebooked hotels, eat with your fellow travelers (sometimes included in the price of your tour, sometimes not), and follow a schedule. A knowledgeable guide can take you places that you might never discover on your own, and you may be pushed to see more than you would have otherwise. Plus, a package tour to Turkey will often be less expensive than independent travel and you'll be spared the trouble of arranging everything yourself. There are, of course, cons, too, one disadvantage being that you'll have less flexibility in being able to choose your hotel.

Whenever you book a guided tour, find out what's included and what isn't. A "land-only" tour includes all your travel (by bus, in most cases) in the destination, but not necessarily your flights to or even within it. Also, in most cases, prices in tour brochures don't include fees and taxes. And remember that you'll be expected to tip your guide (in cash) at the end of the tour.

New York–based **Heritage Tours** is highly recommended as a higher-end, full-service travel company. Heritage can design a trip start to finish, including great hotels, private drivers, and tour guides.

A small yet professionally run agency, **Argonaut Escapades** is based in Cappadocia and İzmir and specializes in cultural tours to lesser-traveled parts of Turkey, including the Black Sea region, northwest Turkey, and eastern Turkey. ☎ *384/341–6255 (in Ürgüp)* ⊕ *www.argonautturkey.com*

Recommended Generalists **Cappadocia Tours** ☎ 384/341–7485 in Turkey ⊕ www.cappadociatours.com. **Credo Tours** ☎ 212/254–8175 in Turkey ⊕ www.credotours.com. **Heritage Tours** ☎ 800/378–4555 in U.S. and Canada, 212/206–8400 in New York ⊕ www.htprivatetravel.com. **Istanbul Life** ☎ 212/638–1215 in Turkey ⊕ www.istanbullife.org. **Pacha Tours** ☎ 800/722–4288 in U.S. and Canada ⊕ www.pachatours.com.

SPECIAL-INTEREST TOUR COMPANIES

Biblical Tours Turkey celebrates Turkey's historic richness as a cultivating ground for some of the world's most prominent religions. Different itineraries will take you to historical churches and pilgrimage sites that are awe inspiring, regardless of your religious affiliation. Other tours focus on the country's many other assets. **Blue World Travel** organizes a number of tours that vary in length and region, all geared toward learning about Turkey's indigenous bird species. **Breakaway Adventures** leads guided walking tours with stops at archaeological sites, along the Mediterranean coast, and elsewhere. **Kirkit Voyage** has tours ranging all over the country, with a special focus on hiking and horseback riding trips. **Peter Sommer Travels** is a UK–based company that provides academic, yet friendly, guided archaeological tours of Turkey on *gulet* (wooden sailing boat) cruises. **Runner Tourism and Travel** runs archaeological, botanical, culinary, and photography tours, in addition to organizing gulet cruises. **Wildflower Tours** organizes tours for nature lovers; tours typically start in one major city and end in another, stopping to enjoy Turkey's remarkably diverse scenery and flora along the way.

Biblical Tours Turkey ☎ 256/618–3268 in Turkey ⊕ www.biblicaltoursturkey.com. **Blue World Travel** ☎ 232/369–4500 in Turkey ⊕ www.birdwatchingtoursturkey.com. **Wildflower Tours** ☎ 542/413–1293 in Turkey ⊕ www.wildflowertours.com. **Breakaway Adventures** ☎ 800/567–6286 in U.S. ⊕ www.breakaway-adventures.com. **Kirkit Voyage** ☎ 212/518–2282 in Turkey ⊕ www.kirkit.com. **Peter Sommer Travels** ☎ 01600/888–220 in U.K. ⊕ www.petersommer.com .**Runner Tourism and Travel** ☎ 242/425–2361 in Turkey ⊕ www.runnertourism.com.

▌ VISITOR INFORMATION

There are tourist information offices in most of the main cities in Turkey; ⇨ *check the listings in the individual chapters.* These offices can provide info on sights and cultural events, and some have accommodation-booking services that can be useful if you arrive in a destination without a hotel reservation.

Contacts Turkish Culture and Tourism Office ⊕ www.goturkey.com.

INDEX

PHOTO CREDITS

Front cover: Zubin Shroff/The Image Bank/Getty Images [Description: Man carrying tray of tea]. Back cover (from left to right): Antony McAulay/Shutterstock; Turkey Ministry of Culture & Tourism; muharremz/Shutterstock. Spine: Sailorr/Shutterstock. 1, DoreenD, Fodors.com member. 2, Mikel Bilbao/age fotostock. 5, Sailorr/Shutterstock. Chapter 1: Experience Turkey: 8-9, DoreenD, Fodors.com member. 10 (top), Fatih Kocyildir/Shutterstock. 10 (bottom), Svetlana Kuznetsova/iStockphoto. 11 (left), Amer Kapetanovic/iStockphoto. 11 (right), Turkey Ministry of Culture & Tourism. 12, vacationwhipple, Fodors.com member. 13 (left),Siobhan O'Hare.13 (right), LouisaN, Fodors.com member. 16 (left), Sibel A Roberts/iStockphoto. 16 (top center), Antony McAulay/Shutterstock. 16 (top right), rm/Shutterstock. 16 (bottom right), Maksym Gorpenyuk/Shutterstock. 17 (top left), Turkey Ministry of Culture & Tourism, 17 (bottom left), maza, Fodors.com member. 17 (top center), wikipedia.org. 17 (right), bartoleq/Shutterstock. 18, Bartlomiej K. Kwieciszewski/Shutterstock. 19 (left), TravelChic13, Fodors.com member. 19 (right), nddavidson, Fodors.com member. 20, Miroslava/Shutterstock. 21, Micke77023, Fodors.com member. 22, rayner, Fodors.com member. 23 (left), Zeynep Mufti/iStockphoto. 23 (right), Gail2000, Fodors.com member. 24, TravelChic13, Fodors.com member. 25 (left), Sufi /Shutterstock. 25 (right), curiousgal, Fodors.com member. 26, dgunbug, Fodors.com member. 27 (left), rward, Fodors.com member. 27 (right), Micke77023, Fodors.com member. 32, Eray Haciosmanoglu/Shutterstock. 34, ariena missche/iStockphoto. 35, Sylvain Grandadam/age fotostock. 36 (top left), Images&Stories/Alamy. 36 (bottom left), Klaus-Peter Simon/wikipedia.org. 36 (right), Andreas Praefcke/wikipedia.org. 37 (right), Robert Harding Picture Library Ltd/Alamy. 37 (left), joearena99, Fodors.com member. 38 (left), INTERFOTO Pressebildagentur/Alamy. 38 (top right), PixAchi/Shutterstock. 38 (bottom right), eerkun, Fodors.com member. 39 (top left), wikipedia.org. 39 (bottom left), Hazlan Abdul Hakim/iStockphoto. 39 (top right), Peter M. Wilson/Alamy. 39 (bottom right) and 40 (top left), wikipedia.org. 40 (bottom left), jonbwe, Fodors.com member. 40 (right) and 41 (left), wikipedia.org. 41 (right), Steve Outram/Photolibrary. 42, pvd, Fodors.com member. Chapter 2: Istanbul: 43, Andoni Canela/age fotostock. 44 and 45 (bottom left), Turkey Ministry of Culture & Tourism. 45 (top), Mariam_Hosseini, Fodors.com member. 45 (bottom right), Turkey Ministry of Culture & Tourism. 46, Mark Henley/age fotostock. 47 (top), sila/Flickr. 47 (bottom), Pinguino Kolb/Flickr. 48, nexus7/Shutterstock. 63, Yadid Levy/Alamy. 66, Michele Falzone/age fotostock. 68 (top and bottom), wikipedia. org. 69 (top), Mediamix photo/Shutterstock. 69 (center), dundanim/Shutterstock. 69 (bottom), Erik Lam/iStockphoto. 70 (top), lmcflorida, Fodors.com member. 70 (2nd from top), David Pedre/iStockphoto. 70 (3rd from top), murat $en/iStockphoto. 70 (bottom), Gryffindor/wikipedia.org. 71 (top), Art Kowalsky/Alamy. 71 (2nd from top), Earl Eliason/iStockphoto. 71 (third from top), Robert Harding Picture Library Ltd/Alamy. 71 (bottom), Images&Stories/Alamy. 72 (top), Alex Segre/Alamy. 72 (center), Dennis Cox/Alamy. 72 (bottom), Sibel A. Roberts/iStockphoto. 73 (left), Images&Stories/Alamy. 73 (top right), Danilo Donadoni/age fotostock. 73 (bottom right), Images&Stories/Alamy. 78, queenmab225, Fodors.com member. 81, Super-Stock/age fotostock. 94, Crispin Rodwell/Alamy. 112, Alaskan Dude/Flickr. 128, sarabeth/Fodors.com member. 138, DavidHonlPhoto.com. 140 (top), Dennis Cox/age fotostock. 140 (bottom), Jason Keith Heydorn/Shutterstock. 141, TimTheSaxMan, Fodors. com member. 143,Vladimir Melnik/Shutterstock. 144 (top left), jonbwe, Fodors.com member. 144 (bottom left), Orhan/Shutterstock. 144 (top right), ukrphoto/Shutterstock. 144 (bottom right), Alvaro Leiva/age fotostock. 145 (top left), Johnny Lye/Shutterstock. 145 (top right), rj lerich/Shutterstock. 145 (bottom right), suzdale, Fodors.com member. 146 (top), David Sutherland/Alamy. 146 (bottom all), Steve Estvanik/Shutterstock. 147, GavinHellier/Alamy. 148, Jos. Enrique Molina/age fotostock. 149 (top), julzie49, Fodors.com member. 149 (bottom), hilarieH, Fodors.com member. Chapter 3: The Sea of Marmara & the North Aegean: 155, Peter Horree/Alamy. 156, infocusphotos.com/Alamy. 157, Brian Harris/Alamy. 158, MaxFX/Shutterstock. 165, Rebecca Erol/Alamy. 171, Bruno Morandi/age fotostock. 177, Carlos Chavez/iStockphoto. 187, Sadık Güle./iStockphoto. 194, Alaskan Dude/Flickr. Chapter 4: The Central & Southern Aegean Coast: 197, Turkey Ministry of Culture & Tourism. 198, FAN travelstock/Alamy. 199 (top), twelfth/ Fodors.com member. 199 (center), hilarieH, Fodors.com member. 199 (bottom), Siobhan O'Hare. 200, DavidHonlPhoto.com. 208, eerkun, Fodors.com member. 226-27, Jose Fuste Raga/age fotostock. 228, IML Image-Group Ltd/Alamy. 229, FAN/age fotostock. 230 (left), Kitkatcrazy/wikipedia.org. 230 (center), Turkey Ministry of Culture & Tourism. 230 (right), Nikater/wikipedia.org. 232, JTB Photo Communications,Inc./Alamy. 233, Turkey Ministry of Culture & Tourism. 234 (top), Marie-Lan Nguyen/wikipedia.org. 234 (bottom), wikipedia.org. 235 (top left), Connors Bros./Shutterstock. 235 (top right), Michael Harder/Alamy. 235 (bottom), Dennis Cox/Alamy. 239, sarabeth, Fodors.com member. 253, Tulay Over/iStockphoto. Chapter 5: The Turquoise Riviera: 265, Demetrio Carrasco/age fotostock. 266 (top), rward, Fodors.com member. 266 (bottom), vacationwhipple, Fodors.com member. 267 (top), FAN travelstock/Alamy. 267 (bottom),

ABOUT OUR WRITERS

Jennifer Hattam is a freelance journalist from San Francisco who has been based in Istanbul since 2008 and has traveled extensively in Turkey, mostly by bus, since her first visit a decade ago. Her work has appeared in *California, J Magazine, The National, Salon, Sierra, Time Out Istanbul,* and *Wired,* among other publications. She updated the Experience and Travel Smart chapters.

Vanessa H. Larson has traveled widely in Turkey since she first visited as a student in 1998. From 2007 to 2013 she lived in Istanbul, working as a writer and editor. She has written for the *Washington Post, Time Out Istanbul,* Qatar Airways' *Oryx,* and other publications, and has served as the managing editor of the global food blog CulinaryBackstreets. com. She updated the Istanbul, Cappadocia, and Central Turkey chapters this edition.

Aidan McMahon first visited Turkey in 2007 and has been coming back ever since. In recent years, he has traveled extensively in North Africa and Spain, and currently edits and writes for an Istanbul-based publication. He has contributed to a number of travel and culture websites, including Unanchor, The Expeditioner, and Mashallah News. He updated the Sea of Marmara and the North Aegean chapter.

Scott Newman first set foot in Turkey in 1994 as a wandering Australian archaeology undergraduate and has been filling passports with Turkish stamps ever since. He's currently living in Istanbul again, and when not teaching English and writing for *Time Out Istanbul* magazine, he's out hiking the Lycian Way or hunting for lost ruins. This edition, Scott updated the Turquoise Coast and Excursions to the Far East and Black Sea Coast chapters.

A Fulbright Fellow, **August Siena Thomas** has lived all over Turkey, from tiny Cunda Island to urban Ankara to cosmopolitan Arnavutköy in Istanbul. She is the author of award-winning historical fiction, as well as an illustrator. Researching the Central and Southern Aegean Coast chapter enabled her to indulge her penchant for ruins, bazaars, and figs.